Boosters and Barkers

Studies in Canadian Military History

Series editor: Tim Cook, Canadian War Museum

The Canadian War Museum, Canada's national museum of military history, has a threefold mandate: to remember, to preserve, and to educate. Studies in Canadian Military History, published by UBC Press in association with the Museum, extends this mandate by presenting the best of contemporary scholarship to provide new insights into all aspects of Canadian military history, from earliest times to recent events. The work of a new generation of scholars is especially encouraged, and the books employ a variety of approaches – cultural, social, intellectual, economic, political, and comparative – to investigate gaps in the existing historiography. The books in the series feed immediately into future exhibitions, programs, and outreach efforts by the Canadian War Museum. A list of the titles in the series appears at the end of the book.

CANADIAN WAR MUSEUM
MUSÉE CANADIEN DE LA GUERRE

Boosters and Barkers
Financing Canada's Involvement in the First World War

David Roberts

UBCPress · Vancouver

32 31 30 29 28 27 26 25 24 23 5 4 3 2 1

Printed in Canada on FSC-certified ancient-forest-free paper (100% post-consumer recycled) that is processed chlorine- and acid-free.

Library and Archives Canada Cataloguing in Publication

Title: Boosters and barkers : financing Canada's involvement in the First World War / David Roberts.
Names: Roberts, David, author.
Series: Studies in Canadian military history.
Description: Series statement: Studies in Canadian military history | Includes bibliographical references and index.
Identifiers: Canadiana (print) 20230496741 | Canadiana (ebook) 20230496776 | ISBN 9780774869584 (hardcover) | ISBN 9780774869591 (softcover) | ISBN 9780774869607 (PDF) | ISBN 9780774869614 (EPUB)
Subjects: LCSH: World War, 1914-1918 – Finance – Canada.
Classification: LCC HJ8513 .R63 2023 | DDC 336.3/4097109041 – dc23

UBC Press gratefully acknowledges the financial support for our publishing program of the Government of Canada, the Canada Council for the Arts, and the British Columbia Arts Council.

This book has been published with the help of a grant from the Canadian Federation for the Humanities and Social Sciences, through the Scholarly Book Awards, using funds provided by the Social Sciences and Humanities Research Council of Canada.

Publication of this book has been financially supported by the Canadian War Museum.

UBC Press
The University of British Columbia
2029 West Mall
Vancouver, BC V6T 1Z2
www.ubcpress.ca

Contents

Illustrations

Figures

Tables

Acknowledgments

Boosters and Barkers was begun in 2012 as a retirement project. The subject of Canada's financing of its participation in the First World War grew out of a chapter entitled "Victory Bonds," on the war years of the Ford Motor Company of Canada. Encouraged by the late Professor Robert Craig Brown, I wanted to understand Canada's domestic borrowing for the war on a broader scale and in a fashion that linked investment securities, need, propaganda, and public experience. I saw the gap in the plethora of Great War studies as both an opportunity and a minefield: finance can be daunting, the field of historical appreciation in Canada thin. The manuscript that emerged, despite trying personal circumstances, was heavily empirical, with evidence, perspectives, and questions that I saw as worthwhile. Pathways for future investigations opened up.

As an independent historian, I undertook the research where my pension and vacations allowed: Montreal, Toronto, Ottawa, elsewhere in Ontario, and the Maritimes. Ever-expanding online resources facilitated a national search. So, too, did a generous community of archivists, curators, and private and academic historians. Formative investigations of Canada's public accounts and the Quebec press were undertaken for me by Marie-Michelle Pagé. At the end of the journey, Sarah Glassford gave editorial shape to a bloated manuscript. Others answered queries, shared their expertise and documents, and offered critiques tempered with backing. At the risk of missing some, I extend sincere thanks to David Bartlet, Réal Bélanger, Jane Boyko, Catherine Buck, Maurice Charette, Robert L. Fraser, Stephanie Gibson, Curtis Mainville, Michael Moir, Mora Dianne O'Neill, and Anna Peretiakowicz. Critical readings of all or parts of the manuscript were also undertaken by Jenny Higgins, James Powell, Jonathan Scotland (who equally provided technical support), and Edward Soye. Translations were graciously done by Phyllis Creighton and Sandy Darmagnac. On top of her other jobs, Jesse C. Roberts compiled the bibliography and the index.

My gratitude extends in no small measure to UBC Press for taking on my manuscript – a good fit in all respects. In particular, I thank editors Randy Schmidt and Megan Brand for their patience and professional guidance. In their assessments, the Press's anonymous readers were challenging but constructive. Copy editor Robert Lewis smoothed the rough spots. In a pleasing ending, this book is produced with the generous assistance of the Canadian War Museum's series Studies in Canadian Military History.

Lastly, for her unwavering support, I thank my wife and closest friend, Jane.

Boosters and Barkers

Introduction

In 1916, Sun Life Assurance of Montreal invested $5.5 million in Dominion War Bonds, Canada's first issue of bonds to help finance its participation in "the great war of Europe." The following year, Finance Minister Sir Thomas White circularized Canadians, asking them to invest in war-savings certificates, a low-cost security unknown to most. In response, two women in Quebec said that they could not invest: one had to support her family; the other, a widow, had to work and was often sick. In 1918, after the campaign for the Victory Loan of that year, with its array of enticements for people to loan the government money through another issue of bonds, a farm girl in Alberta bought one with the dollars that she had earned selling pelts. In a rectory on an Indigenous reserve in British Columbia, women chatted about bonds while knitting. To publicize Canada's final appeal to the people during the Victory Loan of 1919, a copywriter matter-of-factly incorporated into advertisements the requisite "'whoop it up' stuff" about soldiers. In Ottawa, politicians and civil servants dealt with the issues of bonds, soaring national debt, and growing wartime need. For the public, masses of publicity and press coverage aimed to answer two basic questions: what were bonds, and why did Ottawa feel compelled to use them?

Global and civil wars have been funded through four means: borrowing in the domestic market, borrowing abroad, taxation, and issuing currency.[1] Canada's bonds financed about a third of its war costs. *Boosters* is an empirical analysis of this remarkable achievement, with arguments made through evidence, focus, and thematic organization. Three themes are interwoven: the linkages between the political and economic spheres of finance; public mobilization in concert with business over the course of campaigns by the Governments of Canada and Newfoundland; and the cultural forms of these campaigns. *Boosters* moves from a conventional institutional study to a contemporary investigation of society, politics, and public finance, where management of the resulting debt would shape fiscal calculations for decades. The cultural and social side of *Boosters* exists within a broad field of histories of Canada's home front, adding fundraising to a rich landscape.

When Canada was pulled into the Great War in 1914, recruitment, avoidance of financial panic, and a war budget were priorities. No one knew how long it would last. White, Canada's financial czar throughout, later professed that he had not anticipated where the necessary money would come from.[2] Adherence to orthodox fiscal policy was understandable.[3] For most participants globally, financial mobilizations were based on the expectation of only a few months of hostility. But for those with no experience of wartime, who resorted to traditional revenue tools, the challenges would mount. Prime Minister Sir Robert Laird Borden stuck by his mercurial minister. In the fiscal year 1916–17, revenue from customs and excise, war taxes, the post office, the railway, and other sources (excluding loans) would total almost $233 million, and the expenditures for the Department of Militia alone would be more than $298 million. Internationally, the war was financed through state votes of appropriation and credit, emergency issues of currency and treasury notes, borrowing, taxation (a subordinate means for most nations), and duties. Domestication of borrowing and debt was seen in virtually all the belligerents. In this spectrum,[4] Canada, not a major combatant, was a low-key participant. The cost of the war to the Dominion would be just above that incurred by each of Belgium, Australia, Romania, and Turkey.[5] Canada's prosperity and distance from the conflict imposed less of a burden compared to European nations,[6] but remoteness made public engagement challenging.

Canada's borrowing entailed issues of treasury bills, reciprocal credit arrangements with Allied nations, loans in the United States, and the public issue of bonds. In 1914, not all of these resources were foreseen. The war presented a daunting test for Canada's Department of Finance, which had to find the right sequential combinations in tight time frames. Tariffs were expected to be a mainstay. Through direct loans and the purchase of instruments of short-term debt such as treasury bills, the banks would be major participants.[7] Initially, Ottawa was blind to public engagement. By mid-1915, with regular revenues proving inadequate, it had come to realize that loans could be sustained only through massive borrowing from the public in the form of bonds, another security new to most Canadians. Calls for subscriptions to six loans would generate an astounding response. For the government, subscriptions created immediate credit.

The national campaigns, notably their culmination in the three Victory Loans of 1917 to 1919, merged fiscal imperative with coercive, modern marketing, including colourful fundraising events to sell the concept of war, sustain morale on the home front, and generate an aura of civilian participation. The loans created a solid, arguably essential, platform for displays of real and professed patriotism. These adjoining needs would be addressed through these campaigns, beginning in 1917, the year of greatest crisis financially and militarily. Companies and financial institutions with large sums to invest found a profitable avenue. This monumental endeavour went beyond the conventional realm of government finance into every sector of Canadian society, from boardrooms to traplines.

The human cost to Canada was staggering: nearly 61,000 killed and another 172,000 injured. Newfoundland, then separate from Canada but linked to it in the mining, fishing, and banking sectors, and with a shared attachment to the British Empire, suffered between 1,200 and 1,300 fatalities and 2,200 wounded. Making sense of these losses, which have burned their way into the Canadian psyche, is a diligence of memory, an industry of books, articles, and countless commemorations. But there is this other cost, one entrenched in government accounts, convoluted international finance, fundraising campaigns, and public engagement that is equally consequential: the financial investment that Canada poured into the war.

Understanding how support on the home front was mobilized is essential to a fuller comprehension of that formative conflict. Market factors impinged, and the prospect of financial gain and waves of organized propaganda stimulated the essential enablement of Canadians. Among the questions asked are: How did those waves work, how did a controlling finance minister versed in orthodox finance get on board with popular campaigning, was there universal appeal, and how did patriotic motivation mesh with a desire for financial return? Insights emerge from noisy circus-like campaigns designed to draw in the public, from rural grinds, from the nuanced meanings of propaganda and patriotism, which were up against cynicism, nativism, and a pandemic, from differences in Quebec, and from other realms of culture. As the country took to bonds, they developed a life between the campaigns: payment instalments became due, past issues were converted, and issues flooded the marketplace. After the loan of 1919, which was regarded as another "war year," where funding turned to demobilization, maturing issues were refunded (refinanced), part of a legacy of massive national debt that lasted into the 1930s. Following the trail has not been fashionable.

War loans and fundraising campaigns were not new phenomena. During the American Civil War, capital had been raised through bonds, short-term loans, and fiat money (money not backed by gold but by the government). Issues had been floated publicly to finance more recent conflicts: by the United States for the Spanish-American War of 1898, by Great Britain for the South African War of 1900, and by Japan and Russia for the Russo-Japanese War of

1904. A notable feature of the loans was their casting as popular loans, in which small investors could participate at low cost to assist their countries.

For decades, in financial columns, ads, and prospectuses, the Everyman investor had been targeted and mythologized as a complement to democracy. In the developing market for securities in Canada, proposals for popular loans surfaced in discussions of public funding in some provinces throughout the 1900s. At the federal level, in April 1909, the budget of the Liberal government's finance minister, William Stevens Fielding, summarized the loan through bonds returning three and three-quarter percent (better than the normal three and a-half percent), which were floated in January in Britain, the traditional centre for Canadian financing. He took pride in having the loan shaped to interest British investors in Canadian affairs, with bonds as low as £10. No fewer than 603 applications – a big figure at the time – had been received for subscriptions of £90 or less.[8] In early 1914, nothing came of a proposal from a Conservative member of Parliament (MP) for $10 government bonds. More important were the bond and stock dealers who trawled Canada between the 1890s and the Great War. During the war, domestic borrowing and small denominations would emerge, influenced not by progressive attributes but by loans in Europe and by fundraising and marketing initiatives in Canada.

Models for the popular style of campaigning and content used in the promotion of the Victory Loans of 1917 to 1919 can be found in the early drives for the National Patriotic Fund, set up in 1900 to support Canadians who had served in South Africa and their families. With contributions ranging from cents to thousands of dollars, the initial campaign in 1900 raised more than $87,000. The methods of national canvassing and publicity were new. Concerts, poetry readings, and other entertainments raised funds. Newspaper coverage was filled with human-interest stories that brought scenes to life and underscored themes that would be propounded during the Great War. Such hyped publicity would carry over in 1914–15 to the campaigns of the Canadian Patriotic Fund, the Toronto and York County Patriotic Society, and the Red Cross Society, and after resistance within the Department of Finance, to the National War Loans. These loans can be seen as a democratization of investment, a perspective taken by a number of historians in their studies of the Liberty Loan undertakings. Historian Julia C. Ott's *When Wall Street Met Main Street: The Quest for an Investor's Democracy* (2011) is especially persuasive, despite its minimal regard for the financial sector and international context.

Advertising entrepreneurs transitioned easily. Proponents of posters and verve took their messaging into the war years, as witnessed in the marketing journal *Economic Advertising* (Toronto). Some federal departments were early advocates but not the Department of Finance, which was initially satisfied with staid black-and-white ads. Newspapers themselves would become staunch recipients and directors of much government advertising, especially as the Dominion War Loans of 1915, 1916, and March 1917 gave way to the Victory Loans. Whereas the loans of 1915 created a fiscal template, the Victory Loans of 1917 were the breakthrough.

Canada's efforts were not limited to the few weeks of official campaigning. The funds resulting from the sale of bonds fed a continuum. Obligations on securities were paid or renewed. Funds and credits were constantly needed to meet the demands of reciprocal financing with the United Kingdom for the purchase of matériel and for the payment of Canada's overseas forces. The loan returns were interwoven with the revenues from tariffs, war taxes, temporary bank loans, and savings certificates and stamps (the low-revenue offshoots of thrift drives). Even with annual budgets, war finance could be volatile. Before long, the Department of Finance became accustomed to planning and spending only a few months ahead, its dealings unfolding in a tightly strung succession shaped by the war's continuation and, at home, by the persistent need to shore up transnational railways. Regional divergences and politics intruded, especially during the divisive election of 1917 and in Quebec, where nationalist perceptions of financial need were cause for debate. By late 1915, this continuum had pushed Canada into domestic borrowing, a form of engagement that necessitated a massive program of propaganda and public subscription. Investment and saving normally meant family reserves of cash, savings in banks, and real estate. Such public engagement contrasts sharply with the economic perspectives that informed early treatments of war finance in Canada.

In his foundational *Financing the First World War* (2004), Hew Strachan observes that war finance has been largely neglected in scholarship, a void that is narrowing. Accounts for Canada, often subsumed under the imperial umbrella, begin with the *Canadian Annual Review of Public Affairs.* Chapters on the situation before and during the war by Bernard Keble Sandwell, editor of the *Financial Times* (Montreal), are in Volume 2 (1918) of *Canada in the Great World War.* Contemporary articles by William Clifford Clark, Oscar Douglas Skelton, Adam Shortt, and others merit attention. In the 1920s, the Canadian section of Sir Charles Lucas's five-volume *The Empire at War* (1921–26) offered financial content. After the publication of White's *Story of Canada's War Finance* (1921), there was some coverage. In the context of the pressing problems of postwar finance, refunding loans and managing debt took precedence. Speakers and letter writers stepped forward to excoriate war propaganda. A concise summary of munitions funding came, unexpectedly and unofficially, from White in 1927. A fresh summary of *Canadian Federal Finance* by James Stuart Prentice of Queen's University in 1928 underlined the value of investment in bonds and loan flotations, a worthy lesson of the war, he claimed, but hardly a new feature in a period of refunding. In 1931, another Queen's economist, Clifford Austin Curtis, published "The Canadian Banks and War Finance" for the Canadian Economics Association. What these early works do not fully capture is the desperation caused by the continuity of financing needed to sustain Canada's war effort and by the necessity of its imposition on society.

White's intent in his much-referenced *Story* is to provide a general treatment of Canada's financial administration. His government-friendly account covers information that only an insider can explain but without the deep analysis that he is capable of. He champions the war loans, deficit financing, and key measures such as the Finance Act of 1914. Tensions are underplayed. His frequent critic, the fractious militia minister Sam Hughes, is praised for his "brilliant organizing power."[9] On his reservations over domestic loans, he believed "the mass of the people did not know what a bond was." Without mention of his hankering for control, he came round to the need for a "nation-wide popular loan."[10] *Story* also falls short of the effusiveness of the American Treasury's secretary, William Gibbs McAdoo, who would claim that "any great war must necessarily be a popular movement. It is a kind of crusade; and like all crusades, it sweeps along on a powerful stream of romanticism."[11] Rates of interest and other basic features of the loan, White wrote, could be downplayed only when the war and the "pitch" of patriotism were sufficiently advanced.[12]

The advent of a new world war brought consideration of finance to the fore.[13] A coterie of economists, among them, in 1940, John James Deutsch, Frank Albert Knox, Frank Herbert Brown, and John Frederick Parkinson, examined the handling of finance during the Great War, stripping out patriotism and social factors, not unlike the securities dealers who no longer had to pitch the war. The article "Canadian War Finance and the Balance of Payments, 1914–1918," by Knox, a war veteran and economist at Queen's, analyzed international payments, expansion of the volume of money, and "the methods of finance." He nonetheless allowed that the flotation of the Victory Loans had been "a real achievement of organization and promotion."[14] In 1940, one seasoned journalist, Alexander McEachern, in explaining the differences in the upcoming war loan, recounted the loans as "the greatest mass selling performances ever achieved in Canada."[15]

More recent financial and economic analysis of Canada's part is a thin field, overshadowed by military and social studies. Treatments in broader historiography draw from early economic studies. R. Craig McIvor's chapter on war finance in his *Canadian Monetary, Banking and Fiscal Development* (1958) remains essential. Studies of finance in operation include the wartime content explored by Ronald A. Shearer and Carolyn Clark in "Canada and the Interwar Gold

Standard, 1920–35: Monetary Policy without a Central Bank" (1984);[16] Christopher Armstrong's *Blue Skies and Boiler Rooms* (1997); and Jeremy Wormell's *The Management of the National Debt of the United Kingdom, 1900–1932* (2000), which has invaluable content on Canada. Further contextualization emerges from Charles Gilbert's *American Financing of World War I* (1970); Martin Horn's *Britain, France, and the Financing of the First World War* (2002); editors Stephen Broadberry and Mark Harrison's anthology *The Economics of World War I* (2005); Ott's *When Wall Street Met Main Street;* Kenneth D. Garbade's *Birth of a Market: The U.S. Treasury Securities Market from the Great War to the Great Depression* (2012); Hans-Peter Ullmann's chapter "Financing Global War," in *The Cambridge History of the First World War* (2014);[17] and the articles in Freie Universität Berlin's *1914–1918-Online: International Encyclopedia of the First World War.*[18] Studies of war finance and propaganda in Australia, South Africa, and India are also rewarding.

In 2017–18, historians Shirley Tillotson, Elspeth A. Heaman, and David Tough came out with fresh examinations of taxation that contained illuminating insights into notions of modernity in politics, including entanglement with the rhetoric surrounding conscription (of men and wealth) and, in Tough, the class inequities of war loans.[19] While benefiting from these works, *Boosters* diverges by asking how taxes and loans worked in the context of funding Canada's war. "'Maximum Slaughter at Minimum Expense': War Finance," a chapter in Niall Ferguson's *The Pity of War* (1999), is a controversial entry on the limitations of purely economic, taxational, or military analyses. All participants in the war, he concludes, had to rely "heavily on the willingness of its citizens to lend money to the war effort by buying war bonds."[20] Such willingness comes out dramatically in *Boosters.*

The integrated approach, in a holistic sense, emerges in Jeffrey A. Keshen's *Propaganda and Censorship* (1996). *Boosters* advances the scrutiny by tracing the evolution of public engagement and the Dominion's financing of its participation as a striking convergence of dire fiscal need, imperial obligation, forms of patriotism, and crafted atmospheres of ideology and investment. Wholly seen, finance was no hidebound exercise in dollars. *Boosters* is admittedly a primer with technical bias. Reflective of the partly economic nature of this study, including my use of financial records, I have opted for exact figures, which can be easily rounded. At the same time, it is informed by scholarly studies and extensive newspaper research. My approach mirrors the fact that loan organizers and publicists saw finance as part of the integrated atmosphere needed to stimulate subscriptions. Support on the home front was cemented through interconnected means: a finance department calculating a loan's terms, bond houses and banks pushing investments, earnest appeals in theatres, canvassers' pleas, jingoistic literature, and the floods of posters that clogged the public view.

Boosters attempts to deconstruct the propaganda. Books on Canada's war posters are largely pictorial, devoid of artistic or psychological analysis. Among the many digitized collections, those of Library and Archives Canada in Ottawa and the New York State Library in Albany stand out. Studies of formal Canadian war art ignore posters and cartoons, although some curators see them as part of the same visual arts continuum. Works on wartime film, music, poetry, and theatre seldom look beyond their bailiwicks. *Boosters* strives to examine the whole environment, going from Newfoundland to British Columbia and aspiring to be cross-representational of society. The rapidity of wire reportage allowed for campaign organizers and newspaper readers in one province to learn of developments in another. Human voices and experiences are used wherever possible, not just as constants in press coverage but also to reflect public opinion and the engagement of attention. The indispensable involvement of women and children is recognized. Francophone expression has been integrated. The needs for propaganda and the forms that it took, along with the shapes of patriotism, connect this analysis to the broader literature on the war and Canada's home front.

An account that moves from public finance and the investment decisions of youth to circus-like parades, posters, and films must come from vastly different records. The primary sources used for finance are Library and Archives Canada, Record Group 19 (Department of Finance); Canada, Parliament, *Sessional Papers,* no. 1 (Report of the Auditor General), no. 2 (Public Accounts), and no. 3 (Estimates); and unpublished sessional papers in Record Group 14. Given their breadth of use here, these sources are cited selectively. Wormell's *Management* provides vital complementary information from Treasury, Munitions, and other collections in Britain. With no demand for national retrieval, the records of most local and provincial loan organizations have disappeared. A handful survive. In one case, John Wardrop Ross, a Victory Loan vice-chair, put campaign records for Montreal into storage at his offices, where they escaped disposal. Some records of the dominion bodies wound up in the hands of the Second World War's Victory Loan organizers. English and French newspapers and financial and trade journals, many of them digitized, have proven invaluable for discerning representative points of view and regional responses, coupled with a need to filter political and cultural biases and excessive exuberance. By virtue of the transmission of news by wire, information cropped up in unexpected sources. Where local newspapers did not exist, many regions went unreported. Statistically, as seen in the tables here, national and provincial data can be marshalled, but local or county tabulation is hit-or-miss; demographic and deep economic frameworks, of the type possible for British War Loans and America's Liberty Loans, are severely limited because of the paucity of sources.

Boosters builds through thirteen chapters over five parts focused on finance, war-loan campaigns, Newfoundland, resistance and consensus, and propagandistic atmosphere. Part 1 details the fundamental task of getting the money to fund the ever-escalating costs of the war while running operations at home, navigating the shoals of taxation and conscription, and adjusting to postwar realities. Succeeding chapters are grounded on this nexus. Part 2 traces the campaigns across the country, with a compendium of activities trimmed to representative incidents and trends. The Dominion War Loans of 1915, 1916, and 1917 set the financial templates; the Victory Loans of 1917, 1918, and 1919 were focused on nationally orchestrated campaigns of a few weeks' duration determined by tight financial cycles, market factors, and rural-urban differences. The biggest achievements of the publicity machine may well have been the education of Canadians about investing in bonds and their seismic landing in society.

Part 3 moves to Newfoundland, where war funding had similarities and differences compared to Canada. With its smaller population – less than 3 percent – Newfoundland's one public war loan was centred on St. John's. A comprehensive account of the loan campaign is confounded by underreporting in the island's few newspapers, particularly on the results from small outports and towns. Clear, however, is Newfoundland's reliance on loan expertise and financing from Canadian, British, and American sources.

Part 4 probes consensus and resistance, both of which were marked by gradations of support. Despite the nationwide nature of the campaigns and the grand aim of a unifying function, not every Canadian understood or bought into the concept of bonds. There was inability to subscribe because of limited means and ill-health, cynicism, political and conscientious aversion, and opposition to mounting national debt. Ethnic, religious, and labour sectors reacted. Coercion intruded. In Quebec, one critical newspaperman, Henri Bourassa, came to endorse bonds within days of the armistice as a nationalist duty. Subscription did not always prevent harassment. Nor did subscriptions for reasons of investment and economic support automatically denote undiluted patriotism. Response was fragmented. Part 5 breaks down war-loan propaganda into complementary components: the visual imagery, the sounds of bells, clanging parades, music (the "noise propaganda," as one Nova Scotian newspaper put it),[21] and literature, both official and unofficial. With varying degrees of effectiveness, these means, which the public could not avoid but could filter, created the atmosphere vital to Canada's war loans.

Amassing dollars was a self-evident goal achieved with difficulty and by intertwined ways to connect huge sums, produce matériel, and save or sacrifice lives.

Although tariffs were a mainstay, new means of revenue and management had to be found; integration with imperial and American funding had to be negotiated; and the public had to be persuaded to come on board. Some economists have argued that market forces were stronger than such pressures as patriotism, which had limits in determining personal financial decisions. Thomas White understood that bonds yielding less than other securities would not sell and that the failure of domestic borrowing could be catastrophic. Nonetheless, patriotism was an integral part of the cold calculation of the loans and related publicity. In cooperation with the many other financial and social means and strategies, these pressures shaped a potent tool of civic mobilization.

Canadians faced countless appeals to donate to a range of causes but never appeals to loan to the government with the promise of monetary return. If the cost of participation in the war was unfathomed, it became evident as the financial crusade unfolded. The six war loans produced $2.225 billion in subscriptions, a major contributor to the national debt, which would climb from $336 million in 1914 to $1.575 billion in 1919. In December 1915, after just a year of conflict, a British official had offered this bleak prospect in talks on reciprocal funding for munitions and Canada's overseas forces: without loans for purchases, Britain could not long survive. If so used, the subscriptions from Canada's loan of 1915 alone would be consumed in 110 hours. Throughout the war, although the government was sometimes at the brink of financial implosion, Borden and White got the money they needed.

Boosters is intended to contribute to the never-ending scrutiny of Canada in the Great War. It may instigate discussions on social cohesion, on the path of war funding and federal finance throughout the interwar era as loans were refunded and Canada grappled with the Great Depression, and on the legacy of debt, culminating in the financial story of the Second World War.

Part 1
Getting the Money to Finance Canada's War

1

Business as Usual, 1914

Canada entered the war against Germany in 1914 as part of the British Empire. The formidable task of funding the Dominion's participation fell to Thomas White, the forty-eight-year-old minister of finance in the Conservative government of Robert Laird Borden. A former Liberal with a background in business and finance, the Ontario-born White had been in the portfolio, and the House of Commons, for less than three years.

After high school, he worked at various jobs, including reporting for the *Evening Telegram* in Toronto. In 1887, he joined the city's assessment department. He left in 1899 to become general manager of the National Trust Company, founded the year before by meatpacker Joseph Wesley Flavelle as part of a web of enterprises that included banking, stockbroking, and bond dealing. Associations with related directors and managers, such as securities experts Alfred Ernest Ames and Edward Rogers Wood, ensued. Wood, a vice-president of both National Trust and the Dominion Securities Corporation and the managing director of Central Canada Loan and Savings, understood bonds and Canada's dependence on the London market for new-issue funding. Before the war, federal borrowing from London was mainly through the sale of government-guaranteed railway securities and issues with interest rates ranging from 2.98 percent in 1901 to 3.56 percent in 1913.[1]

At National Trust, apart from overseeing estate administration, corporate and personal trusteeships, and liquidations, White managed related funds and loans, work that exposed him to real estate and mortgages, to bonds, debentures, and stocks, and to other investments. He was well positioned to engage in a booming market, which brought him into the inner circles of several big companies, including the electrical power and railway operations of William Mackenzie. White and National Trust did well, with net profits rising from $78,097 in 1901 to $160,779 in 1909,[2] the year before he was made a vice-president. After 1901, his duties began to involve him publicly in major arbitration cases. In 1903, he was an expert witness on Ontario's assessment legislation.[3] His part in debates over

Toronto's street railways and electrical power, where he tended to favour private enterprise, added to his profile, as did civic involvements.

Overshadowed by his business engagements, White's Liberal political persuasions were not overt. As early as March 1910, he was reportedly among a group of businessmen disgruntled with the naval initiative of the Liberal government of Sir Wilfrid Laurier. Its agreement on reciprocal trade with the United States, presented to Parliament in January 1911, riled Canadian commercial interests and intensified the rift. White spoke against reciprocity at a gathering of the Sons of England on 23 February,[4] three days after signing a manifesto along with seventeen other Toronto Liberal businessmen denouncing the agreement. At an anti-reciprocity meeting on 9 March, the *Toronto Daily Star* reported, he gave "the speech of the evening," replete with data on tariffs, biblical allusion, and much invective.[5] Not surprisingly, he was made nominal treasurer of the Canadian National League, set up to provide anti-reciprocity propaganda. Capitalizing on this wave, White stepped down from National Trust to help in the federal election campaign. Borden's Conservatives swept the country on 21 September.

Within days, Flavelle and party insiders were lobbying Borden, who recognized the Toronto dissidents' contribution, to name White to his Cabinet as minister of finance and receiver general, a key position. Some dissidents deemed him unworthy. Many furious Tories railed against such "outsiders"; the prospect of having a Toronto apostle of finance capital in office upset Montreal's business leaders. Sir Edward Seaborne Clouston, the general manager of the Bank of Montreal, the government's banker, had reservations. "With the approaching revision of the Bank Act I do not want a Minister who has to learn his business," he told former Conservative finance minister George Eulas Foster, who wanted the job again.[6] Regardless, Borden appointed White, but getting him into Parliament via a by-election was another matter. Four ridings rejected him. Sworn in as minister on 10 October, he gained election in Leeds on 6 November, promising no radical changes to Canada's traditional sources of income – customs and excise duties – which contributed almost 80 percent of the government's revenue. The simple monetary system and policy in place were based on the gold standard, where exchange rates were fixed in relation to an internationally agreed price of gold, and paper money could be converted into gold on demand. As explained by R. Craig McIvor, banks had to maintain this convertibility of their notes and deposits, and the "essential banking feature was that these institutions possessed no means of expanding their legal reserves from domestic sources."[7] Within the Department of Finance, White was surrounded by seasoned bureaucrats conversant with this inscrutable realm of banking, revenues, and expenditures.

Finance Minister Thomas White and the Duchess of Connaught at an equestrian event, 1912 | City of Toronto Archives, fonds 1244, item 569.

In the House of Commons, White was taunted for his switch of parties. Self-assured but not yet given to cut and thrust, he responded with a lengthy deconstruction of reciprocity, a speech that introduced the House to his penchant for detailed analysis. Regardless, long-time Edmonton MP (and former interior minister) Frank Oliver immediately classified White as anti-farmer. Liberal finance critic Alexander Kenneth Maclean, junior MP for Halifax (which he represented along with Borden), posed trenchant questions as a member of key standing committees, one on public accounts and the other on banking and commerce.

The next three sessions of Parliament, to June 1914, involved White in fields that would have bearing on his performance during the war.[8] In 1912, he championed the bill to form a tariff commission to collect "accurate data" for framing fiscal policies, only to see it killed in the Liberal-dominated Senate.[9] Navigating the banking sector brought him into contact with its main players and the Canadian Bankers' Association. From 1911 to 1913, amidst demands for reform, he ushered through the statutory revision of the Bank Act, in part to allow banks to issue notes over statutory limits. He also dealt with the government's costly commitment to two uncompleted transcontinental railways, begun under Laurier as rivals to the Canadian Pacific. Plagued by mismanagement and dwindling credit and crop failures on the Prairies, these projects made demands that would weigh down wartime finance. In 1913, the government began giving special aid to Mackenzie's Canadian Northern and (backed by loans floated in London) the Grand Trunk Pacific. The following year, another loan was secured for public works and for the government's construction of the National Transcontinental (the Grand Trunk's eastern section). Despite his opposition to such deals, White saw that the railways' bankruptcy could ruin the Dominion's credit.

During White's time in the Commons to April 1913, Borden was pleased with his performance. They meshed but not without tensions. That spring and summer, Borden noted in his diary White's "nervous temperament," professions of illness, and disruptive conduct in Cabinet.[10] White's grudging congruence on the railway question weighed heavily. In June, he began moaning about retirement. Borden cajoled and sustained him, just one of Cabinet's crotchety members. In public, he was buoyant, sociable, well briefed.

Despite his optimistic budgets of March 1912 and May 1913, and upbeat statements to the press, the Dominion was caught in a depression that would continue until after the outbreak of war. Both White and Borden, fearful that an unsettled economy could crumble, moved cautiously. Inflation had been evident since 1909. In his budget speech of 6 April 1914, he downplayed the international financial crisis brought on by the Balkan Wars of 1912 to 1913.[11] Calls for government action were passed over, leaving Ontario to eventually form a commission on unemployment. In October 1913, White had cautioned Borden of "a possible falling-off of revenues" and a need to halt tenders on public works;[12] between the fiscal years ending 31 March 1913 and 31 March 1915, customs and excise revenues fell dramatically, from $133,212,143.67 to $97,420,950.51.[13] Liberals hammered White over his increase of tariffs, his misrepresentation of the economy, and the aid for the Canadian Northern, pushing him to a "petulant outbreak" on 20 May 1914.[14] The size of the loan guarantees appalled White. By June, the government was running out of money. To sustain funding, manage sinking funds, and meet a growing national debt ($335,996,850.14 as of 31 March 1914),[15] including railway funding and maturing treasury bills and government loans from the 1870s and 1880s, the finance department secured loans totalling £17 million on the London market between September 1913 and June 1914. These loans, which met with varying market interest – only 12 percent of the loan of June 1914 was taken up by the public – illustrated government financing as a continuum from one fiscal year into another.

Even with White's close watch on revenues, accountability was imperfect. In his first year, Borden had tried to clamp down on unauthorized spending. White was most concerned with railway spending and the rampant growth in military and naval outlays, thanks to the minister of militia and defence, Samuel Hughes, whose disregard for formal tendering and contracts frustrated White. Hughes's upset of pre-war defence plans had funding implications.[16] His department's expenses rose from $7,580,600 in the fiscal year 1911–12 to $11,151,398 in 1913–14.[17] (By comparison, in Canada's last military engagement, where soldiers' pay was split with Britain, the contingents sent to the South African War had cost Canada less than $2.9 million.)[18] When a conference of deputy ministers and others met in Ottawa in January 1914 to begin preparing a "general Defence Scheme," the Department of Finance was not directly represented. Moreover, Hughes would ultimately replace Canada's wartime mobilization scheme with his own. There was no conscious financial anticipation of war. In discussing White's budget of 6 April 1914 in the Commons, critics saw that militia estimates for 1914 and 1915 had flatlined. Debate in June on military affairs focused on training and naval defence.

1914

The Commons broke for the summer that month. In July, with tensions in Europe set to explode, White was in New England on vacation, returning once to Ottawa and making plans to accompany the prime minister on a western tour that fall. When Austria declared war on Serbia on 28 July, financial crisis ensued across the Continent, forcing the closure of the London Stock Exchange (currency differentials) and the paralysis of the London market, which was slow to appreciate the full risk of war. The closure of the Toronto and Montreal exchanges (the securities markets) had already sparked fears of panic in Canada; doubts arose as to the government's capacity to sustain the convertibility of its currency into gold; there were heavy withdrawals of the metal from banks. Without a lender of last resort (a central-bank function), historian James Powell explains, the possibility of bank runs was potentially serious since banks were required to close if they were unable to meet depositors' demands for gold or dominion notes (paper money).[19] On 2 August, an alarmed White, aware of bankers' fears of losing gold reserves, rushed back to Ottawa to deal with the situation. The capital seethed with patriotic enthusiasms. With rhetorical flourish, public discourse immediately began fabricating Canada as a democracy in opposition to German authoritarianism,[20] a dichotomy that would carry through to the Dominion's calls for domestic finance of war, where popular investment in government securities was viewed as a complement to democracy and an emulation of soldierly sacrifice. Anti-German sentiments rooted in pre-war notions of British superiority flared.

At midnight on 4–5 August, when Britain's ultimatum to Germany expired, Canada also went to war. On Parliament Hill, departments scrambled to meet their priorities, although the government initially expected a conflict of short duration that could be financed using traditional pre-war methods. When the chair of the Civil Service Commission, economist Adam Shortt, returned from England in September, he reported that London financiers predicted that the conflict would be over by Christmas. Internationally, financiers feared that continued conflict would be unaffordable and disrupt trade.[21] As the war progressed, the anticipated end would creep forward. For purposes of financing, such incertitude was deeply problematic.

Fearful of public panic and further runs on gold, White had acted on 2 August. He called Bank of Montreal president Henry Vincent Meredith, who would become a key advisor on wartime finance.[22] White requested a meeting in Ottawa the following day with Montreal's most powerful bankers. His primary concern was the lack of provisions in the Bank Act to deal with the possible draining of deposits to meet demands for currency. At the same time, knowing the banking network well – its small size and head-office control made it "an ideal system to direct"[23] – he did not completely trust the Canadian Bankers' Association, a diverse group with spotty authority. Instead, he called on a quickly formed, four-member "advisory committee": Sir Frederick Williams-Taylor, general manager of the Bank of Montreal; Edson Loy Pease, general manager of the Royal Bank of Canada; Daniel Robert Wilkie, president of the Canadian Bankers' Association; and Herbert Barber Walker, manager of the Canadian Bank of Commerce in Montreal.[24] They arrived on 3 August, met with White to discuss how to handle the "atmosphere of incipient financial panic,"[25] and drafted the substance of the order-in-council that would become the Finance Act. They were joined by Borden. That evening, Cabinet addressed, along with the need for emergency war powers, the financial crisis through five orders-in-council: two amended customs and inland revenue acts, another increased the amount of dominion notes to boost the supply of money, and two others were more substantive. A roughly calculated $50 million would be authorized under a war appropriations bill to defray costs to year-end 31 March 1915.

The Finance Act effectively took Canada off the gold standard, thus allowing the Canadian dollar to float against other currencies. (The dollar would trade in a narrow range against the American dollar before beginning to weaken in 1918, whereas it gained on the British pound sterling almost from the outset of the war.)[26] Meant to conserve gold and allow Ottawa to advance funds and facilitate credit,[27] thus stabilizing bank credit, the bill suspended the conversion of Dominion and bank notes into gold, authorized the chartered banks to pay their liabilities in their own notes and issue them to depositors, and introduced the creation of national credit by establishing a discounting mechanism that allowed the government to advance dominion notes to the banks on securities pledged to the minister of finance. The government was thus allowed to act as a lender of last resort – one means of increasing the money supply. By breaking the link to gold, it would have more latitude to finance war since it could essentially increase the fiduciary issue of notes (notes not backed by gold) and issue more notes backed by Britain's treasury bills. Moreover, the government felt compelled to assure the public that all of Parliament's powers were to be utilized to prevent "any avoidable interruption of stable business conditions."[28] These measures, whose contravention of the Bank Act and other statutes would be overridden by emergency legislation, were announced on the morning of 4 August, the day that war was declared, effectively forestalling any runs on banks. On 10 August, a further order-in-council suspended the redemption of dominion notes into gold. Although the Finance Act would establish an agency of inflation, notably through the issue of dominion notes, White would refuse to recognize any such intent. But as one authority would observe, "The printing presses had pumped out currency, and some at least of the war's cost had been carried by deliberate inflation."[29]

The emergency session of Parliament that lasted from 18 to 22 August gave statutory form to the resolutions and brought forth the authoritarian Emergency War Measures Act. On 20 August, White tabled a budget. Intended as a temporary measure, the Finance Act, officially the Act to Conserve the Commercial and Financial Interests of Canada, became law two days later. In discussing it in the Commons, White had acknowledged his advisory committee, its proximity, and its role in assessing securities offered by banks.[30] It was a pragmatic way to face crisis. The committee would subsequently dictate policy to the Canadian Bankers' Association.[31] What the committee could not do was control ongoing problems within the banking system, notably the persistence of competing interests and, in the fall of 1914, a troubled mortgage market. Nor could it find the money needed to finance the war. The demands facing White in his budget were double-edged. In addition to war needs, if he hoped to meet the government's requirements for the remainder of the fiscal year, he also had to address the imperial loan of £5 million from June, the retirement of £1.7 million in treasury bills in November, and the projected need for another £3 million that fall. The Finance Act ended the monetary crisis, but White still faced the looming costs of military commitment, with revenues insufficient to fund nonwar spending in a period of recession.

The short wartime budget tabled by White was a statement of desperate need and rough calculation. Before the war, he had been confident that the £5 million loan secured in June, together with another for £3 million in the fall, would carry the government until the end of the fiscal year, but this plan was dashed. Along with the Finance Act, two other bills were introduced on 20 August: one to replace the Dominion Notes Act and another on customs and excise duties to raise the taxes on spirits, tobacco, coffee, and sugar. The new Dominion Notes Act would authorize an increased fiduciary issue of notes to allow the government to increase the money supply required to support the war effort.

For the appropriation of $50 million, the calculations were probably the best that could be determined. Small steps had been taken: in the spring of 1914, the militia department's budget was double that of 1911. In August 1914, increased duties were expected to generate $7 million, with more than $36 million to come from borrowing. Using figures hastily supplied by various departments, Borden estimated $13,275,000 for mobilizing and equipping an overseas contingent. On 21 August, speaking on the appropriation, based on a division of 22,318 soldiers, Borden forecast that it would cost about $1,000 to maintain a soldier in the field for a year.[32] Other costs, including civil and naval defences, as well as flour for England, brought the total to $30 million. Debate in the Commons was muddled, with a flood of questions about contracts, naval procurement, the assembly of a contingent, and other specifics. White was compelled to delve into tariffs, dominion notes, banking matters, and the uncertainties of borrowing.

In June, the government had floated an imperial loan of £5 million, which, with an anticipated further loan of £3 million, would have met requirements until the end of the fiscal year, including the retirement of treasury bills in November. However, in light of special expenditure for wartime defence, continued commitment to public works under construction, and declining trade and revenues, Parliament passed the appropriation for $50 million. Determining how much of this sum would be expended before the fiscal year-end was, to White, problematic. Assuming expenditures of $60 million, and allowing for the June loan, treasury bill retirement, and increased duties, he calculated that Canada would still need an additional $36 million. Other elements entered the debate, some setting the stage for major fiscal initiatives in 1916–17. Not only did the Liberals question White's assumed ceiling, but Michael Clark, MP for Red Deer, Alberta, who believed that White was attempting to meet "the extraordinary and the abnormal by very ordinary and very normal proposals," called for "direct taxation" to mitigate Canada's inevitable debt load. Frank Broadstreet Carvell, a New Brunswick MP, advocated a graduated income tax.[33] The calls were turned aside.

In late August, White acted on the need for both accountability and the immediate flow of funds. On 27 August, Auditor General John Fraser, on instruction from White (and he from Borden), joined a group of deputy ministers and the Department of Militia's paymaster general to draft rules for war expenditure, notably a system of credit vouchers (against the appropriations) and Cabinet approval.[34] Within months, this unwieldy accord would founder, sidetracked by irregular and surging spending in the militia department but also by White's propensity for executive control. Accountability, such as it was, shifted from the auditor general to the public accounts committee, which in 1915 would begin to delve into the murky world of contracts.

At the outset, the stark need for war funding, to meet military needs and dominion treasury bills maturing in November 1914, was highlighted by urgent telegrams exchanged between Borden and Canada's acting high commissioner in London, George Halsey Perley, on the matter of further imperial assistance. On 26 August, White had asked Borden to cable Perley:

> Consult Imperial Government confidentially regarding prospect of our floating in London a war loan of eight or ten million pounds early this Fall. Impossible to make issue here as funds could come only from banks which are endeavouring to meet commercial demands and take care of Canadian maturing Treasury Bills in London. United States Government unfavourable to issue there. If direct loan not feasible would Imperial Government loan us amount in exchange for or upon security of our standard debenture stock which is British Trustee Security.[35]

The request raised concerns over the loan's immediacy, its demands from other dominions (South Africa and New Zealand),[36] and its aggravation of "prevailing financial conditions." The release of dominion notes would help the banks to deal with maturing provincial and municipal securities, but with finances "almost paralyzed" by the restriction of funds from England and the United States, "we must however get the loan," a frantic White told Perley on 31 August.[37] Within days, the British chancellor of the Exchequer agreed to provide a loan, although unsure how to do so. On 19 September, acting under authority of the War Measures Act, and still doubtful of any domestic loan, Canada's Privy Council confirmed Perley's arrangement with the Bank of England, as agent for the British government, for a loan of £7 million before war closed the new-issue market in Britain. The rapidly mounting costs of mobilization – Canada's first contingent arrived in England in October – necessitated approval on 17 October of Perley's negotiation of a further loan of £5 million, altogether making £12 million, to run to 31 March 1915. The loans were facilitated through securities issued under Britain's National War Loan in November of £350 million ($1,750,000).[38] This loan, publicized in Canada and to which Canadian banks subscribed heavily, included raising funds for the dominions and was meant to carry hostilities for only a few weeks. The militia expenditure to 31 December 1914 amounted to $26,221,980; another $18 million was estimated to 31 March 1915.[39] Almost from the beginning of the war, reflecting borrowing by other belligerents, speculation over Canada's issuance of dominion bonds had begun surfacing in the press, with White hinting in October, in a release published in newspapers countrywide, of "a Canadian permanent funding war loan,"[40] a radical departure in funding. The financial crisis was already having severe regional repercussions, notably on the Prairies, where the threat to the credit structure on the eve of the fall harvest brought hardship and calls for debt moratoria.[41] In the two or three years before the war, little business was done in Winnipeg in stocks and bonds, with investment and speculation largely restricted to real estate and grain.[42] In Quebec, farmers liked mortgages. Traditional preferences existed in other provinces. Within months, a few newspapers and analysts, among them outspoken journalist Arthur Hawkes, believed that White was grossly underestimating the cost of war.[43]

With Parliament not set to resume until February 1915, the government moved to find millions more from conventional sources. During the fall and winter of 1914, new issues of dominion notes were made to provide "the domestic liquidity,"[44] temporary loans were secured from the Bank of Montreal, and more treasury bills and dominion stock were issued in London. Within Canada's securities markets, the exchanges were settling. Toronto and Montreal reopened for limited trading in October 1914 and Winnipeg in February 1915. But another source of funding was being scrutinized. Although the United States would not enter the war until 1917, its involvement was evident from the start, as Britain and France both came to New York seeking to finance purchases and to place bond issues, and the capital market for Canadian industry gradually shifted to Wall Street.[45]

The international context of Canada's war finance was illustrated in August 1914 when White, as trustee for the Bank of England in an arrangement negotiated by Perley, announced that a stockpile of gold from abroad and American sources would be built up in the vaults of the Royal Mint in Ottawa, thus reducing shipping expenses and the risk of loss at sea. The gold would come principally from Britain, South Africa, the United States, and Russia, with lesser amounts from Brazil and Borneo, via armed ships to Halifax or Vancouver. It would be checked by Department of Finance personnel and thence sent on trucks and guarded trains to Ottawa or New York. This pool of coins and bullion, along with smelting and further refinement, would meet a number of interconnected needs, helping to fund Canada's expenditures, facilitating remittances for British purchases in the United States, allowing for the use of gold in Ottawa (to cover both the payment of Canadian and American indebtedness in Britain and the sale of American securities there), and balancing exchange. As British purchases in America grew, and the rate of exchange turned, gold would move to vaults and accounts in New York. From a European perspective, as historian Martin Horn demonstrates, Canada had only a peripheral, custodial role in the fractious development of Britain's and France's financial relationship and in later dealings with America.[46]

Between 12 August and 16 December 1914, Ottawa received 288 consignments worth $104 million (£21 million). By May 1917, between $1.2 and $1.3 billion had been deposited. The Bank of England would later calculate the amount of gold received in Ottawa between 1914 and 1921 at £323,303,235 (roughly $1.376 billion). In the Commons and in his *Story*, White identified management of gold as one of the two major "duties" that devolved on his department, the other being domestic borrowing. Although reports of shipments criss-crossed the country by wire, the department's oversight and the mechanism for transatlantic payments were negligible functions to most Canadians, but they nonetheless constituted primary components in the evolving sphere of Entente-American finance, whose significance was not fully comprehended in 1914.[47]

In speaking engagements in late 1914, White's messages were meant to reassure. On 14 December, he claimed that "nowhere in the world has the shock of sudden financial restriction been met and adapted so quickly and so smoothly as in Canada."[48] Pushing the government's "Made in Canada" message, he urged Canadians to produce more, a plea that permeated public and commercial discourse,[49] with the duty of thrift entwined with sacrifice. The thrift movement had been around since before the war,[50] but it derived intense meaning in wartime. Newspapers could not fail to notice White "hammering home the truth that Canada must greatly increase her production of things the world needs if she is to make good the great drain caused by war borrowings and by the large excess of imports."[51] In his address that December, he speculated that "Canada would borrow $100,000,000 a year during the course of the war," although he would still be looking to London for most of it, confident that the city would be able to resume lending "within a few months."[52] Heightened public engagement would in time become a fulcrum of war finance, but at this point White was not seriously anticipating any large-scale domestic loan. Skeptics believed that it would impinge on commercial credit and cut into bank deposits. White himself would cite adverse exchange in funding military expenditures, Canada's sluggish productivity at the war's outset, and competitive securities as factors that discouraged any experimentation with a loan.[53] Moreover, the government's borrowings from the public through dominion and post-office savings banks had been falling. At the same time, it was managing the maturing of government securities issued from 1884 to 1912. Although White notified London in November that he had been offered a loan in New York – he had gone there late that month for this purpose (and in the hope of meeting the British Treasury's departing advisor, Sir George Paish) – he was averse to American aid, largely because of the higher interest rates. It was a balancing act. With the London market closing temporarily, Ottawa was obliged to explore the domestic market.[54] Indeed, the domestication of wartime debt was a common theme among all belligerents.[55]

In Britain's low-interest war loan of November 1914, the targeting of commercial investors (including Canada's banks), not the general public, would prove instructive, as would its successful loan of June and July 1915. Another telling feature of Britain's loan of 1914 was how it was spun as oversubscribed, a boost to the war effort, when in fact the Bank of England had to buy in great amounts to cover up failure. The use of oversubscription would not be lost on the planners and publicists of later war loans in Canada: any loan had to be seen as successful. What was not contemplated in Canada, even as the traditional means of raising money were being implemented, was mass, voluntary investment in bonds as a means of financing and cultivating civilian identification with and support for the war, a track parallel to recruitment. Working- and middle-class Canadians were inclined to put their savings not into securities, which were expensive because of their large denominations and were an unfamiliar field, but into property, mortgages, banks, building and loan societies, penny banks, and the emerging credit unions in Quebec.

2

Inching Toward Innovation, 1915–16

Popular predictions that the war would end by Christmas meant little to the minister of finance. As Thomas White indicated in his budget of February 1915, the open-ended task of finding the money for requirements at home and overseas had been "onerous." The prospect of launching a "Canadian war loan" was not a hypothetical. Questions of borrowing, monetary supply, and taxation were pervasive, and references to Britain's experience were frequent. Canada's initial waves of patriotism and enlistment did not readily open the door to civilian finance of the war.

By early 1915, the stream of articles on the war finance of belligerents was underway. In his analysis in October of Canada's course, William John Alexander Donald of McMaster University admitted that White's task would "not be an enviable one." The solutions to fiscal problems were new taxes and tariff revisions, he believed, and so a committee of the country's "best financiers" should tackle the problems. There were few professional economists in Canada, Brandon College's William Archibald Mackintosh would observe,[1] and their advice to the government was mostly admonitory, not practical.[2] White would be more inclined to listen to the prime minister, businessmen such as George William Allan of Winnipeg, Harry Alden Richardson and other banking kingpins, and Toronto capitalists.

In January, White had faced critiques of his issuance of domestic notes by William Stevens Fielding, editor of Montreal's *Journal of Commerce* (and a former Liberal minister of finance) and by the *Globe* (Toronto).[3] No criticism stuck. Parliament resumed sitting in early February, and even before White's budget speech, Liberals turned the spotlight on government accountability in the militia department – White's bane. The surge of spending and unauthorized expenditures there, notably for the hastily established Valcartier Camp of the Canadian Expeditionary Force, had produced an accounting mess, not totally the fault of the militia minister. "It was difficult for the Militia Department to conduct business in wartime," said White's deputy in March, leaving the minister, in place of contracts, to get orders-in-council to cover unapproved disbursements.

At year-end 31 March 1915, spiralling "War Account" expenditures, spread across the entire government, stood at $60,750,476.01,[4] a sum that White could not have anticipated. Of equal concern were cost-sharing arrangements between his government and the British War Office and Treasury for the maintenance of Canada's forces overseas. To pay its soldiers, for instance, Colonel Walter Reginald Ward had been sent with the Canadian Expeditionary Force as overseas paymaster in London, where for a short time the militia department placed sums to the credit of the Canadian high commissioner's office. Requisitions were made on that office by the paymaster, who in turn transmitted sums to the regimental paymasters. In March 1915, discussions began between the War Office and the high commissioner for arrangements that would lead to reciprocating advances. Until August 1915, the high commissioner was also the starting recipient of the funds advanced by the War Office for the purchase of Canadian munitions.[5]

Throughout the year, views on the sources and amounts of loans ranged widely. Analysts such as Canadian-born (but American-domiciled) journalist Agnes Christina Laut saw American financiers and manufacturers as the mother lodes, the focus of attention by the joint Anglo-French loan mission formed in August 1915. As agreement on this loan approached – it was announced on 13 September – some Canadian bankers still saw the wealth that would flow from a "splendid crop" as the basis for internal borrowing. Hanging over all the views was the question of when war funding would stop. Laut believed that unimaginable costs and America's pre-eminence, even in 1915, would lead to the "automatic financial exhaustion" of all others. In Ottawa, fresh from talks with Wall Street bankers about Allied loans, she told a "finance official" that Canada's war debt would eventually exceed a billion dollars. "He gave me one look of contempt and almost called me a fool," she recounted.

White faced financial demands from all quarters. Domestically, western MPs called for the relief of farmers caught without seed grain as a result of drought and crop failure the previous fall. This unexpected need brought on another "paroxysm" in Cabinet from White.[6] In the Commons, he spearheaded the passage in March of a bill that would provide for more than $10 million for seed grain and other relief. His lengthy budget speech of 11 February, a lucid "business statement" in Borden's opinion,[7] had been delivered just as Canadian troops were reaching France. The budget was cautiously based on a continuing drop in revenues, existing financial obligations (notably the coverage of maturing treasury bills), and the upward pattern in military expenditure. Dawning public realization of a protracted war with high expenditures likely fostered greater acceptance of new and higher taxes. Under the authority of a second appropriation act, this one for $100 million, White proposed a series of measures for both war and nonwar needs, much of it to provide interim funding: more temporary loans from the Bank of Montreal, imperial advances, more dominion notes, a new issue of treasury bills, and issues of dominion stock in London. As well, in addition to a war-tax stamp (hastily printed only in English) on mail, taxes were levied on the transactions of financial institutions and on cables, telegrams, and transportation tickets. A tax on wine, effective 12 February, through overprinted postage stamps by the Department of Inland Revenue, was not a big revenue tool; it created public confusion and drew reaction from the Department of the Post Office.[8] The 1915 budget did include the only major change on tariff duties to be made during the war: increases of the general and intermediate schedules and of the British preferential tariff. These revenue sources, light and evenly spread, were contained in the Special War Revenue Act and the Customs Tariff War Revenue Act, both of which received royal assent on 8 April.

The tariff would provide the biggest share of tax financing throughout the war. In 1915, direct means such as income taxation were again rejected for being politically unacceptable, administratively too costly, and constitutionally off limits as a provincial and municipal preserve. "It is not a question of raising a few millions by stamp taxes, by income tax or other minor means of supplementing revenue," White stated in his budget speech. Upwards of $30 million would be needed.[9] By 31 March 1916, the war tax on financial institutions would amount to only $2,083,943.78. At the same time, contextually, war funding for provincial use was being generated in other jurisdictions. In April 1915, Ontario instituted a broad provincial war tax; Nova Scotia initiated one in 1915; and Alberta, Manitoba, Ontario, and Quebec would introduce amusement taxes in 1916, followed a year later by British Columbia.[10]

By early 1915, finding the money for domestic needs and war was proving supremely difficult. Response to White's budgetary proposals from the Opposition, which understood the basic call for more money, ranged from outrage over military spending and corruption in procurement to critiques of White's self-crediting manner, his secretive handling of public finance,[11] and his protectionist leanings. Many MPs wondered where large sums would come from. Large sums, White maintained in his budget, would have to come from foreign borrowing over the next fourteen months. He was thus calculating the payment on long-term securities for another year of hostilities and beyond. In March 1915, a combative minister sparred in the Commons with Alexander Kenneth Maclean over the inflationary effect of new currency issues, a consequence that White and other ministers resolutely denied. On 26 March, White introduced a new dominion notes bill, different from that of the previous year. It gave statutory authority to orders-in-council passed in 1914 that authorized the release of $26 million in notes guaranteed to the Canadian Northern and the Grand Trunk Pacific, both struggling under the burden of building transcontinental lines. Since they were needed to move men and wartime supplies, the government had little choice, nor could it risk any diminution of its own security. As well, the bill authorized a fiduciary issue of $10 million in notes, which White maintained was possible under the Finance or Dominion Notes Acts. Arguing that it was required as an exigency of war, he rejected the claim that the bill asked Parliament "practically for a blank cheque."[12] (Tellingly, the amount of dominion notes in circulation would jump from $157,656,118.91 as of 31 March 1915 to $298,058,697.67 at 31 March 1919.)

That same month, March 1915, a government bond issue for £5 million, the first such since the outbreak of war and underwritten by the Bank of Montreal, was floated in London for port, canal, and channel work and for "other Capital outlays." It was oversubscribed by British investors, White happily reported,[13] even as military costs persisted. By the time the 1st Canadian Division, a force of some 17,800 soldiers, arrived in France in February 1915, war costs had surpassed $100 million, forcing Canada to borrow £2 million monthly in London.

Over the spring, as a long war appeared inevitable, the pullback of British sources from development funding in the dominions marked the beginning, historian Ian MacDonald Drummond explains, of pressure for a more creative use of North American capital markets, with White, "to a remarkable extent, willing and able to run the national finances himself."[14] In a sluggish economy, he believed that the time was not right for a domestic war loan. Such a source was being bandied about in the press and in financial circles familiar with the war bonds of other belligerents. The finance department was investigating the possibility of a domestic loan,[15] but as late as July, White was not fully prepared to test Canada's capital market, despite imperial pressures to do just that. In June, Britain had already launched a second war loan, with a return of four and a-half percent. With an economic upswing, but still facing negative reports from parts of the country, White was stubbornly reluctant, despite his budget's anticipation of war loans. He was not alone: McMaster economist Donald, in his examination that fall of Canada's financial problems, considered many sources of potential revenue, but domestic borrowing was not a clear option.[16]

As war conditions steadily closed the London market, a loan from a New York syndicate was arranged for domestic spending by Sir Frederick Williams-Taylor, via his bank's New York agency, and was authorized by an order-in-council of 27 July. The loan for $45 million, Canada's first in the United States, was to be raised by the issue of one- and two-year notes in denominations of

$1,000, dated 1 August. Secured just ahead of some Ontario and municipal issues in New York, the loan had the approval of British officials, then mired in their own exchange crisis and negotiations for an Anglo-French loan from a syndicate led by J.P. Morgan and Company of New York, the financial and purchasing agent for Britain and France.[17] Aware of America's neutrality (although Germany was still floating money there), White had initially worried whether "the Government or public opinion in the United States would favour a public offering by one of the belligerent nations." Accordingly, like the London loan, it was proclaimed to be for public works and other domestic needs, thus taking "the loan out of the category of a war issue."[18] However, neither White nor Williams-Taylor liked the New York option. It carried risk. The market there charged high commissions (three-quarter percent on this loan) and demanded short-date maturities and collateral requirements that differed from those of London's market. Morgan's was nonetheless America's largest, best-connected private bank, the credit broker to the Entente alliance of Britain, France, Russia, and Italy. At the same time, there was little choice for governments in Canada but to go to New York; over the course of the war, more provincial and municipal loans and credits were negotiated in the United States than by the Dominion. As White would later explain to Parliament, the New York loan was carefully planned, but there were limits to what he could accomplish internationally. And, as with other major loans, the loan took time to discharge: $19,394,000 was outstanding as of 31 August 1917, with a number of investors having converted to bonds maturing in 1935.

As White prepared to test the waters of borrowing in New York, it was with hesitation that he considered a Dominion War Loan. The government seriously doubted that a large issue could be raised. Some outside financiers questioned Canadians' willingness to lend. Others disagreed. After analyzing Canadian public and commercial finance, including a market slump and the option of Anglo-French bonds, Montreal's financial *Chronicle* favoured the international trend toward investment in domestic securities, especially if bolstered by patriotic impulse and an "educational campaign," to bring funds out of savings accounts and the "old stockings."

White understood that for Canada, like other states participating in the war,[19] taxation would not be enough and that the war would have to be funded mainly by borrowing. Raising taxes was also politically perilous. White sounded out High Commissioner George Halsey Perley about imperial thoughts on borrowing in New York, and with the dominions being pushed toward internal borrowing by the British Treasury, White's thinking began to shift as his department monitored Britain's war loan. On 29 July 1915, the *Globe* called on the government to issue twenty-year debenture stock at four and a-half or five percent to "small investors." What such advocacy did not advance was informed calculation of the magnitude of Canada's financial resources or its place in the international strata.

In the fall, British commissioners went to Washington and New York to resolve sterling-dollar problems. They did not come to Canada, as anticipated, forcing White to make quick visits to New York in September and November in order to confer with them about Canada's relations with the British Treasury and the London market, as well as about the high-profile Anglo-French loan (the foreign-credit loan), and to consult financiers about another loan to offset the abrupt drop in Canada's revenues. The foreign-credit loan was successfully placed by Anglo-French commissioners through Morgan's, which spread it over a syndicate of sixty-one financial houses. The loan received attention in Canada, both for and against. A by-product was heightened awareness of borrowing.

Although announced in the press as a participant in the negotiation of the foreign-credit loan, White was excluded, leading some sources to amplify the call for a domestic loan. To many Americans, the Dominion was a small player; one Wall Street wag thought that Britain should offer Canada as collateral.[20] But, recognizing the importance of international factors in his own financial planning, White made the most of the New York negotiations: any improvement in exchange rates as a result of spending by the Allies in the United States would help Canada, he believed. In his postwar summary of Canada's New York loan, White would boldly claim that it had revived a "dead" securities market in Canada.[21] Profound impact came, too, from Canada's experience on the Western Front, where, during the Battle of Ypres in April 1915 alone, more than 6,000 had been captured, wounded, or killed. Such reverberation, including the earliest waves of soul-crushing casualty lists, would play out in Canadians' perception of their engagement on the "home front."[22]

Pressing need, plus the examples of Britain and other participants in the war, would lead to a significant change of direction for White and his department by the autumn of 1915. As it became evident that the usual means of finance would not suffice, there was reluctance to take dramatic steps; White would not make changes until it became necessary. After arguing against domestic war loans for roughly a year, he would turn around and pursue exactly that, setting a new course of policy and methodology that would dramatically influence not only how Canada's war would be paid for but also the propaganda that would shape the solution.

Further appreciation of domestic borrowing was heightened by news of Britain's second war loan, launched in late June 1915. Meant to counter inflation by attracting "small investors" and to steady international exchange by drawing in American funds, Britain's bonds sold for £5, £25, and £50, and it also offered vouchers for 5s. The four-and-a-half percent interest rate was attractive. An advertising agency was engaged to popularize the loan's terms, and government committees were formed to promote thrift and small-scale investment, significantly through continuous saving and through promotions not tied to short, fixed-term campaigns. The loan was deemed successful, even though over half of the million-plus subscribers bought units of £100 or more and the banks contributed a third of the new money. As historian Martin Farr explains, too much had been expected of "inexperienced small investors."[23] Canada's major newspapers followed the loan. A portion was sold in Canada, where there were also offerings of Anglo-French and Russian war bonds; on the Western Front members of Toronto's 48th Highlanders would subscribe for $35,000 worth of British bonds.[24] The collective response led the *Globe* to conclude in June that a domestic loan in Canada "might be surprisingly effective."[25] There was already a new-issue market. The proportion of domestic and private bonds absorbed in Canada between 1904 and 1914 had averaged 18 percent, nothing of the magnitude that would be spurred by the war. The figure would climb to 67 percent by 1920.[26]

Equally attentive to the British loan was the Department of Finance. In June, White was expressing his preparedness to sell bonds to institutions as well as individuals, but the government vacillated. Apart from the British experience and market pressures, there were more direct factors in White's timing. A railway bailout was one. Imperial funding was also problematic because of the decline in sterling exchange. The last war appropriation was proving insufficient. Canada's trade balance and economy were improving, and over the summer (as White did a turn as acting prime minister), record crops were maturing across Canada. Britain, which was now borrowing in the United States, continued to pressure Canada to borrow domestically. Speaking to the Toronto Board of Trade on 7 October 1915, White announced that Canada would float a National War Loan after the crop had been harvested.[27] Positing a favourable trade balance and signs of prosperity, coupled with unfavourable exchange rates, he believed that the time was right for Canada to "finance in part her own expenditure."[28] In commenting on the announcement, the *Lacombe Guardian* (Lacombe, Alberta) reasoned, "It was not the intention to bring it [a loan] on during the period of heavy financing of Canada's crop movement, as such action would result in curtailment of credit to the farming communities. There was no need for haste."[29] Nor did White focus exclusively on the loan.

A popular platform speaker, he deftly positioned loans and borrowing in the category of government achievement and himself as a major spokesman. In his address to the Board of Trade, White was at his best: "I always arrange my financing months in advance. I get the money, and I never worry over the interest,"[30] although in the realm of bond issues and international exchange, certain things that did matter, such as the cost of borrowing in the United States, interest payments, rates, and fractional points. Behind the scenes, his alter ego showed. Unlike the British Treasury, which felt that Canada could foot its own costs, White told Perley in London that the Dominion's capital market was tight and that internal funding would limit its ability to field troops. On 3 November, Robert Laird Borden would note, "Discussed Finances in Council. White greatly perturbed says war will cost us 250 millions next year."[31] The day before, White had told the Canadian Club of Montreal of his intention to launch the loan, which would come with risk. The Department of Finance had no experience with such a venture, and no one yet had a genuine understanding of the limits of Canadians' possible contributions. The market already contained war bonds from other countries at good rates. The Ontario government offered 5 percent bonds that were tax-exempt, a rare feature at the time.[32] Throughout the summer, newspapers had published accounts of the British war-loan apparatus and public engagement. Response to the Anglo-French bonds also illustrated the pragmatic belief of the *Financial Post* (Toronto) in early October that "there is little sentiment in the bond business." A segment of dealers "scent a healthy demand among loyal British subjects in Canada for the loan and, being in the business, they are going to facilitate the gratifying of that demand. The general feeling is that such bonds as reach Canada will sell like wildfire."[33] Competitive offerings concerned White, who did understand the motivational balance between patriotic drive and investment, a parity that he repeatedly proclaimed.[34] He would later explain his rationale behind the loan's intended appeal:

> That so large an issue should be made attractive to investors was apparent. The investment community was still in a discriminating mood. The war had not advanced so far nor patriotism aroused as yet to such a pitch that rate of interest and other features of a loan became of secondary importance. Although a war loan, it was regarded ... as an investment issue to be critically examined and compared with other investments available on the Canadian and New York markets.[35]

Definitions of such "practical patriotism," a term in use since the nineteenth century,[36] varied from civilian contribution to corporate sentiment.

Resisting calls for small-denomination bonds and definitive explanation, White proceeded cautiously. In the estimate of financial analyst Bernard Keble Sandwell, "the results accruing from failure would be of a most disastrous character as concerned the public credit."[37] In his address to the Canadian Club of Montreal on 2 November 1915, White declared that Canada should not only count the cost of "sending forth men" but also begin to shoulder more of the burden by boosting production, a harbinger of the eventual merger of borrowing and self-sufficiency. Further, he proposed a domestic loan at the end of the month. Under the authority of the War Appropriation Act, Canada's first Dominion War Loan (known in French as the Emprunt de guerre dominion du Canada) was launched on 22 November with minimal promotion but much advance preparation to safeguard the result. From 2 to 4 November, White had the Canadian Bankers' Association agree to subscribe half of the $50 million loan through twenty-two member banks. As Sandwell put it, the banks "practically, though informally," underwrote the loan.[38] Local branches, some 3,000 of them, would process loan applications, distribute bonds, and cash interest coupons. Uncertainty among members, especially smaller banks, about the effect of this imposition on their business would force a reduction of the amount to $21.7 million.[39] Together with $10 million from insurance companies and other large commitments, advance subscriptions totalled $40 million. The official period for public purchase was tight, from 22 to 30 November.

The widely published prospectus for the loan laid out its terms and steps to show what people faced after they had grasped the concept of loaning money to the government. The issue, consisting of ten-year bonds, was priced at 97 and a half (meaning 97 and a-half percent of a bond's face or par value) and paid 5-percent interest,[40] with an eventual yield on maturity on 1 December 1925 of about 5.48 percent. (The calculation of a bond's yield involved the purchase price.) The bonds themselves, beautifully engraved in colour, were issued in denominations of $100, $500, and $1,000 for bearer bonds with interest coupons attached, which anyone could hold and cash, and in $1,000, $5,000, and multiples of $5,000 for registered bonds, on which interest cheques were mailed out to registered holders by the Department of Finance. Applications could be submitted through the banks and recognized brokers, who would be allowed a commission of one quarter of one percent. Applications and 10-percent deposits would be followed by the issue of provisional receipts and, if desired, instalments, which could be paid up to 1 May 1916. As an added attraction, the interest on the bonds was tax-exempt,[41] and they could be converted into other denominations or future issues. Once the loan closed and the government's overall allocations had been determined, the receipts would be exchanged at a bank for scrip certificates. Once they had been fully paid up, these would be turned in for actual bonds, which, at maturity, would be redeemed in Ottawa or any regional office of the assistant receiver general.

The terms of the issue had been decided in a narrow time frame within the Department of Finance. The yield was low compared to other high-grade securities available in New York (such as the Anglo-French bonds of 1915), but it was offset by the exemption from taxation, a feature that "New York interests" had demanded from both Ottawa and London.[42] The results of the loan astounded many. In eight hours, economist Oscar Douglas Skelton claimed, this "radical venture" was oversubscribed,[43] with 24,862 subscribers committing $103,729,500. On 3 December, White moved to accept on allotment $100 million, which went immediately to the government's credit in its consolidated fund. In making this allotment, or allocation of subscriptions, the government professed to favour, as it had throughout the campaign, the smaller subscriptions, which it identified as sums up to $5,000. In a deft move to take all of the oversubscription, and with little thought to consequent debt (a near doubling), White explained that the "patriotic reasons" of the large subscribers – the banks, corporations, and municipalities that had already planned their investments – could not be dismissed. The allocation plan reflected this decision.[44] There would be three categories. First, subscriptions of $50,000 and under would be accepted in full. Second, subscribers (other than the banks) of amounts over $50,000 would receive allocation in full but would be allowed to withdraw or reduce their subscriptions. Third, the banks, which subscribed an aggregate of $25 million, would be allowed to take whatever portion of their subscriptions they wanted, as long as the total did not exceed $100 million. The impact of allocation was minimal. Of the $103,729,500 subscribed, $100 million was allotted.

Even though the loan received minimal promotion, mainly in the form of published prospectuses, it had been "snapped up" in a heady jingoistic environment. Readers of the *Toronto Daily Star*, for instance, learned of the Allied offensive at the Dardanelles, opposition to Cecil B. DeMille's film *Carmen* (1915) because of star Geraldine Farrar's alleged "pro-German tendencies," and the joyous reception in Toronto of 143 invalided soldiers on the first day of the loan's issue. Contemporary discussions of debt, currency inflation, the effect of the loan on bank deposits,[45] and thrift and economy were overshadowed in the press by gushing accounts of civilian involvement. Through mass marketing, the gospel of thrift and sacrifice would nevertheless become embedded in campaigns for engagement.

Building on the fabrication of democracy thrown up at the start of the war, emphasis was placed on the ideal of "financial democracy," personified by the rhetorical figure of the "small investor," a term that could never be consistently defined but had been tossed about since at least the 1860s. Anecdotal accounts pointed to the farmer, "investors of small savings," the small company, and school children who raised money for a bond. The analysis of war finance in

January 1916 by young Queen's economist William Clifford Clark questioned the use by many belligerents of taxation, currency extension, and loans. However, in light of the avenue opened by Canada's fall loan, he saw long-term potential in tapping "smaller investors," with this proviso: "If the borrowing is done within the country, it would seem that if the Government can retain the unquestioned confidence of the people the limit is set only by the people's power to lend."[46] Whether official direction was influenced by the concurrent work of Britain's Committee on War Loans for the Small Investor is uncertain.

Canadians did have a tradition of saving in small accounts in government and post-office savings banks. The concept may also have been promulgated as a social and political ideal.[47] Small investors, including rural folk, were the group that White wanted most to publicly identify and credit. His idea from the first was for the loan to be a "popular one," the *Financial Post* observed, but it understood the core drive: "There is good reason to believe that many or most of the big banking and financial institutions have already given the Finance Minister an intimation of the amounts they will subscribe for. This probably accounts for the optimistic sentiments expressed by Mr White as to the success of the loan."[48] On 22 November, White told Borden that financial experts said the price was right. "There is therefore no danger to apprehend that the securities will go to a discount after allotment – a most important factor," he explained. A pleased prime minister pledged to subscribe $25,000 himself.[49] The successful drive was read as a demonstration of strength on the part of both the government and the banks.

The success of the loan, which White proclaimed on the second day of the campaign, was no miracle. The result was virtually guaranteed. From the savings accounts reported in bank and government returns, White knew of the potential for investment. While passing through Toronto after a trip across Canada, undertaken to feel "the pulse of the people," he slyly avoided calling the banks' subscriptions "underwriting." As he told one reporter, the oversubscription "was why I considered it unnecessary to underwrite the loan, although in ordinary issues I am a firm believer in the principle of underwriting. Underwriting usually costs one and a-quarter percent, which on a loan of $50,000,000 would mean $625,000. Consequently, by dispensing with the underwriting the Government was able to give the public a price that is most attractive."[50] At the same time, bonds were not the kind of investment made by people capable of contributing only cents or a few dollars to war charities, such as those with minimal bank accounts, farmers unfamiliar with securities, or workers and clerks earning less than $500 a year. As would be evident in subsequent war loans, many Canadians did not understand what a bond was.[51] The amounts subscribed by denomination suggest preferences for the larger bonds: $100 bonds ($4,099,500), $500 ($8,699,500), $1,000 ($58,876,000), and $5,000 or multiples ($28,325,000).[52]

Although actual money from subscription instalments would take time to materialize, White was overjoyed by the windfall, which had been secured at an initial cost to the government of only $3.4 million, including the $2.5 million expense of discounting the bond price by 2.5 percent. To illustrate the low promotional scale, printing costs ($40,107.88) for the prospectuses, scrip certificates, and bonds exceeded advertising expenses ($36,023.16).[53] Less enthused were the brokers. Although pleased to sell bonds at a time when unrestricted share trading was still prohibited, they had a tough task competing with the network of bank branches, which processed applications, bond distribution, and coupon cashing. The banks pulled in more than three times the commissions earned by the securities community. Some banks reportedly laid claim to the application forms issued by bond dealers, with the finance department refusing to intrude or even to direct a splitting of commissions. Despite such concerns, bonds quickly entered the market and government thinking. The 1915 loan put in place a durable keystone of Canadian war finance. The government borrowed from the banks on treasury bills, Clifford Austin Curtis would explain after the war, in expectation of "floating long-term loans, and, indeed, the banks' holdings of government securities move in close relationship with the government's issue of war loans, showing plainly that a large proportion of each war loan was used to liquidate debts already incurred. Thus, the government's system of financing may be summarized as being a method of issuing short-term bills and then making refunding loans."[54]

For White, even while dealing with the conundrums of railway finance and military spending, the challenge after the war loan was how to use the $50 million oversubscription. In an interview on 30 December, he declared the Dominion's finances to be satisfactory, with enough money until the coming summer. (Imparting calm and confidence was part of his job.) Sidestepping the question of funding beyond that point, he said that the question of more borrowing would be examined in the spring. Despite the success of the November loan, he was unsure that it could be repeated.[55] In the meantime, he urged Canadians to "work harder, save more." Other Cabinet ministers echoed this call, among them George Foster, who, more forthrightly than White, spoke at year's end of the need for more domestic war loans.

White did know where the extra $50 million had to go: imperial credits. Canada's position on Atlantic shipping routes and adjacency to the United States facilitated Britain's purchases of wheat and munitions, a process that had started early in 1915, but the related financial relationship was far from smooth. Imperial purchases of munitions in Canada, a scandal-racked system, had reached crisis levels that fall. Imperial funds were channelled to Canada's Shell Committee, formed in September 1914, from the British War Office through the Department of Finance, which sent the payments to the militia department. By 15 February 1916, £27 million had thus been advanced to Canada, a course with accounts "full of anomalies."[56] In late November 1915, the committee was replaced by the Imperial Munitions Board (IMB), the Canadian arm of the British Ministry of Munitions. Based in Ottawa and chaired by Joseph Wesley Flavelle, who White knew well, the IMB would be responsible for purchasing in Canada.

The funding process faced scrutiny. From the British perspective, cost containment was a priority. Banker, astute treasury advisor, and soon to be the IMB's representative in London, Robert Henry Brand, already saw ways to address exchange problems and to relieve Britain's load. While he and William Lionel Hichens, an industrialist authorized by the British government, were in Canada setting up the IMB, they "formed the opinion" that to cover its expenditures Canada should advance "credits for war purchases," a plan that Brand urged on the government and in speeches to Canadian Clubs in Toronto and Ottawa in December. Credits were needed for the "long struggle," he claimed. But a one-time use of $50 million would last Britain "just 48 hours" and all subscriptions to the loan "just 110 hours."[57]

The form of imperial credits quickly took shape. Following the conclusion of the war loan on 30 November, White had pivoted to its use, exactly as the critical state of munition funding came to a head. That day, White's department issued a release indicating that the excess would be advanced to Britain. On 2 December, he met with a committee of the Canadian Bankers' Association to discuss establishing credits. Two days later, he offered to lend the British $40 to $50 million in instalments, Canada's first credit to the imperial government,[58] an advance that underlined when and how future loan campaigns would be conducted. On 16 December, in a preparative address to the Toronto Board of Trade on financing war orders, White broached the idea of a "co-operative plan" whereby Canadian firms that made munitions or supplied matériel to Britain or France would accept British exchequer bonds in "part payment," due after the war, a means that would bypass unfavourable exchange rates.[59] As details were thrashed out over the coming months,[60] White, who disclaimed long-term financial responsibility, would repeatedly deny that he was under any constitutional obligation to furnish funding, arguing that such funds, provided on moral grounds of imperial solidarity, would be best arranged on a basis of clear understandings of Canada's capabilities.

The loan to Britain was viewed in Britain as a complete reversal. "Thus after having figured year after year as our constant and heavy debtor, Canada has suddenly transformed herself into a creditor of Great Britain," the *London*

Economist observed on 18 December. "That perhaps is the most surprising economic *volte face* caused by the war."[61] Parallel to munition funding and the creation of "reciprocal accounts" was the first imperial advance to Canada in the fall of a £30 million loan for paying and maintaining Canada's overseas forces, to be doled out at the rate of up to £2.5 million a month.

1916

The funding from Canada's loan was spread over December 1915 to February 1916. By March, Canadian advances had absorbed almost all the available loan funds, just as Brand and Britain's chancellor continued to push the Dominion. White then closed the door to Flavelle on further funding, with the recommendation that he approach the banks, an arrangement that White facilitated. As a result, a renewable loan would fund production from April through June. The first direct munition loan by Canada's banks provided $50 million under an agreement of 31 March 1916 between White as minister of finance and the Canadian Bankers' Association, representing twenty-one banks; another $26 million was divided between 1 May and 1 June. Essentially, the finance department advanced millions in treasury bill certificates to the banks to fund production on the strength of short-term British treasury bills held at the Bank of England to the order of the minister of finance.[62] Such was one reality of transatlantic war finance.

The arrangements for these munition loans were difficult for White, too, because of pressure from the banks to sustain their liquidity before a second domestic loan. A key piece of reciprocal funding had fallen into place in June, when Britain offered to advance $150 million for the use of Canada's army in Europe followed by White's support for a munitions credit.[63] A second munition loan from the banks was made on 30 June, with $12 million paid out on 1 July and the same amount paid out on 1 August. To make the loan attractive to the banks, White was later persuaded to drop the rate of repayment on the British Treasury's bills deposited with his department from the 5 percent set in the Finance Act to three and a-half percent. The treasury's requests in August for continued funding were again refused by White, just as he was concluding arrangements to pay down Canadian indebtedness to Britain in a plan that he had put to the treasury's representatives in New York the previous fall during the Anglo-French loan talks.

A complication was the matter of exchange rates. Since Canada had raised loans in New York, and given that munition contracts in Canada often involved American subcontractors,[64] the exchange rate between the British sterling and the American dollar was strongly affected by Canadian actions. Pressed by the Allies' ongoing financial demands, the British Treasury, at the peak of the crisis, called on Canada to assume the entire cost of the Imperial Munitions Board's production. It launched a campaign through Brand to bring White to Britain so that he might gain a fuller understanding of the treasury's financial problems, sort out the IMB's needs, and discuss the triangular arrangements involving the use of Canadian securities in purchases from the United States.[65] White was loath to go. Running through the campaign were efforts by Brand and Flavelle to accommodate a sensitive minister's notions of personal control, Canadian priority, and need for consultation while, in Brand's case, explaining to treasury officials Canada's positions and separating them from American needs in the context of inter-Allied finance. From the time the IMB had been formed, Flavelle and Brand had both monitored federal finances and the capabilities of Canada's banks.

Munition funding was just one of the substantial challenges facing Canada in 1916. Reluctant to call the election due that year, Borden had the imperial government extend the life of Canada's Parliament to 1917. In Europe, the Battles of St. Éloi Craters in April and of Mount Sorrel in June, along with the failed offensive on the Somme from July through November, would consume vast tonnages of shells, necessitating another major munition drive, for which there was inadequate capacity in Britain. At home, the Somme rendered more floods of casualty lists, in turn generating ingenious appeals for new enlistment. On 31 December, Borden announced an expansion of Canada's military forces to half a million. There would be financial consequences.

At the beginning of 1916, the newly knighted Sir Thomas White grappled with a host of internal problems: his conflict with Samuel Hughes over spending and the militia minister's growing distance from the government over substandard equipment and procurement;[66] railways at the brink of failure; and the demands on the Department of Finance, which had to add staff mainly to process the September war loan. Despite the formation of the IMB in November, much criticism of war profiteering landed on White's doorstep.[67] In the Commons, which resumed sitting on 12 January, the Opposition also began pressing him for an accounting of Canada's share in paying the Canadian Expeditionary Force overseas. Canada bore the cost (paid through Britain), but since Britain and Canada (which paid for Britain's munitions and foodstuffs) worked through a system of reciprocal credits, many costs and adjustments could not be determined. The costing of supplies was a distant matter handled in Britain by the War Office and Canada's high commissioner (and later by Canada's Ministry of Overseas Military Forces). Moreover, the IMB, even with a new system of accounting, was a British body, beyond scrutiny in Canada. White disclaimed any responsibility for its expenditures.[68] Complicating the situation was the ineffectiveness of Parliament's public accounts committee and the overworked office of Auditor General John Fraser. In support of White's claim on Canada's cost load, Borden would state in May that all expenditures had been authorized by orders-in-council, a position undermined by Fraser's critical testimony on unauthorized sales of munitions and White's seeming disregard.

Financial strain showed. White's erratic behaviour in Cabinet, including, Borden observed in February 1916, his "mania for talking,"[69] did not deter his focus on his next war budget, his third. In the lead-up, praise and cover for White were provided in the Commons by Borden, his bulldoggish solicitor general, Arthur Meighen, and others. In the prior estimates, the government had included funding for military pensions, certain to be a factor in long-term financial calculations. As usual, White first floated his budgetary proposals in Cabinet; on 12 February, Borden noted, "White's budget quite radical in its retrospective taxation of war profits. He expected Council to balk but on the contrary they urged him to go farther."[70] In the budget, presented on 15 February, White reminded the House that the previous year, the second War Appropriation Act had been for $100 million. Now, another was needed in order to authorize $250 million. With imperial funding shut down, financing would have to be found in Canada. Future prosperity, he rationalized, would allow Canada to place the costs of the war – debt accrued from interest payments on bonds and domestic loans – in the hands of posterity "as a legacy and reminder of the waste of war." The economic argument here, which was questioned in the press in 1915 by experts such as Brand, would be further challenged at home by finance critic Alexander Kenneth Maclean and by Oscar Douglas Skelton in 1918.[71] His 1915 article on federal finance had already brought the decades-old debate over income taxation into a wartime context.

On matters of war taxation, the government "followed, rather than led," historian Shirley Tillotson observes.[72] In a disputation that went back at least to Liberal arguments in the 1870s, White expressed his belief that "heavy individual taxation" would discourage immigration and penalize success. But in the government's first, cautious foray into the field of direct taxation – a partly politically inspired innovation that reflected the war-profits tax introduced in Britain in September 1915 and that could not have been contemplated in the slow economy of 1914–15 – business profits would be taxed retroactively. The tax would go on to produce 80 percent of direct-tax revenue during the war. The *Globe* thought the move "revolutionary."[73] Designed more to meet criticism and to show the government's displeasure with profiteering and less to generate revenue, the tax was to be calculated by a new bureaucracy from self-assessments submitted by businesses. Business contributions did not end with this tax. "To provide a market for the securities of Canada issued in consequence of the war," insurance companies would be obligated to maintain fixed levels of investment in Canadian securities, which could include war bonds and debenture stock. In debate over the Life Insurance Companies Investment Act, White countered Liberal revulsion over such "compulsion" with the easy retort of wartime necessity. In addition, to facilitate saving and investment by the public between war loans, short-term debenture stock would be authorized in sums of $100 at 5 percent for "war purposes." The issue would be strategically launched in early October as part of the finance department's program of small investment.

Wrangling over the budget lasted into April 1916. At one point, White floated the view that in wartime "the minister finds himself in the position of simply doing the best he can." In a fierce defence of spending, he extolled the merits of domestic war loans, an option that he had left open in the budget. Maclean agreed with domestic borrowing, but calling a spade a spade, he concluded that the 1915 loan, "while widely subscribed, was not in the real sense a popular loan," a view that had many adherents.[74] White's input ranged from the intricacies of taxation, to his expansive thoughts on policy, to market-shaped views of the domestic and New York loans, to the necessity for public debt. Bank holdings of war bonds, he noted with satisfaction on 16 March, had been reduced "because there has been a good demand for the loan, and it has gradually been absorbed."[75] That month, the Canadian Bankers' Association had agreed to remove the minimum price on the sale of bonds. In Parliament, White, who was also the government's House leader, ignored opposition calls for financial reorganization, including a "national bank of re-discount"[76] (an incipient central bank). According to finance journalist and White admirer Wellington John Jeffers, the minister long believed his department functioned as a "central bank" during the war.[77] Nor does he appear to have been swayed by the arguments and alternatives voiced in business circles on the profits tax.

Sticking to known avenues, including borrowing, White articulated a policy on war finance based on three guiding principles:[78] borrow well in advance, even at high interest; avoid short-date loans wherever possible; and curb expenditures. In March 1916, he claimed in the Commons that he had never believed in a short war, although one, two, or three more years would be catastrophic, culturally and economically. In practical terms, he stated in his February budget that "the Government is financed until the beginning of next summer."[79] In short, he was thinking ahead four months, with an eye on future maturities and debt payments and conforming, as he later explained, to the maxim "that nations pay for wars as they go along."[80] With the budget tabled, the government passed statutes authorizing its main financial measures: the Public Service Loan Act (the New York loan), the War Appropriation Act, and the Business Profits War Tax Act. Subsequent orders-in-council authorized specific funding. In March, part of the $75 million loan, to be negotiated in New York through the Bank of Montreal, was to cover one-year government notes coming due on 1 August. In July and August, temporary loans were made from the banks. A £22.3 million imperial advance was secured in August for conversion into a bond issue in dollars for use as collateral on the imperial account in New York.[81] September would see another Dominion War Loan, this one for $100 million, to be followed the next month by dominion stock of $50 million and in December by a $50 million loan through the discount of treasury bills. In addition, there were more imperial advances for munitions, aircraft, ships, and rails, as well as for the recurring conversion of loans. Throughout 1916, the New York money market was being heavily tapped by Britain and France, with Canada in the mix both as an issuer of bonds to the British Treasury (against Canada's indebtedness), which were sent to New York, and as a holder of gold reserves on which a portion of Allied purchases were predicated.[82]

By the spring of 1916, with the munition funding crisis building and uncertain that the success of the first domestic war loan could be duplicated, White had accepted the necessity for more New York money. The one-year notes from the 1915 loan there had to be refunded. Publicly, he called it "one of the most useful loans that had ever been placed by the Government of Canada,"[83] an estimate, he felt, that situated Canada well for the New York loan of March 1916. It was quickly taken up, although he had to agree to take no more New York issues until after 31 March 1917. Critics felt that White had priced part of the issue too low, a misstep that he attributed to the fickleness of the New York market. Normally, he paid close attention to pricing and interest calculation, although Flavelle, a vigilant analyst, saw risk in the minister's focus on just getting the money. He suspected that White sometimes, "while desirous of being of service to us, wants to preserve the strength of the banks for his own loan." Moreover, he told Brand, "His policy is to keep liquid, electing to take money when he can secure it, and treating as inconsequential the interest he will have to pay on unused balance."[84]

Administratively, both the war-profits tax and the domestic loan had repercussions for the Department of Finance, where the needed staffing continued to grow. Business profits required time-consuming ascertainments of capital and earnings, as well as assessments. By early May 1916, to begin determining profits and working from commercial agency publications, it had begun listing firms likely to be assessed. Tax officers fanned out across Canada. The retroactive feature – any accounting period ending after 31 December 1914 – meant additional work. The tax generated mixed reaction in the financial press, but the majority of businesses were supportive. Conversely, the financial contribution of this and other direct taxes would meet only a small portion of

Canada's war expenditures. By 31 March 1917, war-tax revenue had increased sevenfold over the course of a year to $14,242,654.33. (Not until 1920 would the public accounts begin to break down the sources of such revenue.)

Major components in this structure were the crisis over railway finance and ownership and the unrelenting need to sequentially fund munition production. To address the railways issue, in July the government appointed a royal commission that included Sir Henry Lumley Drayton of the federal Board of Railway Commissioners.[85] For munitions, imperial advances to Canada required ongoing, behind-the-scenes adjustments of accounts and conversions, partly to redirect funding to Britain's account in New York. On 1 September, Canada converted £22,324,295 11s. of its debt into two Canadian bond issues of three and a-half percent and four and a-half percent, together worth $107,612,029.53. These arrangements, which would also fund Canada's indebtedness created by imperial advances reaching back into 1915, were detailed in an order-in-council of 28 August 1916:

> In view of the necessity in which the Imperial Government finds itself of obtaining dollar securities as collateral for bankers' loans in the United States of America, the Minister of Finance has effected an arrangement under which the above temporary indebtedness will be funded and the Canadian Government give to the Imperial Government bonds of the Dominion of Canada bearing the same rates of interest and having the same maturities as the three and a-half percent and four and a-half percent war loans against which the advances are earmarked.[86]

The bonds in turn were sent to Britain's agents in New York. After July, focus had shifted to the next domestic loan.

In Toronto, the *Globe* was not alone in its claim in August that "there are few in Canada who do not yearn for some opportunity of helping to smash the enemy."[87] Editorials, social columns, analyses of bank deposits ready, and advertisements by security firms all anticipated the loan's announcement. Sir Frederick Williams-Taylor had urged White to go the domestic route. The pushy president of a major insurance company, Thomas Bassett Macaulay of Sun Life, pressed the minister for a discount on the issue price that White expected, claiming that only "intense patriotism" would compel his company to pass up more profitable mortgage lending. White resisted such requests.[88] In July and August, to shape the loan and its market, he had first contemplated a special income tax on all non-Canadian securities held by Canadians. Apart from probing the viability of an income tax, the measure, which would never materialize, was meant to benefit the exchange situation, force the liquidation of foreign securities, and "preserve the Canadian market for purely Canadian securities."[89] White urged investors to forgo foreign securities, including Anglo-French bonds and the upcoming British War Loan, in order to save for the dominion loan, which was finally announced on 9 September.

To ensure its success, White had called on the banks to commit in advance. On 5 September, the executive of the Canadian Bankers' Association obliged, agreeing to $50 million, "if required," as White would explain in the Commons.[90] However, underwriting would prove to be unnecessary. (Actual subscriptions from the banks, twenty-three in all, would be $52,025,600 before allotment.)[91] The details of the loan, what the *Globe* called "Canada's financial mobilization" and Borden dubbed "White's loan," were made public on 9 September. By then, he was wed to deficit financing and borrowing from the public as the primary thrusts of the government's revenue structure. Bolstered by the eager involvement of the newly formed Bond Dealers' Association of Canada (BDAC), whose interests included direct negotiation with White on advertising, marketing, and commissions,[92] the campaign to raise $100 million ran from 12–23 September. From the perspective of the British Ministry of Munitions, the loan was crucial. (By November, 40 percent of Britain's war expenditure was being spent on supplies from North America.) From the loan, White "offered to assume part of the burden on munition expenditure by an advance of $50,000,000 to be paid in equal instalments in November and December."[93] On 27 September, following more talks with the bankers, White cabled the British chancellor of the Exchequer informing him of the advance.

The issue was for $100 million, with an allotment limited to that amount. Bonds would be sold in denominations of $100, $500, $1,000, and $5,000. The issue price of 97 and a half (meaning 97 and a half cents on the dollar) and rate of 5 percent (with an expected yield of 5.30) were the same as 1915, as was the tax exemption, but some terms changed. Instead of a ten-year maturity, the bonds would be for fifteen years, an attractive feature for long-term investors. Unlike the 1915 bonds, which were payable in silver, principal and interest would be payable in gold coin, a new attraction also meant to shield investors from any devaluation of currency. However, whereas the 1915 loan payment could be paid over six instalments, the option in 1916 was tightened to four, the last being due on 15 December 1916. Fearful of any interference "with possible operations later on"[94] and keenly attuned to the bond market, White declined to include any conversion privilege in the issue (an option that would be allowed in the issues of March 1917, 1918, and 1919).

Once again, Canadians, mostly institutions, responded: 34,526 subscribers (10,000 more than 1915) subscribed a surprising $201,444,800, of which the government, with a preference for those in the lower ranges, allotted $106,706,200,

Dominion War Bond with interest coupons attached, 1916. This bond features vignettes of the Governor General the Duke of Connaught and his wife. | Bank of Canada Museum, NCC 2002.072.004.

at a cost of $3,539,410, including an increase in advertising costs and, noticeably, a doubling in the commissions paid to banks and brokers. The price of the issue and the longer term had been attractive – too attractive, White later reflected.[95] Unlike in 1915, the loan was scrutinized by the financial press and local newspapers eager to publicize regional response. In 1916, as in 1915, the most popular bond denomination by far was the $1,000 bond, not the smaller ones aimed at the small investor. (Today, the $1,000 bond would cost $20,920.)[96] With allotment completed, active trading began. The *Financial Post* had already concluded that it would take time for it to be absorbed, with millions being bought for resale and dealers taking large blocks to meet anticipated demand.[97] As well, financial institutions began melding bonds into their portfolios of assets and operations,[98] with the Manufacturers Life Insurance, for one, advertising its readiness to accept bond interest as payment on insurance policies and banks offering loans to purchase bonds. White would later explain his department's rationale on the loans of 1916 and 1917: "In each case we took only the amount asked for ... This policy kept the market firm and enabled us to obtain better prices for succeeding issues than would have been possible had we accepted all subscriptions and left no residue of buying power on the market."[99]

Throughout the campaign of 1916, which consumed just part of White's time, his attentions bounced between the threat of railway bankruptcy, tensions within Cabinet, and the formation of the Ministry of Overseas Military Forces, which would lead to new financial arrangements abroad. During and after the campaign, White's department expanded yet again to handle the loan. In October, before leaving on a trip to England, he hosted a meeting on the formation of a special committee of bankers for the systematic promotion of savings and a meeting of the National Service Board of Canada to broadly promote agricultural and industrial production, savings and thrift, and recruitment. Intended to support this thrust were the introduction of war-savings certificates (a new class of government security) and the sale of the debenture stock announced in the February budget. On 24 October, prior to embarking and without a hint of the tortuous path of munition funding, White's address to the Halifax Board of Trade firmly tied this funding to public engagement through the thrift program: "If we can give them the money we can get all the orders we want and more, but we must save."[100]

White had a busy time in England: a visit to the Royal Navy's Grand Fleet, his investiture at Buckingham Palace, a meeting with the newly formed Canadian Army Council, and an interview by the *Times* on Canadian finance and the Imperial Munitions Board. He was accompanied by Flavelle and Lord Thomas George Shaughnessy of the Canadian Pacific Railway, whose securities and advances were part of the schemes that made up White's big picture. At a luncheon in his honour at the House of Commons, Chancellor Reginald McKenna (who feared Britain's financial collapse) heaped praise on his handling of reciprocal finance.[101] Among other conferences, he attended a meeting with High Commissioner Perley, who learned of White's plan to launch an adjunct "savings Campaign" to raise money.

In a letter to Flavelle in November, White saw only two viable methods of public finance: the "dangerous" route of overdependence on the banks, which were accustomed to issuing short-term securities, or what he now saw as the "sound method" of citizen investment, as he had explained in Halifax and seen in two domestic loans.[102] During a side trip to France, he got the vague impression from General Sir Douglas Haig that "all is well on the western front." Less conspicuous than White during the visit to England was Canada's auditor general, the aging John Fraser, who, probably with White's involvement, aimed to address the tangled state of accounting that surrounded Canada's share of the cost to supply its troops. Supply and pay were beyond White's purview, except where they occurred in calculating offsets and balances in dominion-imperial advances. Negotiations, and the sheer difficulty of ascertaining true costs, led to an agreement that fall to lower the troop per diem from 9s. 4d. to 6s., which would be announced in Canada the following February.[103]

On the return trip to New York in December, White regaled Flavelle with his changing views on finance and the Imperial Munitions Board. Although he had been held back from the front lines in France, his visit would lend gravitas to his subsequent speeches on finance. Back in Canada, where Cabinet turmoil had included Borden's sacking of Hughes, White faced talk about the formation of a national "coalition" government and rumours of him becoming prime minister should Borden resign.[104] At the same time, few were as staunch in their support of the government or publicized Canada's financial needs in such relatable terms as White. At his meeting with bankers on 11 December, it was understood that another domestic loan would be needed in 1917. Four days later, the Canadian Bankers' Association, on behalf of twenty banks, agreed to provide munition funds of $50 million over the months of January, February, and March – the banks' third munition loan. In exchange for dominion notes, they accepted as security "tailor-made" one-year treasury bills payable in gold. They could not be sold, but if pledged elsewhere, they first had to be offered to the department.[105] In fiscal 1916–17, the government would utilize treasury bills totalling more than $130 million.

Following his return, White, in addition to mounting the thrift campaign, resumed discussions with a vital new ally, the Bond Dealers' Association of Canada. Jumping at his suggestion that it form a consultative committee on financial matters, the association boldly proposed on 19 December that it should handle the next war loan on an underwriting basis. On 4 January, it laid out features to be put to White: a loan of $150 million, a doubling of the commission rate to half of 1 percent, one quarter of 1 percent for American brokers but only on applications through Canadian brokers, and confirmation of "recognized brokers." Although White was pleased with the December accords, his correspondence from the last weeks of December and into January is tense: mediating between the banks and imperial officials, defending Canada's financial position, and explaining the intervals of three to four months between funding drives. On 28 December, Borden, back from a tour of western Canada, found his changeable minister in "good form."

At a crowded assembly sponsored by the Toronto Board of Trade at Massey Hall on 18 December, White, whose repute in Ontario now bordered on celebrity, had again made the case for Canada to bear its own burden. The audience was receptive, but Flavelle found his call for public saving wanting. The minister, he wrote, had missed the chance to tell people how they could "share in war service at home ... White is one of the able men who wants to do all the work himself." There was some truth there, but Flavelle concluded that "White seems to centre finally about the right place, but in the process of getting to that point he is a sore tax upon those who have to live with him."[106] Although White was preparing to spend more money than ever in 1917, he remained resistant to the swell of advice on how to make domestic loans into popular loans. His speechifying and incremental steps nonetheless were serving to nudge Canadians toward closer engagement. In the international context, Allied borrowing in the United States was being constrained by America's Federal Reserve Board, a tremor that, in Canada, intensified recognition of the need for more internal borrowing.[107]

The movements for thrift, savings, and greater production had taken hold on the home front early in the war. Governments at various levels began promoting food production to boost output amidst calls for thrift and the integration of Canadians into the war effort,[108] but these campaigns met with indistinct results. As early as December 1914, White had been hammering in the message of greater production. In January 1915, the Department of Agriculture launched a series of lectures, newspaper advertisements, and publications to push that goal. Its booklet *Patriotism and Production "More Than Usual": Agricultural War Book* contained an article by White on thrift as a duty.[109] However, belief in its salvationist value was not shared by all. In 1916, Henry Taylor Ross, an assistant deputy minister in White's department, found thrift campaigns of minimal practical use; brassier methods were needed.[110] Through 1915 and into 1916, agriculturists and rural Liberal politicians derided generalized lectures on improved farming, citing a range of impediments. Still, some rural regions did see greater production, and some households responded to the thrift gospel. Parallel paths of promotion and reservation will be detected in the public's response to finance.

Within the Department of Finance, White faced a flow of letters and editorials calling for small investment, something less than a $100 bond. Additional pressure came from public awareness of Britain's war loan of June 1915. In Canada, the first appeal was made to private saving. In March 1916, the Department of Agriculture issued another "war" booklet, *Production and Thrift: Agricultural War Book*, which, with quotations from White and through other means, linked production, thrift, and national finance. The following month, the Departments of Finance and Agriculture began a joint advertising venture in the newspapers for thrift and production. "Your savings will help Canada to finance the war," read one ad.[111] In October, White, connecting the dots, announced his own committee of bankers to formulate plans for a dominion-wide campaign that would urge savings and thrift as well as to promote the war-savings certificates, designed to attract "those of slender means." (A £1 certificate selling for 15s. 6d. had already been introduced in Britain in June.)[112]

On 7 October, the finance department had begun the sale of debenture stock, not in units of $100 but $500, prohibitive for many. The three-year 5 percent stock could be converted into any future war-loan issue and was designed as a middle-range investment, a complement to the unreleased war-savings certificates. The debenture stock was in part meant, reasoned the *Journal of the Canadian Bankers' Association* (Toronto), to prevent war bonds from rising above a price of par (100).[113] According to one optimistic departmental release, September's war loan, the debenture stock, and the certificates "should bring to the Treasury a steady supply of funds sufficient to meet all war demands without recourse to any future loans outside."[114] The following month, arrangements were completed with the Canadian Bankers' Association for banks and post-office savings branches to create war-savings accounts for deposits made toward the purchase of certificates.

Whatever reservations White may have had, it was publicly acknowledged at the end of 1916 that sustaining reciprocal funding required ever-greater public mobilization. In his grandiloquent speech at Massey Hall in December, White conveyed the sobering conclusion of Sir William Robertson, chief of the Imperial General Staff, that the war was not half over.

3

Crises and Victories, 1917–18

White would describe 1917 as "probably the most trying period of the war."[1] The national issues of conscription, the formation of a coalition government, and a bitterly divisive election loomed large. On the Western Front, momentum swung, even as the Canadian Corps's famed capture of Vimy Ridge in April spurred a wave of nationalistic enthusiasm. Germany's campaign of unrestricted submarine warfare, to starve the Entente of supplies, was devastating, with shipping losses peaking in April. The United States entered the war that month, with no ready army. As part of the Imperial War Cabinet that met from March in London, Borden faced the stark need for more men. At home, he had to deal with hard-pressed ministers and other officials wanting to retire. In the session of Parliament that sat from 18 January to 20 September, the Liberals relentlessly attacked government spending, which was contaminated, they claimed, by profiteering and graft. Various war-savings and taxation methods, including a single tax on land values (a means that would be dismissed by the finance department in 1918), were expounded in the press and at conventions. Persistent funding crises, including the financing of wheat and cheese purchases for Britain, challenged White, forcing him to embrace amplified means. At the beginning of 1918, he left Ottawa for three months of rest in California.

In the early months of 1917, spurred by news of Britain's much-promoted war loan in January (its so-called Victory Loan), White was hounded by proposals for greater war-savings initiatives. Campaigns in Montreal and Toronto, going back to the fall of 1916, for the donations of "One Day's Pay" by workers helped to set the tone. In March, Joseph Wesley Flavelle lamented White's refusal to let local committees "go among the workpeople" in order to drum up support through wage-deduction plans for his domestic loan that month.[2] In September, in advance of another loan, Flavelle was baffled by White's "disinclination to have a thorough-going war savings organization constantly at work. He has been so persistent ... that I know it must arise from some fairly well considered opinion."[3] White did have his reasons. In February, in the midst of a "quietly" conducted campaign to sell war-savings certificates, he explained his disinclination to use the One Day's Pay campaigns as a model for selling them. "I am considering a large domestic loan and I do not consider it advisable that interest in this should be diverted by any special financial campaign ... I am not in favour of these spectacular and sensational campaigns. They are effectual for a day or a week but afterwards interest is likely to subside."[4] For the minister of finance, the job was to manage the confluence of market factors and domestic buy-in. Within months, his position on "spectacular" campaigns would pivot.

In January, as part of a national thrift campaign, White had launched the sale of the three-year war-savings certificates at banks and money-order post offices for $21.50, $43, and $86, redeemable in three years for $25, $50, and $100. Government advertising, through small newspaper ads, postal cancellations, leaflets, and posters, demonstrated modest promotion. Approved by an order-in-council of 26 July 1917, a three-year $10 certificate selling for $8.60 would be introduced on 22 August to reach even smaller investors. By the spring of 1917, the National Service Board's advertising was pushing food conservation and thrift as steps to saving for investment in war-savings certificates. The response of the banking and securities communities was tepid: the issue would raise only small amounts unless it came with substantial promotion. Moreover, not all investors of minimal means were likely to commit to no returns for three years. As the *Financial Post* reasoned,

> It is doubtful whether the laboring class which has not the bond buying habit will be a large buyer of these certificates and certainly not unless the certificates are well advertised and backed up by the efforts of the bond dealers who by the way would make little or no profit on sales of small denominations to persons whom it would be hard to find and to whom it would be hard to sell. The new issue is by implication an admission that it is the well-to-do class that is going to benefit from the system of financing the war by war loans.[5]

But there were sales, as high as a thousand a day, some reports claimed. By 31 March 1917, 79,509 certificates had been sold, producing $5,072,237 at a cost of $43,723.58, and debenture stock brought in $8,634,500 at a cost of $66,097.02.[6] The monetary contribution was small, but the potential for continuous investment, moral suasion, and advertising was becoming clear.

The certificates and related messages of thrift had political value, both as humble anti-inflationary devices (theoretically as people cut consumption to buy bonds, stamps, and certificates)[7] and as a way to offset charges that it was the elites who were receiving interest on tax-free bonds. White would address the utility in the Commons on 1 February, explaining that with certificates "we do not expect to obtain very large sums in terms of Dominion finance; they are large sums but not relatively to our requirements, but it is of the greatest importance that the individual citizen should save his money by investing in these certificates."[8] A case in point was the letter written to the "Playtime" column of the *Globe* in August 1917 by eleven-year-old Lillian Plewman of Port Credit in Mississauga, Ontario: "The money I made from strawberries I am going to put with what I have in the bank and buy a war loan [savings certificate]. This will cost $21.50."[9]

Conservation and other measures of thrift went hand in glove with war savings, all promoted by overlapping programs to manage public opinion. Moral suasion was inherent, too, in the government's initiation of extraordinary regulatory controls over the economy. In 1916, the Imperial Munitions Board (IMB) had already begun to set up a "national factory" system for munitions, and a food controller, William John Hanna, was appointed in June of that year to deal with severe shortages, followed in July by a fuel controller, Charles Alexander Magrath. Facing spiralling war costs, and with its traditional revenue sources maximized, the Department of Finance focused on the fall loan with desperate expectation and ingenuity. Canada's jubilee celebration of Confederation offered the public some relief from war news, but for the finance department the event was of little consequence. In May 1917, White had offered to consider special designs for dollar bills, but they never materialized. In March, a new $1 bill had already been issued featuring a number of patriotic symbols, including a picture of the hugely popular Princess Patricia, a daughter of former governor general the Duke of Connaught.

Funding the production of munitions would require extraordinary effort, particularly over the summer of 1917, to the point of financial breakdown. Within a month of America's declaration of war in April, Britain's foreign secretary went to the United States to secure new loans and increased material aid,[10] an approach that would engage Canada. The Dominion's industrial contribution, notably in munitions and ships, was peaking: its factories would provide between a quarter and a third of all the ammunition used in France by British guns.[11] In dealings with the British Treasury and IMB representative Robert Henry Brand, White was pressed and cajoled, his grasp of the broad financial picture questioned, his skills in Allied finance challenged.[12] Ottawa's gossip mill picked at his working relationship with Flavelle.

By the time of Borden's return to Canada in May 1917, after attending meetings of the Imperial War Conference and the Imperial War Cabinet, he had a sombre sense of the crisis facing the Allies, including Britain's dire need for munitions and food, and a determination to elevate Canada's contribution to a total war footing. Within days, he introduced two radical responses. On 18 May, faced with a dramatic fall in voluntary enlistment, he jolted the Commons by announcing compulsory military enlistment (conscription). To implement it and forestall opposition in Quebec, on 25 May he proposed to Sir Wilfrid Laurier the formation of a union government, a move that White initially opposed. The passage that summer of the Military Service Act and two franchise bills further charged the political climate, which in turn would influence the Victory Loan campaign. One of these bills, the War-Time Elections Act, extended the vote to army nurses and female relatives of servicemen overseas. Widely supported, it disenfranchised citizens born in enemy countries and naturalized after March 1902, legitimizing the widespread hostilities toward foreign "aliens" that would permeate the forthcoming loan campaign. Increases to soldiers' pensions, which were in the supplementary estimates tabled in September, would be approved by an order-in-council and announced by White on 22 October, adding to the government's financial load. On 20 September, Parliament was prorogued. The new Unionist Party, officially introduced on 12 October, was an amalgam of Conservatives, Liberals, and some western farm leaders; the election held on 17 December, won by the Unionists, was the most virulent in Canadian history.[13] The imposition of conscription was fiercely opposed in French Canada. Implicit in Borden's determination was success in funding and in stimulating public acquiescence and participation on the home front.

In many areas of finance, as in past years, 1917 would see the rollover of obligations and maturations and new financing, including the banks' provision of short-term loans. In the first three months, the banks advanced $50 million: $18,925,000 in January, $17,805,000 in February, and $13,270,000 in March, each segment due in twelve months. That summer, they took up short-term Canadian and British treasury bills to meet the Dominion's grain credit of $100 million to Britain. Treasury bills were highly expedient tools: between August 1916 and October 1919, there were no fewer than seventy-eight issues, most to the banks. The size of this support and the resulting expansion of credit were evident during the fiscal year 1916–17, when the banks bought Canadian treasury bills worth a total of $205,105,000. Bills or longer-term government notes, often called "Temporary Loans" in the public accounts, were used for refunding purposes, for conversions, or as cash-management tools in anticipation of war loans. Banks would use the bills' interest and principal payments to fund depositors' withdrawals for their down payments and instalments. Without such ongoing credit, the Dominion War Loans could not have happened.

On top of this support, debenture stock issued in October 1916 was still being advertised by the government in February 1917. That month, broader authorizations received assent: the War Appropriation Act for $500 million[14] and the Public Service Loan Act for $100 million to meet loans and obligations and to fund public works and ongoing government. White's handling of national finance met with the approval of two figures who mattered, Borden and Flavelle, the latter commending his domestic loans and general preference for long-term obligations. Thus finance rolled on, consolidating a key substructure for winning the war. On the troubled railway front, a government takeover, which White supported, would come as the unavoidable conclusion to years of subsidization.

While White was government leader during Borden's absence, he launched the Dominion War Loan, Canada's third. Feverishly devised by his department and announced on 14 February to facilitate funding for three or four months, the campaign for the loan of $150 million ran from 12 to 23 March. For weeks, the market had been holding back on new investments until the loan's terms were announced. There were timing factors besides the cyclical nature of war and munition funding, among them the end of seasonal grain credits and shipping, an expected cancellation that led to the contraction of dedicated loans.[15] Other factors considered by White, in the crowded New York market, were the British loan arranged there in January and the anticipated sales of Canadian municipal securities. For marketing reasons, Canada's loan preceded America's first Liberty Loan, enacted in late April. Notably, restrictions were put on the use of the loan's proceeds for imperial transactions or to support the franc or sterling, adding to the pressures facing Canada in a financial triangle. Much was done by White's department to ensure the Canadian loan's success: the minister had lined up contingent backing from the banks, which again stood to gain a bounty of business as a conduit for subscribers, while his department pushed the sale of debenture stock, which could be converted into war bonds. In addition, the loan would be payable in both Canada and New York to discourage leakage into the United States.

Whatever the patriotic framing of the loan, it was understood in pragmatic terms by the financial community. The details were carefully arranged in co-operation with the Canadian Bankers' Association. With an eye on the banks' control of domestic credit, the goal was to minimize the imbalance or relative "displacement" in bank portfolios of commercial bills by treasury bills that were paid by the government from the new loan to liquidate temporary loans from the banks (covered by four-month bills) at the start of the year. "This is new work for the Canadian banks," journalist Homer Mark Philip Eckardt explained, "as prior to the war the Dominion Government was accustomed to placing its short-date Treasury bills in London." In addition, the twenty-year term of the new issue offered "greater speculative possibilities" (with greater risk) than the ten-year bonds of the 1915 loan or the fifteen-year bonds of 1916.[16]

Despite mixed predictions of marketability, and the availability of other securities, including provincial and municipal bonds, brokers and bank branches were receptive. The Bond Dealers' Association of Canada was again highly involved.[17] The objections of two bankers, Edson Loy Pease and Sir Frederick Williams-Taylor, to the size of the loan and of J.P. Morgan and Company to payment in gold in New York as well as Canada "shook White for a day or two," Flavelle observed.[18] Enthusiasm was generated, too, by the wildly successful British Victory Loan of January and February and by the prospect of exemption from federal taxation on the Canadian one. With thoughts of mirroring the British loan, the issue informally became known as Canada's "Victory Loan." Its prospectus offered the expected terms: a price of 96, tax-exempt interest of 5 percent, instalment payments, a twenty-year term (up from fifteen years in 1916), and an expected yield of 5.4 percent. Despite a flurry of correspondence over the prior winter calling for low-denomination bonds, March's denominations were the same as 1916 – $100, $500, and $1,000 – emulating the British example. With changing market conditions, conversion privileges from past war bonds were restored.[19] Slightly lower advertising costs – $46,493.39 compared to $50,963.87 – were augmented by brokers' ads, newspaper headers, and a stream of press releases and rosy projections from the Department of Finance. One clever release on 7 March announced the distribution of 14 tons (1-and-a-half million pieces) of application forms, literature, stereotyped advertisements, and other material.[20] Newspaper headlines made the appeal simple: "Canada's War Loan Will Help General Haig to Keep Advancing."[21] Pushed by the Bond Dealers' Association and anchored by strong institutional applications, including a contingent $60 million from the banks, more than 41,263 subscribers committed to $260,768,000, up from $201,444,800 in 1916. The government cancelled the banks' underwriting and raised its allotment to $172,926,800, which included conversions of some $20 million from past loans. Expenses jumped from $3,539,410 in 1916 to $8,550,552. The banks subscribed heavily ($61 million), as did life, fire, and other insurance companies ($28 million). Flush with new business in a rising economy, life insurance firms found government securities particularly attractive.

Typical of all of Canada's war loans, which pulled in funds in a gradual flow, the loan had brought in $18,100,232.48 by 31 March 1917. And the amount would rise to $154,826,567.52 by 1918. The loan, however, was not the largest source of revenue in the consolidated fund: temporary loans from other sources – imperial government loans, New York temporary bank loans, and treasury bills – put $516,864,999.97 on the books, and customs and excise generated $171,341,074.97. White professed to be overjoyed with the results of the March loan. Another domestic loan would not be needed until the fall, he told the *Montreal Daily Mail.* What rarely surfaced were the internal bureaucratic problems that plagued all the war loans, notably in staffing and processing. The sudden resignation of the chief clerk of advertising in the office of the King's Printer, for instance, created delays in sending out and processing contracts for the loan and the production campaign.

Predictably, White's budget of 24 April gave prominence to rising military costs and the increase in the national debt.[22] War expenditure for April 1916 to January 1917 stood at $216,901,822.68, but for the fiscal year 1917–18 the government was estimating $415,171,000. The success of March's loan, he told the Commons, would enable munition funding only until June, a short period that never seemed to fully register with the public. To continue funding, he anticipated that "treasury bills will be temporarily negotiated, until the proceeds of the next public loan are available" in the fall. Since Canadians could pay only part of the principal of its war expenditure, White explained, government policy had been "directed along two main lines: first, to fund the war indebtedness so as to postpone its maturities to periods well beyond the end of the war, and secondly, by increased taxation on the one hand and the reduction of current expenditures on works on the other."[23] Reduction on public works, a perennial target, did materialize, but against that attainment were the dramatic costs in the public-railways sector. In the tariff realm, White fended off changes, leaving customs and excise revenues to rise from $158,456,190.20 for fiscal year 1916–17 to $171,341,074.97 for 1917–18. Although always defensive of profits, a position that riled many, the cautious minister proposed to extend the business-profits tax, but (until July) he remained reluctant to tax income, around which debate swirled heatedly among financial experts, politicians, economists, and advocates of the vague "conscription of wealth," a tough pill for capitalists to swallow.[24] In an editorial in June, the *Bella Coola Courier* (Bella Coola, British Columbia), an advocate of conscripting wealth, observed that the government "has followed the path of least resistance. Sir Thomas White has pinned his faith on the Customs Tariff and unlimited borrowing at high rates of interest," thus placing "upon the masses the weight of the burden." "Pressure of public opinion has forced him to make a pretence of taxing war profits, while forgoing income taxation."[25] At the same time, while the government weighed its options, the business sector kept pushing back against the business-profits tax.[26]

Despite growing support for an income tax, White continued to believe that it would produce little revenue; moreover, incomes earned through joint-stock companies were already subject to the business-profits tax. For months, he had been mulling over the costs and arguments, the work needed to expand the bureaucracy, and any infringement on provincial and municipal jurisdictions. Some provinces were already making tax assessments for the private Canadian Patriotic Fund. It was conscription, notions of equity, and expediency that tipped White's scales; the war's costs and reformist demands necessitated response. On 25 July, the day after the third reading of the Military Service Act, White brought in the Income War Tax Act, long in the wings, his fiscal counterpart to the conscription bill. The tax bill was one area where government policy aligned with the advocacy for greater taxation voiced by fiscal and social analysts, including such academic economists as Oscar Douglas Skelton and Stephen B. Leacock. As White explained, a sentiment had arisen over the conscription bill that those with substantial income should also contribute to the war's financing.[27] He had been inundated with letters and advice on taxation, all of which, he noted in the Commons, pinned the charge on the "other fellow." Income tax placed White in a no-win situation. Critics who lamented the lack of labour representation in the government chastised it for placing the tax burden of war expenditure on the masses. In 1917, the stressed minister was being pushed away from fiscal conservatism and toward more democratic taxation, a path intensified by complaints[28] that the government's fiscal policies were actually threatening the war effort, including the buildup to the thrust of the first Victory Loan.

Supposedly a temporary measure, the tax bill, which was passed on 17 August and received assent on 20 September, applied to the year ending 31 December 1917, with returns due in February 1918. Although White would later cite war costs to justify the tax, as would the press, he had long understood that at best only a few million dollars could be gathered at great expense, a small return that would be manifest only as tax revenues materialized in 1918 and 1919. Moreover, with reference to the New York loan of 1915 and the war loan of 1916, he also refused in his budget to consider taxing the income on war bonds, a deterrent to investment, in his opinion. On 2 July, the *Globe* had speculated that the prospect of income-tax legislation and exemption would spur investment in a fall loan, particularly in light of the tax-free bonds of the American Liberty Loan. In any case, from a market perspective, on 1 August the *Globe* announced that "the glut of war bonds is pretty well removed."[29]

Angry debate in the Commons over finance carried through the spring and summer. Liberal MP Edward Mortimer Macdonald believed that the grab of government securities by capitalist investors would create a "bonded aristocracy."[30] Sharper criticism came from Alexander Kenneth Maclean, whom White sometimes took seriously, partly because they agreed on such issues as the government ownership of railways. On the borrowing bill in February, Maclean had called in vain for a broad appeal to the public. At the same time, the minister was beginning to comprehend the need for support from Canadians who had been donating their small coins, their knitting, and untold hours to patriotic causes. In terms of real need, however, their monetary support was slight. The purchases of war-savings certificates starting at $50, he stated in the Commons on 29 May, "represent for the most part subscriptions by those of comparatively slender means."[31] Few MPs quibbled; debate drifted into wages, the employment of women, or the military service of munition workers. White shunned complicated explanations of exchange and munition funding. Mentions in the public accounts for fiscal 1917–18 were brief: of the $504,566,272.84 advanced to the British Treasury, the Imperial Munitions Board took $441 million. Behind this ongoing process, however, were convoluted deliberations, at no time more critical than in 1917.

The trail of munition funding is complex. The IMB had begun to negotiate in November 1916, while White was in England, for an extension of Canadian credits to meet its requirements in 1917, starting with more than $250 million of shipments from January through June. Britain expected that Canada would advance the necessary funds, a commitment that White would not accept in late 1916, much to Flavelle's exasperation. The IMB head found him overly cautious, vacillating, unwilling to curb Canadians' excessive purchasing abilities through income taxation or to tap their savings through aggressive domestic loans.[32] In December, White did secure an agreement for bank assistance; in January, Cabinet authorized him to borrow $50 million from the banks to advance to the IMB for the first quarter. The domestic loan in March allowed him to promise another $25 million for each of April and May, with the likelihood of the same amount for June. But in June, the IMB's *monthly* disbursements peaked at $52.5 million, partly to address its shipbuilding program, where White's opposition fell before the threat posed by the submarine menace.[33]

The entry of the United States into the war on 6 April 1917, weeks before White's budget, shook the course of Allied war funding, with power shifting to America. Its involvement complicated the procurement of munitions and ships, largely because of the exclusion of purchases for Canadian war production and because the United States halted Canadian borrowing and British borrowing in New York to discharge Canadian obligations.[34] With White holding firm at $25 million a month for the IMB, and its demands on the British Treasury mounting, the situation forced him to confer over new cessation of options, including the use of Canadian corporate securities in the mix of British-American funding (possibly the use of railway sterling securities for use by the Canadian Pacific Railway as collateral with which to borrow in New York).[35] The United States' ingress also led to its own $2 billion war loan (soon to be called the Liberty Loan).[36] In a campaign begun in May, it offered bonds to the public at three and a-half percent in denominations as low as $50. The American Treasury's secretary, William Gibbs McAdoo, took pains to publicize the loan as "a popular one" and to ensure that it was oversubscribed in order to bolster confidence. White watched these developments closely, aware that a Canadian loan had to come after the Liberty Loan's surge and after the second Liberty Loan of early October.

That summer, the IMB faced the bleak possibility of cessation of munition funding as the British Treasury ran short of Canadian dollars.[37] This likelihood played out against the turbulence created by conscription, taxation, and re-election, a loan of $7.5 million to the Grand Trunk Pacific, and White's closure of a stormy debate on the bill to take over the Canadian Northern.[38] The grounds there had been set by the report tabled on 2 May by the railway inquiry appointed the previous year.[39] By then, the British Treasury had begun pressing the government to take on more of the financial burden of munition purchases. Even with a $75 million loan from the banks, Brand and others at the Ministry of Munitions, notably its minister, Winston Churchill, found Canadian funding utterly inadequate. Last-ditch dispatches from Britain in July and August affirmed Britain's inability to buy cheese, hay, oats, and flour unless Canada provided further credits. Over the summer, a hard-pressed White shuttled between Ottawa, Washington, and New York, representing Canada's contribution to Allied purchasing and negotiating with American and British officials new arrangements for the funding of munitions and cheese.[40] Failing to secure enough bank funding in Canada, and after securing an exemption from the American embargo, he lined up a $100 million loan from Morgan's in a deal that had been projected as early as February. White had delayed the issue of dominion notes, hoping instead to use the proceeds from a New York loan and other monies,[41] but in order to create a reserve of currency, an issue of $50 million worth of notes was authorized in July. Initially, he had approached the American Treasury's secretary for a loan. The best that McAdoo was prepared to offer was short-term credit and his authorization of a loan in New York. The issue there failed. The British Treasury had to underwrite $25 million of the loan, and in early August, historian Jeremy Wormell explains, White was forced to deposit money with Morgan's in order "to help carry some of the unsold securities. He was thus taking, or was financing, nearly half the issue."[42] Any admission of failure would have undermined public confidence, future Canadian borrowing, and American banks' interest in carrying British loans then under negotiation. Upbeat accounts appeared in Canadian newspapers, with the *Globe* reporting the deposit of $96,111,111 to the New York branch of the Bank of Montreal for use by the Department of Finance, said to be "the largest single payment to pass through the New York Clearing House."[43]

Sobering details nonetheless emerged. The *Financial Post*, a critic of the federal system of war finance, estimated that interest and commissions on the loan cost the government 8 percent, a "big price to pay."[44]

The loan produced stinging reprimands of White in the Commons. On 8 September, cognizant of the risks faced in New York, he defended the loan: "In war time you face war conditions, pay war rates of interest, and war rates of Commissions."[45] He would later recognize the loan as the "least successful of the public flotations made by the Government during the war."[46] But he got the money. The emotional toll of the crisis on White, along with the other crossroads facing the government, appears to have been acute. In testimony before a commission on a bank failure during the war, he would read from *Story* on how he had been tormented by the problems of war, with nightmares of German submarines. In 1917, he continued to take heat in both Parliament and Liberal newspapers. The *Island Patriot* (Charlottetown), for one, found his performance "scandalous."[47] On 3 September, in the Commons, while the funding crisis was playing out, he could still speak at length, with confidence, giving numbing explanations of the supply vote for $150,000 to cover the cost of administering the war-profits tax and of the need to enlarge his staff to collect the new income tax. On 14 September, Borden witnessed his minister's private struggle:

> In Council [Cabinet] discussed reply to British note as to purchases in United States and afterwards drafted reply. White went in the air, said he was over wearied and must get out, that his duties and responsibilities were undermining his health. I soothed him as best I could and arranged for his work while absent in Washington to meet British envoy Lord Reading.[48]

The loan was not the only tool used to mitigate the funding crisis. Although conscious of the need to control monetary expansion, in late August, through an order-in-council under the War Measures Act, White obtained a special rate of three and a-half percent for borrowing the growing sums needed to advance to the imperial government, secured by British treasury bill certificates.[49] Never easily spelled out to the public or Parliament, the tools of munition funding included a bewildering mix of orders-in-council, guarantees, bank loans, gold reserves, British credits in the United States, and American advances. Manoeuvres ranged from standard renewals to desperate negotiations through flurries of letters and cables, White's trips to Washington and New York, British missions, threats and counter-pressure, blunt Canadian refusals, and personal impugnment. Transactions between Canada and Britain, White would later explain, effectively turned his department into "a bank for the purpose of financing the Imperial Government in carrying out the purchase of our commodities" and the British Treasury into "a bank to finance our heavy expenses in Great Britain and on the continent." The United States, in the view of Flavelle and probably others, did not regard Canada as a "principal country," whose use of any American funding had to go through Britain. Fortunately for Canada and White, he had functional relations with the Canadian Bankers' Association, notably its president, Edson Loy Pease, and its secretary-treasurer since the beginning of 1917, Henry Taylor Ross, White's former assistant deputy minister.[50]

Munitions were not the only matériel in play. The temporary cessation of cheese purchases in June 1917, when the treasury ran out of Canadian dollars, had thrown the cheese industry into turmoil, a crisis resolved only through an American loan to Britain.[51] To repay an advance made in 1916 for wheat, a shipment of Russian gold destined for Ottawa (for Britain's account) was sold. Untangling trade imbalances was at the core of Lord Rufus Isaacs Reading's special finance mission to the United States in September through November. With the Canadian wheat crop coming to market (a determinant in the timing of war loans), Reading also visited Ottawa to persuade bankers to help facilitate its purchase. In September, the *Globe* reported an advance by the banks of $80 million for wheat, in addition to another $75 million for meat. By early October, White and the bankers had agreed to lend $100 million for wheat on the condition that the American Treasury provide the balance.[52] After convoluted talks that were partly driven by American demands for more Canadian funding for wheat (in exchange for American contributions), a final agreement for $100 million (the "Royal Wheat Loan") was reached on 1 November between the minister of finance and the Canadian Bankers' Association, representing twenty-one banks.[53] Under this agreement, the department issued one-year "Imperial Treasury Bill Certificates" (certificates evidencing ownership) to the banks against a deposit of £22.2 million ($108.2 million) in one-year British sterling treasury bills at the Bank of England for the account of the minister of finance as its trustee. The agreement would run to May 1918 and then be extended the following November and again in 1919 and 1920. How much of the funding was used is unclear, especially given the vagaries of climate and marketing: crop yields and shipments from western Canada declined in 1917–18. Millions more for munitions were provided in October 1917.

By November, the immediate crisis of funding had lessened, levels of munition production had declined, and the shifting balance in Canadian-imperial accounts had tilted to the Dominion's favour. More broadly, in November, the Imperial Munitions Board reached an arrangement with the United States' Ordnance Department to bring orders to Canada.[54] As summarized by the *Canadian Annual Review of Public Affairs* at year-end,[55] advances to the British

Female munition workers milling shell fuses, Toronto, 1917. The Russell factories employed 2,942 men and 3,016 women, with women doing 70 percent of the work on fuses. | Shaw Newton and Russell Motor Car Company, *The Second Line of Offence* (Toronto: Southam, 1918), 38.

Treasury by the Canadian government, the banks, and the Canadian Pacific Railway (secured with Canadian treasury bills) came to some $550 million, against an imperial advance to Canada of $300 million (a fluctuating figure) to maintain its forces overseas.

Even with this trend, White and Borden understood the clear need for another domestic war loan in the fall of 1917. One had been mooted for months, partly to pay down bank loans.[56] There was no consensus on when the war would end, but preparations were already underway for postwar demobilization. The Military Hospitals Commission had been created in 1915 to deal with medical care, retraining, and pensions, and by 1917 the number of repatriated wounded soldiers had grown substantially. It was the funding crisis of that year, which called for millions, that forced White to accede to amplified borrowing through restructured means. The "sudden intimation" of July and August, he wrote,

> completely upset our financial plans and made it imperative for us to not only provide a loan campaign on a national scale, with the object of raising at least three hundred million dollars to carry us until the spring. We found part of the money immediately required by issuing fifty million dollars in Dominion notes secured by approved collateral lodged by the British Treasury to our credit with the Bank of Montreal in London. Later, we called together the leaders in the

investment world of Canada and discussed with them the making of a nation-wide appeal through the medium of an organization which would cover every section of Canada.[57]

Market analysts believed that "one huge selling organization" would reduce duplication of work and commissions. What was new about domestic borrowing that fall would be its reframing not just for greater financial return but also for social and political purposes in the midst of the government's course on conscription and re-election. In this crucible, extreme propaganda would be an absolute necessity in securing public collaboration. In the weeks before prorogation on 20 September, White said nothing in Parliament about the loan except its timing.[58]

Designed to generate more funds than ever before, by engaging Canadians in unprecedented ways, the loan of November to December 1917, officially named the Victory Loan (Emprunt de la Victoire in French), was by 6 October rooted in the calls for forms of grand promotion that emerged from the thrift campaign and from the British and American war loans of early 1917. Canada's Victory Loans of 1917, 1918, and 1919 were also emphatically predicated,[59] operationally, on the experience of the Dominion War Loans of 1915, 1916, and 1917, but White saw a distinction. "There was increased production, higher prices, large sums of money coming to the people who produced and sold supplies and commodities," he would explain.[60] Bank reports and the press supported this comprehension of a reservoir of savings. Organization of the loan had started with much haste in August 1917, with White juggling the railway and munition issues and negotiating with the Bond Dealers' Association of Canada to create a national organization consisting of a dominion executive with provincial and local bodies to publicize and sell Victory Bonds. Modelled after the large-scale drives of the Canadian Patriotic Fund and the Red Cross, mirroring the aggressive sales techniques of a host of other patriotic and war-relief organizations (what one observer called "war philanthropy"), the Victory Loan drew not just the brokers, bond dealers, and bankers into the campaign but also the press and, tellingly, the commercial advertising profession.

The issue of $150 million (the same target as March) was announced by White on 6 November. The issue price of par (100), higher than the 96 of the March loan, was offset by a five and a-half percent rate of interest and exemption from federal taxation, as White continued to maintain that such taxation would drive down bond prices. The maturities were 1922 (five-year bonds), 1927 (ten-year), and 1937 (twenty-year), with conversion privileges, down payments of $10, instalments between January and April, and expected yields ranging from 5.61 percent on the twenty-year bonds to 5.81 percent on the five-year. To the usual denominations of $100, $500, and $1,000, a $50 bond was added on the advice of the Bond Dealers' Association and others, to reach the "thousands of little savers anxious to help," as the *Globe* called them.[61] Touted as a selling feature, the bonds' negotiability in the marketplace would prove to be a can of worms for many first-time investors. As added incentive, some municipalities and provinces waived their income taxes on bonds. Also in play was the oft-found disconnect between patriotism and market forces. (In examining the placement of bonds, some economic analysts downplay the roles of patriotic motivation and sales techniques.)[62] The campaign sold bonds hard from 12 November to 1 December. Compared to the March loan, vastly more money was expended on promotion: $162,821.95 by the newly formed dominion publicity committee and $435,202.24 on advertising by the Canadian Press Association and the affiliated Dominion Press News and Feature Service, based in Toronto.

The loan was not conducted without risk. In 1939, on the verge of funding a new war, Henry Herbert Stevens, a Conservative backbencher in 1917, would recall the emotions surrounding the Victory Loan: "It was done with fear and trembling. We had no idea what the resources of the country were in that regard. We feared it might be a failure." Its success came as "a surprise to every financial authority in the country, and it was not until after the first victory loan that we obtained some realization as to the reserve resources of this country."[63] Much was done, however, to mitigate the risk.

The propaganda campaign and national organization, although hastily constructed, were unprecedented. Canada's past loans, those of other nations, and Canada's financial potential were sounded in advance. Carefully mounted to maximize large institutional subscriptions, without bank underwriting as a guarantee, the loan delivered $566,327,500 from 869,300 subscribers, with $149,741,700 coming from conversions. The government boosted the size of the issue and allotted $546,156,300, at a cost of $4,714,150, far less than the March loan. Bank commissions claimed $991,678.76, and bond dealers received $732,304.67. It would take months – until July 1918 – for the finance department to deliver all of the bonds to subscribers. The proceeds also took time to come in, especially where instalment payments and procrastination were involved. (Only 10 percent of the amount subscribed would be passed to the credit of the finance minister on 1 December.)[64] A chunk of the proceeds was applied to loans from the banks, which were learning to manage the enormous impact of the loans, including the deposits that subscribers drew on for bonds. In the opinion of the deputy postmaster general, Robert Miller Coulter, increased withdrawals from post-office savings accounts and a greater number of account closures in 1917 (and greater again in 1918) were likely due to people pulling out

E.N. ("Newt") McConnell, "A Solid Quebec Will Vote to Rule All Canada/Only a Solid Ontario Can Defeat Them," *Globe* (Toronto), 17 December 1917. In this cartoon, one of a number of warnings from the vitriolic Citizen's Union Committee on the eve of a divisive election, a block of ice ("A Solid Quebec") flattens "Old Man Ontario," knocking aside his bundles of Victory Bonds.

their funds to buy bonds. In January 1918, the Canadian Bank of Commerce anticipated a drop of $3 to $4 million over the next four months. Made attractive through waves of publicity, the Victory Loans did tap into Canadians' earnings but not at the long-term cost of savings, which, one trust company official reckoned, jumped 75 percent between 1914 and 1919, and not even to the detriment of retail sectors willing to treat bonds as currency or promotions. The results of the loan relieved many. "It invigorated our efforts in the war," proclaimed Edward Rogers Wood of its dominion executive.[65] Exuberant accounts of campaign, public enthusiasm, and positive spins in the press on the war front hardly drowned out Canada's deadly serious election campaign. The anti-Quebec vitriol of the election negatively impacted canvassing in French Canada and produced, in the English Canadian press, skewed, offensive accounts of Quebec's contribution.

At the same time, Germany's submarines and the collapse of the Italian and Russian fronts were sending shock waves through the financial markets. On Canadian exchanges, in an arbitrary move meant to regulate the capital market and to lessen competition with dominion issues, the imposition of minimum prices on shares in October was followed on 22 December by an order-in-council that required federal approval of any provincial, municipal, or corporate borrowing through issues of securities. Strong provincial and opposition objections on constitutional grounds were initially met by White's war-measure retort, although he would soon back off through orders-in-council that allowed for exemptions and retroactive approvals. To assess corporate, provincial, and municipal applications to borrow, White had Toronto's finance commissioner and treasurer, Thomas Bradshaw, appointed in January 1918. The *Financial Post* would later claim that few applications for exemptions were refused. Ontario's treasurer, Thomas William McGarry, frustrated that his province "had been cut off in the floating of bonds by the Victory Loan," met with White in February and was easily granted permission to issue a loan at six and a-half percent. And there were other cases, public and corporate. Another concern was the dramatic impact of war bonds in the market. To keep interest rates low, war issues had to trade as near to par as possible. Discounting and pre-maturity sales, inflation, and military reverses in Europe all pushed bonds onto the secondary market at reduced prices. The third war loan, that of March 1917, had dipped to a low of 91.75. Inflation also led to rising yields on bonds traded, although the impact on real rates of return after inflation is unclear. The cycle was undoubtedly hard for laypeople to comprehend. On 22 January 1918, in advance of their actual delivery and exchange listing, the controlled trading of 1917 bonds began. With these bonds starting to flood the market, historian Christopher Armstrong observes, "The task of stabilizing secondary trading became more and more important."[66]

Early in January, a group of bond dealers contemplated forming a syndicate to buy bonds on the secondary market in order to support prices. Discussions among dealers, the banks, and the finance department, beginning in December 1917 over trade stabilization, would lead to a more potent control mechanism, the Victory Loan Special Committee, chaired by George Herbert Wood of Wood, Gundy and Company (of no relation to Edward Rogers Wood). Operating out of Winnipeg, Toronto, and Montreal, and using finance department advances through the Bank of Montreal, this committee would buy and resell Victory Bonds and set market prices (up and down), beginning on 22 January. Based on Britain's market-control operation (the Currency Note Redemption Account at the Bank of England) and foreshadowing the American Treasury's bond purchase fund,[67] Canada's Special Committee had originally been mooted as a means to provide "market protection" for new, "uneducated" bondholders and to shield them from "trafficking" by wheeler-dealers. The emphasis, however, quickly shifted to the controlled marketing of the large blocks of war bonds being shed by major investors and institutions. Between then and 20 January 1919, the committee bought up $70,329,050 worth of bonds and resold them, except for $5,779,650 worth of short-term maturities or small denominations ($50 and $100), "such bonds not being saleable in that form." These bonds would later be purchased by the minister of finance for sinking-fund purposes.[68] Another unsettling diversion was the devastating munition explosion in Halifax on 6 December 1917,[69] which precipitated appeals for heavy municipal and provincial loans, special warrants from the governor general, and nationwide relief drives. Portions of the Victory Loan went to Halifax.

Even with market disturbance, imperial funding had settled down after the fall of 1917 as production and finance shifted to the United States.[70] In November, the Imperial Munitions Board needed to draw on White only for $16 million,[71] but abatement did not bring him complete peace. He faced lobbies from many supply sectors – munitions, shipbuilders, food producers, leather manufacturers – all anxious for Victory Loan money and market access. A balanced, justifiable distribution of the loan's proceeds was vital; within days of the federal election on 17 December, he was planning allocations. As he cabled Sir George Halsey Perley in London on 20 December, "it is idle for our Food Controller to urge the farmers to raise hogs unless a market is provided for their product. Inform Chancellor [of the] Exchequer of my desire that he give the whole question his personal attention."[72] White also faced adjustment in the securities market as it absorbed the Victory Loan. Politics were a constant.

In the Unionist government formed by Borden in October, White had continued as minister of finance and receiver general, one of three ministers to retain his portfolio. In the bitter election, where the Unionists secured an enormous majority in English Canada, he was easily re-elected in Leeds on a conscriptionist, pro-suffragist, anti-Quebec platform. His year of heavy lifting had nevertheless taken a toll. That winter, as he was mulling over some form of "market protection" that culminated in the Special Committee and short-term borrowing payable from another Victory Loan, exhaustion and bronchial problems pushed him into one of his near collapses. When Borden visited him in January 1918, the bedridden minister wanted to resign. "He gave me his reasons, physical, financial, domestic." A worn-out White left in January to recuperate at the Los Angeles Country Club and elsewhere in California, without his wife, Anna Isobel. The *Globe* reported his condition (never clinically diagnosed) as a "temporary physical breakdown" and later as a "serious nervous breakdown." It had taken some effort to bring Maclean, the Liberal finance critic, into the coalition government as acting finance minister, and he needed time to adjust, especially in a department bursting with employees doing Victory Loan work. He reminded a demanding Borden of the expertise that White had wielded.

Borden, like Flavelle, felt that White was a one-man show. The prime minister noted in his diary on 4 February that he found Maclean "of little use."[73] Maclean could nonetheless rely on the seasoned experts in his department, notably Thomas Cooper Boville (deputy), Robert Walker Breadner (taxation), and James Anthony Russell (tariffs).

1918

In early 1918, the Allied line on the Western Front was perilously pressed. The tide would not turn until August. At home, the government faced reaction in French Canada to the election and to the enforcement of the Military Service Act. The war pervaded daily life, but tensions translated only indirectly into financial outlay. The government's merchant-shipbuilding program, announced in January 1918,[74] came with a hefty estimated cost of around $65 million for 1918–19. Of mounting significance, the Military Hospitals Commission was superseded in February by the Ministry of Soldiers' Civil Re-establishment, with much the same cost, over $11 million. As well, as legions of soldiers returned, the settlement board set up in 1917 to put veterans on farms through a scheme devised by the finance department and the Canadian Bankers' Association, was reformed in 1918 to be funded by the war loan.

Routine matters of finance carried over from 1917, such as the use of Victory Loan funds to repay bank loans. Demands, and more trade missions, continued to arise, too, from the involved financial arrangements between Canada, Britain, and the United States. Lord Reading persuaded the American Treasury's secretary, McAdoo, to advance $50 million, payable in New York, for purchases of Canadian foodstuffs by Britain, France, and Italy. Munition funding also continued into 1918, with Canada's finance department advancing $25 million or more to the Imperial Munitions Board. Adding to this flow was the IMB's release of credit to buy foodstuffs, notably the next wheat crop. These purchases and advances, along with the munition industry's purchases of supplies from the United States, exacerbated the trade deficit. White's deal with McAdoo in 1917 to shift portions of America's loans to Britain, earmarked for the purchase of American materials used in Canadian munitions, contributed to the imbalance. In February 1918, a Canadian delegation, including Borden, Maclean, and Flavelle, met in Washington with American and British representatives to thrash out solutions. Flavelle already knew from Canada's deputy minister of finance that Canada's revenues during the fiscal year ending in March would provide sufficient revenue to meet expenditures in Canada. But that was internal. In addition to a flow of American orders to help balance payments as well as American loans to Britain to buy Canadian goods, Flavelle wanted Britain to provide credits to cover Canadian obligations maturing in London.[75]

The inconclusiveness of the Washington meetings, and his own restored vigour, brought White back from California. He joined Borden in New York in April. They then went to Washington for further talks on Canadian credits for purchases in Canada on Britain's account (using US funds) and on ways to address the Canadian-American cash imbalance. White stayed on until mid-May, lobbying for more American orders of munitions and other supplies for Canadian fulfillment, to be paid for in US dollars,[76] and for more financial aid from Britain. He would return to Washington in June.

In Ottawa, Parliament had resumed on 18 March. As acting finance minister, Maclean knew that the government's war accounts were held in twenty-four banks, the sums paid to brokers and bond dealers in commissions on the Victory Loan, and that 77 percent of the allotments on the loan had been paid in full. However, all the facts on bank subscriptions and payments on war loans eluded him. Despite his grasp of such thorny issues as railways, his handling of international negotiation and budget making found him wanting. At several points, Borden was forced to consider other candidates should White actually quit. White had encouraged Maclean to get Flavelle's input on the plans for 1918. Flavelle had to adjust the financial statements that Maclean had drawn up for the Washington talks and coach him on handling British officials; his budget proposals were rewritten by Cabinet veterans. When White came to New York, he and Borden vetted the budget. In Parliament, Liberal wits concluded that, in the Maclean-White duo, "we have an internal Minister of Finance in Ottawa and an external one in the United States." Much of the financial representation fell to Borden. On 12 March, in fending off provincial demands, he had told Prince Edward Island's premier, Aubin-Edmond Arsenault, "Perhaps you do not fully realize the tremendous strain upon the financial resources of the country."[77]

In 1918, as in all war years, finances were divided between civil costs and war expenditures. The latter, under the authority of annual appropriation acts and many orders-in-council, were spread over all government departments. The bulk of the war funding went to the Department of Militia and to meeting Canada's advances to Britain. The size and escalation of these obligations can be seen from a comparison of costs for the fiscal years 1916–17 and 1917–18. For the year ending 31 March 1917, the war account totalled \$306,488,814.63, of which the militia department spent \$298,291,030.66; to 31 March 1918, the account totalled \$343,836,801.98, of which the department spent \$316,669,871.95.[78] In the government's war estimates tabled by Borden in the Commons on 10 April, \$155 million was allocated to the Dominion's troops in England and France. This cost in itself was complicated, subject to change. The troop per diem of 9s. 4d. to be paid by Britain had been reduced to 6s. in the fall of 1916 with recognition of the likely need to adjust upwards. (The capitation was restored to 9s. 4d. as of 1 September 1917.) To help offset the actual cost, a matter of continuing negotiation with the War Office – arbitration on pay would continue into 1919 – the militia headquarters in Ottawa had sent $73 million to the imperial government in the fiscal year 1917–18.[79] The estimated expenditures overseas came to $225,162,500 and in Canada to $217,887,500. By year-end 31 March 1918, these "reciprocal accounts" – advances by Canada amounting to $504,566,272.64, less $384,466,666.67 "written off by agreement" on advances in London to Canada, along with other costs – had gone to Canada's favour for $111,708,045.39,[80] figures that would change over the next year. The means of getting money to Canada's forces varied. Much involved labyrinthine reciprocal accounting. For instance, in September 1917, the *Globe* reported that White had sent about $112 million in dominion bonds to the British government "in part settlement of balance due for pay and maintenance of Canadian Expeditionary Forces overseas, and since that settlement another large balance has piled up against us in this account." Within months, more than $100 million in bonds, also earmarked for pay and maintenance, were sent to New York to be held as collateral on an American loan to Britain.[81] After the formation of the London-based Ministry of Overseas Military Forces of Canada in 1916, the existing reciprocal payment arrangements underwent much negotiation and change. According to the ministry's report of 1918, credits were being issued by the finance department to the paymaster general through the London branch of the Bank of Montreal.

During the 1918 session of Parliament, which ran to 23 May, financial matters were not always front and centre. Debate on the War Appropriation Act, which presaged a bewildering expenditure of half a billion dollars, was brief. Conscription dominated, notably the impassioned debate on 19 April to deal with the crisis in military enlistment and the cancellation of exemptions though an order-in-council rather a formal bill. Still, finance proceeded, just as signs of war fatigue began appearing on the streets. Guided by the estimates that Borden tabled on 10 April, Maclean gamely presented his war budget to Parliament on 30 April, while White was in Washington. Confident that an order-in-council of 22 December, this one prohibiting nonfederal borrowing through securities, had given the government the muscle "to expropriate the money market," Maclean continued the search for revenue. The income and other taxes, along with duties, were raised, and the range of companies subject to the war-profits tax was extended. Imperial advances, the trade balance, and the credits with the United States then under negotiation were also addressed, but it was the Victory Loan of 1917 that was highlighted. With an estimated shortfall of $700 million, Maclean's budget pointed to further borrowing.

For the first time, he gave the Commons a full statement on the 1917 loan's organization and results. The budget and explanation underlined the government's revenue policy, which was intended to exploit the lesser political cost of borrowing compared to taxation, while capitalizing on patriotism and moral suasion.[82] With a view to immediate funding, Maclean explained, "The unexpended balance of the Victory Loan will finance our war expenditure and advances to the Imperial Government until July next, when Treasury bills will be temporarily negotiated [with the banks], until the proceeds of the next public loan are available." Resorting to melodramatic realism, he insisted that even in the face of plummeting enlistment, Canadians could step up at home to engage the enemy: they "must, year after year, purchase Victory Bonds. There is no other way."[83] Some Liberal MPs nonetheless pressed him for a more thorough breakdown. In Quebec, the county of Nicolet's persistent Arthur Trahan, who found the government's accounting incomprehensible, asked how much the banks had subscribed and what proportion of subscribers had defaulted. Maclean brushed the questions off as "too indefinite to permit an answer."[84] Trahan further opposed constant borrowing and monetary expansion through the continuing issue of dominion notes. "The Government should cease to finance this country on paper," he argued in vain.[85] Other Liberals attacked Maclean with equal vigour. Much wind was vented on notions of giving. "This Victory bond business is not an example of sacrificing," claimed Red Deer's Michael Clark, now a Liberal-Unionist. "It is an example of selfishness and shirking of duty. The man in the trenches is sacrificing." Old arguments were run out: the loan's cost was said to be outrageous, and Joseph Archambault, the member for Chambly-Verchères, lambasted its use as a "political step-ladder" in the December election, despite its backing by Laurier and Quebec's premier.[86]

What politicians did not fully grasp was the direction of funding in 1918. Through a budget that introduced increases in a broad base of direct and commodity taxes, along with the formation of the Canada Food and War Trade Boards and the Dairy Produce Commission in February and the Board of Grain Supervisors in September, the government was moving to recognize the "'full logic' of a wartime economy," as explained by tax historian J. Harvey Perry. "At the peak of the war," he writes, "it had been finally realized that the basic problem of a wartime economy is the marshalling of men and materials for the single purpose of winning the war, and that after a strategic point is passed direct controls must supplement others measures to achieve this purpose efficiently. The 1918 budget was in keeping with this lesson."[87]

Largely finished in Washington and New York, White returned to Canada on 15 May. Although Maclean would continue for a time as acting minister, White resumed control. In June, with funding from the last war loan due to end, he met with the executive members of the Canadian Bankers' Association to secure bridge funding for August and September. That same month, he announced a new issue of debenture stock, which he promoted as a good reinvestment of the interest payments then being released on war bonds. Largely unsold, most of the issue would be converted to the Victory Loan in the fall. Later in June, White went back to Washington to address the persistent problems of trade imbalance and foreign exchange and the question of issuing Canadian securities in the United States. His endeavours had two results. First, British gold was shipped to the American Sub-Treasury in New York and placed to the credit of the local Federal Reserve Bank, with transfers of gold to Ottawa in order to facilitate any loan to Canada by the American Treasury and "as a further means of lessening the premium on New York exchange at Canadian centres."[88] Second, the Capital Issues Committee of the Federal Reserve Board agreed to lift a ban on the placement of Canadian securities in the New York market. This outcome produced a reciprocal agreement, announced on 29 June, for joint Canadian-American control of the sale of private and public securities.[89] For Canada, such sales, which required ministerial approval, had two key goals: first, facilitating and controlling provincial loans and the "gradual absorption" of securities; and second, through the listing of securities (along with Canadian government issues) in New York, relieving an exchange situation where the American dollar was currently trading at a 2 percent premium against its Canadian counterpart.[90] After the Capital Issues Committee requested that banks and investment houses withdraw public offerings of securities, ostensibly to make way for the Liberty Loan of October, the Department of Finance followed suit in Canada to "conserve" funds for its upcoming Victory Loan. White's work in the United States registered with few Canadians.

Rejecting rumours of another loan there, White encouraged Canadians, in his old refrain, to "pinch and scrape" for the next domestic loan.[91] Practical matters claimed his attention in August, including financing the western grain crop, commandeering British Columbia's salmon pack for Britain's Ministry of Food (with the cost to come from the fall loan), and stabilizing the markets for Victory Bonds and provincial and municipal securities. White's "roseate review" of financial stability and his defence of tax-free bonds, the *Globe* cautioned, "may not be altogether unrelated to the next Victory Loan appeal."[92]

The finance department's preparatory statements on the fall loan had started coming out as early as June 1918. It was authorized by an order-in-council on 5 July, plans geared up the following month, and White announced its terms in Winnipeg on 8 October, during a western speaking tour. He had already dismissed as unworkable calls for an unlimited issue of war-loan bonds[93] (as would be offered in France), and on 13 August, he had released a forceful statement defending, among other attractive features, the continued exemption of bond interest from taxation to keep investment money in Canada. Nor would tax-free securities restrict the flow of capital to other enterprises, an argument that he based on America's experience with Liberty Bonds. His defence elicited strong retorts from a number of Montreal financiers, notably the Royal Securities Corporation's president Izaak Walton Killam, whose published letters to Borden and White caused a brief stir. Long a supporter of a graduated income tax who wanted finance capital to do its part for the war, Killam argued that tax-exempt bonds favoured the large investor and would tend to nullify future income tax. As an incentive, exemption nonetheless had other support. Some provinces moved to eliminate their income tax on Victory Bonds, as they had on provincial and municipal bonds. In October, Ontario had also announced its intention to let municipalities assess only the net income from such securities and not to impose succession duties on Victory Bonds. (Some sources had argued to no avail that since the bonds emanated from an Ontario city, Ottawa, they would be dutiable.) Elsewhere, from Winnipeg, the *Grain Growers' Guide* feared future taxation to compensate for the exemption. Complicating this debate, there were misconceptions of how the 1917 Victory Loan would be used. Approved by an order-in-council in July and announced in Regina the following month, $1 million was advanced to Saskatchewan for use in loans to farmers. However, private loan organizations, the *Edmonton Bulletin* reported, were "indignant that funds raised for the use of the Dominion Government ... are being used in this national way to unfairly compete."[94] The linkage was false, but the loan could sometimes be seen as everyone's treasure chest.

White further reasoned that tax revenue had to be weighed against returns based on carefully calibrated selling prices and interest rates for bonds.[95] Returning to an old argument, if an income tax had been levied on Canada's combined past issues, which totalled $750 million, the return would not have been worthwhile, only a million or a million and a half. Moreover, taxation would have necessitated a higher interest rate by half a percent, which would have increased the interest charge to the government by $3,750,000, "and we should now be facing a 6 percent rate upon our next loan, instead of floating it at five and a-half percent, as we shall." Looking to the future, exemption would reduce the interest charges on refunding the loans. Overall, taxing bonds would be a rash "experiment." In one of his clearest statements on the separation of patriotic support and investment, White concluded, "While it is true that patriotism plays a great part in the successful flotation of war loans, it should be kept in mind that prices must reasonably conform to market conditions."[96] The financial press, notably the *Monetary Times* (Toronto), agreed: market conditions came before patriotism.[97]

In mid-August, when the Victory Loan Special Committee advanced the price of bonds, White capitalized on the move in order to promote bonds and the upcoming loan.[98] His public preoccupation with the loan coexisted not only with market considerations but also with his behind-the-scenes work to keep the banks engaged.[99] They were essential to war finance, especially as more and more of it, particularly short-term financing, had been placed on the banks' shoulders after the dark days of 1917.[100] With no reference to the difficult negotiations involved, White would later describe this relationship as easy as picking up the telephone. In 1924, in the investigation of the collapsed Home Bank, he would claim that any exposure of bank weakness leading to failure "would have been disastrous" to the 1918 loan.

With the end of the war in sight, the loan campaign, from 28 October to 16 November, was tumultuous, despite the horrendous influenza epidemic and initial fears that peace would dampen interest. News of the Allied offensive in Europe, notably the Canadian Corps's capture of Cambrai, had a positive impact on the market for past Victory Bonds, commonly called "Victories" or "Victorys." They dominated bond-market news; bank deposits had surged in anticipation of the new issue. News of the loan had created a "bare security market," as the *Monetary Times* put it, with few new issues appearing and investors holding back, leaving the field open for Victory Bonds. Smaller in size to conserve paper and labour, they were issued in the same denominations as 1917: $50 (blue), $100 (green), $500 (olive), and $1,000 (brown).[101] Sales and the armistice of November 11 magnified each other. The war's end, the *Financial Post* reasoned, did not mean the end of "war financing." With the goal of bringing in $300 million, the loan was sold at par with an attractive five and a-half percent tax-exempt interest, which some analysts likened to "mortgaging the future."

The 1918 loan was once again driven by experienced local sales teams and advertising on an unmatched scale, as will be seen in Part 2. The dominion publicity committee would spend $305,560.36 (almost twice its expenditure in 1917), and advertising came to $277,958.42 (slightly more than 1917).[102] Propelled by masses of propaganda, the results exceeded expectations: in the only war loan to attract more than a million subscribers, 1,140,057 applied for $707,117,550, at a cost of $5,762,091. (Conversions accounted for $66,261,166.) After due consideration of various market factors, including an assessment of monies remaining in public hands for other government and municipal bonds, the government would allot $682,302,900, a slightly higher proportion than

1917. Once again, subscribers showed a preference for the $50 and $100 bonds and for subscriptions under $500. The monumental consequence was the impact on the national debt, which grew daily; by nighttime on 31 August 1918, deputy minister Thomas Cooper Boville reported, the net debt had risen to $1,196,239,346.04.[103] But the debt, even with the morass of railway liabilities, was not the government's primary concern; with funded debt, White took the long view.

By the end of the war, the economy was enduring extreme highs and lows. Industrial momentum had let up, big railways were moving toward government takeover, and prices continued to skyrocket. Share and bond trading had fallen in 1917 and 1918, but after the 1918 Victory Loan, the number of new bondholders and trading were impressively high. Victory Bond issues, as Armstrong puts it, "dwarfed anything ever imagined in Canada before the war."[104] At the end of November, to build on the momentum created by the campaign of 1918 and the armistice, the government named a National War Savings Committee, which would emulate like movements launched in Britain in 1916 and the United States in 1917 and adapt savings campaigns to postwar needs. Chaired by Sir Herbert Brown Ames of Montreal, the committee released $5 war-savings stamps, building on British and American initiatives, Canada's $10 war certificate of July, the $50 Victory Bond, and the omnipresent thrift program. Placed on sale on 2 December for $4, the stamp, initially printed only in English, could be redeemed for $5 in five years. (Design essays for the stamp, dated 1 July 1918, had actually been prepared before the formation of the committee. Essays in French for both the thrift and war-savings stamps would follow on 24 January 1919.)[105] Also in December, picking up on a savings-stamp plan proposed for release in September 1917 but postponed (partly on the grounds that the war certificates sold at post offices met the needs of the small investor), 25¢ "thrift stamps" were issued to complement the war-savings stamps; sixteen of them saved on a "thrift card" could be exchanged for a war-savings stamp. Based on a drawing in *Punch* in 1915, the device was modelled after British and American thrift stamps.[106]

For fundraising purposes, the Canadian stamps may not have been worthwhile, but they caught on. One of the larger holders of war-savings and thrift stamps, to 31 March 1919, was Canadian Government Railways, with $35,142.88. The contribution of these stamps to war finance was minimal; bankers were skeptical. By 31 March 1919, only $1,640,166.28 worth of war-savings and thrift stamps had been sold, with $116,132.40 redeemed; by 23 October 1919, $2,792,558.74 worth had been sold, with $287,717.14 redeemed.[107] Still, as the *Globe* and others had predicted, their value in terms of public engagement was

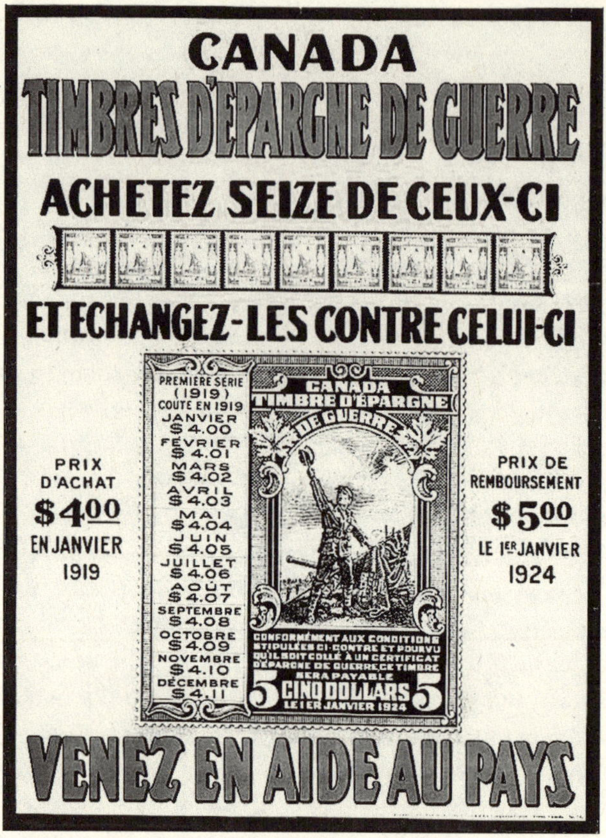

Poster for war-savings stamps (French version), 1919. In English, it advocates "Canada / War-Savings Stamps / Buy Sixteen of These [25¢ stamps] / and Exchange Them for This / [$5 stamp] / Help Pay for the War." The small image of a flag-waving soldier on each stamp comes from a ubiquitous drawing honouring Canada's part in the Battle of Ypres | Library and Archives Canada, R1185-67-0-E, box A142/X3, e010697535.

substantial. Commenting before the Victory Loan campaign of 1918, Oscar Douglas Skelton stated his belief that the stamps program, although under-utilized, would "assist the larger loan campaign" by "making saving a habit."[108]

Midway between the Victory Loans and the savings stamps and certificates were the war taxes. Income tax returns for 1917 had fallen due at the end of February 1918 (a deadline extended to 31 March), but they took time to materialize, with extreme difficulty getting returns from some parts of the country. On 5 May 1919, White would report the cumulative results in the Commons:

- Number of assessments approved to 31 December 1918: 22,293
- Amount assessed: $4,570,140.77
- Payments received: 13,009
- Amount paid: $1,698,445.37

- Number of assessments approved to 30 April 1919: 42,145
- Amount assessed: $10,031,094.28
- Payments received: 32,715
- Amount paid: $6,865,047.10.[109]

He noted that "many firms which would otherwise be assessable for income under the Income War Tax Act are not liable to assessment by reason of their paying a larger amount under the Business Profits War Tax Act." Farmers and stock raisers, who were exempt from the business-profits tax, formed a subcategory. For taxes on 1917 income, 5,885 farmers were assessed for $417,349.10, with 3,623 paying $219,826.84. Information on the locations of farmers assessed and how many paid completes White's report, giving substance to the tax in practice.

As late as the fall of 1919, taxes on 1917 income were still being calculated. In October 1919, deputy minister Boville reported that tax had been levied on 51,558 people, with assessments totalling $12,221,669, but he noted that only 47,021 had paid, with just over $10 million being collected. Firm numbers from the public accounts to 31 March 1919 appear in the *Sessional Papers,* showing that of the $56,177,508.33 collected as "War Tax Revenue," $32,970,061.81 came from the business-profits tax, whereas $9,349,719,80 came from income tax.[110] As a revenue tool, the income tax was more symbolic than substantive. In no

Table 3.1

Assessments of farmers for income tax

Province	Number assessed	Number paid
PEI and Nova Scotia	12	7
New Brunswick	4	3
Quebec	30	27
Ontario	396	342
Manitoba	1,454	1,281
Saskatchewan	1,084	564
Alberta	2,826	1,325
British Columbia	79	74

combatant country did taxes keep up with war expenditures.[111] For fiscal 1918–19, Canada's revenues remained heavily dependent on borrowing, at a ratio of 2.5 to 1 over taxation.[112]

After the armistice, as taxation unfurled, war loans were applied to new uses besides reconstruction. Adding to White's responsibilities as minister were his duties as acting prime minister during Borden's absence in Europe between November 1918 and May 1919 for peace talks, duties that had financial implications. These undertakings included Canada's unpopular participation in the Allied military intervention in northeastern Russia (Siberia) by British, French, and American forces after the Bolshevik Revolution, as well as the related but fragile forging of Canadian-Siberian trade links through an economic trade commission. The invasion brought the forces into the civil war on the side of the "Whites" against the Communist "Reds" – the Bolsheviks. Canada's military contribution, mooted since at least June 1918, had been approved by an order-in-council on 12 August.[113] Cabinet had been reticent, but British pressure was relentless.[114] In a cost-sharing agreement with Britain, the total expense to Canada of the military expedition, as reported in the Commons, would be $2,823,960.98.[115] A credit of $1 million for goods to Siberia was approved by another order-in-council on 20 February 1919, to be channelled through a company operating under the auspices of the Canadian Economic Commission to Siberia, but this plan fizzled out.

In November 1918, Edward Rogers Wood, chair of the Victory Loan's dominion executive, had recognized the trade potential. Trade commissions, he noted, were on their way to Europe to negotiate credits. "This is the situation which justifies the present Victory Loan," the *Globe* concluded.[116] The link was never highly promoted. In December, a London-based trade commission was set up. Subsequent credits for Britain, Italy, France, Belgium, Romania, and Greece, established from the loan, backed up this goal, although a "nervous and cautious" Department of Finance reduced the credits.[117] Allied aid to Romania was also meant to protect it from Bolshevik aggression. Victory Loan money appears to have been kept away from the Siberian front, certainly from the cost of the military intervention. On the home front, fears of the phantom menace of Bolshevism were rampant.

In the aftermath of the revolutions in Russia, White's angst over the "red scare" brought out his hyper-fretfulness. Hitting home above all was the state of Canada's debt, which stood at $335,996,850.11 on 31 March 1914 but had exploded to $1,574,531,032.44 by 31 March 1919, with the war costs amounting to $446,519,439.48 for the previous year.[118] Annual interest on the debt would climb to $142,281,057.51 for 1920–21. For White personally, the load, including the war loan, once again set off his urge to retire, although he had promised that he would continue as acting prime minister until Borden's return. On 10 November, the day before the armistice, White gave a press interview on the upcoming problems of postwar readjustment and reconstruction. He was not prepared to relax his calls for citizen funding. In his address in Montreal on 11 November, amidst the wild celebration of the peace and the loan, he mentioned "armistice terms" only in passing. Major funding was his preoccupation. In December, the underused war-savings certificates of 1917 were discontinued, although the sale of war-savings and thrift stamps carried on.[119]

On 16 December, White issued a crafted statement that vaunted the achievements of the Unionist government in its first year in office. His assertion of prosperity blended well with the optimism found in the press and voiced by various Cabinet members. But White was no partisan apologist. Close observers, such as the Ottawa correspondent for the *Commercial and Financial Chronicle* (New York), held that he was probably "the least deceived man in Canada." He faced a decline in the volume of customs imports, "the chief reliance of Federal finance," the correspondent rightly claimed.[120] Moreover, in 1918, wheat exports had plummeted and incomes fallen; in hindsight, getting out of a wartime economy was complicated.[121]

White understood, as did other authorities and the financial press, that 1919 would have to be treated financially as yet another "war year."[122] Still, there was some abatement of wartime controls: at the end of November, the finance department relaxed its control over provincial and municipal borrowing and security issues; and on 21 December 1918, the Victory Loan Special Committee permitted open exchange listing of the 1917 loan. On 20 January 1919, it allowed listing of the 1918 loan and suspended its price-support operations altogether. Although some in the bond-marketing community questioned the value of control, the committee had helped to stabilize the market. The minister of finance believed so,[123] as did its chairman, George Herbert Wood. In a review released on 3 February, he claimed that the committee's interventions had allowed the 1918 loan to be issued at par, saving the country "perhaps $10,000,000" on pricing.[124] The *Monetary Times* saw the delayed listing of the 1917 issue through a different lens: "The issue was so large and the market so weak that it was thought the publication of sale prices would result in panicky sales."[125] Also evident was the significant shift in the placements of Canadian bonds over the course of the war. Revenue from the volume sold in Canada jumped from $45,603,000 in 1913 to $727,446,000 in 1918, whereas the amounts sold in the United Kingdom and the United States fell dramatically.[126] The operation of the Special Committee following the armistice also served to cloud whatever impact peace, and with it the deflation of patriotic motivation, may have had on the war-bond market.

On 19 November 1918, during Borden's absence, White had welcomed provincial premiers to Ottawa for a conference. On the table were issues of higher subsidies, the prairie provinces' demand for natural-resource transfers, and land settlement by soldiers. The premiers heard much of the government's bleak estimates of revenue shortfall as the economy faced a downturn, with White emphasizing the problems of reconstruction. Three months later, he confided to Prince Edward Island's premier that the war had been so costly that any increase in provincial subsidies was highly unlikely.[127] In December 1918, the government had nonetheless initiated loans to the provinces to provide housing for veterans. Not until mid-1920 did the money materialize, and for some Liberals, White's belief that it could come from the Victory Loans did not meet the definition of wartime need.

War finance faced new realities. The Canadian Bankers' Association proved itself ill-prepared to deal with postwar politics and protests. Although the annual reports of the big banks showed that they had done well during the war and in 1919, there were strands of tension between the Canadian Bankers' Association and the Department of Finance.[128] Its deputy minister, for instance, wanted the banks to pay interest on the large deposits that had been made during the loan of 1918. The banks countered that, because the money market could not absorb all the short-term funds coming in for bonds, they could not generate revenue from it and pay interest. Here was the department's alternate milieu, the counterpart to its promotion of war loans to the public and its entry into another "war year." After one more Victory Loan, in 1919, the focus of finance would shift to debt management, refunding, and the dissipation of wartime enthusiasm for financial engagement.

4

Legacies in Peacetime, 1919–20s

"CANADA IN 1919 WAS IN FLUX, hovering uneasily between war and peace." So concludes the introduction to a collection of essays on that transitional year.[1] Financially, it was seen as another "war year." By the end of fiscal 1918–19, according to American economist Ernest Ludlow Bogart, Canada's war expenditures amounted to $1,665,576,032 against revenues of $1,898,792,191. By this calculation, the government had got the money for Canada's participation in conflict. Even as the economy did well, war costs nonetheless extended throughout 1919 and into the early 1920s. The decisions, innovations, and debt experienced in 1914–18 would have far-reaching implications. A return to the pre-war financial order would be impossible.

The fiscal year ending 31 March 1919, was the most expensive year of the conflict,[2] with "War Account" expenditures of $446,519,439.48 spread between seven months of warfare, the war costs of departments at home, and the final stages of repatriating Canada's forces, some 350,000 soldiers and dependants. In the fiscal year 1919–20, demobilization costs amounted to $346,612,954.56, of which the militia department spent $323,360,987.33. The mélange of service gratuities and pensions, medical, welfare, and employment programs, vocational training, and land-settlement grants added to the debt.[3] Reconstruction came with labour tensions, radical social prescriptions, and political crisis. Among Canadians facing high unemployment and steadily rising prices, there was unease.[4] With a view to reconstruction overseas, the government found it impossible at the start of the year to determine what portion of the last Victory Loan could be apportioned to credits for European purchases in Canada. In January, White was still meeting in Ottawa with British officials and the bankers to discuss food credits. One such credit was the renewal of the $10 million instalment due on 1 January 1919 on the imperial loan of $100 million for the wheat crop of 1917. As collateral on this advance by Canada (through the banks), the secretary-treasurer of the Canadian Bankers' Association, Henry Taylor Ross, told deputy minister Thomas Cooper Boville that £2,225,000 worth of treasury bills had been deposited with the Bank of England, a transfer facilitated by Canada's high commissioner in London.[5]

Administratively, the finance department had greatly expanded, from 162 employees in 1912 to 833 in 1920, 669 of them women, including temporary clerical staff. The office processing income and business-profits taxes was large, as was that of the comptroller of currency, which handled the war loans.[6] The taxation branch grew to include inspectors and offices across Canada. Heavy burdens fell on the regional bureaus of the assistant receiver general; offices dedicated to the income tax would open not just in Ottawa but also in Halifax, Montreal, and Nelson, British Columbia. The harmful personal impact of the load on White was clear, and in 1921–22 cracks would appear in stressed-out employees. There was spillover to other departments, with a flow of referrals and decisions on bonds and war taxes, for instance, between the finance and justice departments.

In the session of Parliament that ran from February to July 1919, White, doubling as acting prime minister, faced a host of finance-related delegations and questions on taxation, the takeover of the Grand Trunk Pacific, gratuities, and tariff policy, increasingly a focus of discontent among western farmers and MPs. In the aftermath of the Victory Loan of the previous fall, he fielded a barrage of queries on tax exemption, commission and advertising costs, the use and adequacy of proceeds, and their origins by province and even class. With condescension, he dismissed criticisms of his propensity to administer by order-in-council.[7] Sir Wilfrid Laurier lamented White's failure to consult with him as leader of the Opposition, as per British convention. Liberal MP Rodolphe Lemieux rejected the view of 1919 as another "war year" and condemned the government's "free-hand in spending" during the war. White, like his whole department, was keenly aware that blocks of Victory Bonds had been dumped onto the market. Price variations, factors of influence, and the activity of the various bond issues were tracked in the business sections of newspapers. In 1913, the Dominion-funded debt payable in London had stood at $258,679,819.47 and in Canada at $2,190,767.60. By 1919, a strong reversal had occurred: $362,703,312.40 in London but $1,475,883,312.40 in Canada, with $75,873,000 in New York.[8]

Despite the cessation of conflict, White believed that Canada faced unsettled conditions warranting the retention for another two years or so of wartime financial measures. Due mainly to declines in munitions and wheat, the value of exports had fallen in 1918, contributing to a chain of economic reverberations.[9] Customs and excise revenues had increased only marginally between fiscal 1917–18 and 1918–19, but war-tax revenue more than doubled. Reported in the public accounts, the receipts to year-end 31 March 1919 puts revenues in context. The Victory Loan of 1918 was the largest generator.

Table 4.1

Government revenue, 1918–19

Consolidated fund	$
Customs	147,169,187.98
Excise	30,342,034.26
Post office	21,603,542.09
Revenue from public works	317,546.94
• Minor public works	79,117.08
• Railways	37,967,550.84
• Canals	387,654.90
Interest on investments	7,421,001.58
Patent fees	275,708.85
Casual	2,910,189.73
Ordnance lands	4,819.27
Fines and forfeitures	228,815.17
Premium, discount, and exchange (e.g., on New York funds sold)	532,848.90
Mariners' fund	69,243.65
Electric light	88,071.25
Steamboat inspection	2,774.61
Gas inspection	55,701.45
Weights and measures	134,889.70
Cullers' fees	1,229.49
Law stamps	8,628.10
Penitentiaries	132,958.13
Insurance inspection	64,683.98
Fisheries	123,114.29
Canada Gazette	29,413.70
Superannuation fund	26,068.67
Lighthouse and coast service	335.00
Dominion steamers	13,620.92
Military college	54,428.13
Militia	35,954.84
Civil service examination fees	11,568.00
Dominion lands	3,539,927.50
Militia pensions	23,840.96
Inspection of staples	1,082,069.63
Royal North West Mounted Police officers' pensions	4,030.26
Chinese revenue	2,026,669.00
War-tax revenue (inland revenue, business profits, income, misc.)	56,177,508.33
	312,946,747.18

Loans	$
Temporary loans	
• Imperial government	214,133,333.31
• Treasury bills	214,121,250.00
5 percent debenture stock, 1919	107,500.00
War-savings certificates	647,661.70
Victory Loan 1917	780,470.99
5½ percent debenture stock, 1919	11,454,550.00
5½ percent debenture stock, 1920	929,250.00
5½ percent debenture stock, 1921	1,222,550.00
War-savings and thrift stamps	1,640,166.28
Victory Loan 1918	575,048,267.54
5½ percent debenture stock, 1919, on school lands	3,876,000.00
	1,023,960,999.82
Savings banks	*16,761,819.73*
Dominion notes	*193,245,500.00*
Trust funds	
Bank Circulation Redemption Fund	206,951.65
Common School Fund	4,427.39
Indian Fund	1,569,663.54
	1,781,042.58
Other revenue	*2,378,328,285.00*
TOTAL	*$3,927,024,394.31*

With the exception of the war-tax revenue and the war loans, all the other sources of revenue were conventional pre-war means. Of the wartime sources listed here, the Victory Loan of 1918 was the largest generator, producing 15 percent of the total. The sum for Victory Loan 1918, $575,048,267.54, compared to that shown as allotted in Appendix 1, $682,302,900, could indicate preliminary calculation on the former and eventual growth through conversions.

Public reaction to the loan was mixed. On 4 March 1919, in response to the throne speech outlining the government's intentions, Sir Sam Hughes, the dismissed militia minister but still an MP protected by parliamentary immunity, blindsided his government with a rambling attack not just on Sir Arthur W. Currie (Canada's military commander in Europe) but also on past war loans, bringing to the floor complaints that rumbled throughout all of Canada. Commissions constituted theft, interest rates were exorbitant, and price-fixing was extortionate. The 1918 issue, he ranted, "is for the benefit of the speculator, and not for patriotic purposes. Five and a-half percent is a little high for patriotism," especially when American bonds yielded less. According to Hughes, Victory Loan advertising was no less odious: "Imagine the absurdity of the placards that were distributed about the country: 'Help our boys in the trenches,' when there is hardly a man of them who has a son in the trenches. The thing is absurd on the face of it. It is camouflage; it is propaganda; it is deceiving the public." Hughes's broadside irked both White and Alexander Kenneth Maclean, the former acting finance minister. Maclean would be the first to rebut, doing so on 7 March. Hughes's figures were "palpably in error," Maclean said, a misinterpretation of the public accounts and auditor general's report. He would be followed on 18 June by White, whose rebuttal came in his remarks on finance after his budget, although bigger issues, such as the receivership of the Grand Trunk Pacific, were on his plate.[10] Not evident here was the public's lingering skepticism over patriotic posturing and rake-offs by loan advertisers and bond sellers.

During the 1919 session, giving substance to the preparations for a "war year," several appropriation bills were enacted, notably the Demobilization Appropriation Act. White had introduced the resolution to vote $350 million for this bill on 10 April. It contained his most thorough exposition of war expenditure, with little varnish: expenditures going back to 1914, broken down by department, totalled $1,225,098,122.36 to 31 March 1919, a sum that would rise to $1,323,803,748.61 by later accounting. He claimed that "our debt is pretty well funded," by which he meant long-dated securities, coverage of interest from the consolidated fund, and sinking funds. Supported by continuing war-tax incomes and by customs and excise revenues, the government had funds to deal with the costs ahead, although he anticipated the need for a domestic loan in the fall.

Table 4.2

Advances between Canada and Great Britain

Advances by Canada to Great Britain	$
Agriculture department: hay, oats, etc.	15,342,398.65
Canadian cereal crop	68,500,000.00
Dairy Produce Commission	34,748,119.62
Finance department, "Special Account"	19,466.66
Foodstuffs	17,500,000.00
Marine department, "Requisitioning Boats"	801,852.27
Militia department	135,572.43
Munitions Board	315,207,458.20
Munitions Workers Separation Allowance	43,747.09
Interest Account	5,500,000.00
Naval Service department, "Shipbuilding"	2,273,594.47
Railways and Canals department, "Rail Account"	4,331,416.13
Royal Air Force	1,863,269.79
Addition to the Royal Mint	39,369.52
Russian Clothing Account	977,954.59
Salmon pack	8,467,144.85
Siberian Account	271,285.81
Trade and Commerce department, "Paper Account"	7,492.70
	476,030,143.80
Less	
Militia department, sale of gov. property at Halifax	209,985.00
Agriculture department, "Flax Seed Account"	100,000.00
Finance department, remittance from New York	30,581,250.00
Bullion Special Account	13,063.12
	30,904,298.12
Total	*445,125,845.68*
Advances by Britain to Canada	
Temporary loan, London	187,366,666.65
Temporary loan, February and March, not yet posted	26,766,666.66
	214,133,333.31
Balance in favour of Canada	445,125,845.68
	– 214,133,333.31
	$230,992,512.37

Note: The statement explains that £80,679,204 19s. 7d., or $392,638,797.39, comprised advances to Britain written off against advances received from Britain as per agreements of 29 June and 15 November 1918.

Foreign trade, undermined by a "demoralized" state of international exchange, had suffered. As for demobilization, he referred to the public estimates for the cost of pensions arising from the "European War and active militia" ($15 million for the fiscal year 1918–19, $25 million for 1919–20). Given the positive state of the government's credit accounts with Great Britain, he included the statement of advances by Canada since the outbreak of the war, "as entered in the books of the Finance Department."[11]

As an example of an advance, White cited the sale in 1917 of Canada's cheese, a main export along with wheat. An unhailed component of imperial procurement, cheese represented 67 percent of the Allied war supply in 1918. In April 1919, other advances were being arranged to cover the cost and export of wheat and flour.[12] What White could not clearly calculate, but could anticipate in the estimates, was the final cost of maintaining Canada's troops in Europe, which in April 1919 was under arbitration. The newly appointed auditor general, Edward Davenport Sutherland, had gone to England for that purpose along with accountants from Price, Waterhouse.[13] The matter would be concluded with Canada's agreement in April 1920 to pay $252,567,942.03.[14] Britain would still remain in Canada's debt: in March, an adjustment of accounts had shown that Britain owed $214,684,439, a debt that would be paid off in the 1923–24 fiscal year.[15]

Over the spring of 1919, as labour and agrarian protest swept into Ottawa, western MPs and some Unionists challenged the protectionist tariff provisions of White's budget, which was presented on 5 June. Farmers' advocate Thomas Alexander Crerar, who had resigned as agriculture minister on the previous day, saw the need for more nontariff revenue, such as increased income taxes and inheritance and land taxes, to deal with the staggering war debt. As he had argued before, White insisted that such taxes "would not meet a fraction of the deficit." He also had to deal with tariff requests from specialized sectors based on Victory Loan expectations. In March 1919, for instance, marine-equipment producers petitioned for greater support, citing the subscriptions of manufacturers and employees, on the grounds that official advertising had created the impression that proceeds would go toward domestic shipbuilding.[16]

White's budget did make concessions to farmers, notably in tariff reductions. In response to western grievances, he even ventured to have a tariff commission formed. Recognizing the hardships caused by increased costs of living, customs duties were reduced by repealing the five-percent rate on the British preferential tariff and extending exemptions on certain commodities. The budget also raised corporate and personal income taxes and continued the business-profits tax. Overriding calls for a central bank,[17] the Finance Act was extended (and its provisions related to bank advances would be made permanent in the Finance

Act of 1923). The demobilization and other appropriation bills would receive assent a day later. Satisfied that most of Canada's debt could be handled through refunding and redemption, White was equally pleased that most of the debt was owed in Canada: $1,510,000,000 versus $326,700,000 in Britain and $150,873,000 in the United States. What he also saw, in a war year, was the need not for tax tinkering but for another domestic war loan, which he formally announced on 8 May. In the two weeks after the budget, White endured much pointed debate about the Victory Loans. He responded on 18 June with another aggressive defence. Tax-free issues, he maintained, had been necessary to compete with Anglo-French bonds offering 7 or 8 percent. In addition, the cost of flotation was greater in proportion than in the United States, whose war bonds had been sold free of charge, whereas in Canada salesmen charged commissions. "We needed the money and could not have got so much on a voluntary basis," he would later claim. In the early morning hours of 19 June, his budget passed, with twelve Liberal Unionists joining the Opposition. The dissidence left a fractured government.[18]

Following the budget, White turned to other ongoing matters. Debenture stock was converted into 1918 Victory Bonds; as in every war year, more temporary loans were obtained from the banks, secured by treasury bills. British war bonds from 1914 to 1915 were cancelled and credited to the British Treasury against advances by Canada. In July, a sterling obligation of some $20 million was paid off in London. That same month, a new loan of $75 million in two- and ten-year bonds had to be negotiated with a syndicate of New York bankers organized by J.P. Morgan and Company to refinance Canada's loan of 1917, maturing on 1 August, which "represented about as heavy a loan as Canada could raise there."[19] Although White had few options, he was deemed reckless. The rate of upwards of 6 percent caused disbelief in financial circles: "This sounds a good deal like war-time, when, in fact, the war ended over six months ago," a hostile *Globe* professed.[20] Reports from New York delighted in the loan's oversubscription. For White, the London settlement and New York loan marked turning points. With them, he told a reporter on 9 July, all of Canada's external maturities were arranged "for a long time to come,"[21] meaning into the 1930s. With the prime minister back from peace talks in Paris, a worn-out White once again tendered resignation, citing the decline of his health and "personal affairs."[22] Borden accepted, and White left office (but not the Commons) on 2 August 1919. The day before, a new Victory Loan (a "Peace Loan," the *Globe* called it, "without the patriotic impetus of previous campaigns") was announced. There was never any doubt that it would be a domestic loan. Informal talk of floating another loan in the United States foundered on the recent experience in New York and on the Canadian dollar's weakness. During a conference on the loan on 1 August at the Château Laurier hotel, White was reflective, his remarks consistent with past realizations: "In war time, the treasury loses control to a large extent over expenditures ... Finance becomes secondary in war time; the money must be found."[23]

Sir Henry Lumley Drayton

To the surprise of many outsiders, White was succeeded by the stolid Sir Henry Lumley Drayton, chief commissioner of the federal Board of Railway Commissioners. Borden had been considering him as a replacement since at least February 1918. His work on the board had immersed him in railway operations and finance, maritime transport, and the nationalization debate. For his first three months in the finance portfolio, he was almost constantly involved in the Victory Loan campaign, starting on 3 September with an address to the directors of the Canadian National Exhibition in Toronto. The *Financial Post* and many others saw a dramatic difference in the demands faced by White and Drayton. "In the maelstrom of war and war expenditure," the former's "mandate was not to count the cost." But, facing retrenchment and scrutiny by soldiers and farmers alike, Drayton, in the estimate of Sir George Foster, the minister of trade and commerce and a former finance minister, "will feel inclined to handle the proceeds of this new loan, not as though it were drawn from inexhaustible supply, but as though it were coming from near the bottom of the barrel."[24] Elected in October in a by-election, Drayton remained overshadowed for much of the fall and winter by White, who, after a short holiday, had returned to the Commons as a backbencher on 11 September, greeted by cheers.

The following month, White, still an indispensable authority, was called to testify on Canada's financial condition before a parliamentary committee on re-establishment problems, notably the demand of veterans' organizations for increased gratuities and bonuses, a debate that was dividing the nascent veterans' movement. He had already seen dependant and disability pensions escalate from $2,447,375.03 in the fiscal year 1916–17 to $16,598,601.06 in 1918–19. His summary of debt and obligations supported the government's intention not to increase gratuities, a decision meant to demonstrate its resolve to control the debt. White expounded on the next war loan (and the need for another in 1920) and on funds for re-establishment. Of the 1919 loan, he claimed, $225 million would be needed to meet past expenditures and bank loans; any balance would carry the government "for a very few months afterwards." In White's opinion, money could not be found for costlier cash gratuities on top of pensions; the issue of special bonds to soldiers, as proposed by one breakaway veterans' group (the United Veterans' League, headed by the truculent John Harry Francis Flynn and backed by a handful of MPs), would "demoralize the market for securities and bonds." Calls in other forums by Flynn and some Progressive MPs for a "tax on wealth," much debated in Europe, was just too radical. The committee also heard from deputy minister Thomas Cooper Boville and federal tax commissioner Robert Walker Breadner.

Boville's sweeping review, dense with figures, explained the web of loans and financial commitments, including demobilization and credits for Britain and other Allies, and confirmed the absolute necessity for borrowing. His testimony underscored the utility of short-term borrowing from the banks on the security of treasury bills, usually for four months or so, when loan proceeds had been exhausted. In 1919, this bridge funding totalled about $240 million. Overall, Boville stated on 27 October, on the eve of the new Victory Loan for $300 million, "We must constantly look forward to money raised by loans to meet our obligations." In short, the loan was already spent. In anticipation, the department had borrowed not only the $240 million from the banks but another $35 million elsewhere. He foresaw the need, in addition to the Victory Loan, to borrow further large sums in order to meet government estimates and commitments on railways, shipbuilding, demobilization, and other major expenditures. Failure to get $500 million in 1920 meant cutting appropriations or undertakings already launched.

These testimonies, rife with wisdom accepted by loan publicists, backed White's conclusion but left some frustrated. "Boville's examination was just cold-blooded figures," committee member Edward Walter Nesbitt confessed. Charles Grant MacNeil, counsel at the hearings for the Great War Veterans' Association, was especially perplexed. "I have here the newspaper report of Mr. Boville's evidence, giving his figures; Sir Thomas White's Budget speech, and the Victory Loan Campaign literature," he concluded, "and I find that there are many discrepancies. It is impossible for the man who is not a financial expert to reconcile these discrepancies."[25] Whereas Boville was found to be obscure and was not well liked among his staff, who dubbed him the "Kaizer," White was respected within the civil service, grudgingly so in the Commons.

There, seemingly re-energized, he debated the takeover of the Grand Trunk Pacific's operations with William Stevens Fielding, who had returned to the house as a Liberal-Unionist in the election of 1917. He also helped Drayton to organize and campaign for the Victory Loan, the formal terms of which were announced on 21 October. The prospectus of 27 October called for $300 million at five and a-half percent and an issue price of 100, in five- and fifteen-year bonds. Conversions from past loans were allowed, and for the first time, in a reversal dictated by White under political and agrarian pressure before leaving office, the interest on bonds would be taxable. The risk there, much debated in the newspapers and elsewhere over the previous months, was the removal of one inducement for large corporations and banks to subscribe. The proceeds would help to pay off Canada's indebtedness, cover the costs of demobilization and industrial reconstruction, including shipbuilding, and establish credits necessary for purchases of grain, foodstuffs, and timber by Britain, France, Belgium, Italy, and Greece. (As of 31 March 1920, Canada's funded debt payable stood at $2,066,856,126.23 in Canada, mostly in war loans; at $336,001,469.72 in London; and at $135,873,000 in New York, a substantial increase in a year.) Debt in the United States would be intensified by Britain's use of Canadian and Newfoundland securities to pay down its debt to America.

The Victory Loan campaign that ran from 27 October to 15 November 1919 faced headwinds. Although Drayton and experts such as Lloyd Harris, head of the Canadian trade mission to Britain, promoted the loan's benefits for trade, the *Globe*'s skepticism over financing foreign purchases of foodstuffs while the Dominion faced debt was common. Some cynics feared that loan funds were going toward the purchase of the Grand Trunk Pacific's rail network. Without the impetus of war, and facing reaction to the taxation provision and par pricing, as well as stiff competition in the bond market (including a drop in the price of "Victories"), the results fell off from 1918 to 795,463 subscribers (344,594 fewer) and $653,475,550 ($53,642,000 less). The amount allotted was $616,999,000. As in most war loans, new money merged with conversions, and some subscribers took time to pay up.

As with all of Canada's Dominion War Loans and Victory Loans, market factors impinged, with ups and downs. Prior to the 1919 issue, there was heavy liquidation on the stock exchanges of all the loans, causing price declines that, it was feared, would have a "depressing effect" on the new flotation. After the war had ended and patriotic sentiment subsided, small holders of bonds and war-savings certificates had started to redeem them, with some impact on public confidence. As a result, and faced with "tight money" conditions immediately after an exchange-rate shift,[26] the Victory Loan Special Committee was reactivated on 16 August 1919 to stabilize prices in the purchase and resale of bonds, especially the large quantities being unloaded by major investors. Reactivation was needed in the opinion of Edward Rogers Wood because the market in Victory Loan securities "has been sagging off quite noticeably." Wood, the Special Committee, and the press were familiar, too, with unease in financial markets elsewhere, part of the aftershock of the financial disequilibrium caused by the war. As well, the American Treasury was struggling to refinance short-term certificates, long-term loans were suspect, interest rates were fragile, and the resale value of Liberty Bonds was problematic.

The committee's transactions were facilitated by the trading account established at the Bank of Montreal in the aftermath of the 1917 Victory Loan. Periods varied for the restriction or open trading of the different Victory Loan issues. Those of 1917 and 1918 were delisted from the Toronto and Montreal exchanges on 22 January 1920, with control going back to the Special Committee, a move that upset many dealers. Calm market conditions would allow the committee to cease operations on 29 November 1920, when open trading on all issues resumed and bonds still in department hands went into the government's sinking-fund account.[27] The relisting of Victory Bonds caused some disruption in the market.[28] Under a special agreement, the committee would continue to deal in 1919 maturities until 31 December, after which, along with the removal of the embargo on securities, prices began to conform to market conditions. The volumes of bonds that went through the committee were substantial: between 24 November 1919 and 30 November 1920, it purchased $289,482,400 worth, but to the end, there was argument over the value of control.[29] Not surprisingly, White remained unofficially involved in its operation. He was also a prime defender of both the loan and his past financial administration. In May 1920, when Fielding had questioned an apparent loss in the Victory Loan trading account, an affronted White interrupted to say that it had actually made money in 1918 and that stabilization "did not cost the Dominion one cent."[30] There were grounds for both views. The trading committee made a profit of $123,998.31 on 1917's Victory Bonds, according to the public accounts for fiscal 1920–21, but at the conclusion of the committee's operations, the $95,007,950 worth of bonds remaining unsold were cancelled and deducted from the government's funded debt.

1920–22

Throughout the war, changes to the revenue structure had been determined by stupendous requirements. In November 1919, the *Vancouver Daily Star*, long a proponent of heavy taxation, voiced the sentiment that White's methods of finance had been "hand-to-mouth."[31] But the charge was becoming irrelevant. By 1920, war finances were shifting into ongoing market considerations, refunding, and different revenue streams as Canada dealt with its postwar debt. Victory Bonds nonetheless remained a commonplace feature of Canadians' financial holdings, but with costs of living spiking – followed by deflation, the dimming of patriotic incentive, and persistent misunderstandings about investment – finance department officials scrambled to tell malcontents why they could not get full value for their bonds before maturity. In some out-of-touch quarters, notions took hold that farmers and industrial workers were cushioned by their Victory Bonds during the "high-price years" of 1919–20. All outstanding issues peaked at above par in June 1919,[32] but as the prices of services and goods rose, the real value of bonds eroded. White's suggestion in 1919 of another war loan in the fall of 1920, which never took shape, drifted into the realm of rumour, with speculation arising not that a new issue was coming but that a campaign for the wider distribution of existing issues was planned. Any ideas, however, faced market realities and were subsumed in the work of the market-stabilizing committee. The removal of control in November 1920, which caused ripples as the market adjusted, would be a factor. Not until 1923 would long-term bonds, with maturities from 1925 to 1937, begin to trend again above par on the market, where other factors had been in play.[33]

Throughout 1918, the Canadian dollar had been weakening vis-à-vis the American dollar, which was riding an economic boom, a trend that would continue after the war. Following excessive monetary expansion during the war, inflation, and trade imbalances linked to the war effort and demobilization, and facing a falling British pound, the Canadian dollar would slide to a record low of just over US$0.84 in early 1920. In the Commons, in March of that year, White again refused to acknowledge inflationary causes and touted his efforts to stabilize exchange while maintaining confidence in Canada's financial institutions. Interventions in the exchange market to smooth out daily fluctuations through the government's agent bank, the Bank of Montreal, had minimal effect.[34]

Internationally, the slide of the British pound against the Canadian dollar had led to the worrisome selling of Canadian securities held in Britain, notably railways, a movement that depressed security prices in Canada, including war bonds, in the last half of 1919. As a result, in February 1920, in two other (and related) moves to support the prices for Victory Bonds, a worried Drayton had the banks, bond dealers, and brokers place an embargo on acquisitions of Canadian securities from overseas because such purchases were depressing the price of Victory Bonds. Under pressure from heavy sell-offs and discontented financiers, some of whom vented to White, the embargo would be lifted in January 1921, allowing trading to resume and the government to liquidate its holdings of bonds. And on 23 February, the Special Committee, which Drayton would vigorously defend in Parliament, lowered the prices for Victory Bonds.

The embargo and price drop temporarily shocked the financial community. In protest over the embargo, the Royal Securities Corporation withdrew from the Bond Dealers' Association of Canada, Greenshields and Company offered "severe criticism," and the *Globe* denounced government interference "to bring about political ends."[35] To some dealers and large investors, the drop occasioned buying opportunities, but many bondholders felt deceived, convinced that they could never recover their money before maturity because of both the cut – up to 3 and a-half points on some issues – and the sales fees mandated by the Special Committee. Between February and September, widows, veterans, dealers, companies, banks, fraternal organizations, and other fault-finders inundated Drayton's department with letters. Betrayal of patriotic motivation, misrepresentation by canvassers, and mismanagement were among the grievances. D.C. McIntyre of Brockville, Ontario, wrote to Drayton on 25 February 1920, "I, like many others, to help the loan along, bought these bonds, but not to hold them," and then, "like a bolt from the blue," prices fell. On 17 April, F.A. Burlington of Wellington, Ontario, wrote,

> I very foolishly read all that fool literature about the great security and safe investment of Victory Bonds and took out $5,000.00 of 1934 issue of 1919 not being in a position to take former issues where the investor was insured from any tax but still being damn fool enough to think Dominion of Canada could not go below par after reading that great and expensive publicity literature and playing into the hands of bond brokers and special salesmen who raked down a nice commission like Wood Gundy of 50,000 or better and in this place men who kept 4,000 miles from that battle front although of military age and looking fit.

Burlington knew his letter might not reach Drayton if "some stool warmer sees fit to throw it in the waste basket."[36]

Not every protester was a small investor. Large corporations were also affected by the price downturn. William Allan Black of Ogilvie Flour Mills in Montreal laid out his case on 13 March. In 1919, his company had purchased a volume of Victory Bonds for patriotic reasons, knowing that it would have to dispose of them at later dates with "some sacrifice." It had gradually worked off $700,000 worth but still had about $1 million to dispose of. When the company tried to sell, it was told by the Special Committee that Drayton wanted large owners to hold off. Within ten days, the price dropped from 99 to 96, Black claimed, posing a potential loss of $30,000. Drayton's reply likely provided little comfort. He understood that many bond investments had been made not purely for patriotic reasons but "more in the character of an underwriting than anything else and an underwriting with but little opportunity of profit. This has always been then case," hence the formation of the Special Committee to control disposals and "restrain sales as much as possible until the offerings could be absorbed." Such stabilization, he continued, was proving difficult due to the dumping of high-interest Canadian securities, such as railways, by overseas owners and due to "depreciated foreign exchange." Without stabilization, prices would have fallen further.

There was a common thread in these letters. Many subscribers, especially those professing no understanding of the "intricacies of finance," never intended or were unable to hold their bonds to maturity. Many had been led to believe that there would be little or no depreciation. Market stabilization, with the consequent impositions of sales fees and the fall of prices, worked as a management strategy but did not sit well with investors who had to sell. Drayton seems to have been less perturbed by such complaints than was White, who had been imbued with the need to sustain public confidence during wartime. Responsibility for responding to all these letters fell to department solicitor Robert Botsford Viets and secretary Bennet John Roberts. Drawing on set explanations, they cited the factors in play: supply and demand, the impact of foreign exchange, the government's original promise of return at maturity, the likelihood of rebound, low prices internationally, and the claim that Canadians were better off with bonds.[37] Such a response must have been galling.

In addition to bond pricing, other wartime programs were transformed. In early November 1919, the *Financial Post* had anticipated the cancellation of the war-savings and thrift stamps as a weak revenue source and had suggested their replacement by a savings certificate, "leaving out the war idea." The Canadian Bankers' Association pulled bank branches out of the program, finding the expense and work involved "out of all proportion to the results."[38] In December, on grounds of administrative expense (14 percent), the sale of the 25¢ thrift stamps was discontinued, except through schools and post offices; the stamps' influence in schools, the government recognized, "has been good in promoting thrift." These 25¢ stamps, and their accumulation in a booklet, encouraged and inculcated scores of schoolchildren and low-income families; merchants found them to be handy promotional giveaways. The thrift stamps and the $5 war-savings stamps, with a maturity of 1 January 1924, continued to be sold for some months. The savings movement was being wound down; the National War Savings Committee was discontinued on 1 January 1920. As of 31 March 1920, outstanding war-savings and thrift stamps (always accounted for together) amounted to $2,576,549.65. With the 1917 issue of war-savings certificates discontinued in December 1918, the government introduced three-year Dominion of Canada War Savings Certificates in December 1919 under an order-in-council, offering them in denominations of $5, $10, $25, $50, and $100 at banks and money-order post offices, purchasable at the rate of $85 per $100. But there, too, sales and revenue were modest: only $531,636.75 by 31 March 1920. What did pick up, even in a falling postwar economy, were receipts from war-tax revenues (inland revenue and income and business-profits taxes), which doubled between 1919–20 ($82,079,801.58) and 1920–21 ($168,385,327.50). Like the income tax, the Business Profits War Tax Act, which was to expire at the end of 1919, lingered on and was amended in 1920, part of the new fiscal state.

During the parliamentary session of 26 February to 1 July 1920, White, although no longer finance minister, continued to be targeted for his wartime initiatives, especially the Victory Bonds, including their market control and tax status. In a spirited defence on 8 March, he reiterated the essentials for any minister launching a loan: "In the first place, he must get his money – the offering must be a success; and in the second place, he must consider the market situation after the loan, especially if he is going back for another loan."[39] Indeed, in 1919–20, discussions of Victory Bonds had moved from the patriotic, win-the-war realm to a purely market context. In the House of Commons, White and Drayton fielded questions on the securities embargo, the Victory Loan Special Committee, the amount of outstanding bonds, the mechanics of the loan, and regional annoyances. On 7 April, in response to one Unionist MP, a comprehensive statement was tabled of all Canadian loans since 1911, including issues of treasury bills.[40]

In his budget of 18 May, Drayton, turning the corner on borrowing, launched a program of fiscal reorchestration. The first finance minister since Confederation to call for debt reduction in a budget,[41] he had already started to scrutinize the government's books to determine the "exact position" of Canada's debt. He understood that winning the war had "required raising large sums of money in the easiest possible way,"[42] but with the war won, Canada faced maturities on several major, long-term obligations. Out of the proceeds of the 1919 Victory Loan, a floating debt of $247 million had been paid off, but much remained. At the close of the fiscal year on 31 March 1920, Canada's net debt stood at $2,248,868,623.79 (an increase of $647,337,591.35 over the previous year).[43] Annual estimates and spending would continue to climb, but in his budget Drayton bravely announced a halt to further loans, although he would later attempt to authorize oversubscriptions on past war loans. In a bid to counter inflation, the amount of dominion notes in circulation was reduced. Turning to taxes, he repealed the war-tariff increase and the tax on films in theatres. He continued, at lowered rates, the business-profits war tax, placed a surtax on individual and corporate incomes, increased luxury taxes, and introduced Canada's first general sales tax on consumer goods except food and coal. For the next six weeks, taxation dominated debate, with the Liberals waiting for the Conservatives to collapse.[44]

Despite Drayton's focus on the debt, military spending did not abate. Estimates called for $12,498,506 for the Department of Militia, an increase of $4,128,953.98. Andrew Ross McMaster, the Liberal MP for Brome, Quebec, felt compelled to ask: "Are the people of Canada sane folk or are they continuing the mad race which has been carried on in Europe" since the end of the war? In reply, he was told by the minister of militia that the increase was needed to deal with "internal unrest in the country." Perhaps, he meant the bogey of industrial unrest, although the real cost lay in military reorganization.[45] By the summer of 1920, the agitation over soldiers' gratuities had died down, but many veterans' organizations remained resentful. Drayton was easily able to ignore the radical calls by Flynn, as president of the United Veterans' League, for the conscription of war profiteers' hoardings and the use of the oversubscriptions on the last Victory Loans for the soldiers. Debt filled the big picture. During the early 1920s, discussions of a wartime finance policy based on need gave way, shaped by the agrarian-based goals of the newly formed National Progressive Party and the depression of 1920–21, to broad analyses of taxation, debt, worldwide depression, the government's role in the economy, and the Finance Act. Professional and academic economists, among them William Clifford Clark, came forward to scrutinize postwar realities. From September 1920, Drayton travelled widely while chairing a tariff commission, where he heard earfuls about goods and issues, from shoes to the contentious luxury tax.

Early in 1921, to gain a true understanding of the debt, including war loans and other public flotations since 1914, he initiated an audit. With the federal audit office and the public accounts committee in states of flux, the job was given to the private accounting firm Edwards, Morgan and Company, which reported in 1922. (A prominent accountant, George Edwards had worked closely with Joseph Wesley Flavelle at the Imperial Munitions Board.) The accounts of the Victory Loan Special Committee had already been audited in 1919 by another private firm from Toronto. Over the years, the auditor general had cursorily reviewed the finance department's summary figures on the war loans; some accounts had been "examined" for both White and Drayton by Thomas Bradshaw; Alfred Ernest Ames had begun reporting in early 1918; the Special Committee had kept track of its own accounts from 1918 to 1921; and other accounts had been audited for the Dominion and regional executives. But nothing comprehensive had been done. The clean report produced by Edwards, Morgan and Company was briefly marred in late 1921 by a finding of embezzlement of bond coupons worth some $33,000, a finding disavowed by James Ernest Rourke, the department's overworked comptroller of currency (and acting deputy minister), who had internal control of bonds, gold stores, and notes. He committed suicide during the night of 10–11 December, an unfortunate "war casualty," White lamented. Within days, department accountant John Godfrey was arrested for the embezzlement.

White himself had already withdrawn from politics. Borden had been succeeded as prime minister in July 1920 by his bulldog, Arthur Meighen, White having resisted the call. He would claim that he had never intended to be a career politician; the accolades that had started to come his way after the war brought no recompense.[46] The Commons's speaker announced White's resignation of his seat on 6 April 1921, two months before the end of Parliament and the call for an election in December, which the Liberals would win, resoundingly, with the Conservatives trailing the second place Progressives, led by Thomas Alexander Crerar. The former minister nonetheless remained active, and better paid, as a municipally appointed arbitrator and as a member of corporate boards and the federal Grand Trunk Pacific arbitration board, to which he had been appointed in July 1920. His report, which would hold the railway's capital stock to be valueless (and the whole railway ill-conceived), gives open substance to his reputation as an analyst.[47] After April 1921, he faced flak over his past handling of western grain matters and a contentious case of corporate tax evasion, as well as his lucrative Grand Trunk arbitration work, and he gave a few election speeches in support of the Conservatives and his own past performance in the finance department. In 1927, as will be seen in Chapter 13, he stood up to the charges of Winston Churchill. a wartime minister of munitions. As late as the 1930, in response to taunts by Liberal prime minister William Lyon Mackenzie King over postwar debt, White was still defending his recourse to borrowing.

Canada's total debt and funded debt would eventually decline during the 1920s, with debt management achieved primarily through refunding and conversions. Debt reduction could also be realized through outright repayments. To pay the $25 million instalment due 1 April 1921 on the Public Service Loan of 1916, Drayton described the means of discharge in the Commons: "By shipping to New York 'free' gold purchased from time to time from Canadian miners and paid for in cash out of ordinary revenue $19,500,000; balance provided for by flotation of temporary treasury bills."[48] In 1920, the Liberals, under King, had been coy about the prospect of launching a new loan. In 1921, Drayton saw the need for refunding, although the Victory Loans' cachet had faded. The European credits arranged in 1919 produced a stream of contracts for Canadian manufacturers, but the biggest borrower, beleaguered Romania, also became the worst defaulter, and in 1921 Meighen closed the Canadian Trade Commission.

Following the Liberals' return to power that year, it fell to a long-time critic, Finance Minister William Stevens Fielding, to deal with maturing Victory Loans and other obligations, beginning in 1922 with a $100 million loan in New York and a conversion loan at home on the 1917 issue, followed in 1923 with a conversion and refunding loan taken up by a Toronto syndicate. The new continuum is illustrated by this loan. In September 1923, tenders had been called by the government for a loan to refund five-year bonds of the 1918 Victory Loan that would mature on 1 November, amounting to $172,459,650. The resulting issue consisted of five- and twenty-year bonds that would mature on 15 October 1928 and 15 October 1943 respectively. More refunding issues were made by Liberal governments in 1924, 1925, 1926, and 1927, such that by 1929 the bulk of the debt was owing to the Canadian "people."[49] Canada's small share in the fiscal year 1925–26 of the sums awarded as wartime reparations, an evolving balance, did little to alter the debt. By late 1927, Canada had paid off $161 million of its war debt, but the remaining load was immense. The conflict had cost almost $1.7 billion in direct war expenditures; related costs, which included interest and pensions, pushed the figure to an estimated $6.6 billion.[50]

Refunding loans came almost annually in the 1930s. The successful dominion conversion loan of 1931, which dealt with maturities between 1931 and 1934, was cast by Prime Minister Richard Bedford Bennett as a response not to the war but to the Great Depression – the "Dirty Thirties." (Even then, Victory Bonds were being bought as safe investments by various organizations, one being the Ontario Hockey Association.) Newspapers exaggerated the "mammoth machine" formed to market the bonds of 1931, with the *Globe* claiming that the "feverish activity of dealers is reminiscent" of past Victory Loan campaigns. Even White came forward to praise the loan.[51] The last of the wartime issues to mature was that of March 1917, which came due in 1937. It, too, was refunded. The fifteen-year bonds of the 1919 issue were refunded in 1934, during the Depression, through a new issue of two- and fifteen-year bonds, thus extending the obligation, for the last time, to 1949.[52] The war debt and its impact continued to overshadow public finance throughout the 1930s, as seen not just in the public accounts but also in evidence such as that presented to the House of Commons's Select Standing Committee on Banking and Commerce in 1933.[53] Overall, in terms of the international perspective, Canada came out of the war in relatively good shape financially.[54]

A new pattern of finance had thus been set, with the urgency and grand publicity of the Great War years reduced,[55] although, when the first publicly offered war loan of the Second World War was launched in January 1940, it was clear that operational lessons and informative documentation on publicity had been drawn from the issues of 1915–19.[56] The apparatus of the loans during the second conflict was much the same,[57] with the National War Finance Committee calling up records and films of the dominion publicity committees for 1918 and 1919 to inform the advertising of the Victory Loans of the second war.[58] With reference to the first conflict, studies were undertaken in 1939–40 in the finance department in preparation for a different war.[59] In October 1939, to set up Canada's forthcoming loan, Finance Minister James Layton Ralston wanted nothing "like the generous terms prevailing during the Great War." Outside economists such as John James Deutsch, Frank Albert Knox, Frank Herbert Brown, and John Frederick Parkinson came forth with articles related to the Great War. Parkinson, in a view with much hindsight, revived the debate of taxation versus borrowing and argued that finance could not be separated from politics, resource capability, and public will. He compared the fiscal realities and balance of payment problems in trade resulting from the agrarian-based economy of Canada during the first war to the greater emphasis on manufacturing war goods (guns, aircraft, vehicles, and so on) during the second. A few journalists posited that during the first war, because of its unknown duration and outcome and for market reasons, including interest rates in Britain and France that reached 6 percent, Canada had needed to offer competitive rates.[60]

In 1914–20, Canada dealt with finding money, reciprocal financing, the pushing of political boundaries, and public engagement. Part 2 examines how this combination unfolded.

Part 2
From Broadside to Vaudeville in the War-Loan Campaigns

5

The Dominion War Loans, 1915–17

IMPLORING POSTERS AND RACKETY parades, with much participatory appeal, would be introduced in the radical reframing of national publicity for the first Victory Loan in the fall of 1917. Such boosterish techniques were generally uncommon before then as tools of public financial engagement. Although the Department of Finance did not turn to ordinary Canadians to fund the war effort in 1914, a host of charities did, among them the Canadian Red Cross. Citizens anxious to help were greeted everywhere by requests. The campaign in Toronto for the British Red Cross's Trafalgar Day Appeal in October 1915 (which raised $231,500) featured parades, concerts, bunting, posters, and all manner of promotions. In the newspapers, word pictures of brutality and human-interest stories (a neglected aspect of war studies)[1] were brought forward. At the beginning of the year, a *Globe* columnist had captured the new atmosphere: "Even the least patriotic cannot evade the posters, glaring headlines and war talk we hear on every street corner, in every business and social circle." On the Red Cross cause, *Globe* columnist Peter McArthur proclaimed a "need of immediate and full publicity."[2] It was in this milieu that the concept of public funding of the war emerged.

Throughout 1915, the press began drawing Canadians' attention to the Allied war loans, particularly Britain's in June, France's Emprunt de la défense nationale (of interest in Quebec), and the Anglo-French loan secured in New York in September. In July, the *Globe*, for one, saw much practical value in a domestic loan.[3] The *Regina Morning Leader* also claimed to have been an early proponent, only to see its advocacy ridiculed.[4] Although his department followed the British loan, White was unprepared to commit. By October, enabled by a favourable trade balance and market conditions, he was ready. In his "I get the money" speech in Toronto on 7 October,[5] he announced Canada's first domestic loan, with war bonds to be sold through bank branches and brokers, but without emulating Britain's popular techniques or the canvassing networks then being used by the Canadian Patriotic Fund and like organizations.

On 2 November, White met with the executive committee of the Canadian Bankers' Association in Ottawa.[6] After confirming the government's commitment to borrowing, he pressed the banks on what they could subscribe "to ensure the success of the loan" and began sorting out such mechanics as the interest rate, the balance of patriotism versus investment, and the role of the banks in delivering temporary receipts and bonds as well as the payment of interest coupons. With the campaign set for 22–30 November, there was much work to be done, including printing the bonds and distributing application forms to brokers and banks. There were 3,159 bank branches operating in Canada in 1915, ready to accept commissions on subscriptions and to take on new clients, which necessitated renting safe-deposit boxes for bonds and assisting foreign-born residents wishing to access the bonds of their home countries. (Pre-war issues from Germany were still trading in 1914–15.) The brokers, too, were active, although not yet in an organizational capacity. Wood, Gundy and Company of Toronto and Saskatoon, "the largest purchasers of Canadian Government and Municipal bonds," circularized its clients, distributed postcards soliciting subscriptions, and advertised with standard propagandistic twists such as: "Do you want to see the War at an end?"[7] Emanating from the Department of Finance and the government's printing bureau, advance notices and prospectuses were sent to newspapers, all eager for advertising revenue. Without question, wire-fed newspapers were the most efficient tool of communication.

At the same time, how many Canadians read newspapers, saw war news or war-loan advertising, or were swayed by patriotic pressures? Historian Robert S. Prince suggests a link between the slumping circulations of popular dailies (such as the *Toronto Daily Star*) and cost-of-living pinches or a readership drawn away by service.[8] Patriotism is a complex sentiment – an expression of genuine national feeling or superficial rhetoric. Historian David Silbey explains that British workers enlisted for reasons other than nationalism. Loyalties based on geography or personal attachments, for example, counted. Workers could display skepticism about government propaganda both before and during the war. Traces of such distrust lurk in accounts of Canada's war-loan campaigns and Patriotic Fund operations, along with such prohibitive factors as illness or low income. Some of the households approached by canvassers expressed doubts. In letters, some soldiers took exception to the shallow patriotism that was generated by the better wages offered in factories, that was lapped up by people with "time and money on their hands," and that was displayed by haughty after-dinner speakers with no knowledge of a soldier's life or by the "bluffing flag waving patriotic type."[9] For many citizens, some elements of propaganda worked; others did not.

To many rural newspapers, the quarter-page prospectus for the 1915 loan was novel; the *Chinook Advance* (Chinook, Alberta) made room for this "big war loan advertisement."[10] In addition to such direct promotion, White had toured to gauge interest. On 7 November, foreshadowing future loan promotions, he spoke in florid imperialistic language at a recruitment rally at Massey Hall in Toronto, where he was joined on stage by, among others, Lieutenant George Reginald Forneret, who had been wounded in France at the Battle of Neuve-Chapelle in March. Before and during the campaign, newspapers would monitor each other, picking up distant news. The finance department would issue statements by wire service and press release, flashing updates along with messages from White, the government's most newspaper-friendly minister.[11] He understood the medium; journalists in turn reported his propensity for deep analysis. He would cultivate close relationships with a coterie of reporters and have his budget speeches released in manageable parts: his substantive statements for immediate release and then the dry stuff of duties and tariffs. White nevertheless had foes as well as friends in the parliamentary Press Gallery: Wellington John Jeffers of the *Globe* was a fan; John Knox Munro of Toronto's *Evening Telegram* and *Maclean's Magazine* downplayed him with gossipy aplomb; and in Montreal, *Le Devoir*'s Ernest Bilodeau lambasted him.

Equally as important in 1915, in the absence of any organized campaign and overt propaganda, newspaper reports on the loan's progress insinuated a community of contribution. To the *Phoenix Pioneer* (Phoenix, British Columbia), the loan was "a well-made silver bullet in [the] hide of Prussian militarism." The moral imperatives of thrift, saving, and eliminating "superfluous expenses" such as drink were also put in place, buttressing patriotism and corporate desires to demonstrate support. Throughout the coverage, the heralding of the hypothetical small investor enhanced a nascent democratization of the loan, although identifying investors of slight means is difficult. (Only the listing of large subscribers in the newspapers carried social weight.) Little account was taken of the competing demands of the Canadian Patriotic and other relief funds, which offered no investment return. Still, there was anecdotal support of brisk subscriptions on opening days, along with catchy stories of personal experiences. In some regions, interest was slow to develop. Vaguely reported trends in one region (on farmers' interest, for instance) were contradicted in another, and there were logistical challenges: reports of weak canvassing of bank clients, the late arrival of application forms (nothing reached the Yukon), and the delays caused by sending applications to Ottawa. Many brokers, feeling outdone, charged that the banks had received prospectuses days before them. For the most part, brokers and bond dealers recognized the unequalled opportunity for new business, and they were quick to tell the press as much. In Saint John, James MacMurray of the Eastern Securities Company reported on

> some of the smaller people who had never even looked at the possibility of city and other securities, nothing outside the post office savings bank in fact, who are taking out applications. These are some of the people that I understand the financial advertisers of the government desire to get; it means bringing the realization of the war home to them in a new way and emphasizes the necessity for whole hearted patriotic effort.

Among applicants known to MacMurray were an "old lady of seventy, small tradesmen and even girl stenographers."[12]

The campaign of November 1915 was nonetheless a quiet, short affair. With no centralized organization or strong promotional apparatus, it lacked the spate of events and displays of public enthusiasm that would enliven the campaigns of late 1917, 1918, and 1919. The subscriber target for canvassers was never precise; in some communities, such as Moose Jaw, bank customers were singled out. In some provinces, the campaign overlapped with Patriotic Fund canvassing. For the most part, the loans of 1915–16 flew above partisan lines. During the 1915 campaign, two Liberal newspapers in Quebec, *L'Autorité* (Montreal) and *L'Avenir du nord* (Saint-Jérôme), endorsed the loan, although the latter bashed the government over its handling of munition funding.[13] The English-language financial press deemed the loan a success, a boon to the securities industry. In a step toward granting White celebrity status, the *Monetary Times* (Toronto) profiled him as the "Man Behind the Loan." In the end, during the week of the campaign, war bonds pushed business in other securities to the side. Even with limited publicity, applications swamped the Department of Finance, and the loan was vastly oversubscribed, as anticipated.

Lessons were learned, notably about where money could originate, which included the businesses that invested heavily, the municipalities, boards of trade, and school boards, the fraternal and social organizations, the Women's Institutes and other bodies looking for a sound place for their monetary reserves and sinking funds (their floating capital), and the many anonymous individuals with $100 or more in savings accounts. Of the large subscriptions, the International Nickel Company, enriched by war production, subscribed for $1 million as well as $1 million of the Anglo-French loan, and the Canadian Bank of Commerce took $3,426,000, on top of blocks of the British and French War Loans. Hundreds of wealthy individuals also stepped forward. Within weeks of the campaign, war bonds began entering the secondary market.

With much investment capital seen as untouched, there were analysts who found the 1915 campaign insufficient. Many Canadians still remained unclear about bonds, their use as collateral for loans, and the concepts of maturity and long-term investment. "Beyond the daily announcement of the terms of the loan," the *Globe* concluded on 25 November, "no official effort is being put forth to induce people to subscribe, but apparently no stimulus is necessary." Toronto's crustily analytic *Financial Post*, which questioned the loan's popularity, had reported mixed reaction on the desirability of the Anglo-French loan and the value of canvassing for small investors, which would become a perennial debate. Some labour newspapers questioned public borrowing; the spectre of debt and inequality loomed. As early as October 1914, *The Voice* (Winnipeg) had presciently identified bond issues as the major source for war finance but one that would produce massive national debt, which would benefit only "the investing class."[14] On 19 December 1915, at the People's Forum held at Vancouver's Labor Temple, Samuel Pearson Panton, a peripatetic real-estate agent, ridiculed the war loan: only the banks would profit.[15] For reinforcement, the *British Columbia Federationist* (Vancouver), feeling knowledgeable, underlined people's general ignorance of money matters.[16] In the House of Commons, Liberal critic Alexander Kenneth Maclean would claim in February 1916 that the loan, "while widely subscribed, was not in the real sense a popular loan," White's preparations having been poorly thought out: "A campaign widespread and enthusiastic by various mediums should have been undertaken."[17] In context, the government's recognition and use of advertising as a promotional tool in 1914–15 was having mixed results, with only a few ministers on board.[18] In November 1915, one trade journal, *Economic Advertising* (Toronto), in its critique of a densely printed ad for the Anglo-French loan, had lamented the languid state of Canada's official war-loan publicity.[19] The same journal would conclude in March 1916 that the matter was still up for debate.[20] These opinions were partially offset by the estimates of such investment authorities as Thomas Bradshaw, Toronto's finance commissioner and treasurer, who saw an upswing in Canadians' investment in borrowing by federal and provincial governments, municipalities, public utilities, railways, and other private corporations.[21]

Over the nine months between November 1915 and September 1916, White would hear from Canadians, who were being bombarded with the thrift message, that the 1915 loan had lacked scope and vigour, that the next one needed to be run by a broadly based organization, that the methods of commercial advertising should be brought to bear, and that, following British models, small-denomination securities (starting at $5) should be offered. In women's columns in newspapers, domestic saving was extolled, and challenges were hurled by letter writers with an eye to another loan in the fall of 1916. Echoing complaints in other newspapers, the *Gleichen Call*, east of Calgary, lamented that in 1915 the "wage-earner and small investor" had been sidelined by the "great financial corporations." The 1916 loan "is not only for the purpose of raising money but also for allowing a patriotic people, the common people, to exercise their patriotism as best they can."[22]

In 1916, two organizations stepped up to engage public contribution: the Bond Dealers' Association of Canada (BDAC) and the Canadian Patriotic Fund. Both would have significant impacts on the government's war loans. In February 1916, the bond dealers' section of the Toronto Board of Trade met with its counterpart in Montreal with a view to forming a "national" organization that could "standardize practices." White had not bothered to approach the Toronto section when launching the first loan. Formally organized on 16 June with William Hanson (of Montreal's Hanson Brothers), the BDAC moved to inform the minister of the "troubles" experienced by members in the last loan and how they could participate in that of 1916, where commission rates, advertising, and their identification as "recognized" brokers would also be concerns. The "troubles" included brokers' unease over the placement of subscriptions directly by insurance companies (as they had done in 1915) rather than through "regular investment channels," a grievance discussed with White by Alfred Ernest Ames, the eminent Toronto broker and a vice-president of the association. There matters stood in early September when the BDAC prepared to distribute the loan circulars delivered to the assistant receiver general's office in Toronto.[23]

First established as a private fundraising organization during the South African War, the Canadian Patriotic Association had been recast in 1914 as the Canadian Patriotic Fund (CPF) and charged with providing aid to soldiers' families. With White as honorary treasurer, it was headed by Herbert B. Ames, a progressive businessman and MP from Montreal, a productive centre of charitable fundraising. As Desmond Morton explains, Ames believed that the CPF was partly designed to show how systematic thrift, along with counselling and other components, were meant to keep working-class families, especially those with their breadwinners overseas, out of poverty.[24] Rarely inclined to articulate sociological goals, White saw thrift and saving as a platform for the financial enablement of the war, even when early attempts to sell the public on voluntary thrift met with varied response. Working from the organizational model developed for the CPF branch in Montreal, Ames understood the mechanics of national and local organization, systematic canvassing, modern advertising, and conducive entertainment, when wed to patriotism, maternal sacrifice, and other forms of social pressure.

Such organizational and motivational factors faltered at the fracture lines in Canadian society, such as in Quebec, and unlike the war loan, the CPF offered no investment incentive. What it did demonstrate, as in the campaign in Saskatoon in November 1915 and the January 1916 "On to Victory" campaign of the Toronto and York County Patriotic Fund, was the effectiveness of tight local campaigns built on central offices, lists of potential donors, organized canvassers, rallies and parades, Barnumesque stunts and entertainments, and colourful paraphernalia, including "glaring posters" and contribution gauges in the form of clocks and "thermometer" poles. Cutting-edge advertisements for the campaign appeared in Toronto's newspapers, which enthused over the "whirlwind campaign," the "progressive policy" of the daily canvasses, and the "riot of enthusiasm" evident in the windup rally at Massey Hall.[25] Such fervour was found in recruitment rallies, too, and in related bodies such as the Speakers' Patriotic League, formed in March 1915 to push recruitment. By comparison, the war-loan campaign paled.

Preoccupied in early 1916 by the New York loan in March and by implementation of war-profits taxation, White remained cool to the CPF model. He rejected calls to popularize the next loan, which, he claimed for many months, was not a certainty. In 1916, the work being done by volunteers for the CPF, the Red Cross, and other organizations devoted to fundraising and serving dependants was showing signs of stress. The work was exhausting, in many regions funds were being tapped out, and social prejudices against the "unworthy" were appearing. In Alberta, civic leaders worried that voluntarism was falling off.[26] For some, new means to stimulate public engagement were called for. In March, George Augustus Warburton, an experienced fundraiser as secretary of Toronto's Young Men's Christian Association (YMCA), urged White to organize the next loan through the provinces, with voluntary committees and door-to-door canvassing, much as the innovative British Red Cross Society campaign of October 1915 had been run.[27]

When, on 13 July, White finally announced the loan, planned for September, it was clear that it would be conducted along the lines of the 1915 loan and largely out of the Department of Finance, where the minister was reluctant to relinquish control to nongovernmental operators. The King's Printer costed out advertising in the country's newspapers, and the finance department, to determine the terms of the loan, scrutinized market conditions and advice from outside experts. Simple departmental advertisements extolling the combined virtues of winning the war and securing an investment "of the highest class" began appearing in newspapers in August. Editorialists repeated the message. The *Northern Advance* (Barrie, Ontario), for one, reasoned that money had to be found: "Our own war loans [constituted] an investment rather than a contribution, but it is an investment which is patriotic through and through."[28] A strong ally, the financial press, on to a sure trend, churned out articles on the loan from a market perspective, focusing on the formative experience of 1915, the interest rate, other bonds, and the returns from the western crop, always a factor in Canada's war loans. Investors did face choices, with French, British, Russian, and even German war loans being advertised. Publicly, White called on Canadians to invest not in foreign bonds but to save for their homeland, although creating a loan within the range of the small investor – still the target – remained illusory.

From the bank returns submitted to his department, White had evidence of the savings of small depositors and of the possible appeal of small-denomination subscriptions.[29] Over the course of 1916, he heard from Canadians who called for them. They were disgruntled with the restrictive nature of the last loan, which some felt favoured the wealthy. At the same time, securities of less than $100 were administratively impractical, White candidly told Francis A. Williams of Summerland, British Columbia, in September 1916. Citing the small units available to the public in Britain, Williams had confessed, "It hurts me as a loyal Canadian not to be able even in the smallest way to help the country win the war."[30] Within months, White would relent by authorizing the issue of war certificates starting at $25. In August, Henry Victor Franklin Jones of the Canadian Bank of Commerce's head office had advised him to better broadcast the war-savings message by stirring up the "ordinary wage-earner" and "reaching the largest number," not through newspapers or spoken incitement but through the commercial means of posters, pamphlets, and dodgers (small handbills). "I am afraid that admonition, whether by speech, advertisement or poster is of little value," he wrote. As a former manager of his bank in London, familiar with British War Loans, Jones had had first-hand experience.

People here "are so remote from the war," White responded,[31] while attempting to connect with people through bonds and in the light of emerging patterns of advertising by other government departments, not to mention the reams of recruitment, cinematic and commercial posters, and casualty lists confronting people.[32] The gung-ho *Monetary Times* had no doubt about the need for "real advertising salesmanship to distribute" the war loan.[33] Recruiting efforts were showing the way, even as advertising largely remained the purview of local regiments, battalions, and military districts. Newspapers described the uncoordinated profusion of recruitment devices encountered across Ontario: clever slogans, bold posters, signs, inserts, and all manner of pitches to enlist.[34]

White disliked advertising where content could not be directed, even in light of the promotions in the Departments of Trade and Commerce (apples to offset curtailed markets in Britain), the Interior (immigration and settlement),

Agriculture and Finance (production and thrift), and Naval Service (for the Royal Naval Canadian Volunteer Reserve).[35] Some work for the militia department was done by private printing firms through the King's Printer.[36] Nor was White inclined to use advertising agencies, despite their access to advances in market research and poster design and the psychology of advertising. Hence, for the war loans, the finance department and bond houses released statements, the King's Printer prepared letterpress notices such as prospectuses, and the Canadian Press Association coordinated accounts. Graphic content was nonexistent, and commercial advertising agencies were largely sidelined, much to their dismay. The resulting separations and feuding tensions would be seen in 1916 and early 1917 in the *Printer and Publisher*, a trade journal of MacLean Publishing in Toronto (which also put out several other such journals and the *Financial Post*), and *Economic Advertising*, the creative vehicle of the Norris-Patterson Agency in Toronto.[37]

The campaign of September 1916 was a sedate event, bereft of visible promotions but with the benefit of tested machinery. The King's Printer placed the advertising copy, some of it provided by such agencies as J.J. Gibbons Limited of Toronto.[38] At the outset, to avoid discouraging new and small investors, White cautioned the newspapers to avoid announcing big advance subscriptions, but within days he was all for such publicity; it provided social recognition of subscribers and had coercive value. The *Montreal Daily Mail*, for one, obliged, with dozens of corporations and rich individuals receiving mentions. The Bank of Montreal subscribed for $7,091,800 (the largest of any bank), and Montreal-based Sun Life Assurance went in for $5.5 million.[39] Such reporting became a national trend, despite some corporate grumbling about being bombarded by investment-company mailings. In comparing the 1915 and 1916 campaigns, the *Financial Post* saw a greater efficiency in the rollout of the latter. The government poured more money into advertising and the printing of prospectuses, bonds, and scrip than in 1915. Many newspapers eagerly cooperated, with the *Monetary Times* producing a "Special War Loan Bulletin." Some publications promoted the loan to specific sectors. The *Farmers' Magazine* (Toronto) and the *Grain Growers' Guide* (Winnipeg), for instance, pushed it in columns on investment for farmers,[40] who were largely unfamiliar with such securities, just as many of them felt removed from the war and suspected that generating capital for investment or even machinery could be problematic. Although many invested in war bonds, many were likely more attuned to the matter of rural credits, whether on land, machinery, or returns on crops or from banks.

Based largely on newspaper reports, bond dealers, anxious to corral business and legitimize their new (largely eastern Canadian) association, figured more prominently in the campaign through circulars, which clogged the post offices and newspapers promoting "practical patriotism." Cooperation between the brokers, banks, and insurance companies was also evident. At the end of the campaign, White was effusive in his praise for the brokers and bond dealers. Leading their charge was Wood, Gundy of Toronto, which secured $22.5 million in subscriptions. Some large houses reportedly had devoted themselves exclusively to the loan for weeks – in many cases, in collaboration with advertising agencies. The Gibbons firm solicited southern Ontario newspapers, offering to try to get an ad from A.E. Ames and Company to go alongside any government advertising. Backing came, too, from Ontario's Organization of Resources Committee, whose broad mandate included support for recruitment, thrift and economy, and finance.[41]

Complementing the entry of advertising were catchy human-interest stories, not unlike testimonials in advertising. As advertising copywriters and canvassers knew, these stories humanized the loan narratives. Long a staple of popular journalism, such snippets, usually devoid of depth, were meant to foster interest. Entertaining and idiosyncratic, stories reported by canvassers to their headquarters found their way into the newspapers. The *Montreal Daily Mail* understood this draw when it published a "Special" from Brockville, where a hotelkeeper born in France – likely Antoine Wendling of the Commercial Hotel – had subscribed for $10,000. Following the Franco-German War of 1870–71, he had fled Alsace-Lorraine "to escape the German yoke" and was now subscribing to do so again.[42] But the appeal of "human interest" was hardly unique to the loan campaigns. During the war years, reviews, reports, and audiences often found elements of such interest in films, theatrical productions, books, poetry, and inspirational talks about the war and the "boys." Vaudeville had come into the era facing challenges, including audiences thinned by enlistment, but its time-tested variety programs offered the "light entertainment" that they wanted – tricks, comedic acts, music, dancing, acrobatics, motion-picture and glass-slide interludes, and slots for fundraising. The combination of entertainment and financial advocacy was telling.

Support for the loan of 1916 looked uniform. Many, however, still did not grasp the concepts of borrowing by the government and bond maturity. Others, unused to fluctuating market prices, were misled by promises of full cash value at any time. Prospectuses may not have been clear, relief-fund drives continued to claim support, and on-the-ground factors of accessibility (the small-investor debate) nagged a campaign striving for popularity. Bond dealers noticed that most subscribers were in urban areas. Savvy investors needed no encouragement; from the start of the campaign, reports pointed to the $1,000 bond as the most wanted. Regional undercurrents were also developing. Subscriptions by the western branches of large corporations and banks were claimed by their

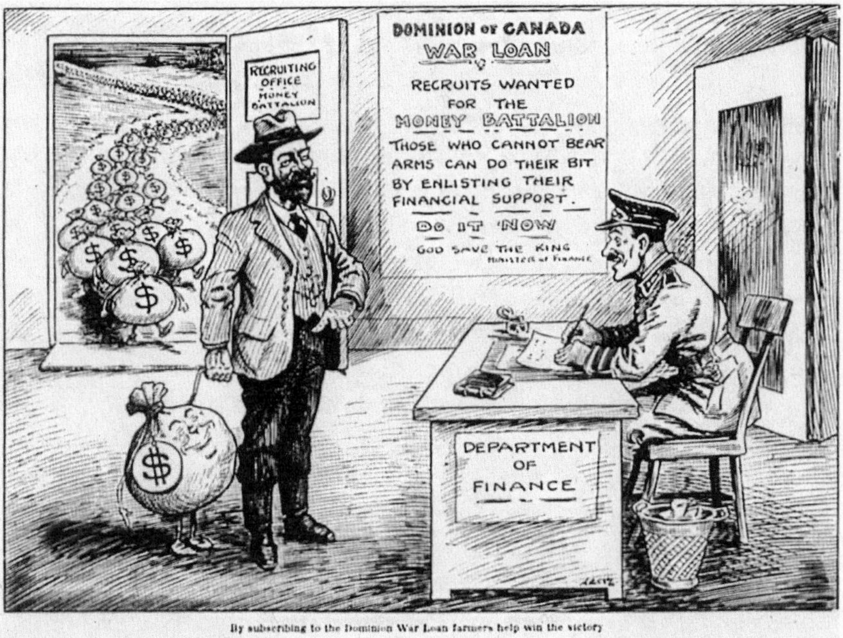

Arch Dale, "The Money Battalion." Western farmers who did not bear arms could do their "bit" by subscribing to a mutually beneficial cause: the loan would be used to purchase produce for the war effort. | *Grain Growers' Guide* (Winnipeg), 20 September 1916.

eastern headquarters. Quebec newspapers such as *Le Canada* (Montreal) separated their support for the loan from their partisan hostilities against the vitriol coming out of Ontario over Quebec's contributions to the war. Among the retorts was the fact that, among the provinces, only the Governments of Quebec and Manitoba subscribed to the loan. In *Le Nationaliste* (Montreal), long an advocate of borrowing, not only was the loan supported but a $50 bond payable monthly was also called for, mirroring the war loan of France, an issue by the Crédit Foncier de France, and the New York loan to the City of Paris.[43]

Driven by the bond houses and improved promotion, the campaign attracted a rise in subscribers to 34,526, up from 24,862 in 1915, and saw a near doubling of the amount taken, a trend that generated valuable publicity. Here were the "recruits" who made up the "Money Battalion" depicted in a cartoon by Arch Dale in the *Grain Growers' Guide* (Winnipeg). In Ottawa, in a move that cut to the core purpose of the loan, White, after conferring with the bankers, cabled the British chancellor of the Exchequer on 27 September that Canada was ready to advance $50 million from the loan to the imperial government for the purchase of munitions and supplies in Canada. Within days, in a familiar tie-in,

White also had the Canadian Bankers' Association form a committee for the national promotion of thrift, a thrust that needed frequent recharging. White's committee – Henry Victor Franklin Jones of the Canadian Bank of Commerce, Clarence Atkinson Bogert of the Dominion Bank, and John P. Bell of the Bank of Hamilton – was tasked with formulating plans for an organized, dominion-wide campaign. Following the "British example," posters and placards were to be widely used. At a meeting of the committee on 4 October, it was asked: "Can you make people save?" A member responded, "We can't make people save," especially in a time of high unemployment, but the goal was to begin directing "minds to the practise of thrift."[44] If a different audience was intended for the debenture stock introduced that month, starting at $500, the advertising sector was set to partner with the government on thrift.

On 23 September, the E.L. Ruddy Company Limited of Toronto, an aggressive outdoor advertising firm, had presented White with "the idea of Government using the great power of poster publicity throughout Canada as a foundation for such propaganda as may go forth on this important subject of thrift."[45] As a result of subsequent meetings with representatives of publicity and printing firms, the minister began thinking of posters and billboards but was unready to relinquish control. Echoing his remark about Canada's remoteness from the war, he was also cautious about how sacrifice should be framed: advertising should be prepared with care, "as there is always a danger of alarming the public."[46] What White deemed alarmist is unclear, although he was quite ready to exploit alleged German atrocities on behalf of the Patriotic Fund, just as scenes of cruelty had crept into recruitment advertising.[47] Publicly, from rural townships to large cities, the evidence of warfare was pervasive: enlistment drives, the dreaded casualty lists, injured returnees, bees for knitting socks, food conservation, and small-donation relief funds.

On domestic sacrifice and fortifying resolve, White was on sure ground. During his trip to Britain from October to December 1916, as the payment of loan instalments temporarily emptied bank accounts,[48] steps were being taken toward the war loan predicted for 1917. The thrift campaign launched on 2 January 1917, along with engagement by the Bond Dealers' Association with White, charted the way. In January, to replace an assistant secretary who had enlisted, White brought in Newfoundland-born Bennet John Roberts, a twenty-four-year-old dynamo whose efficiency would help the department to deal with its "exceedingly heavy" demands in the coming year, including two war loans. He had worked in Toronto for the *Financial Post* and *Daily Star* and then in campaigns for the Patriotic Fund, recruitment, and the British Red Cross, and he had been a member of the Speakers' Patriotic League and the Organization of Resources Committee, gaining experience in both urban and rural campaigning. Not unrelated was the growing sophistication of campaigning by the Canadian Patriotic Fund. Its drive in Montreal in January 1917 (among other cities) had been cutting-edge: outdoor advertising in the form of posters and large signs and the inclusion of French Canadians as canvassers.

Roberts was put in charge of his department's thrift and war-savings campaigns. The department was swamped with correspondence calling for low-denomination securities, after the British example. Roberts collaborated with the King's Printer to inject eye-catching colours and large size into otherwise staid posters for war-savings certificates, and he had masses of posters and flyers distributed to banks, businesses, and government offices, including the military pay branch. Throughout January and February, newspaper advertisements calling for people to begin saving for the next war loan retained simple word formats. Unfortunately, Roberts was caught in the crossfire between the press, through which the government directly placed its advertising, and advertising agencies that wanted in on the business. Emulating perhaps the direct mailing used in the 1916 American election and for store catalogues, a mass mailing of circulars signed by White promoting war-savings certificates was sent to homes. Roberts's work also put him in touch with a host of social organizations, advertising and poster company executives looking for an in,[49] and bankers anxious for an externally organized body to aggressively promote war-savings and the next war loan.[50] In Parliament on 1 February, Alexander Kenneth Maclean called for just such a body in order to reach more than corporate investors. White, however, remained reticent. His broadened efforts were meeting this goal, he argued. Moreover, his secretary should handle the campaigns, not any local group. If Roberts were to sanction any such committees, he risked offending others, the minister told Donald A. Cameron of the Canadian Bank of Commerce in January 1917, "and in addition I should lose the power to regulate the movement,"[51] a rare expression of White's power dynamic. By February, Roberts was sending out to postmasters bundles of posters and pamphlets on war-savings certificates.

Both he and White understood that few local organizations had national reach. Typical in early 1917 was the Canadian Household Economic Association's Housewives' League of Toronto, where Susanna Mary Loosemore's high-minded thrift campaign for food conservation, aimed at battling waste and the high cost of living, was meant in part to generate savings for war loans and savings certificates. Occasionally, chippy opinions were expressed about the upper-crust composition of some thrift groups, and some bankers were dubious about the effectiveness of thrift propaganda. At Ontario's Lakehead, in another illustrative instance, meeting food crises and controls was a primary challenge with unclear results, any financial valuation being a lofty abstraction, and the responsibility for saving fell to the women of the households, Canada's "kitchen soldiers."[52]

There were many pronouncements on war savings and thrift, their moral imperatives, and how they should complement the war loans. On 25 February 1917, White addressed St. James Methodist Church in Montreal on the movement's tenets of self-sacrifice and denial. Others joined the chorus. Privately printed in early 1917, *National Organization for War,* a pamphlet by Stephen Leacock, brought his social criticisms of extravagance to bear in a blunt call for unselfish commitment in a true war economy. The nation did not need more manufactured goods or public works but a "blast of taxation" and "a succession of Government patriotic loans, not money-lenders' loans at market and super-market rates, but patriotic loans in the real sense, at a low rate of interest, let us say four percent, and issued in bonds of twenty-five dollars, with a dollar a year as interest," Leacock believed. If "a national campaign for thrift and investment is set on foot," he continued, "if we give to the ideas all the publicity that our business brains can devise, if we advertise it as commerce advertised its healing oils and fit-right boots and its Aphrodite corsets, then the people will subscribe, tumultuously, roaringly, overwhelmingly." The goal would be a "nation of war-workers."[53] Not surprisingly, Leacock's pamphlet, along with pieces by White on sacrifice and by Vernon Henry Mottram (a lecturer in physiology at the University of Toronto) on nutrition, would soon be seconded by the National Service Board for its booklet *How to Live in War Time.*[54]

The mass-mailed dodgers on war-savings certificates, in both English and French, were probably the first nonelectoral communication received from a government minister by Canadians at all social levels. Direct-mail advertising was a well-known commercial practice, one used, too, by provincial departments of agriculture. How many invested as a result of White's circulars is impossible to know. Hugh Day Scully, secretary of the Russell Motor Car Company in Toronto, which also produced shell fuses, wanted more of the large blue and yellow posters for war-savings certificates for his factory.[55] In many respects, the war-savings campaigns were providing a foundation for the high-pressure Victory Loan campaigns that lay ahead.

By the time of its first annual meeting on 5 February 1917 in Montreal, the Bond Dealers' Association of Canada was anticipating a new war loan and consultation with the minister, who was also lining up bank support. He had some trepidation about turning over more responsibility to the bond dealers. Going into a meeting with White the following day, Alfred Ernest Ames professed to be "somewhat at sea" as to the terms of any loan and what greater role the association would play. Over the next three weeks, in a flurry of telephone calls, letters, and meetings, several issues were discussed: the terms and timing of a loan, including any boost to be gained from a possible American bond issue; brokers' commissions, on which White moved up to three eighths of 1 percent, while prohibiting the splitting of commissions with purchasers; payment in the United States in American dollars at par to address the adverse exchange rate, to which White agreed; an earlier delivery of prospectuses, which would be delayed; and White's commitment to "advertising extensively." The negotiations drew three key Toronto dealers to the forefront: James Henry (Harry) Gundy and William Norman McIlwraith of Wood, Gundy, along with the innovative Ames. All shared an astute appreciation of the market potential of dominion securities.[56] "The plans of the Finance Minister include the use of the efficient distributing machinery of the larger bond houses," the *Globe* would conclude, even as it speculated about the possible tie-up of investment capital in the United States due to the submarine crisis and the backup of munitions and foodstuffs on the seaboard.[57]

On 27 February, the Department of Finance announced the terms of the $150 million loan, with a campaign to run from 12 to 23 March. The "extensive advertising campaign" rapidly launched by the department constituted a greater, exclusive use of newspaper advertising and bond dealers' promotions, which White called "private propaganda."[58] A new, nationalistic enthusiasm pervaded the larger newspapers. The department's widely published press statement, emphasizing the sheer amount (1 and a-half million pieces) of material sent by the government to 3,500 bank branches, post offices, financial houses, newspapers, and regional offices of the assistant receiver general, was clearly meant to grab attention, as was the increased volume of departmental reports and updates. Similarly, the perennial small "wage-earner" to whom the loan was pitched took on a promotional identity. The populist ethos that emerged was typified by coverage in the *Saint John Globe*, where articles and security-firm advertisements highlighted the "Grounds of Patriotism and Good Business" and the targets: working men and women, factory labourers, clerks, stenographers, artisans, domestics, and "toilers in all lines." Some Toronto investment dealers reported downtown "business girls" coming in to buy bonds. An "elderly woman" wishing to subscribe $10 was turned away at the offices of Wood, Gundy – $100 was the minimum – but her "spirit" was praised.[59] The *Toronto World*, an effusive supporter, confirmed the $2,000 subscription on 23 March by the Toronto Newsboys' Union through its shrewd twenty-five-year-old president, Harry Roher.[60] Other reports in the *World* lamented a weak response from "wage-earners," although no statistical evidence was offered. Only rarely were small subscribers identified, once again leaving the impression that they provided more democratic promotion than financial underpinning. Nonetheless, investment value could not be ignored. A worker in manufacturing with a yearly salary of $1,315 who purchased a $100 bond would get an annual return of $5.[61]

At the high ends, corporations and other big subscribers, some of them wishing to avoid unwanted investment-house solicitations, made the most of their nominal listing, which was required by White from the large newspapers in 1917. Another motive in his direction was his department's inability to cope with the demands from some corporations that it publicize their large subscriptions. Long lists, from $10,000 to several million, became commonplace in the major dailies. In a pattern that would mark all the war loans, trade journals with vested interests showed no shyness about publicizing the big subscriptions of related corporations and their officers. *Canadian Railway and Marine World* (Toronto), for instance, saw dual value in subscribing for private investment and to sustain imperial purchases from transportation industries. In April, to illustrate the need and willingness to commit, it published its first long list of subscriptions, from the Steel Company of Canada's $2 million down to the $20,000 of Bell Telephone's Charles Fleetwood Sise. At the same time, branches of some banks and insurance companies were reticent to reveal their own subscriptions, likely because they were claimed by their head offices, often in eastern Canada. Since the United States was not yet in the war, with no war loans of its own, American representatives of Canadian investment houses, the *Montreal Gazette* reported, actively canvassed stateside.[62] Institutional subscriptions from the United States were openly publicized.

Newspaper advertising for the war loan of March 1917 was the most extensive to that point. The *Toronto World*'s fulsome support and coverage were matched or surpassed by other large dailies, including Toronto's *Globe* and *Daily Star*, Saskatchewan's *Regina Morning Leader* and *Saskatoon Phoenix*, and Montreal's *Gazette* and *Daily Mail*, the latter run by White's half-brother, Mark Edgar Nichols. Extensive publicity was called for, the *Daily Mail* argued, to outpace other promotions on the "street" and the "live wires" who were pushing other investments. Prospectuses were published everywhere, although word ads and application forms from securities firms provided the dominant publicity. Reports of regional coverage were widely shared, fabricating a sense of commonwealth of contribution. Newspaper promotion also brought forth, in addition to lists of subscribers, company advertisements that pushed the loan. Not unexpectedly, the campaigns for war-savings certificates and bonds overlapped in many communities. In Edmonton, during the loan drive, the branch of the Canadian National Service League promoted employee programs for both securities. In the fast-changing field of advertising, spurred by twenty-some federal and provincial campaigns, the newspapers led by the Canadian Press Association (CPA) had been lobbying hard since 1915 to corner government contracts, with minimal involvement from the advertising agencies, although some did make inroads, among them J.J. Gibbons Limited of Toronto and McConnell and

Fergusson of London, Ontario.[63] During the March campaign, the *Edmonton Bulletin* issued typical refrains. Government advertising should go directly to newspapers, with the costs of any placements through agencies being paid by the governments. Governments, CPA manager John Mills Imrie told various gatherings, should make advertising a "necessary function" and even publish ads in "tabloid form."[64] Entwined issues included high newsprint costs, printing and commission rates, and the particularly contentious matters of unpaid advertising, publishers' allowance of free publicity, and placement of government advertising through ad agencies. What this rough road could not obstruct was the mounting case, in the design of war-loan campaigns, for national, multimedia advertising of commercial quality. Even then, with the particularized campaigns for recruitment, food, fuel, thrift and war savings, and loans, there was, as historian Jeffrey A. Keshen notes, no comprehensive, "publicly-funded propaganda network" before 1918.[65] (The Victory Loan of late 1917 undermines this conclusion.) But there was buildup. Distinctly absent from the campaign of March were official networking and graphics.

The hawking of the March loan brought in more than expected. The banks' initial subscriptions were rendered unnecessary. Patriotic and relief-fund drives suffered from the diversion of public attention, but their constituency of small investors remained intact, with the CPF in some provinces pushing for more systematic and aggressive drives, especially in rural areas. Advance predictions of "huge success" fuelled the war-loan drive, and steady reports fanned its "brilliant close" in Montreal and elsewhere, along with the need for stronger campaigns, which would start, White anticipated, the next fall. The result also supported the expertise brought to the campaign, notably the greater participation of BDAC members. The bond dealers, who were mostly based in Toronto and Montreal,[66] sold between 44 and 60 percent of the loan (with accounts varying). Among the larger investment houses, lessons had been learned in 1916 about how to stage a campaign through mass mailings and direct solicitations and by, as the *Montreal Gazette* described the process, "establishing communications" early and "bringing up artillery preparatory to a big drive later on."[67] Big subscribers, in turn, learned from past allotments how much to subscribe. Another trend, that of ebbs and flows, also appeared. In Toronto, the *Globe* remarked, after the subscription list had been open for a fortnight, that "the response by small investors seems to lag at some time or other."

The pace of the campaign varied from region to region and from urban to rural districts. In Regina, for example, it was slow to take off: investors, the *Morning Leader* explained, preferred short-term loans, and some were put off by the initial absence of a conversion privilege from the 1916 issue. Proclamation of the campaign's last week as a "Win-the-War Week" – a final push also found elsewhere – helped.[68] At the same time, bonds were finding a niche in the host of government securities being amassed by boards of trade, municipal councils, and other public organizations. A columnist in the *Grain Growers' Guide* listed a typical selection shortly after the campaign: Anglo-French, dominion, provincial, and municipal bonds; rural telephone-company bonds; and British gold notes (receipts for deposits of gold). In the wake of the loan's assurance of new funding, additional publicity came from mentions in industrial and trade journals on its spending. In April, to give one application, *Marine Engineering of Canada* (Toronto) noted the transfer of $10 million to the Imperial Munitions Board to start a program of building wooden ships.[69]

Despite increased subscriptions, observers still found the campaign lacking. *Saturday Night* (Toronto), through the lens of the much-hyped British War Loan, which had closed in February and drawn Canadian investment, concluded that Canada's campaign in March 1917 lacked "ginger."[70] In his address on loans to a convention in St. Louis in June, James Murray Allison would allude to the absence of commercial advertising like that used to push food and other products.[71] Henry Victor Franklin Jones of the Canadian Bank of Commerce, who had pressed White and Roberts before on higher-profile promotions, asked Roberts on 12 March whether he had seen the advertising for the British loan. "It seems to me something like it might be got out here in connection with the present War Loan," he wrote, "as there does not appear to be the same interest taken in it as in the last."[72] In response, Roberts talked up the advertising matter on war-savings certificates.[73] And as he would have known, White was satisfied with the broad advertising in the press for debenture stock, the thrift campaign, and the war loan. Although bonds remained terra incognita to many, the level of familiarity was rising.

Critical response came, too, from those dissatisfied with a perceived imbalance in war funding. The sometimes contrarian *Financial Post*, which did not fully endorse the government's war finance (but still ran a "Special War Loan Section"), wanted increased taxation of "abnormal profits."[74] The call for higher taxes was mounting. Readers of the *Toronto World* may have been amused by the work of its acerbic cartoonist Samuel O'Brien Hunter, who, although he liked the loan, pinpointed in his ink drawings the contradiction between White's appeal for public thrift and his perceived failure to tax piggish profiteers to the hilt. Such cartoons – including work from Arch Dale in Winnipeg, William Noakes ("Noax") in Regina, and Fred Pegram (reproduced from London's *Punch*, that great incubator of war-loan enthusiasm) – began adding a new and catchy graphic element to the loan campaigns. There were also those who recognized the worth of placing savings in war bonds but were skeptical of the "propaganda of the Thrift Campaigners." In a letter to the *Globe*, "True Thrift," although appalled by government waste, thought that "some girls professing thrift might better forgo silk stockings and invest it in war bonds."[75]

Such critiques parallelled political discourse on Parliament Hill, where in the early months of 1917 the Liberals continued to attack government waste. *Le Canada* supported the war loan but, given its virulent anti-Borden stance, hoped that the loan's proceeds would not be misused. In the tense partisan climate of 1917, as well as reporting on the funding crisis in foodstuffs and munitions production, newspapers of all partisan stripes carried government advertising for the war loan, food conservation, and the Royal Naval Canadian Volunteer Reserve, often alongside political critique. In the realm of fundraising, especially in such large cities as Montreal, by that summer, a profusion of organizations, some of them fraudulent, were competing for patriotic dollars, often leaving potential donors perplexed.

In June, in an innovative sequence of text-only and illustrated advertisements placed in newspapers by the A. McKim advertising agency, the National Service Board, under director Richard Bedford Bennett, aggressively pushed war-savings certificates, bonds, thrift, and food conservation. A corps of speakers was put on the road to tout their merits. Bennett would explain the aim of his board's propaganda simply: "to arouse and organize public sentiment" through direct appeal, particularly to women. The final word went to the Department of Finance and its stream of releases and statements by White, for whom thrift and the war loan were inseparable. On 26 March, three days after the closure of the loan campaign, he applauded the success of the loan and how it homed the war's determination. Canadians relied first on patriotism but second on the "merit of the securities and the attractiveness of the rate at which they were offered."[76] Such fiscal euphoria, which drew on the imagery of bonds as silver bullets and canvassing teams as the "Massed Battalions of Finance," blended easily with the romanticized portrayals of national grit that followed the triumph at Vimy Ridge in France in April. Even Vimy had an established war-loan component: subscriptions from soldiers before they went over the top.[77] Indeed, Canadian soldiers overseas, including the British-born and their families, had been ploughing pay back into British and Canadian war bonds for some time.[78]

In the aftermath of the loan, advertising executives rushed to proclaim the inadequacy of pre-war methods: the single columns of newspapers, text-only broadsides and posters, and the rare use of bold colours. Needed was a radical makeover in design and implementation, with verve and subliminal intent, to keep pace with the "crash of events at the front" and to sell war needs as if selling chewing gum. The call would stir up the debate between newspapermen (the CPA) and advertising agents and associations not only over practicalities such as rates and commissions but also over the primacy of responsibility and planning in new campaigns. The gospel of advertising was not lost on governments. Through late March and April, in trade journals such as *Economic Advertising, Printer and Publisher,* and *Printers' Ink* (New York), attention remained focused on the growing use of advertising by federal and provincial departments. With their launch of twenty-six advertising campaigns since the start of the war, the ball was rolling in Canada, CPA manager John Mills Imrie told the Bureau of Advertising of the American Newspaper Publishing Association in New York in April and the Associated Advertising Clubs of the World in St. Louis in June. On a converging course, White's budget and his missions to Washington and New York for further funding were grounded in the sober reality of monetary need.

Between White's budget of 24 April and the loan called for the fall, many market factors were in play, but they were hardly at the fore of parliamentary debate. Conscription, railways, and the prospects of a union government held sway. The budget confirmed indebtedness as government policy. With finance in place only till June, the underwhelming New York loan, upcoming issues of treasury bills, dominion notes, and debenture stock, and munition funding all loomed large that summer. Also important were the price fluctuations of past war bonds in the marketplace and how they would shape the fall loan. For the banks, recuperation from withdrawals of money for instalment payments and repayment of loans to the Imperial Munitions Board would allow them to focus on any new loan and on funding the crop movement, which involved grain bills of exchange on the New York market. At the same time, some newspapers reasoned, the banks also had to deal with bond dumping by investors and the uneven distribution of issued securities.

Having witnessed the New York loan close-up, the handful of Canadian analysts who reported from the United States, among them Agnes Christina Laut of Wassaic, New York, were pessimistic about how a new loan would be received south of the border.[79] Many bond dealers also had reservations. In July, Russell D. Bell of Greenshields and Company in Montreal and a critic of loan advertising in 1916, offered a trenchant critique. The March loan, he claimed, had not been widely distributed, in spite of warnings from bond-merchandising authorities. Any loan would fail if "offered at a complicated price in a technical prospectus, unsupported by any widespread propaganda in modern result-getting advertising and salesmanship. War loans are bound to go begging if you continue to force them into the same hands and neglect to get them out in small lots throughout the mass of the people." Canada should copy the rousing, tightly organized campaign of America's second Liberty Loan of May and June, along with the advertising council behind Britain's successful sale of bonds, he argued:

"Great Britain actually sold its bonds in the same way that our big manufacturing companies have found it necessary to adopt in order to sell anything – the way Pears sell their soap and Heinze [sic] his pickles."[80] There were lessons, too, to be learned from the "formula for organized selling" employed by the Ford Motor Company of Canada to sell its Model Ts, using municipal assessment records, voters' lists, telephone books, calculations of potential sales, and local consultations to pinpoint customers.

Absorption, congestion, overreliance on bank credit to buy bonds, and recovery would all impinge on the fall loan. It was partly to sustain investor engagement that White, in July, announced the conversion privilege from past loans and exemption from the new income tax, where political timing was a concern. Even if bonds and war-savings certificates were becoming known to many and had a market niche, there was growing consensus that more Canadians could be enticed to buy into the war. Articles extolling Canada's financial self-sufficiency had appeared in western weeklies in April. It was clear, too, from the contingencies facing the Department of Finance – market variables, loan distribution, the stresses of a terrible war year and conscription, and calls for a brassy approach – that a decidedly different kind of campaign was needed for the fall. G.A. Stimson and Company Limited, a Toronto investment-banking firm, would conclude in its annual review that the year had been a dismal one for Canadian bonds: "It seemed to be the general opinion that some new method of selling the loan must be invoked."[81]

In early June 1917, picking up from discussions in February, White went to Toronto to meet with Alfred Ernest Ames and Harry Gundy of the Bond Dealers' Association of Canada to resume discussion about domestic borrowing. In progressive fashion, he proposed that "the country be organized and canvassed in the same way as the Patriotic Fund was organized and raised in the various Cities." Two other ideas were floated: a prohibition on Canadian purchases of foreign bonds, to boost internal investment, and a bond issue payable annually for up to twenty or twenty-five years. Later that month, recognizing the grand opening before them, the BDAC began looking at other options, including handling the loan like the American Liberty Loan, where no commissions were collected. The idea was soon shelved. What would not be lost in the planning were the Liberty Loans' creation of local quotas for subscriptions, advanced sales techniques, gimmickry, and aggressive pressures.[82] What moved White to finally consider the Patriotic Fund model is uncertain, but retaining control was paramount, the time for setting up a new campaign tight.

6

The First Victory Loan, 1917

Over the summer of 1917, the finance department began preparing in earnest for the fall war loan. The past three loans held a "firm spot" in market buying, a presence attributed by the *Globe* (Toronto) to investors' preparation for the income tax, and there was every need for firmness to continue. However, estimates of market conditions varied. The *Monetary Times* (Toronto) would maintain that a big push was necessary to meet expenditures in the face of unspecified "adverse market conditions." On 11 August, White brought seven members of the Bond Dealers' Association of Canada (BDAC) to Ottawa to continue hammering out the new loan: Alfred Ernest Ames, George Herbert Wood, John W. Mitchell, and William Norman McIlwraith from Toronto; and J.M. Mackie, Edwin Hanson, and Ralph A. Stephenson from Montreal, the latter an investment banker who had experience with past war loans. White made two things clear. First, his "main obligation" was repaying the $75 million borrowed from the banks the previous spring and due in October. Second, he said "he was laying his financial plans irrespective of the question of an election." Because of the supercharged political climate, the BDAC, as well as life insurers and others, were also uneasy about any branding of the loan "along patriotic lines" that could result from a nominal association with the Patriotic Fund,[1] however instructive its mechanics. Taint would nonetheless be hard to avoid. Efforts to ensure an apolitical loan would be severely tested in Quebec, where reaction to the "agitators" in the Ontario press was strong. So, too, was anti-conscriptionist feeling, which burst out in disturbances in Montreal in late August.[2]

As a Borden minister with strong anti-Quebec sentiments, White carried baggage. During the summer, Henri Bourassa's Nationaliste newspaper, *Le Devoir* (Montreal), had ridden White hard on finance, including the New York loan. Since White's budget of February 1915, Bourassa had been a stern critic of the government's spiralling spending on the war. A writer in *Le Nationaliste* (Montreal) had rebuked him as one of the "vilest" members of Cabinet.[3] Like most other Quebec newspapers, *Le Nationaliste* and the Liberal *Le Canada* (Montreal) still ran income-producing government advertising. Even in the event of a concurrent election campaign, White believed idealistically, at least in the press, that candidates and the public would keep the loan neutral. But at this point, political factors did not dominate its shaping, which carried throughout August and into September. Taking precedence over all else was the immediate need for imperial credits.

On the vital matter of handling the loan, White yielded a degree of management to the bond dealers – who had the most experience with distributing securities – while moving to balance the BDAC's involvement with that of the Canadian Press Association, the advertising agencies, and the banks. On 6 September, White, who said little about the loan in Parliament, told the press "that between now and November a nation-wide organization would be instituted to make the loan a success." He offered to cover the costs of an intensified "professional" organization, as well as expert publicity, to educate "such investors by personal canvass as had not responded hitherto." He would have final approval on publicity. Some in the press saw his heavy hand at work, consistent with his "power to regulate" comment, made earlier in the year.[4] Ames would later recognize the minister's systematic analysis of past loans and his use of force in "commandeering" members of bond firms and stock exchanges. Going from such indicators as the size of savings accounts, both the BDAC and White believed that Canadians had accumulated enough wealth for another loan, with untapped potential in remote villages and farms. But investors faced options. In September, for instance, the Saskatchewan Greater Production Loan, meant to extend credit to farmers for the cultivation of more land, offered bonds at 5 percent.

Floated and rehashed, different organizational proposals were put before the minister by the BDAC, including the "amateur" Patriotic Fund model, itself under refinement at the provincial levels. Recognizing the need for professionalized management and the elimination of competitive effort, he settled on a grand composite plan (the "county plan") for a national, nongovernmental executive drawn from various bond houses and exchanges. Committees would work down through provincial, county, and local subcommittees and teams of commissioned canvassers made up of bank managers, stockbrokers, bond men, and insurance salesmen. White felt that it was vital to enlist canvassers who could "project considerable knowledge of financial matters."[5] Lists of prospective subscribers, slates of speakers, and records and communication systems connecting the local committees and provincial headquarters, "as used in the patriotic fund campaigns," would ensure a "scientific distribution." Wire and telephone networks would be essential, including the initiation of a federally subsidized, national news service over leased wires promising rapid communication and tabulation.[6] All manner of publicity would be scrutinized for optimal effect: floods of departmental releases, newspapers, official and sponsored advertisements, promotional literature, posters, postal cancellations, and telegram forms bearing slogans. On 10 September, a joint national publicity committee of twelve members was named by the Canadian Press Association (CPA) and the Canadian Association of Advertising Agencies.[7] To distribute the press publicity, the Department of Finance contracted with the CPA in late September.

The CPA relished the prospect, the "first time the entire press of Canada has been harnessed efficiently to a single enterprise," enthused one newspaperman.[8] A "master plan" with consecutive stages was worked out. Media were divided into "circuits," among them newspapers and religious, farm, technical, and trade publications. Government advertising would be supplemented by "donated" but "controlled" advertising sponsored by the bond dealers, private individuals, firms, and organizations. Guides and designs for donated content would be provided or created locally. One full-page newspaper ad donated by the Toronto members of the BDAC addressed the basics: "Q. What is a Victory Bond? A. A nicely engraved document on distinctive paper. It is called a Bond. It is Canada's promise to pay you your money back at a certain rate and to pay you interest." In addition, the CPA ran a news service to spread pieces produced by its stable of writers. Working with the dominion publicity committee, a special CPA committee, in turn, secured the services of five advertising firms, which were paid by the newspapers.

By 17 September, a dominion executive, or Setting Up Committee, had been formed under Alfred Ernest Ames, who understood large-scale marketing. It worked fast. On 21 September, its members met at Ottawa's Château Laurier hotel and took part in a conference that included bankers, press, bond dealers, and advertising representatives. Their talks were wide-ranging, from campaign organization and publicity to further bank advances. Throughout the more focused discussions with the BDAC, several related matters arose, including estimates of cost, the name of the loan, bankers' involvement, and the discouragement of Canadian investment in foreign securities. The recommendation of the Dominion Securities Corporation's Joseph Alfred McQuesten for a $10 war-savings certificate, which could be exchanged for bonds, was immediately acted on by White, who had already had it approved. All shared McQuesten's belief that Canada was "not a bond-buying country," a condition that only an "active campaign" could alter.[9] After the conference, committees were formed by the Montreal Stock Exchange and by the eastern (Quebec) section of the BDAC, as well as among the bankers, and White brought on board the fire underwriters, life insurers, fraternal insurance societies, and other potential sources of investment and canvassers. Local organizations took shape. White's office was bombarded with recommendations for appointees and with requests from advertisers. The government's printing bureau, the King's Printer, handled the production of prospectuses, and Bennet John Roberts got Liberty Loan posters for review, the start of a useful practice of exchange. Formally launched on 1 October, the Liberty Loan, America's second, would opt for intense publicity and "spectacles" meant to grab public attention.[10] Despite such cross-fertilization, White was anxious to avert any interference with the Liberty issue and would try to avoid Canadian promotion on American soil, but solicitation there was heavy (as had been the case in March), and bonds would be snapped up in large volumes.[11] Conversely, in Sarnia, Ontario, a border town with a population of 11,676, the Liberty Loan subscriptions taken up by the third week of November totalled 2,021.

On 26 September, John Mills Imrie of the CPA told White that "advertising agents are hard at work on the copy and plans for the campaign."[12] The following day, the minister presented its outlines to Governor General Victor Cavendish, 9th Duke of Devonshire, for his approval. The headquarters would be in Toronto. A confrère there of Ames was Edward Rogers Wood, a Methodist millionaire, one-time treasurer of the Toronto and York County Patriotic Association, a veteran campaigner, and president of Dominion Securities. At the organizational stages in September and October, he liaised with the banks. In meetings with the executive council of the Canadian Bankers' Association, he secured a cooperative committee of bankers and brokers. Less successful were his requests, first, that no calls on loans by brokers (who would set normal business aside during the campaign) be made by the banks until the loan had closed and, second, that the banks disclose deposits to show "how much might reasonably be expected for subscriptions."[13] Ames would also meet with resistance from the association in early November. Once lists of applications began coming into the banks, tensions developed when they declined to share them with the loan's local committees, which were eager to identify the untapped. As head of the dominion special subscriptions committee, a group of connected financiers and businessmen, Wood would lead the drive to secure major subscriptions from corporations and the rich. Through further meetings, organization and coordination proceeded at a whirlwind pace – unduly fast, Ames later admitted. From White's perspective, the haste was justified: the loan had to be executed quickly, he explained, so as "to meet the unexpected demand for large British credits for the purchase of munitions and foodstuffs in Canada."[14]

The tone of the loan, the carny barker's language, was evident in White's statements and in the press's early reportage. "The main idea is to make this a popular loan in every sense of the term," *Economic Advertising* (Toronto) proclaimed, giving pep to an old refrain.[15] Organizers pushed the need, most often defined as engaging subscribers for the new $50 bond or creating consensus. On the new publicity committee, the *Globe* reported, "the plan of the Minister will be to cover the entire Dominion with a propaganda which will emphasize the necessity of national saving and subscription to the war loan." The organization to be created would be "the largest single piece of business machinery ever created in Canada," White boasted with folksy zeal on 7 October. "Wherever dollar bills are hidden in Canada there will be a 'dollar-detective' on its trail to politely 'arrest' the attention of its owner – and lay before him the attractive proposition of Jack Canuck. Jack Canuck, in other words, is out to borrow money from his folks."[16] In social commentary, tabloids, and cartoons, the allegorical "Jack" was the manly counterpart to "Miss Canada" and "Janey Canuck," whose many manifestations during the war included their use in war-loan promotions.

On 6 October, on the heels of Lord Rufus Isaacs Reading's funding mission in Ottawa, White had announced the loan. Its terms, including the easy target of $150 million (the same as the March loan), would be formally given out on 6 November, with the campaign set for 12 November to 1 December. Names for the loan continued to come in from an intrigued public. Prosperity Loan, Democracy Loan, Great Democracy Loan, Win-the-War Loan, People's Loan, and Support-the-Boys Loan were some of them, but the government chose Victory Loan, picking up on past labelling. The time frame for campaigning was tight. The dominion publicity committee set to work immediately. One obvious organization essential to coordination was the National Service Board. On 22 October, Charles Wesley Peterson, its secretary, would tell White that the work of his staff selling war-savings certificates had needed to be stopped until the United States' latest Liberty Loan campaign ended on 28 October. (Overlap could be problematic in promotional and marketing terms.) Only then could he assign his teams to the Victory Loan in Ontario. They had met with some success in industrial establishments, where another hurdle had been discovered: "Only a very small proportion of these people had ever saved a cent before."[17] This finding, if true, may be suggestive of low wages or working-class hardship.

By early October, the loan's apparatus was in place. It reflected the framework of the Canadian Patriotic Fund and Red Cross drives. Men constituted the organizing groups at every level; women were dominant in the local field and clerical corps. Constituting the "supreme command" desired by White, five dominion committees were formed: an executive, special subscriptions (the only committee with coast-to-coast representation), finance (to apportion and distribute operating funds), publicity, and business (to tabulate and release the results wired in daily, prepare forms and records, and standardize accounting).[18] In Toronto, a contingent of more than 250 women and men, on loan from banks, financial houses, and other offices, would work voluntarily to compile results nationally for daily release. "We could not have produced our organization in such a short time if we had had to depend upon people we could hire," admitted William Sefton Hodgens, chair of the business committee. Not surprisingly, three members of the executive – Ames, Wood, and James Henry Gundy – came from the three firms that would gain the most in commissions from the loan. In addition to the dominion and provincial committees, there were backbenches of honorary committees, which conferred prestige on legions of citizens.

Advance publicity in the newspapers was a valuable prelude in a campaign seeking to engage noninvestors. Looking back in December, the editor of the *Bow Island Review*, in rural Alberta, understood this dynamic: "The press publicity created an atmosphere and a knowledge of the situation that in addition to securing large numbers of subscribers without personal solicitation made it possible for the personal workers to do their work quickly and effectively and with infinitely greater results."[19] But soliciting rural sign-ups, given the vagaries of weather and farmers' financial habits, was demanding work, often dependent on the reach of newspapers and pamphlets.

Little promotion was openly geared to generating large subscriptions. Arranged beyond the limelight, such subscriptions, which made up about a quarter to almost a third of the total (and maybe more),[20] were pragmatic investments of sinking funds, reserves, war earnings, and capital, with varying shades of patriotic motivation. They were never simply guided by devotion. These special subscribers, officially for $25,000 or more (statements of the threshold varied), included wealthy individuals, companies, boards, associations, municipalities, provinces, estates, and unions. The regular appearance in the newspapers of lists identifying big subscribers and their commitments, some starting at $5,000, brought public recognition, a mainstay of press coverage. White counted on these subscriptions. Commitments took shape behind the scenes, with ministerially approved privileges on the timing of payments, some to the end of 1920. Among the largest holders were Sun Life Insurance ($8,475,750), National Trust ($4,684,700), and Toronto General Trusts Corporation ($2,853,000). Individuals included Edward Rogers Wood ($150,000), Joseph Wesley Flavelle ($100,000), and Liberal up-and-comer William Lyon Mackenzie King ($40,000). The randomly ordered lists now held at Library and Archives Canada, which identify a fraction of the bondholders, point to a pattern of frequent acquisitions and sales by financial institutions, or "capital recycling."[21]

Before the campaign opened on 12 November, heavy industrial subscriptions were anticipated. Delegates had spent the preceding week sounding out possibilities and corporate attitudes, lining up subscriptions, and devising plans to maximize employee subscriptions, with the companies reaping the publicity.

At Imperial Oil, for example, which had a sizable workforce nationwide, the plan was geared to salaries and capacity, starting with $50 bonds on instalment. By the end of November, 2,294 employees had signed up.[22] What could not be fully anticipated anywhere were employee departures and defaults, one possible indicator of pressured subscriptions.

Preparations for the campaign had continued throughout October and into early November, with an impressive degree of coordination. The office of the dominion publicity committee and the publicity bureau of the Canadian Press Association were side by side on the third floor of the Dominion Bank Building in Toronto. The brazen boosterism on display in the newspapers and on the campaign trails was extraordinary.[23] Published photographs of the loan's heads became commonplace; weekly newspapers started bulging with ads. Ames and White talked up the loan wherever possible. Ames met at least twice in Montreal with Gilbert B. Bogart and John J. Schumann from the distribution committee of America's Liberty Loan. In late October, letters went out to Ontario's municipal officials from Professor Albert Holden Abbott as secretary of the province's Organization of Resources Committee. Credits for Allied purchases in Canada, he explained, could be secured only through support for the local Victory Loan Committees.[24] On 10 November, two days ahead of the campaign, White mass-mailed an appeal "To The People of Canada": a letter, brochure, prospectus, and application form.

Other advance publicity, including coast-to-coast newspaper coverage, took different forms. Sequenced official advertisements, some 116 in total (although no one newspaper published them all), began appearing in the last week of October. Published in Ottawa, Wood's *Some Facts and Figures Regarding Canada's Victory Loan, 1917,* emphasized that the loan's proceeds would be spent in Canada only for war purposes.[25] One critical observer, the *Financial Times* (Montreal), believed that the Department of Finance forwent press releases on the vital wheat credit agreement of 1 November "lest the prospects of the Victory Loan might be affected adversely."[26] The jumpy *Financial Times,* however, was wrong. The *Edmonton Bulletin* and the *Munson Mail* (Munson, Alberta),[27] and perhaps other western papers, had been picking up statements on the wheat purchase, along with official advertisements for the loan. Published in several western newspapers, they beseeched farmers to subscribe in order to give Britain the money needed to buy their wheat.

In a widely publicized address to the Insurance Institute of Toronto on 23 October, Ames reiterated his explanation of the loan's organization and primary goal: "to get the money in Canada because there is nowhere else to get it."[28] To that end, he was later cleverly echoed, the financial community was "willingly conscripted."[29] As the loan was being put together, its organizers could not help but notice the productive impact of unrestrained publicity in the country-wide campaign of the British Red Cross Society in October, despite the obstacles to voluntary donation. In Toronto, campaigners "recognized that the hugely-increased cost of living, the many worthy patriotic calls, the pending war loan, and the new income tax were all factors which contributed to the problems confronting a generous citizenhood."[30] But such professions of understanding also worked to gain advantage. Abetted by a mass rally, church and school teams, banners, and aggressive canvassing in a campaign of "unprecedented scale," the target there was exceeded. In Edmonton, advertisements with cartoons of Miss Canada helping Mother Britannia and war-infused poetry by Robert William Service, author of *Rhymes of a Red Cross Man* (1916), enhanced promotion.

In English-speaking Canada, such language and imagery were not new. Propaganda films, war-themed performances at theatres, and public addresses were already imbued with such discourse. On 12 November, *Globe* managing editor (and recently returned war correspondent) Thomas Stewart Lyon told Toronto's Canadian Club that Canadians were doing their "splendid share" to push the war to a "triumphant finish."[31] New propaganda, calculated targets, and the fundamentals of professional advertising, such as repeated exposure, worked, as did the government's control over advertising. Much of the campaign's parlance would be couched in the dialect of military precision. According to Montreal's Victory Loan vice-chair, John Wardrop Ross, an accountant, "the machinery must be set-up with scientific accuracy and let loose at the physchological [sic] moment," with the strategy of a "drive on the western front," starting with an "opening barrage of publicity – the surprise attack by the over-the-top troops."[32] Such language and identity were pervasive. Proficiency in munition shops was sustained by female "soldiers," and just as "women soldiers" drilled as home guards, countless women toughed it out as foot soldiers in the loan campaigns. The legions of actual veterans who served as canvassers brought credibility. Canvassers were "armed with unanswerable arguments." Boys and girls were "mobilized." So, when the *Globe* described loan workers and subscribers as "Toronto's Great Battalion in the War Loan Campaign Army,"[33] people were attuned to the simile.

The loan's apparatus and tone were also being shaped by the toxicity of political events: the formation of the Unionist government and writs for an election on 17 December. The loan campaign, to be conducted from 12 November to 1 December, would occur entirely during the election campaign, with White taking time out to stump his own riding and bash Sir Wilfrid Laurier and Quebec.[34] At a rally in Toronto, he had predicted that once Canada was three weeks into the loan campaign, "I shall be surprised if we do not make a sideshow of the Dominion election."[35] His proposal to ask candidates to make nonpartisan

Victory Loan appeals yielded pitches on the hustings, but more often the request got mixed into the conflicting rhetoric of Liberals and Unionists, recruiters, and win-the-war crusaders.

Despite White's call for a separation of loan and election, there was linkage. Few drew the threads together better than the prime minister. In a much-publicized address to a rain-drenched crowd in Millbrook, Ontario, on 30 November, he said that there would be no market for produce if Canada did not raise credits for Britain, regardless of cost. "Far better that we should repudiate our national debt than we should repudiate the debt that we owe to the men fighting our battles,"[36] he explained. More effective than any candidate's promotions was the sheer showmanship brought to bear by the Victory Loan web in a masterwork of overlap. One integral device was Lieutenant-Colonel John McCrae's iconic poem "In Flanders Fields." Published in 1915, it became a "pivotal tool" in both the loan and election campaigns. Committees nationwide found that it provided the "best appeal" for bonds, although it went unused in Quebec. In 1917, it was used against Laurier and francophone Quebecers to promote the campaign through repetition and imitation.[37] Portrayed, too, in graphic imagery, this set piece worked its way into anthology, parliamentary debate, patriotic letters, addresses, and the English Canadian psyche.

To implement the web, campaign districts and subdistricts had been mapped out in fast order, using the county model. In rural areas, transportation and knowledge of farming cycles and modes of finance were vital. Montreal, whose surviving campaign records may be unique, was one of the most sophisticated districts in terms of organization, with French and English teams and a strong reserve of expertise from past YMCA and Patriotic Fund campaigns. The English-speaking teams operated out of thirty offices with thirty telephones, seventy-five workers, a separate office for publicity, employee canvassing (1,500 businesses were earmarked), and seventy-plus multilingual speakers (sixteen of whom were assigned to speak at cinemas), twenty women's committees, and forty teams of canvassers. Equally well equipped, but still seeking volunteers in the early days of the campaign, the French-speaking committee worked out of its own flat. Contact lists were compiled for specific sectors of potential subscribers: special subscriptions constituted one list, which was handled in consultation with White. Contact was expected to be made with 125 labour organizations, thirteen railway organizations, fifty-two Jewish societies, and several fraternal bodies. A special meeting for women was expected to pull in 1,000 attendees. To reach prospects for $50 bonds, Montreal, like the rest of the province, scoured telephone directories through the kindness of Bell Telephone. The result was 6,000 prospective names for the English-speaking teams alone. Other expertise was brought to bear on Montreal's office buildings and suburban and island communities.[38] In New Brunswick, similarly effective use was made of voters' lists. Ambitious targets were methodically calculated elsewhere: whereas only 325 people had subscribed in Calgary to the March loan, organizers now aimed for more than 5,000. With many variables and challenges in play, drawing conclusions about the performance of any one region can be problematic.[39]

In October, the sluice gates opened. Under intense time constraints, in just over a month, masses of materials were produced in French and English and sent out: bonds in both languages,[40] application forms, prospectuses, brochures and envelope stuffers, sequential publicity bulletins for local committees (running from 10 October to 1 November), canvassing kits, and street banners. Broadsides and colourful posters, along with illustrated advertisements for newspapers and periodicals, were released in arranged series for calculated impact. The posters were plastered everywhere, from city streets to rural buildings. Dominion efforts also included quietly conducted contacts by James Henry Gundy and the special subscriptions committee, which narrowed down a list of 1,200 potential contacts nationwide to 700. Determined to provide "great hustling" and "exhaustive canvassing," local committees created imaginative campaigns, with an enormous range of devices and attractions in the large centres. Sensory attraction, guilt and shame, sacrifice, patriotic and religious appeal, investment opportunity, and entertainment were common weapons in the bombardment. The press perpetrated notions of obligation, home-front stability, and democratic freedom. In rare concurrence with military events overseas, reports of Canada's horrendous casualties at the Battle of Passchendaele in Belgium were used by White to boost enlistment and to propel sacrifice at home through subscription. It became impossible to avoid the appeals. In Quebec, bucking this surge, *Le Devoir* argued for a different kind of Canadian national interest and rejected most of these notions, along with any engagement meant to serve European goals. Arguments that paying war's costs through loans should not be the "last word in war finance" or that profiteers should be taxed more heavily fell flat.[41]

Before and throughout the formal campaign period, Canadians could have read about campaigns elsewhere, as reported and shared in newspapers from the Maritimes to British Columbia. Comprehensive canvassing and a huge variety of events were aimed at promoting subscriptions through entertainment and persistent solicitation. The ever-growing list of features included window displays and intriguing novelties such as tanks, aeroplanes, and submarines. Motivational talks were given by veterans, labour, celebrities, and advertising experts. There was a blossoming of pastoral exhortations, commercial and industrial buy-ins, school projects, contests, district competitions, and explanatory materials. Subscription booths and offices, stunts and parades with all kinds of circusy hoopla, and constant newspaper coverage of campaign results and human-interest stories became hard to avoid. The community halls of rural townships hosted outside speakers accompanied by music makers drawn from local Red Cross workers. Common, too, were morale-boosting gatherings for campaign workers and organizers; at one in Calgary, Rotarians paraded about a hall garbed in Ku Klux Klan robes "singing catchy ditties."[42] Barrages of sound, from opening-day bells and whistles to bands, comprised the "significant noise propaganda" described by one Nova Scotia newspaper.[43] A campaigner in Toronto, a gum-company executive, understood that "there are many kinds of noise but if you tie it all up to something it makes great advertising – people are bound to be affected." The links between entertainment, personal relief, investment, and funding were palpable.

Canvasses varied enormously, from loud urban onslaughts to noiseless rural slogs, from door-to-door outreach to contact at special subscription centres, booths, banks, and pay offices. Opinions on effective canvassing varied enormously. Representative of one viewpoint, *Saturday Night* magazine in Toronto, saw publicity "stunts" as no substitute for "personal solicitation." Distances were reduced by automobiles, horse-drawn carts, and railways. The Prince Edward Island Railway, for instance, ran special trains for bond salesmen and offered low rates for prospective investors going to town to subscribe. In British Columbia, the Canadian Northern provided a car for salesmen in the run from Vancouver to Lucerne. In Ontario, canvassers rode the rails out of the Lakehead. Except for Montreal and a few large towns, Quebec was not given to mounting grand parades. If the campaign unfolded quietly in many areas, in others it dominated. The National Service Board suspended its operations, and stock exchanges and security and insurance businesses closed their doors as salesmen went out canvassing. Behind the scenes, assigned targets, quotas, and woeful pleas for finishing drives – all old ploys – were in play. Calculations were made for oversubscription, another surefire publicity manoeuvre, as a shortfall would have been a public-relations disaster. Buttressing came from the thrift and war-savings pushes.

In all of these local drives, the role of women emerges emphatically, but within recognized female-male boundaries. Forceful appeals were made to women. Bonds were cast as providing security. There were women's meetings and canvassing committees, especially strong in Quebec and among society women, and indispensable legions of female support staff worked in makeshift offices, at the bond-printing presses, and in the Department of Finance. Women who faced real need or illness or who were disinclined on principle to subscribe received no attention in the press, whereas women's councils and clubs where bonds were earnestly talked up did receive coverage. One young member of the Canadian Business Women's Club in Toronto "was moved almost to tears" over the prospect of subscribing. Newspaper advertisements encouraged the mothers, wives, sisters, and sweethearts of boys in the trenches to fight "shoulder to shoulder" with them: "You can fight with your money."

The campaign did not always run smoothly. Female canvassers were sometimes relegated to unreceptive neighbourhoods. Relations between the dominion and provincial committees could be tense. Cooperation between the canvassers and the banks, through which applications were funnelled, could be tested: some banks refused to divulge client information to aggressive canvassers, and other banks took credit (and commissions) for unmarked applications. The Canadian Bankers' Association did its best to smooth relations. The banks, of course, stood to gain mightily from Victory Loan business, which included advances[44] to subscribers to buy bonds (emulating the "borrow and buy" practice in the Liberty Loan campaign).[45] Despite the push on $50 bonds, such authorities as broker William Courtlandt Noxon later told the staff of MacLean Publishing that the small bonds would have a soft market, a trend that would continue into the 1930s.[46] Likewise, politics, opposition to the loan, and nativist sentiments had negative implications.

The election campaign, especially the issues of a union government and conscription, complicated campaigning in many Liberal areas, including ridings in the Maritimes and particularly in Quebec and other French-speaking regions. Some Liberal and independent newspapers deftly combined criticism with support for the newsworthy loan campaign and government advertising. Liberal leader Sir Wilfrid Laurier and many of his candidates backed the loan, but such support was not an electoral determinant. In September, Charlottetown's *Island Patriot,* for one, lambasted the finance minister for his "scandalous" record of borrowing $682 million over the past four years and paying out $11,968,597 in commissions.[47] Then, in November and December (and again in 1918 and 1919), it backed the Victory Loan. The *Eastern Chronicle* in New Glasgow, Nova Scotia, while conceding the necessity for war loans, attacked White's record, his reputed support of war profiteers, and the national debt. The concentrated coverage given the campaign by *Le Soleil* (Quebec City) and *La Patrie* (Montreal) was the most effusive and defensive of all the Quebec newspapers examined for this study,[48] although their approaches differed from the methods used by the press outside Quebec. Conscription could never be forgotten. Advertisers in Quebec newspapers tended to avoid sponsored or donated ads for the loan. As historian Shirley Tillotson observes, "with the exception of a few national advertisers, *La Patrie*'s advertisers studiously ignored the whole hullabaloo."[49] Behind the headlines, the status of Montreal and adjacent islands as a semi-autonomous

Victory Loan district, organizationally distinct from the rest of the province, along with its frequent separation from the rest of Quebec in subscription reports, exposed the returns outside of Montreal to ridicule in Ontario and parts of western Canada. Protests over the separation were sent from Montreal and Quebec City to the Victory Loan headquarters. Blame was spread around; the rivalry between Montreal and Toronto did not help. Montreal's men's committee and the moderate *Quebec Chronicle* (Quebec City) complained about the reporting on French Canadians in Toronto's newspapers, where they were stereotyped as unpatriotic misers. Dominion chair Alfred Ernest Ames tried to strike a balance between the reporting of Montreal and Quebec and that of Toronto and Ontario, with mixed results, but harm had been done. Montreal's separation was likely due to its size (according to the *Monetary Times*), its high concentration of major donors, and the city's insular organization for the Canadian Patriotic Fund, headed by investment dealer, YMCA fundraiser, and organizational "live wire" John Wilson McConnell.

The Victory Loan became a demonizing platform in the anti-Quebec charge. Diligent war worker, former secretary of the Speakers' Patriotic League, and chair of Ontario's Victory Loan publicity committee Professor Albert Holden Abbott had no problem in also serving as secretary of the vitriolic Toronto-based, pro-union-government Citizens' Union Committee. It saw Quebec as a drag on Canada and the loan, despite the province's contribution in other areas such as agricultural production and the food effort.[50] The committee's chair, George Augustus Warburton, had long promoted the loan and wanted to keep Ontario's substantial subscriptions out of Quebec's hands. At the same time, when Scottish vaudevillian Harry Lauder visited Canada to lift spirits with his act and push bonds in speeches of Victory Loan "evangelism," his inopportune call, in the midst of the conscription furore, for French Canada to fight for the "Mother Country" sparked scorn in Quebec for Lauder the "clown." The reaction had consequence in Montreal, where at the outset of the campaign, thirty-four theatres (French and English) had agreed to offer time for promotional pitches. The manager of one, His Majesty's Theatre, where Lauder had recently performed, backed his criticism. The city's mayor was outraged, *La Presse* (Montreal) and *La Patrie* refused to run ads for the theatre, and French Canadians boycotted it, leaving the much-loved French actress Sarah Bernhardt to end her critically acclaimed run there before many empty seats. Prior to coming to Montreal, she had thrilled in Hamilton, where, through speeches and autographs, she had generated mounds of subscriptions. Bonds had become polarizing pawns.

In a booklet published in late November by the Union Government Publicity Bureau, *Plain Facts for English-Speaking Electors*, Quebec's Liberals were found wanting on concocted grounds: "Patriotism in truth has been boycotted, subscriptions to the Patriotic Fund have ceased and the Victory Loan is, generally speaking, sneered at."[51] Equally distortional were the newspaper advertisements run by the Unionist Party Publicity Committee. If Laurier was elected, one claimed, Victory Bonds would not be needed, as "there won't be any troops to equip."[52] Such were the "abominable" lies spread by the publicity bureau and decried by *L'Acadien* (Moncton) and the Quebec press. Typical of much sentiment in the western press were the openly biased statements in the *Calgary Daily Herald* on the stark electoral choice and Quebecers' decision to "cravenly withdraw" from the war and the loan.[53]

Despite the swell of patriotic response, undercurrents and local grumbles were also created by late starts, political tensions, and encounters with those unable or unwilling to subscribe. Subscription did not preclude opposition to the war on other grounds, as will be seen in Chapter 11. Canvassers in Calgary later reported that "some people were dubious about investing ... for they were not so sure that we were going to win the war."[54] In the Roman Catholic diocese of Antigonish in Nova Scotia, reports out of St. Francis Xavier University and in the *Casket* newspaper give the impression of a smooth campaign, one supported by Bishop James Morrison. But south of Cape Breton, on Isle Madame, where conscription caused much consternation among largely francophone Acadians, clergymen refused to endorse the loan until Morrison had openly done so, a standoff that degenerated into a brief row with the local committee.[55] In Quebec, where the loan results of counties were published, subscriptions in adjoining Yamaska and Nicolet were extremely low, with rural skepticism and opposition to government decisions being possible factors.

In Montreal, executive chair McConnell, while taking pains to sidestep the loyalty debate, nonetheless understood the range of problems confronting grain dealer Joseph Quintal, head of the French Canadian committee. McConnell reported that Quintal had faced the difficult task of educating French Canadians "in the matter of purchasing Government securities. It necessitated breaking into absolutely new territory; educational methods had to be introduced and developed." For his part, Quintal, who questioned the need for separate French and English committees, claimed that the French Canadian campaign had started late, a problem also found outside of Montreal. At least two months should have been devoted to organization before any campaign opened, he reasoned. Nor had the French Canadian committee any input on publicity. (As one result, the quality of translation on Victory Loan posters suffered and was challenged by *Le Devoir* and others.) Quintal and other campaign leaders also noted the failure to synchronize with patterns of loans by farmers (traditionally made on 1 November), their limited familiarity with securities other than land

Le Comité des dames canadiennes-françaises d'Emprunt de la Victoire, Montreal. Chairperson Élodie Hébert is fourth from the left. The image was originally published in *La Presse* and *La Patrie,* 9 November 1917. | *Coolopolis,* http://coolopolis.blogspot.com/2010/11/more-gorgeous-photos-from-crypt.html.

mortgages, general resentment toward commission-based sales, and the unexpectedly dismal returns in such areas as the St. James Street business section. The effectiveness of women as campaigners in Quebec City was undermined by the refusal of the English-speaking women to organize with the French Canadian women, causing "deep discontent."[56] Further, Madame Élodie Hébert, chair of the often abased French Canadian Women's Committee in Montreal, reported that both "the impending election" and the "political aspect" of the Victory Loan "proved a considerable impediment to us," a claim backed by the small number of applications that the committee was able to secure.[57]

Newspaper reportage reflected both the divides and the propelling urgency of the loan as seen by Ottawa. At a luncheon of canvassers in Montreal on 30 November, White urged them, on the grounds that Canada should expect no territorial gains or indemnity from a defeated Germany, to complete a vibrant campaign to get domestic support, one infused with "more self-denial" and a "spirit of religion." The address was covered in the *Montreal Gazette* but not by Bourassa's *Le Devoir,* which, unlike Hébert, lauded her committee's subscriptions. Its correspondent Ernest Bilodeau continued to chide White as a Toronto henchman, a friend of distortion.

In a complicated coexistence, opposition in Quebec first to a European conflict and later to conscription did not preclude support for the war and patriotic causes. From the earliest months, organizations such as the Fédération nationale Saint-Jean-Baptiste presented an autonomous front separate from English Canadian voluntary societies, allowing them not only to support causes on their own terms, including relief for Belgian refugees, but also to champion Quebec's 22nd Battalion and, in a show of solidarity, to aid injured Franco-Ontarians back from overseas.[58] Similar differences of allegiance and support applied to the war loans.

Characterization of the 1917 loan as a grand stunt, a shill's call, was forcefully put to the Quebec public by Bourassa as part of a biting criticism of the loan and "la maison Borden-White et compagnie" in a scathing eight-page booklet, *L'Emprunt de la "Victoire": La surenchère du "bluff."* It would have been censored had it not appeared in such sensitive proximity to the election.[59] Sent to newspapers in late November and sold for 5¢, it went through two printings. Extracts and commentary, in *Le Progrès du Golfe* (Rimouski) and elsewhere, spread the viewpoint. Bourassa likened the loan to an escalating political bluff defined by lies. War bonds he equated to sticky strips of flypaper, meant to ensnare unthinking investors, especially small investors, who would fall prey to overblown claims of resale value in a war based on deceit, profiteering, uncertain victory, and potential bankruptcy.[60] In its cold intimation, "the *voluntary* subscription to the loan ... is the exact repetition of what was done to organize and stimulate the *voluntary* enlistment of soldiers: it is the same exploitation of jingoism, of the vanity of parvenus, of the gullibility of people, these are the same methods used for reclamation, blackmail and intimidation."[61] Bourassa's utterance of investment pitfalls had merit, but they were slow to surface elsewhere (and they did) and were heavily overshadowed in the fall of 1917. Deeply entangled with the election coming on 17 December, vilification of the loan and condemnation of anglophone ridicule of Quebec quickly spread through the French-language newspapers, even after the campaign had ended, alongside attacks on the government, conscription, and White. Charges of Prussian-style intimidation, pressure on employees, and views of Montreal's Victory Loan parade (on nomination day no less) as a "grotesque circus" (as one French Canadian "mother" termed it) set a strong tone. Even while attacking the Unionist government, a number of newspapers, among them *Le Progrès du Golfe* and *Le Sorelois* (Sorel), separated out and endorsed the loan, which received episcopal and provincial support. Building on *La surenchère du "bluff,"* Omer Héroux of *Le Devoir* castigated the Unionist Party's immoral hijacking of the loan for partisan purposes, arguing that its intended use had been compromised. All accepted government advertising. In other pockets of the country, Liberal newspapers ripped into White.

Elsewhere, practical problems undermined campaign rhetoric and impacted the drives. Geography, the long distances to be covered by some canvassers (especially in the West), language and ethnic differences, and the late-fall weather presented challenges. In Toronto and elsewhere, the campaign wrapped up in cold and often snowy conditions. In many areas, given the tight time frame and distances, campaign materials arrived behind schedule. The campaign reached the Yukon and overseas soldiers even later. Set up through High Commissioner Sir George Halsey Perley in London, arrangements for subscriptions at overseas pay offices (through assignment of pay) and YMCA huts were not implemented until late November and December.[62] But according to a report from the militia department, soldiers subscribed $1.5 million in a two-week period, with "no propaganda or coaxing of any kind."[63] In the midst of the campaign, the *Toronto Daily Star* reported that loan posters were being distributed "among all Canadian units in England."[64] In Canada, closer to timely promotions, members of the Royal Flying Corps Canada training organization subscribed for $350,000 through its pay office.[65]

In addition to operational problems, pockets of apathy and opposition received some attention in the newspapers. Tabloid-style instances of individuals' rejection of Victory Bonds were sometimes deemed newsworthy. Still, the network held together. Professionalized organization, a national master plan, and mass communication prevailed. A template was set. White was ecstatic; congratulatory messages were received and issued. Whereas 41,263 subscribers had bought bonds in March, 869,300 stepped forward in November, subscribing more than $566 million against a call for $150 million. Subscriptions per capita jumped from $23.19 in March to $53.18 in November, the ratio from 1 in 193.5 to 1 in 9.62 (compared to 1 in 23 in Britain and 1 in 27 in the United States).[66] On the Toronto Stock Exchange, trading was suspended for weeks as brokers concentrated on winding up the campaign. Driven by a mix of patriotism, financial opportunity, and the compelling drive, Canadians had responded in a significant way. The larger newspapers gave voice to this response, also seen in private correspondence, a response offset in some quarters by skepticism and by the silence of nonsubscription. Pointing to the investment side, the assertion that the loan "turned profiteers into patriots" has merit.[67] There was demonstrable fervour from a public willing to engage. Typical in many respects, the response in the Anglo-Canadian home of Ruth Caroline Shaw Antliff in Montreal was enthusiastic, as evidenced in her letters to her son, a stretcher-bearer in France. The campaign's launch and parade and her household's subscriptions, including that of "our little ignorant French maid," are described in excited detail. "Everywhere we read about" the loan "and hear people talking about it."[68] The contrast to much of the French Canadian sentiment was stark.

Letters from other servicemen in France and Canada tell of the moral support derived by soldiers from family subscriptions and recount soldiers' own clear-headed investment in bonds.[69] From Vancouver, William Lowry, a former prospector and badly burned veteran, wrote to his mother in Ireland on 20 November:

> We have a big loan campaign in this town at present introducing parades, fireworks, canvassers, boosters barkers and speilers [sic]. The war loan is known as the Victory Loan. Bonds are sold as low as fifty dollars. I thought that one of these bonds might make an acceptable Christmas present for Dorothy so I bought her one tho' on afterthought I believe she would have preferred the cash.[70]

Days later, a store theft – set up as a Victory Loan joke in a "carnival spirit" – was dourly described by the *British Columbia Federationist* (Vancouver) as a "cheap show." The *Federationist* accepted advertisements for the loan but professed disregard for profiteers and canvassers who accepted commissions: "The hustlers for the Victory Loan throughout Canada cleaned up." It gave some voice to the Canadians who did not or could not subscribe, including union members who could afford only life's essentials.[71] Noticeably, estimates of carnival quality shared ground with the pointed ridicule by Bourassa and others in Quebec. Lowry's remark could also reflect the distance that existed between many veterans of real battlefields, on the one hand, and revellers and armchair enthusiasts at home, on the other.

As had happened in March, some Canadians felt compelled to respond to White's mass mailing, sometimes after the close of the campaign and without clear understanding of the loan. Hugh C. Merry of Middlechurch, Manitoba, who could not afford a bond, sent $2 as a donation to the loan. Elderly and incapacitated, G. Ramsell of Nanaimo, British Columbia, had $200 in the bank, which he meant to use to bury himself and his wife. If he put it into bonds, would the government, he asked, bury one or both of them? From Pibroch, Alberta, Albert Couturier claimed that farm losses and expenses prevented him from subscribing, but he was prepared to donate his profit on three cows to the country, maybe the Red Cross. Such were some of the missives that crossed the desk of White's secretary, Bennet John Roberts.[72] Near the start of the campaign, the department claimed to have received hundreds of letters asking for White's advice on bonds. The department took every opportunity to portray him as a busy man and Canadians as eager investors.

Companies and financial institutions were motivated by varying mixtures of patriotism and business calculation. Toronto's largest corporate subscriber, Canada Life, invested $5 million, "practically all our revenue for the coming year" after claims and expenses, its president telegraphed White. Claiming to be keen to support the war effort, it was also, in a banner year, attempting to build its reserves. The big investment firms, such as A.E. Ames and Company and Greenshields and Company, were quick to publish advertisements, in Newfoundland as well as Canada, that promoted their handling of war bonds. Patriotism could be ignited at no cost; the morale built by the loan was incalculable. But, conducted behind the patriotic and promotional glare of the loan, there were cold considerations of the financial incentives. To institutional subscribers for millions (and to some present-day economists examining America's Liberty Loans), these incentives were pre-eminent. In the midst of the 1917 campaign in Canada, choice of bond maturity dates, yields, conversion calculations, and the implications of tax exemptions were significant factors, worthy of serious discussion in the newspapers but likely to be passed over by attention to the holder of a few small bonds.[73]

What emerges from much of the newspaper reportage and the correspondence is the image of a commonality that was sometimes forced and sometimes defined by propaganda. Investment broker Albert Livingstone Crossin, who had criss-crossed Manitoba for the Victory Loan, was convinced that it would "consolidate the country."[74] One captain of an English canvassing team in Montreal, ignoring the fault lines there, believed that the "campaign brought the people together in a common cause and this lending to the Govt't till it hurts ... will make us all better and true Canadians."[75] The *Island Patriot* would see war loans as "the dawn of a fuller and ampler citizenship."[76] White's communications were the epitome, just as there were expressions of Canadianism that refused to be defined by support for the Victory Loan. Financial inability, electoral taint, and the divisiveness of conscription and union government undermined these notions of commonality. Still, White's machinery had got him his money at a critical time. Equally, the Victory Loans, in their call for communal payment, moulded public appreciation of other means such as income taxation.[77]

During the first half of 1918, even with White absent in California and Alexander Kenneth Maclean focusing on his budget and funding matters in the United States, Victory Bonds maintained a striking presence on the home front, mirroring the "almost religious fervour" that one banker saw displayed in the sale of Liberty Bonds.[78] (The concept of the "home front," often found in reference to Germany, was introduced for Britain in 1915, but the term was not found in Toronto's *Globe* or *Daily Star* before 1918.) The impact of bonds took two forms. First, women and others who had given their time to the fall loan turned out in large numbers to canvass for the Red Cross, YWCA and YMCA, and Patriotic Fund campaigns. Commissions from bond subscriptions were frequently given to such drives. Second was the market. Questions about bonds were asked in Parliament; reports were submitted. Despite its promotional value, the new $50 bond proved unpopular among large investors and department officials. The first interest payment to holders of registered bonds, for instance, necessitated the mailing of hundreds of thousands of cheques, each for $1.38, producing "great administrative trouble and expense," the *Globe* reported in June 1918. The banks, security dealers, and the government were all kept busy with purchases of bonds, the issue of interim receipts, instalment and interest payments, conversions, and a host of related tasks. Not wishing to be seen as purveyors of bad business, banks took issue with reports of subscribers who defaulted or struggled to make their instalment payments. Because of the loan and conscription, retail business experienced a "slight depression." As well, because of the "temporary unsettlement" caused by the loan, the government's campaigns promoting thrift and war-savings certificates had been postponed, although the finance department announced in January that they would resume within the "next couple of months."[79] The banks watched their deposits fluctuate temporarily as money was withdrawn for the purchase of bonds and certificates, accumulations of subscribed money were transferred to the credit of the Department of Finance, imperial credits were processed, and short-term government loans were liquidated. The market hummed, seemingly dominated by investments in Victory Bonds, although support was not unanimous. The financial press recognized the element of speculation. Unscrupulous dealers emerged to fleece uninformed bondholders, despite public warnings that they should sell only through the banks, recognized bond firms, or stock-exchange members.[80] Many others were frustrated by low prices on sales before maturity.

The annual reports of banks and trust companies were bullish about the loan and the "reserve power" being found on the home front, with one director declaring, "Canada has found her soul," even as Ottawa faced surging debt.[81] Experts and publications began analyzing component sectors of the loan: investment, the role of the banks, the impact on retail trade, organization, printing, and publicity, including bond and recruiting posters, which were being collected and exhibited, much like battlefield souvenirs. The atmosphere was electric for some, distracting for others. "We live in an age of campaigns," exclaimed Professor Charles Bruce Sissons of Toronto's Victoria College in *Farmers'*

Magazine (Toronto),[82] looking at the array of drives for the Canadian Patriotic Fund, Red Cross, YMCA, Navy League, relief, prohibition, recruiting, farm production, thrift and war savings, and Victory Loan. Newspapermen gave lectures on war advertising. Many weeklies, eager for copy, picked up and spread the same articles, such as those on the application of the loan to the Halifax Relief Fund, the heavy subscriptions of railway employees, and the praise in American newspapers. Duplication of coverage and views emerged, as in MacLean Publishing's loan-friendly trade periodicals. Victory Bond news, laudation, and investment advice filled the press and a host of journals, which relentlessly publicized a linkage between economic prosperity and the loan, with only sporadic mentions of inflation or debt. Every angle garnered attention. The use of "In Flanders Fields" to promote the loan intensified. The public asked questions – such as whether interest coupons could be used to pay taxes. Untold numbers of businesses, companies, government bodies, and civic and private organizations continued to buy bonds for sinking and trust funds and for other reserves. Individuals concealed bonds in vaults, safe-deposit boxes, and home drawers, many to emerge in estates, thefts, court cases, and sales before maturity. Bonds became a form of unofficial currency in retail transactions (one outcome in the tug-of-war between consumerism and saving), and they were used for charitable donations, presents by companies, contest and lottery prizes, and security for bank loans. In October 1918, in negotiations for expanded hospital facilities for veterans in Manitoba, the federal minister of militia even offered to use Victory Bonds to pay, but the province refused.[83]

Throughout the crisis year of 1917, the means of raising war funding were debated with increasing urgency. The president of the Canadian Bank of Commerce, Sir Edmund Walker, convinced that the Department of Finance was too relaxed between the "whirlwind" campaigns of the war loans and too willing to ignore the "small purses," called for implementing the war-savings stamps shelved by the government. He was not alone in this old argument. In a letter to the *Globe,* a "West Toronto Housewife," who saw war-savings certificates being sold to men in factories, wanted the housewives and children at home to be able to save and contribute, too.[84]

Much like the campaign's approach to mothers and widows, the engagement of boys and girls brought gendered viewpoints, familial sacrifice, and sanitization of war. Long shamelessly involved as unofficial recruiting agents, children were called on to save. Toronto's Board of Education was exhorted in the loan campaign of 1917 "to mobilize the child forces of the city" and "enlist" students to work as promoters and canvassers. In 1918, as in 1917, students continued to be cultivated through educational curricula, savings programs, essay competitions, and all sorts of paraphernalia. In New Brunswick, loan committees leaned

Victory Bond posters are displayed by five boys, some of them Boy Scouts, and two men in front of Way's ladies' wear store in Regina, 1918. | Provincial Archives of Saskatchewan, R-B8132 (48).

on principals, and female teachers and students participated in Home Efficiency Clubs geared to selling preserves in order to buy bonds.[85] Students at Sunday schools bought them with money earned doing odd jobs. The plucky responses of youth mirrored those in Britain and Europe, leading historian Niall Ferguson to speculate that "perhaps the grim truth about war propaganda was that it had the greatest influence on the social group which mattered least to the war effort: children."[86]

In contrast, known soldiers' letters between January and May continued to show pragmatic understandings of British and Canadian war bonds. Some reflected what their writers had read about the Victory Loan and related enthusiasms at home. If there was any money left from Christmas, pilot Gordon Budd Irving wrote to his sister in February from London, England, "grab it before the old man buys a war bond with it. Judging by the rapturostical letters I receive from Beamsville [Ontario] you did you[r] duty in that direction." When one soldier learned that his folks had invested his assigned pay in the war loan, "he nearly took a fit," according to a friend overseas. Invective, the dark side of the response in Ontario to Quebec's contribution to the loan and recruitment drives, was also evident. Writing in January from "Somewhere in Muddy France,"

Forestry Corps member Norman Cecil Nayler, a lumberman in Ontario before enlistment, told his brother, "I would like to have about half a million to invest in that war loan stunt. You say they aren't doing very well in Quebec. They aren't apt for those French Canadians must have a streak of yellow up their backs about a foot wide."[87] Victory Bonds thus worked their way into everyday discourse.

Public responses to the loan insinuated a way to contribute, an antidote to anxiety. In the closing months of 1917, a tough war year, a dour mood had settled on Canada, where drafts of soldiers were being asked "to adventure forth in chilly silence."[88] That winter brought fuel and food shortages, regulations, and shrill calls to save. Military turns in Europe in early 1918 forced the government to end exemptions to service, leading to angry demonstrations. The Victory Loan posited a calculated boost: "selling" the war to Canadians through fiscal policy.[89] In many ways, the loan and its publicity committees mirrored, on a much smaller scale, America's four Liberty Loans of 1917 and 1918 and the Committee on Public Information, the American agency established in April 1917 to mobilize public support. Its go-getting head, former muckraker George Edward Creel, would describe the committee as "a plain publicity proposition, a vast enterprise in salesmanship, the world's greatest adventure in advertising."[90] But did such adventure work here?

In the aftermath of the 1917 Victory Loan, *Hardware and Metal* and *Dry Goods Review* (both part of MacLean Publishing's stable of trade journals) would quote a campaign committee executive as saying that he had not met "one man who will admit that the advertising influenced him to buy a bond." Others would point to specific posters as particularly motivating. In response to the executive, the journals argued that advertising had created the atmosphere. The lesson for retailers, as it had been for loan propaganda, was that they should not expect a flood of customers after one's first ad, "but remember, like the Victory Bonds, continual telling of your story will wear its way into the reason of the most obdurate."[91] The loan's publicity committee counted on unrelenting exposure to create the visual and psychological atmosphere conducive to public engagement.

Reaction to loan propaganda, including alarmist promotions and the gamut of commercial advertising, ranged widely. Alleged atrocities portrayed in Victory Loan print, cartoons, donated ads, and speeches, as well as the characterization of fear-filled women, innocent children, and angelic nurses, all needing male and soldierly protection, strived to bring the war's front into Canadian homes.[92] Toronto's Victory Loan publicity committee, chaired by the enterprising heads of the F.W. Woolworth Company and the Wrigley Company, had felt that dramatic emphasis should be tried. The result was a fictitious eight-page tabloid, the *Victory Telegraph*. Issued in November 1917 but dated 28 November 1921 and meant to boost bond sales, it blared out news (with a few tips of its fabrication) of a German takeover of Canada, including the fall of Halifax, Saint John, and Toronto, and it reported the demise of the British fleet. In the "years" after the loan campaign, the *Telegraph* went on, citizens hanged themselves for not subscribing. Similar scare tactics would be used in a handful of loan advertisements and posters in 1918 and for that year's campaigns in Nova Scotia, New Brunswick, and Newfoundland, which emphasized their vulnerability on the edge of the Atlantic. The *Telegraph* reflected the popularity of imagined invasions in pre-war literature in Britain, but in 1917 there were some grounds for legitimacy, among them fears in Canada of saboteurs, spies, submarines, and "half-assimilated German settlers." Perhaps the *Telegraph* boosted sales of bonds, but reaction varied at a time when campaign souvenirs such as this shock-effect paper and posters were becoming collectible and their impact scrutinized. Writing from Halifax to his mother in Toronto on 5 December 1917, George Veals, a wireless-telegraph operator, told her that he and his naval mates had been amused to learn in the *Telegraph* of the city's so-called ruin. The next day, Halifax's massive munitions explosion fatally injured young Veals.[93]

Author Lucy Maud Macdonald (née Montgomery) of Leaskdale, Ontario, one of many obsessive followers of war news and propaganda, was aware of the *Telegraph*, a clever gambit, she noted in her journal, that had nearly frightened some Torontonians "into fits." On 6 December, during a visit to Toronto, on seeing the headline "Halifax City Is Wrecked" in another paper, she dismissed it as a fake, like the *Telegraph*. "I thought a repetition of it was rather silly and wished the government had hit upon a more effective dodge for opening the eyes of Canadians to their peril." She nonetheless bought the paper – it was the *Daily Star* – "out of mild curiosity and opened it. Twenty minutes later I came to my senses upon an uptown [street]car without any recollection of how I got there," stunned by the reality of what she had read.[94] In Toronto, riding the Victory Loan's momentum, the *Telegraph* continued to be sold into January as a souvenir, generating $4,000 for the combined campaign of the Toronto and York Patriotic Fund and the Canadian Red Cross.[95]

Loan publicity was not all of the shocking or curiosity-provoking sort. There were the much-underrated informative pamphlets. Among the self-congratulating pieces was *The Story of Canada's Victory Loan, 1917: A Slight Appreciation of a Remarkable Event* by Edward Rogers Wood of the dominion national executive. Issued in early 1918, it provided summaries of different aspects of the loan, including the reporting and keeping of records and a five-page list of special subscribers of more than $50,000. As president of Dominion Securities, Wood also produced a New Year's review of the bond market, where "Victories" figured prominently. Equally quick to capitalize was the firm of national chairman Alfred Ernest Ames, which in January issued *Canada's War Loans, Including Victory Bonds: Interesting Things about Them,* an investor's guide aimed not just at the "small circle of specialists" but also at "small wage earners."[96]

7

Pandemic and Peace, 1918

By the time the Victory Loan campaign of 1918 was unfolding in Nova Scotia, the influenza pandemic was just beginning to spread. The impact of the disease there (1,789 deaths) would be less severe than in other parts of Canada.[1] In King's County, it would claim sixty-four lives, but the campaign went ahead. On 28 October, it opened boisterously in Wolfville with a street parade led by the Boy Scouts and a band, followed by two automobiles carrying returned soldiers, with another decked out as a tank. Next came a horse ridden by Mary Ellouise Black, dressed in white as Joan of Arc, the saviour of France in a long-ago war. Bringing up the rear were more decorated cars and floats, two of them featuring the Give Service Girls Club, of which Black was president, depicting the Allies and Canada. On the back of a delivery truck was a caged "Kaiser Bill." Children, some on bicycles, wove in and out. The cavalcade travelled to other communities, drumming up enthusiasm before finding its way back that night. In the campaign's first three days, subscriptions for $160,000 were secured in King's County.[2] Parades like this had provided grand kickoffs in 1917, when the Victory Loan had firmly planted bonds, public engagement, and government control.

The stabilizing Victory Loan Special Committee started up in January 1918, just as financial men from Toronto and Montreal met to fix the opening price for trading in war bonds. The Department of Finance was already having trouble keeping pace with the administrative load of the loan, not to mention the forthcoming returns of the new income tax and the arduous task of dealing with lost, stolen, unclaimed, and destroyed bonds. By the fall of 1918, some 28,000 bonds from 1917 were unclaimed, according to the department. (By early 1929, many from 1915 to 1917 and almost 3,000 from 1917 to 1919 were reported as missing or destroyed. In 1955, the finance minister of the day stated that there were more than $200,000 in Great War bonds still hidden away, and the previous year $8,250 worth of bonds had been presented for payment.[3] Whatever the rate of seepage, momentum was strong going into 1918.

The department continued to receive letters offering critiques and ideas for debt management and fundraising, some building on the brassy side of the 1917 campaign. One amusement-company president thought that bonds could be hawked at carnivals and midways. More prominent still was the escalating revival by Toronto's *Marketing and Business Management* (formerly *Economic Advertising*) of the call for advertising and poster outfits to guide the government's war advertising, independently of the Canadian Press Association. Strong criticism was directed at the arrangement whereby the association was again allowed to handle the apportionment of funds for advertising, essentially leaving them "in the hands of those who are to share in it." *Marketing*, which came down hard on what it viewed as the shortcomings of the 1917 loan, offered suggestions to the dominion publicity committee, drawing from America's Liberty Loans and stressing the need for "a strongly emotional appeal," with a wary use of "horror copy." To the public, the tiffs were likely irrelevant. More and more as the war progressed and government advertising grew, agencies, journals, and the newspapers claimed that the war was proving the power of advertising.[4]

Elsewhere at the government level, the Victory Loan and Bonds entered the arsenals of the National Service Board and the War Lecture Bureau, the propaganda mill created in January in the Privy Council Office with jingoistic lecturer Frank Yeigh as secretary, under director of public information Mark Edgar Nichols, who had been appointed to the position the previous November. Meant to channel issues and mobilize opinion, the bureau sent out thousands of newsletters and scripts to campaign volunteers.[5] Its corps of 100 or so speakers, the "Five-Minute Men," was modelled after fast-talking spielers in the 1917 campaign and the "Four-Minute Men" of George Edward Creel's Committee on Public Information in the United States.[6]

Outside of Parliament, members of the Unionist Cabinet also pushed awareness of bonds and loans. On 18 February, Frank Carvell, once a critic of White's policies but now minister of public works, in a speech to Montreal's Canadian Club, censured the state of the government railways but endorsed 1917's Victory Loan. In an address to Toronto's Central YMCA on government achievements, Privy Council president Newton Wesley Rowell repeated the stock argument of the loan's centrality in financing purchases by Britain.[7] All of this attention meshed with the surge in government advertising in the first half of 1918 from the Departments of Finance (explaining the War Income Tax) Agriculture, and Trade and Commerce and from the newly constituted Canada Registration Board and the Canada Food Board, formed in February 1918 out of the Office of the Food Controller. In concert with provincial and local bodies that addressed shortages, the Food Board would extend the federal reach through sweeping regulations dealing with inspection, handling and licensing, rationing, hoarding, and waste prevention. The underlying gospel of thrift infused a complementary panoply of publicity. In late February, the board announced its intention to arrange "an extensive propaganda" through twenty-five districts. Representatives would work with advertisers "to carry on a campaign somewhat similar to that of the Victory Loan."[8] The *Canadian Food Bulletin* (Ottawa), begun by the Food Controller in October 1917, and a succession of speakers and colourful posters made clear the symbiotic connection to the campaign for war loans and to the drives for thrift, savings, and food conservation. The *Bulletin* of 3 November urged readers, "Do your part to ensure the success of the Canadian Victory Loan. You will be ready then for the Production and Conservation Campaign." The issue of 14 December, pushing for greater hog production, ran a compressed pronouncement that may have amused more than one rural household: "The slogan for Canada should be: 'Make a hog buy your next Victory Bond.'" In November, Allied purchases of foodstuffs were described as the "food side" of the loan.

The expertise and data generated by the 1917 loan would provide a solid basis for that of 1918. Although some official accounts on 1917 would not appear for another two years (and no official audit until 1922), reports were tabled in April and May 1918 in the Commons on the costs and distribution of advertising the 1917 loan and on other dominion expenses. A statement on the remuneration paid to 266 dealers and brokers was submitted by a one-time partner in A.E. Ames and Company, Thomas Bradshaw, treasurer of Toronto, part of the city's Victory Loan executive, and a member since the start of the year of White's coterie of securities advisors. Bradshaw, not the finance department, handled remunerations.[9] The final report by Alfred Ernest Ames as chair of the dominion executive, a revealing document submitted to White on 26 April, was congratulatory in feel and factual in content. The ratio of subscribers to population rose dramatically, from 1 in 193.4 in March 1917 to 1 in 9.62. Special subscriptions came in at $132,102,000, or almost a third. The statement included neither the Yukon, where $97,150 had been subscribed, nor overseas subscriptions, estimated at $1.5 million by the Department of Finance. Care was taken, Ames stressed, to report only "new money," although some $3.9 million of conversion money had entered the account. He wanted to avoid double reporting. Overlap with the election campaign, which the dominion executive had wanted to avoid, was spun as a generator of "further energy" within the campaign. His main recommendation for the next loan was more lead time for organization, advice that was widely supported.[10]

The extent of Victory Bonds in investments and rhetoric was widespread but not uniform. Some sectors felt excluded from the loan's beneficence. Veterans began questioning the levels of government aid, grieving families fretted about support, and many farmers saw no clear financial benefit from increased production. In Alberta, inveterate letter writer Mrs. M.E. Graham asked: "Why should not loans [for farmers] to keep up production come in the same class as War Bonds?"[11] Much of the debate was tinged by issues that had surrounded the election. Quebec was singled out for harsh scrutiny. Despite the litany of campaign problems, Montreal was a beehive of activity in the first half of 1918, with dealers also using out-of-town newspapers to buy and sell bonds. In a bid in February to sell Montreal city bonds, with a generous 6-percent interest, dealers launched a campaign, "much as in the Victory Loan."[12] Committees from the 1917 campaign in Montreal and Quebec City turned over their commissions and time to the Halifax Relief Fund and the Red Cross. Attitudes in Quebec had nonetheless become hardened by the perceived impact of the loan on the election, by nationalist censure of Unionist finance, and by mounting antagonisms in the new year toward national registration, conscription, and enforcement of the Military Service Act.[13] Parliamentary debate in the spring of 1918 about troubles in Quebec came amidst critiques of the Victory Loan. How far the 1917 campaign and subsequent boosting went to redress unfamiliarity in Quebec with securities is uncertain. Moreover, the securities field was becoming crowded with competitive offerings; municipal debentures issued elsewhere in Canada also offered 6 percent and Newfoundland six and a-half percent, well above the five and a-half percent for Victory Bonds. Nonetheless, investment advisors and analysts touted the long-term return on the twenty-year Victory Bonds.

The debate and information on the loan presented in the Commons that spring filtered through to newspapers. *The Voice*, a labour paper in Winnipeg and supporter of Canada's war loans since 1916, wondered "how much the newspapers received for their share at the psychological moment of Union Government formation."[14] Newspaper and advertising firms were well aware, however, of the escalation in government advertising. In April 1918, William Elgood Smallfield of the *Renfrew Mercury* in eastern Ontario told a Toronto audience that the most important drives had been Sir George Foster's eat-more-apples campaign in 1914, the production-and-thrift campaign begun in January 1917, and the Victory Loan campaign that fall.[15]

As late as May, the Department of Finance was too preoccupied to make serious plans for the 1918 loan. White's prolonged absence in the United States did not help. The deputy minister of trade and commerce, whose department was the leader in the production of advertising films, urged his counterpart in the finance department to build on its venture into the cinematic field in 1917. Responding on 8 May 1918, Thomas Cooper Boville recognized the use of motion pictures as an "absolute necessity," but he backed off, confessing, "We are too busy getting the old loan off our hands to think of the next one which will no doubt be issued some time in the fall."[16] Indeed, as late as June, bonds were still being sent out. The payment of interest coupons, due on 1 June, required another surge of effort. Throughout the prior month, coupon holders were being urged by security firms and the government to reinvest the money in more bonds, debenture stock, and war-savings certificates, whereas stores wanted the interest to go into purchases. After June, the Department of Finance began hearing that many bondholders, especially of small denominations, were simply unaware that the semi-annual coupons could be cashed. But even with the preoccupation noted by Boville, consideration in some quarters was being given to the next loan. The Victory Loan Special Committee, for instance, was well aware that some subscribers had made only their initial payments, which under the terms of the loan's prospectus could be forfeited. Committee chair George Herbert Wood told assistant deputy minister John Cramp Saunders that such action could hurt the next loan by putting off small subscribers.[17] Refunds were preferable, but the forfeiture clause would be retained.

In late May and June, as White attended to bank funding till September and to exchange and security matters with the United States, he set plans in motion for the fall campaign, two months earlier than 1917's start-up. By early June, prior to his return, his department was well into developing the mechanics. On 1 June, Ames, the former dominion chair, recommended Edward Rogers Wood as his successor. He accepted on 25 June, and over the next few days, letters and telegrams flew out from White's office asking some thirty others to join the executive. White wanted wide representation; for honorary provincial committees, he sought out figureheads. The headquarters for the new loan was moved to Ottawa, closer to White, who would also be concerned that summer with a postal strike (as a negotiator), financing the western crop, imperial supply, railway matters, and ongoing administration of the war-finance juggernaut.[18] In June, the Bond Dealers' Association of Canada met to discuss the terms and conditions of the loan. Throughout July and August, several other organizational and analytic meetings were held. Such early planning was needed, and there were issues to be addressed, among them tax exemption on bond interest. On 22 September, at its annual gathering in Quebec City, the Trades and Labor Congress resolved after hours of "acrimonious debate" that the loan "be placed on the same tax-bearing basis as other securities." One New York journal dismissed such wrangling as a "diverting little passage-at-arms."[19]

Behind such debates lay practical challenges. There were unfounded but lingering perceptions of favouritism in the payment of commissions. Whatever subscriptions were publicly reported from 1917, actual receipts trailed. The response of farmers and rural workers was opaque.[20] At the end of the war, Foster, an astute observer of the war loans, claimed that whereas urban Ontario had reached 111 percent of its quotas, rural areas had not even delivered 40 percent, suggesting imprecise forecasting.[21] Propaganda had primed for more and in other sectors, too. In June 1918, the Toronto Women's Patriotic League posted a notice in the window of its rooms on Bay Street calling for reduced sugar consumption. This plea for economy, the *Globe* (Toronto) observed, "is part of the wide propaganda intended to impress on the individual the importance of his or her own efforts in husbanding resources and financing the allies' part in the war."[22] Whether food conservation measures practically helped housewives is debatable.[23] The link to war funding is clearer. With so much of the loans going to institutions, it can be seen that the publicity aimed at women, farmers, and others was intended not just to generate funding but also to build and stabilize popular support for the war effort. In New Glasgow, Nova Scotia, the president of the East Pictou Local Council of Women, in a tone of shared responsibility, proudly reported the transfer of male organizers' commissions from the loan to the council for "patriotic and philanthropic" distribution. "The obligation is ours as well as the men's."[24]

Commercial and official advertising of the 1918 loan began appearing in July, the Bond Dealers' Association of Canada had drafted a prospectus by early August, and to clear the decks, bond dealers would stop selling the last issue of bonds on 7 September. At the offices of the Canadian Press Association (CPA) in Toronto on 23 August, members of the association, the advertising-copy writing committee, the bond dealers' committee, and the dominion publicity committee met to hear White "outline the reasons for the loan." Editorial writers, summoned by White, produced columns to prepare the public, a "quiet but effective form of propaganda," *Marketing* called the initiative. The loan's provincial chairs met in late August to coordinate plans of action, including pushing subscriptions in the $5,000 to $25,000 range, which had reportedly been weak in 1917. Over the summer, the CPA launched a comprehensive plan of promotion and organization.

As in 1917, press publicity would be handled conjointly by the CPA and the dominion publicity committee, assisted by the Canadian Association of Advertising Agencies. The group's executive committee was chaired by William James Taylor (the CPA's president and the publisher of the *Woodstock Sentinel-Review* in Woodstock, Ontario), and the dominion publicity committee was again headed by Montreal securities specialist Ralph A. Stephenson; thirteen advertising agencies were engaged. An insightful post-campaign summary, likely prepared by Taylor, outlined the group's work in two divisions: official paid advertising as well as press releases and feature service for newspapers.

Official advertisements – 168 in all, more than in 1917 – were released in series of mounting intensity over three periods with specific goals: in the first in a series, beginning on 7 September 1918, ads were issued reminding Canadians to practise thrift so that they would have "as much money as possible to lend to their country"; in the second series, starting on 12 October, the appeal shifted to "educational" content interspersed with "emotional and inspirational advertisements"; and the third series, from 26 October to 16 November, consisted of outright "selling advertisements."[25] The press publicity was managed by Newton Wylie, a *Globe* staffer, who, among other contributions, came up with the slogan "dollars counted as much as bullets." Poster services were handled by the Poster Advertising Association of Canada under the direction of the publicity committee.

Such plans, and all matters of promotion, including items as small as subscription pins, were filtered through the publicity committee. Starting in August, efforts were made to have short films made, including the adaptation of Liberty Loan films. From the sidelines, calls came from publicity extremists who wanted the "circus methods" of America's Liberty Loans, including the zealotry of revivalist Billy Sunday, to "invigorate" any Canadian campaign.[26] Such evangelical appeal would find space in western and maritime weeklies in the form of "Billy Sunday on the Victory Loan," a much-recycled article (likely fabricated) that linked support for the loan with Christ the fighter. Sponsored advertisements would conflate evocations of bond purchases and God's protection for Canada's sons. In one official advertisement, in French in *La Liberté* (Winnipeg), the need to subscribe to support Canada's troops was traced back to Moses the "general" in his fight for the Promised Land. As historian Linda Quiney concludes, the "ideology and imagery of Christian doctrine" deeply infused Victory Loan drives, just as they did recruitment, the volunteer-nursing movement, and calls for donations to patriotic organizations.[27]

On 15 September, visiting English suffragist Emmeline Pankhurst spoke on "what women have done to win the war" at Loew's Theatre in Toronto. Her exhortation to "fight on the home-front, as our soldiers are fighting on the battlefield" mirrored the military ethos and engaging reciprocity of the Victory Loan.[28] Similar warrior rhetoric emanated from pulpits. It is this discourse, especially with reference to the transformation of women's community service into voluntary patriotic work, that helped to reshape the divide between home front and battle.[29] Despite any remoteness, Canadians already knew of the pain of war, just as they encountered the crafted messages of sacrifice, pride, and entertainment in Victory Loan campaigns. What was evident in the messaging was the abstract recognition of slaughter overseas. Equally apparent was the projection of women as the economic bedrock in homes and the subscription's liberating impact on them. In the lead-up to the 1918 campaign, bond purchases were seen by columnists such as Polly Peele (Mona Hazelwood Cleaver) of the *Globe* as invigorating exercises in self-sufficiency.

The finance minister, at his best when trying to manage public opinion, talked up the 1918 loan, pushing the liquidity of bonds, his view of Canada's financial stability, and how the Victory Loan stabilization benefited the terms of the upcoming loan, a spin that would be underlined by campaign organizers.[30] Contests for loan posters, essays, poetry, and cartoons – the more jingoistic, the better – were launched. The confident mood, which shielded public tensions as peace approached, was reinforced by Canada's military offensive in Europe, which would end with the armistice of 11 November, and, in the market, by anticipation of the new issue and successful war-loan drives in Newfoundland (June–July) and the United States (April–May and September–October). Hurdles were addressed directly by the loan conglomerate or disregarded. The public's reported ignorance of bonds and hesitancy would again be a target of official advertising and brochures. Pamphlets aimed to explain how the 1917 loan was spent. Some western newspapers spread erroneous claims that the loan was being used to fund federal loans to farmers through the provinces. Legal actions by businesses challenging municipal assessments of bond interest were left to the courts and the provinces. The possible impact on the campaign of enforcement of the Military Service Act and compulsory registration of all citizens (from 22 June) went to the back burner. On 7 June, at a gathering in Toronto conducted by the United Farmers Organization to demand that the bill be revised to exempt farm workers, a protest proposal "to buy no more Victory Bonds" was rejected, but it reflected one line of thought.

In Ottawa, logistical problems, such as getting blank printing plates from the American Bank Note Company in New York through customs, were addressed by White's department. In some regions, knowledge of bonds still continued to be weak. In a letter to the deputy minister, J.S. Hull, a bank accountant in Biggar, Saskatchewan, lamented the "astonishing amount of ignorance among the public." Despite such anxieties, awareness of Victory Bonds was evident in distant parts of the Dominion. One day during the summer of 1918, in the parlour of the Anglican rectory at Alert Bay, a Kwagu'ł (Kwakwa̱ka̱'wakw) community north of Vancouver Island, a visitor wrote that there was "over the teacups the usual interesting talk, and then one by one a knitter takes her needles in hand and we sit around the fire talking of war and victory bonds."[31] At the same time, the bonds had a growing off-market presence. In Toronto, scammers were ever present, pawnbrokers offered loans on Victory Bonds, and the city accepted bond coupons in payment of taxes.

During the summer of 1918, the financial need for the loan was indisputable. Despite Canadian victories in battle, among them at the Drocourt-Quéant Line and the Canal du Nord, many believed that the war could last another year or more. Canada's financial requirements stretched just as long. Although White would begin talking about postwar adjustment right after the armistice, which happened during the loan campaign, that summer he was not about to alter the driving themes of the loan. Some thought that he should, one being Robert Lorne Richardson, a Unionist MP and manager of the *Winnipeg Tribune.* On 4 September, responding to a letter from White on the loan, he would write,

> I think it particularly desirable that the psychology of the situation should be studied. There ought to be a slogan. The last Victory Loan was made easy because of the power of the cry "Support the boys at the front." I do not think it will be possible to make a new appeal exactly on this line. There ought to be something along the nature of "Secure money to finish the job, and finish it right."[32]

The "psychology of the situation" was a realm of analysis rarely discussed outside of advertising and publicity circles, but White took notice, and some newspapers, especially the Quebec press, would recognize the shift. White would also continue to use the mantra of "Produce and Save," which was espoused by all, from King George to the Canadian National Exhibition in Toronto. One financial journal, the *Chronicle* (Montreal), drawing from the field of social science, had credited the appeal of "street processions" in 1917's campaign to "crowd psychology," a tenet of effective propaganda.

On 24 September, after "exhaustive" discussions, White issued a comprehensive statement of the plan for the loan. On 8 October, at Winnipeg's Industrial Bureau, he announced the $300 million goal, double 1917's target. Larded with clichés, his "stirring speech" touched all the bases. It was prefaced by a cable from General Sir Arthur William Currie, commander of the Canadian Corps.[33] From Winnipeg, White continued westward, stopping along the way to promote the loan. At Vancouver's Horse Show Building on 15 October, he noted that "he used to like to arrange his financial affairs for some considerable time ahead. But now, he said [drawing from an old religious line], 'I do not wish to see the distant scene. One step ahead is enough for me.'" To this the *British Columbia Federationist* (Vancouver), which reflected labour's mixed feelings about the loan, retorted (quoting from the biblical book of Proverbs), "Where there is no vision, the people perish."[34]

Throughout the spring and summer, the loan took shape in a field crowded with fundraisers, expectations, and past experience. Canadians were being dunned for their small change by the British and Italian Red Cross societies, the French Flag Day, the Belgian Relief Fund, the Navy League (for the families of merchant seamen), branches of the Overseas Club, the YMCA Red Triangle Fund, tobacco and prisoners of war funds, and a host of others. Compounding this tumult were the aggressive campaigns of local war-chest funds, an American innovation, which sought to represent many of the other causes. Citizens were amazingly generous. Notions of unequal sharing of the war's burdens, class and gender differences, and resentment of profiteering, hoarding, and consumer extravagance, as well as donor fatigue, could also enter newspaper reports and readers' letters.[35] One tough-minded female teacher in Pembroke, Ontario, diagnosed a "patriotic hysteria," where any questions from women, such as about food economy and suffrage, consigned them to "the ranks of 'Pro-Germanism.'" And how did the loan's spirit of austerity mesh with the onerous circumstances encountered at some homes in contrast to the independence and wages being earned by young female munition workers who spent their money on clothing and good times, a dichotomy that the retail sector tried to nullify? A full answer is clouded. Loan canvassers faced impediments, but propaganda, superior organization, and newspapers' screening tempered blunt assessment. Small coins did not generate down payments on subscriptions. Canadians were inundated with publicity in 1918, more so it appears than in 1917.

In 1918, provincial and local Victory Loan organizations were rapidly formed, many drawing experienced volunteers. Large volumes of newspaper promotion ensued, buttressed by government propaganda, including speakers of the War Lecture Bureau and the overtly propagandistic *Canadian Official Record (Bulletin officiel canadien),* put out weekly by the Office of Public Information in Ottawa. The responsible minister, Newton Wesley Rowell, on the *Record*'s launch in October, claimed that "it is the citizens of Canada who are carrying on the war" – a political assertion that interlocked with loan messaging and, seemingly, with related public engagement.[36] Predictably, the *Record* drew criticism. It was probably the "newspaper" that former Liberal MP George Perry Graham said that the government had started up "to boom themselves" using money from the Victory Loan of 1918.[37]

Partisan transfers of money seem unlikely. White's decisions were driven instead by considerations such as cross-funding with Britain and market forces. In September and October, he conferred closely with Flavelle about purchases by the Imperial Munitions Board and about American sensitivities over business with Canada. Flavelle was buoyed by his expectation of a return of $500 million or more. Apart from some common ground on taxation and domestic borrowing, White rarely engaged on war finance with economic analysts such as Oscar Douglas Skelton and Adam Shortt.[38] Throughout the fall and in the midst of the 1918 campaign, as subscriptions mounted, the minister would fret about reports of people postponing bond purchases and of cases of unsaleability, subpar prices, or disreputable deals. In the middle of the campaign, when Shortt – then with the Canadian Archives' Board of Historical Publications – sent him a draft article on postwar finance, White had him rewrite sentences suggesting circumstances where securities could not be sold or had to be sold.[39] The public did not see this restive side. They would see White's photographs in newspapers, read his direct mailings and press statements, and hear the widely distributed voice recording that he made for the campaign in the studio of the Berliner Gramophone Company in Montreal. Administratively, at his department in Ottawa, four "expert men" from the Victory Loan organizations of Toronto and Montreal were hired in mid-October for supervisory duties until the "final adjustment" of the new loan.

The campaign, set to begin on Monday, 28 October, kicked off in Toronto on a Sunday with a massive gathering at Queen's Park, where celebrities and unknowns mixed with scant regard for the influenza. Back from the West, White was joined on stage by Borden, Rowell, Premier Sir William H. Hearst, and Ontario treasurer Thomas William McGarry. Enlivened by martial music and the positive course of the war, then in its final days, thousands attended.

Back in Ottawa for government business and the opening of the campaign there, Borden (in the absence of the governor general) bought the first bond. In Toronto, he had cautioned against war fatigue, which was surfacing in soldiers' letters and public discourse. To dispel this cloud, newspapers called for a host of fixes, including contrast to Germany's greater exhaustion and the reputed salvations of saving. By May 1918, Henry Milton Walker, editor and manager of the *Okanagan Commoner* (Armstrong, British Columbia), had seen enough: "The average Canadian long since has tired of the childish nonsense dished up day after day under what may be called 'propaganda.'" To emphasize his pique, he quoted from Toronto's *Saturday Night:* "We are told that ... without swallowing a pack of lies every twenty-four hours ... we'd get downhearted, and give up contributing to the Red Cross and the Patriotic Fund and cease knitting and such things." In speeches to branches of the Women's Liberal Associations of Toronto, Helen Ethel Deeks railed against the "temptation" to succumb: "We must keep up the material side of the work, and it will take all our courage to keep up the spirit of the men and women who work behind the lines, away from the stimulus of the actual contact with the war." Such sentiments echoed the grievances sent to White's office about the loans, on top of misunderstandings about bonds. It was the "infection" of weariness that Victory Loan propaganda was meant to counter in order to sustain morale while trumpeting investment. At the core of the propaganda, the most focused Canada had ever seen, were the recognized principles of simplification and repetition.[40]

Starting six weeks before the official opening of the 1918 campaign, Canadians had been inundated with appeals that employed every possible theme – investment, idealism, shame, grief.[41] They came in all manner of mass communication: mailings to homes, newspaper and magazine ads and editorials, banners and flags, pamphlets, posters and broadsides, lapel pins, stamp stickers, films, and more. In cases where ads held up mothers who subscribed or worked and asked others to measure up, female teams and organizers encountered both challenges and successes. Canvassers were taught to frame the loan in the language not of buying and selling but of lending. According to one executive, Thomas Bradshaw, "the time occupied in preparing for the campaign was more than twice that of any previous one." Speakers delivered galvanizing talks. At a gathering of campaign workers at Toronto's King Edward Hotel, Baptist padre William A. Cameron boomed that Canada "had discovered itself."[42]

More systematic organization characterized the campaign. Materials were sent out earlier than in 1917, although in the bottleneck that was Ottawa, it was not until 24 October, after a delay in paper supply (a widespread deficiency), that White was able to approve a specimen of the new bond. His department, in concert with the Civil Service Commission, had started in July to bring in more staff. The civil servants' journal, *The Civilian* (Ottawa), grumbled about the load. The hire of extra stenographers and other personnel surged at provincial and dominion headquarters and at the bigger bond firms, with bilingual stenographers being much in demand in Montreal. Voters' lists once again provided the basis for card systems and canvassers' rolls. Bank deposits were carefully analyzed to ensure that oversubscription to the loan would be possible; local tax assessments and the 1917 loan results were examined to objectively determine quotas. In her study of an "investors' democracy" arising from America's war loans, Julia C. Ott observes that the pressures to subscribe were most effective when committees could harmonize publicity, pageantry, and predetermination of ability to invest.[43] In addition, banks tightened their handling of subscription applications; branches were to have bonds on hand for immediate exchange on full payment. Campaign phases were methodically planned. The special subscription committee prepared lists of potential large subscribers. Big subscriptions were gathered at the front end, allowing organizers to reckon the drive for small subscriptions. The $1 instalment plan offered by banks in 1917 for bond subscriptions was dropped in favour of bank loans with interest.[44]

Headed by George Herbert Wood, Ontario's provincial headquarters and district network were deemed an "immense machine" by the *Toronto Daily Star*, the domestic parallel of the "grim machinery of war." Several executive members brought experience from the 1917 loan and the YMCA's national campaign in May. Supplementing this machine in the large industrial establishments were employers' and employees' committees, groups that "would supervise a systematic canvass of those who are enjoying the benefits of Canada's war prosperity."[45] In Toronto, an employees' committee was formed under automobile and munitions maker Thomas Alexander Russell to canvass 150 concerns. The Ontario Employees Committee had already come up with a "model plan" for plants. Group photographs imparted a sense of cohesion. As in 1917, some municipalities and larger companies set up their own payroll-deduction plans.[46] At others, solicitation at entrance gates could produce pressure to subscribe or shady offers to buy or sell bonds. The government railways had vast networks for canvassing. Imperial Oil and Eaton's department stores exemplified a new manner of corporate donations, namely through district branches rather than head offices, a practice that had generated local complaints in 1917. At the loan's Toronto headquarters, in an office building on King Street, sixty voluntary or loaned recording staff (almost always called "girls"), supervised by Helen W. Cleveland, a clerk with Wood, Gundy and Company, processed returns from some 3,635 canvassers, along with district reports. Returns were wired to headquarters nightly, tabulated, posted on a huge blackboard, and released daily to the newspapers, the Canadian Press Association, and Ottawa. The publication of totals had a powerfully suggestive effect on sales.

Comparable machines were run elsewhere, with regional variations in scale, pace, and results. In British Columbia, which now included the Yukon, provincial organizers were additionally aided by access to the names and locations listed in proof sheets of the new *Wrigley's Directory*, which sent canvassers to "little communities which otherwise might have been overlooked." Early on, the province was given the "full details" of Ontario's "method of organization," which was largely followed. Since British Columbia had only a few general investment firms, it depended once again on canvassers with experience in insurance or merchandising and on the voluntary cooperation of businessmen. Pep talks, luncheons, and inter-team competition helped to sustain momentum. During White's visit early in October to boost the loan, "his personality had a very decided effect on all the workers in the campaign."[47]

Nationwide, the campaign faced two events with major implications: pandemic and peace. The deadly influenza that swept the Dominion, spread in part by infected soldiers returning from overseas, posed the most unexpected challenge. By mid-September, it had Canada in its grip, eventually killing up to 50,000. Over the following month, industry took a hit, and bans would be imposed on public institutions and gatherings. In rural areas, canvassing was hindered by fear of contagion, compounded by bad roads and lack of meetings. Preventatives included masks and the closures of schools, libraries, and places of entertainment. Desperate public-health directives and fake remedies abounded. Peaking around the third week of October, the influenza caught the Victory Loan organization off guard. The death in Washington of the son-in-law of the governor general, the Duke of Devonshire, from pneumonia following influenza forced Devonshire to go to Quebec to be with his daughter, resulting in the cancellation of a Victory Loan flag-raising scheduled for 13 October in Ottawa. The pandemic led to an emergency consideration of cancelling the loan campaign, but even a reduced campaign and loss of control over the loan narrative would have been catastrophic. On 16 October, while in Vancouver, White made plans to return east. He forwent some meetings but spoke in Edmonton, gave interviews, and had releases issued, all boosting the crusade.

On the morning of 21 October, members of the dominion executive met in Toronto and decided not to postpone the campaign. The success of the recently concluded Liberty Loan campaign in the United States, in the midst of the contagion, was a deciding factor in the decision. To give it authority in Ontario (prime territory for the loan), Alfred Ernest Ames, Edward Rogers Wood, and George Herbert Wood met with members of the province's government that afternoon. Provincial secretary William David McPherson immediately notified local health officers: "The extreme importance of the Victory Loan campaign necessitates that no interference with the conferences, organization or committee meetings be made by the local Boards of Health. It is the desire of the Government that every municipality as far as possible facilitate the efforts of the local workers and that their meetings be allowed in all cases."[48] On 27 October, with the scourge maintaining its hold and loan chair Albert Holden Abbott fretting that women could not be found to staff booths, a "monster service of prayer and praise" on behalf of the loan was held in Toronto at Queen's Park.

A number of stalwart health officers pushed back against such liberty, with several towns and cities banning public and campaign-planning meetings in theatres, schools, and churches, with much inconsistency and lobbying. In Regina, 75 percent of the canvassers fell ill. The campaign in the Southern Alberta district was seriously disrupted, with rural subdistricts being particularly hit hard. In Calgary, masks were donned at one loan meeting, and the hall was sprayed; an opening parade and "pyrotechnics display" were cancelled. Alberta's health department nonetheless went so far as to issue an order allowing canvassers to enter homes to solicit. In Winnipeg, it was estimated that the pandemic cost the campaign $10 million. At the same time, laid-off theatre workers there received no income relief. In Vancouver, in the absence of large public meetings, effort was focused on house-to-house canvassing. The local of the International

Victory Loan parade, Hamilton, 9 November 1918. Visible are all sorts of costumes, instruments of music and noise, and a horse-drawn circus wagon. | Image courtesy of David Bartlet, Calgary.

Alliance of Theatrical Stage Employees asked why some stores and saloons there could stay open but not theatres. Campaigns carried on, often through resourceful means, including outdoor screenings of Victory Loan films, greater use of telephones, booths at markets and on the streets, legions of salespeople (often society women), and door-to-door drop-offs of pamphlets. In mid-October, Saint John's Board of Health granted the loan committee permission to arrange street talks. Beginning on the evening of 31 October, the Allen Theatres in Toronto put on open-air showings of some of the 13 Victory Loan films that they had on hand featuring American stars, producing subscriptions for more than $25,000 and inestimable goodwill for the proprietors. In Hamilton, the loan committee asked for the city's Board of Health to lift its ban of 17 October, following Toronto's example, but the board refused. According to the city's medical officer, Dr. James Roberts, "gross inconsistency had been shown by the Toronto board."[49]

On the supposition that the influenza had run its course, some cities began lifting their embargoes within days of the campaign's start. Montreal, where the crisis was as controversial as it was severe, lifted its ban over a period of days, 4–7 November, and on the following day health officials gave the go-ahead for the grand Victory Loan parade slated for 11 November, Armistice Day, as it turned out. The list of attending dignitaries was long, among them White and Sir Wilfrid Laurier. Bypassed were the women, who according to spokespersons

Lady Isobel Brenda Meredith and Élodie Hébert, were not participating in the campaign because of the influenza and their domestic priorities.

Fearing a dampening effect on the loan not just from the influenza but also from the prospect of war needs ending, loan officials issued nationally publicized calls to propel the campaign. On 12 October, Edward Rogers Wood had reviewed Canada's financial situation and need for another year of funding. Two days later, he gave an interview that dripped with hyperbole: "When the Hun first used his poison gas on the battlefield, it was a lone Canadian division that saved the situation. It may be possible for Canadians at home to render a similar service now."[50] Talk of an armistice had been mooted throughout the summer, well before the campaign opened on 28 October. Even then, peace was not a certainty: false reports frustrated both the public and the campaign. On 29 October, Borden's Cabinet discussed the British prime minister's message about an armistice and his request that Borden return to England to help prepare for a peace conference. At Borden's house that night, White voiced his intention to resign at year's end, with the loan behind him. Initially, its organizers had been apprehensive: was the loan even needed with hostilities soon to end? *Le Devoir* (Montreal) believed that the federal censor had held up any premature reports of peace lest they harm the campaign by overexciting public sentiment.

With peace a strong probability, *Marketing* reported, the press publicity group charged with advertising moved "to alter radically its copy policy to conform to a new situation which would ensue from the sudden cessation of hostilities."[51] The group's own post-campaign summary put the challenge more emphatically. Reports of peace, beginning in mid-October and blossoming in November, demanded a change in messaging:

> When the Victory Loan Campaign opened, prospects were that we would be at war for a year at least. Complications immediately developed. Not once but several times during the Campaign the foundations on which the propaganda up to that point had been built, slipped from under our feet like shifting sand. The claim may be justly made for the press that it met the new situations created from time to time almost before they developed, and that thereby it prevented the growth in the public mind of a conviction that because the war was about over the Loan would no longer be necessary, a conviction which would have had disastrous consequences.[52]

Propaganda abruptly transitioned to demobilization and postwar reconstruction. Writing in *Printers' Ink* (New York), Harold Constantine Lowrey saw advertising move from "the circus method" to this year's "simon-pure 'reason-why' appeal." Canvassers would report that the public was in accord, but as hundreds of climactic celebrations unfolded on 11 November, the "most critical day of the campaign" for the publicity committee, all the planned stunts and parades went ahead.

The campaign, unleashed between 28 October and 18 November, featured all the elements seen in 1917 but amplified. Parades were standard fare. None rivalled the extravaganzas mounted in Montreal, where a French Foreign Legion contingent wowed crowds, and in Toronto, where one parade featured 1,500 participants, including costumed canvassers led by a comedian in blackface makeup and a "huge five-ring Athletic Circus." For those involved, the experience was exhilarating. In Sarnia, Ontario, stenographers from the Imperial Oil refinery, garbed as "farmerettes," mounted a float decorated with hay, cornstalks, and Victory Bond signs. One young member of the ensemble enthused in a postcard, "We got 2nd prize ($25.00) for the second best feature in the parade. The Great War vet tank took first. We were one of the floats entered by Imperial Oil. The parade was a hummer, 2 milers long. It was our own idea and we did all the work." In the larger urban centres, thousands were drawn to the cause by stunts that included performances by escape artist "The Mysterious Raffles," by the "Human Fly" (Harry H. Gardiner), who climbed building exteriors in Toronto, Hamilton, and Vancouver, and by vaudevillian Charlotte (Lottie) Fletcher, who, clad in khaki, scaled a firetruck ladder to post the day's returns on a banner outside Vancouver's loan headquarters. Aerial displays in Ontario, Quebec, and Nova Scotia, drops of literature and prizes, and fêtes for young aviators, some from Royal Air Force Canada and American bases, proved exciting. Aircraft and warships built in Canada with Victory Loan funding were profiled. Entertainment prevailed.

Wherever crowds gathered, canvassers awaited. At the St. Lawrence Market in Toronto, for instance, a bunting-decked booth was operated by the Club for the Study of Social Science, headed by Mrs. Ethel Dallas Small and other society women, who swarmed the market aided by some high-powered speakers, selling $5,000 in bonds with "a great deal of propaganda work done as well." Nor could crowds miss the street theatre: the reams of posters, banners, and promotional films; exuberant newspapers, speakers, and window displays with models of soldiers and trenches; and the newly instituted honour flags emblazoned with the governor general's crest and awarded to districts and companies exceeding their quotas of subscriptions.

Human-interest stories, often sentimental and tabloid-like but seldom questioned, were reported in the hundreds by the canvassers, as were people's excuses for not subscribing. Typical are the accounts of the soldier's wife with no means who offered to trade a baby for a bond; the widow with three sons at the front who had framed her bond and coupons, oblivious to their monetary value; the mother who filled out her bond application while on her knees thanking God "that the war is being won ... and that Canada is safe to-day"; and the groom who gave his bride a $100 bond. One of the most poignant stories to emerge was that of Herbert Bond, a young messenger at Canada Life Assurance, and his wife, Emma Fraser, who had a son. They named him Victory – Victory Bond. Ten months later, on 16 September 1919, the infant died at Toronto's Hospital for Sick Children from diarrhea leading to "decomposition." Such accounts blended well with selected testimonials on why people subscribed, invariably in the vein of "too old to fight" or "sons in the forces." Although the pattern was not evident in Quebec's French-language press, journalists elsewhere continued to find that human-interest reporting made good copy.

Whatever the entertainment factor, propaganda was serious business, geared to reinforcing linkages between the loan, business, industry, imperial credits, and regional capability. Advertising highlighted shipping, salmon, and aircraft timber in British Columbia, grain and livestock on the Prairies, cheese, munitions, and aircraft construction in Ontario, produce in Quebec, and shipbuilding in the Maritimes. In the midst of the campaign, Charles C. Ballantyne, the federal minister of marine and fisheries, announced contracts for Wallace Shipbuilding in North Vancouver; "Success of Loan Means More Ships," said the *Vancouver Daily Sun*. In Port Arthur, for patriotic reasons and in light of its loan-funded contracts, the manager of Port Arthur Shipbuilding called on all employees to subscribe at least 10 percent of their annual wage.[53] Official advertisements and brochures spelled out what military items a bond could buy, even as peace approached.[54] In one instance, a photograph in the *Toronto Daily Star* showed a Felixstowe F-5-L – a huge flying boat made at the Toronto plant of Canadian Aeroplanes Limited, easily the most successful of the Imperial Munitions Board's national factories – with the caption "Thanks to the Victory Loan." The plant also turned out about 1,210 of the famous Curtiss JN-4 "Canuck," a training aircraft. No mention was made of the complex cross-border exchanges of technology or funding involved and the shipment to an American naval base of the thirty flying boats made. The import of such production is highlighted by the number of factories, more than 675, that had worked on munitions board contracts by the war's end.[55]

Deftly shifting amidst countrywide celebrations of peace, the loan became a catalyst. In Toronto, parades on 8 and 9 November conflated peace and the loan. In countless assemblies of campaign workers and in editorials throughout English-speaking Canada, speakers eloquently proclaimed that the dominion "had discovered itself." The sentiment built on even more transcendent

The "Dug-Out" Victory Bonds booth, Victoria, 1918. On Armistice Day, it was a hub of raucous celebration, with crowds cheering and bond salesmen calling for subscriptions to bring the "boys" home. | Image courtesy of David Bartlet, Calgary.

advertising, with one Eaton's ad declaring, "We spiritualize our savings when we commit them to the high purposes of the Victory Loan." The chair of the Toronto executive recognized the armistice as a "great stimulus." With the campaign nearing its conclusion, its spontaneity and extraordinary results infused celebrations. In Toronto, newspaper accounts, personal recollections, and photographs captured the turbulence. On 7 November, as peace news swirled, canvassers at the corner of Yonge and King sold $11,000 worth of bonds in two hours. Loan executives were urged by politicians to focus not on peace but on the "great drive." During the celebrations in Toronto on 11 November, aircraft dropped loads of bits of paper inscribed "Lend/Delivered by Aeroplane," creating an atmosphere of ethereal snowfall. The *Globe* claimed that 90 percent of the subscriptions taken on that day were "made in the streets." The jubilant celebration at one corner in Victoria, British Columbia, where veterans sold bonds from an empty lot, across which a model front-line trench had been dug out, complete with sandbags and a machine gun, was also typical. It immediately formed a rallying point, where fireworks and cheers, the *Daily Colonist* reported, "intermingled with the stentorian demands from the enthusiastic salesmen to 'come across' with the money with which the boys will be brought home." Such crazed scenes were witnessed throughout Canada. Bond posters and banners jump out from old photographs and paintings. In the heady aftermath of the war, the *Globe* would see the Victory Loans and their stimulation of the bond market as a crowning achievement "in the most patriotic atmosphere ever created in Canada."[56]

The features presented above are drawn largely from coverage in newspapers, reportage that varied from a loan prospectus in weeklies to saturation in major dailies. In a few small newspapers, such as the *Caribou Observer* (Quesnel, British Columbia), loan advertising squeezed out local coverage or forced the addition of extra pages. Campaigns varied enormously in scale, from urban blitzes to rural districts, whose single canvassers traversed dirt roads in places where posters appeared in a general store or on a barn at a crossroads. In country areas, there were challenges never encountered in urban centres, as seen in Enderby, British Columbia, population 800. From there, campaigners aimed for the remote settlements of Mara and district, Sicamous, Grindrod, Deep Creek, Ashton Creek and Trinity Valley, and Hupel. Canvassing was still coordinated to ensure that every remote homestead was reached, but in Enderby a distribution of subscriber buttons and cards was deemed "impracticable in a district like that of this Unit." Other suggestions from "above" were disregarded as unworkable. Wet weather made roads "very heavy." Extra canvassers were enlisted as needed, one to visit the logging camp at Kingfisher, another to go to Mara on a Sunday, "when the Finlander railway men were at home." Hupel, population 120, yielded one subscription. Steps were taken to avoid any assemblies because of the influenza, but the town's campaign committee still raised $53,650, surpassing its quota of $35,000 to win an honour flag with three crowns, but it came at a cost.[57] In the nearby village of Armstrong, the canvassers and organizers were jaded. When expected to step up again in January 1919 for the Red Cross drive, they were slow to get started, the *Okanagan Commoner* observed. "The Victory Loan committee was fed up on soliciting," so "new blood" was enlisted.[58]

Campaigns were thus shaped by regional circumstances. On the West and East Coasts, canvassers covered visiting ships, including steamships bound for the Yukon.[59] One advertisement in the *Dawson Daily News* claimed, "Victory Bonds Are Better Than Gold." Strong subscriptions came from Dawson ($290,300), Whitehorse ($71,950), and Atlin ($10,250). At Ontario's Lakehead, Frank W. Ross and railway roadmaster Ole Larsen canvassed the Canadian Pacific line as far as Ignace. After signing on as a canvasser at large for two months, Gustav Heinrich (Henry) Schoof, a game warden, itinerant lecturer, all-round fundraiser, and rancher near Claresholm, Alberta, made a "strenuous trip through the Rockies" to levy fines and roust poachers, enduring snowstorms and a broken wagon, during which he sold "thousands of dollars worth of bonds to ranchers and others who could not otherwise have been reached," reported the *Claresholm Review-Advertiser* on 15 November. His perspective was illuminating. On an earlier trip, in June, Schoof had written from Indiana about his encounter with American fundraisers,

> The Yankees can beat us getting money. They comb the country and the cities and let no man or woman escape. First they plead and reason, then they threaten and then they boycott. The committee appointed know almost to a dollar how much a man is worth and it is useless for him to lie to them. They have the people catalogued as Patriots, Hypocrites, Slackers and Skunks, and they never leave a man until, through his own argument, he places himself under one of these headings.[60]

In Calgary, despite the pandemic, a vibrant atmosphere was reported at the loan headquarters, complete with gramophone recordings of war songs and Thomas White's speech. At the kickoff meeting on 25 October, everyone still wore a flu mask. Organizers did their best to overcome disruptions and alarm. The Southern Alberta district experienced a full-blown campaign, even with the late arrival of poster advertising in rural districts. New schemes were devised for a second canvass of Calgary using a card system of record keeping to avoid duplication, the city purchased bonds (some to be resold to employees), and campaign members were proudly profiled. Such recognition was serious business, conducted without critique or satire of the Leacockian sort. Manitoba, too, was hard hit, especially in rural districts with minimal medical aid. Upwards of 100 towns were isolated by quarantine, and parades and films were postponed. In Winnipeg, loan operations were scaled back, but audacity could not be denied. In a public display of Victory Loan firepower, soldiers shot away a map of Germany, one piece after another, each representing a million dollars more in subscriptions. Among the other experiences was this account from a team captain: "I was standing at a counter ... waiting to canvass a man for Victory bonds while he was telephoning to someone the interesting information that he had been suffering from the Spanish 'flu' for a couple of weeks. I nearly died but we sold him just the same."[61] Nonetheless, partly on the strength of outdoor work, door-to-door canvassing, and the lifting of bans, campaign returns across the Prairies rose.

In Ontario, the campaign unfolded much as planned, the dampening effect of the influenza seemingly cancelled out by the armistice. In the absence of a vitriolic election, publicity and press coverage were less toxic, more campaign-oriented. Publishing the names of major subscribers had become de rigueur. The Catholic archbishop of Toronto, Neil McNeil, who had actively backed the loan in 1917, was upset that his subscription for $10,000 on behalf of the archdiocese was not immediately published. The executive committee hustled to comply. Toronto in particular was a hotbed of activity focused on the prospect of peace and joyous spillover. The commissions secured by local security houses were extraordinary. In a bold showing of give and take, not only did the biggest firms – Wood, Gundy; Dominion Securities; A.E. Ames; and W.L. McKinnon – reap the highest remunerations paid to brokers, but most of their principals were also key members of the Toronto, Ontario, or dominion campaign organizations. One Liberal MP from Windsor, Ontario, who would sarcastically label them government "friends" who had been "commandeered," was quick to point out that across the border, brokers levied no charges in the Liberty Loan campaigns. The Victory and Liberty Loans, which claimed tons of paper, even figured in the 1918 hearings of the federal enquiry into the cost of producing newsprint. Arguments were made there that newspapers benefited from rate increases and government-paid advertising for the Victory Loan, in contrast to the American loans, where costs and space for newspaper advertising were sponsored by private enterprise. In June 1919, in a Commons debate on his budget, White would once again have to justify the payment of commissions as part of a broad, self-crediting exposition on wartime finance. Scrutinized alongside Canada's population densities, difficulties in attracting workers, and other efficiency analysis, the voluntarism used in America's campaigns had been found unsuitable. Incentives had always been a must. "We had to have the money," White said, and he had gotten it. "We could have got half the amount if we had a voluntary organization such as they had in the United States."[62]

Even if, in 1918, efficiencies coalesced, political and cultural sensitivities mutated. Quebec experienced sea change. Over the summer and into October, journalists such as Ernest Bilodeau, in his columns from Ottawa for *Le Devoir*, remained critical of government war finance and the hackneyed slogans and claims of the loan campaign. In the parish of Sainte-Anne-de-Beaupré, northeast of Quebec City, many residents cancelled their subscriptions in early November to protest abusive Military Police actions in chasing down defaulters, leading to the dissolution of the campaign committee there. News of the event went beyond Quebec. Overall, however, the campaign was marked by less political antagonism than in 1917 and by greater support in the French-language press and among French Canadian organizations and the Catholic Church. A number of Liberal MPs endorsed the loan. Campaign coverage displayed practical reasons for Quebecers to subscribe and sought to move them toward smart investment and national reconstruction. White boasted that his talks with the French Canadian press in Montreal, "a fine lot of fellows," had helped. As early as June and July, the financial pages of newspapers, based on the strong reception of

A Curtiss JN-4 "Canuck" set to fly from Camp Rathbun (near Deseronto, Ontario) to the province of Quebec to barnstorm for the Victory Loan, 1918. | Community Archives of Belleville and Hastings County, CAMPR-06-22.

City of Montreal bonds by "small investors," had been predicting liberal buying of Victory Bonds in Quebec.

The French Canadian publicity committee proved particularly effective. Shortages of literature in French (but not apparently in other languages) and the flu restrictions (lifted for the armistice) were offset in Montreal by a strong campaign, mayoral support, locally produced brochures, and the loan-dedicated journal *L'Obligation.* The Foreign Legion detachment, members of the 22nd (French Canadian) Battalion (greatly esteemed in Quebec for its participation in the war),[63] "Vive la France" sentiments, touring (and much-fêted) aviators such as Flight Lieutenant Georges-Louis Vézine, and national extolment by *La Patrie* (Montreal), *Le Soleil* (Quebec City), and other journals added vigour. The coverage in *Le Soleil,* a Liberal newspaper, was dense, ranging from a full page of photographs of the local executive to ads that straddled product and bond promotion, such as this simple pitch: "Buy Victory Bonds/Eat Clark Baked Beans."[64]

A key question is how to square support for the war loans in French Canada with the opposition there to conscription and with the arguments, by Henri Bourassa and in current literature,[65] that most French Canadians felt no passionate commitment to either England *or* France. For newspapers such as *L'Echo du Saint-Maurice* (Shawinigan), even before the campaign, support for the loan was purely a practical matter. Recognizing the need for money for foodstuffs, a sentiment that went beyond Quebec, it had reasoned that "the negotiation of a Victory Loan is less a matter of patriotism and sentiment than a business matter." Even as *Le Devoir*'s Bilodeau continued to berate White's financial policies, he conceded that the prospects for the loan looked promising. The clearest endorsement came from Bourassa in his editorial in *Le Devoir* on 14 November, written in a spirit of economic and national equilibrium: "It is in this spirit, with no hesitation whatsoever, that I advise all nationalists, *because they are nationalists*, to subscribe to the Victory Loan, which has become, due to the circumstances, the Loan for peace and for national reconstruction."[66] Similar arguments appeared in other papers that had printed hard criticisms in 1917, including *Le Progrès du Golfe* (Rimouski) and *L'Avenir du nord* (Saint-Jérôme). Noticeably, *Le Progrès* also ran ads from the Crédit Anglo-Français in Quebec City and from Versailles, Vidricaire, et Boulais, a Montreal brokerage business, for corporate and municipal bonds offered at six to six and a-half percent, more than Victory Bonds. A number of French-language newspapers also ran the prospectus, submitted by the French Consulate in Montreal, for France's latest war loan, the 4-percent Emprunt de la Libération. The rhetoric of a "Peace Loan," which appeared in other French-language newspapers, had also been appearing in journals since the summer and would carry forward into the postwar campaign of 1919. The drive of 1918 in Quebec was all the more remarkable, it seemed to the English-language *Quebec Chronicle*, because of the simultaneous unfolding of three other campaigns by the Canadian Red Cross, the Navy League of Canada, and the Canadian War Contingent Association.

In every province, international boundaries were not insurmountable. Loan organizers went to some lengths not to infringe on the American Liberty Loan that ended on 19 October, with Canada's set to start on 28 October. Canadian bond dealers were prohibited from advertising or offering bonds in the United States, but volumes were sold through "private" offerings and by banks without advertising. Despite official sensitivity over advertising Canadian bonds in the United States, loan officials exchanged visits and publicity materials, mutual support emerged in the newspapers of Detroit and Windsor, and campaigners criss-crossed the border, just like the loan workers who moved between Seattle and Vancouver. In the Niagara region of Ontario, soldiers from the Welland Canal Field Force and the Polish camp at Niagara-on-the-Lake had been allowed by both Ottawa and American authorities to cross over to Niagara Falls, New York, to participate in the Liberty Loan campaign. Aided by a favourable exchange rate, many large American corporations and touring theatre companies took out subscriptions, including $5,550,000 by Metropolitan Life Insurance of New York, $1,100,000 by Travellers' Insurance of Hartford, $50,000 by the Brotherhood of Railway Carmen of America, which had lodges in Canada, and $25,000 by the International Brotherhood of Carpenters. Overseas, too, at military headquarters and camps, accredited canvassers were put to work, with publicity and subscription results from England and France published abroad in field journals such as the *Canadian Daily Record* in London.

Of any war loan, that of 1918, riding the road to peace, produced the largest number of subscribers (1,140,057) and the greatest amount ($707,117,550).[67] Edward Rogers Wood's announcement of the countrywide totals at a packed Massey Hall in Toronto on 18 November met with a "tremendous outburst of popular enthusiasm." Congratulations were thrown out like confetti. The *Toronto World,* for one, likened White to Alexander Hamilton (d. 1804), the celebrated secretary of the American Treasury, of whom Daniel Webster had written, "He smote the rock of the national resources and abundant streams of revenue gushed forth. He touched the dead corpse of public credit and it sprang upon its feet."[68]

Unquestionably, the intense publicity – a milestone in Canadian propaganda – and carefully planned organization were key factors. Analysis of the returns by province or subdistricts requires caution due to innumerable variables, the lack of centralized collection of records, and the scarcity of socio-economic evidence of the kind found for the Liberty Loans. In many areas, there were no newspapers to report results. Analysis by sector is spotty. One Ontario historian believes that the farmers of Grey County understood the loan "a good deal better than the previous year,"[69] but such a conclusion is rare. On the Prairies, agrarian organizations recognized the loan's anticipated impact on the grain market. So, too, did the *Grain Growers' Guide* (Winnipeg), while grumbling about the national debt and standing up for rural areas unable to put up a good showing because of the influenza. Upwards of 100 towns had been isolated by quarantine, it claimed after the campaign. By contrast, the success of the special subscription organizers – the back-channel sector of the loan – was telling. The Canadian Pacific Railway, for instance, subscribed $17 million, with other huge sums coming from life- and fire-insurance companies. Required by law to invest heavily in Canadian securities, these companies, after their scrutiny of past loans, were able to make the largest subscriptions possible. By early January 1919, for example, Canada Life Assurance would hold an astounding $11,586,000 in bonds. Special subscriptions easily achieved $270,259,950, near its quota, about 38 percent of the loan's total and a doubling of 1917.

In some provinces, vague trends emerged. The two with the greatest increases in subscriptions were British Columbia (94.7 percent) and Quebec (91.3 percent). Some analysis, such as regards corporate backing and the shift in support, seems possible for Quebec. It jumped from $94,287,250 in 1917 to $180,363,450. Montreal, the "principal feeder" accounted for $143,433,050 as of late November, but most notable was the increase in all districts, including those that were predominantly rural. The province's response would be trumpeted in the

DISCO Victory Loan Committee, Dominion Iron and Steel Company, Sydney, Nova Scotia, 1918. | Beaton Institute, Cape Breton University, 80-180-4360.

Commons by Aimé-Miville Déchêne, the Liberal MP for Montmagny.[70] In contrast to the flu-devastated areas of the Prairies, there were other rural regions of the country that did well, such as in Ontario and the Maritimes, among them the predominantly French-speaking county of Madawaska in northwest New Brunswick (where France's fourth war loan had competed for Acadian subscriptions) and the rural, western district of Pictou County in Nova Scotia. The Acadian response in New Brunswick to the war and the war loans was complex, just as it was in Cape Breton and Quebec. In the Maritimes, newspapers could recognize Acadians' support for the loan but could also disregard their overall contribution to the war effort (as in agriculture), localized resistance to the loan, and anti-conscription sentiment.[71]

Company and employee subscriptions, often noted in the newspapers, are almost impossible to collate. Canvassers found office buildings tough to cover. Small businesses were mostly handled by assigned canvassers. At one such business, Municipal World Limited, a publishing company in St. Thomas, Ontario, the canvasser got twenty-two employees to subscribe, most for $50 bonds.[72] Industries for which information exists include automobile manufacturing, munitions, oil refinement, life insurance, and shipbuilding. Speakers and campaigners are known to have worked the yards of William Lyall Shipbuilding (North Vancouver), Port Arthur Shipbuilding (Thunder Bay, Ontario), Collingwood Shipbuilding (Collingwood and Kingston subsidiary, Ontario), and Shelburne Shipbuilders (Shelburne, Nova Scotia), some of them recipients of loan funding through contracts. Investments in Victory Bonds, initially made perhaps for public-spirited reasons, became integrated into companies' financial structuring. On 16 November, two directors of Shelburne Shipbuilders telegrammed its manager, "Consider best interest of company requires subscriptions [of] victory bonds to amount of paid up capital at least[.] Strongly urge this action."[73] At Port Arthur Shipbuilding, there was a growing level of Victory Bond "assets," rising from the $5,000 in the accounts in January 1918 to $398,509.67 in April 1920, after which, by June, the holding was liquidated.[74] At Collingwood Shipbuilding, plans for canvassing employees through instalments and payroll deductions were implemented in October and November at the request of local loan organizers. Following the campaign, the plant secretary in Kingston reported that employees had subscribed for $17,600, of which $8,850

> was taken out on the regular Government plan leaving the balance of $8,750.00 to be carried on the instalment plan ... At first there seemed to be an inclination on the part of the men to hold aloof as they saw the work on the Trawlers being completed and were doubtful about constant employment. The announcement however of the contract for the Government Freighter tended to relieve this feeling and enabled us to procure the highly satisfactory result shown above.[75]

Although no official evaluation of the campaign appears to have been made by the dominion executive, there was ample recognition of its organization and grand result. White sent out loads of congratulatory letters and telegrams. It fell to the newspapers and journals to examine the campaign, often from self-crediting angles. The *Abbotsford Post* in British Columbia, for instance, boasted that "it was the press that made the Victory Loan of 1918 the grand success that it was."[76] In *Maclean's Magazine* (Toronto), William Byron would see it as a major achievement in the government's use of advertising after 1916. Toronto's fusty *Financial Post* praised the campaign but deplored the "horseplay," which did not take into consideration "whether the 'prospect' was 'sold' on the proposition ... The idea of getting the people into the street by Barnum and Bailey stunts and endeavouring to sell them bonds as some sort of return for the entertainment is belittling the national credit."[77]

Some columnists separated genuine support for the loan from the exploiters and the frivolous celebrants who tagged along. In Toronto, Ida Louise Webster lauded the response of the "real" workers. What upset her was the example set by the officer who strutted onto a stage and harangued the audience to buy bonds so that his son could be brought home from the front. "Now with all due respect to both him and his son," Webster claimed, "there was not a person in the whole audience who really and truly cared whether his son came home ... Every person in the house had troubles of their own, and they were not at all impressed by listening to this officer screaming about his only boy." Webster railed, too, against the "fellows and girls" who drove up and down Yonge Street professing to sell bonds but really searching for the "limelight," with one young lady "yapping" at a male canvasser. But such complaints were not openly expressed nationwide. In contrast, Harry Lauder, speaking on the same Toronto stage in 1917 about his son's death in France, had met with great success generating subscriptions. Different war-related causes drew different audiences: a discriminating number disdained the deluge and the dreary "impromptu speechifying"; others favoured the elevated appeals of noted philanthropists; audiences connected to some veterans better than others; theatre patrons, moviegoers, and parade enthusiasts wanted entertainment with the fundraising; and explanations of investment registered differently. After the campaign, one celebratory account, *Toronto Victory Loan Campaign, 1918: A Souvenir with Views of a Remarkable Achievement* lavished praise, with no mention of the politics of influenza.[78]

What the *Financial Post* and columnists such as Webster did not fully recognize was the jubilant atmosphere and the campaign organizers' savvy understanding of entertainment as a tool for selling and coping in wartime.[79] After the campaign, a number of executives, organizers, and canvassers were drawn into charitable associations, where their skills and networks would prove invaluable. James Henry Gundy, for one, became active in the Federation for Community Service in Toronto. On sure ground over the weeks following the campaign, the *Financial Post* assessed the loan's impact on the market. What could not be tracked as easily was action on the street, where "scalpers" and dubious transactions confounded innocent bondholders. In Toronto, some fly-by-nighters and part-timers ventured to run classified ads. "All Victory and other bonds bought for cash; no waiting; best price paid," wrote "Wood" from a transient address. At one point, the *Globe*, offended by opinions that no one believed the newspapers, took out its affront on holders of small bonds. Not reading warnings in the press, they had only themselves to blame when they sold their bonds prematurely or were hoodwinked or robbed.[80]

A GROUP OF WILLING SUBSCRIBERS TO WAR SAVINGS CERTIFICATES AND VICTORY BONDS

"A Group of Willing Subscribers to War Savings Certificates and Victory Bonds," Russell Motor Car Munitions Factory No. 3, Toronto, 1917. Of Russell's 6,000 employees, 500 invested $80,000 in bonds, with an unspecified number taking certificates for $100,000. | Shaw Newton and Russell Motor Car Company, *The Second Line of Offence* (Toronto: Southam, 1918), 76.

The *Globe*'s condescending characterization was just part of the debate that swirled around "Victories." As extreme as the commentaries that freely assigned praise and blame in the scramble of postwar thought were the commentaries that predicted easy adjustment for Canadian workers sustained by wartime employment. Some pundits, anticipating the layoffs of munition workers, naively looked at Victory Bonds as stopgaps. The government would see to their reabsorption. On the day after the armistice, the *Globe* thought that the government was optimistic about the integration of munition workers, who, while seeking employment, must "live on their Victory Loan bond interest and other savings if they did save."[81] In some quarters, views on the savings and investment habits of workers were marked by elitist tones. In January 1919, for example, the manager of the Canadian Bank of Commerce speculated that its issue of more dollar notes may have been caused by a "certain class" of munition worker who hoarded savings.

Many "munition girls" – the "munitionettes" – and other working women, wives, and mothers did invest in bonds, often through employee programs, with a resulting sense of self-reliance. The women at Russell Motor Car's munition factories in Toronto could be an optimistic group, their matron, Miss Moore, reported at war's end. A large group of them, "willing subscribers" for bonds and war-savings certificates, were photographed late in 1917 for the company's publication *The Second Line of Offence.* An invaluable record of production, this book, like the related loan publicity, nonetheless overlooked the workplace hazards common to the industry, including explosions. *The Second Line of Offence* lauded one woman for enduring chemical poisoning.[82]

If many women worked to hold homes and families together, others saved to subscribe for bonds, often scrimping to do so by taking up secondary work. A number would face disappointment when they tried to sell their bonds prematurely. Untold numbers quietly stashed them away, and some novel uses were reported. One hotel proprietor in Toronto, a subscriber himself, felt that female war workers deserved a just return on Victory Bonds in the form of government support for a boarding hotel for women supported by women.[83] For some payroll-based subscribers, the armistice was ruinous. The sudden closure of Willys-Overland's aircraft-engine plant in West Toronto at the end of November threw its workers, women and men who had been "canvassed finely" to subscribe, out of work, terminating their payroll deductions, putting the bonds out of reach, and producing "a good deal of feeling among those affected that the company has acted in a peremptory manner."[84] Expectations that laid-off women, until they found new employment, could live off their bond interest, were ludicrous. Some saw the government maintaining a stance that workers would be absorbed. At year's end, Willys-Overland gave gold badges to 180 women with two or more years of service. Conspicuous in the long debate over the collapse of women's wartime employment was the absence of any support from the Victory Loan, as was the case for soldiers' rehabilitation. Within months of the armistice, veterans' organizations would lay claims to the government's loan funds for enhanced gratuities. Such were some of the narratives attached to Victory Bonds after the armistice.

The onset of peace had necessitated quick adjustments in promoting the loan. Editorialists could be nimble. Witness this piece from the *Saint John Globe* of 11 November:

> Shout, sing, dance, wave flags, ring bells, blow whistles, give expression, in whatever way you will, to satisfaction at the good news; but never for a moment forget that our heroes are still in France and cannot come home for many a long day. Sober, serious reflection on that thought will bring its own conviction that what-

> ever else you do to show your pride and satisfaction in the country's achievements, you have failed in the all-important thing if you fail to place at the country's service some of the money needed to finish the great task.

Adjustment, too, was required from the government. Politicians and planners, anticipating an expansion of world trade that would demand more Canadian products, predicted the absorption of veterans and war workers, often using Victory Loan platforms at rallies and luncheons for their bullish claims. At Montreal's parade on 11 November, White had made his case for war funding for demobilization and "to continue to furnish credits for the purchase of our agricultural and other products required to meet the food demands of Great Britain and her allies, and for reconstruction work in France and in Belgium."[85] This focus on funding would continue into 1919.

8

Thrift, War Savings, Markets, and the Clean-Up Campaign of 1919

TRAINLOADS OF SOLDIERS WERE joyously welcomed home in early 1919. In January, clergy could call for a "war spirit" in work on the home front for men still overseas, and Harry Lauder could fire up support for the campaign of the Salvation Army Fund. In May, however, a four-day "repatriation campaign" in Toronto, replete with a corps of canvassers, a parade, and stunts, fell short of its goal. People were "tiring of campaigns," the *Globe* (Toronto) observed.[1] Earlier in the year, a women's committee had tried to launch a national campaign for thrift and war-savings stamps, but the effort fizzled out, leaving the government as the main purveyor.

Within weeks of the conclusion of the loan campaign of 1918, and after some delay caused by the war's end, White had announced on 29 November the formation of the National War Savings Committee to promote thrift and specifically to handle the sale of the $5 war-savings stamps and the 25¢ thrift stamps, beginning on 2 December. Already authorized on 4 October by an order-in-council, the program was meant to tap those unable to participate in war loans and to keep war funding moving forward in the public eye. The committee sought to emulate the network set up in 1916 in Britain, where local associations pushed savings stamps, certificates, and war loans all together.[2] The campaign for these colourful stamps, nicknamed "baby bonds" (like the savings certificates of 1917), was intense; posters, newspaper advertisements, and flyers were all employed well into 1919. One official-looking newspaper advertisement, echoing commercial overlap from 1917, urged stamp purchases with the money saved by using Gillette Safety Razors rather than visiting barbershops. The introduction of the stamps was not uniformly smooth. Their actual financial return would be minimal. In Quebec, concerns over bilingualism had already afflicted past war-funding devices. Apparently designed only in English, the stamps were boycotted by the Cercle catholique des voyageurs de commerce de Québec, which, on grounds of racial harmony, called in January for the issue "en français des timbres d'épargne et d'économie de guerre." Alfred Ernest Ames backtracked, and translated stamps were produced. Reaction in the anglophone press, when the concern even registered, was surly.[3]

In another initiative of related propaganda, in late 1918 a summary of the war was put together for teachers by the National War Savings Committee, the *Canada War Thrift Book,* and issued under various titles (with provincial inserts) by provincial Departments of Education. A semi-monthly *Thrift Magazine* was also put out for children. Hardly traditional children's fare, the book and magazine were addressed to youngsters and educators, with chapters in the book on the war's costs, its financing, investment, and bonds and savings stamps. These small books and magazines were among the most exhortative, unapologetic pieces issued.[4]

By 1919, bonds were mainstays, but they faced a changed environment. Many of the marketing concepts of past loans were obsolete. Journalists' impressions of past campaigns ranged from good to cynical. One, the Ottawa correspondent for *Le Devoir* (Montreal), Ernest Bilodeau, in his report of Sam Hughes's rant of 4 March, claimed that Cabinet had "sweetened" the press with paid announcements and advertising in order to reduce criticism. From this perspective, newspapers had missed out on the revenue from loan promotion. At the same time, in British Columbia and likely other provinces, exhausted Victory Loan teams were hesitant to work on Red Cross and other campaigns. The war-shaped economy did not easily shift back to peacetime, when deflation and recession set in. On the Prairies, wheat prices fell. Tides of discontent rocked the labour and agricultural movements, and the cost of living had risen an estimated 75 percent during the war as real wages lagged. Wartime taxation became entrenched. The maintenance of high tariffs sparked a wave of western populism. And the use of public funds faced intense scrutiny. The Canadian Manufacturers' Association railed against both the government, over the enormous gap between revenues and needs, and the Western Grain Growers' Association, over its call for massive taxation. *Toronto World* cartoonist Sam Hunter portrayed one of his favourite targets, Thomas White, as a fisherman trying to hook the Grand Trunk Pacific Railway. During the loan campaign in the fall of 1919, the contentious purchase of the Grand Trunk would pose serious distraction. The opposition of Quebec industrialist and political eminence Georges-Élie Amyot and his consequent decision to stop subscribing to the loan received nationwide attention. Past loans, in their pan-Canadian intent, had been promoted as a means to smooth competing interests and thereby to shape a consensus, not unlike food production and thrift,[5] a goal that would be tested in 1919. In the months after the war, patriotic sentiment seeped away. It was in this milieu that the Victory Loan of 1919 was bravely cast as transitional.[6]

The fiscal year 1918–19, given the costs of demobilization, reconstruction, and ongoing purchases for the Allies, would prove to be the most expensive year of Canada's engagement in the war. In April and May, the government's War Appropriation Act and budget, as war costs and the long-term redemption of debt were calculated, anticipated a new war loan – a "Peace Loan." In Parliament, the Victory Loan and Bonds of 1918 lost their patriotic allure, with debate focusing on the old issues of tariffs and tax exemption and on the costs of the past loan. On a quieter but larger stage, the securities market, bonds still maintained a prominent place. The Victory Loan Special Committee was in hiatus from January to August, with bond prices rising and then falling over the summer before control was reinstituted, in part to deal with corporate off-loading. During the first half of the year, Victory Bonds shifted from the realm of supercharged campaigns to the realistic spectrum of the market.[7] Appearing on 15 March 1919, the *Globe*'s following report on the bonds maturing in 1932 and 1933 is typical in its perspective:

> After a week of easier tone, war bonds returned to the centre of the stage on the Toronto Stock Exchange yesterday with the establishment of a new high for the 1933 Victories of 104 and three-quarters. Sales in this bond alone amounted to $558,900 of the total of $605,600 for the day in war bonds. The demand for the 1933's was strong and continuous all day and though the close was easier at 104 and three-eighths on a broken lot, the last full lot was at the high for the day. At Montreal this bond touched 105 during the afternoon. The 1932's are now rapidly approaching a five-percent basis, and need only go to about 105 and one-quarter to reach it. All the longer-term bonds developed strength yesterday, and showed gains from one-eighth to a full point. An analysis of the sales shows comparatively few fifty- and one-hundred-dollar bonds in the trading, which confirms the impression which has gained force of late that the selling of small bonds by individuals is pretty well over.

Students, however, still wrote letters and essays on bonds, and Sunday schoolers still earned money from odd jobs to buy them.[8] One "prize letter" written in early 1919 by a fourteen-year-old farm girl near Rockwood, Ontario, Madeleine Taylor, reflected the undiminished enthusiasm of youth, which campaigns were quick to capitalize on. Perhaps with adult coaching, Madeleine wrote that since she was not old enough to be a nurse, she had contributed to the war effort through household chores, food production, and being the "proud possessor" of Victory Bonds. "When the boys come home I shall be able to look them bravely in the face, knowing that I have done my 'bit' to support them and bring liberty to the world."[9] Letters sent during and after the war to the Pathfinders Club in the *Free Press Prairie Farmer* (Winnipeg), among other newspapers with children's sections, could be forthright, with matter-of-fact mentions of bonds. In January 1918, Ethel Place, age fourteen, who hoped to join the club, wrote from near Viking, Alberta, "We live two and a half miles from school. Our school is closed now on account of the flu. We have traps set for coyotes and we got one this morning. Last year we sold $50 of coyote and muskrat hides, so we bought a victory bond." Writing from near Admiral, Saskatchewan, in February 1919, an eleven-year-old said that he had grown some wheat on a patch on the family farm, plus "I was in the Boys' and Girls' Pig contest this summer and I got 7th prize. The prize was $4. I bought a $50 Victory Bond with my money. I have a brother that enlisted in 1916. He was killed in action on Oct. 30. He was 25 years old. [Signed] Kenneth Lyon."[10]

With the war over, many patriotic holders of bonds and war-savings certificates moved to redeem them, a trend also impelled by public disillusionment over their values before maturity and the wheeling and dealing of swindlers. In the handful of such cases reported from the street, "Hebrews" and "foreign Jews" were named in instances in Glace Bay, Nova Scotia, and in Hamilton. In February and March, concerned over new investors who had dived into Victory Bonds and "strange securities" only to encounter exploitative dealers (an area where the finance department proved powerless), a committee of the Bond Dealers' Association of Canada looked into promoting legislative protections but found that counter-advertising by "legitimate bond dealers" was the only answer.[11] Default on subscription payments was becoming more evident, and government accounts began recording arrears. The failure of many subscribers to claim their bonds continued to be a problem, too. At the branch of the Merchants Bank in Shawville, Quebec, for instance, $30,000 in bonds remained unclaimed in March 1919, with the bank calling on subscribers to bring in their receipts for exchange. Opposition politicians were quick to pounce on the many hitches. Even among the well-intentioned bondholder, immediate need could arise. In Winnipeg, the Reverend Charles William Gordon (familiar to many as noted author Ralph Connor) sold his Victory Bonds to meet a mortgage payment of $42,000.[12] For others, the postwar boom did not shield them from the spiralling costs of living and other inflationary squeezes; for some, especially laid-off workers, sustaining instalments became a challenge. In February, the Canadian Business Women's Club in Toronto offered to line up help for "business girls who had taken Victory Bonds and were unable to keep up payments."[13] For some soldiers still overseas, challenges of readjustment were on the horizon. Tones of sarcasm surfaced. Walter Henry Liddiard, a twenty-four-year-old gunner, was upbeat when he wrote from Jandrian, Belgium, on 2 February to his parents in Victoria, "You must have felt good when the armistice was signed to go and buy that $50 war bond, I hope you took the money out of my assigned pay. I will have lots of money and bonds when I get back, think I will have to retire."[14]

Government attempts at controlling prices (other than on bonds), including the Board of Commerce, constituted in August 1919, would prove largely ineffective. (Prices would not break until the summer of 1920.) In this environment of social and labour unease, thrift and saving, represented by Victory Bonds, could simplistically be seen as both solutions and obstacles. Hard-pressed wage earners grumbled about large bondholders who evaded taxation. During the Winnipeg General Strike of May and June, when tensions broke loose, an economics professor, with a nod to the last Victory Loan, told a retail merchants' convention in Regina that thrift, "not any proletariat autocracy," was a pillar of democracy. Labour leaders from afar, some of whom had supported past loans, came to Winnipeg to remind listeners that they had backed the "boys at the front" while lambasting both war and capital. In the wake of the strike, *One Big Union Bulletin* (Winnipeg) classified the 1919 loan as "another flood of Government of Canada I.O.U.'s." In Ontario, Herbert Hartley Dewart, an outspoken Liberal member of the provincial Parliament, believed that the "new fortunes" carved out of patriotic sacrifices and Victory Loan savings served only to intensify class consciousness. Bonds thus became multidimensional.[15]

The government's program of thrift and war-savings stamps, its processing of bonds, and its New York loan in July claimed attention. Within his department, White would report in July, 221 temporary clerks were busily employed registering and transferring bonds, issuing interest cheques, and redeeming and adjusting with the banks more than 6 million bond coupons. At bank branches and regional offices of the receiver general (part of the finance department), bondholders asked to exchange bearer bonds for registered bonds, to transfer them to other people, or to convert bunches of $50 bonds into a $1,000 bond in order to increase their market value. Some customers wanted to convert debenture stock into Victory Bonds.

With the war ended but not the costs, the identity of the fall loan needed to be rethought. Actual conflict had motivated a selling milieu at home; funding demobilization, reconstruction, and foodstuffs would prove to be a much different need. From Vancouver, Lionel Waterlow Makovski, a one-time waiter, land speculator, self-described authority on Russia, newspaperman, and secretary of British Columbia's committee for the 1918 Victory Loan, wrote to White on 26 July of the new setting, where there were no patriotic grounds for any loan's appeal.[16] The minister did not fully agree. On 1 August 1919, the day before he retired as finance minister, he convened a conference in Ottawa of key financial men, brokers, representatives of the Canadian Press Association

(CPA), and members of the new dominion executive, including Edward Rogers Wood and Alfred Ernest Ames (who also chaired the dominion administration and finance committee), to discuss the preliminaries of the "Peace Loan." The meeting found White at his persuasive best. He had long feared the dire financial consequences and "moral effect" of a failed flotation. Only another "popular appeal" would work. To that end, the CPA's display-advertising committee made arrangements with five advertising firms experienced in war-loan campaigns.[17] Later in the month, determined to stay in the game, White would again address the executive to extol its absolute responsibility to "find the money" for financial needs ahead.[18] Amidst Victory Loan speaking engagements, his return to private business was confirmed in November when he was appointed to the boards of the Steel Company of Canada and the National Trust. On 5 August, within days of the conference, Wood summoned the dominion publicity committee. Under the direction of its new head, William Norman McIlwraith, an investment-publicity specialist with Wood, Gundy and Company, it worked fast. On 24 August, he reported back to Wood on its progress on a gamut of features, among them moving pictures, display advertising (in cooperation with the CPA), prizes of big guns (in cooperation with the War Trophies Commission), and "forceful pamphlets." Despite the proclamation of 1919 as another war year, the campaign would abandon many of the win-the-war concepts of past drives.

To some observers, the buildup seemed disconnected from a tired government's efforts to deal with Canada's economic and social problems, including the cost of living and complications in its reconstruction program. Testimonies at the National Industrial Conference, the offspring in September of the Royal Commission on Industrial Relations, touched on past loans. Praise there for White's wartime policy was mixed with labour's laments for the resulting load of national debt and failures to deliver the contracts for work promised by loan propaganda. But by October, preparations for the loan were under way, despite any cynicism.

The new finance minister, Sir Henry Drayton, lacked White's skill in selling. A snappy satire in *Maclean's Magazine* (Toronto) would contrast the two. Whereas White could use the "soothing phrase" and skate around "air holes," Drayton met problems with blunt practicality, as in his budgets, regardless of the political reaction, as in the tariff commission hearings. The satire saw a postwar Canada "teaming with war money," credits for European countries, high wages, desires for luxuries, and wearisome calls for people's money: "The great organized orgy was over, when the dollars followed the drum and the drum thumped at every cross-road; when a Victory Bond in every top commode drawer was more necessary than a bottle in every cellar. The whole nation, four times tagged [canvassed] for Victory, was once more tagged for reconstruction."[19] Whatever the climate for another domestic loan, Drayton took it seriously.

He had his first meeting with loan workers in late August and gave his first loan address on 3 September. That same month and in early October, drawn into the campaign's practical arrangements, he met in Toronto with the dominion executive, provincial organizers, the Bond Dealers' Association of Canada, and the Canadian Bankers' Association, and he approved the posters and sixteen newspaper advertisements that the CPA proposed for release at intervals between 2 and 25 October, the "Educational Period" prior to the campaign's start on 27 October. CPA manager John Mills Imrie, knowing how a good number of veterans and their association felt about the government's tight-fisted support, stressed the "delicate nature of the direct appeal to the returned soldiers to support the loan." He had Drayton write an advertisement that appeared in *Veteran, Khaki Call,* and other publications for veterans.[20] Their sentiments on the loan varied. In New Westminster, British Columbia, for instance, veterans were for the loan, which Comrade Thomas Wiedeman, a reporter by trade, termed "a real democratic innovation" in the floating of loan issues generally in Canada.[21] The facade of democracy thrown up in 1914 was nonetheless proving resistant.

Without the win-the-war wind behind him, Drayton's explanation of the loan proved to be a hard slog.[22] Conscious of the sensitivities surrounding veterans' expenses, the minister was "emphatic" that one brochure be changed from "three-fifths for the Soldier" to "three-fifths for War Costs." It was White, however, along with deputy minister Thomas Cooper Boville, who outlined the rationales for loans, market stabilization, and the impossibility of increasing soldiers' gratuities in statements before the parliamentary committee on soldiers' civil re-establishment in October, just as the Great War Veterans' Association was pushing for cash grants to be drawn partly from the loan. (In fact, the government would increase certain gratuities in December.) Much of the forthcoming loan "has already been expended," White claimed, and another would be needed in 1920, an idea that never materialized. Other proposals, by some veterans' groups, for special bonds for returned soldiers were dashed by White. He was sure that dedicated bonds would "demoralize the market for securities and bonds."[23] In early October 1919, official advertising and press releases began stressing the specifics and costs of demobilization.

By this point, Drayton was being told by some large manufacturers that, because of problems arising from reconstruction, they could not be part of the highest class of subscribers. Still, he remained convinced, as White had been, that corporations must lead with substantial subscriptions (from $500,000 to several million), knowing that any in excess of actual need would be disposed of by the market-stabilizing committee, that "special arrangements" could be made with him (mostly for large Canadian and American insurance companies) for an extension of payments to the end of 1920, and that big American pledges would receive special processing. They were to be taken through designated agents, among them the Merchants Bank of Canada in New York. Since the last Liberty Loan had ended in May, the field was clear.

Just as the campaign's mechanics were being shaped in August, September, and October, with much troubleshooting by the minister's secretary, Bennet John Roberts, negative trends were surfacing. The lingering impact of another wave of influenza created a drag in some regions. Getting eminent personages to appear on the loan's behalf was proving difficult, and political partisanship was beginning to stand in the way of clear endorsements. Spats over alleged profiteering and graft in past loans broke out in the campaign leading up to the Ontario election of 20 October. Federally, the new Liberal leader, William Lyon Mackenzie King, would back the loan only if the campaign's organization was "entirely non-political." So assured by Drayton, King issued his approval on 1 October. In Toronto, Sir Allen Bristol Aylesworth, a prominent lawyer, agreed to join the honorary committee there but refused to subscribe on the grounds that the loan's terms did not appeal to him.[24] Gathering support in Quebec also proved frustrating. Sir William Price and Sir Georges Garneau declined to serve as joint chairs of the loan committee for Quebec City and district, and Premier Sir Lomer Gouin turned down the invitation to stand as an honorary chair. In Montreal, John Wilson McConnell, the "live wire" of past campaigns, refused to head the drive there.[25]

In Quebec, Dominion Police actions against defaulters under the Military Service Act had been a flashpoint of protest in 1918. Similar actions and resentments would continue into 1919. The chase and conscription of farmers' sons, who were needed to work at home, was especially resented. Default was occurring in every province that summer and fall, but in Quebec the bill's prosecution had ramifications for the forthcoming loan campaign. On 16 September 1919, the provincial co-chair, investment dealer Albert-Pierre Frigon, told Drayton that police had stepped up their actions between Montreal and the Gaspé. Not only was such conduct hurting the workforce during cropping season, but it was also "apt to create some bad feelings and put obstacles in the work of our organizers." Frigon asked Drayton to get the government to back off. As police actions escalated, district campaign meetings were cancelled, and Frigon, with the support of at least two Quebec politicians, pleaded for "a little diplomacy." His indifferent co-chair, Frederick G. Donaldson, the manager of Montreal Trust, thought that the whole issue should be put off. After referring the matter to the minister of justice, Drayton did little; apart from his knowledge of the transportation sector, his old beat, his understanding of Quebec was shallow. The loan's benefit to Quebec's production and marketing was the priority, he believed. Federal authorities had already shifted blame, ascribing "defiance" of the Military Service Act in Quebec to "evil teaching or influences."[26] What did unite Frigon and Donaldson were press reports beyond Quebec of its low levels of subscription and enthusiasm, reports that they vigorously protested.[27] Once again, the Montreal organization, dominated largely by anglophone businessmen, operated separately from the rest of the province, a dissociation that did not help.

The Military Service Act, views on Quebec, and veterans' benefits were not the only public measures to become controversially enmeshed with the loan. When Drayton was in Montreal on 23 October to launch the campaign there, speeches were dominated by the government's contentious purchase of the Grand Trunk Pacific's rail network. In Toronto, the rejection of prohibition's repeal in a referendum on 20 October, the same day as the provincial election, rebounded on the loan. At some east-end factories "No Beer, No Bonds" posters were countered with "No Beer, No Bums." This spat, in Hamilton as well as Toronto, was dismissed by the loan's publicity committee as a minor distraction, "confined for the most part to foreigners." On 5 November, at the YMCA's Red Triangle Club in Toronto, Victory Loan speakers, including the mayor, were heckled by veterans over gratuities and wages. One returned soldier doubted "if the Federal Government should be entrusted with the expenditure of the loan."[28] Such were the ways that the loans became injected into public life.

On 21 October, six days before the start of the official campaign, Drayton had announced the terms of the loan. For the first time, bond interest would be taxable, a feature that would spur new responses from armchair economists and advisors in Canada's dailies and weeklies, from professors in Nova Scotia to agrarian columnists in the West. Four days later, Drayton set out to promote the loan in a tour of the West. Interviewed in British Columbia on 5 November, he said that he had taken on his portfolio on short notice and almost immediately "had started out on this Victory Loan campaign, not that he relished the job."[29] And he did make some missteps. In Cabinet, he had tried to have 2 November proclaimed a day for citizens to reflect on their obligations, specifically to fund the loan. To publicize the day, he tabled a sample letter to Quebec's clergy that ended tactlessly with lines from John McCrae's poem "In Flanders Fields," which enjoyed little popularity in the province. Cabinet rejected the proposal.[30] More effective was Frigon's lobbying of Quebec's bishops.[31]

Organizers saw every sector, including labour and Ontario's new United Farmers–Labour coalition government, as being on board. "If you ever tried to finance a strike in the third week, Sir Thomas White's task would sink into insignificance," stated Alfred C. Mance of the *Industrial Banner* (London, Ontario) and an ardent loan speaker, but "we are with you to assist until the Victory Loan goes over the top."[32] Despite the support of the leadership of the United Farmers Organization, there was lingering resentment in its ranks toward the tax exemptions granted on past loans.[33] Not all farmers may have had the means to subscribe. The high prices set for wheat by Canada's new Wheat Board drew resistance from millers, prompting Liberal MP Archibald Blake McCoig to tell the Commons that unless western Ontario farmers could dispose of their crop, "it was going to seriously interfere with the sale of the Victory Bonds."[34]

Prior to the campaign, which ran from 27 October to 15 November, organizations were reactivated and fine-tuned. Canvassers would be paid on a salary basis rather than commission, and many districts would be recanvassed two or three times. Advertisements would be handled by the Canadian Press Association in cooperation with the dominion executive committee and the dominion publicity committee. For press publicity, three divisions were laid out: display advertising paid for by the government, display advertising donated by firms and individuals, and a Press News and Feature Service to support news and editorials, including the provision of cartoons and a "boiler plate." An outline, *Plan and Organization of Press Publicity for Canada's Victory Loan, 1919*, published after the campaign, provides an overview. On formation, the publicity committee understood the challenges that it faced: a "general attitude of critical enquiry, and, in some quarters, of antagonism" and "a partial demobilization of patriotic feeling, as well as a demobilization of armed forces." Planning also had to adjust to the election in Ontario, its referendum on prohibition, public misunderstandings over the loan's taxation features, and a reported decline in the number of small investors. On 2 October, to surmount such hurdles, the committee had launched an initial phase of "educational work," with an injection of "human interest" content.[35] As the *Globe* had once reported before imparting a string of such stories,

> The lot of the canvasser selling Victory Bonds is not an easy one. In some places he is received with open arms, in others he has to put into force his oratorical efforts in order to persuade the prospective purchaser that it is a business deal worth while, and not a question of receiving no return for the money he is asked to invest. There is a touch of human interest brought to the surface invariably in the consummation of every sale.[36]

A second phase, selling advertisements, began with the start of the campaign; some inspirational ads were used to strike "the high note of patriotic obligation,"[37] particularly on Armistice Day.

Victory Loan Headquarters, Owen Sound, Ontario, 1919. The staging here combines posters, local artwork, and boards with district data. | Archives of Ontario, F 507-1-2-0-222.

Records of the 1919 press publicity committee reveal even more of its inner operations, from the timed release of advertisements and statements to wordings and designs, including the use of French Canadian content in posters destined for Quebec rather than co-opting such icons as "In Flanders Fields."[38] The display-advertising divisions worked with the bond dealers, advertising firms, and artists to prepare copy and plates, have posters designed and pamphlets drafted, and handle printing contracts and distribution, an arrangement that required coordination with both the King's Printer and the loan's dominion publicity committee, which had the final say. The press publicity committee also issued bulletins, billboards, pay-envelope fillers, blotters, automobile stickers, sample bonds, some eleven films, small coloured cards for school children, and other paraphernalia, from bottle caps to bread pans and wrappers. Publicity committees once again analyzed population and school-attendance figures for distribution purposes. The Dominion Press News and Feature Service provided assistance and copy for papers to use for their news and editorial columns. Recognizing that organizers, workers, and salesmen would face "certain very specific lines of resistance in the coming campaign," propaganda was designed to meet any obstacles. Much of the literature was translated into twelve or more languages. The largest numbers were in Hebrew in Toronto and French in Quebec and New Brunswick. Overall, working relationships within this advertising brain trust, although sometimes tense, were productive. Midway through the campaign, Edward Rogers Wood, chair of the dominion executive, summarized the vital role of press publicity: "The effect is going to be to create an atmosphere that will put the loan over."

An inside, and more entertaining, look at the process of producing advertisements appeared in *Marketing and Business Management* (Toronto) in October, written by an unnamed copywriter. When called together in August, the team had minimal enthusiasm: "Everybody was fed up." Telling the public why the government needed money after the war would be difficult: "Nobody loves a War Government – after the war is over." A professional spark was kindled when this "pearl" was suggested: compressing demobilization into a tight time frame and one coherent package of advertising. In addition, there was the need for "the 'whoop it up' stuff on behalf of the soldiers and the usual line of dope about keeping industry prosperous." Proposals for advertising the educational period went back and forth between the "copy hounds" and the committee, a case of the "same conferences, same beating over of the platitudes"; sixteen advertisements were finalized, some of them illustrated in this article. The copywriter still found basic educational ads "blooming logical" and "banal in spots." Official ad number 115, "Miss Canada Gives Account of Her Stewardship," which concerns expenditures, is shown as an example, but news of public interest and the possibility of reaching $500 million energized the team. The campaign needed the boost. Then, for the vigorous selling period of the campaign, the team turned out some "syrup and painless publicity" that could be easily approved. The account ends there.[39] For these copywriters, producing propagandistic publicity was not a dour exercise of patriotic application but an arm's-length feat of working collaboratively with a committee and illustrators while maintaining a sense of humour and detachment. "Whoop it up" was certainly part of the language of war-bond hucksters, cartoonists, event organizers, and trade journals in both Canada and the United States. In the context of shaping advertising, the Victory and Liberty Loans stirred copywriters to turn out narratives around war themes, often enhanced by illustrations, that dramatized actions needed from citizen-consumers.[40]

The goal in 1919 was to produce what Drayton called a "clean-up loan" in order to deal with remaining war costs and demobilization and to facilitate economic prosperity. Harking back to a metaphor used in 1917, slogans and imagery portrayed a sweeping broom but without the support-the-boys rhetoric.

One banner in Toronto had a racehorse dashing to the finish. Posters and other publicity proclaimed this theme of reconstruction relentlessly. At a music-infused pep rally on 23 October at Toronto's King Edward Hotel, Sir George Foster, old but still eloquent, reminded a primed audience,

> You are going up against a psychological condition different to that of 1917 and 1918. There must be a different appeal to that of the war ... Today the war is won in one way – the fighting is done. The human factor has been removed, but the keeping and favorable success of the country remain. Today the loan is largely a business proposition. The soldiers have done their bit, and we are no men unless we do ours.

He then hammered home the points of thrift, greater production, and investment.[41]

Teams of canvassers were so coached on the new themes, often in the misguided belief that the loan was risk-free, with no hint of market variables and controls or of the economic downturn to come. Some teams, as was the case in Saint John, were exhorted "to get after American capital" because of their closeness to New England and the high exchange rate reportedly being paid on the American dollar: 4 percent versus one-eighth of a percent before the war. In West Pictou, Nova Scotia, the campaign chair reported that the Department of Finance, to stabilize exchange, had authorized a fixed rate of 3 and a-quarter percent, thus removing the "element of speculation" in US funds paid by American subscribers. American-owned operations in Canada, most with Canadian-dollar accounts (such as shipyards in Port Arthur), faced problems only of market-price fluctuation and asset management. Holding bonds and other Canadian securities in anticipation of rate equalization, as advocated in one industry journal,[42] would have been risky.

Advertising also pushed the investment angle. The one-year anniversary of Armistice Day provided an ideal point for promotion, from solemnity to revelry. In the big cities, the campaign was once again characterized by a proliferation of sales booths, sponsored advertising, posters and banners, parades, and circus-y events. The entertainment factor could not be neglected. The sight of a trapeze artist in London, Ontario, throwing out pamphlets while swinging was novel but not strange.

The campaign received even more of a boost from the visit to Canada, between 15 August and 10 November, of the celebrated Prince of Wales, who privately ridiculed his scripted speeches as "pompous stunts." The tours of Drayton and the governor general, the Duke of Devonshire, who subscribed for $10,000, also drew attention. On 1 September, before setting out on tour, the prince had laid the cornerstone of the tower of the new Centre Block of the Parliament Buildings (the original block having burned in 1916) and unfurled the Victory Loan's new honour flag. The idea for the flag began with William Norman McIlwraith of the dominion publicity committee. Like the honour flag of 1918, the prince's banner, awarded for district achievement in the loan, became a coveted prize and a driving force in local campaigns. It bore the Union Jack in the upper left and the prince's coat of arms; over-quota achievement was marked by added badges in the form of his plumed crest. The lists of recipients would be long, from the remotest areas to the big cities. Visited by the prince for fishing, Cameron Falls, a rough hydroelectric-construction settlement north of Nipigon, was the first place in the vast Lake Superior district to win one. A flag and seven crests were won by a tool-die factory in Galt, Ontario, where, in the first week of November, "everyone is talking Victory Loan and Victory bonds," *Canadian Machinery and Manufacturing News* (Toronto) reported. In arrangements worked out with the federal Commission on War Records and Trophies, formed in December 1918 (the so-called War Trophies Commission), other prizes in district competitions included war mementoes, often heavy German guns brought back to Canada. Captured tanks and a submarine, the *UC-97*, drew curious crowds. Photographs of these curios flashed across the country. During the campaign, there was keen competition for guns in eleven communities, from Kamloops in British Columbia to Yarmouth in Nova Scotia.[43] In Prince Edward Island, in a contest that drove up subscriptions, Summerside beat out Charlottetown for a gun. Spirits ran high. At one munitions plant in Toronto, a "shell buster" (a temporary worker) subscribed "right to the neck." In Sussex, New Brunswick, fourteen-year-old Elda S. Carleton won a dollar for her slogan "Every Miser Helps the Kaiser: Buy A Bond." Events, banquet menus, lyrics, essays, and amateur verse and republished poems and stories were all laced with loan lingo. Commercially, bonds continued to be treated as unofficial currency. In northwest Ontario, for example, Miss Alvira May Bishop, a young milliner in Fort Frances, put on a fur show and offered to accept bonds as cash.

Throughout the campaign, the themes of remaining war costs, re-establishment, and prosperity were pumped out at every turn. Echoing Sir George Foster, one sponsored ad in the *Port Arthur News-Chronicle* pulled no punches: "Our soldiers are watching you. It was great to 'whoop it up' and send the boys away to fight. Everybody was a patriot then. There is some paying to be done now, and it is the money raised by this Victory Loan that must do the paying." The taxing of interest on bonds caused some confusion, but brochures sidestepped the complex questions of taxation and enforcement, offering up the popular explanation that the burden "is placed on the shoulders of those best able to bear it." Early in the campaign, press releases noted the distribution of 20 million pieces of literature with such messaging. The means of distribution included mailings, handouts, door-to-door deliveries, and aerial drops, although not without risk. In a bond contest in Truro, Nova Scotia, a boy scrambling to pick up flyers that had been dropped from a plane was struck and killed by an automobile. Near Eganville, Ontario, a Victory Loan aeroplane crashed, killing its occupants. At the same time, official pamphlets sewed confusion about disposing of bonds "for ready money."

The campaign utilized all of the promotional apparatus of past loans: the competitions and contests, company plans, the targeting of children and women, the parades, and sales during theatre performances. In Antigonish County, Nova Scotia, a Victory Loan concert band toured the countryside, performing in parish halls and schools. At a masquerade ball in Cumberland, British Columbia, Mrs. P. Myers flaunted a costume representing Victory Bonds. In a touring vaudeville show at the Pantages Theatre in Edmonton, "Robinson's Military Elephants" wore loan posters in performances. "The aid of other theatrical performers is to be requisitioned as well, and the Victory Bond atmosphere is to be intensified by every possible device," the *Edmonton Journal* reported. Victory Loan shtick thrived. Among the grander recognitions of the armistice were Toronto's supercharged celebrations from 7 to 15 November, the last day of the campaign. In a letter asking Ontario's clergy to cooperate, Drayton, claiming that patriotism was still "essential," recited "In Flanders Fields." On the night of 11 November, an "Armistice Night Carnival and Community Dance" was launched, to run each evening. Attendees were treated to a variety of sights and entertainments, among them five French tanks and a simulated air raid over Yonge Street, complete with anti-aircraft fire and two "illuminated" German Fokker D.VII fighters,[44] one piloted by the much-decorated William George ("Billy") Barker.

Indoors on 11 November, at Massey Hall, the keynote speakers were Solicitor General Arthur Meighen, the Reverend William A. Cameron, and the United Farmers of Ontario's premier-designate, Ernest Charles Drury, in his first major appearance. He spoke bluntly, to Meighen's apparent discomfort, about wartime inflation, the "pinch of hard times" ahead, and the perils of "continued borrowing" through loans. Nonetheless, he recognized the need for the Victory Loan and its value for subscribers "as a business proposition," a position upheld by the United Farmers' secretary, James J. Morrison. In a mass mailing to farmers, Morrison had pointed out that more than $200 million, or 34 percent, of the 1918 loan had been advanced to Britain and its allies for the purchase of Canadian wheat and other foodstuffs. Hence, for farmers to receive good prices in 1919, it was essential that the loan be oversubscribed.[45] United Farmers in other provinces, along with United Grain Growers Limited, agreed, although with some differences between the East and the West and some localized quarrels over taxation on the loan and over farmers' commitment.[46] The benefit was pushed by both White and Drayton. One official advertisement announced that $24 million would be used to make loans for land to "soldier farmers," a sum that would prove grossly inadequate.[47]

Postwar realities produced shifts in focus and reaction. Although general support came from labourers, farmers, veterans, fraternal organizations, tradesmen, and retailers, there were departures. Veterans' groups continued to differ on how support and gratuities should be funded. The loan was often chastised as insufficient, and spokesmen were targeted as government shills. At the YMCA's Red Triangle Club in Toronto, vets heckled loan speakers. The positions of corporations, despite their heavy investments, are far more difficult to track. With market and value determinants dominating patriotic motivations in the long run, dominion securities were bought and sold at a steady pace, although in the largest companies, such as Sun Life, those securities comprised only a small fraction of overall assets. Coverage of the 1919 loan never failed to mention big corporate subscriptions – which did form a third or so of subscriptions. Except in the reports that insurance companies made to the government, coverage seldom delved into the fluidity of asset management. Starting in 1915, war bonds had surged in the reported asset mixes of insurance companies, where patterns of calculated disposals and conversions subsequently emerged. Two other trends also emerged. Responding to pressures from their branches in past campaigns, a number of corporations had their subscriptions credited to the local campaign districts of their branches instead of to head-office locations elsewhere, in defiance of the Victory Loan's dominion executive. The *Regina Morning Leader* lambasted the executive's "autocratic decision" as contrary to the loan's aspiration to create a "national sentiment." A second trend was the thrust of the loan's special subscriptions committee into the United States.

America's last Liberty Loan had ended in May, leaving many companies to look north for investment opportunities. Stabilization of the exchange rate helped. In October, dominion chair Edward Rogers Wood went to Montreal and New York to confer with key financiers and corporations. Within weeks, special subscriptions were outpacing the individual subscriptions secured by canvassers, a trend that undermined promotions of a people's loan. (Wood himself subscribed for $250,000.) Drayton would try to downplay the volume of American subscriptions, but they were substantial.[48] By 8 November, these large subscriptions had reached $27,281,550, or so the *P.E. Island Agriculturist* (Summerside) reported, another instance of the swift spread of loan news. A delegation from the special subscriptions committee subsequently went to New York, hunting for another $30 million. James Henry Gundy, the committee's chair, called the venture "a collection, not a canvass." His committee was able to clean up in the northeastern States, where subscriptions in the range of $300,000 to $600,000 by major financial institutions were common. On 31 October, the Canadian National News Service reported authorization by Sir Frederick Williams-Taylor, general manager of the Bank of Montreal, of the announcement of a $1 million subscription through the bank's representatives by J.P. Morgan and Company of New York, its first direct subscription "to any of the public issues made by the allies." To remove any guesswork by American subscribers, the Department of Finance gave them the option of paying in American or Canadian funds and at a fixed exchange rate of 3 and a-quarter percent. As for the labour perspective of cross-border involvement, shipbuilders in Seattle had supported Canada's loans, and in 1919 at least one yard, Skinner and Eddie, invested heavily in Victory Bonds. Other campaigns took advantage of their proximity. One canvasser from Beebe, on the Quebec border, had "considerable success" soliciting subscriptions in Newport, Vermont.

Corporations were not the only institutional participants. Most major religious denominations endorsed the loan, alongside sermonizing and Sunday school participation. Whether building on grounds of practical investment or religious veneer, publicity correlated the loans with Christian belief. The largest subscription, $250,000, came from the Methodist Church's superannuation fund, an investment that it intended to cover from its upcoming national campaign. At an interfaith convention at Massey Hall on 25 November, the chairman of Victory Loan Special Committee, George Herbert Wood, a Methodist who had headed Ontario's Victory Loan campaign, would bring his experience to bear: "It remains to be seen whether the nation can make the same response to God's call as they did to that of a Finance Minister in the Victory Loan campaign." The Presbyterian Church, which bought bonds for its investment funds, saw the loan as a model for its own fundraising, "God's Victory Loan." In past loans, the *Presbyterian Record* (Toronto) had run official advertisements that featured biblical exhortation (Moses "knew" that all must do their share in wartime, citing Numbers 32:6) and claims of righteous cause, as well as an article that conjoined "Christ and the Victory Loan." On the street, canvassers could spout pious sentiment to sway the doubtful, but it was the physical environment that often posed the greatest impediments in fall campaigns.

In 1919, perhaps more than in 1918, vast distances and the vagaries of climate could be inhibiting factors. In November, as harsh weather swept the Prairies and most other provinces, canvassing became increasingly difficult. Other factors for canvassers and potential subscribers alike, such as drought (in Alberta), poor crops, unemployment among veterans, relief schemes, and financial hardships – the worst, some said, since the winter of 1906–07 – seldom crossed over into the coverage or rhetoric of campaigns. In the Southern Alberta district, many rural canvassers were farmers who understood the obstacles, although some areas, such as Raymond, still exceeded their quotas. Aware of such difficulties, Drayton had the terms for western farmers' loan instalments relaxed to allow for the disposal of the next season's crops. As well, privileges were extended on lines of credit based on Victory Bonds. In Halifax, the campaign was slow, as the *Financial Post* (Toronto) reported, for two reasons: the "lack of war incentive" and consumer spending. Not to be thwarted, Josiah Clifford Stredder, a veteran and an insurance manager, developed the highly successful practice of canvassing docked ocean liners. Ports canvassed by others included Fort William (now part of Thunder Bay), Ontario. In some distant areas, campaigning continued past the official deadline of 15 November. William Harold Malkin, British Columbia's chairman, asked the finance minister to telegram the chair in Yukon "to take applications from remote districts after the fifteenth so that banks may receive such applications without questions. Please instruct Bankers Association to notify branches in Yukon accordingly."

News flowed fast, with the results of provincial and local campaigns appearing via wire with great rapidity in newspapers. Still, opinions were often shaped with minimal analysis of regional circumstances. The fallacies of propaganda and misleading anecdotal reports could be exposed. In the dailies of Montreal and Quebec City, coverage was strong, even as outbreaks of influenza persisted. In Montreal, the speakers' circuit was particularly busy, with public meetings out of doors at all kinds of events – football matches, public parades, street-corner "attractions," and after-church gatherings. "The importance of these meetings for the purposes of creating a Victory Loan atmosphere," the speakers' committee would report on November 19, "could not be over-estimated." At the same time, the late arrival of publicity materials in Montreal proved detrimental; having them a month earlier would have been much better. "This is very very important," the responsible committee claimed. "We were badly handicapped by [this] not being done this year and last."[49] Organizers found merchants less enthusiastic about store and window decorations, newspapers less willing to cooperate.

Rural response, as reported in *Le Soleil* (Quebec City), was appreciable. The visit by the Prince of Wales appeared to help; the awards of much-cherished honour flags fuelled morale and expectations. Other newspapers in Quebec and elsewhere attempted to separate political stances on the Grand Trunk Pacific and other issues from support for the loan. *Le Colon* (Roberval) believed that subscriptions would help to sustain the province's credit. *L'Acadien* (Moncton) did not back the government or conscription but still saw the advantages of investing. *Le Devoir* saw some change on a cultural front. In an opinion piece on 18 November 1919, it praised translations of advertising done in-house by the loan's French publicity office in Montreal:

> Around this time last year we congratulated the French Advertising Bureau of the National Loan Office in Montreal for the intelligent advertising campaign created under their supervision. We congratulate them this year again for the same reason. We did not get stupid and word-for-word translations from ads written in English, which might have meant something to an English-speaking audience, but was completely irrelevant to the small French Canadian capitalists and investors. Everything from ads, billboards, flyers, inserts, posters were home-made, and written in a very good French, and the editors in chief of this French advertising campaign presented economic plans explained in a very clear fashion to encourage our French Canadian buyers to purchase 1919 Victory bonds. They left aside the same old militaristic and imperialist rhetoric, and jingoism that we've been fed from Toronto for a couple of years to use only meaningful and understandable arguments. Let's congratulate them right away this time. Ottawa and Toronto might finally understand, from the experience of the past two years, that the best way to get what you want from French Canadian people is to treat them fairly and respectfully in their own language and according to their own mindset.[50]

Although the key figures in the loan organization for the Island of Montreal were predominantly Anglo-Canadians – the president was Percy Parsons Cowans, a broker – pains were taken on translation.[51] One English organizer nevertheless grumbled about "too many French" posters.

Divisions emerged, and rhetoric could flare. As the campaign progressed, dissections followed. *Le Devoir* supported the loan but remained ready to challenge wartime shibboleths. Henri Bourassa pointed out the contradiction between the prince's praise for Canada's part in the war and its subservience to imperial wishes. Distaste for a worn-out federal government, the polemic surrounding the Grand Trunk Pacific, and the reported reticence of the "big capitalists" to subscribe may have had dampening impacts. A lack of enthusiasm, and the police actions censured by Albert-Pierre Frigon, were part of the mix. In Montreal, *L'Autorité* and *Le Canada* slammed the government for its continuing dependence on loans, Drayton's inexperience, and evidence of unabated government by order-in-council. In *L'Autorité,* "Flambeau" condemned the supposed incompetence of Frigon and the anti-government newspapers that took advertising, calling the loan a fiasco sustained only by Anglo-Canadian capital. Subscriptions in Quebec fell by $18 million, the most of any province.

In which sectors of Canadian society results fell or rose is unclear: some pointed to the corporations, some to the agrarian sector, and others to the small subscriber. Throughout the campaign nationally, publicists and many newspapers had striven to champion the "little guy," soldiers and civilians alike, but their subscriptions did evidently decline in the postwar doldrum. In Saint John, canvassers reported difficulties getting people to withdraw their bank savings in order to buy bonds. Despite canvassers' efforts to push $50 and $100 bonds, there was a falling-off of subscriptions from "small investors," according to Edward Rogers Wood and other organizers.

In the midst of this hazy decline, some of the elusive modest subscribers can be identified. Many acted in the fervour of celebrations, without clear understandings of how bonds worked, but most were serious undertakings. On 23 October, on the verge of a marriage that would never happen, Jessie Margaret O. Henderson, a teacher of limited means in Spirit River in northern Alberta, wrote to a friend, "When I do take the plunge there will be no wedding, just go to the preacher's and get tied. I bought $150 victory bonds today. I'll have $400 altogether. Not bad, eh?" Although the war had ended, soldiers still subscribed, often through payroll deductions, a gradual method that slowed the flow of actual money to the government's coffers. Lieutenant William Errol Boyd Starr in Halifax, for example, made payments between 21 November 1919 and 6 August 1920 for $150 in Victory Bonds.[52] Another Halifax soldier, Corporal John James O'Brien, unable to continue payments, got a refund of his instalments when he was demobilized in 1920. Such withdrawals, along with civilians' premature disposal of bonds, could complicate accurate calculations of loan statistics, as well as raise questions about the reasons for termination. Elsewhere in Canada, at the end of the campaign on 15 November, the City of Toronto began taking subscriptions by its employees. The rare surviving ledger for five departments – architects, assessment, city clerk, fire, and health – records the fortnightly or monthly payments of hundreds of small-investing staff by name, address, and choice of denomination. Payments stretched over a year, with some cessations and surrenders. Not every employee subscribed; of the 522 members of the fire department, for example, only 184 signed up. The ledger entries, combined with directory listings, are revealing. May O'Connor, a telephone switchboard operator at the city clerk's office who lived at home with her mother, paid $1 a week for a $50 bond, and Edith Kathleen Russell, a public-health nurse who lodged at the residence of Mrs. Edith Atkin, a teacher, signed up for a $100 bond.[53] These were some of the actual people in the corps of small investors. Elsewhere within the municipality, the Toronto Police Benefit Fund was on a course of purchasing and converting war bonds on a much larger scale.

The overall results of the campaign fell off from 1918. Postwar times were different. The momentum of wartime had dissipated. Many organizations had been reticent or financially exhausted, and individual subscriptions appear to have dropped off. The campaign in Quebec, as noted, suffered from multiple factors. In Ontario, special subscriptions led the field in Hamilton, London, Toronto, and industrial centres like the northwestern mill town of Rainy River. Large subscriptions from Toronto and Montreal alone generated almost a third of the national total at the end of the campaign's second week, according to James Henry Gundy, chair of the dominion special subscriptions committee. In its later examination of accounts, a committee headed by Thomas Bradshaw put special subscriptions in 1919 at 39 percent, more than 1917's one-third. In some ways, special subscriptions did not comfortably fit the drives to democratize the loans.

Not only did the Victory Loan tail off in 1919, but arrears and defaults would also continue. Fundraising by other patriotic organizations also experienced declines or had been superseded by government and other national programs, although the Victory Loan, with its opportunity for investment, had claimed most people's available dollars. The district of Quesnel, British Columbia, for instance, by March 1919, had witnessed the following allocations: war loans ($57,450), Canadian Patriotic Fund ($6,458.05), Red Cross ($3,850.59), tobacco fund ($689), war-comforts fund for knitting, parcels, and the like ($676.33), Belgian Relief ($550), and YMCA ($385).[54]

On the Victory Loan, only two provinces, Ontario and Prince Edward Island, the latter reporting a strong rural response, exceeded their 1918 results. Analysis of returns by rank, rate of participation, or average subscription can be tricky, with a number of factors in play. In 1917, for example, Prince Edward Island exceeded its quota twofold, but with the second lowest rate of participation in Canada and the smallest purchase per capita. The island's average subscription ($440) put its investors fifth among the country's provinces. In 1918, the participation rate was the lowest (1 in 17.33, compared to 1 in 4.65 in Ontario), but the average subscription (about $557) was the third highest. On a proportional basis, fewer Islanders bought bonds, "but those who did made relatively large investments," and they were likely from Charlottetown or Summerside.[55] Comparable breakdowns can be made for all nine provinces, but in all cases, the effectiveness of local campaigns, economic well-being, and ingrained perceptions could sway results. Once again, without comprehensive campaign records and newspaper reports, local results resist easy explanation. In the district of Pictou County, Nova Scotia, for example, results were reported in 1918 for the following places, most of them extended rural communities: Pictou town ($308,200), Pictou Island ($3,200), Caribou ($15,850), Cape John ($15,450), River

John ($41,100), West Branch ($21,750), Dalhousie and Roger Hill ($27,350), Lyons Brook and Scotsburn ($39,250), and Toney River ($17,500). Of the named places, five won honour flags, and in Pictou town the subscriptions for $50 and $100 bonds were the most popular by far.[56] It is nonetheless impossible to identify subscribers and their socio-economic circumstances – a frustrating conclusion.

Within days of the campaign's end, and despite the smaller return, Drayton, newspapers, and loan organizers were lauding the results. Committees issued congratulations and hosted celebrations, giving out scrolls and, in Quebec, even gold medals. Newspapers and advertising agencies were never more ready to brag that the war had proven the virtue of advertising.[57] One agency, McConnell and Fergusson of London, Ontario, boasted that the Victory Loans had amply demonstrated the power of advertising "to mould public opinion into one enthusiastic whole." But under the weight of postwar realities, war loans may have become passé in terms of public engagement. In November, *Le Canada* (Montreal) immediately called for an end to the "loan policy."[58]

9

The Aftermath, 1919–20s

After 1919, Victory Bonds shifted to the course of the marketplace. As the *Financial Post* (Toronto) observed in November, Victory Bonds bought in 1917 and 1918 were "finding their way into the innumerable small brokerage shops that have sprung up all over the country," an expansion reflected in newspaper advertisements and directory listings.[1] In Toronto, A.E. Ames and Company offered other bonds but still with "special attention given to War Loan Business." Following the 1919 loan, it published *Comparative Table: Canadian Internal War Loans, Showing Essential Details* to allow investors to navigate the options. Similar brochures came from other Toronto firms, including that of Walter L. McKinnon, former secretary of Ontario's Victory Loan organization, and Wood, Gundy and Company, with a brochure on tax and Victory Bonds. In Montreal, the ads and publications of Versailles, Vidricaire, et Boulais, by differentiating between English Canadian clients and more cautious French Canadian investors in Victory Bonds, promoted what Joseph Versailles's biographer terms "a certain kind of French Canadian economic nationalism."[2] Here was a perpetuation of "Quebec's distinct fiscal culture during the war years," as described by historian Shirley Tillotson.[3] At the same time, Montreal's *Le prix courant* expressed the authoritative view in February 1920 that the market for Liberty and Victory Loans had become saturated.[4] There were traces of resentment toward the stay-at-home politicians who had led the loan parades.

Although campaign stories and fiscal forecasts from 1919 faded from the press, Victory Bonds still maintained a public presence, not just in the market but also in public consciousness as prizes in school-essay competitions throughout the winter of 1919–20, in children's costume contests (where posters made stiff outfits), in war-trophy competitions, and in memorial poles, towers, and plaques funded by Victory Loan commissions. Although student essays were too few to allow broad interpretation, one is illustrative, that of May Meek, whose "The Victory Loan" appeared in the magazine of the Literary Society of a high school in Richmond, Ontario. The story contains familiar components:

a young girl, Mary Osborne, decides to use her birthday-gift savings of $50 during the campaign of 1919 to buy a bond, which has been explained to her by her father. Her brother, killed in the war, "was now sleeping in Flanders Fields." The piece ends, "Mary felt glad that she had a share, however small, towards making her country stronger and better in the years to come."[5] Any contrivance here is hard to filter from genuine sentiment, which contrasts with the less noble handling of bonds by some. Thefts, including $100,000-plus in bonds from Toronto's missing millionaire Ambrose Joseph Small, were reported, with many poignant testimonies of personal loss. In 1922, Jean Craig, a single bookkeeper in Toronto, talked about the theft of her $950 in bonds: "You know, those bonds really mean the savings of a lifetime, I have worked hard for them. It is really the money saved during my fifteen years' service with the Harry Webb [baking] Company."[6] Throughout the 1920s, thievery and fraud involving bonds were rampant.

In the fade-out of the 1919 campaign, the government still crowed about its achievements. Writing in *The Rotarian* (Chicago), W.G. Cates of the Office of Public Information boasted that during the war Canada had surprised itself by flexing its financial strength. "It was with a certain amount of anxiety that Canada first began to raise money for war purposes," but with the Victory Loan of 1917, it was "decided to adopt up-to-date war loan campaign methods in which the spectacular found a place."[7] War bonds, Cates added, were not in the hands only of the banks but also of the public, the sort of broad view that Sir Thomas White had promulgated. In a postwar society and market needing stability, bonds represented permanence, even as price controls, dumping, fraud, and price fluctuations tested their worth. Puffing came easily from the brokerages and sympathetic press, especially MacLean Publishing's interrelated trade journals. Harvey H. Black of the *Financial Post* remained bullish about long-term "Victories," especially the twenty-year bond of 1917.[8]

Some investors continued to be vexed by pre-maturity prices and by circumstances that forced them to sell, and they told the finance department as much in the early 1920s. Counter-arguments swirled: the government, bond dealers, and a host of newspapers continued to urge subscribers to hold their bonds. A.E. Ames and Company, in an advertisement in October 1920, appealed to holders to hang onto the securities in order to reap the "golden harvest": among the many examples, a $100 bond costing $95.52 would return $179.75. Many listened, but others could not. As the *Toronto Daily Star* editorialized in November 1920, "Their value is down at the present because so many are selling these bonds – they are passing from the hands of the many into those of the few. It's a pity. But some bought more bonds than they were able to pay for, and others paid for more than they could afford to keep."[9] Inevitably, bonds changed hands at a rapid rate; large financial firms scooped up many. Occasionally, cynicism entered the debate. From London, Ontario, a businessman, too young to have served, would write,

> During the late war a heavy subscription to the Victory loan was an accepted badge and index of patriotism ... Would one of your correspondents tell me just what is patriotic about investing money with absolute security at a liberal rate of interest? The sacrifice, it seems to me, is all with the man who couldn't afford to buy bonds.[10]

Some letters spoke to the sentiments of the thousands who were silently holding their bonds.

Within the finance department, where the corps of temporary clerical assistants swelled to over 1,000, work on bond transfers, exchanges, refunds, and conversions became integral; the employees who dealt with the business profits and income taxes constituted another contingent. In May 1920, during its last year in operation, a "special campaign" was conducted by the Victory Loan Special Committee to sell bonds that it was holding from large sell-offs. Evidence points to large companies in both Canada and the United States pulling out of Victory Bonds altogether.[11] Many of them knew that, regardless of any original patriotic motivation, they would have to unload, convert, or redefine their investment strategies. After 1921, insurance companies, whose substantial investment and use of Dominion War Loan and Victory Bonds can be tracked, began selling off higher-priced tax-free bonds to buy cheaper taxable issues, divesting, and re-entering the mortgage-lending field, where business had declined because of the war loans and good crops. Such restructuring occurred worldwide. And there were other consequences in Canada. At the convention of the Canada Mortgage Loan Association in Winnipeg in May 1921, Victor Evan Gray, Ontario's superintendent of insurance, explained that "the exploitation of the Canadian field by Victory Loan campaigns and tremendous issues of Provincial and municipal securities at attractive rates of interest had put [conventional] loan companies at a disadvantage."[12]

Whatever the business impact, Victory Loan campaigns lingered in the public consciousness as a sign of bond house expertise and sometimes as a model for security sales and for the campaigns of organizations as varied as the National Council of Education and the Forward Movement of the Protestant churches. In an address in Toronto in July 1920, Major Frederick James Ney, executive secretary of the National Council of Education, wished that the energy of the Victory Loan campaigns could be applied to the cause of education. In 1921,

Saskatchewan's sale of farm-loan debentures was conducted through a newspaper push similar to the Victory Loan campaign "but on a smaller scale." British Columbia contemplated, and then abandoned, the idea of a domestic loan "along the line of the Victory Loan campaigns." By 1921, a market-centric overview of all the war loans was possible. In its annual review at the beginning of 1921, the *Monetary Times* (Toronto) published "The Market Record of Canadian War Loan Issues," complete with a tables of prices and observations far removed from campaign propaganda.[13] Through the early 1920s, numerous authorities attested to the public's interest in securities.

Following the Liberals' defeat of the exhausted Unionist government in December 1921, accounts emerged in Commons debates of plutocratic bond hoarders and tight rural credit, with western farmers hard-pressed by an agricultural downturn selling their Victory Bonds to save their farms, in some cases because the bonds were rejected as security for loans. Large amounts of bonds continued to be held by the public, but their appeal had changed. The new minister of finance, William Stevens Fielding, had no interest in the persistent recession but sought only to table a noninterventionist budget, balanced by sharply reducing government expenditure and by doubling the federal sales tax.[14]

Beginning in 1922, coverage of the government's conversion and refunding issues referred to loan "drives" and special "campaigns," but these reports were limited to published prospectuses, upbeat newspaper accounts, and dealers' advertisements – a purely market realm without the visual and sonic publicity of 1917–19. At the same time, perspectives on war "propaganda" seemed to have shifted. In trade-journal coverage from the early 1920s, propaganda was regarded as "disinterested" or "evil" news, or it was treated as simply informational. Clearly, financial need had moved from conflict to providing "credit to the Dominion in these times when money to keep the country's business going 'is not growing on the lower branches.'" The success of the conversion loan of 1922, open only to the holders of five- and ten-year bonds from 1917, the *Globe* (Toronto) observed, "signifies a lively appreciation by the country of 'The Little Grey Man's' [Fielding's] concession to wartime patriotism." But the remark seems offhand. The excitement was gone. Discussing the refunding loan of 1923, *Saturday Night* (Toronto) concluded, "All the machinery which accompanied the popular campaigns during the war is left out of the present appeal."[15] Refunding mattered, not just to a new government, which could not ignore it, but also to those who, for whatever reason, had invested in their country. Various accounts, financial and otherwise, attest to the societal impact of war bonds. In his annual report in 1928, Ontario's minister of agriculture, John Strickler

Martin, himself a farmer, claimed that farmers preferred bonds over farm mortgages for their "greater convenience." Bonds were "a new field opened up to the farmer by the educational processes of the Victory Loan campaign during the war."[16] The claim may be feasible. At the federal level, publicity for the several conversion and refunding loans, as well as for the National Service Loan of 1931, tried to evoke the spirit of the Great War loans, but the atmosphere could not be duplicated.

Part 3
Newfoundland and the Canadian Connection

10

Finance in Newfoundland and the Campaign of 1918

Prior to the Great War, public finance in Newfoundland, a self-governing dominion, had one foot in Britain and the other in North America. Major loans were traditionally placed in London.[1] In 1894, after the crash of commercial banks in St. John's, the Bank of Montreal opened a branch there and soon became the government's banker and source of temporary loans. Newfoundland's securities were listed alongside those of Canada's provinces in Canadian stock exchanges and newspapers. There were affinities, too, between the Maritimes and Newfoundland in shipping and industry.

As in Canada, the eruption of war created immediate financial demand. In early September 1914, through the Volunteer Force Loan Act, Newfoundland's legislature authorized a $250,000 loan to raise a regiment, believing that the war would last for only a few months. In December, the *Evening Telegram* (St. John's), citing a weak investment climate, reported the inadvisability of any loan.[2] What did come to Newfoundland that fall were advances from Britain's National War Loan and the Bank of Montreal. After the first year of war, the government benefited from financial surpluses resulting from increased exports and customs duties.[3] As well, a death duty had been introduced in 1914. A business-profits tax would follow in 1917 and an income war tax in 1918; on the latter, Newfoundland's Department of Finance referenced Canada's Tax Act. In June 1916, with war expenditures doubling, the government of Sir Edward Patrick Morris secured a three-year loan at 5 percent for $5 million from an American-Canadian syndicate to fund the war and Newfoundland's branch railways and to repay the British Treasury and the bank. Launched by a syndicate comprised of Lee, Higginson and Company of Boston, A.E. Ames and Company and Dominion Securities of Toronto, and William A. Read and Company of New York, the issue, Newfoundland's first venture into the American market, sold within a day of its public offering. Much of it was disposed of in Canada, the *Globe* reported, suggesting that Newfoundland's public may have seen little of the issue, which would be refunded through Wood, Gundy and Company of Toronto in 1919.[4]

In 1917, after the 1916 money was exhausted – demand was incessant – the government secured a further imperial loan for £400,000 ($1.5 million) and authorized a $3 million loan for military and naval purposes.[5] To pay down debt, Newfoundland purchased Britain's treasury bills, among other assets. Fearful of high interest and exchange rates and possible local reluctance to invest, Morris had rejected calls to float a loan domestically.[6] In August 1917, he asked Sir Robert Laird Borden for advice from Canada's Department of Finance on a loan in the United States.[7] He went there in November, only to be turned back by a market committed to America's own war effort and second Liberty Loan. Throughout, there was politicking.[8] Writing in the *Evening Telegram*, "Patriot" blamed Morris for not raising a loan in Newfoundland when Canada aimed to raise $150 million at home, "but instead the Premier is sent to the States or England to borrow the money."[9] With reportage on British War Loans in the local press and with Canada's 1917 Victory Bonds being sold by brokers in Newfoundland, the concept of a domestic loan was not unknown.[10] A more concrete, if unheralded, instance of the monetary link to Canada, because of the war, was the switch in the production of Newfoundland's coinage from the Royal Mint in England to its branch in Ottawa in the latter part of 1917.

Following Morris's resignation at the end of 1917, finance and customs minister Michael Patrick Cashin went looking again in the United States and Canada. He was deterred by the costs and by Newfoundland's weak position internationally, despite its surging economy. In April 1918, he returned to St. John's from Canada, where he had spent "several weeks" negotiating a loan. Facing a gross funded debt of more than $34 million, in the House of Assembly on 11 May, when he presented his budget, he enthused over Canada's war loan of the past fall. Along with announcement of taxes on business profits and income and increased excise duties, a war-loan bill was passed authorizing $6 million to fund the war, to refund Morris's New York loan of 1916, and to repay the imperial advance of 1917. The tax-exempt bonds came in denominations of $50, $100, $500, and $1,000, with principal and interest payable at the Treasury Office in St. John's, the Bank of Montreal in Montreal or Toronto, or the bank's agency in New York. Applications could be made through the minister of finance in St. John's, the Bank of Montreal there, the office of any other bank, or the postmaster at any of twenty named outports and settlements. Strong bank deposits of more than $16 million, large sums in life-insurance policies, gold and silver hoarded by the public, and war-loan experiences elsewhere led the government to believe that the loan would meet with success, but it reasoned that, given Newfoundland's low standing in international finance, the loan had to have attractive terms.

Known as the "Victory Loan," it would be released in two blocks. The first, for $2 million, was taken up by a syndicate of three Toronto bond houses, key players in Canada's war loan of 1917: Wood, Gundy, Dominion Securities, and A.E. Ames. Formally issued on 1 June at par with an exceptionally high interest rate of six and a-half percent in a competitive market, it had been taken up the day before by the syndicate. It promptly took another $1 million, most of which was absorbed within days. The offering in Canada, made with the permission of its finance minister, was the "centre of attraction in financial circles in Toronto."[11] The second block, for $2 million, was seen by the *Western Star* in Curling (now part of Corner Brook) as "the first Government loan placed upon the Newfoundland market." Looking to display self-sufficiency, the government recognized calls for Newfoundland to pay its way. The *Evening Telegram,* which grumbled about the press censor's surveillance of loan stories, stoutly called for support for the "local loan." Ignoring the syndicate's takings, Cashin claimed that money would be hard to come by "outside the island."

Newfoundland's Victory Loan drive of 18 June to 27 July was conducted by Cashin and a special committee (mostly newspapermen) assisted by the Women's Patriotic Association, a representative of the Toronto syndicate, and a Victory Loan organizer from Canada. The campaign brought in almost $3,509,000 from 1,838 subscribers, about half of them from St. John's, where brokers and banks were eager to offer bonds, with merchants happy to buy them. Not every broker had been enthusiastic. J.J. Lacey and Company initially disliked bonds and, with nationalistic pride, the prospect of so much of the loan going to "outsiders." Seeing the results, however, the company came around to the idea of them. By 27 June, $2 million had already been subscribed, and the government moved to increase the loan and to accept the oversubscription, which it had anticipated.[12]

In early 1919, to meet the maturity of the New York loan of 1916, Cashin sought a refunding loan in Canada or the United States. Tenders were called that spring. On 1 June, the government issued a twenty-year loan at five and a-half percent for $5 million through Wood, Gundy, acting for a Canadian-American syndicate. This loan by Newfoundland was "the largest individual Government bond issue ever offered to Canadian bond houses for tender," the *Globe* reported.[13] It is estimated that in total the war cost Newfoundland about $35 million, including the war loans, interest, pensions, and demobilization expenses. The loans totalled $13,400,000, and the Newfoundland Regiment consumed more than $16 million. The total expense did much to boost the country's debt from $30.5 million in the fiscal year 1913–14 to $42 million in 1918–19, a lasting load that would be a major factor in Newfoundland's loss of self-government.[14] At the same time, alongside other Newfoundland securities (which had a pre-war presence in mixes of assets in Canadian hands), volumes of 1918 and 1919 bonds quickly appeared in the portfolios of Canadian corporations, notably insurance companies.[15]

Dragged down further by economic collapse and then the Depression, the debt hit more than $97 million by the time of Britain's 1933 Newfoundland Royal Commission (known as the Amulree Commission after its chairman, William Warrender Mackenzie, 1st Baron Amulree), which recommended Britain's temporary takeover of Newfoundland's government. Between 1918 and 1932, to stay afloat, it had been forced to scramble for loans annually, often engaging Canadian, London, and New York financiers while facing domestic questions about its ability to even pay interest and about the shocking prospect of defaults. At least one proposed loan was abandoned after there were no tenders to handle it. The financial manoeuvring, including the retirement of wartime loans, was desperate and perplex, as were the entwined straits of St. John's city bonds. Newfoundland's wartime funding of military involvement and the costly Newfoundland Railway left a legacy of enormous consequence, including dependence on Canada's financial sector and bank branches in Newfoundland. Commenting in 1933 on its financial crisis of 1932, Canada's prime minister, Richard Bedford Bennett, observed that "Newfoundland is served by Canadian banks and has long been regarded as being within the Canadian banking zone."[16] During the second war, riding a wave of prosperity, Newfoundland was able to loan money to a beleaguered United Kingdom in 1941 and 1942,[17] in remarkable contrast to the island's years of precarious financial survival.

Campaign of 1918

The marketing of Newfoundland's war loans had drawn from Canadian and British experience, but the island's small population, sea-bound geography, and limited advertising resources posed challenges. So, too, as in Canada, did the concept of security ownership. The degree of public participation in Newfoundland's early loans is unclear. On the verge of the 1916 loan, which was sold offshore through a syndicate, Bonavista's member of the House of Assembly, William Ford Coaker, who supported the war effort, asked "how many of our local Croesuses have ever subscribed to our war loans?"[18] Newfoundland's loan of 1918 was orchestrated by finance minister Michael Cashin, who had gone to Canada that spring. The trip not only generated $3 million, and then another $1 million, but also opened up access to Victory Loan personnel and publicity materials in Canada. Back in Newfoundland, Cashin also launched the loan for $2 million that would run from 18 June to 27 July, including one extension. It was heavily oversubscribed, as were Canada's patriotically fuelled domestic loans. Like much of Newfoundland's war effort, partly because of the scattered

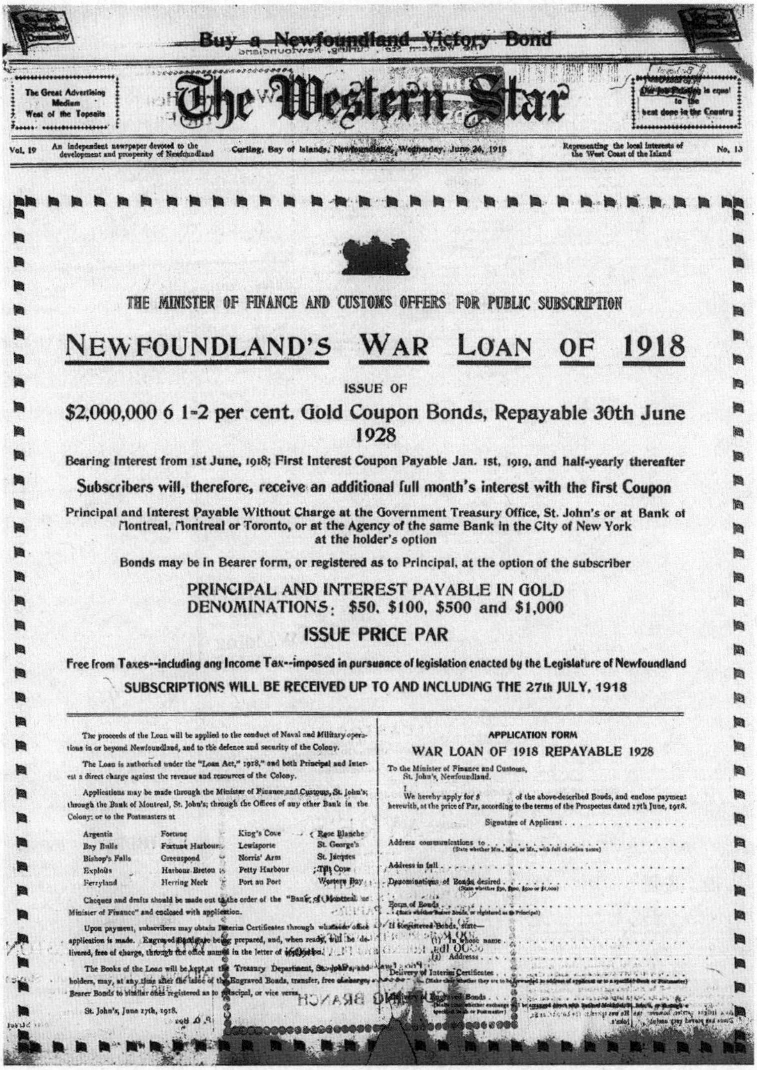

Buy a Newfoundland Victory Bond

The Great Advertising Medium West of the Topsails

The Western Star

Our Job Printing is equal to the best done in the Country

Vol. 19 | An independent newspaper devoted to the development and prosperity of Newfoundland | Curling, Bay of Islands, Newfoundland, Wednesday, June 26, 1918 | Representing the local Interests of the West Coast of the Island | No. 13

THE MINISTER OF FINANCE AND CUSTOMS OFFERS FOR PUBLIC SUBSCRIPTION

NEWFOUNDLAND'S WAR LOAN OF 1918

ISSUE OF

$2,000,000 6 1-2 per cent. Gold Coupon Bonds, Repayable 30th June 1928

Bearing Interest from 1st June, 1918; First Interest Coupon Payable Jan. 1st, 1919, and half-yearly thereafter

Subscribers will, therefore, receive an additional full month's interest with the first Coupon

Principal and Interest Payable Without Charge at the Government Treasury Office, St. John's or at Bank of Montreal, Montreal or Toronto, or at the Agency of the same Bank in the City of New York at the holder's option

Bonds may be in Bearer form, or registered as to Principal, at the option of the subscriber

PRINCIPAL AND INTEREST PAYABLE IN GOLD
DENOMINATIONS: $50. $100, $500 and $1,000

ISSUE PRICE PAR

Free from Taxes--including any Income Tax--imposed in pursuance of legislation enacted by the Legislature of Newfoundland

SUBSCRIPTIONS WILL BE RECEIVED UP TO AND INCLUDING THE 27th JULY, 1918

The proceeds of the Loan will be applied to the conduct of Naval and Military operations in or beyond Newfoundland, and to the defence and security of the Colony.

The Loan is authorized under the "Loan Act," 1918," and both Principal and Interest a direct charge against the revenue and resources of the Colony.

Applications may be made through the Minister of Finance and Customs, St. John's; through the Bank of Montreal, St. John's; through the Offices of any other Bank in the Colony; or to the Postmasters at

Argentia	Fortune	King's Cove	Rose Blanche
Bay Bulls	Fortune Harbour	Lewisporte	St. George's
Bishop's Falls	Greenspond	Norris' Arm	St. Jacques
Exploits	Harbour Breton	Petty Harbour	Tilt Cove
Ferryland	Herring Neck	Port au Port	Western Bay

Cheques and drafts should be made out to the order of the "Bank of Montreal ac Minister of Finance" and enclosed with application.

Upon payment, subscribers may obtain Interim Certificates through whatever office application is made. Engraved Bonds are being prepared, and, when ready, will be delivered, free of charge, through the office named in the letter of application.

The Books of the Loan will be kept at the Treasury Department, St. John's, and holders, may, at any time after the issue of the Engraved Bonds, transfer, free of charge, Bearer Bonds to similar ones registered as to principal, or vice versa.

St. John's, June 27th, 1918.

APPLICATION FORM

WAR LOAN OF 1918 REPAYABLE 1928

To the Minister of Finance and Customs,
St. John's, Newfoundland.

I/We hereby apply for $ of the above-described Bonds, and enclose payment herewith, at the price of Par, according to the terms of the Prospectus dated 27th June, 1918.

Signature of Applicant . . . .

Address communications to . . . .
(State whether Mrs., Miss, or Mr., with full christian name)

Address in full . . . .

Denominations of Bonds desired . . . .
(State whether $50, $100, $500 or $1,000)

Form of Bonds . . . .
(State whether Bearer Bonds, or registered as to Principal)

If Registered Bonds, state—
(1) In whose name . . . .
(2) Addresss . . . .

Delivery of Interim Certificates . . . .
(Make clear whether they are to be forwarded to address of applicant or to a specified Bank or Postmaster)

Delivery of Engraved Bonds . . . .

Bond prospectus as front-page content and advertising. | *Western Star* (Curling, NL), 26 June 1918.

nature of the outports, the loan was centred in St. John's.[19] Even then, Burin's member, John Stewart Currie, called for a "vigorous campaign." Reaction to the strong participation in the loan by St. John's merchants, alongside public support for the taxes on business profits and income, were factors in what historian Michael R. Westcott perceives as a "renegotiation of class in wartime Newfoundland."[20]

In May, Charles Alexander Cheves Bruce (a St. John's bond and investment dealer and a manager at Canada Life in Newfoundland) had taken samples and information for Wood, Gundy in Toronto for use in producing the bonds. He represented the lead underwriter in the syndicate, Dominion Securities, which agreed on 20 May not only to pay a price of 95 (the public price being par, or 100) but also to help Cashin with any local campaign. In an undated telegram (likely 1 June) to Bruce, Dominion Securities, speaking for a pleased syndicate, anticipated the placement of the additional $1 million, for which federal approval was expected: "We have undoubtedly struck psychological moment for flotation as Montreal will offer six million dollars issue next week and two or three other provincial and municipal issue of substantial amounts are to follow immediately thereafter."[21] By contrast, even with the economy doing well, the local campaign would have to face the wavering popularity of the war effort – conscription had been implemented in April – and edgy debate over Cashin's financial management. As historian Sean T. Cadigan explains, political rhetoric during the summer of 1918 was geared to strengthening resolve.[22]

John T. Stevens of Montreal, an officer at the Bank of Montreal and a knowledgeable participant in Canada's latest Victory Loan, arrived in St. John's on 5 June to conduct Newfoundland's campaign. Over the following weeks, he met with Cashin's committee, local newspapermen, the Board of Trade, and the Women's Patriotic Association, whose members were prepared to circularize its outport branches using "propaganda and any other means in our power." (Financially open-minded, the association also invested in American Liberty Bonds.) Stevens understood that in formulating any campaign, geography and conditions were different in Newfoundland. "Some of the methods followed in Canada were not workable here," he told one meeting on 12 June. No explanation was recorded.[23] The campaign would have to be centred in St. John's and taken to the outports in the form of prospectuses, application forms, and posters at post offices and plants along with the circulars of the Women's Patriotic Association. What Stevens did bring with him for distribution were bundles of Canadian Victory Loan posters that bore no Canadian identifiers, just exhortations.

The short summertime campaign included standard ingredients. Lantern slides, made of glass, were produced locally and shown in theatres in St. John's, Harbour Grace, Carbonear, Heart's Content, and Grand Falls. The small number of outport newspapers obliged with advertising; inquiries came into Cashin's department from communities such as Harbour Breton, Bay Bulls, Wabana, Brigus, and Grand Falls. Support was encouraged in sermons. Recruiters hustled to link support for the loan to calls for manpower. Advertisements and editorials, in turn, saw subscription as a form of enlistment. In the face of any German invasion (a ploy also found in Canada's Maritimes), subscription put up a defence. Display cards and posters were placed in factories and the stations of the Newfoundland Railway; banners and streamers were hung. In addition to the Canadian posters, all of which were distributed, small (28 × 21.5 cm) text-only posters were printed. Boilerplate illustrations were adapted for use in newspapers, a number of them exploiting alleged German barbarity. Newspapers still ran the usual explanatory releases, promotional plugs, and loan-related poems, and businesses sponsored advertisements and offered bonds as prizes. Some ads, just as in Canada, were of the bandwagon variety: "You bought a Victory Bond/To Help win the war and to make money/Buy a bag of Basic Slag [phosphate fertilizer] for the same good reason." Photographs of events or dignitaries elude discovery.

The *Western Star* (Corner Brook), on the island's west coast, accepted the ads and published the loan's prospectus on an entire front page, but owing to distance, it refused to submit any promotional articles or editorials to the government's newly appointed press censor.[24] Because of censorship,[25] other newspapers threatened to "refrain from a full support of the Victory Loan." Cashin, who faced grumbling that he had shown favouritism in selecting papers for advertising, was solidly supported in St. John's, especially by its business community. One company, Canada Life, which backed Cashin and Bruce, subscribed for $200,000. Bonds were also bought, among others, by the Coopers' Union and by St. John's Lodge of the Society of United Fishermen. On 1 July, to capitalize on patriotism, campaigners took full advantage of national celebrations of the Royal Newfoundland Regiment's part in the war, notably its devastating losses at Beaumont-Hamel, France. Local newspapers reported that the outports responded well, much as Canada's press had smiled on farmers and the rural districts; participation likely varied by region. Specific results from the outports and towns other than St. John's were scarcely reported, although over the spring, summer, and fall, the city's newspapers followed war loans in Canada, Britain, the United States, and Australia.

Evidence of individual action is scant. St. John's tinsmith William J. Clouston subscribed on a modest scale. At his death, John Francis Williams, a planter (fisherman) in Bay Bulls, would leave a $1,000 bond to his sisters. Grand Falls businessman Josiah Goodyear left bonds from both Newfoundland and Canada to his wife. Overall, the success of the loan, which had been carefully calculated, was roundly applauded. To the *Evening Telegram*, it showed the world that Newfoundland was in the war to the finish, even if much of the loan had been taken by "outside investors."[26] At the same time it added considerably to the country's debt. Apart from this impact, Newfoundland's bonds found their way into society. In the spring of 1919, for instance, an enterprising group of children proposed to buy one and use the proceeds from its coupons to repair a playground. The previous November, a request had come in from Detroit for posters and advertising matter for one school's "historical collection." After 1918 and 1919, Newfoundland's scramble for financing was devoid of much public campaigning.

Part 4
Consensus and Resistance

11

The Limits of Patriotism

The national campaigns for Canada's war loans advanced new boundaries for civic inclusion and resolve, the counterpart to the "new national imaginary" seen by historian Julia C. Ott in America's loans.[1] Canada's loan publicists and the federal government interpreted oversubscription as countrywide consensus. As one campaigner in Manitoba put it, the Victory Loan was meant to "consolidate the country," a mythic gloss at cross-purposes with established strains of nativism and cultural difference. In Montreal, at odds with nationalist sentiments, one English-language team captain believed that the loan would pull people together in a "common cause" and "make of us all better and true Canadians." In such views, the loans represented forceful shows of national determination, marked by grand and virtuous messages to Germany of democratic defiance. Campaigning on regional interest, be it British Columbia timber or maritime shipping, stressed a community identity. Thomas White had proclaimed this ideal of unified purpose and voluntary effort in a speech on the launch of the Canadian Patriotic Fund's campaign in February 1917: "We have imposed on ourselves heavy taxation, pledged the national credit, subscribed the loans to amounts which before the outbreak of the war we would have regarded as beyond the utmost of our power; and it has all been done voluntarily, without compulsion, without constraint, without even persuasion on the part of any external authority." But, as historian Doug Owram explains, the voluntarist urge was being challenged by "direct compulsion to ensure maximum effort to win the war," starting with the War Measures Act.[2] Maximum effort clothed as voluntarist backing would fully show in the Victory Loans in the form of social pressures and relentless propaganda.

In reality, the response was not one of total unity. As state intrusion in civilian life intensified, resistance mounted. Some Canadians offered only conditional support to the loan campaigns, others rejected them outright, and some subscribed but objected to the war effort on other grounds. The loans were interventionist in the securities market and relied, in the war's hyper-nationalist climate, on social coercion through shaming and patriotic exhortation, strategies that raised hackles in some quarters. The steady publicity given to the so-called small investor and enthusiasms for the loans masked a diversity of response. Substantial efforts, both official and nongovernmental, were initiated "to withdraw ideas from public discussion."[3] Wartime censorship probably suppressed much opinion and effort against the loans, and some outspoken critics met with harassment. Often, instances of criticism, resistance, or nonconformity were held up to the sanitizing light of financing and winning the war. An examination of the surviving evidence of resistance offers a window into how the campaigns strove to build consensus or fell short, especially where they reinforced the isolation of minority groups or communities. Dissent came to be heard in vastly different ways: there was no one avenue in a context where the machinery for containing and suppressing dissent far outweighed the means of expressing it.

Criticism of wartime funding emerged early. In October 1914, the Winnipeg labour journal *The Voice* asked how the war would be paid for. Its prophetic answer was framed by class: "To a large degree by government loans in the shape of bond issues, which future generations must stagger under ... One class will profit. That is the investing class, the people with ready capital."[4] In April 1915, convinced that increased tariffs would hurt consumers, the *Globe* felt that borrowing would further "burden the Canadian people and deceive them into believing the war responsible."[5] Such sentiment would simmer. Instances of refusal to contribute to the Canadian Patriotic Fund and the Red Cross became entangled with charges of seditious utterance.[6] The communal goals of the war loans did much to obscure complaint or nonparticipation, a screen that would persist in the early histories of the conflict, where, historian Robert Teigrob observes, "many of the less consensual aspects of the Great War story" are downplayed.[7] But there were objections and reservations, as evidenced by the disgruntled letters sent to the Department of Finance and by unproductive canvassing. There were complaints about the circusy methods employed in campaigns but nothing that constituted a solid wave of dissatisfaction. By and large, grievances published in the English-language press dealt with the mechanics and terms of the loans and with their impact on the national debt. Then there was the inconsistent application of federal censorship in loan matters. French-language and Liberal newspapers and labour journals tested the limits, as did some outspoken small-town papers. In 1918, the *Burk's Falls Arrow* (Burk's Falls, Ontario) objected to any expectation of free promotion for the Victory Loan, explaining that "expense accounts have never yet been satisfactorily liquidated by wind and hot air," and it criticized the huge sums spent on advertising bonds, "the demand for which was created wholly and solely by the press." In Newfoundland's campaign that year, the *Western Star* (Corner Brook) baulked at the prospect of censorship in its response to the government's request for support of the loan.

Starting in 1915, the war loans generated a stream of negative, often passionate, comment from within varied sectors: the financial community, labour, and an assortment of socialists. Although improved incomes would gradually allow workers to subscribe in large numbers, labour voices such as the *British Columbia Federationist* (Vancouver), amidst skirmishes with Canada's chief press censor, opposed the burden being laid on posterity and the benefit to "financial agents." The high costs of White's New York borrowings in 1917 were prime targets. Allied loans secured there, even when backed by the "gilt-edged securities" of capitalist financiers, could not go on forever, argued the Socialist Party of Canada's *Western Clarion* (Vancouver), which would be shut down by the censor in 1918. Other voices persisted. The *Canadian Forward* (Toronto), the journal of the moderate Social Democratic Party, consistently opposed war loans as capitalist platforms.

Rarely did socialists and objectors find untrammelled expression in the mainstream press. During Victory Loan campaigns they could be easy foils, the stuff of human-interest stories but with no cohesive narrative. James Marren, a Toronto barber and avowed Marxist, was able to express his view through the *Globe* on 2 September 1916: all "true Socialists" should reject any loan. Suppression and public shaming were potent tools, which could make for smug patriotic reports. In one instance, during the lead-up to the armistice in 1918, the intersection of King and Yonge Streets in Toronto teamed with people anxious for news and emotional release, along with bond canvassers eager to hook subscribers. One evening, a busload of returned soldiers stopped to play patriotic music in support of the loan drive, whereupon an unnamed woman exclaimed, "Look what they are doing to get the people to buy bonds. The miserable Government." She bravely added, "I am a Socialist, I am." Admonished by a female reporter from the *Toronto Daily Star* the woman backed off, but the reporter trailed her to ensure that she would not rail "against the Government and the boys at the front again."[8]

Whereas the Dominion War Loans of 1915–17 had generated little discernible opposition outside of Parliament, in part because of their relatively low-key promotion and weak public familiarity, the Victory Loans, like the Military Service Act and conscription, became lightning rods for intense sentiments. In addition to logistical problems, there was partisan antipathy in the newspapers, and encounters with indifference and outright hostility among the population.

Domestic borrowing on the principles that prevailed at the start of the war – the healing of social divisions, voluntarism, short duration, and the temporary diversion of capital – broke down as the war dragged on.[9] Underlying much grumbling was the inequitable distribution of its burdens. In some quarters, the loans of 1917–19 generated debate over social inequalities. One newspaper reported in October 1918 that because the influenza put strain on the savings of "workingmen," greater responsibility for subscription was placed on the shoulders of the "well-to-do." In November 1917, the *Alberta Non-Partisan*, a leftist newspaper in Calgary, had argued that the failure to conscript wealth degraded the sacrifice of human life. Further, it deplored the protrusion of the loan into the schools, where campaigning and the distribution of subscribers' buttons shamed "the poor boy who could not afford a nickel towards the loan."[10] Similar complaints surfaced elsewhere, but with little effect. Trenchant critiques would come later, notably from such economists as John James Deutsch in 1940 and R. Craig McIvor in 1958, both of whom saw the inequality resulting from the shift of income from low-level earners to business-profit surpluses, which in turn were poured into the war loans.[11] Inflation was an expedient necessity that would help the country to get the money for the war, although with a dampening impact on real incomes. In September 1939, harking back in the government's budget for another war, acting finance minister James Lorimer Ilsley rationalized, "It was this reduction in the real income of one section of the community and the creation of large surpluses in the hands of other sections willing to lend to the government that in considerable part at least made possible Canada's remarkable record in mobilizing public savings through the various war and victory loan programs."[12] Sacrifice and national unity of purpose were paramount, ran this reasoning.

Opposition to or support for the war loans did not follow clear-cut lines, resulting in a ragged pattern that confounded notions of consensus. Dichotomies could be found in many sectors. Reaction in the labour movement was particularly diverse. In October 1918, on the invitation of White, who wanted broad, symbolic support, the loan's dominion executive was joined by the president of the Trades and Labor Congress of Canada, Thomas Moore, and its secretary treasurer, Patrick Martin Moore, even though days before Thomas Moore had protested an anti-strike order-in-council.[13] At its annual convention in November, the congress resolved to urge workers to subscribe, and many labour groups did or backed employee subscription programs.

Local circumstances could influence positions on the loans. A bitter strike in 1917 at a smelter in Trail, British Columbia, over the eight-hour day for workers, led to refusals to subscribe and, on 13 November, a symbolic bonfire of Victory Loan literature. In the federal election that year, insurance-claims adjuster James H.H. Ballantyne, the Labor candidate in East York, Ontario, took issue with loan canvassers who complimented each other on their patriotism while pulling in $500 apiece for three weeks of work. In British Columbia, the 1918 anti-strike order set back the provincial loan committee's appeals to labour.[14] Writing in October 1918 in the *British Columbia Federationist* about support among mine workers at Fernie and Michel, stationary engineer Walter Head offered this pithy summary: "They are patriots when they boost the Victory Loan, and alien enemies when they strike for fair working conditions."[15] In Vancouver, the local boilermakers' union, in response to the mayor's letter for support of the loan, stated that "as the members of the organization were only earning barely sufficient to enable them to live they could not see their way to participate in the loan." The musicians' and the hotel and restaurant employees' unions, however, voted to lend their support. At Lyall's Shipyard in North Vancouver, workers blocked MP Sanford Johnston Crowe's entry to speak about the loan because of his opposition to a recent strike by laundry workers. In contrast, Liberty Loan workers from Seattle's shipyards and labour organizations, as well as James A. Duncan, secretary of Seattle's Central Labor Council, went to Vancouver at their own expense to help in the Victory Loan campaign. News of this aid spread to newspapers in eastern Canada. In 1919, a host of French and English labour organizations sponsored advertising for the loan. The loan was decried by workers Roger Ernest Bray and James Shaver Woodsworth, participants in the Winnipeg General Strike, who believed that war loans and growing debt were inflationary and fuelled the costs of living. In the aftermath of the strike, the radical press disparaged the loan, although ironically the *British Columbia Federationist* and the *Western Labor News* (Winnipeg) urged workers to buy Victory Bonds in order to pay the legal expenses of prosecuted labour leaders.[16]

Among military veterans, responses also varied. During the war, many served effectively as loan spokesmen and representatives of soldierly sacrifice. In 1919, veterans' support continued, but inflammatory issues such as benefits and gratuities could generate heated reaction at Victory Loan meetings. Continuing calls for the conscription of wealth (long a solution in the eyes of radical labour and farmers) came with outright opposition to the loan in Alberta from the strident Great War Next-of-Kin Association and some branches of the Great War Veterans' Association.[17] Opinions on the Victory Loans, especially in the aftermath of the war, were not always black-and-white. Veterans reflected the range, as did those social reformers who paid lip service to the loans but felt that they diverted support from needy causes.

Even in the midst of patriotic flurry, debates and reproaches over indifferences to the loans and food conservation belied doubts and social inequalities. White and food controller William John Hanna, like countless recruiters, recognized the problems of engagement that were posed for their campaigns by the war's remoteness, which they valiantly tried to overcome through propaganda.

For the first Dominion War Loan in 1915, 1 in 321 subscribed. For the Victory Loan of late 1917, the ratio moved to 1 in 9.62,[18] a stunning increase, but a number of Canadians still did not subscribe: small-wage earners, migrant workers, the young and the elderly, and the outright objectors for philosophical, religious, or political reasons. After White's mass mailing to push war-savings certificates in early 1917, some in straightened circumstances had felt compelled at least to respond. Madame René Belisle of Saint-André-Avellin, Quebec, wrote the minister on 1 March, "I have a family and then I am obliged to get my money for their living and instruction." From Montreal, Marie-Laure Thérien, a widow, explained on 21 March that she would not be buying since she had to work and was often ill. Arthur Cholette, an Ottawa Valley merchant, claimed that farmers had no spare money to invest. Other respondents, some from remote places, provided a variety of feedback. E. Appleton of the Indian Lake Lumber Company at Osaquan, in northwest Ontario, stated that foreign-born employees were likely to take their savings with them after the season.[19]

The reasons unearthed also included subsistence wages, rising costs of living, misunderstanding of investment, or preference for less expensive forms of support, such as tobacco, sock, and relief funds. In a number of factories, employees who signed up to subscribe moved on or defaulted. And, as canvassers discovered, some segments of the populace were simply indifferent to the war.[20] As in drives for other causes, canvassers met with peripheral, deflective reasons for not subscribing.

A multitude of bond-related grievances were recounted in Parliament and the press. Whereas MPs expressing grievances in Parliament enjoyed immunity, citizens with complaints could be shamed or put down. At the end of the 1919 campaign in Regina, for instance, the *Morning Leader* did just that to unnamed skeptics of its lament over lagging subscriptions, a common practice meant to get them over the top. The critics felt that this lament was crying wolf, but the paper huffily dismissed them by throwing up a shield of dollars pledged. In his travels across Saskatchewan for the Victory Loan, real-estate agent and grain-trade expert John Heber Haslam encountered districts where attitudes toward the war and the Victory Loan were "very apathetic."[21] Often, such a response was explained in ethnic or linguistic terms.

Although never precisely articulated by the architects of the Victory Loan campaigns, the ethnic strategy, common in America's Liberty Loan drives,[22] was one way to bring people "together in a common cause," as participants in Canada's loans put it in 1917. Reaching for every dollar, loan organizers embraced groups otherwise marginalized. The results of the strategy are patchy, most often filtered through campaign reports in the press. Canvassers in

WORKING FOR VICTORY LOAN

These Chinese citizens are on the special committee appointed by Fred Hess, chairman of the teams committee of the local Victory Loan executive, who are working for subscribers to the loan among the Orientals in Chinatown. Reading from left to right: Ho Lem, Louie Khong, Wong Man Chung and Charlie Yee Yock Sam.

Chinese Special Committee, Calgary, 1917. It was formed to canvass "the Orientals in Chinatown" for Victory Bond subscriptions. One member, businessman Louis ("Luey") Kheong (second from left), had been active in the debate over its relocation in 1910 and was a vocal critic of racial discrimination. | *Calgary Daily Herald*, 19 November 1917.

Toronto's clothing-trade district, for instance, stated in 1917 that "the response from the Jewish element has shown a high degree of patriotism among this class of the community." There was nothing in the Department of Finance or the loan organization like the foreign-language division of the American Treasury, which tabulated subscriptions by ethnic and language groups. It was able to track the astonishingly high percentage (46.5) of subscribers of foreign birth or parentage in the fourth Liberty Loan in 1918.[23] Despite this evidential vacuum, some anecdotal evidence exists. The *Regina Morning Leader* reported subscriptions by Belgians, Germans, Galicians, Austrians, and Doukhobors. In Vancouver, the Japanese were approached, as were Mennonites in Ontario and on the Prairies, Ukrainians in Winnipeg, Austrians in Sudbury, Greeks in Vancouver, Toronto, and Quebec City, Poles in Toronto and Calgary, Italians in Sault Ste. Marie, Chinese in Victoria, Vancouver, Calgary, Winnipeg, Toronto, Brantford, and Fort William, and Jews in Toronto, Montreal, Winnipeg, and Regina. Even after federal legislation stripped many Ukrainian Canadians of their right to vote in 1917, *Ukrains'kyi Holos* (Winnipeg) was still ready to urge the purchase of Victory Bonds.

In a few communities, financial objectives were assigned to those religious or ethnic groups whose members did their own canvassing and organization, with minimal, sometimes patronizing, commentary in published reports. Court and immigration-agency interpreters were employed, linguistic and cultural differences could create barriers, and churches and societies were often sponsoring bodies. Support of the loans could draw attention to organizations such as the Zionist Federation of Canada and the Red Magen David Association (a Jewish women's wartime charity) in Montreal, the Chinese Empire Reform Association in Vancouver, the Toronto Chinese Christian Association, and the Chinese Nationalist League, which had branches in a number of Canadian cities. Undoubtedly, much of the response also had patriotic, investment-driven motivation. "Sure, me good Canadian Austrian," Mike Yustuk, who was "known" around the Canadian Northern Railway docks, told the *Port Arthur News-Chronicle* after he had subscribed for $2,400 in 1918. Communities such as the Greeks in Toronto had their own organization, and the Poles there contributed through St. Stanislaus Kostka Parish and the Polish National Society, even with its socialist elements. Others had go-betweens. In 1917, Toronto's "Chinese organization," which involved intermediaries, was headed by John Hammond, J.P. Sam, and Mark Moon, who brought in 200 applications for $50 bonds. It was only after "considerable" inducement by bond salesmen, however, that the "race" had signed on. Victoria's Chinatown was canvassed in 1918 by hustler Harry Hastings, an anti-racist businessman whose mother was Chinese. He raised $40,000. Responses could mix with racist tone. In 1918, Chinese subscribers in Toronto were regarded as "wise Celestials," a reference perhaps to the ancient Celestial Empire. During the 1919 campaign in Fort William, with mention of the subscription of local laundryman Jim Lee, the canvass of the city's "Chinamen" was expected to bring "surprising results." A parodic quotation in the *Daily Times-Journal* read, "Victly bondee allee samee good buyee." The subscription by the Toronto branch of the Union Insurance Society of Canton warranted this stretch of a headline in the *Vancouver Daily Star:* "Arm of Victory Loan Reaches to Land of Orientals."[24] In all the communities where Chinese subscribed, they did so despite the infamous federal head tax on Chinese immigrants.

Not every ethnic or religious group received sympathetic attention during the loan campaigns, during which racist prejudices were only thinly veiled. In British Columbia, on the Pacific Rim, discriminatory immigration policy was particularly strong.[25] Hindu, Chinese, and Japanese residents had been denied voting rights, on top of the head taxes for the Chinese. Provincial loan chairman William Harold Malkin appealed to the small Hindu community for support in November 1918, only to hear back of their grievances with the post office over the disappearance of money orders that they were trying to send back to India. An oblivious Malkin wondered why Hindus should press such "supposed grievances" when they enjoyed "a prosperity never before known to them." More to his liking were the subscriptions from other ethnic groups, which he reported at campaign's end in a conventional narrative: "A word must be said as to the work done and the subscriptions made by the foreign element of the population. A rough analysis of the subscriptions shows that $529,000 was subscribed by European foreigners and $308,200 by Asiatics, chiefly Japanese."[26] Omission in reportage sometimes spoke volumes. "All the white employees of the Hastings sawmill, Vancouver, bought Victory Bonds," noted the *Western Lumberman* (Winnipeg) in December 1918, with no mention of the ethnic groups employed there.[27] Such groups were only marginally represented in the ranks of the loan organizations as translators and team leaders. In a climate of hostility, insinuations flew. After the campaign of 1919 in British Columbia, John Nelson of the *Vancouver World* and chair of the press and news-feature committee prepared a congratulatory analysis of the campaign work of the press province-wide, except for one missing sector that he identified in an open letter: "The racial press – Chinese, Japanese, Scandinavian, etc. – all of whom did wonderfully well, are not included in this compilation owing to the difficulty of getting measurements [of the inches of space] of their copy." The letter gives rise to questions about, among other possible factors, cooperative intent and newspaper composition.[28]

In contrast, the pacifist Mennonites of Ontario and the Prairies were defended by their MPs and received special attention from the Department of Finance. They had contributed to the humanitarian work of the Red Cross Society and the benevolent efforts of the Patriotic Fund, but the Victory Loans – to fund the waging of war – proved a sticking point. In November 1917, the Mennonites of north Waterloo County in Ontario refused to subscribe on the conscientious grounds that the loan was equivalent to taking part in the war. To "combat this view," local loan officials pointed out, in conventional campaign language, that Canada's prosperity depended on the "success or failure" of the loan.[29] When he got wind of the situation, and hoping to connect with the group's philanthropic leanings, White immediately telegrammed their head, assuring them "that the large proceeds of the loan will be spent for humanitarian purposes connected with the war, as, for instance, in payment for foodstuffs for Great Britain."[30]

Saskatchewan's Mennonites were divided in their response both to national registration and to funding drives. Some, on pacifist grounds, were willing to have their contributions used for foodstuffs and relief efforts but not military purposes. Mennonite objections to the Victory Loan were nonetheless unpopular with the wider population and generated criticism. When the *Steinbach Post* (Steinbach, Manitoba) initially refused to accept a paid advertisement for the loan in 1917, Canada's chief press censor, Ernest John Chambers, and the Canadian Press Association, which saw the Mennonites as "alien enemies in our midst," took offence. Yet a cautious justice department refused to take action. In light of Chambers's clampdowns elsewhere, the conclusion of historian Adolf Ens – that the government, fearing backlash, "wanted as little of the mailed-fist approach in censorship as possible"[31] – seems incomplete. In November 1918, loan advertisements in the *Steinbach Post* would explicitly target the Mennonites.[32]

In December 1917, White had received from the Sommerfeld congregation in Manitoba its semi-annual donation, in lieu of a loan subscription, for the benefit of war widows, orphans, and cripples. The money was placed with the Board of Pension Commissioners for Canada. At the start of the 1918 campaign, moving to resolve Mennonite objections, the finance minister recognized the "conscientious scruples" of the Hutterite and Mennonite colonies in the Magrath district of Alberta and authorized their subscriptions, made even in the midst of devastating crop failures, to go into a trust for disbursement to the Red Cross and other organizations. "Special accommodation," including donations to convalescent homes and hospitals, was also extended in Saskatchewan, Manitoba, and Ontario, and in the Tofield district of Alberta, the Mennonites subscribed directly. Such mixed practices were continued in 1919 through negotiations involving White's successor. Despite purchases estimated at $600,000 to $700,000, Ens figures that Mennonites, for the most part, rejected the loans.[33] Some of the religious minorities that contributed drew little attention. With high financial expectations but much lower returns, the loan's Rosthern subdivision in central Saskatchewan was canvassed, because of its mostly foreign-born population, according to "faith": Mennonite (New Church, Old Church, Brethren), German Lutheran, German Evangelical, German Roman Catholic, Swedenborgian, Adventist, Jews, "Galicians," "French," and "English-speaking." In the Yorkton district, foreign-born residents, largely farmers, also subscribed, with the communal Doukhobors at Veregin in for an impressive $25,000.

An overall view of opposition or support in Canada's ethnic and cultural groups is almost impossible to construct. How the loans fared in the Black communities of Ontario and Nova Scotia or in many farming regions not surveyed by newspapers, for example, awaits deeper local research. Responses among First Nations are rarely noted in Victory Loan campaign reports. Indigenous peoples gave generously to the Canadian Patriotic Fund and other war charities (some $45,000), doing so with little expectation of return, as families could not receive payments from the fund because formally they were wards of the government. The Department of Indian Affairs rejected the requests of many bands to invest their trust funds in bonds on the grounds that the money belonged to the Crown. In southern Ontario, the Six Nations Council's attempt in 1917 to have its funds invested in Victory Bonds met just that fate, despite the *Globe*'s claim that residents there were buying "readily" as individuals. Elsewhere, some, such as Ga'axsta'las (Jane Constance Cook) of the Kwagu'ł society and Chief George Baptiste of the Osoyoos (Nk'Mip) Reserve, both in British Columbia, purchased bonds. Collectively, the Ojibway bands at Garden River and Batchawana, near Sault Ste. Marie, were awarded a Prince of Wales honour flag for reaching the objective of $3,000 in subscriptions. Victory Loan promotions mobilized instances of Indigenous support to spur others to contribute. According to the deputy superintendent of Indian Affairs, Duncan Campbell Scott, "The Indians responded well within their means to the Victory Loan appeal. Many of them invested their savings in this fund, and thus the part played by their race in the great struggle was rounded off by participation in every phase of war activity."[34] By the end of the war, First Nations had given enough to various war funds to be made a source of (often racist) propaganda for donations from all Canadians.[35]

Subscriptions by non-Anglos were seen as demonstrations of patriotism, but displays of resistance were used to paint them as unpatriotic, foreign, and dangerous. Demonizing, anti-German sentiment ran even higher, historian Margaret MacMillan argues, among civilians on the home front than among fighting soldiers.[36] In 1918, the government moved to suppress enemy-language publications. In areas of the country where Germanic names and ancestries were prevalent, antipathies were exacerbated by the patriotic surge of loan campaigns. Confrontations were not unusual between canvassers and Germans who declined to subscribe on grounds of homeland affinity. At the same time, in many communities with residents of German origin, there was plenty of support for the loan, among them the captains of schooners in Lunenburg County, Nova Scotia.[37] But those were not the communities that attracted attention. In September 1918, Samuel James Williams, a manufacturer in Kitchener (formerly Berlin), Ontario, told White that it was hard to sell bonds in a city with so many German "sympathizers."[38] Numerous residents of surrounding Waterloo County did indeed speak German or Pennsylvania German, many of them Mennonites, but they did not necessarily support the enemy. In Alberta, supposed German sympathies figured among the reasons given for low subscriptions. From Ladysmith, a coal-mining town on Vancouver Island, one campaigner reported in November 1918 that its 100 or so Finnish residents were reluctant to support either the Red Cross or the loan, prompting a call for action against "these pro-Germans (for they are nothing else)."

Throughout Canada's loans, there was an array of prejudices in play. At one point in the campaign in Winnipeg, 334 women working in twenty-three teams were given the undesirable job of canvassing residential districts that were "financially the least productive," an "exhausting task" made more difficult by the conscientious objectors and "German folk" they encountered.[39] That same month, during the campaign in Alberta, the Mennonites in Tofield, already hit by influenza, had to work to "dispel the race feeling that was growing up between them and their neighbours."[40] The town of Irvine, which subscribed well, still had to contend in 1919 with the "unjust impression" that it was "pro-German."[41]

On 29 October 1919, almost a year after war had ended, an article appeared in the *Toronto Daily Star* entitled "Germans Buy Bonds." It was sparked by a dominion pamphlet printed in German and circulated by the Manitoba committee of the Victory Loan. The circular was seen by Frank Albany Rowlatt, an English-born advertising agent, who wrote to ask the *Star*, "Why allow German to be printed in Canada or British territory – you can bet your boots that those old Germans who cannot read English will not subscribe to the loan." His opinion was followed by statements from George Herbert Wood, the loan's chair in Ontario, and from Alfred Ernest Ames of the dominion executive, both of whom understood the challenges of practical outreach. The release of pamphlets in several languages in targeted provinces was meant to "get the money from all classes pf people," Wood indicated, including German speakers. "We must remember that there are quite a few Germans in Canada who are loyal to this country. I don't think it is wrong for them to subscribe." The pamphlet was printed not only in German, Ames added, but also in other languages to appeal to western communities. "There are some thrifty Germans in the West, and they are good investors. There are over forty languages spoken, and circulars are printed for every tongue."[42] Ames would have known the number. The languages encountered for this study included French, English, Russian, German, Ukrainian/Ruthenian, Croatian, Armenian, Syrian, Japanese, Chinese, Polish, Hebrew, Yiddish, Finnish, Norwegian, Icelandic, Swedish, and Italian. Some languages were grouped as "Oriental" or Cyrillic. In contrast to the production of such pamphlets were the chief censor's prohibition orders against foreign-language newspapers.

Throughout much of Ontario and the West, fuelled by past swells of prejudice, the loyalty and conformity of foreign-born residents were denigrated. For the Finnish community at Ontario's Lakehead, the war enflamed a turbulence of labour activism, socialist organization, ethnic factionalism, and nativist hostility. The conservative *Canadan Uutiset* (Port Arthur) supported the war loans, even though it was banned by federal order in October–December 1918, and many Finns did subscribe. Some loan organizers were unsure how to navigate this fluid mix. At the end of October, although Fort William's committee planned to inform the district's Finnish and Ukrainian residents about the loan, the town's *Daily Times-Journal* reported that "it is not quite clear how they are going to understand this notice."[43]

Ethnic response, and its reception, varied wildly. Historian Shirley Tillotson documents depictions by nativist loan enthusiasts of foreigners carrying "wads of cash" and the ways that were construed to get at that money.[44] The use of pamphlets in multiple languages could be seen in this light. Reports of subscriptions could be inconsistent. Jews, Chinese, Greeks, Austrians, Doukhobors, Mennonites, and other sectors were branded as "foreign elements" and enemy aliens regardless of their support for the loans. In Alberta newspapers, Doukhobors were taken to task over their preference for acquiring land and Mennonites for their pacifist objections. In Toronto, the expulsion of a drunk, crippled veteran from a Greek restaurant sparked riots in August 1918. Some sources blamed "Pro-German Greeks," despite a consular statement of community loyalty and support for the Victory Loans. Elsewhere, press coverage was complicated by stereotypical or pejorative identifications, with a Ukrainian being called Austrian, foreigner, alien, Slav, Ruthenian, and, after the Russian Revolution of 1917, Bolshevik.[45] In November 1918, citing bitter feelings among organizers in one labour hot spot, Ontario's Lakehead, newspapers there praised "pro-British subscribers" but lambasted the "foreign born," the "Austrians," and "other alien classes" who worked at local grain elevators for their meagre response to the loan.[46] Redemptive undertones were not uncommon in snippets in English-language papers. An instance perhaps was the case of Peter Hellevichk of Cochrane, an "Austrian," who on his release from an internment camp in northern Ontario (likely Kapuskasing) bought $300 of Victory Bonds with the wages that he had received during internment.[47] Perhaps, too, there was the resentment of bondholding by "foreigners." Among the so-called aliens swept up by police in the aftermath of the Winnipeg General Strike in 1919 was Steve Prycun, an unemployed Pole, who in an interview at the Kapuskasing camp stated his assets: a mortgaged house and a $50 bond.[48] All through 1919 and into the 1920s, anti-German sentiments continued to be fanned by, among other provocative sources, gloating newspapers, reports from peace treaty negotiations, veterans' testimonies, and accounts from correspondents in Europe. One, on the German Savings Premium Loan of 1919, trashed its rubbishy "loan propaganda literature."

As in the realm of recruitment, coercion was widespread in the Victory Loan campaigns. In earlier loans, discretionary requests had prevailed, but in 1917 financial need intensified, and voluntary appeal merged with forcible methods. Irresistible pressures, humiliation, and hardships caused by hasty subscriptions were well known in the American loan campaigns.[49] In Canada, both before and after conscription, pressure tactics were used to boost enlistment.[50] Similar compulsion was employed in the war loans. Coercion happened directly, whether through shaming, group conformity, and challenges to masculine identity or under the guise of humour. Advertisements could be blunt. "Do You Know Any Bond Slackers?" asked one in the *Regina Morning Leader.* In Toronto, the *Globe* reported instances of low-paid shopgirls who were "being forced to buy a bond. One girl with two brothers overseas, and an invalid father to care for, was told by the manager who employs her that if she did not buy a bond she was pro-German and a slacker." Such taunting was found throughout editorial comments and official advertisements. In Belleville, Ontario, the local newspaper urged readers to confront any man not wearing a subscriber's button, an action comparable to the "white feather" pinned on men who did not enlist. After witnessing the campaigns of 1917 and 1918, the *Globe* concluded that "it is well known that some bonds were bought under pressure, or enthusiastic people bought more than they could well carry, and a proportion of them were bound to find their way into the market," producing "mischievous traffic" by "sharpers."[51]

Not all coercion was overt. At a gathering of provincial civil servants in Edmonton in November 1917, it was announced that obligatory payroll deductions for the Canadian Patriotic Fund were cancelled, much to the crowd's delight. In the Victory Loan pitches that followed, Alberta's treasurer claimed that "nothing in the way of coercion" was intended, but the hint was there. More commonly, aggressive canvassing, shaming, job loss, and legal action were put to use against those who exhibited objections, intemperate utterance, or a perceived lack of enthusiasm. Many saw such tactics, amidst all the stunts and noises of the campaigns, as legitimate. In newspaper coverage, instances abound, often with the levity found in the loans' tradition of popular human-interest reportage. At an office building in 1918 in Vancouver, where the campaign was conducted at a furious pace, even surrounded by the flu epidemic, canvasser John Wallace Mackenzie, a veteran, approached a woman who, refusing to subscribe, quoted the Bible. Mackenzie shot back with his own interpretation: "To my mind Jesus Christ was about the finest fighter the world has ever known. He had nerve." The woman was reportedly swayed, a bond was sold, and readers of the encounter in the *Vancouver Daily Sun* may have nodded without sensing the simplistic reduction. Elsewhere in Vancouver, another canvasser sold bonds to a husband whose wife immediately called him a "piker," forcing him to take more.[52] In advertising in 1918, the Manitoba General Committee threatened, "If you have money or credit and do not buy Victory Bonds public opinion will mark you and the boys will not forget."[53] There was also one case of attempted coercion in reverse. In 1917–18, Winnipeg harness maker Elisha Frederick Hutchings, possibly the biggest individual subscriber in 1916 (for $550,000), offered to buy another $500,000 if his intended-successor son was exempted from military service. He was not.

The failure of a campaign district to go over the top on subscription – the quota set-up – could bring only "humiliation and disgrace," the *Regina Morning Leader* preached in November 1918.[54] Some newspapers threatened to forward the names of nonsubscribers to the "authorities in Ottawa." The more aggressive war-chest campaigns threatened to expose delinquents. Reluctant foreigners should be "leaned on," said the *Empress Express* (Empress, Alberta). Readers of the *Morning Bulletin* (Edmonton) in May 1918 were made aware of tar-and-feather reprisals during the Liberty Loan campaign in South Dakota, just one instance of vigilante activity in the United States.[55] French Canadian textile workers in Woonsocket, Rhode Island, felt pressured, although the Union Saint-Jean-Baptiste d'Amérique there, with an element of American identification, willingly bought $25,000 worth of Liberty Bonds.[56] In Quebec, where perceptions of the loan were divergent, the loan became entangled with the federal election, Unionist hostility, and anti-Quebec vitriol. The head of the French Canadian campaign in 1917, Joseph Quintal, called in vain for Montreal's mayor to launch an inquiry into the "shameless pressure methods" used by some employers.[57] Quintal's complaint gave substance to Henri Bourassa's nearly censored pamphlet on the "forced loan." During the 1919 loan in Quebec, as joint chairman Albert-Pierre Frigon had demonstrated in vain, the persecution of military defaulters had disrupted both the campaign and the harvest season.

In November 1917, the month before the election, White had tried to deal with a flurry of telegrams and letters from the West complaining about canvassers who told farmers that "they must subscribe."[58] In the 1919 campaign, complaints about "coercion," often by employers against labourers and factory workers, continued to be received by a largely unresponsive Department of Finance. At factories in Ontario and elsewhere, through obligatory payroll schemes and at exit gates, workers faced intimidation, sometimes producing financial "hardship" and a high rate of default, occasionally under the guise of fun. On the final day of campaigning in Vancouver in 1918, "jovial" policemen and firemen cruised the streets encouraging people to subscribe or risk false "arrests."[59] The stunt was both productive and entertaining. At the Calgary Gas Company in 1918, mandatory bond purchases by employees were administered through payroll deductions. In 1919, at the main gate of the Swift packinghouse in Toronto, where an unofficial loan "bureau" was set up, workers were met by two workers costumed as John Bull and Jack Canuck; for its mounting response, the "foreign element" was praised. In Hamilton and Toronto, "Austrian" workers who refused to subscribe were fired or prosecuted. Acting on "well grounded fears," including knowledge of tactics used in Seattle, the Trades and Labour Council of Vancouver voiced its intolerance of coercing workers into taking bonds.[60] In a strike at Trail, loan literature was burned. At the same time, many workers and civic employees benefited through affordable payroll deductions. In 1919, the *Canadian Mining Journal* (Gardenvale, Quebec) cited claims by miners that deductions were the only way that they could save, even as some of the "younger men" and those "who unfortunately could not help themselves" sold their bonds, sometimes at a loss.[61]

Campaigns were driven best by positive responses or gloss. Reports of repression or nonsubscription served as both deterrents and fodder for human-interest stories. In some cases, as with the Mennonites and German speakers, bondholding did not always forestall hostility. The six profiles that follow demonstrate that subscription did not necessarily prevent maltreatment or accusations of disloyalty. Although too few such instances are recorded to permit broad conclusions, all reveal individual circumstances met by uneven treatment. Whatever the official Victory Loan strategy was, and regardless of the legal authority, people sometimes took coercion into the public domain. The profiles begin at a barbershop.

Joshua Swan, Toronto[62]

What actually transpired at Joshua Swan's shop one day during the campaign of November 1917 is unclear. A campaign worker asked him to put up a Victory Bond poster. The worker said that Swan refused on the grounds that he did not approve of the loan as a means of funding. Swan, who favoured "conscription of wealth," said that he put up the poster that evening. According to the worker, who was about to enlist, Swan further claimed that men in Montreal were not signing up and expressed his belief that the worker and others should not be compelled to do so, that enlistment was "foolish." In denying such statements, Swan claimed that he was talking about newspaper articles on Quebec. Sentiments collided. Swan's supposed obstruction of the operation of the Military Service Act was reported to campaign organizers, who had instructed canvassers to disclose such encounters. He was arrested and brought before George Taylor

Denison on 28 December, one of the 130 cases that the police magistrate faced that day. The poster issue was deemed to be of no legal consequence, but it had set up the exchange over enlistment.

Found guilty and sentenced to one year, Swan was taken by rail in frigid cold to the Burwash prison farm south of Sudbury. The day after his arrival, he was returned to Toronto and released on bail. Although he was supported by the press, which at the same time attacked the censor's suppression of the *Sault Express* (Sault Ste. Marie, Ontario) in 1916 but not *Le Devoir* (Montreal) in 1917, and despite backing from the local Trades and Labour Council (Swan belonged to the barbers' union) and the aid of experienced counsel, his sentence was upheld in the York County Court in February. On appeal to the federal minister of justice, he was released on 4 March on a ticket of leave (a pardon with restrictions) and returned to work, with one hand impaired from his time in the cold. Although his responses on the Victory Loan had not figured in his trial, the loan, by shaping the forum, had demonstrated the weight that it could bring to bear. In April, the *Globe* was still asking why authorities had come down hard on Swan but not on Henri Bourassa.

Albert Arnold, near Drumheller, Alberta[63]

On 11 November 1918, with anti-German sentiment rampant, a boisterous group celebrating the armistice in Drumheller turned into a mob. They had been driving around in high spirits and had gone to a cafe to sign bonds and kiss the Union Jack. They then decided to terrorize German-born residents said to have refused to support the Victory Loan and the Red Cross. After taking two of them to a poolroom and compelling them to buy bonds and apologize for their origins, the gang, not all of them official bond salesmen, dashed off into the countryside. After forcing subscriptions from an elderly farmer and his son, the pack, led by Edward A. ("Tip") Blain, a barber, arrived at the farmhouse of Albert Arnold. A single, thirty-five-year-old native of Germany and reportedly an army officer there, he had come to Canada and was naturalized in 1914, although to the *Drumheller Mail* he was a "Hun." According to a neighbour, one of the gang shouted in reply to Arnold's call as to what they wanted, "We've got you now, you son-of-a-bitch." After first stoning the house and then knocking but receiving no answer, they entered. When Blain, who was wrapped in a Union Jack, approached an inner door, he was shot by a terrified Arnold. The rest of the party fled but would later return for Blain's body, upon which Arnold bolted. He gave himself up the next morning. At his trial for murder in Calgary on 20 January, it was heard that the gang had meant to force Arnold to buy bonds and that he had acted in self-defence. He was acquitted.

Herman Penzloff, near Claresholm, Alberta[64]

Born in Germany, Herman Penzloff came to Alberta in 1902, and he and his family built up a prosperous farm there. In 1918, he ran afoul of the nativist sentiment enflamed by the local Victory Loan campaign. According to the *Western Globe*'s (Lacombe, Alberta) account of what happened on 5 November, Penzloff refused to subscribe to any patriotic fund, claiming that contributions could be used to kill relatives in Germany. The community was "exceptionally patient with his conduct," but the campaign was the tipping point. He was seized, draped in the Union Jack and the Stars and Stripes, paraded around under the threat of being tarred and feathered, told to kiss the British emblem and subscribe for a $2,000 bond, and taken to the campaign's committee rooms, where he was given a choice. "Penzloff's reformation was so complete that after taking the $2,000 Victory bond," the *Western Globe* reported, he also wrote a cheque for $200 to the Red Cross. "The committee has the names of a few more such German residents in the district and they will be sent warnings that they had better subscribe at once." The *Claresholm Review-Advertiser* acknowledged Penzloff's subscription but made no direct mention of any coercion or humiliation: "A man is not to be blamed because of the place of his birth, but every man should be patriotic to the land of his adoption and to the country where he made his wealth." Claresholm won an honour flag for its level of subscriptions, and the Penzloffs continued to farm.

Gregory Syronty, Hamilton, Ontario[65]

A Russian-born factory worker, Gregory Syronty popped up in Hamilton's labour ranks in November 1918. When his superintendent approached him on 31 October to buy a Victory Bond, he refused. According to the *Hamilton Spectator*, he held that "Russia was better than Canada." Asked if he was "one of the Bolshevski," he said that he was. At the time, in the wake of revolution in Russia, Hamilton had a core of Bolshevist proponents. Following Syronty's refusal, he was charged with "seditious utterances." The police court's docket that week was filled with the foreign-looking names of individuals who had breached the Military Service Act. On hearing Syronty's case, magistrate George Frederick Jelfs, in a surprising expansion, turned to court interpreter Anthony A. Yarosh (a Russian and an employee of the Hamilton Foreign Steamship Agency) to discuss whether Russia was a country, whether it was at war with the Allies, and what "Bolshevski" actually meant. Reminded of Syronty's claim that Russia was better than Canada, Jelfs defended his right "to stick up for his country." On the bond matter, the magistrate concluded that he had a right to refuse. "Because he doesn't take a bond doesn't signify that he is antagonistic toward the country. He may have good reasons for not doing so, from a financial

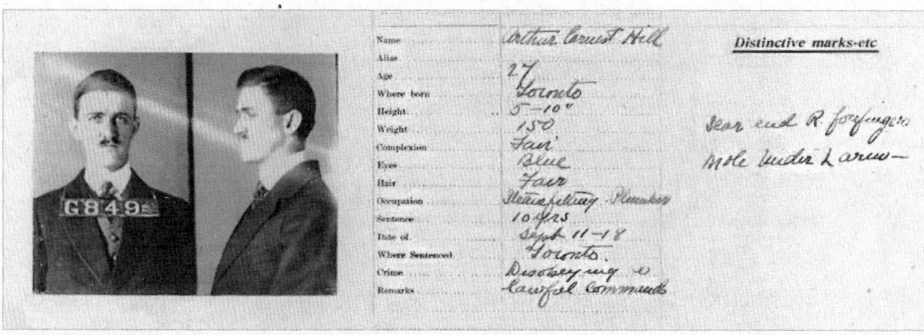

Arthur Hill's convict card from Kingston Penitentiary, 1918. | Library and Archives Canada, RG 73-C-6, vol. 561. Courtesy of Canada's Penitentiary Museum, Kingston, Ontario.

standpoint." Moreover, Jelfs reasoned, "people should not be persistently importuned to buy bonds after they had refused." Lacking evidence to detain or reprimand Syronty, Jelfs let him go.[66]

Arthur Ernest Hill, Port Credit, Ontario[67]

Victory Bonds were part of Arthur Ernest Hill's response to the war. A twenty-seven-year-old bachelor, he was a steamfitter-plumber and a foreman in his father's plate-glass plant in Toronto and, like his family, a member of the pacifist Christadelphian sect. Called up for service under the Military Service Act, he and his brother Alfred Thomas claimed exemption as conscientious objectors. The judge at the presiding tribunal on 2 April 1918 reserved his decision (although that same day, George Taylor Denison, the magistrate in the Swan case, sentenced another Christadelphian to six months in prison). The decision went against the brothers, and they were conscripted. Alfred was discharged because he had tuberculosis. Arthur continued his resistance, even as he fought off the flu, demanding a private medical examination and claiming that "he was not a soldier." On 11 September, he was sentenced to ten years in Kingston Penitentiary. Public opinion swirled around the case and the inconsistent attitudes toward "slackers." One defender said that Hill had "invested the bulk of his savings last year in Victory bonds," but this support and his factory's work for the Imperial Munitions Board carried no weight. Hill entered jail on 9 November as convict G-849. Early in 1919, a general pardon for inmates sentenced for conscientious objections was granted, and Hill was pardoned on 10 March.

Phoebe Osborne, Sophiasburgh Township, Ontario[68]

During the campaign of 1918 in Prince Edward County, a complaint by a canvasser led to the creation of a file at the attorney general's office in Toronto. The incident began when Thomas Franklin Spafford called at the farmhouse of Jacob and Phoebe Osborne to solicit subscriptions. He likely expected a positive response; the Osbornes' teenage daughter, Inez, had subscribed the year before. Instead, he faced a tirade from Phoebe, evidently with input from Inez. Spafford reported them to the county's campaign organizer. The file's extracts from his one-sided letter make for fascinating reading:

> Mrs. Osborne made the statement that more than half the Red Cross proceeds did not reach the proper channels; that all V.B. advertising was just to give someone a rake off; that our soldiers were not properly fed; that she and her husband, Jacob Osborne, and the daughter, Inez Osborne, had money, but they would have nothing to do with V.B.'s ... The family lives directly in front of the Church and are out of sorts with about everybody. I could not wedge in a single argument in favour of V.B.'s on account of the torrent of abuse that Mrs. Osborne poured forth like the River Styx full of pollution and filth. They certainly ought to be gently looked after. For my part I kept my patience most serenely.

In a second document, a copy of Spafford's "blue card" on the Osbornes, he remarked,

> Rank, traitorous, libellous abuse of V.B.'s. Red Cross and the Government with flat refusal accompanied by insults. [On back:] The Osbornes did not buy Bonds last year. The daughter, Miss Inez Osborne bought $500 last year. I received the most scurrilous, unpatriotic, libellous, false and Germanic (pro) abuse of V.B.'s, Red Cross, the Government you could possibly imagine. I earnestly wish you would send someone after them.

His complaint went up and down the ladder of authority, reaching the county organizer, George Herbert Wood as chair of the loan's provincial executive, and Ontario's attorney general and his deputy, before being sent back to the county's Crown attorney, Richard H. Hubbs, for action. As recommended by Wood and the loan's executive, Hubbs sent "warning" letters to Phoebe and Inez. There, the file goes silent, but it raises questions. Although Phoebe held contrarian views, her side of the incident is muted. Were her views as "adversely" influential as the deputy attorney general suggested? Her remarks, as related by Spafford, could reflect the rumours and misinformation that dogged the Red Cross and other sectors of the war-loan machine.[69] What can be seen is the part played by the Victory Loans in the public's assessment and expression of positions on Canada's needs. Phoebe Osborne's claim of rake-offs in the Victory Loans echoed criticisms of the costs paid for the war loans found in newspapers such as the

British Columbia Federationist and expressed in the House of Commons. One is mindful here of Sir Sam Hughes's description in March 1919 of speculation masquerading as patriotism.

There were other incidents that undermined loan organizers' aims of national consensus. Given Canada's diversity of viewpoints and means, this proviso should come as no surprise. Ordinary people were swept up, as well as ignored, in the war-loan campaigns with minimal trace. Resistance permeated the loan process at every level for different reasons. As the cases recounted above attest, subscription did not obviate objection on various grounds. These and other cases, the dissentient letters sent to the Department of Finance or published, the reports of low-yield neighbourhoods and office buildings, the stories of persuasion, and less than optimal employee response are presented as illustrative, if not quantifiable, possible antidotes to the imaginary of unity in Canadian society in 1915–19. The financial results and the eventual reach of the war-loan campaigns remain indisputable, a testament to their integrated components and atmosphere. Still, Canadians reacted in different ways to the tools used to shape that atmosphere.

Part 5
The Images, Sounds, and Words of the War Loans

12

Selling through Posters, Cartoons, and Illustrations

Some understood that finance and propaganda had to be connected. On 13 August 1914, journalistic gadfly Arthur Hawkes was interviewed by a reporter. "The time has come to organize, unify and express the national sentiment about the war," Hawkes stated. Asked for an example, he picked finance:

> Parliament will vote scores of millions for the war. It cannot lightly borrow from London. War taxes are coming. They won't provoke loud cheers. The tax-collector cannot promote the spirit which causes women to offer their jewels at the national altar. There will be funds of different sorts, but they won't be enough. There must be propaganda for the war, and it must be implemented. A Patriotic League would crystallize the sentiment ingeminated by a newspaper press.[1]

In his journal *Canadian War* (Toronto) in February, he argued that federal estimates were far below the costs certain to emerge.[2] Although his league never took shape, the linkage of propaganda and finance were prescient. Canada's newspapers would became the primary vehicle for the messaging that created the environment needed for efficient dissemination. War-loan content was easy to come by, particularly in the form of reportage and official notices and advertising defined not by the war's events but by predetermined phases of publicity and sales. The press's role as purveyors complemented the deluge of visual imagery.

In pre-war years, the term "propaganda" was applied to different forms of publicity, from innocuous information on sewers and playgrounds to the promotion of political, military, and social causes. In the early stages of the war, propaganda often meant posters. A recognized medium, they advertised an array of products, services, and events. Many were utilitarian broadsides, although theories of design, messaging, and marketing were also in circulation. Curator Maurice F.V. Doll explains that the war "marked the first time governments became directly involved in overseeing the use of propaganda in the form of the poster." Its language and art were energized, communications historian Pier Paolo Pedrini adds, "to create and sustain the war." Without the persuasive mechanisms employed, "there would have been neither reason nor will to fight. For many, war is indeed distant in kilometres and interest."[3]

After war broke out, the need for official propaganda first emerged not in the realm of finance but in recruitment and agriculture. Some work was paid for through the Department of Militia, but it did not exercise national oversight. Recruiting posters were produced by individual regiments, battalions, and military divisions. In response to requests from Canadian towns, posters from Britain's Parliamentary Recruiting Committee were brought in for unofficial distribution as of October 1914 and carrying into at least 1916.[4] This influx overlapped with the entry of the militia department into the production of posters in fiscal 1915–16, adding to the visual surge, often with copy supplied by advertising firms. Canadians began seeing the names of Canadian battles such as Saint-Julien and Festubert, along with the names of Quebec's past military heroes. Within months of August 1914, propaganda was also being called for in the agricultural sector as a means to push the consumption of apples and to promote greater farm production and the Made-in-Canada movement, where Hawkes had also been advocating vigorous propaganda. The Department of Finance, with little to push, had not yet entered the fray.

From early 1915, exhibitions of Allied war posters and cartoons, collected as souvenirs for their artistry and humour and often shown to raise funds for relief work,[5] were popular. Together, they became a new, respectable genre distinct from commercial and film posters. Appeals for Belgium, which had been overrun by German forces, came early in Canada, as did the related work of London-based Louis Raemaekers. His poster of a mother and child against a background of flames was "one of the most remarkable and certainly the most heartrending of all the 'War Posters,'" claimed one Ontario newspaper. Official propaganda attacked Germany's "cruel militarism," although Canadians, even in the face of demoralizing casualty lists, did not fully grasp front-line horror.[6] The servicemen who wrote graphic letters that passed censorship and the journalists who had battlefield access, such as Philip Gibb of the *Globe* (Toronto), were able to describe bodies "slain like rabbits." At home, audiences were more likely exposed to sanitized, censored war films from France and Britain. After the United States entered the fray in 1917, audiences would be inundated with American film propaganda.[7] Used to attract enlistees and customers, poster campaigns could generate controversy. In Britain, one historian argues, by mid-1915 the public was steeling itself against commercial and recruiting posters.[8]

Even as government-sponsored advertising grew, war-loan publicity would emerge as a dramatic departure. The loan campaigns of 1915 and 1916 were sedate affairs in terms of visuals; corporate subscribers responded best to investment argument. Letterpress posters and newspaper advertising were the mainstays. The committee of bankers charged with implementing the national savings campaign announced by White in September 1916 had new ideas. Since Canadians did not know how to save, they professed, posters could be used to direct "peoples's minds," following Britain's example. Responsibility for the campaign soon shifted to the National Service Board, which would employ A. McKim Limited of Montreal for the advertising. Hesitation about how to publicize loans began to melt in early 1917 in the face of mounting financial need and public pressures. One catalyst was the campaigns for thrift and war-savings certificates launched out of the Department of Finance, where Bennet John Roberts was busy with posters. Even then, they were of the standard letterpress variety.

Poster styles and functions, 1917. On the left, a letterpress poster from January 1917 gives information, meant to be read, on war-savings certificates. On the right, the lead-off poster in the Victory Loan campaign of November, W.P.1, makes an eye-catching pitch for people to buy Victory Bonds | Library and Archives Canada, R1185-67-0-E, box A145/X2, e010697261, and box A146/X3, e010779189.

Issues and professional interests got tangled. John Nelson McKim, of A. McKim Limited, told Roberts that the government's direct placement of advertising with the press was the "least efficient method of bringing the matter" before Canadians. Eager for business, newspapers nevertheless championed thrift. How it should be packaged was hotly debated. At a meeting of the War-Time Thrift Committee in Toronto on 7 February 1917, one of the society women present proclaimed, "It is not enough simply to save for your own use. We want you to save for the Government." Citing a cartoon in *Punch* from 17 January, which shows the kaiser being snowed under with British war-loan applications, she asked: "Don't you think we could make a pretty big drift about the old boy?"[9]

Opinions on visual impact varied. In Toronto, *Economic Advertising* and *Printer and Publisher*, both of which wanted more vigour and resented the sidelining of agencies, saw the government's word-only posters as a handicap and lamented the "cold formality" of thrift advertising.[10] In January 1917, M. Scarth Stevenson of Molson's Bank in Montreal made a pitch for full-page newspaper advertising, which would eventually be adopted in the Victory Loan. Unfortunately, in *La Presse* (Montreal) and in posters meant to reach and educate "the poorer class of French Canadians," he used for illustration the graphic depiction by the Comité de recrutement canadien-français of the slaughter of a woman and child. The proposal was rejected by White, who was selective in his condonation of negativity.[11] The committee did play to French Canadian sensibilities in a colourful poster featuring Adam Dollard des Ormeaux, the "saviour" of New France, at the Battle of Long-Sault in 1660.

Where industry journals such as *Economic Advertising* honed the edge of publicity was in their promotion in 1915–17 of "red-blooded, human copy." Newspaper advertising of the Canadian Patriotic Fund and Canadian Red Cross Appeal of 22–26 January 1917 (the "Victory Campaign") was a case in point. One ad asked readers to picture a "German Lunatic" atop the Canadian Pacific Railway Building in Toronto, with the intersection below a "Flanders mudhole." Although the plea was fear-based, *Economic Advertising* reasoned that "the aim seems to bring the trenches, the needs of our soldiers and their families as close to the heart of patriotic Torontonians as is possible by any form of presentation." Thus, referencing campaign illustrations by Carlton ("Carl") George Beal, the paper said that "the illustrations should abound in human interest." Beal, a member of the campaign's committee, was a freelance artist and sales manager at a local advertising agency. He also drew the brilliant, perhaps too brainy, series of newspaper illustrations for the recruiting campaign of the 109th Regiment in February and March.[12]

Despite the buildup of pressure, the Dominion War Loan of March 1917 lacked publicity with ginger. In contrast to developments in recruitment and the poster barrage of the Canadian Patriotic Fund, loan advertising was almost exclusively restricted to the newspapers, with the King's Printer turning out some stereotyped posters.[13] With stables of artists, writers, and salesmen, firms in Hamilton, Toronto, Ottawa, and Montreal were well positioned to produce posters, as were the larger newspapers.[14] The move from broadsides to lithographed posters, art historian Robert Stacey concludes, was "surprisingly swift."[15] With the greater involvement of professional poster makers and advertising firms, the text-only look of posters gave way to new styles and purposes.

Most of the Victory Loan lithographs, from 1917 to 1919, reflect commercial art of the period; artists likely saw European magazines on print and design. In their content and form, curator Mora Dianne O'Neill writes, posters by three creators, Frank Lucien Nicolet, Arthur Keelor, and Malcolm Gibson, show "a modernist approach that sets them apart from most graphic design in Canada." In much of the work for the loans, as in the posters of most belligerents, one can visualize such authoritative explanations: integrated pictorials and geometric approaches replace drawing, colouring and lettering are dramatic, and figures are placed within "planar renditions of landscape."[16] Few wartime viewers articulated close scrutiny, but in many of the posters, subliminal communication is evident: heavy lines and swaths of colour focus the eye, figures make visual contact, diagonals activate perusal, shifts in scale signify depth and narrative purpose, and the coordination of image and text confirms the messages.[17] Cultural historian Jane Potter holds that "the impact of the visual was enormous,"[18] a brave, sweeping conclusion that ranges over a host of factors, from individual sightings to the conglomerate of atmosphere. "Posters need to be read not just visually," multidisciplinary historian Pearl James adds,[19] but considered within political, social, and financial contexts on the home front, including a disentanglement of war myths and an understanding of campaign structuring.

The design and intent of Victory Loan posters evolved over three stages: the launch and hard sell of 1917, the transition over the armistice of 1918, and re-establishment in 1919. Throughout the spring and summer months of 1917, that year of hardship and fervid debate, a visual and psychological atmosphere was shaped.[20] The posters used in campaigns near and far, many known to Canadians, including America's first Liberty Loan drive, were unavoidable. Writing in July 1917 to the *Globe* on Britain's Eat Less Bread campaign, a result of food shortages caused by the submarine blockade, a correspondent reported, "The poster reached its highest expression in this crusade."[21]

There was much to be seen and heard, too, from Ottawa. The National Service Board was known through its campaigns on farm labour, food conservation, and war-savings certificates,[22] with much of its publicity handled by advertising firms and commercial printers. The National Council of Women, through its local councils, put up 100,000 small posters (called "hangers") on conservation and certificates in factories, stores, and post offices. More came from the federal Office of the Food Controller. By the start of the Victory Loan of 1917, amidst such an atmosphere, the manner of visual and experiential propaganda could range from full-on blatancy – both American historian Ann P. Linder and Pedrini call it "emotional blackmail"[23] – to operation on "subtle linguistic and emotional levels."[24] Given the existence of two main languages in Canada, nuance was a factor in the translation of posters.

Victory Loan materials had different translators, depending on language and type. In November 1917, one translator of posters and other materials was Sosthène-Louis-Émile Durantel, an employee in the census and statistics branch of the Department of Trade and Commerce. His work on posters between October and December caught the critical attention of *Le Devoir* (Montreal).[25] At the Food Board, office staff did the translating; the Commons, the Senate, and various departments had their own permanent translators. Although pamphlets were translated into multiple languages, posters were issued almost exclusively in French and English, with some exceptions. On the launch of the campaign in November, Victoria's *Daily Colonist* reported, "Plans are being made to have Chinatown plastered with Victory Loan posters in Chinese [dialects]."

Recognition of atmosphere, including the language and placement of posters, is vital to an understanding of Canadians' response. Letters from overseas flowed, soldiers were everywhere, and war news was a staple in the press. In the weeks before the Victory Loan campaign, the Hippodrome in Toronto screened the British version of *The German Retreat and the Battle of Arras* under the auspices of the British War Office. Advertising for the film and succeeding productions promised depictions of the "valiant rush of heroic Canadians" and "insight into the actual operations at the front." In truth, according to historian Nicholas Reeves, *Retreat* was selective, with few dead bodies.[26] Over the summer, other cinemas had screened British propaganda films. They did not likely change attitudes, Reeves argues, but in their elicitation of sympathy and support, they helped to bridge the home front and the battlefield through entertainment tinged with a modicum of reality. Such imagery, in posters and films, added a visual dimension to the atmosphere of the campaign.

Organization for the Victory Loan began under intense pressure in early August 1917 amidst the continuous debates over the expected federal election and conscription. To succeed, enhanced visual propaganda would be needed. The dominion publicity committee consisted entirely of securities and finance men from Toronto and Montreal, a media-savvy lot headed by Ralph A.

Stephenson. The campaign, he explained, "was intended to produce the largest number of mental pictures in the minds of the greatest possible number of people."[27] Its primary job was to distribute posters, banners, educational pamphlets, postcards, glass slides to illustrate talks, small stickers, and a film. As banker Henry Victor Franklin Jones had told White in 1916, posters, not newspapers, were the most practical way to reach the largest number. By virtue, too, of their national goals and public placements, war-loan posters reflected a respectability not accorded film and other purely commercial placards.[28] By late September, sources for posters were being considered, and in White's office Roberts was working to get Liberty Loan posters from the United States for review. The Committee on Public Information was a mighty force in America's "conscription" of art, as committee head George Edward Creel put it.[29] Canada's smaller but coordinated program, like that of the National Service Board, nevertheless smoothed out "the uneven quality of the propaganda material issued by private firms."[30]

Responsibility for copy and graphic materials rested with the newspapermen and advertising firms, all under the auspices of the dominion publicity committee, a fractious but productive union. Everything was rushed. Initial orders for posters went in only twenty days before subscriptions were to open. The posters, six designs in each language (three would be added later), were shipped to local committees around 1 November, a mere eleven days before the campaign. Organizers were encouraged to change them over the course of the campaign "to keep the matter fresh." In total, 460,000 window posters and 15,350 for billboards would flood the country.[31] One Montreal mother wrote to her son overseas, "The ferries are decorated with some very clever posters and everywhere we read about it."[32] Local campaigns were pushed to put up posters everywhere. Placements were difficult in rural areas, but even there, any surface was sought out.[33] The posters, Pedrini observes, thus "redefined the limits of public space, introducing nationalistic imperatives into private," educational, industrial, commercial, and "ecclesiastical environments."[34]

After the campaign of 1917, and throughout 1918, the Poster Advertising Association of Canada, two Toronto trade journals (*Economic Advertising*, soon to be renamed *Marketing and Business Management*, and *Printer and Publisher*), and a host of firms were emboldened to boost the "power of posters" and aesthetic design. Nothing surpassed pictures, the association claimed, for their "extreme conspicuousness, intensity of appeal and ability to reach everybody in the most effective way." Recognizing the opportunity, the Chicago-based Poster Advertising Association, which published *The Poster: War Souvenir Edition* and had many Canadian members, had few rivals in selling the medium. Some of Canada's Victory Loan posters, it would claim, "were outstanding examples of publicity force that will never be forgotten ... Canada was turned into Posterland."[35]

In lockstep, newspapers such as *La Patrie* (Montreal) and *Le Soleil* (Quebec City) splashed their front pages with Victory Loan news and photographs of committee groups and members. They were not alone. To maximize the visual effect, the *Hants Journal* (Windsor, Nova Scotia) overprinted its entire front page with "Buy Canada's Victory Bonds," and in Toronto the *Daily Mail and Empire* trumpeted the loan in huge red and black lines. Whatever the circulation of these newspapers, everyone would see posters. Some were meant to be seen in passing, with rapid registration; those with only a few words employed other devices, such as vibrant colours. Looking at the volume of posters appearing across Canada, the *Calgary Daily Herald* observed that the Department of Finance has "taken a leaf from the experience of the British, French and American governments."[36] Together, the posters of 1917–19 exhibited several strategies of persuasion, among them emotional appeals, dialogism, the them-us divide, national symbolism, and regional scenery.[37] Those of 1917, which represented a marked departure from most of Canada's recruiting and government posters,[38] reflected up-to-date commercial, artistic, and psychological sensibilities. They were the leading visual edge of the campaign. Some broadcast fundamentals such as the five-and-a-half percent interest (better than the interest on bank accounts). Meant to transform sentiment into action, all were invitational.

Analysis of three of the posters issued in 1917 reveals their radical departures in design and strategy. The striking leadoff billboard poster, which came in various sizes and versions, featured a helmeted Canadian soldier with an outstretched arm, pointing finger, and riveting gaze against a dull yellow background. His message was simple: buy Victory Bonds. Its design was taken from other famous posters: the 1917 Italian war-loan poster by Achille Luciano Mauzan, Britain's finger-pointing Lord Herbert Kitchener recruiting poster of 1914 by Alfred A.C. Leete, the United States' pointing Uncle Sam of April 1917 by James Montgomery Flagg, and one or more Liberty Loan posters from 1917.[39] (There was rarely talk of plagiarism in advertising and propaganda.) The Canadian finger figured prominently on Toronto's streets on the opening day of the campaign, 12 November. "No citizens, excepting the deaf and blind, can now pretend that they have never heard or seen anything about the Victory Loan," reported the *Globe*. "If they could not hear the bells, they could not miss seeing the posters. The pointing finger and fixed, piercing eye of the helmeted warrior arrested them at every corner." Labelled "a poster with a soul" by one reviewer, it was so well regarded that takeoffs appeared in loan advertisements in newspapers, they were blown up on giant "aerial signs" (billboards where size, strong design, and colouring mattered to the outdoor advertising crowd, among them the E.L. Ruddy Company,[40] Williams-Thomas Limited of Montreal, and the Canadian Street Car Advertising Company), or they were reduced to stamp-sticker size. The tenets of repetition and visibility were widely sustained.

The first window poster released (marked "W.P.1" for War Poster No. 1)[41] featured a standing soldier leaning toward the viewer, arms outstretched against a vivid reddish-orange background. Imploring gestures and forceful colours were regarded as important.[42] The urgency of the message was clear: "Now! Victory Bonds." The artist was Joseph Ernest Sampson, a designer with Rolph-Clark-Stone Limited, a Toronto lithographing firm that had done several modernist recruiting posters in 1914. His use of gesture, solid background (a departure from cluttered recruiting posters), and emotional tension was evident, too, in his iconic design for W.P.3: a young girl with golden curls, a red bow in her hair, and a white frock against a grey-blue background. She begs, "Oh please do! Daddy" and stands in front of teetering toy blocks that spell out the rest of her plea: "Buy Me a Victory Bond." The poster, which oozes vulnerability and manipulation, in part from its imposition – it did not ask – was originally meant to be distributed among schoolchildren, but its seductiveness struck a chord with the public. Anticipating a strong reception, the publicity committee authorized a print run of 75,000,[43] a high number for Victory Loan posters.

The golden-haired girl was three-year-old Faith Berry of Toronto, daughter of Leslie L. Berry, advertising manager of the Cowan Cocoa Company, whose older daughter had also gained publicity as a "'poster' girl" ("Little Miss Canada") in company ads and labels. He showed a snapshot of Faith to one of the heads of Rolph-Clark-Stone, after which it was passed along to Sampson, who brought it to the publicity committee. After the campaign closed, Faith, in a much-publicized presentation, was given a bond and flowers in gratitude by a delegation that included Alfred Ernest Ames and Ernest Lawrence Ruddy. Ruddy was the go-getting head of an outdoor signage firm, originator of gimmicky stunts, and a director of the Poster Advertising Association of Canada. For the Victory Loan, Faith's image, which was widely copied, was a godsend: it gave substance to the call for human interest in advertising.[44] The poster was followed up by an official advertisement that portrayed a curly headed girl begging her daddy to buy her another bond. To make the message crystal clear, the girl cheerfully points to her subscriber's button and doffs her HMS *Victory* cap, an oft-used link between the loan and the nineteenth-century flagship of Sir Horatio Nelson, the victor at Trafalgar.[45]

Further insight into the impact of the Faith Berry poster and into the heavy degree to which children were mobilized and symbolically used emerges from its reception nationwide. In Ontario, at a loan meeting in Belleville's city hall, attendees were struck by the many "Liberty [sic] Bond posters which adorned the walls. One in particular is worthy of special notice among the many artistic designs which testified to the power of publicity, the one depicting the little girl who had arranged her alphabet blocks."[46] London's chief librarian, Fred Landon, in an article encouraging public libraries to preserve ephemeral records of the war such as Victory Bond posters, singled out the poster as an ideal means "to be used in explaining to children of the future what the war meant to Canadians of today."[47] In Vancouver, the loan's director of publicity, a securities professional, arranged for the distribution in schools of 13,500 miniature reproductions of this "favorite 'kiddie' poster, that has taken the public heart by storm." Children, the *Vancouver Daily Sun* claimed, were "natural enthusiasts" and gifted canvassers, quite capable of dissecting the "mysterious slogans" on posters.[48] The adulation did not end there. The *Daily Sun*'s "Children's Column" published Margaret Esther Crosfield's entreating poem "O! Please Do Daddy." Daddy's girl would continue be a ploy in Victory Loan advertising in 1918 and 1919. The poster also found its way to Australian and American publicists.

Visually, the posters of 1917 were impressive. Apart from contributing to the loan atmosphere, there is some evidence of spur-of-the-moment reaction. In November 1917, a widow in London sold her engagement ring to buy a bond after viewing W.P.6: "Bring Him Home with the Victory Loan." Still, in the spring of 1918, undercurrents of exasperation were surfacing, in the *Okanagan Commoner* (Armstrong, British Columbia), *Saturday Night* (Toronto), and elsewhere, over the deluge of "childish nonsense" called propaganda. Moreover, Canadian war-loan posters did not dominate the interest of collectors and exhibitors; recruiting posters continued to be popular as mementoes, collectibles, and prizes. In May 1917, at the Hudson's Bay Company store in Edmonton, the YMCA's reconstructed Red Triangle Hut concluded its fundraiser with an auction of a grenade and a collection of recruiting posters. In December, Sir William Mulock made his fashionable Toronto home available for a musical and an exhibition of French war posters, with the proceeds from ticket sales going to the Franco-British Aid Society to help wounded French soldiers. The war-loan poster had nonetheless captured public attention. As late as August 1918, the image of the finger-pointing soldier was still prominent in ads.

The work of the poster artists brought some of them specific recognition. For his work on display cards for a glove seller, Sampson would be identified in *Dry Goods Review* (Toronto) as "Samson [sic], of Victory Loan fame."[49] The Toronto firm of Rous and Mann, among others, was churning out chromolithographed posters for the Canada Food Board, and war-related posters and cartoons from the United States and thrift posters from Europe were also coming to Canadians' attention. The medium's prominence was furthered by the war loan anticipated in the federal budget of April 1918. That summer, bundles of 1917 Victory Loan posters – those with no mention of Canada – were sent to Newfoundland for its campaign.

Even though the Canadian Press Association would again be intimately involved in advertising Canada's loan of 1918, there were inner tensions – and not just with advertising firms or over rates. In early June, for instance, the *Western Canada Press* (Winnipeg), the new journal of the Manitoba division of the association, complained in print and to the minister of finance about the exclusive use of eastern Canadian printers and lithographers for the production of loan materials, including posters. Ample facilities existed in the West, it argued. *Printer and Publisher* agreed, but the grievance was brushed off in Ottawa.[50] The same day that the new Victory Loan was authorized by an order-in-council, 5 July 1918, the old publicity committee met. On its agenda was the initiation of a poster competition, with prizes, the first of the loan's popular exercises in public engagement. Submissions were to be based on sketches provided by the publicity committee.[51]

The contest experienced problems. It was announced quietly, with a tight time frame. The deadline for submissions was 1 August (some newspapers and trade journals, confusingly, gave 25 July and 15 October), the winners would be announced on 15 August, and printed posters were needed by mid-October. The contest committee declined to show any of the original drawings submitted until the start of the loan campaign at the end of October, when it intended to exhibit them.[52] In July, it was believed that the unveiling would happen at the Canadian National Exhibition, slated to open at the end of August. According to *Marketing and Business Management*, the uncertainties left artists confused.[53] Nonetheless, more than 600 entries reportedly arrived.[54] A viewing by the contest's judges took place at the newly completed Art Museum of Toronto, where they were awarded up to 66 and two-thirds points for their ideas on bond selling and 33 and one-third points for artistic merit.

Judging from the entries that have survived, including two award winners, the results displayed a cross-section of amateur and professional talent, along with raw sentiment.[55] Submissions came from veterans, a teenager, a single woman in Saint John, a Montreal decorator, a farmer's wife in Lake of the Rivers, Saskatchewan, and others. The poster painted by Arthur Moore Goodden of Hamilton, a railway-car builder before the war, veteran, and sign painter, vividly displayed a statue of Lady Justice, her scales weighing money (Victory Loan funds) against an overflowing pan of blood.[56] The entry of Hilda M.

Neville, an electrician's wife residing near Waltham Station, Quebec, was a crowded homemade collage with a photo of a soldier holding a baby, pasted maple leaves, slogans and loan details, and a cut-out of a military badge. On the reverse was this call:

To all our allies
O, Canada shall we forget
The nurse's and baby's killers
Let us of we who left behind
Make this the fifth and greatest –
Victory Loan
And comfort them so freely
Have given us their all.

The twelve posters produced for the campaign of 1918 were printed in runs of up to 65,000 each and were being distributed by 18 October. The two that kicked off the campaign, W.P.1 and W.P.2, combined aggressive propagandistic intent and artistic punch. Entitled "Victory Bonds Will Stop This –/Kultur vs. Humanity," W.P.2, which took the poster contest's second prize, depicts the sinking of the Canadian hospital ship *Llandovery Castle* on 27 June by a submarine and the killing of survivors, "a near-perfect propaganda opportunity" according to the Canadian War Museum.[57] The branding of German culture as marked by a predisposition to destructiveness pervaded the loan publicity. The poster's composition is ingenious, with the viewer's gaze guided to the victims in the centre. The artist, Lorne Kidd Smith of R.G. McLean Printing in Toronto, accentuates the frigidness of the water through his use of dark blues and tossing waves; a soldier holds a nurse's limp body and shakes his fist at the surfaced submarine, its gun blazing. The nurse, an army sister, is changed in the poster to a nurse of the Voluntary Aid Detachment, the Red Cross emblem on her uniform accentuating the pathos.[58] The outrage occasioned by the sinking, a sentiment that built on newspaper ads for war bonds in 1917 that had featured the sinking of the *Lusitania* ("Lest We Forget!"), was sustained on the home front by reports of other maritime destruction and by the Sailors' Week campaign, managed by A. McKim Limited.[59]

The posters for 1918, all prepared before the armistice, promoted Victory Bonds in different ways. Some contemporary reviews, comparing them to the posters and advertising of 1917, suggested that there was more of an emphasis on lending,[60] with the arguments of investment and sacrifice constituting a "weapon of reciprocity."[61] Caricatures of German notables – Kaiser Wilhelm, Field Marshal Paul von Hindenburg, Crown Prince Wilhelm, and Admiral

Submission by Hilda M. Neville of Waltham Station, Quebec, in a poster competition leading up to the Victory Loan campaign of 1918. Raw in messaging and cluttered in composition, it was rejected. | Canadian War Museum, Ottawa, George Metcalf Archival Collection 19770066-003.

Alfred von Tirpitz – seen in a British poster in 1915 were the four reasons to buy in W.P.12, by F.L. Shields of Montreal. W.P.11, which portrayed two beavers gnawing at trees, called on citizens to "Keep All Canadians Busy," the farms and industry going, by investing in the Victory Loan. (In an official newspaper advertisement, a gang of beavers did double duty by chasing the kaiser across Europe.) Although one poster showing women ploughing in France was the only one with direct female depiction in 1918, gender was front and centre.

The theme of women's needs and contributions, as portrayed in numerous posters and other visual propaganda showing nurses and mothers, built on a slew of articles and photographs of women knitting, working at factories and

"Commander and Chief of Accounting Dept." George Webster presides over a "Victory Loan Chest" and female clerks who, we are told, adore him. | *Calgary Daily Herald*, 5 November 1919.

on farms, nursing, and sustaining grassroots fundraising.[62] Interlaced with publicity and roiling patriotism, the Victory Loan campaigns were heavy with gendered initiatives. Official publicity played to and off women, often to connect them to a distant war; posters and advertisements could stress maternal sacrifice and obligation. One journalist called Canada's food-producing women part of the "second line of defence" if Germany took England. Many women who saw bonds as investment opportunities subscribed as students, employees, and relatives holding the fort. Analysis of women's portfolios and estates in Ontario, along with a survey in 1915, supports a receptivity to securities.[63] Women marched in parades, donned costumes and uniforms, and offered kisses to prospective subscribers. Stars of American stage and screen shone. In gender-based divisions of labour, women were dominant in teams of canvassers and at recording centres and bond-printing plants, usually under male oversight. Sometimes, women were assigned to low-yield districts and employee groups (as occurred with telephone operators), or they were among the office workers at local campaign offices and in the Department of Finance.

By early 1920, within the federal bureaucracy, the finance department, including its war-loan branch, had grown exponentially to 833 people, 669 of them women in mostly clerical positions. The opportunities for the employment and engagement afforded by the loan and thrift drives, as in industry, were huge, if fleeting, but seldom framed in explicit feminist terms. At the same time, several women's organizations endorsed the loans. Even with women's loan committees in some centres, where society ladies were prominent and received adulatory press, there were no national women's organizations of the kind involved in America's Liberty Loans, likely for reasons of scale, with only an understated connection to the "new woman" trend evident in the American campaigns.[64] In 1919, the women's division of Canada's National War Savings Committee was Ontario-centric and short-lived. Examinations of the food conservation movement, which offered women meaningful roles, are mixed in their conclusions. Like many men, a number of women had reservations or principled objections to the war loans. Others evolved in their thinking. Prairie feminist ("women are our last reserves") Nellie McClung, for one, moved with agony from pacifism to support for the war effort after her son enlisted. She wrote of reformed holdouts on the Canadian Patriotic Fund, and in her 1919 article "Men and Money" she lauded Victory Bonds.[65]

The roles and depictions of women and girls in the loans deserve in-depth study, with cultural differentiation. If any of the French-language versions of 1918's posters gained particular attention in Quebec, it may have been W.P.7, which depicts three women pulling a plough in France, based on a photograph by Jean-Baptiste Tournassoud (appropriated by Brown Brothers of New York). It had already been used to promote food conservation by the United States Food Administration and by the Canada Food Board in its *Canadian Food Bulletin* (Ottawa) in April.[66] As will be discussed, it was the poster that replaced an American poster in Mary Pickford's promotional short film *100% Canadian*. In newspapers – the *Omineca Miner* in Hazelton, British Columbia, the *Regina Morning Leader*, and Fort William's *Daily Times-Journal* are three examples – the photo appeared with this line: "Women of France are Doing This: What are YOU Doing?"[67] In the United States, the photo was turned into a famous poster by Edward Penfield, and from Maine to the rural South, it was used in appeals to women. For Canada's poster, the picture – adapted in Montreal by W.T. Taylor and worded "They serve France/How can I serve Canada?/Buy Victory Bonds" ("Elles/servent/la France/Tout le monde peut servir/Souscrivons à/l'Emprunt de la/Victoire") – may have complemented the prevalence in Quebec newspapers of photographs and articles depicting French dignitaries such as Prime Minister Georges Clemenceau and General Ferdinand Foch, visiting French Legionnaires, and Quebec's "glorious" 22nd Battalion. The theme of maternal sacrifice may have registered with those who had seen Sarah Bernhardt's 1917 film *Mères françaises*. Surmise aside, these references to France may have had limited effect. The poster itself stresses inclusiveness, sacrifice, and physical service, which it equates with the purchase of bonds. As Ann P. Linder observes, the French-language version's replacement of "How can I serve Canada?" with "Tout le monde peut servir" implies that subscription is service while omitting any mention of Canada and avoiding the stated question. Like most posters involving food production and conservation, Linder concludes, "women were targeted because they controlled the household economy. Total war was waged at the kitchen table for the egg money."[68] Similarly, one official Victory Loan advertisement in the newspapers in October, during the "save" phase of the campaign, called on female factory workers to put money aside: "The money is *yours*! You have earned it, But –."[69]

Of all the 1918 posters, the most popular in English Canada was W.P.1, which featured "In Flanders Fields," the famous memorial poem by the late John McCrae of the Canadian Army Medical Corps. It is also the most reproduced. In the contest, the poster won first prize for commercial artist Frank Nicolet, a resident of London, Ontario, and an artist with the printing company Lawson and Jones Limited (some sources place him in Montreal with Regal Press). His poster featured the wording "'If ye break faith –/we shall not sleep,'' followed at the bottom by "BUY VICTORY BONDS." The poster itself is visually arresting – reds draw the eye – and manipulative; the composition is striking, with graphic contrasts and unavoidable emotion. At the centre, a Canadian soldier pays his respects before a wooden cross, a blasted farmstead in the background. Across the poster stretch masses of scarlet poppies. It is one of the few posters to dwell on the human cost of war, although an alternate interpretation seems plausible. The absence of McCrae's words "with us who die," one literary specialist notes, serves to repress the human costs and redirects the expression of faith to its financial costs.[70] In the view of another historian, the poem identifies a gap (between the living and the dead) or an absence (of action to join the military) that only the reader could address by buying bonds in an act of "substitution and consolation."[71]

Nicolet's design gave visual representation to a poem that had exploded in popularity since it was published in *Punch* on 8 December 1915. "In Flanders Fields" was used "with tremendous effect" in the Victory Loan of 1917.[72] Laced with romantic sentiment, the poem appealed powerfully to fear. In the poster, subscription offered absolution. The imagery of "blazing" red poppies also emerged in other poems of the time, as in Frank Oliver Call's "In a Belgian Garden" (1917), but it was "In Flanders Fields" that captured the most attention. Quoted, imitated, adapted for various fundraising campaigns, used by the Unionist cause, and even set to music in the United States (by both Charles Ives and John Philip Sousa), it surged in the months leading up to the loan of 1918.

In the estimate of the *Winnipeg Free Press,* it "has done more for the civilian morale of this country than any other written or spoken contribution to the cause." Some letter writers held it as "almost sacred" and "flawless"; a few were insulted by the "parodies and adaptations" and by its appearance on billboards.[73] Others, however, saw the poem and Nicolet's rendition as master strokes. In a typical expression of the combination, George Goldwin Smith Lindsey's address on the loan to the Toronto Women's Liberal Association was covered by the *Globe:* "'Do what you can,' said the speaker, 'for the living at the front and for those who lie beneath alien soil,' and ended his talk with the beautiful 'In Flanders' Fields.'"[74] Both the poem and the poster continue to captivate English-speaking Canadians through reproduction and commemoration.[75]

The *Globe* would call Nicolet's poster "one of the best posters" used for the loan,[76] a centrepiece in countless window displays and postwar exhibits. More copies would be distributed than was the case for any other Canadian war poster. Segments would appear in official advertisements for the loan and in commercial blurbs. During Thrift Week at the Hudson's Bay store in Calgary, a "Bond Booth" offered every purchaser of a $100 bond the chance to enter a contest that involved guessing Calgary's total subscriptions, despite the influenza tearing through the city. For the campaign's window-dressing contest, the Bay excelled: "The leading display in the corner window is undoubtedly one of the greatest human interest ever seen in this city. It is a reproduction of 'In Flanders Field the Poppies Grow.'"[77] The contest was won by the Diamond Clothing Company, where one of its salesmen and a window dresser built a display around the poster and Flanders. If the poster left any doubt, official advertisements spelled out the message of duty to the dead: buy bonds.[78]

In French-language newspapers, the poem received minimal attention, the poster none. In the translated debates of the House of Commons, "Flanders Fields" or parts of it remained in English. As with the poster of women ploughing, the translation of the Flanders Fields poster merits attention. "If ye break faith – we shall not sleep" is replaced by "Pour que la terre leur soit légère," often translated as "So that the earth may lay lightly on them" or "May they rest in peace." The French phrase, which softens the consolatory reaction (to buy bonds) and does not beatify McCrae's challenge, reaches back to a passage from an early-nineteenth-century tribute by French poet Alfred de Musset: "Que la terre leur soit légère – Ils ont aimé!" For the Victory Loan propagandists, the graves of Flanders, like the sinking of the *Llandovery Castle,* provided a golden opportunity.

The posters of 1918, as in 1917, did not exist in isolation. As major components of the war-loan atmosphere, they appeared along with, often in coordinated fashion, the long series of illustrated newspaper advertisements, press releases,

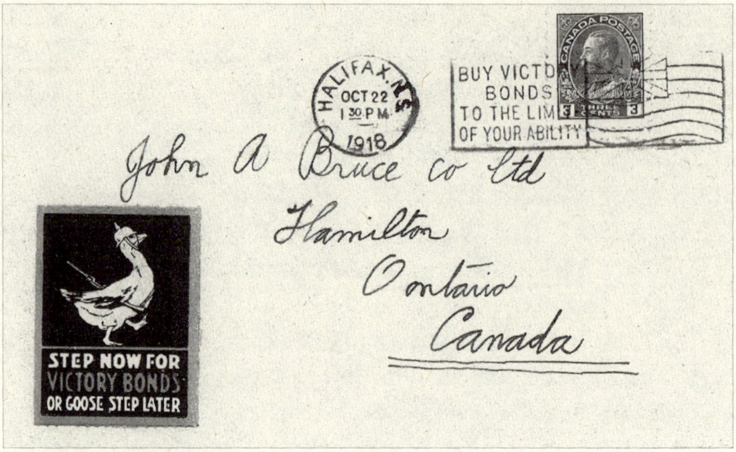

Postal cancellations and cartoon stickers extolling the Victory Loan of 1918 were seen on mail. The stickers were also affixed to letters, photo albums, and anywhere that fancy dictated. | Image courtesy of David Bartlet, Calgary.

pamphlets, buttons, and window cards attesting to subscription, as well as other ephemera, including widely used stamp stickers. These bore logos and designs such as "Step Now for Victory Bonds or Goose Step Later" below a marching, German-helmeted goose. On another, featuring the pointing soldier, the meaning of "Stick It Canada! Buy More Victory Bonds" puzzled some.[79] Soldiers understood; as one wrote in August 1918, until the war is over, "we have got to 'stick it'" in a show of fortitude. The stickers – not unlike Christmas Seals (for anti-tuberculosis campaigns) and the "poster stamps" used in advertising – appeared everywhere, including on correspondence, envelopes, and parcels. Reproductions emerged in donated advertisements in newspapers.[80] The propagandistic atmosphere was enjoyed by some, and that was part of the intent. From Montreal, an enthusiastic Ruth Antliff sent some of the stickers to her son overseas: "Posters which are most artistic are everywhere and these stickers come home on our parcels from the stores."[81] The stamp of 1917 with the finger-pointing soldier even found its way to Australia for possible adaptation the following year.[82]

In hundreds of donated advertisements, there was commercial crossover, another component of atmosphere. As its contribution to the loan campaign, the E.G. Gillett Company of Toronto had its well-known billboard for Magic Baking Powder redesigned by Rous and Mann, the printing firm. In the original, designed by English illustrator John Hassall and captioned "A Great Catch,"[83] a policeman leads away a crying boy and his terrier, apparently for illegal fishing; in one hand, he holds the boy's rod and worm can (a Magic Baking Powder can). In the background is a miniature billboard advertising Gillett's powder. In its own ads, the Poster Advertising Association of Canada touted the billboard poster, at 10 by 25 feet, for its "conspicuousness" if placed every few blocks. In the adaptation, where humour is wonderfully displayed,[84] the policeman leads away a little Paul von Hindenburg, the German military leader. The distant billboard is reworded "Victory Bonds/Shorten the War" and the caption is changed to "Help to catch Huns." *Marketing and Business Management* called the adaptation "One of the cleverest stunts in the Victory Loan Campaign ... This has not been without value to the advertiser, of course." *Printer and Publisher* claimed that it "probably ranks amongst the best known of Canadian posters."[85]

The atmosphere on the home front at the time of the armistice, much of it intensified by the war-loan campaign, is hard to capture in words. The sight of 3,000 posters in Montreal's monster parade on 11 November contributed to a "kind of street theatre."[86] On the impact of posters, different theories were expounded, including immediacy of message and constancy of repetition – the atmosphere that campaigners aimed for. Three Liberty Loan campaigns in the United States brought critical attention to posters, and exhibits there gave exposure to Canada's Victory Loan posters secured on exchange or by collectors. Bundles came and went across the border, some officially and some through personal and institutional networks. In an exhibition by the Buffalo Historical Society in early 1919, Nicolet's Flanders poster was singled out as "perhaps one of the most appealing."[87] Seeing it at a show at the New York Public Library, another reviewer described it as "beautifully colored and skilfully executed."[88] The war-poster show held in March 1919 at Toronto's Forum Hall, in aid of a veterans' fund, drew from the all-country collection of James C. Heerey, an Australian mining entrepreneur, who attended to supervise.[89] Among the avid collectors at home was Captain Louis Keene, an artist and author, who loaned his "patriotic posters" to the Women's Art Association of Toronto for exhibition in November. In Point Grey, Vancouver, Theodore Elizabeth Wright, the daughter of an insurance agent, showed her noteworthy collection. Many of the posters at the Nova Scotia Archives came from Violet Black, whose father, William Marshall Black, had opened the Opera House, which doubled as a cinema, in Wolfville in 1911.[90] Posters thus joined the ranks of war trophies and other souvenirs.

Aesthetically, Canadian posters land between those of the United States and Europe. Like American works, they use strategies from commercial advertising and printing, but they are largely without sensationalist depiction and echo the realism of English, French, and German posters, which emphasize sacrifice and civilian contribution.[91] Cross-border flows and comparisons led some observers to note the reticence in Canadian (and British) work to use sensual, glamourized "girls" in the graphic style (and feminized messaging) of American artists such as Charles Dana Gibson, Howard Chandler Christy, and Władysław Teodor Benda, although some depictions at home and overseas of the allegorical Miss Canada and Miss Toronto came close.[92] One *Globe* reporter had mused about such depictions back in 1915, stating that if Gibson or Christy "wanted to make a picture of the best type of Canadian military nursing sister he would consider himself lucky to secure Mrs. George Eedson Burns [Anne Louise Mills] for a model," on the basis of her "smart uniform."[93] Starting in 1917, as discussed below, film and live theatre would help to fill the demand for appealing figures.

The poster industry in both Canada and the United States took full advantage of this visual prominence to extol its medium, often in hyperbolical language and promotions. Store windows and walls became filled with Victory Loan posters and displays, a few featuring military gear and models of soldiers mixed with store products. Some displays were professionally executed, including one in Montreal by noted New York dioramic specialist Dwight Franklin. Prizes were offered for best displays. All kinds of retail promotions involved Victory Bonds, with merchants acting as surrogate agents. Given Canada's role as a supplier of produce to Britain, thrift and food-conservation posters from the Canada Food Board were part of the array.

Throughout 1918 and into 1919, Canadians continued to see, along with the war-loan posters, those put out by the Ministry of Soldiers' Civil Re-establishment, the National Service Board, the Canada Food Board (dissolved in early 1919), and the National War Savings Committee (discontinued in January 1920) to push thrift and war-savings stamps and certificates.[94] In 1919, in exhibitions held in New York, Montreal, Ottawa, Toronto, and London, war posters from many countries were shown alongside war souvenirs and formal war art, much of it sponsored by the Canadian War Memorials Fund, which had been set up in Britain three years prior. Two exhibitions illustrate the new environs and popularity of posters, whether seen as propaganda, affirmation of victory, or artifacts. In October, at the Canadian National Exhibition, a major show hosted by the fund attracted thousands to see guns and aeroplanes, sculptures, posters, war photographs, and paintings of torn corpses and blasted battlefields, many of them done in Europe by Canadians.[95] Viewer response varied, but the show was deemed an extraordinary success.[96] Viewer curiosity was a big factor, as it was in Victory Loan events. Signage for the Victory Loan peeks out in two paintings done on the home front: George A. Reid's *Armistice Day, Toronto* (1919) and Stanley F. Turner's *A War Record* (c. 1919), depicting a view there of "Wizz-Bang Corner" (Yonge Street and Davisville Avenue) near a military orthopaedic hospital. Posters may not have impressed in mixed shows, but their validity as artistic mementos was clear. By the time of the Victory Loan in late October 1919, they remained a primary medium. At this point in Britain, in the view of *Punch*'s satirists, the "universal eruption" of war-loan and thrift posters pointed to "a new Art – that of Government by advertisement," a development mirrored in Canada.

News of the fall loan had peaked the interest of prospective artists. On 19 July, Private Graham Craigie Norwell, a student before the war and a budding artist, had written to White from Sir Sandford Fleming Military Convalescent Home in Ottawa, asking if posters would be designed. His letter was acknowledged, but there would be no public contest. In the first three weeks of August, following on the heels of the Victory Loan organizational conference, the dominion publicity committee moved rapidly to get posters designed and printed; eighteen were commissioned. The themes, consistent with the campaign's sweeping-broom logo, were industrial and agrarian growth, reconstruction, re-establishment, and export trade (imperial purchases mainly), needs that did not easily convey, in graphic form, the urgency of the war years. Artists who had provided designs in 1917–18 submitted sketches based on specified "lines of appeal." Those found favourable were returned for completion by 18 August. "In almost every case," committee chair William Norman McIlwraith reported, "some alteration needed and sketches now back with artists. Instructed to return completed sketch by the 22nd. It is intention to immediately thereafter place orders with the lithographers." By 16 September, the posters and "other colour work" had been placed with printers in six cities in three provinces. Printers in Montreal and the West who had been left out complained.[97]

The campaign's first appeal would be strong in western Canada, where a poster showing grain would resonate, and then stronger still in the urban centres of the East, where posters of industries would be floated. Basic instructions were also offered. "Picture" posters worked best in store windows, whereas wordy posters were used in places that they could be easily read, such as railway stations, banks, lunchrooms, hotel lobbies, barbershops, marketplaces, and factories. To counter the anticipated "lines of resistance," local publicity committees would receive printed suggestions and the ubiquitous informational brochures.[98]

For many of the posters, rationales were offered in the publicity committee's bulletins. W.P.1 moved a worker, a flag-bearing soldier, and a winged Victory figure over a cross-and-poppy-filled Flanders field to an industrial landscape. Designed by Malcolm Gibson of Color-Craft Limited in Toronto, W.P.4, the only poster with a "negative appeal," featured idle factories – the result of not buying bonds. The gloomy message here is furthered by flat colours. The committee worried that such pessimism could backfire. Just as military officials had deplored shaming in recruitment posters aimed at women,[99] fearmongering was generally avoided in Victory Loan propaganda. With a few exceptions, such as the *Victory Telegraph* (Toronto) and official advertisements that warned of German invasion, the alarmism of many American posters was shunned.[100] One advisory pamphlet issued to speakers encouraged them, when talking of soldiers dying, to say that they did so without agony, happy with their sacrifice.[101] W.P.5, designed by Arthur Keelor, a commercial artist with Rous and Mann, featured a smiling soldier taking off his coat and saying, "Come On!/Let's finish the job/Buy Victory Bonds." It so impressed the committee that they also made it into a billboard as the "get-ready poster." Featuring a farmer with produce and a farm, a bond in the background, W.P.11 stated, "Let's facilitate the sale of our products by subscribing to the Victory Loan." Issued only in French for distribution in Quebec, it reflected the province's wartime prominence in agricultural production and the nationalist emphasis on farming peculiar to Quebec.[102] Other posters – W.P.12, 13, 14, and 15 – offered, in utilitarian fashion, the "specific selling arguments" of security, income, and saleability. Two more featured the Prince of Wales honour flag, suitable for his visit, and the employees' honour banner, both much sought after.

Although most of the posters of 1919 lacked the emotionalism of the 1917–18 issues, several displayed fine composition, where manipulation, information, and familiar cultural norms could all be in play. Arthur Keelor's modernistic W.P.8 ("For Industrial Expansion/Buy Victory Bonds") and W.P.7 ("Our Export Trade Is Vital/Buy Victory Bonds") are characterized by "dynamic composition with strong vertical and diagonal thrusts, bright primary colours and bold lettering, and pictures of powerfully grouped labourers" building Toronto's Bloor Street Viaduct against a backdrop with trails of steam or smoke.[103] Emotional pressure comes out fully in W.P.18, "Do it again/Daddy/Please!/Buy Me a Victory Bond," a reiteration of the "Oh please do! Daddy" poster of 1917. In an instance of commercial overlap (or encroachment), Fry's Cocoa of Toronto claimed that the little girl in some of its print advertisements was the model for "Do it again."[104]

The distribution and placement of posters could be slightly less arduous than door-to-door canvassing. Newspaper reports nevertheless vested the job with urgency. In Toronto, for example, publicity meant for factories was mailed, and "a full set of posters" was sent to each school.[105] On 23 October 1919, seventy-five businessmen in cars blanketed the city's stores and banks with posters. The task was done in six hours, "thanks in many cases," the *Toronto World* reported, "to the wives of owners of cars who took over the work when their men folk found it impossible to do so." Once the campaign was over, posters were unceremoniously torn down. Some were saved by collectors, museums, and libraries. The loan's publicity chair, McIlwraith, asked Roberts in the finance department if it or the dominion archives would take the original sketches for the posters. Send them in, Roberts replied.

As in past drives, posters were not a fixture that viewers commented on publicly in 1919, nor did they have the momentum of war behind them. In December, *Marketing and Business Management* was extra skeptical: "The critically inclined will pass up most of the latest Victory Loan posters as not being posters at all, but merely coloured, some illustrated, bulletins."[106] Except for some archives, museums,[107] and collectors, the posters – "the poor man's picture gallery" to some academics of the time (a view now questioned)[108] – were all but forgotten until the Second World War. In the interval, however, the advertising industry did not hesitate to proclaim the value of its contribution. Whereas some saw the medium as a vehicle of propaganda, others saw it as opportunity, among them Herbert Andrew Williams, manager of the Canadian Poster Company.[109] One large agency, McConnell and Fergusson of London, Ontario, gave the achievement mythic proportion in a newspaper advertisement where it declared that the Victory Loan campaign "provides an excellent example of the power of advertising, properly directed, to mould public opinion into one enthusiastic whole."[110] An article by Rufus William Gould, secretary of the Canadian Manufacturers' Association, drove home this perspective with great boastfulness in August 1920:

> In Canada, White advertised for a new Victory Loan. He got it ... Posters and newspaper advertisements put more stalwart Canadian fighting men in the trenches on the western front than did all the fevered oratory of the mayors, municipal councillors and county constables throughout the length and breadth of this country, and I do not attempt to belittle their efforts ... The picture burned into the memory of the eligible by a clever poster, cleverly worded and drawn was well nigh impossible to ignore.[111]

Praise of a sort also came from two British curators, Martin Hardie and Arthur Knowles Sabin, in their decidedly anglophile *War Posters Issued by Belligerent and Neutral Nations, 1914–1919,* published in 1920. Of the British "colonies," Canada, Australia, and South Africa "produced posters of quite a high standard," they wrote. Canada's W.P.11 of 1918 – the beaver poster – "shows what promise there is, and indeed attained, among the Western children of our race."[112]

The finance-related posters reveal the predominance of the investment and economic pitches and of the emotional and moral appeals. In his study of propaganda posters, historian Terry Crowley argues for caution: "It would be difficult to retrieve the meanings attached to these posters by contemporaries on the basis of the images alone." Evidence from British documentary sources, he finds, can reveal disdain for the "mawkish sentiment of these posters and their attempts to provoke feelings of guilt,"[113] a conclusion close to contemporary disparagement of Canada's war-loan circus. Regardless of the claims of the poster and advertising industries, posters cannot be given full credit for the success of the loan campaigns but were part of a larger flow of information. In looking at the parallel success of the Liberty Loans, marketing historian Donald F. Dixon maintains, in a statement that could apply to Canada, that success was not "the achievement of advertising alone. The sale of Liberty Bonds was embedded in a more general campaign to convince a divided public of the merits of the war effort and to stifle dissent."[114] Posters were far from being the only form of visual propaganda.

In *Brushes and Bayonets: Cartoons, Sketches and Paintings of World War I,*[115] Lucinda Gosling makes a case that in Britain the Great War was "an illustrators' war," apart from the work of "fine" artists, a category that in Canada would include those studied by historian Maria Tippett.[116] Although illustrators were more prolific in Britain and France than in Canada, the field here was not barren. Through pen-and-ink sketches, editorial cartoonists had satirized the Borden government over railway nationalization, profiteering, the election of 1917, and broad social concerns. Sam Hunter of the *Toronto World* did not hesitate to pick on a "young" Tommy White, suggesting that he was not up to adult responsibility. Working for the *Grain Growers' Guide* in Winnipeg, Archibald Dale on 24 February 1915 lampooned him in "How Canada Becomes Rich by Taxation," where the nervous minister's consumer taxes outweigh poor crops, unemployment, and low wages. In one cartoon in November 1918, the *British Columbia Federationist* (Vancouver) looked at a local labour conflict and saw democracy under threat from government by orders-in-council, industrial autocracy, and Germanic "militaryism," and elsewhere in the issue, there appeared an official advertisement touting "Labor's Interest in Victory Loan 1918."[117]

In the first months of conflict, Canada's few full-time cartoonists had been caught between revulsion for war and imperial duty. In the *Grain Growers' Guide* on 12 August 1914, Dale's "The Angel of Death Is Abroad in Europe" was stark. On 14 October, his "The Dance of Death" featured a drum-beating skeleton leading figures labelled Armaments Trust, Famine, Powder Maker, Cannon Maker, Pestilence, and Ruin. Other artists expressed similar abhorrence, but the national cause won out. In August, cartoons in the *Edmonton Journal* and Montreal's *Star* and *La Presse*, among others, had Canadians set to fight; throughout the early months, many of the front-page cartoons in the humour weekly

A.E. Gleed, "The Bonds of Love." Using clever wordplay, an amateur artist in St. Catharines, Ontario, has a uniformed "Jack Canuck" reaching out from a Victory Bond poster to thank a grateful "Miss Canada" for buying bonds. Such use of poster imagery was common. | *Globe* (Toronto), 4 December 1917.

Le Canard (Montreal) were anti-German. In Britain, the War Propaganda Bureau was engaging artists and writers, among them Louis Raemaekers,[118] the masterful illustrator of atrocity, to blend humour with messaging through distortion and ridicule. By late 1916, Raemaekers's less-shocking cartoons were being seen in Canada.

Canadian newspapers pulled cartoons from various British sources. Reproductions from *Punch* were noticed seriously, if not widely. A reproduction of Sir Bernard Partridge's famous depiction there on 5 May 1915 of "Canada!" – a propagandistic tribute to the Battle of Ypres in April in the shape of a heroic, flag-waving Canadian soldier – appeared in the *Globe* in June. Well regarded by Canadians, Partridge's original was acquired by Sir George Perley in England and presented to Borden "for preservation in Canada."[119] The drawing would have extended life in the advertisements of department stores and manufacturers,[120] and it was the basis for the final design of Canada's thrift and war-savings stamps and war-bond coupons of 1918–19, where small-scale obscured recognition of the link to Ypres.[121] In his coverage of the British War Loan,[122] William Lacey Amy, the prolific Canadian writer, pointed to *Punch*'s famous cartoon by Frederick Pegram, "A Plain Duty," where a soldier greets a man about to buy a war bond, a cartoon reproduced in Canadian newspapers.[123] With foreign cartoons attracting attention, too, artistic sparks slowly began to emerge from the pens of local cartoonists in various newspapers, seldom with viciousness.[124]

Cartoons about the war loans entered this bag of topics. Known for artistic finesse and political bite, Sam Hunter, who satirized White over his failure to boost taxes on profiteers, had Jack Canuck rolling up bags of dollars for a war loan in another sketch. In Winnipeg, Dale of the *Grain Growers' Guide* beckoned farmers and other "recruits" for the "Money Battalion" and placed John Bull, the personification of Britain, at Canada's sales wicket. In his simple "To-day's Hero" segment in the *Montreal Daily Mail* on 15 March 1917, George D. Lawrence had a stout cigar smoker looking at a sign that read, "Do It Now/Invest in New Canadian War Loan."[125] Although few in number, with none of the brutal edges of Raemaekers and others, these cartoons would help to place war loans in the home-based realm of humour and entertainment, which the first Victory Loan would exploit so effectively as part of the drive to fund supplies for Britain. A cartoon in an Ottawa paper in April 1918 praising the farmer as "the man to win the war" stirred comment in the Commons and the press over the delinquency of wheat shipments to Britain.[126] In British Columbia, the Victory Bond pieces of James Brian Fitzmaurice for the *Vancouver Daily Province* were a mainstay in his cartooning of the war and the home front, a class-bound, male-oriented oeuvre explored by Robin Anderson (a rare instance of historical examination of the form in Canada). For the 1918 loan campaign, with the war's end in sight, "Fitz" adopted an upbeat approach, where his "multi-panel style increased comic potential by embedding absurdity within commonly experienced situations."[127] Contextually, viewers appreciated cartoonists, like Britain's famous artist-author-playwright Bruce Bairnsfather, who could turn battlefield horror into cheerfulness, a preference reflected in Canadian cartoons and staged comedies and cinematic interludes featuring his famed anti-hero, soldier Old Bill.

The fraternity of cartoonists in Canada was small, with viewership restricted mostly to the large dailies. Although cartoonists would continue to address domestic politics, it was recognized that attacks on the enemy, slackers, and war profiteers could be effectively blended with humour. Increasingly, too, national symbols began appearing, among them the maple leaf and the allegorical figures Johnny or Jack Canuck, Janey Canuck, Miss Canada, and Winged Victory. The pre-war Miss Canada, once a graphic model for women's fashion and a national symbol, moved into her patriotic alter ego during the war, decked out in a white gown and flag.[128] She appeared everywhere – in songs, plays, films, sculptures (including the gigantic figure by Frances Loring for the Canadian National Exhibition in 1917), exhibition appearances, cartoons, and Victory Loan ads – much like the symbolic Marianne in France, Britannia in Britain, Miss Liberty and Miss Columbia in the United States, and Joan of Arc in Britain, Canada, and America.

Some of the humour that ran throughout cartooning resembled that in the far-off, front-line trench newspapers. The *Listening Post* (7th Canadian Infantry Battalion) had been a bemused observer of Britain's second war loan in 1915. It calculated that carrying the equivalent gold to the national war chest would take a 38-mile procession of 200,000 soldiers, stretching the distance from Vancouver to Nanaimo. It was in this journal that one commentator, in 1917, spoke of "our grand, last, and final Victory War Loan," far in the future, in 1965. Such humour had counterparts in Canada, where it blended with the wryest of cartoons and with the quips of at least one humour newspaper, Montreal's *Le Canard,* which (usually) supported the war loans. With reference to Quebec's premier, it mused, "Sir Lomer [Gouin] bought $10,000 worth of Victory bonds. That's what accelerated the signature of the Armistice."[129]

Cartooning had been absent from the war-loan drive of 1915, but so were most forms of visual propaganda. In September 1916, Dale's "Bringing in the Sheaves," which called for "marshalling agricultural resources to the war loan," appeared in the *Grain Growers' Guide* and the *Financial Post* (Toronto). The loan of March 1917 saw slightly more cartoons: "A Plain Duty" from *Punch* appeared in the *Montreal Gazette;* one in the *Montreal Daily Mail* featured a subscriber; William Noakes drew for the *Regina Morning Leader;* and Raemaekers appeared in the *Saskatoon Phoenix* and the *Morning Leader.* During the campaign of March, when many newspapers accepted official prospectuses for publication, the *Toronto World*'s Hunter did not hesitate, while also turning out his anti-German cartoons, to take more jabs at the finance minister.[130] In the *Grain Growers' Guide* of 2 May 1917, just weeks after Vimy Ridge, Arch Dale portrayed White chasing the figure of "Corporations" for their untaxed wealth. Viewers, however, were being exposed to the range of perspectives and venues possible in a deluge of other cartooning and illustrated ads for recruitment in newspapers and magazines; comic strips; illustrated

Frederick H. Varley, "Laura Secord Risked Her Life for Her Country – To-day – Canada Asks Her Women To Lend Their Money – Victory Bonds." | For this advertisement, donated by sixteen businesses, Varley, then a commercial artist, links the War of 1812 heroine and Canada's financial need during the Great War. Evocation of Canada's past was frequent. | *Toronto Daily Star,* 27 November 1917.

public lectures by cartoonists, among them Arthur George Racey of Montreal and Thomas Lewis Skuce of Toronto; public exhibitions of cartoons, posters, and paintings; and sharp critiques in *Le Nationaliste* (Montreal) and the *Toronto World.*

The Victory Loan campaigns of November–December 1917 and 1918 drew on a large number of promotional cartoons. In Quebec, *La Patrie* offered the highest number, some from regional sources and others reproduced from New York newspapers. English Canadian admen and cartoonists found inspiration and authority in the much-memorialized heroes of the War of 1812 (among them Laura Secord and Charles-Michel de Salaberry), Great War battlefields, and Nelson's flagship *Victory.* "Laura Secord Risked Her Life For Her Country

Mutt and Jeff adaptation, "To the Bond Buyer Belongs the Victory." *Mutt and Jeff* was Bud Fisher's widely seen comic strip. Here, Mutt has Jeff use his dividends to buy more bonds. | *Regina Morning Leader*, 13 November 1918.

... Today – Canada Asks Her Women To Lend Their Money" boomed an advertisement from sixteen financial companies below a drawing of a resolute Secord emerging from the woods, done by Frederick H. Varley, then an artist with Rous and Mann in Toronto. In a handful of large dailies, caricatures of local loan officials brought smiles and social recognition. The majority of the nonlocal cartoons appeared in multiple publications, many drawn from large American dailies. Several pieces were commissioned by the Victory Loan Committee. The types varied, from single frames to comic strips, an indispensable feature from around 1915, aided by syndicated distribution. From the newspapers examined here, almost thirty known and unknown cartoonists can be identified, including the creators of famous strips such as *Pop Perkins, Bringing Up Father, The Doo-Dads,* and *Mutt and Jeff.*

In addition, newspapers – the *Halifax Herald* being a good example – had access to the reproducible work of American syndicates, and artists were employed to illustrate official and donated advertisements. The dominion publicity committee readily supplied the newspapers with samples; one that called for sacrifice, in its depiction of a physician waiting over a dying child, drew from Sir Luke Fildes's famous painting *The Doctor* (1891). Like the posters, these ads were geared to the stages of the campaigns and regional targets, and they were adjusted with the onset of peace. Typical themes and images were employed: soldiers' sacrifices, the grieving wife, Flanders, German enslavement, beavers, children, Miss Canada, industrial and economic growth, and end of the war. Since no publication published the full series, strategic goals were undoubtedly lost on most readers. The repetition and reworking of images and themes were likely noticed by interested viewers. A number of the official and sponsored advertisements were echoed in the superb cover of the *Canadian Home Journal* (Toronto) in November 1918. Painted by Frank Downey, an artist with the Advertising Service Company in Toronto, it portrayed a young widow – a motif and shaming technique in much propaganda[131] – with a maple-leaf banner in the background and this caption: "She Gave Her All/You're Only Asked to Loan/Buy a Victory Bond."

Publicists played all the angles of marketing. In the midst of the 1918 campaign, the Dominion Press News and Feature Service announced the winner of a cartoon contest, which had opened at the beginning of October: the entry of Winnipeg artist Malcolm Daniel Charleson, "Victory is OURS." Not unlike the Ypres stamp, it was judged on its merits "as publicly calculated to assist in the selling of Victory bonds" and was widely published, but the conventional image of a soldier charging forth with a flag drew little comment. Some propaganda could fall flat. What also emerges from Victory Loan advertising is the business substructure. As noted, not every official advertisement could be published in a single source, especially weekly newspapers. Not only did publishers have to juggle submitted advertising and news releases against local material, but costs and revenues also entered every calculation, and printing plates and permissions for cartoons had to be secured. The publicity committee, in addition to official advertisements, sent out samples for newspapers to offer to potential sponsors. In October 1919, for instance, the publisher of Charlottetown's *Island Patriot* offered "Victory Loan ads all ready on hand" whose size and wording could be adjusted.[132]

Whatever adaptations or exclusions were made, partisan intent could intrude, especially during the overheated election campaign of 1917. On voting day, 17 December, the *Globe* ran a cartoon by Elisha Newton McConnell. In a blatant anti-Quebec sketch sponsored by the Citizens' Union Committee of Toronto, a sneering Henri Bourassa stands atop a massive block of ice called "A Solid Quebec" that has been violently dropped on "Old Man Toronto," his hat and

Victory Bonds knocked to the side. "Only a Solid Ontario Can Defeat Them," the piece blared. In Winnipeg, cartoonist Benny Batsford took leave from the army to work on the loan for his old employer (and supporter of the Unionist government) the *Free Press,* where he set out to boost conscription and to "lampoon the opposition forces." The result, *Cartoons Magazine* (Chicago) noted, was a series in which he "rapped the anti-war element in Quebec, showed the folly of party spirit in war time, and made clear the duty of Canadians to their men overseas."[133] During the election, cartoonist Arthur George Racey also designed a poster urging viewers to vote for the Unionist government. Foreshadowing the famous war-loan poster of 1918, his call drew a direct link to "Our Glorious Dead" through lines from "In Flanders Fields." Retorts in the Quebec press often came in the form of pointed editorials and blistering letters castigating the Toronto mindset.

Following the war, cartoons drifted back to the mainstays of comics and social and political criticism. In early 1919, the National War Savings Committee sponsored a cartoon contest, but it received little publicity; the $50 prize was won by C.F. Sauverburn of Montreal. Poster exhibitions, such as that at the Forum Hall in Toronto in March 1919, often included cartoons as kindred work, although their content is unknown. The cartoons produced for the war-loan campaign of 1919 lacked wartime verve. Many, in keeping with the campaign's themes, publicized "sensible" investment and reconstruction – dry stuff for cartoonists, but they made the most of the situation. In an unsigned cartoon in the *Port Arthur News-Chronicle* depicting a horse race, a steed named Prosperity was "an easy winner against Luxury and other opponents" (a gloss on the real tensions between consumerism and restraint). Viewers of an illustrated, official ad in *Hardware and Metal* (Toronto) probably chuckled over the title, "The Kaiser Is Canned." Wilhelm, with his spiked helmet and potential for facial exaggeration, was a caricaturist's dream. Other official ads displayed regional sensibility. One, released at the start of the campaign, featured soldiers marching along. In the English version of 1914 to 1915, a song sheet in the background proclaims, "When They Went Away Singing 'Tipperary,'" with reference to the much-beloved British music-hall song. In the French version, the song and words are replaced by "Le Glorieux 22ème," about the French Canadian battalion. For acerbic cartoonists such as Sam Hunter of the *Toronto World,* war loans no longer had much attraction. It was the political and social issues of the day that guided his pen: railway nationalization, United Farmers politics, proportional representation, and prohibition.

As with posters, a question arises: what impact did cartoons have? Admittedly, they were sparse overall. Illustrated talks by cartoonists and their confreres, the vaudevillian "chalk-talkers," drew crowds eager to hear banter and to see live drawing and projections on screens from glass slides. In 1916, Skuce of the *Toronto World* gave illustrated talks at theatres using his "facile pencil" and slides. During the 1918 campaign in Toronto, in shows to boost the loan just before the armistice, *Daily Star* cartoonist Harry Beamer Moyer projected amusing images drawn quickly on smoked-glass plates. Caricatures of the kaiser drew laughs; drawings of the king, British prime minister Lloyd George, and American president Woodrow Wilson were enjoyed. "But it was when Mr. Moyer depicted a lonely field in Flanders, with the solitary figure of a fully equipped Canadian soldier doing homage at the grave of a dead comrade, that the patriotic fervour of the audience was seen and heard on every side."[134] Slides were also in circulation among theatres in Newfoundland in 1918. Newspapers there adapted lithographic sketches originating with the *New York Tribune,* done by illustrators such as William Balfour Ker and Jay Norwood ("Ding") Darling.

"Bucking the Kaiser / Buy a Bond / In the Good Old Western Style." In this action cartoon, which appeared in many western newspapers, a horse named "Buy a Bond" throws off the German Kaiser. Many Victory Loan cartoons had such regional flavour. | *Red Deer News,* 13 November 1918.

Like the many Victory Loan entertainments, cartoons offered humour and strove to boost morale. Letters to the *Toronto News* in November 1917 made this point with reference to the cartoons of Newt McConnell, who contemporaries also recognized for his crude but powerful style and for his mastery of facial caricature. Historian Eberhard Demm broadens the assessment: "Cartoons form an integral part of propaganda; they cannot be isolated from other forms of it. Thus, one cannot distinguish precisely if it was a cartoon, a speech or a newspaper article which led to a certain reaction of the addressees."[135] A contemporary source, *Canadian Bookman* (Montreal), offered this summation of combined effect in April 1919: "The newspaper cartoon ... long recognized as a powerful weapon, was, during the war, ably supported by the poster, showcard, and painting."[136] All were brought to bear.

Although by far the most conspicuous, posters, advertisements, cartoons, and other illustrations were not the only forms of visual propaganda for war loans. Throughout the campaigns of 1917 to 1919, there was hardly a major newspaper that did not feature photographs of executives, teams, and committees, with those depicted garnering no small amount of social prestige. The dominion and provincial publicity bodies matched this display with countless photographs of Sir Thomas White and even pictures and articles on the campaigns' recording offices, switchboards, and bond printing by the American Bank Note Company in Ottawa (all dominated by female workers). Published in French and English newspapers, one photograph shows White, who had already gone on film in 1917, engaging in another modern medium on behalf of 1918's campaign: making a promotional, four-minute recording in the studios of the Berliner Gramophone Company in Montreal for its series His Master's Voice/Le Voix de Maître. The medium was widely in use, from the British election of 1910 to America's Liberty Loan campaigns.[137]

Alongside recordings and other paraphernalia, bonds were always a focus of tangible propaganda. Official pamphlets, press releases, and advertisements never stopped explaining them, beginning with a simple definition: they were pieces of paper with value. Made smaller as paper supplies became scarce, they were created with the technical expertise accorded postage stamps and dominion dollar bills. Regardless of their contribution to the war-loan atmosphere, they seldom drew commentary on their own. Issued in different sizes, they could contain vignettes of the king, the queen, and the governor general, as well as allegorical figures, the Parliament Buildings, Canada's coat of arms, and trains, warships, merchant vessels, or factories. The attached interest coupons could feature images of Britannia and, in the issues of 1918–19, miniaturized engravings of Bernard Partridge's Ypres-soldier picture from 1915, also reproduced on the war-savings and thrift stamps released in December 1918. But the bonds,

SCIENCE AND INDUSTRY AID VICTORY LOAN

As an instance of how science and industry have co-operated in helping to win the war, it is interesting to note that Sir Thomas White, K.C.M.G., Minister of Finance, has made a special "His Master's Voice" Record for the purpose of actually informing the Canadian Public in his *own voice* concerning the need of the second Victory Loan.

Science has thus made it possible for the voice of the Finance Minister to be heard in thousands of places in every part of the Country at the same time.

The illustration shows Sir Thomas "caught in the act" as he made his special recording at the laboratories of the Berliner Gram-o-phone Company, Limited, Montreal.

A master of media, Sir Thomas White records a speech for gramophones. "Science has thus made it possible," the caption ran, "for the Voice of the Finance Minister to be heard in thousands of places in every part of the Country at the same time." | *Regina Morning Leader*, 6 November 1918.

coupons, and stamps, not unlike posters, were ephemeral: once redeemed or converted, they were destroyed or hidden away. Lost to us, too, were perhaps the eight life-size sculptures of a "typical Canadian soldier" done for 1917's Victory Loan by three Eaton's employees for placement throughout Toronto's downtown. The soldier, not unlike Partridge's figure, surges forward, a rifle in one hand and a flag in the other.

Visual and aural connection mattered in fostering public engagement.

13

Selling through Film, Theatre, Music, and Words

AFTER THE START OF THE WAR, theatre proprietors faced audiences thinned by enlistment. The numbers of travelling performance companies had been in decline for some years, forcing proprietors to innovate, some by playing more films. Vaudeville and movie houses, where promotions could dovetail with entertainment, were natural venues for the war loans. From the early months to well into 1916, charitable fundraising and benefits appeared alongside commercial fare and war films. It was not until the high-powered publicity of the Victory Loan of 1917 that loans hit the stages, with local campaigns kicking off in crowded theatres. In October 1918, many were shut down because of influenza, but the start of the campaign in early November brought extraordinary pressures to reopen and entrepreneurial inventiveness. In Toronto, following the "Flu Vacation," crowds thronged back on 5 November to see American actors in new Victory Loan films as well as other loan films "showing some of our troops at the front," and to hear the likes of Canadian-born baritone George MacFarlane sing these lines:

> Every bond that we are buying
> Helps our boys to the Rhine,
> Buy bonds, buy bonds,
> For your boy and mine.

Subscriptions ensued, thus making the patron into "an active war-citizen," as one study frames the engagement.[1]

Driven by the surge of nationalism, the Canadian silent-film industry experienced a flurry of production, with governments and cinema owners seeking to reconcile the burst with censorship and warfare. Sanitized war films were labelled as realistic depictions. The public appetite was keen but not without backlash. In Toronto in November 1915, *Carmen*, with American star Geraldine Farrar, drew reaction because of her alleged "pro-German tendencies." That same month, Canada's militia department released *Canada's Fighting Forces.* It avoided any scenes of warfare – the department worried about the possible impact on enlistment – and the Battle of Ypres in April was portrayed only on a map. Films depicting broad aspects of the war, made officially through the Canadian War Records Office in Britain, started to arrive in cinemas early in 1917, but they met with mixed reviews, weak ticket sales, and disputes over censorship.[2] War films of any kind never dominated distribution and programming, and like newspapers, theatres did not exist everywhere.

In the larger centres, cinemas, theatres, and vaudeville houses were bringing in dozens of films and live performances. In March 1917, audiences at Griffin's Theatre in Belleville saw *The Canadian Army in Action and the Appearance of the Tanks* (filmed in September 1916 at the battle of Courcelette), a presentation by the pioneering impresarios Julius (Jule or Jules) and Jay Junior Allen of Toronto and the "first official film of the Canadians in action" by the Canadian War Records Office. Such glimpses were more often the stuff of escapist entertainment or curiosity. More common were the kind of films and variety shows being seen on one random day, 3 September 1918. Shea's vaudeville theatre in Toronto featured an American dramatization of Jack London's *The Sea Wolf* (1904) and two acts: a singer and a violinist. At the Regent Theatre in Calgary, ticket holders could see the American films *The Claws of the Hun,* on "the inside workings of the German spy system," and *The Woman in the Web,* about the overthrow of Russia's czar and the "red scare."

In wartime Quebec, French-language films were often either melodramas or documentaries, some featuring Belgian independence and French dignitaries and places. Screenings of graphic war content were shunned. Despite censorship and clerical criticisms of American influences, audiences were drawn to fictionalized action, the machines of war, invasions in Europe, romance, and sacrifice, creating what one historian of film in Quebec and Ontario regards as "propagande patriotique."[3] Sarah Bernhardt's hugely popular *Mères françaises (Mothers of France)* (1917), for one, stressed maternal sacrifice. *La scene française pendant la guerre,* made in Paris and billed at Théâtre Passe-Temps in Montreal as beautiful and revelatory, appeared along with George M. Cohan's comedic *Hit-the-Trail Holliday,* straight from New York.

Screenings of war films, meant to stimulate the war effort, were frequently combined with lectures, appeals, and accompaniments such as maps, features that would eventually include relief-fund and war-loan promotions. In March 1916, the proceeds from the American film *The Battle Cry of Peace,* a box-office success in the United States, went to the Toronto and York Patriotic Association. Film as a means of promoting loans had been adopted in Britain as early as 1916.[4] After the United States entered the war in April 1917, the industry there mobilized as a powerful ally, especially for the Liberty Loan drives beginning in May.[5] Canadian audiences quickly became inundated with American film propaganda, a tool permeated with women in nonpassive roles.[6] *The Little American,* a fourteen-minute war drama made in July with Toronto-born, Hollywood-championed Mary Pickford,[7] came to Toronto in November to highlight the opening of the Allen Theatre at Richmond and Victoria, with music by local maestro Luigi Romanelli. Pickford was equally popular in Quebec, where her film came out as *La Petite Américaine,* and for her fashionable attire.

Film in Canada during wartime is ably recounted by historians.[8] In addition to commercial fare, the medium was being used by several federal and provincial departments. Charles Tepperman, in his examination of the Ontario Motion Picture Bureau, formed in May 1917, looks at rural audiences and the use of film for education about farming practice, highways, and public health.[9] Such films were often exhibited on recreational occasions, including at patriotic gatherings and, later, at concerts in aid of Victory Loan drives. In September, the federal Food Controller set up a Motion Picture Distribution Committee. In 1918, the publicity branch of the Ministry of Soldiers' Civil Re-establishment issued the poster series Canada's Work for Wounded Soldiers, along with a film of the same title. Both the posters and the film were bolstered by the appearance of wounded soldiers in Victory Loan advertising.

Aware of other departments' use of film, the publicity committee of the Victory Loan drive of 1917 grasped the medium. *Victory Calls to You, Canada,* a minutes-long film with intertitles, was made and distributed by Regal Films of Toronto (a film-rental company formed in 1916) to promote Victory Bonds. White played himself as finance minister in the film. Miss Canada was portrayed by Gwendolyn Darling Haynes, a twenty-one-year-old clerk recruited from an Eaton's store. The storyline is known. While walking along a Toronto street, she sees "something unusual" – a Victory Loan advertisement. Inquisitive, she goes to Ottawa to question White. He explains what the money is for and outlines Canada's duty, its needs shown "in graphic manner" on the screen; one of the "many thrilling moments" is the scene showing the return of soldiers. The film concludes with Miss Canada buying a bond.

Released just before the campaign, *Victory Calls* was heavily promoted. The necessary waivers by censors had posed no problem. Newspapers flashed photographs of a fashionably attired Haynes, "said to be one of the most beautiful women in Canada." White was dubbed a "screen star." Advance notice of the film went out by 3 November. Three days later, White attended a private screening at the offices of Regal Films. On 9 November, it was premiered during a grand public gathering at Massey Hall, where White, accompanied on stage by Haynes, Lady White, publicity chair Ralph A. Stephenson, and dozens of other big names, announced the loan. In his opening remarks, the chairman of the event, John W. Mitchell (head of the loan in Toronto), "touched on the unsatisfactory war news, and declared that the nation needed a strong presentation of the kind they expected from the Minister of Finance." He did not disappoint, and his cinematic novelty was well received. The *Globe* (Toronto) said of the film, somewhat stiffly, "It set out the elemental facts in that newer style of instruction in a commendable way."[10] What Mitchell meant by "unsatisfactory war news" is unclear; perhaps it was Germany's submarine warfare, revolutionary implosion in Russia, or mutiny in the French army. Even with the Canadian seizure of Passchendaele, a brutal ordeal, the loan was best propelled by critical need.

Prints of the film were distributed from Nova Scotia to British Columbia. Partly because of its originality, reviews were positive; its Canadian production was stressed. At the same time, it appeared in a campaign filled with other novel entertainments and aggressive promotions, competing for attention in theatres with commercial releases, vaudeville shows, and British war films. At the Hippodrome in Toronto, during the week of 12 November, it screened along with a western, a super-horse film, a musical comedy, and live song-and-dance numbers. Whatever the impact of *Victory Calls* on audiences, theatre operators upped the incentive and goodwill factors through tested promotions such as prize tickets for Victory Bonds, an inducement that would blossom in the middle of the influenza epidemic of 1918. For the prize draw at Griffin's Theatre in Belleville, Ontario, at the end of the 1917 campaign, the "theatre was packed." At the same venue, to support the local publicity committee, members of the Only Girl Company went among the audience and secured pledges for nearly $1,000 in subscriptions. The committee's work was actively backed by theatre manager George J. Forhan, who made his stage available for key announcements and also served on the committee's "Stunts Sub-Committee."[11] In Montreal, 445 addresses were given in cinemas and theatres. The French Canadian committee, because of its late campaign start, delivered addresses at only 27 public meetings and nothing in theatres.

The cost of making *Victory Calls,* $7,368.91, did not escape political notice. In May 1918, in the House of Commons, Liberal MP William Costello Kennedy, a regular thorn in White's side, would criticize the expense, along with a snide reference to the absent minister's newly bestowed fame as a "star." Commenting on this brickbat, Regal Films's secretary, A.S. Aronson, stated in *Canadian Moving Picture Digest* (Toronto) that there was no need for the company to defend White for his appearance. He had done so reluctantly, "from a high minded patriotic viewpoint only." By chance, the cost was put in perspective later in the session when Sir George Foster at trade and commerce reported that his department had spent $18,000 in 1917 on a number of films advertising Canada.[12]

The deputy minister of finance agreed in May 1918 that the use of film for advertising "is now becoming an absolute necessity," although processing the 1917 loan was still claiming all of his department's efforts. Preparatory statements on the next loan began coming out in June, followed by official authorization the next month and the start-up of organization in August. Sound and screen were among the new forms of promotion attended to by Stephenson that summer. Scenarios were explored. At least one Victory Loan newsreel was initiated, a depiction of Saint John's shipyard by Pathéscope of Canada Limited. Censor waivers were dealt with. Knowing the limits of the filmmaking business in Canada, Stephenson moved to engage American expertise and stars. The National Association of the Motion Picture Industry had already thrown its resources behind three Liberty Loan drives and mobilized the support of several well-known names.[13] As explained by one zealous star, Ontario-born Marie Dressler, who worked crowds into frenzies of subscription, "Sometimes, I scolded, sometimes, I coaxed."[14] Pickford's *Little American,* with scenes of what audiences thought was happening at the front,[15] had already come to Toronto the previous fall. Stephenson got White to contact Pickford, a guaranteed draw, about doing a film for the Victory Loan, to be shown alongside feature presentations. "America's Sweetheart" (also known as "Canada's dainty moving picture artist"), who had already boosted the Liberty Loans and was a favourite in Canada, accepted. She wired White, "Kindly outline story or suggestion you would like used for a picture and we will see what we can produce for Canada." White thanked her on 8 August, and the wheels were in motion.[16] The result would be *100% Canadian,* an easy adaptation, as it turned out, of her *100% American,* made for the 4th Liberty Loan and released in early October. In Quebec, the Canadian adaptation would be blandly billed as "Une Vue [film] pour l'Emprunt de la Victoire."

Soon afterward, apparently on behalf of the publicity committee, and citing an absence of Canadian producers, Toronto's Allen brothers reached out to the president of the National Association of the Motion Picture Industry about adapting other Liberty Loan films for the 1918 Victory Loan by doing retakes and inserting identifiable Canadian content.[17] Stephenson also arranged for White, the voice of the war loans, to make his Berliner Gramophone recording when the minister was in Montreal on 10–11 September. Sent out to be played at loan meetings,[18] it meshed with the recordings of patriotic and music-hall songs and Liberty Loan pitches being heard and sold publicly. That same month, Stephenson met with the Motion Picture Exhibitors' Protective Association of

A frame from the silent film *100% Canadian.* Sitting in an ice-cream parlour, Mary Pickford's character, Mayne, fixates on a Canadian war-bond poster, which confirms her resolve to save and buy a bond. *100% Canadian* was an adaptation of her *100% American,* and the same frame appears in each film. | *Treasures III, Social Issues in American Film, 1900–1934,* National Film Preservation Foundation, San Francisco, and Library of Congress, Washington, DC.

Ontario, the Toronto Exchange Managers' Association, and dominion publicity's subcommittee for moving picture distribution, which included the Allens, to discuss an expanded distribution of the American shorts expected soon for the Victory Loan drive.[19] The distribution went ahead despite the widespread closures of theatres in the second week of October because of the influenza. In Toronto, the municipal ban on theatres began on 21 October, the very day that the Victory Loan films were to open, but the show went on.

On 22 October, seventeen films were previewed in Toronto by a group of businessmen. According to the *Globe,* ignoring any lighthearted scenes, they were sobered by the "horrors of war" and the role of Victory Bonds "to mitigate those horrors." The use of American stars and their adapted films was proudly announced by White. Of the seventeen films, thirty-three prints were made of each (over 500 in all) and distributed: fourteen for Toronto and Ontario, six for Montreal and Quebec, three for the Maritimes, and "due proportion" for the West. Screenings took place throughout the first week of November, just days into the campaign, and ran for four weeks. Undeterred by the flu, which closed many theatres, operators resorted to outdoor screenings (a recent innovation within the industry), with added attractions. Few excelled at such opportunism, and generated publicity, as successfully as the Allens' chain, which showed films and hosted speakers every night, set up Victory Bond booths, and offered passes as prizes for subscribers. On one night, almost $25,000 worth of bonds was sold. In Guelph, the front of an empty theatre was plastered with posters. During the campaign, Pickford came to Toronto from New York to subscribe for $100,000, a gesture that she would repeat in 1919.[20] Outdoor screenings were not strictly urban events; ingenuity took them on the road. In November 1917, the Ford Motor Company of Windsor, Ontario, for instance, outfitted two cars as projection platforms "and is covering Essex county with the Victory Loan pictures." Despite their brief promotion by the Allens and others, the adapted films may have been a splash in the pan for moviegoers. A few continued to play in Toronto, squeezed in after popular fare such as *Green Eyes,* a drama with Dorothy Dalton, or *In Pursuit of Polly,* a comedy-drama with Billie Burke.

Whatever their impact, what do we know of these adapted films, of which there may have been twenty-one in all, a number compiled from the exuberant coverage in newspapers, motion-picture journals, and advertisements? Extant examples reveal typical storylines, a blend of Manichean struggle, sacrifice, and slapstick. In *A Victory Loan Appeal,* Dorothy Dalton, a nurse in a hospital under bombardment, dies dramatically, praying that Canada will answer with Victory Bonds. In William Duncan's *The Decision,* "horrors" are portrayed as imagined German barbarity on the home front. Pickford's *100% Canadian,* a clear repudiation of "business as usual" in favour of investment,[21] has her working-class character forgo ice-cream sodas and public transit to buy a bond. The Canadian inserts include a Union Jack and Pickford's resolute gaze at Victory Loan poster W.P.7, which depicts women pulling a plough in France. The *Intelligencer* (Belleville, Ontario) reported that the film "has taken the crowds by storm wherever shown." In *The Maple Leaf Forever,* another thinly disguised adaptation, Douglas Fairbanks plays Democracy, "who is assured by his servant, Propaganda, that the time had come to strike" at the flames of "Prussianism," using a lot of firehoses. The adaptation for *His Extra Bit,* with Wallace Reid and Dorothy Davenport, may have struck audiences as particularly vaudevillian. In the film, a scheme for buying bonds is concocted by a family with Black servants. "Even Mandy, the cook, prevents Rastus from buying a watermelon so as to save [for] the bonds," explained *Moving Picture World* (New York).[22] Some films needed little modification to be popular. D.W. Griffith's *Hearts of the World,* a war-propaganda film set in France, sold out at the Allen Theatre in Toronto. In July 1918, management there, with one eye on ticket sales, called it a godsend that would preserve morale in Canada and pave the way for future Victory Loans. Canadian audiences would not have seen the film's scenes of combat, cut by the chief censor.

Live-performance theatres were in on the frenzy, which was heightened by the armistice of 1918. Like film, vaudeville and music halls had the advantage of appealing to loosened-up attendees, building on the pre-war popularity of military themed plays. Some plays and films seen in Toronto from 1915 addressed serious war issues dramatically; some had fundraising speakers for the Red Cross and Victory Loans, but it was the lighter fare, with laughs, dancing, and singing, that loosened the purse strings. If anyone represented the link between vaudeville and the war loans, it was the vivacious, British-born teenager Kathleen ("Kitty") Herbert, part of the Herbert Sisters, who performed in circuit on stages in New York, Saint John, and Toronto between about 1916 and 1919. Encapsulating Kitty's aura, a review in the *Evening Times Star* (Saint John) in November 1917 stated that the "Jolly English Girls"

> danced, sang new patriotic songs – British songs too – and after the audience applauded them back to the stage for repeated bows Miss Kathleen Herbert stepped to the foot-lights and gave one of the best Victory Bond speeches (purely extemporaneous) that one could wish to hear. She told of her father lying wounded in England, her two brothers in France and Mesopotamia – her thirty-two other relatives in the fight and five having paid the supreme sacrifice. While she talked the other sisters walked on stage with a Union Jack and the orchestra played We'll Never Let the Old Flag Fall [a Canadian composition from 1914]. The audience broke loose.

Having been a Liberty Loan campaigner in New York, Kitty canvassed for the 1918 loan on the streets of Toronto, where the "Division B Whirlwind" reportedly raised more than $22,000 in bonds by early November, with an ambitious target of $250,000. Along with Captain Joseph ("Joe") Martin Lawson, a veteran, zealous recruiter, and fellow campaigner, she spoke to a Polish audience at Occident Hall, among other venues; her live performances complemented many star-studded film promotions.

Like Kitty Herbert, who would resurface in Hollywood films in the 1920s using the name Kay Deslys, numerous other performers and theatre-company managers promoted war loans with flair and savvy. At Toronto's Royal Alexandra Theatre in 1918, Grace Daniels, the prima donna of the play *Oh, Lady! Lady!!* – performed by a Comstock and Elliott troupe out of New York – bought $2,000 worth of bonds. During one performance of this light comedy (with music by Jerome Kern), $7,000 worth was sold between acts. The cast, the *Globe* reported,

Vaudevillian and vibrant Liberty Loan campaigner Kitty Herbert at Toronto City Hall, 1918. | City of Toronto Archives, fonds 1244, item 969.

was "enthusiastically determined to win one of the Governor-General's 100 percent honor flags, as was done by the *Ask Dad* and *Chin Chin* companies."[23] At the Star Theatre, "The Home of Real Burlesque," known for musical comedy and vaudeville, chorus girls went into the audience, mostly men, and sold bonds. In November 1917, actress Dolly Lewis, in Edmonton for a vaudeville revue at the Pantages, got light applause, but she did better on the street giving out loan applications and yellow chrysanthemums.

During the war, moviegoing took on a "veneer of nationalism," an interpretation advanced by film historian Paul S. Moore, as ordinary folk, by paying amusement taxes, viewing films, listening to guest speakers, and purchasing bonds on-site, joined in the war effort.[24] So, too, was this the case with the live-theatre and vaudeville houses. Here was the theatrical-cinematic component of Julia C. Ott's concept of "investors' democracy," part of the shield of democracy thrown up at the start of the war.[25] The films of 1918, although often fillers, had strengthened the profile of White and made the medium a key component of loan propaganda, largely through its value in sustaining atmosphere. Less conspicuous, but clearly part of the wartime film culture, were the newsreels that complemented the loan, the now lost footage of local campaign parades, and the instructive films pouring out of provincial agriculture departments, the

Department of Trade and Commerce, and the Canada Food Board, which had come on the scene (as the Office of the Food Controller) in November 1917 to make films for agricultural instruction.[26]

Goodwill accrued to theatre owners for their support of relief funds, educative newsreels, outdoor entertainments during the flu, and war films, as well as the War Lecture Bureau's speakers, military pitchmen, and loan promotions. The "movie-men" nevertheless faced hurdles. When Thomas Scott, secretary of the Motion Picture Exhibitors' Protective Association of Ontario, went to Ottawa in April 1919 to lobby for the removal of the federal tax on reels, an effort that would carry past the loan campaign that fall, he claimed that the expenses of operating a moving-picture theatre during the war had escalated 300 percent.[27] Audiences, too, had sensitivities. A "Mother of Six," after attending a film on behalf of the "Liberty Loan drive" (probably the Victory Loan), told the *Globe* that she found it "excellent and educative, but there were scenes calculated to arouse men's worst passions."[28] The depiction of an American flag on Vimy Ridge in an American propaganda film *The Heart of Humanity* got reaction. Another, *The Common Cause,* was hailed in the *Toronto Daily Star* as "a war film that does not picture the United States as the one nation that won the war."[29] When it came to shorts for the Victory Loan, the dominion publicity committee still looked south, except for one distraction.

Film work for the campaign of 1919 started early, with the visit of the Prince of Wales, one of the first important cross-country events to be caught for newsreels, and with examinations of the Liberty Loan films. On 1 September 1919, the prince, in Ottawa to lay the cornerstone for the new Peace Tower at the Parliament Buildings, unfurled the Prince of Wales honour flag, to be given out as awards in the upcoming loan campaign. The filming of the ceremony was done by Mervin LaRue of Pathéscope, which would follow the prince across Canada. William Norman McIlwraith, head of the publicity committee and the flag's originator, took particular pains: other "picturemen," he telegraphed, were to be kept in the background to prevent them from "prematurely" filming the ceremony.[30]

Adaptation of Liberty Loan films once again proved to be an expeditious route. As one publicity committee chair in Alberta put it, "it has been found almost impossible to secure films of the class needed in Canada."[31] Evidently, neither Pathéscope nor the filmmakers used by the trade and commerce department could fill the call for ready-made, star-studded shorts. The department's Exhibits and Publicity Bureau, however, did produce one film, *The Victory Loan,* possibly for foreign distribution. By 20 August, members of the publicity committee had viewed sixteen Liberty Loan films from 1918 and within weeks had adapted a number of them. Some were simply retitled. The distribution of the resulting Victory Loan films was entrusted to the Allen brothers in Toronto, who commanded a chain of fifty-seven theatres and were working free of charge. McIlwraith worked closely with them, including a trip to New York for a showing that they had planned, and with Pathéscope, apparently to create something distinctly Canadian along industrial lines, which would fit with the campaign's theme of economic growth.

Which films were selected was discussed in the *Calgary Daily Herald* by Ernest Willis, chair of the Southern Alberta district's publicity committee and manager of the Calgary Bill Posting and Advertising Company.[32] He was well aware that in 1918 films had been prepared but theatres had been closed because of the flu. Along with the films – and there may have been up to eleven, including seven retitled Liberty Loan shorts – there were two or three that showed "heroic deeds," from the battlefield to demobilization. Regardless of the wide distribution, intent, and featured stars, among them Fairbanks and Dustin Farnum, the films were no longer carried by the momentum of war, the armistice, or opportunistic promotions such as outdoor viewings. Theatres and vaudeville houses were already bustling with new productions. In Toronto, for example, in the midst of the campaign, theatre critic Edwin Rodie Parkhurst needed much space on 4 November to describe Kitty Gordon's live variety show at the Royal Alexandra. Sandwiched between acts, the short loan films received only passing mention.[33] Elsewhere, before screenings at theatres in Fort William, female speakers took the opportunity to articulate their perspective on the loan and to impress on audiences how "the women can and will vindicate their citizenship in the 1919 campaign,"[34] a merger of suffrage and finance.

As in 1918, it was not always the proffered films that inspired theatre goers in 1919. The plight of the loan campaign in Verdun, Quebec, is illustrative. With the city slow to meet its campaign quota, the local committee approached the manager of the Park Theatre, who agreed to turn it and its vaudeville performances, from the B.F. Keith and Loew circuits, over to the loan for a dedicated show, which generated $100,000.[35] This is not the only instance of live-theatre support. American impresario Alexander Pantages made sizable subscriptions through the managers of his chain of Canadian theatres, an act that generated extra local publicity. Jules Brazil, a Toronto concert-banquet-parlour "entertainer" and musical director for Victory Loan events in 1918, including an open-air "community" songfest, made a tour of western Canada in November and December 1919, during which he took "the opportunity of doing propaganda work" on behalf of the loan.[36] Once the campaign wound up in November, it was back to the American-dominated business of entertainment for the film industry. In a year-end column in the *Globe,* satirical humourist Peter Gilchrist McArthur, having heard of British government plans for new films, pined for releases "not stuffed with propaganda. I had hoped that moving picture propagandas would pass with the war."[37]

The operation of venues that drew on war loans for content had underlying structures, not unlike newspapers. The entertainment business could be precarious, a fact evoked in vaudeville magazines such as *New York Clipper*. The Victory Loan enhancements of the Allen brothers' cinemas, among others, most certainly impacted their box offices through mutually beneficial performance. Although loan promotions enhanced receipts, during the official push for American investment in Victory Bonds in late 1919, at least one vaudeville-company owner, Gus Hill (Gustave Metz) of New York, understood the exchange factor that bedevilled Canadian finance ministers and cross-border business. Faced with a four and a-half percent exchange rate on remittances to New York from his four companies touring in Canada, he considered instead investing his Canadian take in Victory Bonds at five and a-half percent. Frank Flesher, a "shrewd Yankee business man" whose theatre company mounted the play *My Soldier Girl*, made a $3,000 subscription while in Truro, Nova Scotia. Such investments, behind the fronts, were common within America's commercial sector from October through December.

What effect did visual propaganda, including stage acts and films, have on the responses of everyday audiences? Certainly, the propaganda was blended, as in variety shows at theatres. Recent studies question how far the British public could be influenced. Historian Catriona Pennell finds that success needed a synergistic relationship with popular attitudes – that is, a coincidence of propaganda and sentiment. Like marketing experts of the war era, Eberhard Demm calls this relationship "receptivity." Adrian Gregory downplays the mythic effectiveness of propaganda. Historians of war propaganda James Aulich and John Hewitt nonetheless hold that British war-loan posters "gave a visual unity to the campaigns and cumulatively they contributed to a sense of common purpose, of the effective translation of personal investment into military power."[38]

How do such views apply to the campaigns for Canada's loans? In selling bonds and educating the public, the Department of Finance oversaw efforts that had the dual appeal of investment and support for the war. There was receptivity as well as skepticism. Of equal consequence was the creation of atmosphere through the various means of propaganda and the methods that worked in different sectors. For canvassers who traversed rural roads or went door-to-door, on-the-spot explanations and informational pamphlets did more than posters, films, or stunts. In early November 1917, before the start of the first Victory Loan campaign, the department saturated the press with a promotional ad containing a mail-in coupon for a pamphlet, *Canada's Victory Loan – All about It*. In the large centres, entertainments and theatrical gimmickry, rallying viewers to the cause, also worked. Institutions that outwardly professed patriotic motives were very conscious of the investment factor, which needed accounting acumen, not pitch.

Atmosphere required profusions of sound. The Great War was a "singing war," a war that inspired the publication of some 300 patriotic songs.[39] Soldiers sang music-hall favourites, sentimental ballads, parodies, and irreverent ditties. In Britain, music and war loans were interwoven.[40] On the home front in Canada, and in its loan campaigns, music was the audible component of the entertainment spectrum. The artistic community in Canada responded with unreserved enthusiasm to the outbreak of war.[41] The public was equally inclined through popular fare, church singing, classical choral work, and patriotic numbers, what Vancouver's *Western Clarion* called "the usual dizzy headed doggerel of patriotic song."[42] Campaigns for the Canadian Patriotic Fund and the Red Cross Society in 1915 and 1916 used music to good effect. Music could be laden with regional sensibilities and prejudices. In 1918, *The Week* (Victoria) picked up the report of a Saskatchewan teacher who had been dismissed for insisting on teaching patriotic songs to the children of German parents. The government should have supported the teacher, this journal of temperance and "sane socialism" maintained, not the "aliens."[43] In Quebec, if "Tipperary" was heard in any quarters, it had to compete with classical music and operetta, along with sheet music and songs that pitted French soldiers (the *poilus*) and Zouaves against the "Boches." Francophone artists and recordings in French were largely unfamiliar beyond Quebec, where little loan-associated music has been found. In Toronto, patriotic music was given shape by popular performers such as the Great Lakes Naval Training School's band, led by America's "March King," John Philip Sousa, who had signed a contract in 1915 with local amusement kingpin Lawrence ("Lol") Solman and in 1917 had recorded a medley of "Canadian National Airs." Sousa's last shows under contract were at Solman's baseball stadium in July and August 1917, shortly before the launch of the first Victory Loan. His fundraising performances and recordings also aided the United States' Liberty Loan campaigns, and his compositions, such as "Liberty Loan" and "In Flanders Fields the Poppies Grow," were known to Canadian audiences.

Music was an expected component of war-loan publicity. A vibrant, sometimes dissonant, means of exploitative entertainment,[44] music figured in the bells-and-whistles "noise propaganda" of the campaigns, as the *Truro Daily News* (Truro, Nova Scotia) would describe the milieu.[45] In campaigns for the Victory Loan of 1917, music was found in places small and large. Amateur bands blared, small volunteer ensembles preceded speakers in rural halls, soloists and choirs sang out, parades passed loudly, and military tanks rumbled. At a loan meeting in Wardner, a railway and mill town in British Columbia, speeches were interspersed with patriotic songs performed by local schoolboys. In Empress, Alberta, where Arthur L. Sifton, a federal minister and former premier, pushed electoral causes at a meeting at the Grand Theatre, patriotic music was performed by the Empress Orchestra. The gatherings and music in larger centres were the most resplendent. On 9 November 1917, before the premiere of the Victory Loan film at Toronto's Massey Hall, a "rousing song review" was led by a talented bank messenger, Duncan R. Cowan, accompanied by the brass band of the 109th Regiment. The program included stirring speeches by White and war correspondent Stewart Lyon and a performance by Frank Oldfield, "the [John] McCormack of Baritones," who sang one of his signature pieces, "Sussex by the Sea," a British marching song from 1907. Two weeks later, at the reception for Colonel (and former American president) Theodore Roosevelt at Toronto's armoury, the band of the 48th Highlanders warmed up the large audience with a "song Rally and Concert."[46] In Windsor, the publicity apparatus of the Ford Motor Company arranged performances by Sousa's band and British entertainer Harry Lauder, who had fizzled out in Quebec but had pulled in heavy subscriptions in Toronto. In Vancouver, noted performer and teacher Ida Winnifred Fahey sang for the loan campaign at the Orpheum Theatre on 18 November, and four days later, before a large Unionist electoral rally at Calgary's Grand Theatre, a Victory Loan song was performed by Miss Doris Gilbert, a "little girl" in a white dress with a red sash emblazoned with "Buy a Victory Bond for the Baby."[47] Elsewhere in Canada, "A Loan Lyric" appeared in newspapers.[48] In countless examples, the messages were clear and audible.

Patriotic music did not trail off as a war-loan component after the campaign of 1917. In July 1918, Sousa and his band were back in Toronto, where his program included the marching song "We're from Canada," composed and performed by teenager Irene Humble, who had been writing and singing locally since the first year of the war. For the campaign of 1918, patriotic music was applied in earnest. At a loan-launch service in Queen's Park in Toronto on 27 October, there was prayer and singing. In Calgary's loan headquarters, campaigners were "spurred on" by "war songs" played on a gramophone, along with White's recorded speech, after which they sped off in automobiles to canvass outlying districts. In Fort William, Saint John, and Regina, among other centres, newspaper readers saw, and maybe played, the score and words to "Victory Loan Chorus/Buy More Victory Bonds," contributed to the cause by Gordon Vincent Thompson, the Toronto songwriter and publisher who had moved into patriotic composition. His "For the Glory of the Grand Old Flag" was a recent hit, and he had also written the music for a sentimental recruiting song by Captain Joe Lawson. "Victory Loan Chorus" was pushed in 1918 for its "swing," with the brio typical of the whole campaign.[49] The piece nonetheless fleeted away. In

October and November, there was much competing noise, with armistice celebrations becoming clamorous affairs, especially in the cities, where music was punctuated by the loud hawking of bonds.

The music that accompanied the Victory Loan of 1919, like the whole campaign, lacked wartime urgency, although the entertainment component continued. In both Canada and the United States, many a Victory Loan song appeared in newspapers, sheet-music form, and music halls, most of them jingoistic ditties. The themes of re-establishment, economic prosperity, and bond sales were not easy to musicalize, but efforts were made. In July, Charles Albert Edwin Harriss, an Ottawa composer and conductor, was asked to organize a musical demonstration to celebrate the "'Joy' (victory) loan."[50] During the campaign, other compositions emerged. At a rally at Toronto's King Edward Hotel on 23 October, addresses pumping the loan were energized by lusty join-ins featuring "songs sung by men who last year were fighting in the trenches." A new composition, "Selling for Victory" by literary editor and columnist Peter Donovan of Toronto's *Saturday Night* magazine, was performed by Frank Oldfield. The audience gave it an "enthusiastic interpretation," the *Toronto World* reported.[51] Victory Loan numbers were also sung at luncheons and banquets for campaign workers. In Saskatchewan, the publicity committee arranged for the composition of a two-part song, "The Victory of Peace," by composer-manufacturer Jonathan Hughes Arnett, arranged by young Alma Wynfred Ward of Regina. Like Thompson and others, Arnett had been successful in the patriotic-song business as the publisher of "Three Cheers for Foch" and "Canadian Marching Song." "The Victory of Peace" went heavy on Canadianism and emotion in its lyrics: "We will not fail to cover the Victory Loan, for widower and children and men."[52] The use of "Tipperary" as backdrop in one English-language official ad for the loan would have been instantly recognizable. That old standard would outlast the war, but the special war-loan compositions would disappear, relics of outworn propaganda. Popular music in French associated with the loan, if any, is elusive. In the wide spectrum of popular music, loan-related content was a drop in the bucket.

The sheer amount of visual and audible propaganda was nevertheless substantial. So, too, was the response in other modes of expression: poetry, essays, financial columns, and storytelling, not unlike the cartoons, comic strips, film plots, and human-interest accounts that accompanied the campaigns. Florid poetizing was prominent on the home front and overseas in diaries, correspondence, newspapers, and invitations to relief-fund events. A modern blog identifies the "commonality of recourse to rhyme in everyday language" during the war.[53] In its first months, like other belligerents, Canada saw its papers and magazines deluged with amateur patriotic verse, and poetry quickly became a staple of wartime literature. It served "a very public role."[54] Some newspapers, such as the *Globe,* already had dedicated columns for "The Daily Poem." Most of the contributions were jingoistic but emotionally expressive. In Toronto, critics in *Maclean's Magazine* and *Saturday Night* in 1915–16 found most of the early crop simply bad poetry.[55] By 1917, seasoned authors were weighing in, and serious anthologies by Canadians, among them Carrie Ellen Holman and Robert J.C. Stead, were appearing. Canada's war loans stimulated new levels of clichéd, patriotic propaganda in verse form, demonstrating a "dialogic" relationship between propaganda and poetry with a degree of public participation not unlike that seen in the poster, cartoon, and window-dressing contests.[56]

The energized publicity brought to the loan campaign of 1917 provided ample opportunity for poetic enhancement. The "Oh please do! Daddy" poster, for instance, was an ideal platform. In its "Children's Column" on 18 November, the *Vancouver Daily Sun* published an entreating poem, "O! Please Do Daddy," by local widow (and future Women's Freedom candidate) Margaret Esther Crosfield. An early entry into amateur poem writing on the loan, it had already been recited, in a smart piece of publicity, outside the loan office "by one of the Patriotic Pierrot troupe" from a local theatre.[57]

Similar exhortations appeared in newspapers and journals across the country: Charles Lambert de Roode's "L'Emprunt de la Victoire" in Montreal (published in *La Patrie* as a tribute to Joseph Quintal and in a separate volume slanted toward France), W.H. Lloyd Roberts's "Buy!" in Saint John, and Austin A. Briggs's "If Nelson Could Return" (an amusing play on the victor at Trafalgar) in Toronto. Even Rudyard Kipling's imperialist ode to Canada, "Our Lady of the Snows" (1897), was resurrected and adapted in the middle of a question-and-answer piece on the loan in *Everywoman's World* (Toronto). In Montreal's Liberal *Le Canada,* a publication targeted for vicious attacks in Toronto newspapers, a poetic creed of lofty support appeared just weeks ahead of the divisive federal election. Ending with "I am the Victory Loan, the pleasure of God and the disappointment of Kaiser and Satan," the poem appeared above this boldly printed line, "Win the War with Laurier and Freedom."[58]

All through 1918, amateur war poems from all parts of Canada appeared almost daily in the *Globe.* During the loan campaign of July in Newfoundland, a lone poem appeared in the *Evening Telegram* (St. John's). Like the use there of generic Canadian posters, "The Victory Loan" was an adaptation of the poem in the *Globe* written the previous November by the Reverend Charles D. Baldwin of Addison, Ontario. In this version, names of significance to Newfoundlanders were substituted: Newfoundland for Canada, "July the first" for St. Julien, Gallipoli for Ypres, and Monchy for Vimy Ridge.[59] (July 1 was the anniversary of the decimation of the Royal Newfoundland Regiment.)

During Canada's loan campaign of October and November, related poetry continued to blossom in the newspapers, much of it anonymous, some of it signed by local scribes such as Steve Matthews and Hope A. Thomson in Saint John, Douglas Malloch in Toronto, J. Baldwin Bryant in Barrie, Ontario, and Elspeth Honeyman in Vancouver. All of it implored and stressed the "buy" and the sacrifice. Some of it was meant to shame; a few pieces were combined with quotations from Sir Thomas White, were shaped as prayers or prefaces to Victory Bond "catechisms," or were contained in sponsored advertisements. Typical of the doggerel was this verse from a shaming poem published across North America and attached in Canada to a quotation from White's Winnipeg speech of 8 October 1918: "Over in France where the death shells scream/The boys are fighting as in a dream;/A glorious dream of blood and hell,/While I stay home and prosper well." The poem ends with a call to the "Stay-at-home Canadian" to subscribe.

Absent was the disillusionment found in the work of the famous soldier poets and a few Canadian anthologies. Easily turned to propaganda, popular poetry nonetheless had a place, as proponent Jessie Pope was proving in Britain with her work, which romanticized war. Canadians were happy to write. The Dominion Press News and Feature Service understood this penchant and in late September 1918 launched a poetry contest. It would close on 15 October and be judged by committee chair Charles Fenwick Crandall of the *Montreal Daily Star* and University of Toronto professor Malcolm William Wallace. First prize would be a $50 Victory Bond. In imitation of the poster contest, the directives for submissions were explicit: they would be judged on their "ability to sell bonds." So coached, contestants from Canada, England, and the United States submitted between 1,100 and 1,300 poems; twenty-four entries by twenty-two contributors, all from Canada, received honourable mentions, and they came from everywhere: Montreal, Saskatoon, Neepawa in Manitoba, Ottawa, Calgary, Toronto, Winnipeg, Hamilton, Vancouver, Saint John, Brantford, HMCS *Niobe* in Halifax, and the base of the Royal Air Force Canada near Toronto.[60]

The winning entry, "Then Grudge Ye Not," was written by George Hearn Maitland, municipal editor of the *Toronto Daily Star* and an avid amateur poet. He wondered whether the voices of the "dear lost lads" could be heard:

> If such could be, would these not ask
> (Vague voices down the wind)
> That we should help – ah, humble task –
> Their comrades left behind?
> Then grudge we not the yellow gold
> To beat the foemen down,

Where the Red Prussians pitiless hold
Sacked city, pillaged town.[61]

Maitland's formulaic poem appeared in newspapers nationwide in the first two weeks of November and found its way into talks by Frank Yeigh and others from the War Lecture Bureau. It was even inserted that month into the brochure put out by the Department of Trade and Commerce to promote Canada's participation in the trade fair at Lyons, France. The poem's "yellow gold," which represented the cost of Victory Bonds, must have impressed the judges, as Maitland reinforced obligatory response in the conventional fashion of "In Flanders Fields." His "The Boy Who Lies Out Yonder" and pieces by Blanche Murison of Vancouver, who had garnered an honourable mention, would appear in *Canadian Poems of the Great War* (1918). Also earning mention, from within the civil service came "Shall We Not Give Our Gold" by Jack Cadden, dubbed the "Kipling of the Railway Mail Service" by *The Civilian* (Ottawa). In his introduction to *Canadian Poems,* editor John William Garvin expressed his respect for poets of "minor qualities" who "reflect and influence their own generation."[62] Whether propagandistic war-loan poems achieved much in that direction, or even compelled subscriptions, is unclear, but they did contribute to the desired atmosphere.

Although poetry fell off sharply in the campaign of 1919, some amateur pieces found their way to the Department of Finance and popped up in newspapers. John D. Leitch, a machinist and keen promoter of past loans in his factory in Hamilton, had sent in names for the loan ("Peace Loan, 1919," "Your Loan, 1919," "Thanksgiving Loan"), as well as corresponding poems. In the *Globe*'s "Daily Poem" section, old themes predominated (nostalgia, nature, music, and yearning), along with some verses on the Prince of Wales and Margaret Clarke Russell's "Post Bellum Medley." Official advertising continued to perpetuate the message of obligation. In one ad, beside the image of a soldier's wraith rising up from a field of crosses and poppies, a mournful poem, "The Soul of a Vision," leads the reader "To Pay Debts of Honour" through a loan intended to cover the costs of medical services and vocational training for veterans.[63]

War-loan essays and stories were complementary forms of writerly mobilization. Public and secondary school students were ardently engaged through talks, fundraising activities, official lessons, and contests. Information on locally and provincially sponsored contests is particularly rich for Ontario, from the Grand River in the south to Jackfish on Lake Superior's north shore. Surviving essays contain the standard, patriotic rationales. In the competition of fall 1918 in the province's secondary schools, on the topic "Victory Bonds – Why Canadians Should Buy Them," a pamphlet prepared for the schools by three educators, *The*

Victory Loan and What It Means, was issued as a guide. (Where it ranged into abstract discourse such as gold versus paper money, some readers may have been perplexed.) Nonetheless, students from 187 schools would respond, with prizes to be awarded after 1 January. The language of the surviving entries reflects not only the guidelines but likely some coaching. In one essay, Frances Loretta Fagan, an eighteen-year-old from a farm near Caledonia, where she attended high school, expressed views inculcated all over the English-speaking home front: "On the shell-torn fields of Flanders ... Canada's young manhood are fighting and dying ... In return for these sacrifices are we to do nothing? ... The ownership of a Victory Bond is proof that the investor has bought a share in the triumph of victory over defeat, of civilization over barbarism."[64] Jessie Kerr of Toronto, who at twelve was too young to have her entry considered, concluded her essay with "Our brave men have fought ... to free us from a tyrannical foe, and so now we must do our bit and pay the price by lending our money to the Government." The Victory Loan headquarters was so impressed that it had her composition published.[65]

The proliferation of unofficial articles and editorials on the loans hammered in the same themes. MacLean Publishing's string of trade journals was particularly attentive. *Farmers' Magazine* (Toronto) and *Everywoman's World* offered investment advice. Articles came from known (and some unknown) authors, including Marjory MacMurchy, Elizabeth C. Hazelton (who wrote a short romantic piece called "Love in a Victory Bond"), Hector W. Charlesworth, John C. Kirkwood, Victoria C. Ratcliffe, Elizabeth Clare, Ethel M. Chapman, and "A Woman at Home." Just as the comics, cartoons, campaign parades, and theatrical productions used humour and entertainment, some columnists – Peter McArthur was one – could cause a smile. In the *Toronto Daily Star*, in October 1918, "Margaret Lillian" described the loan rally at Queen's Park through the folksy vernacular of the cartoon characters Maw and Paw, ending with Maw's reverential nod: "An' every time I see the beautiful picture an' the dear Cross an' the poppies, I jest breathe a prayer soft like to myself an say – An ye who sleep in Flanders Fields,/We shall not fail you now." So motivated, Maw got Paw to put his pay raise toward a bond.[66] Elsewhere, in other short pieces, bonds got mentioned as fixtures of everyday life.[67] In Calgary, noted writer and director of publicity for the Canadian Pacific Railway's immigration department, Robert J.C. Stead, served as head of loan publicity in the Southern Alberta district in 1917. In support of the campaign there, he produced a booklet, a "story in verse," to be sold in Edmonton and Calgary by the Edmonton Boys' Victory Loan Association. (In ads, it goes unnamed.) Discussing Stead's *Kitchener and Other Poems* (1917), William T. Allison, a college professor in Winnipeg, noted its avoidance of "the hip-hip-hurrah, superficial style of patriotic verse."[68] Stead's experiences and concerns over the war's outcome would be reflected in his novel *The Cow Puncher* (1918).[69]

When the dominion publicity committee decided to add fiction to its programming in 1919, it wanted promotional stuff. Material from Elizabeth Hazelton of Vancouver arrived too late to be used, but the committee did get a piece from Arthur Stringer of Chatham, Ontario, a popular novelist with a knack for eerie twists. Illustrated by Charles William Jefferys, *The Stranger* appeared in newspapers and as a sixteen-page booklet. Reaching for inspiration from the imperial past, Stringer has John Hardy's automobile colliding with the ghostly barouche of General James Wolfe, whose army had captured Quebec in 1759. In their subsequent talk in Hardy's office, Wolfe tells him that he died for Canada on the Plains of Abraham. The conversation shifts to aid for the Great War, and Wolfe, called back to the dead, leaves Hardy ready to subscribe and get his workers to do the same. Hardy tells them, "We belong to the land of the Beaver, which is the wisest and the hardest worker on four legs. So show 'em what the sons of the Beaver can do."[70] Although Stringer's story was officially "calculated to prove an effective appeal to all true Canadians," it received little critical attention; as propaganda pulp, it was a novelty. Unlike Toronto's *Victory Telegraph* souvenir, it generated no monetary return.

The pamphlets and circulars issued by dominion and provincial committees, by contrast, were the most intensive form of publicity, the unsung backbone of the whole crusade. They could be distributed anywhere. There were dozens – more when the translated versions are counted. As educational fact sheets, they spread basic information: definitions of bonds, their value as investments, simple statements of war finance, civilian support, and blatant propaganda such as the need for vengeance. Recognized as effective tools for canvassers facing "lines of resistance," they were part of the total marketing effort, itself a component of the war's "major impact on the process of investor education" internationally.[71] In Canada, other materials came from a host of agencies. Banks and bond houses channelled information. Brochures and flyers appeared in French in Quebec, including a release from the Conseil de la Chambre des notaires.

The flow began in 1917 with White's mass-mailed package, followed during that year's campaign by several pamphlets, along with the first issue of posters. The pamphlets of 1918 – 115 tons of material – featured accounts of expenditures. Specific audiences were targeted, among them women, farmers, students, and American subscribers. In a typical question-and-answer format, *The ABC of the Victory Loan, 1918* included the standard particulars, plus a response on this question: "Can my wife help too?"[72] The War Lecture Bureau issued instructive bulletins, and newspapers published their own catechisms. In 1919, the heaviest year of pamphlet issue, postwar features entered the mix: taxation, reconstruction, and memorialization. An official statement released on 24 October indicated that 20 million pieces had been printed, including 2 million of *How Our Last Victory Loan Was Spent, 1918* and 3 million of *What You Want To Know about the Victory Loan 1919*. In terms of enablement, pamphlets were a crucial weapon in the war-loan onslaught.

Following the campaign of 1919, as Victory Bonds became permanent fixtures in the marketplace, they retained a place in the brochures of bond firms and security reporting companies. They did not disappear totally from works of humour, fiction, and recollection. One letter, seemingly written to a local businessman or newspaper editor, spread like wildfire across North America in 1919–20. Versions such as this one appeared in Canada's weeklies, trade journals, and labour convention proceedings:

> Sir, –
>
> For the following reasons, I am unable to send you the cheque asked for:
>
> I have been held up, held down, sand-bagged, walked on, sat on, flattened out and squeezed, first by the Government for War Tax, the Excess Profits Tax, Victory Bonds, Thrift Stamps, Capital Stock Tax, Merchant's Licence and Auto Tax, and by every society and organization that the inventive mind of man can invent to extract what I may or may not possess.
>
> From the Society of John the Baptist, the G.W.V.A., G.A.C., United Veterans' League, the Woman's Auxiliaries, Navy League, the Red Cross, the Black Cross, the Purple Cross, and the Double Cross, the Children's Home, the Dorcas Society, the Y.M.C.A., the Y.W.C.A., Salvation Army, the Boy Scouts, Jewish Relief, Belgian Relief, Tarring the Avenue, and the Fraternal Order of Weary Willies.
>
> The Government has so governed my business that I don't know who owns it. I am inspected, suspected, examined and re-examined, informed, required and commanded, so I don't know who I am, or why I am here. All I know is that I am supposed to be an inexhaustible supply of money for every known need, desire or hope of the human race; and because I will not sell all I have and go out and beg, borrow or steal money to give away, I have been cussed, discussed, boycotted, talked to, talked about, lied to, lied about, held up, hung up, robbed and nearly ruined; and the only reason I am clinging to life is to see what in hell is coming next.[73]

Chuckles and relatability aside, readers looking for war content in books had choices, from Harry Milner Wodson's *Private Warwick* (1915) to William A. Bishop's *Winged Warfare* (1918), works meant to bolster resolve, stoke hatred, and feed a public looking for adventure and "true" stories on the front.[74] In such company, *The Stranger* underlined the weakness of fiction as a vehicle for Victory Loan propaganda. But one well-known author did realistically work the loan into one of her novels.

In a chapter of Lucy Maud Montgomery's *Rilla of Ingleside* (1921), part of her fabled *Anne of Green Gables* series,[75] the scene is the loan drive of November 1917 in rural Prince Edward Island, where young Marilla Blythe, Susan Baker (the family's politicized housekeeper, "a perfect dynamo of patriotism"), and others have been "furiously" campaigning. One old man who had refused to invest (and was suspected of being a spy and pacifist) was "converted" by the electrifying speech at a meeting by Susan, who ordered taunters "to march up to the platform and subscribe." Most did. The old man also understood the value of investment at five and a-half percent, Marilla reasoned, "even when a militaristic government pays it." *Rilla* was one of a few fictional accounts of young women's views of the war on the home front. The *Globe* found its depictions plausible; Montgomery knew about them from experience. *Rilla* does not display the propagandistic intent or jingoism of the newspaper stories, *The Stranger*, or much of the poetry. Throughout the twenties, Victory Bonds occasionally emerged in popular literature as small props, like paper money, as in Douglas L. Durkin's *The Magpie* (1923). Written attention to the Victory Loans and Bonds mostly remained rooted in financial realities.

Outside political forums, articles on Sir Thomas White had already started to burnish his achievements.[76] While still in the House of Commons, although not a minister, he began to write his own account of wartime finance. It began as a series in the *Montreal Gazette*. Announced there at the end of 1920, the articles appeared between 1 January and 5 March 1921 and were reworked and published in Montreal as *The Story of Canada's War Finance*, a seventy-page booklet. It was in the hands of newspapers by June but was ignored by much of the press, including *Le Devoir* (Montreal), the *Toronto Daily Star*, and the *Globe*. *Le Canada français* (Saint-Jean-d'Iberville) merely noted White's transition to "écrivain." Copies were distributed to libraries and the Conservative faithful. An incisive review, by Gilbert Edward Jackson, a professor of political economy at the University of Toronto, did appear in the *Canadian Historical Review*. He found White's handling of inflation lacking, regardless of his wartime concerns over debt: "He does not attempt a strict analysis of the delicate but obscure reactions between an excessive issue of fiat money, the level of prices in the markets, interest rates, and exchange rates. From his account of what happened, it is doubtful if he had worked out those relations for himself." What Jackson, a veteran, did fully recognize were the pressures that White had faced: "War is always a series of emergencies."[77] At the same time as *Story*, the financial press could be counted on for reports and articles. In January 1921, for instance, *Monetary Times* (Toronto) had published "The Market Record of Canadian War Loan Issues," a valuable summary stripped of promotion. It acknowledged, given the novelty of the loans, that "mistakes" had been made, official controls had limited market movement, international factors had intruded, and taxing the 1919 issues had been a "handicap."[78] Such reportage filled the gaps in *Story*.

Little else was written on Canadian war finance during the 1920s. In the context of the pressing problems of postwar finance, it was superseded by refunding, the manifestation of what Julia C. Ott calls the "investor-centred theory of political economy."[79] White never spoke in such terms. After the war, few seemed inquisitive. Speakers and letter writers stepped forward to excoriate war propaganda. After *Story*, White wrote a shorter, follow-up account about federal financial administration and the banks,[80] highlighting their critical role and his own part. In 1927, now lauded by Sir Reginald McKenna, a former chancellor of the Exchequer, White caught notice of statements in a volume of Winston Churchill's epic *The World Crisis* denouncing what the former munitions minister regarded as Canada's underfunding of munitions during the war. White took umbrage. Drawing on his own knowledge (and *Story*), his former department, and Toronto neighbour Sir Joseph Flavelle, he had three authoritative letters published detailing the course of munition funding, the desperation of 1917, and the shifts in Canadian-American production.[81] Subsequent jabs by the Liberals also brought informative retorts; refunding loans spurred remarks from the former war minister. Reflecting in 1929 on the immediate postwar period, he mused about the wisdom of denying veterans cash bonuses, believing that they would undermine Canada's credit abroad, and he fretted about America's dominant holdings of Canadian debt.[82]

Throughout 1918–19, the concepts of propaganda and atmosphere permeated trade journals, agencies, and government departments in contexts ranging from war-loan advertising to promotions of mercantile goods. Of course, not everyone experienced the full sensory panoply of war-loan promotions; in some rural areas, a canvasser at one's door was it. Into the 1920s, the public at large saw the lessons debated and applied with vigour in new visuals, economic studies, and ad planning. The advent of the Second World War brought war finance to the fore in amplified form, with new generations of posters and literature, emotions, and pressures.[83] Economists looked back on how finance was handled during the Great War, just as they would provide analysis of economics, the market, and government refunding after the Second World War.

Conclusion

Through its finance minister, the Borden government got the money that it needed for the Great War, a result that was never preordained. At the start, it had been essential to avoid financial panic. Under the vaunted Finance Act of 1914, significant powers were given to the Department of Finance. Sir Thomas White and Canada's banks were not reluctant to use them. In the waves of propaganda that shaped Canadians' perceptions and involvement, both military and civilian, finance loomed large. Over the period 1915–19, six war loans, which generated almost $2.5 billion in subscriptions, formed a major component of war funding, roughly a third, on top of conventional revenue streams and taxes. No stand-alone source of funding, the loans were calculated and launched in complex interplay with other loans, short-term securities, taxes, and other revenues, interlaced with the gospels of thrift, sacrifice, and national engagement. Even with adjustments necessitated by politics and the markets, financial planning was projected in monthly chunks as maturities rolled over, new sources were found, and parallel matters such as railways were debated. Finance and annual budgets did not always materialize in synchronization with military or political events. Much of the web was woven away from the public gaze in the finance department, the head offices of banks, and the channels to London and New York. As British historian Adam Tooze observes, although propagandized war bonds were vital to the "collective war effort" and "bulked large in the popular imagination," unpublicized treasury bills did not grip the public's consciousness, however much they counted.[1] Views of the government's methods as expedient, unsatisfactory, inequitable, or coercive do not recognize the collective effort or the extraordinary demands.

In the unprecedented propaganda that carried the loans and war-savings measures, Canadians were seldom inundated with the financial constituents thrashed out in the Department of Finance under intense pressures, supervised by a nervy but masterful minister. The incessantly repeated message was kept simple: one's dollars would help to win the war and would provide a sound personal return. Informational pamphlets and door-to-door canvassing conveyed the investment benefit in persuasive fashion.

From the beginning, loan propaganda spelled out the meaning of bonds; only rarely did publicity focus on the intricacies of imperial funding and exchange. Equally prominent was the selling of the war and national solidarity: why finance was significant, why it had to be a personal goal, and how recruitment was dependent. Among the personnel of the loan, the steady presence of security professionals jumps out, as does their aptitude for propaganda. Equally evident was White's initial reluctance to use modern forms of advertising, his conversion, and his obdurate sense of control.

Canadians and their institutions came forward to invest, drawn by a mix of personal interest, forms of patriotism, and media promotion. Navigation of the financial needs of wartime, not always with clear understandings or complete acceptance, took Canadians through the shoals of imperial obligation, interaction with the American behemoth, cultural divisions, and appeals from other relief causes. Patriotism, whatever its motivation and manifestation, was a factor in wartime borrowing. Following the war, as the sea of propaganda-driven sentiment drained, individuals moved to sell their bonds, institutions recalculated their portfolios, and the government refunded its debt, which would carry on for decades. War bonds maintained a strong presence, in large part through the control exercised by the Victory Loan Special Committee over two periods in 1918–20 but also as the market carried bonds past 1919. In the securities field and society at large, the loans were formative and interventionist, like so much of government policy and legislation. Shortly before the armistice, the *Globe* (Toronto) could say that the prospect of peace removed the patriotic rationale for subscribing: "The Victory bond stands at the top as an investment."[2]

With his pillars of finance, the war loans, White proceeded along two paths of public engagement – marketability and social calculation – where major campaigns would bolster confidence, generate support for the war, and entertain. The campaigns gave rise to oversubscriptions that supposedly demonstrated the broad civilian backing and emotional commitment needed to prosecute the Great War. The pooling of the loan proceeds did speak to a kind of common purpose, although it was not always maintained in some regions, whether for ethnic, political, or national reasons. In Quebec, distinctions were made between Canada's economic welfare and its entanglement in an imperial conflict. But everywhere, as Kenneth D. Garbade of the Federal Reserve Bank puts it for the United States, in an assessment that can also apply to Canada, success required supporters "up and down the economic ladder to buy into the effort."[3] Hence, both small investors and big subscribers were courted, from vaudeville audiences to corporate offices. Coordinating the two paths of prosecution required discerning market boundaries, introducing the public to the concept of securities, demonstrating need, steering voluntary support around coercive pressures and taxes, and integrating Canada's finance with that of Britain and the United States. Although Canada's costs were modest compared to the outlays of other Allied nations, the point of integration should not be underestimated. Funding munition production is a primary example. Whether inter-Allied loans made any decisive difference to the war's outcome cannot be determined with certainty, but as German historian Hans-Peter Ullmann concludes, undoubtedly "they contributed to a more integrated economic effort than the Central Powers managed and helped funnel war supplies to the Allied effort."[4] Moreover, Canada was the only imperial domain to engage in reciprocal funding with Britain.[5] In these respects, the contribution was appreciable. In similar fashion, equally meaningful was the implementation of fundraising practices, from bonds to vaudeville, in Britain, the United States, and diverse jurisdictions in Canada. In this context, understanding the effort as a whole is vital. Viewed from any angle – fiscal policy, economics, mass investment, investor-centred theory, political climate, interventionism, or cultural strain – the government secured money through a broad, coordinated effort. It was in this effort, despite its often-fragmented components, that finance, public mobilization, and cultural forms coalesced to shape an unprecedented atmosphere and to influence fiscal realities in the 1920s and 1930s, with the world marching toward another war.

White's *Story* of war finance received new attention in the tightly focused, unrelenting tax debate and formulation of funding for the Second World War. Some analysts saw merit in his claim that direct taxation had not been possible before 1917.[6] His comment that taxation should be a provincial responsibility would later fuel federal-provincial disputes over jurisdiction. In 1940, John James Deutsch, then at the Bank of Canada, claimed that "the circumstances of 1914 to 1918 required, in large part, only an intensification and slight adaptation of normal peace-time activity"[7] for the government to draw on Canadian resources. The economy, it was argued, was simpler then. Compared to the demands of the new war, the Great War had required less; during the second conflict, there would be two war loans in 1940 and nine Victory Loans between 1941 and 1945. Overall, they brought in about $12.5 billion, six times the Great War loans. All were replete with coercion. The publicity campaigns for the loans of 1940 suffered at the hands of "amateurs," in the estimates of some financial journals, but it was clear that the lessons and records of the issues of 1915 to 1919 were considered by the second war's National War Finance Committee, which targeted institutional and corporate investors more directly and got 52 percent from that sector. Present-day economist Livio Di Matteo concludes that the debt-finance program created during the Great War "was also largely followed during World War II" and that "the stage was set for the future expansion of the income-tax system."[8] He makes other useful comparisons. During the first war, the ratio of deficit to gross domestic product (a standard measure of the manageability of debt) jumped from 4.3 percent in 1914 to 8.6 percent in both 1918 and 1919, although compared to the second war, government finance was modest relative to national output. For each war, the government of the day generated high defence spending, with war loans emerging as "satisfactory," if expedient, solutions.[9]

In the 1920s and 1930s, commentators spoke of the disappearance or revival of a war atmosphere, even in the midst of the war's expansion of government activity and services. Economists aside, few recalled the atmosphere of the Great War, which had enabled public engagement at home. In the 1940s, in different circumstances and economies, Victory Loans were employed to fund needs vastly greater than those faced in the previous conflict. The fiscal and promotional means – the campaigns, the propaganda, the public appeals – nevertheless came from the playbooks of Canada's Great War. The loans, then, also left a mark on charitable fundraising of the 1920s to the 1940s,[10] where social advertising, public recognition, and enjoyment were linked, as in the holistic culture fashioned in the Great War. The Victory Bonds of the second war, which would be refunded and converted at maturity, were replaced in 1946 by Canada Savings Bonds, which Finance Minister James Lorimer Ilsley hoped would continue Canadians' wartime habit of saving, without the parades, the displays, or the roving salesmen of years past.

Appendix 1

Dominion War Loans 1915–19: Results

Loan		Campaign period	Amount of loan ($)	Number of subscribers	Amount subscribed ($)	Amount allotted ($)	Expenses ($)
Dominion War Loan	1915	22–30 Nov. 1915	50,000,000	24,862	103,729,500	100,000,000	3,408,358
	1916	12–23 Sept. 1916	100,000,000	34,526	201,444,800	106,706,300	3,539,410
	1917	12–23 March 1917	150,000,000	41,263	260,768,000	172,926,800	8,550,552
Victory Loan	1917	12 Nov. to 1 Dec. 1917	150,000,000	869,300	566,327,500	546,156,300	4,714,150
	1918	28 Oct. to 16 Nov. 1918	300,000,000	1,140,057	707,117,550	682,302,900	5,762,091
	1919	27 Oct. to 15 Nov. 1919	300,000,000	795,463	653,475,550	616,999,000	6,448,249

Note: There is no definitive statement of war-loan results, which were always in a flux of calculation. In the important categories of numbers of subscribers and the amounts, marked variance occurred. The variables include incomplete accounting, inclusion (or not) of sums converted from past loans, government buy-back, use of estimates or unofficial summaries, unpaid subscriptions, remittances and sales over time, and failure to distinguish between amounts subscribed and those allotted (accepted) by the government.

Sources: The most accurate results of the war loans probably come from the records of the Victory Loan Special Committee in Library and Archives Canada (LAC), RG 19, E-2-e, vol. 588, file 155-1D and vol. 592, file 155-28-1T, part 1. The following were also examined: other files of the Department of Finance (LAC, RG 19, vols. 588, 592, 4006, 4013, 6074); records of the National War Finance Committee of World War II (Bank of Canada Archives, Ottawa); published *Sessional Papers;* unpublished *Sessional Papers* (LAC, RG 14, D2); parliamentary *Debates;* the United States Federal Reserve's *Bulletin; Monetary Times* (Toronto); Canada, Dominion Bureau of Statistics, *Canada Year Book, 1915–20* (Ottawa: Census and Statistics Office, 1916–21); *Canadian Annual Review of Public Affairs;* and John Castell Hopkins, *The Province of Ontario in the War: A Record of Government and People* (Toronto: Warwick Bros. and Rutter, 1919). The results appeared in various other published studies, among them Ernest Ludlow Bogart, *Direct and Indirect Costs of the Great World War,* 2nd ed. (New York: Oxford University Press, 1920), 43–51; Clifford Austin Curtis, "The Canadian Banks and War Finance," *Contributions to Canadian Economics* (Toronto) 3 (1931): 7–40; and Douglas H. Fullerton, *The Bond Market in Canada: A Study of the Institutions, Machinery, Techniques, and Problems Involved in the Issuing and Marketing of Bonds and Debentures* (Toronto: Carswell, 1962).

Appendix 2

Victory Loans 1917–20: Subscriptions by province

Province	*1917*	*1918*	*1919*
Alberta	16,515,150	18,979,250	17,178,900
British Columbia	18,814,700	36,633,900	36,411,915
Manitoba	32,326,600	44,030,700	41,642,200
New Brunswick	10,463,350	17,002,550	15,635,050
Nova Scotia	18,588,150	33,321,550	28,521,900
Ontario	204,185,400	336,055,350	355,739,050
Prince Edward Island	2,331,350	3,011,050	3,158,400
Quebec	94,287,250	180,363,450	162,032,150
Saskatchewan	21,777,050	26,072,450	21,712,650

Note: In the absence of a dominion system of accounting, introduced for Victory Loan 1917, the Dominion War Loans of 1915 to 1917 were not reported by provincial totals. Rather, the newspapers published lists of major subscribers and sectors: insurance companies; industrials; provinces and municipalities; American banks, insurance, and finance houses; individuals and firms; trust, loan, and mortgage companies; banks; public service corporations; and miscellaneous. See, for instance, *Globe,* 20, 24 March 1917.

Sources: Library and Archives Canada (LAC), RG 14, D2, vol. 46, no. 186 (unpub. Sess. paper, 1919, no. 186); vol. 70, no. 138 (unpub. Sess. paper, 1920, no. 138). As for Appendix 1, the figures for Appendix 2 vary. See, for example, Alfred Ernest Ames's "Final Report" for Victory Loan 1917, submitted on 26 April 1918, LAC, RG 14, D2, vol. 37, no. 131a (unpub. Sess. paper, 1918, no. 131a).

Appendix 3

Victory Loan 1918: Subscriptions, applications, per capita, ratios by province

Province	*Subscriptions ($)*	*Applications*	*Per capita ($)*	*Ratios*
British Columbia	36,633,927	80,315	91.58	1:4.98
Alberta	18,999,250	56,813	37.26	1:8.98
Saskatchewan	26,072,450	77,323	40.11	1:8.40
Manitoba	44,030,700	86,792	79.34	1:6.40
Ontario	336,055,350	542,648	131.26	1:4.72
Montreal and Islands	146,302,250	114,535	–	–
Quebec (outside Montreal)	34,061,200	47,278	80.91	1:13.78
New Brunswick	17,002,550	31,957	48.58	1:10.90
Nova Scotia	33,221,550	61,040	70.24	1:7.75
Prince Edward Island	3,011,050	5,406	32.13	1:17.33
Totals	*695,389,277*	*1,104,107*	*88.91*	*1:7.08*

Note: In 1920, after the Victory Loan of 1919, Thomas Bradshaw reported on subscriptions per capita by loan: Dominion War Loan 1915, 10.01; Dominion War Loan 1916, 18.37; Dominion War Loan 1917, 23.19; Victory Loan 1917, 53.13; Victory Loan 1918, 88.12; Victory Loan 1919, 86.43. See Library and Archives Canada (LAC), RG 14, D2, vol. 70, no. 138, 9.

Sources: Published in the *Globe,* 24 January 1919, 12, this "new and perhaps final table of the subscriptions to the 1918 Victory Loan" was submitted by William Sefton Hodgens, secretary of Dominion Securities, acting as chair of the loan's dominion business committee. Some variation from Appendix 1 is noted. The census of 1911 appears to be the basis for the calculation of the per capita figure for each province. The absence of per capita and ratio figures for Montreal and Islands, not explained in Hodgens's report, may be a result of late reporting. See LAC, RG 14, D2, vol. 46, no. 186. The question of separate reporting for Montreal, within Quebec, is addressed in Part 2.

Notes

Introduction

1 So summarized in Pablo Martín-Aceña, Elena Martinez Ruiz, and María A. Pons, "The Financing of the Spanish Civil War, 1936–9," in *Convergence and Divergence of National Financial Systems: Evidence from the Gold Standards, 1871–1971,* ed. Patrice Baubeau and Andres Ögren, 145–70 (London: Pickering and Chatto, 2010).

2 Sir Thomas White, *The Story of Canada's War Finance* (Montreal: Canadian Bank of Commerce, 1921), 3.

3 Robert Craig Brown and Ramsay Cook, *Canada, 1896–1921: A Nation Transformed* (Toronto: McClelland and Stewart, 1974), 229; John James Deutsch, "War Finance and the Canadian Economy, 1914–20," *Canadian Journal of Economics and Political Science* 6, 4 (1940): 537.

4 For comprehensible summaries, see Adam Tooze, *The Deluge: The Great War, America and the Remains of the Global Order, 1916–1931* (New York: Viking, 2014), 36–49; and Nicholas Mulder, "War Finance," in *1914–1918–Online: International Encyclopedia of the First World War,* ed. Ute Daniel, Peter Gatrell, Oliver Janz, Heather Jones, Jennifer Keene, Alan Kramer, and Bill Nasson (Berlin: Freie Universität Berlin, 2018), https://encyclopedia.1914-1918-online.net/home.html.

5 "The Cost of War: World War I," *Owlcation,* 13 July 2022, http:/owlcation.com/humanities/World-War-1-The-Cost-of-War.

6 Stephen Broadberry and Mark Harrison, "The Economics of World War I: An Overview," in *The Economics of World War I,* ed. Stephen Broadberry and Mark Harrison (Cambridge, UK: Cambridge University Press, 2005), 14–15.

7 R. Craig McIvor, *Canadian Monetary, Banking and Fiscal Development* (Toronto: Macmillan, 1958), 108, 116.

8 Canada, House of Commons, *Debates,* 20 April 1909, 4563.

9 White, *Story,* 14.

10 Ibid., 24.

11 William Gibbs McAdoo, *Crowded Years: The Reminiscences of William G. McAdoo* (Boston: Houghton Mifflin, 1931), 374.

12 White, *Story,* 25.

13 See Robert B. Bryce, *Canada and the Cost of World War II: The International Operations of Canada's Department of Finance, 1939–1947,* ed. Matthew J. Bellamy (Montreal and Kingston: McGill-Queen's University Press, 2005).

14 Frank Albert Knox, "Canadian War Finance and the Balance of Payments, 1914–1918," *Canadian Journal of Economics and Political Science* 6, 2 (1940): 226–57.

15 *Financial Post* (Toronto), 6 January 1940.
16 Ronald A. Shearer and Carolyn Clark, "Canada and the Interwar Gold Standard, 1920–35: Monetary Policy without a Central Bank," in *A Retrospective on the Classical Gold Standard, 1821–1931,* ed. Michael D. Bordo and Anna J. Schwartz, 277–309 (Chicago: University of Chicago Press, 1984).
17 Hans-Peter Ullmann, "Financing Global War," in *The Cambridge History of the First World War,* 3 vols., ed. Jay M. Winter, vol. 2, 408–33 (Cambridge, UK: Cambridge University Press, 2013–14).
18 Ute Daniel, Peter Gatrell, Oliver Janz, Heather Jones, Jennifer Keene, Alan Kramer, and Bill Nasson, eds., *1914–1918–Online: International Encyclopedia of the First World War* (Berlin: Freie Universität Berlin, 2018), https://encyclopedia.1914-1918-online.net/home.html.
19 David Tough, "'The rich ... should give to such an extent that it will hurt': 'Conscription of Wealth' and Political Modernism in the Parliamentary Debate on the 1917 Income War Tax," *Canadian Historical Review* 93, 3 (2012): 382–407.
20 Niall Ferguson, *The Pity of War* (New York: Basic Books, 1999), 384.
21 *Truro Daily News* (Truro, NS), 13 November 1917.

Chapter 1: Business as Usual, 1914

1 A.W. Blue, "Conversion Loan Success Reflects Faith in Canada," *Maclean's Magazine* (Toronto) 44, 13 (1931): 64.
2 *Globe* (Toronto), 27 December 1910.
3 Elspeth A. Heaman, *Tax, Order, and Good Government: A New Political History of Canada, 1867–1917* (Montreal and Kingston: McGill-Queen's University Press, 2017), 261–62, 269.
4 *Globe,* 24 February 1911.
5 *Globe,* 10 March 1911; *Toronto Daily Star,* 10 March 1911.
6 *Globe,* 11 October 1911; W. Stuart Wallace, *The Memoirs of the Rt. Hon. Sir George Foster, P.C., G.C.M.G.* (Toronto: Macmillan, 1931), 161.
7 R. Craig McIvor, *Canadian Monetary, Banking and Fiscal Development* (Toronto: Macmillan, 1958), 101.
8 An overview of the Department of Finance near the beginning of White's tenure is in Robert MacGregor Dawson, *The Civil Service of Canada: A Special Issue of The Civilian* (Ottawa: The Civilian, 1914), 47–52.
9 Canada, House of Commons, *Debates,* 1 April 1912, 6808–20; *Canadian Annual Review of Public Affairs* (1912): 228–33.
10 Library and Archives Canada (LAC), Sir Robert Laird Borden and Kathryn Rose, "The Diaries of Sir Robert Borden, 1912–1918: Transcription by Dr. Kathryn Rose," 25, 29 April, 1, 22, 30 May 1913, digitized by Memorial University of Newfoundland, http://research.library.mun.ca/id/eprint/2428 (hereafter cited as Borden diaries).
11 Canada, House of Commons, *Debates,* 6 April 1914, 2446.
12 Robert Craig Brown and Ramsay Cook, *Canada 1896–1921: A Nation Transformed* (Toronto: McClelland and Stewart, 1974), 199.
13 Canada, Parliament, *Sessional Papers,* 1914, no. 2, 8; 1916, no. 2, 8.
14 *Globe,* 21 May 1914.
15 Canada, Parliament, *Sessional Papers,* 1915, no. 2, xii.
16 Desmond Morton, *A Short History of Canada,* 7th ed. (Toronto: McClelland and Stewart, 2017), 175–76; James A. Wood, "Pre-war Military Planning (Canada)," in *1914–1918–Online: International Encyclopedia of the First World War,* ed. Ute Daniel, Peter Gatrell, Oliver

Janz, Heather Jones, Jennifer Keene, Alan Kramer, and Bill Nasson (Berlin: Freie Universität Berlin, 2018), https://encyclopedia.1914-1918-online.net/home.html.

17 Canada, Parliament, *Sessional Papers,* 1913, no. 1, O-2; 1913, no. 2, 9; 1915, no. 1, P-2; 1915, no. 2, 9.

18 Canada, Parliament, *Sessional Papers,* 1903, no. 35, 5–6; 1903, no. 35a, 94–95.

19 James Powell, *A History of the Canadian Dollar* (Ottawa: Bank of Canada, 2005), 37; Richard Roberts, *Saving the City: The Great Financial Crisis of 1914* (Oxford: Oxford University Press, 2013); William L. Silber, *When Washington Shut Down Wall Street: The Great Financial Crisis of 1914 and the Origins of America's Monetary Supremacy* (Princeton, NJ: Princeton University Press, 2007).

20 On democracy, see Doug Owram, *The Government Generation: Canadian Intellectuals and the State, 1900–1945* (Toronto: University of Toronto Press, 1986), ch. 4; and Julien Mauduit and Jennifer Tunnicliffe, "Introduction," in *Constant Struggle: Histories of Canadian Democratization,* ed. Julien Mauduit and Jennifer Tunnicliffe (Montreal and Kingston: McGill-Queen's University Press, 2021), 18–19.

21 *Globe,* 11, 25 September 1914; *Toronto Daily Star,* 18 January 1916; Margaret MacMillan, *The War That Ended Peace: The Road to 1914* (Toronto: Penguin, 2013), 634.

22 Duncan McDowall, "Meredith, Sir Henry Vincent," *Dictionary of Canadian Biography,* vol. 15, http://www.biographi.ca/en/bio/meredith_henry_vincent_15E.html.

23 Clifford Austin Curtis, "The Canadian Banks and War Finance," *Contributions to Canadian Economics* (Toronto) 3 (1931): 7.

24 Canada, House of Commons, *Debates,* 21 August 1914, 64–65; *Monetary Times* (Toronto), 14 August 1914, 9.

25 Canada, Royal Commission on Banking and Currency in Canada, *Report* (Ottawa: Privy Council Office, 1933), 22.

26 Powell, *History of the Canadian Dollar,* 38 (Chart 2), 97 (Chart C1).

27 *Globe,* 19 August 1914; McIvor, *Canadian Monetary,* 102–3; Duncan McDowall, *Quick to the Frontier: Canada's Royal Bank* (Toronto: McClelland and Stewart, 1993), 151, 153; Robert B. Bryce, *Maturing in Hard Times: Canada's Department of Finance through the Great Depression* (Montreal and Kingston: McGill-Queen's University Press, 1986), 31–32.

28 Sir Thomas White, *The Story of Canada's War Finance* (Montreal: Canadian Bank of Commerce, 1921), 9. On dominion notes, see White's address of 22 January 1922 to the Toronto Bankers' Educational Association, published as "The War Finance of Canada," *Annals of the American Academy of Political Sciences* (Philadelphia) 107 (May 1923): 210–12. See also *Evening Citizen* (Ottawa), 4 August 1914; Curtis, "Canadian Banks and War Finance," 8–9; Frank Herbert Brown, "The History of Canadian War Finance, 1914–20," in Frank Herbert Brown, James Douglas Gibson, and Arthur Fitzwalter Wynne Plumptre, *War Finance in Canada* (Toronto: Ryerson, 1940), 3–7.

29 J.L. Granatstein, "Afterword," in Robert B. Bryce, *Canada and the Cost of World War II: The International Operations of Canada's Department of Finance, 1939–1947,* ed. Matthew J. Bellamy (Montreal and Kingston: McGill-Queen's University Press, 2005), 327.

30 Canada, House of Commons, *Debates,* 21 August 1914, 64–65. White would later regard the Finance Act as "one of the most important measures that was ever placed upon the statute books of Canada." White, "War Finance of Canada," 209.

31 John Anthony Turley-Ewart, "Gentleman Bankers, Politicians and Bureaucrats: The History of the Canadian Bankers' Association, 1891–1924" (PhD diss., University of Toronto, 2000), 195, 220–21.

32 Canada, House of Commons, *Debates,* 20 August 1914, 23–26; 21 August 1914, 52; Robert Craig Brown, *Robert Laird Borden: A Biography,* 2 vols. (Toronto: Macmillan, 1975–80), vol. 2, 11–12.

33 Canada, House of Commons, *Debates,* 21 August 1914, 72. Taxation is traced in Shirley Tillotson, *Give and Take: The Citizen-Taxpayer and the Rise of Canadian Democracy* (Vancouver: UBC Press, 2017).

34 Canada, House of Commons, *Journals,* 1915, app. 3, 9–17; Canada, Parliament, *Sessional Papers,* 1915, no. 122; Norman Ward, *The Public Purse: A Study in Canadian Democracy* (Toronto: University of Toronto Press, 1962), 148–49.

35 Canada, Department of External Affairs, *Documents on Canadian External Relations,* 29 vols. to date, ed. Robert Alexander Mackay et al. (Ottawa: Queen's Printer, 1967–), vol. 1, 44; Roy MacLaren, *Commissions High: Canada in London, 1870–1971* (Montreal and Kingston: McGill-Queen's University Press, 2006), 168–71.

36 For comparison to war finance in other dominions, see Karin Pallaver, "War and Colonial Finance (Africa)," and Jatinder Marn, "War Finance (Australia)," both in *1914–1918-Online: International Encyclopedia of the First World War,* ed. Ute Daniel, Peter Gatrell, Oliver Janz, Heather Jones, Jennifer Keene, Alan Kramer, and Bill Nasson (Berlin: Freie Universität Berlin, 2018), https://encyclopedia.1914-1918-online.net/home.html; David S. Waller, "War Loans Bonds in Australia, 1915–1921: Patriotism or Propaganda?" *Journal of Nonprofit and Public Sector Marketing* (Binghamton, NY) 3, 1 (1995): 81–96; H.T.B. Drew, ed., *The War Effort of New Zealand* (Auckland: Whitcombe and Tombs, 1923), ch. 14; "Finance, Public – First World War," in *Encyclopedia of New Zealand,* ed. A.H. McLintock (1966), https://teara.govt.nz/en/1966/finance-public/page-2. Finance in Newfoundland will be treated here in Part 3.

37 Canada, Department of External Affairs, *Documents on Canadian External Relations,* vol. 1, 46. See also Turley-Ewart, "Gentleman Bankers," 243–48.

38 On Britain's war finance and National War Loans, see *Globe,* 18, 20–21 November 1914; E. Victor Morgan, *Studies in British Financial Policy, 1914–25* (London: Macmillan, 1952), 106; Jeremy Wormell, *The Management of the National Debt of the United Kingdom, 1900–1932* (New York: Routledge, 2000), 65–66, 70–88; G.C. Peden, *The Treasury and British Public Policy, 1906–1959* (Oxford: Oxford University Press, 2000), ch. 3; Martin Horn, *Britain, France, and the Financing of the First World War* (Montreal and Kingston: McGill-Queen's University Press, 2002); Hew Strachan, *Financing the First World War* (Oxford: Oxford University Press, 2004), 147–48.

39 Archer Fortescue Duguid, *Official History of the Canadian Forces in the Great War, 1914–1919,* 1 vol. in 2 parts (Ottawa: King's Printer, 1938), vol. 1, part 1, 116–17.

40 Among other newspapers, see *Globe,* 17 October 1914; and *Regina Morning Leader,* 17 October 1914.

41 Jeremy Adelman, "Prairie Farm Debt and the Financial Crisis of 1914," *Canadian Historical Review* 71, 4 (1990): 491–519.

42 Roderick George MacBeth, *Sir Augustus Nanton: A Biography* (Toronto: Macmillan, 1931), 35, 50.

43 See Arthur Hawkes, "Notice to Pay," *Canadian War* (Toronto), 27 February 1915, 1–9; and *Globe,* 5 April 1915.

44 Ian MacDonald Drummond, "Debt and the Dominion Government, 1914–1920," [4], paper presented at the 18th Conference on the Application of Quantitative Methods to Canadian Economic History, Vancouver, 2 October 1992. Since this paper could not be located, I have used the incomplete version in the Drummond Papers at the University of Toronto Archives and Records Management Services, B1995-0013/017(25).

45 Strachan, *Financing,* 60–61, 187–88; Gregory P. Marchildon, "'Hands Across the Water': Canadian Industrial Financiers in the City of London, 1905–20," *Business History* (Cambridge, UK) 34, 3 (1992): 69–95; Horn, *Britain, France,* ch. 3.

46 An account of the movement of gold from Halifax to New York, taken from the *New York Evening Post*, appeared in the *Beacon* (St. Andrews, NB), 18 November 1916; Horn, *Britain, France*, 52–53, 102, 120, 145, 173, 216n14.

47 John Osborne, *The Bank of England, 1914–21*, 4 vols. (1926), vol. 2, chs. 4 and 5, Bank of England Archive, London, M7/157, https://www.bankofengland.co.uk/archive/bank-of-england-1914-21-ww1; Canada, House of Commons, *Debates*, 29 May 1917, 1796–97; *Globe*, 13, 19 August, 26 October 1914; Sir Thomas White, *The Story of Canada's War Finance* (Montreal: Canadian Bank of Commerce, 1921), 15–16, 40–41; Roberts, *Saving the City*, 172–74; John Milton Cooper Jr., "The Command of Gold Reversed: American Loans to Britain, 1915–1917," *Pacific Historical Review* (Berkeley, CA) 45, 2 (1976): 209–30.

48 *Montreal Daily Mail*, 15 December 1914.

49 For insight into the thrift and "mass philanthropy" phenomenon, some of it applicable to Canada, see Joshua J. Yates and James Davison Hunter, eds., *Thrift and Thriving in America: Capitalism and Moral Order from the Puritans to the Present* (New York: Oxford University Press, 2011); and Olivier Zunz, *Philanthropy in America: A History* (Princeton, NJ: Princeton University Press, 2012).

50 See, for example, Hartley Withers, *Poverty and Waste* (London: Smith, Elder and Company, 1914); and Ann K. Perry, "Manliness, Goodness, and God: Poverty, Gender, and Social Reform in English-Speaking Montreal, 1890–1929" (MA thesis, Queen's University, 1998).

51 *Globe*, 16 December 1914.

52 *Globe*, 15 December 1914.

53 *Globe*, 22 October 1914; Canada, House of Commons, *Debates*, 11 February 1915, 80–88; White, *Story*, 12, 22–26; Turley-Ewart, "Gentleman Bankers," 252.

54 Canada, Parliament, *Sessional Papers*, 1916, no. 2, 3; 1915, no. 2, 3; Albert W. Kimber, ed., *Kimber's Record of Government Debts and Other Foreign Securities, 1922* (New York: A.W. Kimber, 1922), 227–33; Robert Bothwell, Ian MacDonald Drummond, and John English, *Canada, 1900–1945* (Toronto: University of Toronto Press, 1987), 182. Drummond's authorship there of the pages on war finance has been confirmed by John English.

55 Strachan, *Financing*, 218–19.

Chapter 2: Inching Toward Innovation, 1915–16

1 Hugh Grant, *W.A. Mackintosh: The Life of a Canadian Economist* (Montreal and Kingston: McGill-Queen's University Press, 2015), 67.

2 Robert Craig Brown and Ramsay Cook, *Canada 1896–1921: A Nation Transformed* (Toronto: McClelland and Stewart, 1974), 229; Hew Strachan, "Economic Mobilization: Money, Munitions, and Machines," in *The Oxford Illustrated History of the First World War*, 2nd ed., ed. Hew Strachan (Oxford: Oxford University Press, 2014), 135–37; Benjamin H. Higgins, *Canada's Financial System in War* (New York: Financial Research Program, National Bureau of Economic Research, 1944), 63–64.

3 *Journal of Commerce* (Montreal), 7 January 1915; *Globe* (Toronto), 11 January 1915.

4 Canada, Parliament, *Sessional Papers*, 1916, no. 2, xv.

5 For an overview, see Keith Neilson, "Canada and British War Finance, 1914–17," in *Forging a Nation: Perspectives on the Canadian Military Experience*, ed. Bernd Horn, 109–22 (St. Catharines, ON: Vanwell, 2002).

6 Library and Archives Canada (LAC), Borden diaries, 26 January 1915.

7 Ibid., 11 February 1915.

8 *Globe*, 25 March, 2, 14, 16–17, 22 April 1915; Christopher D. Ryan, "Canada's Provisional War Tax Revenue Stamps," *Canadian Revenue Newsletter* (Toronto) 61 (2008): 7–10.

9 Canada, House of Commons, *Debates*, 11 February 1915, 84.

10 *Globe,* 24 February 1915, 8, 14 March, 27 April, 6, 10 May, 7, 13 July, 21 November 1916; Canada, Dominion Bureau of Statistics, *Canada Year Book, 1915* (Ottawa: Census and Statistics Office, 1916), 681–83; *1916–17* (1917), 680.

11 When finance critic Alexander Kenneth Maclean asked in the Commons for copies of the correspondence on imperial loans to Canada, Borden responded that, according to White, most of the correspondence was confidential and could not be tabled. Canada, House of Commons, *Debates,* 1 March 1915, 522.

12 Ibid., 26 March 1915, 1528–39; Canada, Parliament, *Sessional Papers,* 1919, no. 2, xxvi; *Globe,* 27 March 1915.

13 Canada, Parliament, *Sessional Papers,* 1917, no. 2, xi; *Globe,* 25 March, 15 April 1915.

14 Ian MacDonald Drummond, "Debt and the Dominion Government, 1914–1920," [6], paper presented at the 18th Conference on the Application of Quantitative Methods to Canadian Economic History, Vancouver, 2 October 1992; Hew Strachan, *Financing the First World War* (Oxford: Oxford University Press, 2004), 217.

15 LAC, MG 27, II, D18, vol. 3, file 11(a).

16 William John Alexander Donald, "Canadian Financial Problems," *Journal of Political Economy* (Chicago) 23, 8 (1915): 753–90.

17 Canada, Parliament, *Sessional Papers,* 1917, no. 2: xi–xii; Robert D. Cuff and J.L. Granatstein, *Ties That Bind: Canadian-American Relations in Wartime from the Great War to the Cold War* (Toronto: Samuel Stevens Hakkert, 1977), 23–25; Martin Horn, "A Private Bank at War: J.P. Morgan and Co. and France, 1914–1918," *Business History Review* (Cambridge, MA) 74, 1 (2000): 85–112; Kathryn Kemp, "House of Morgan," in *1914–1918-Online: International Encyclopedia of the First World War,* ed. Ute Daniel, Peter Gatrell, Oliver Janz, Heather Jones, Jennifer Keene, Alan Kramer, and Bill Nasson (Berlin: Freie Universität Berlin, 2018), https://encyclopedia.1914-1918-online.net/home.html.

18 Sir Thomas White, *The Story of Canada's War Finance* (Montreal: Canadian Bank of Commerce, 1921), 19. See also *Globe,* 22–23, 26–27 July 1915.

19 Strachan, "Economic Mobilization," 135–37.

20 *Evening World* (New York), 16 September 1915.

21 Canada, House of Commons, *Debates,* 16 March 1916, 1818–32; White, *Story,* 20; Christopher Armstrong, *Blue Skies and Boiler Rooms: Buying and Selling Securities in Canada, 1870–1940* (Toronto: University of Toronto Press, 1997), 80.

22 According to David Welch, *Propaganda: Power and Persuasion* (London: Bloomsbury, 2013), 90, the concept of a "home front" emerged in Britain in 1915. The term does not appear with regularity in Canadian newspapers until later, sometimes with reference to Germany's home front but also to Canadian civilians as part of the battlefield.

23 Martin Farr, *Reginald McKenna: Financier among Statesmen, 1863–1916* (London: Routledge, 2008), 291–92.

24 *Globe,* 7 October 1915.

25 *Globe,* 24 June, 2 October, 12 November 1915. On Britain's first and second war loans, see E. Victor Morgan, *Studies in British Financial Policy, 1914–25* (London: Macmillan, 1952), 106–10.

26 Ian MacDonald Drummond, *Capital Markets in Australia and Canada, 1895–1914: A Study in Colonial Economic History* (New Haven, CT: Yale University Library, 1974), 178–87; Lance E. Davis and Robert E. Gallman, *Evolving Financial Markets and International Capital Flows: Britain, the Americas, and Australia, 1865–1914* (Cambridge, UK: Cambridge University Press, 2001), 465–66.

27 Some understanding of the postponement of the loan until after the financing of the western wheat crop is offered in the *Western Globe* (Lacombe, Alberta), 13 October 1915;

the *Canadian Thresherman and Farmer* (Winnipeg) 22, 10 (1917); and the *Globe*, 17 September, 17 December 1915, 26 January, 30 June 1916. The editorial of 30 June 1916 provides information on the facilities for discounting and credit expansion successfully set up (under the Finance Act) in the fall of 1915 "for the financing of the western grain crop." The postponement, it was noted, also gave farmers the opportunity to subscribe to the loan. The traditional period for moving the crop, according to White, *Story*, 8, was September to February.

28 *Globe*, 8 October 1915. White also announced his preparedness to borrow domestically in an address to the Canadian Club of Montreal on 2 November. Thomas White, *Canadian Trade and Finance During the War* (Montreal: Canadian Club of Montreal, 1915).

29 *Lacombe Guardian* (Lacombe, Alberta), 15 October 1915.

30 *Globe*, 8 October 1915.

31 LAC, Borden diaries, 3 November 1915; Robert Craig Brown, *Robert Laird Borden: A Biography*, 2 vols. (Toronto: Macmillan, 1975–80), vol. 2, 43–44.

32 *Globe*, 31 October 1914.

33 *Financial Post* (Toronto), 2 October 1915.

34 White, *Story*, 25. White would repeatedly remind Canadians of the value of balancing patriotism and investment, as in *Globe*, 14 August 1918.

35 White, *Story*, 25.

36 The term assumed urgent meaning during the early weeks of the Great War. See, for example, the editorial on "Practical Patriotism" in *North Battleford News* (Saskatchewan), 27 August 1914.

37 Bernard Keble Sandwell, "Financial Measures," in *Canada in the Great World War*, 6 vols. (Toronto: United Publishers of Canada, 1917–21), vol. 2, 125–26.

38 Ibid., 126.

39 Clifford Austin Curtis, "The Canadian Banks and War Finance," *Contributions to Canadian Economics* (Toronto) 3 (1931): 12; John Anthony Turley-Ewart, "Gentleman Bankers, Politicians and Bureaucrats: The History of the Canadian Bankers' Association, 1891–1924" (PhD diss., University of Toronto, 2000), 254.

40 The accounting impact of discounts and interest rates is explained in Marie-Michelle Pagé, "Les Emprunts de guerre et les Emprunts de la Victoire dans les comptes publics du ministère des Finances du Canada (1915–1937)," unpublished report, 2014, 6–11.

41 A search for applicable federal taxation at the time of the loan has been inconclusive, although summaries of federal taxes suggest none. See Canada, Dominion Bureau of Statistics, *Canada Year Book, 1916–17* (1917), 543–45, 677–68; *1920* (1921), 10–13, 555, 729. The prospectus for the 1915 loan (e.g., *Globe*, 22 November 1915) suggests exemption from future taxation: "The issue will be exempt from taxes – including any income tax – imposed in pursuance of legislation enacted by the Parliament of Canada." Some provinces moved to exempt the 1915 bonds from provincial income taxation, succession duties, and other taxes, as seen for instance with British Columbia in March 1916.

42 White, *Story*, 26; *Globe*, 18 November 1915.

43 Oscar Douglas Skelton, "Canadian War Finance," *American Economic Review* 7, 4 (1917): 822.

44 *Globe*, 4 December 1915.

45 Curtis, "Canadian Banks and War Finance," 13–15; *Financial Post*, 4 March 1916.

46 William Clifford Clark, "Financing the War," Part 1 of *Economic Aspects of the War*, 1–64 (Kingston, ON: Queen's University, 1916).

47 On saving as an ideal and movement in America and Britain, see Sheldon Garon, *Beyond Our Means: Why America Spends While the World Saves* (Princeton, NJ: Princeton University Press, 2013).

48 *Financial Post,* 20 November 1915.
49 From the notes of Borden biographer Robert Craig Brown, University of Toronto Archives and Records, B80-0009/022 (49 R), noting White to Borden, 22 November 1915, and Borden to White, 23 November 1915.
50 *Globe,* 23 November 1915.
51 White, *Story,* 28–29.
52 *Financial Post,* 10 March 1917.
53 Canada, Parliament, *Sessional Papers,* 1917, no. 2, 17.
54 *Globe,* 31 December 1915; Curtis, "Canadian Banks and War Finance," 21, 36–37.
55 Armstrong, *Blue Skies,* 82.
56 Great Britain, Ministry of Munitions, *History of the Ministry of Munitions,* 8 vols. in 4 (London: Ministry of Munitions, 1922), vol. 2, part 4, ch. 6, 56–57.
57 University of Oxford, Bodleian Library, uncatalogued papers of R.H. Brand, Baron Brand (hereafter cited as Brand papers), file 35, Brand to Milner, 27 August 1915; Brand to McKenna, 2 September 1915; related but undated memoranda; and file 57-2, Brand's "Introduction to the History of the Imperial Munitions Board," 7–8; *Globe,* 6–7, 9, 28 December 1915.
58 *Globe,* 3 December 1915; *Toronto World,* 3 December 1915; Jeremy Wormell, *The Management of the National Debt of the United Kingdom, 1900–1932* (New York: Routledge, 2000), 288, 291, 293–94.
59 *Globe,* 17 December 1915.
60 Peter E. Rider, "The Imperial Munitions Board and Its Relationship to Government, Business, and Labour, 1914–1920" (PhD diss., University of Toronto, 1974), ch. 5.
61 Quoted in Roberts, *Saving the City,* 223. See also *Globe,* 4 August 1916; White, *Story,* 21–22; and Wormell, *Management,* 291, 293.
62 Wormell, *Management,* 289; Michael Bliss, *A Canadian Millionaire: The Life and Times of Sir Joseph Flavelle, Bart., 1858–1939* (Toronto: Macmillan, 1978), 269–70; LAC, MG 27, II, D18, vol. 8, 5235, Flavelle to White, 13 December 1915; "A Resume of War Financing" [going back to 1916], *Journal of the Canadian Bankers' Association* (Toronto) 25, 2 (1917–18): 140–42, also reported in the *Globe,* 11 February 1918.
63 Rider, "Imperial Munitions Board," 197.
64 Queen's University Archives, Sir Joseph W. Flavelle fonds, box 4, Favelle to White, 26 June 1917: "We find it advantageous to have the Treasury put us in funds in New York as we pay our American bills by cheque in New York."
65 Keith Neilson, "R.H. Brand, the Empire and Munitions from Canada," *English Historical Review* (Oxford) 126 (2011): 1430–55.
66 *Canadian Annual Review of Public Affairs* (1916): 362–63.
67 One company in question was Steel and Radiation, a Toronto firm headed by Sir Henry M. Pellatt. Its profitable move into shell production attracted attention in the Commons. Canada, House of Commons, *Debates,* 20 January 1916, 141; 21 January 1916, 177; 9 March 1916, 1555. This move was also noted in the tabloid *Jack Canuck* (Toronto), 4 December 1915, which felt that White should confiscate the excess profits of "Sir Hank Pellatt and His Brother 'Profiteers.'"
68 Great Britain, Ministry of Munitions, *History of the Ministry of Munitions,* vol. 2, part 4, ch. 6, 57; G.W.L. Nicholson, *Canadian Expeditionary Force, 1914–1919* (Ottawa: Queen's Printer, 1962), 359–61.
69 LAC, Borden diaries, 10 February 1916.
70 Ibid., 12 February 1916.
71 White, *Story,* 59. See also Oscar Douglas Skelton, *Canadian Federal Finance – II* (Kingston, ON: Jackson, 1918), which first appeared in *Queen's Quarterly* (Kingston, ON) 26 (July

1918): 195–228; and Barry Ferguson, *Remaking Liberalism: The Intellectual Legacy of Adam Shortt, O.D. Skelton, W.C. Clark, and W.A. Mackintosh, 1890–1925* (Montreal and Kingston: McGill-Queen's University Press, 1993), 176.

72 Shirley Tillotson, *Give and Take: The Citizen-Taxpayer and the Rise of Canadian Democracy* (Vancouver: UBC Press, 2017), 22–23.

73 *Globe,* 16 February 1916.

74 Canada, House of Commons, *Debates,* 17 February 1916, 891.

75 Ibid., 16 March 1916, 1844.

76 Ibid., 16 March 1916, 1814–15, 1834.

77 *Globe and Mail,* 11 March 1940, 14 December 1944, 2 January 1950, 18 February 1955.

78 Canada, House of Commons, *Debates,* 6 April 1916, 2625.

79 Ibid., 15 February 1916, 808.

80 White, *Story,* 59.

81 This funding was announced in the *Toronto Daily Star,* 4 August 1916, as an issue of three-and-a-half-percent and four-and-a-half-percent dominion bonds, maturing in 1928 and 1945, to pay off temporary imperial debt.

82 Wormell, *Management,* 221–26; Strachan, *Financing the First World War,* 198–201; Kathleen Burk, "The Diplomacy of Finance: British Financial Missions to the United States, 1914–1918," *Historical Journal* (Cambridge, UK) 22 (1979): 351–72.

83 Canada, House of Commons, *Debates,* 16 March 1916, 1819–22.

84 LAC, MG 30, A16, 24, file: R.H. Brand, Flavelle to Brand, 10, 23 June 1916; *Globe,* 25 March 1916.

85 *Globe,* 27 June 1916, 14, 24 July 1916.

86 Canada, Department of External Affairs, *Documents on Canadian External Relations,* 29 vols. to date, ed. Robert Alexander Mackay et al. (Ottawa: Queen's Printer, 1967–), vol. 1, 137–38. See also Canada, Parliament, *Sessional Papers,* 1918, no. 2, x; LAC, RG 14, D2, 46, no. 167 (unpub. Sess. paper, 1919, no. 167); and Burk, "Diplomacy of Finance," 355.

87 *Globe,* 26 August, 6 December 1916.

88 LAC, MG 27, II, D18, vol. 4, file 14(a).

89 *Globe,* 25 July, 5 August 1916; *Toronto Daily Star,* 4 August 1916.

90 Toronto-Dominion Bank Archives, Toronto, Canadian Bankers' Association, Executive Council, Minutes, 5 September 1916; Canada, House of Commons, *Debates,* 28 June 1917, 2775.

91 *Montreal Daily Mail,* 16, 21, 25 September 1916.

92 Investment Industry Regulatory Organization of Canada, General Counsel's Office, Toronto, box 58516184, Bond Dealers' Association of Canada, vol. 1, Minutes 1911–16; vol. 2, Minutes 1916–17.

93 Great Britain, Ministry of Munitions, *History of the Ministry of Munitions,* vol. 2, part 4, ch. 6, 62.

94 *Globe,* 23 August, 13 September 1916.

95 White, *Story,* 21, 25–26, 31; *Globe,* 12 October 1916.

96 Calculated as of 27 May 2019 using the Bank of Canada's inflation calculator at https://www.bankofcanada.ca/rates/related/inflation-calculator/. The dollar of 1916 would be worth $20.92, and the dollar of 1918 would be worth $15.81.

97 *Financial Post,* 30 September 1916.

98 See, for example, Manulife Corporate Archives, Toronto, Board of Directors, Minute books nos. 11 and 13.

99 White, *Story,* 28.

100 *Financial Post,* 25 October 1916.

101 *Prince Rupert Journal* (Prince Rupert, BC), 12 November 1916.

102 LAC, MG 27, II, D18, vol. 8, 5354–59, White to Flavelle, 9 November 1916.
103 Canada, House of Commons, *Debates,* 1 February 1917, 356–58; 10 April 1918, 576–77; 10 April 1919, 1347; *Globe,* 11 April 1918; Nicholson, *Canadian Expeditionary Force,* 359–61; Norman Ward, *The Public Purse: A Study in Canadian Democracy* (Toronto: University of Toronto Press, 1962), 151–53.
104 LAC, Borden diaries, 15, 19, 22, 27 December 1916, 31 May 1917.
105 LAC, MG 27, II, D18, vol. 8, 5375–5402, 15–26 December 1916; Wormell, *Management,* 289.
106 University of Oxford, Bodleian Library, Brand papers, file 9-1, Flavelle to Brand, 29 December 1916.
107 Wormell, *Management,* 226–33; *Globe,* 28, 30 November, 2, 5, 8 December 1916; Hew Strachan, ed., *The Oxford Illustrated History of the First World War,* 2nd ed. (Oxford: Oxford University Press, 2014), 61–62, 147.
108 Mourad Djebabla, "'Fight the Huns with Food': Mobilizing Canadian Civilians for the Food War Effort during the Great War, 1914–1918," in *World War I and Propaganda,* ed. Troy R.E. Paddock, 65–88 (Leiden: Brill, 2014).
109 Thomas White, "Canada's Duty – Production," in Canada, Department of Agriculture, *Patriotism and Production "More than Usual": Agricultural War Book* (Ottawa: Department of Agriculture, 1915), 6–8; Joshua J. Yates and James Davison Hunter, eds., *Thrift and Thriving in America: Capitalism and Moral Order from the Puritans to the Present* (New York: Oxford University Press, 2011).
110 Turley-Ewart, "Gentlemen Bankers," 282.
111 *Globe,* 19 April, 3, 19, 24 May 1916.
112 *Globe,* 5, 11, 17, 19 October, 28 November, 6 December 1916.
113 *Journal of the Canadian Bankers' Association* 24, 2 (1916–17): 98–99: "This stock will prevent the war loan bonds from rising above 100. If the bonds rose above par the yield on them would be less than 5 percent, and an investor could get the full 5 percent for the time being by buying the stock." The *Journal,* 24, 3 (1917): 253, also indicated that debenture stock was seen by investors as a temporary investment while awaiting a long-term dominion loan bearing a higher rate. See also *Globe,* 12 October 1916.
114 *Globe,* 10 October 1916.

Chapter 3: Crises and Victories, 1917–18

1 Sir Thomas White, *The Story of Canada's War Finance* (Montreal: Canadian Bank of Commerce, 1921), 52.
2 University of Oxford, Bodleian Library, Brand papers, file 6B, Flavelle to Brand, 19 March 1917.
3 Ibid., file 9-2, Flavelle to Brand, 11 September 1917.
4 Queen's University Archives, Sir Joseph W. Flavelle fonds, box 4, White to Flavelle, 21 February 1917.
5 *Financial Post* (Toronto), 13 January 1917.
6 Canada, Parliament, *Sessional Papers,* 1918, no. 2, xi, 15.
7 The diversion of money from consumption to war-savings devices is almost impossible to trace. White's calculations of interest rates are equally opaque, with nothing comparable to Richard Sutch's probing examination of America's early Liberty Loans in his "Liberty Bonds: April 1917–September 1918," Federal Reserve History, https://www.federalreservehistory.org/essays/liberty-bonds. Clearly evident is the propagandistic campaigning.
8 Canada, House of Commons, *Debates,* 1 February 1917, 344–45.
9 *Globe* (Toronto), 25 August 1917.
10 Hew Strachan, ed., *The Oxford Illustrated History of the First World War,* 2nd ed. (Oxford: Oxford University Press, 2014), 132, 147–48, 238–51.

11 Jeremy Wormell, *The Management of the National Debt of the United Kingdom, 1900–1932* (New York: Routledge, 2000), 297; Michael Bliss, *A Canadian Millionaire: The Life and Times of Sir Joseph Flavelle, Bart., 1858–1939* (Toronto: Macmillan, 1978), 317.
12 Keith Neilson, "R.H. Brand, the Empire and Munitions from Canada," *English Historical Review* (Oxford) 126 (2011): 1430–55.
13 Patrice Dutil and David MacKenzie, *Embattled Nation: Canada's Wartime Election of 1917* (Toronto: Dundurn, 2017).
14 Apart from imperial credits, direct war costs to the government by department can be followed in the "War Account" expenditures listed in the "Public Accounts" in the *Sessional Papers.* For example, for 1915–16, the accounts totalled $166,197,755.47, of which $160,433,416.42 (96.5 percent) was claimed by the militia department. Canada, Parliament, *Sessional Papers,* 1917, no. 2, xiii-xiv.
15 *Globe,* 1 March 1917.
16 Homer Mark Philip Eckardt, "The War Loan," *Journal of the Canadian Bankers' Association* (Toronto) 24, 3 (1916–17): 251–53. For a comparable consideration in Britain, see Benjamin H. Higgins, *Lombard Street in War and Reconstruction* (New York: National Bureau of Economic Research, 1949), 16. (Lombard Street was London's financial centre.)
17 Investment Industry Regulatory Organization of Canada, General Counsel's Office, Toronto, box 58516184, Bond Dealers' Association of Canada, vol. 2, Minutes 1916–17; Toronto-Dominion Bank Archives, Toronto, Canadian Bankers' Association, Minutes 1913–17; *Journal of the Canadian Bankers' Association* 23 (1916) and 24 (1916–17); *Financial Post,* 3, 10, 17, 24, 31 March, 7 April 1917; Christopher Armstrong, *Blue Skies and Boiler Rooms: Buying and Selling Securities in Canada, 1870–1940* (Toronto: University of Toronto Press, 1997), 84–5.
18 University of Oxford, Bodleian Library, Brand papers, file 6B, Flavelle to Brand, 23 February, 27 March 1917.
19 *Globe,* 17, 26 March, 9, 12 July, 1 September 1917; *Journal of the Canadian Bankers' Association* 25, 1 (1917–18): 20. The restoration of the conversion privilege, which would not be done until the passage of an order-in-council in July, produced a surge of reinvestment. See the list of amounts converted from the 1915–17 loans in Library and Archives Canada (LAC), RG 14, D2, 46, no. 167 (unpub. Sess. paper, 1919, no. 167).
20 *Globe,* 8 March 1917.
21 *Globe,* 17 March 1917.
22 Canada, House of Commons, *Debates,* 24 April 1917, 718–21; Clifford Austin Curtis, "The Canadian Banks and War Finance," *Contributions to Canadian Economics* (Toronto) 3 (1931): 19.
23 Canada, Parliament, *Sessional Papers,* 1919, no. 19, xvii.
24 In the context of explaining war loans, bonds, and business taxes, White had to confront the belief that "conscription of wealth" meant the confiscation of bank deposits, which it did not. White, *Story,* 53. In a deft combination, he stated in July 1917 that it was not the government's intent to conscript "the people's legitimate savings through thrift and economy." *Globe,* 11 July 1917.
25 *Bella Coola Courier* (Bella Coola, BC), 9 June 1917.
26 See, for instance, *Business Profits War Tax Act: A Criticism* ... (Toronto: n.p. [1917]), copy in Archives of Ontario, Toronto, F 895-1-0-388, box B862153.
27 Canada, House of Commons, *Debates,* 25 July 1917, 3760; *Globe,* 14 June 1917; Robert Craig Brown, *Robert Laird Borden: A Biography,* 2 vols. (Toronto: Macmillan, 1975–80), vol. 2, 95. W. Irwin Gillespie, *Tax, Borrow and Spend: Financing Federal Spending in Canada, 1867–1990* (Ottawa: Carleton University Press, 1991), 79–80, 84, 89, 92–93. 96–97, 113–17, 123–24, 299. For recent analyses of White on income taxation, see David Tough, "'The

rich ... should give to such an extent that it will hurt': 'Conscription of Wealth' and Political Modernism in the Parliamentary Debate on the 1917 Income War Tax," *Canadian Historical Review* 93, 3 (2012): 382–407; Shirley Tillotson, *Give and Take: The Citizen-Taxpayer and the Rise of Canadian Democracy* (Vancouver: UBC Press, 2017); and Elspeth A. Heaman, *Tax, Order, and Good Government: A New Political History of Canada, 1867–1917* (Montreal and Kingston: McGill-Queen's University Press, 2017).

28 Heaman, *Tax, Order, and Good Government,* 410–19.

29 *Globe,* 2 July, 1 August 1917.

30 Canada, House of Commons, *Debates,* 25 July 1917, 3777.

31 Ibid., 29 May 1917, 1800.

32 Michael Bliss, *A Canadian Millionaire: The Life and Times of Sir Joseph Flavelle, Bart., 1858–1939* (Toronto: Macmillan, 1978), 275, 315, 327.

33 Henry Hague Vaughan, *The Manufacture of Munitions in Canada* (Ottawa: Engineering Institute of Canada, 1919); Chris Madsen and Michael Moir, "The Imperial Munitions Board and Merchant Shipbuilding in Canada," in *Turning Point 1917: The British Empire at War,* ed. Douglas E. Delaney and Nikolas Gardner, 51–77 (Vancouver: UBC Press, 2017); Bliss, *Canadian Millionaire,* 312, 316, 386; Garth Wilson, *A History of Shipbuilding and Naval Architecture in Canada* (Ottawa: National Museum of Science and Technology, 1994), 50. See also Canada, House of Commons, *Debates,* 11 May 1917, 1320–43.

34 Robert D. Cuff and J.L. Granatstein, *Ties That Bind: Canadian-American Relations in Wartime from the Great War to the Cold War* (Toronto: Samuel Stevens Hakkert, 1977), 27–30; Madsen and Moir, "Imperial Munitions Board," 69. On war finance in the United States, see Adam Tooze, *The Deluge: The Great War, America and the Remains of the Global Order, 1916–1931* (New York: Viking, 2014), 78, 206–7; Charles Gilbert, *American Financing of World War I* (Westport, CT: Greenwood, 1970); Kenneth D. Garbade, *Birth of a Market: The U.S. Treasury Securities Market from the Great War to the Great Depression* (Cambridge, MA: MIT Press, 2012), part 2; Robert D. Hormats, *The Price of Liberty: Paying for America's Wars* (New York: Times Books, 2007); Allan H. Meltzer, *A History of the Federal Reserve,* 2 vols. (Chicago: University Chicago Press, 2003–09), vol. 1, ch. 3.

35 Toronto-Dominion Bank Archives, Toronto, Canadian Bankers' Association, General Managers, Minutes, 31 May 1917, 10; Wormell, *Management,* 246–47.

36 Sutch, "Liberty Bonds."

37 White, *Story,* 60; G.C. Peden, *The Treasury and British Public Policy, 1906–1959* (Oxford: Oxford University Press, 2000), 111; Wormell, *Management,* 297; Heaman, *Tax, Order, and Good Government,* 416–18.

38 *Globe,* 28–31 August 1917. Railway nationalization is covered in Brown, *Robert Laird Borden,* vol. 2, 95–98; Robert Craig Brown and Ramsay Cook, *Canada 1896–1921: A Nation Transformed* (Toronto: McClelland and Stewart, 1974), 245–47; R.B. Fleming, *The Railway King of Canada: Sir William Mackenzie, 1849–1923* (Vancouver: UBC Press, 1991); and Roger Graham, *Arthur Meighen: A Biography,* 3 vols. (Toronto: Clarke, Irwin, 1960–65), vol. 1. White, who had supported government ownership since at least 1915, but with reservations about the huge subsidies, had assistance from Solicitor General Arthur Meighen and others in disentangling the web of railway financing.

39 Canada, Parliament, *Sessional Papers,* 1917, no. 20g; *Globe,* 3 May 1917; Larry A. Glassford, "Meighen, Arthur," *Dictionary of Canadian Biography,* vol. 18, http://www.biographi.ca/en/bio/meighen_arthur_18E.html.

40 The mood of desperation here is reflected in University of Oxford, Bodleian Library, Brand papers, file 8, Brand to Keynes, 6 June 1917. Summations of the financial positions in June are in file 9-2, Memos, Ottawa, 8, 12 June 1917.

41 *Globe*, 23 April, 7, 12–18 May, 18, 26 July, 1 August 1917; Kathleen Burk, *Britain, America and the Sinews of War, 1914–1918* (Boston: Allen and Unwin, 1985), 150–51. The convoluted dealings of the spring and summer of 1917 are best understood by combining Burk with the narratives in Canada, Department of External Affairs, *Documents on Canadian External Relations*, 29 vols. to date, ed. Robert Alexander Mackay et al. (Ottawa: Queen's Printer, 1967–), vol. 1, 169–72, 174, 176–77, 179; Neilson, "R.H. Brand"; Wormell, *Management*, 289–90, 295, 298–302; Cuff and Granatstein, *Ties That Bind*, 29–30; and Bliss, *Canadian Millionaire*, 315–16, 326, 364–5. A base plan put first to Borden by White is in Queen's University Archives, Flavelle papers, box 4, White to Borden, 20 July 1917.

42 Wormell, *Management*, 301–2; Neilson, "R.H. Brand," 1449–50; Cuff and Granatstein, *Ties That Bind*, 33–35, 154–55. In 1919, White would acknowledge that part of the loan "was got in and cancelled." *Globe*, 30 June 1919.

43 *Globe*, 23 August 1917.

44 *Financial Post*, 28 July 1917.

45 *Financial Post*, 8 September 1917, 5525.

46 White, *Story*, 56.

47 *Island Patriot* (Charlottetown), 27 September 1917.

48 LAC, Borden diaries, 14 September 1917; *Globe*, 13 September 1917; *Canadian Annual Review of Public Affairs* (1917): 298–99; Wormell, *Management*, 304.

49 Robert B. Bryce, *Maturing in Hard Times: Canada's Department of Finance through the Great Depression* (Montreal and Kingston: McGill-Queen's University Press, 1986), 32.

50 Sir Thomas White, "The War Finance of Canada," *Annals of the American Academy of Political and Social Science* (Philadelphia) 107 (May 1923): 211–12; John Anthony Turley-Ewart, "Gentleman Bankers, Politicians and Bureaucrats: The History of the Canadian Bankers' Association, 1891–1924" (PhD diss., University of Toronto, 2000), 281–301.

51 The use by Wormell in *Management* of Treasury and Ministry of Munitions records and other archival records in Britain complements the Brand papers at Oxford University, the Flavelle and White papers in Canada, and key newspapers. For more information on the cheese and wheat advances, see *Globe*, 28 August, 22, 26 September 1917, 11 February 1918.

52 *Globe*, 22 September, 4, 6, 8 October 1917; Homer Mark Philip Eckardt, "Banking Became New Business in 1917," *Globe*, 2 January 1918; Wormell, *Management*, 290, 302–5; Kathleen Burk, "Wheat and the State during the First World War," in *Strategy and Intelligence: British Policy during the First World War*, ed. Michael Dockrill and David French, 119–38 (London: Hambledon, 1996); Burk, *Britain, America and the Sinews of War*, 61, 132, 172–74; Martin Horn, *Britain, France, and the Financing of the First World War* (Montreal and Kingston: McGill-Queen's University Press, 2002), ch. 8; Bliss, *Canadian Millionaire*, 363–72.

53 Wormell, *Management*. The marketing context is explained in Mitchell W. Sharp, "Allied Wheat Buying in Relationship to Canadian Marketing Policy, 1914–18," *Canadian Journal of Economics and Political Science* 6, 3 (1940): 372–89.

54 Cuff and Granatstein, *Ties That Bind*, ch. 2.

55 *Canadian Annual Review of Public Affairs* (1917): 301. The Canadian Pacific Railway's involvement is detailed in *Commercial and Financial Chronicle* (New York), 23 June 1917.

56 The bank loans of 1917 are summarized in *Globe*, 11 February 1918, with reference to data tabled at the annual meeting of the Canadian Bankers' Association.

57 White, *Story*, 58. The same rationale and wording appeared in White's defence of munitions funding in 1927 in response to charges from Winston Churchill, a former British minister of munitions.

58 Canada, House of Commons, *Debates*, 13 September 1917, 5777.

59 This predication is a key conclusion of Marie-Michelle Pagé, "Les Emprunts de guerre et les Emprunts de la Victoire dans les comptes publics du ministère des Finances du Canada (1915–1937)," unpublished report, 2014.

60 White, "War Finance of Canada," 213.

61 *Globe*, 3 September 1917.

62 For an examination of this perspective in American war finance, see Hugh Rockoff, "Until It's Over, Over There: The U.S. Economy in World War I," National Bureau of Economic Research, Cambridge, Massachusetts, June 2004, https://www.nber.org/papers/w10580; and Sung Won Kang and Hugh Rockoff, "Capitalizing Patriotism: The Liberty Loans of World War I," National Bureau of Economic Research, Cambridge, Massachusetts, January 2006, http://www.nber.org/papers/w11919. On France's war finance, see Irene di Jorio, Kim Oosterlinck, and Veronique Pouillard, "Advertising, Propaganda and War Finance – France and the US during WWI," paper presented to the European Business History Association, 12th Annual Meeting, University of Bergen, Norway, 21–23 August 2008.

63 Canada, House of Commons, *Debates*, 12 September 1939, 148.

64 Eckardt, "Banking Became New Business."

65 *Canadian Annual Review of Public Affairs* (1918): 485.

66 Armstrong, *Blue Skies*, 88.

67 United States, Department of the Treasury, *Annual Report of the Secretary of the Treasury ... for the Fiscal Year Ended June 30, 1918* (Washington, DC: Department of the Treasury, 1919), 14–15.

68 Investment Industry Regulatory Organization of Canada, General Counsel's Office, Toronto, box 58516184, Bond Dealers' Association of Canada, vol. 3, Minutes 1917–19, 65–116, 161–63; LAC, RG 19, E-2-e, vol. 592, file 155-28-1T, parts 1 and 2; LAC, RG 19, E-5-h, vol. 4006, file: Misc. 1917–21, Sir F. Williams-Taylor to White, 3, 28 December 1917; LAC, RG 19, E-5-h, vol. 4012, file Exchanges 1918–20, Special Committee to White, 15 August 1918; LAC, RG 14, D2, vol. 70, no. 168 (unpub. Sess. paper, 1920, no. 168); LAC, MG 27, II, D18, vol. 5, files 17(a), 18, 19(a); Armstrong, *Blue Skies*, 87–88. The origins and accounts of the Special Committee for the 1917 loan are outlined in Canada, Parliament, *Sessional Papers*, 1920, no. 168. These accounts were audited by three private accounting firms, which in turn were examined by the chief accountant of the Department of Finance. It is important to note that accounting was undertaken by quasi-official firms and individuals as well as by the department. On the Special Committee, the minutes taken at regional and annual meetings of the Bond Dealers' Association of Canada are also essential. The stabilizing work of the committee was closely examined by the United States in the formation of its War Finance Corporation in 1918. United States, Treasury, *Annual Report* (1918), 14–15; LAC, MG 27, II, D18, vol. 5, file 17(a), 2972, 2989, 2997, correspondence with Clarkson Potter, assistant director, United States Treasury, July 1918; *Globe*, 14 December 1918; *Wall Street Journal* (New York), 12 December 1918; Julia C. Ott, *When Wall Street Met Main Street: The Quest for an Investor's Democracy* (Cambridge, MA: Harvard University Press, 2011), 67.

69 *Halifax Herald*, 6–12 December 1917.

70 Bliss, *Canadian Millionaire*, 364–67.

71 Great Britain, Ministry of Munitions, *History of the Ministry of Munitions*, 8 vols. in 4 (London: Ministry of Munitions, 1922), vol. 2, part 4, 72.

72 Canada, Department of External Affairs, *Documents on Canadian External Relations*, vol. 1, 187–88.

73 LAC, MG 30, A16, vol. 24, file: R.H. Brand, Flavelle to Brand, 15 February 1918; LAC, Borden diaries, 4 February 1918; Bliss, *Canadian Millionaire*, 371.

74 Canada, Parliament, *Sessional Papers,* 1919, no. 21, 15–28; 1920, no. 1, app. O-101-5, 109; Madsen and Moir, "Imperial Munitions Board," 70–71; Kenneth S. Mackenzie, "C.C. Ballantyne and the Canadian Government Merchant Marine, 1917–1921," *Northern Mariner* (Ottawa) 2, 1 (1992): 1–13.

75 Canada, House of Commons, *Debates,* 8 May 1918, 1647; *Globe,* 11 February 1918; Bliss, *Canadian Millionaire,* 371–72; Brown, *Robert Laird Borden,* vol. 2, 126–27; Wormell, *Management,* 295–305; Cuff and Granatstein, *Ties That Bind,* 70–71.

76 Great Britain, Ministry of Munitions, *History of the Ministry of Munitions,* vol. 2, part 4, ch. 3, 41–43; *Globe,* 6 March, 22 April, 22 May, 14 September 1918. Writers for the *Globe* saw the large picture, as on 6 March: "The exchange created by shipments of munitions to the United States should be available during the summer months, a season in which grain bills [of exchange] may not be plentiful." An article on 14 September, filed from Washington and citing US Treasury reports, spoke of America's loan of $400 million to Britain being spent in Canada for wheat and munitions, thus contributing "materially to improving the exchange."

77 LAC, MG 30, A16, vol. 24, file: R.H. Brand; Canada, House of Commons, *Debates,* 20 March 1918, 50; 2 May 1918, 1303; 3 May 1918, 1429. Borden's letter to Arsenault is quoted in Mary Janigan, *Let the Eastern Bastards Freeze in the Dark: The West versus the Rest since Confederation* (Toronto: Vintage Canada, 2013), 216.

78 Canada, Parliament, *Sessional Papers,* 1918, no. 2, xii-xiii; 1919, no. 2, xiii.

79 Canada, House of Commons, *Debates,* 10 April 1918, 575–78; 10 April 1919, 1347; 5 May 1920, 2008–9; Canada, Parliament, *Sessional Papers,* 1919, no. 1, ZZ-62; 1919 no. 2, xiv; G.W.L. Nicholson, *Canadian Expeditionary Force, 1914–1919* (Ottawa: Queen's Printer, 1962), 359–61.

80 Canada, Parliament, *Sessional Papers,* 1919, no. 2: xii; Canada, Ministry of Overseas Military Forces, *Report of the Ministry of Overseas Military Forces of Canada, 1918* (London: Ministry of Overseas Military Forces, 1919), 417, 426, 431.

81 *Globe,* 17 September 1917, 5 January 1918.

82 As analyzed by economist W. Irwin Gillespie in *Tax, Borrow and Spend,* ch. 6.

83 Canada, House of Commons, *Debates,* 30 April 1918, 1255; Curtis, "Canadian Banks and War Finance," 18–21. Maclean's budget speech of 30 April would be largely reprinted in *Bankers Magazine* (New York) 97, 5 (1918): 542–43, 545–51.

84 Canada, House of Commons, *Debates,* 15 April 1918, 741. Detailed information on unpaid subscriptions and lost or damaged bonds would not emerge until the audit undertaken by Edwards, Morgan and Company in 1921–22.

85 Canada, House of Commons, *Debates,* 1 May 1918, 1322; Curtis, "Canadian Banks and War Finance," 29–33. On dominion notes, bank notes, and coinage issued and in circulation, see Canada, Parliament, *Sessional Papers,* 1921, no. 2: 143–45; and 1923, no. 2: 167–68.

86 Canada, House of Commons, *Debates,* 8 May 1918, 1627–29, 1638–39.

87 J. Harvey Perry, *Taxes, Tariffs, and Subsidies: A History of Canadian Fiscal Development,* 2 vols. (Toronto: University of Toronto Press, 1955), vol. 1, 160–61.

88 Ibid.; Canada, House of Commons, *Debates,* 3, 22, 27 May, 19, 22, 29 June 1918. Detailed information on foreign exchange and movements of gold can be found in LAC, MG 27, II, D18, vol. 6. For one view of White's work expressed by the American press, see "Financing Canada a Hard Job," *The Sun* (New York), 8 September 1918.

89 Canada, House of Commons, *Debates,* 20, 22, 28 June, 1 July 1918.

90 *Canadian Annual Review of Public Affairs* (1918): 482–83; *Globe,* 10, 13 August, 4, 16, 20 September 1918. Securities approved by White for sale in New York included Manitoba provincial bonds and Riordon Pulp and Paper.

91 *Globe,* 25 June 1918.

92 *Globe,* 6 August 1918.

93 *Globe,* 19 September 1918. An unlimited issue – one with no fixed terms or period of sale – would not, White argued here, generate the large sum needed at one time. Moreover, an unlimited issue would create "a vast body of securities which, by reason of being out of conformity with investment conditions[,] would speedily, upon our narrow markets, go to a heavy discount, causing dissatisfaction ... and necessitating the payment of a much higher interest rate upon succeeding issues."

94 *Edmonton Bulletin,* 21 August 1918; Canada, Parliament, *Sessional Papers,* 1920, no. 2, 2.

95 Interest rates were carefully tracked in the financial press; see, for example, *Monetary Times* (Toronto), 4 January 1918, 78; 5 July 1918, 9.

96 *Globe,* 14 August 1918.

97 *Monetary Times,* 25 October 1918, 9–10.

98 *Globe,* 14 August, 28 November 1918. In the lead-up to the Victory Loan campaign, there were official claims as to the Special Committee's expiry on 31 July and proposed extension to 31 December 1919, but there was no discontinuation. *Globe,* 10 September 1918. On the American experience in maintaining market prices, see Gilbert, *American Financing,* 132–36; Garbade, *Birth of a Market,* 79; and James L. Butkiewicz and Mihaela Solcan, "The Original Operation Twist: The War Finance Corporation's War Bond Purchases, 1918–1920," *Financial History Review* (Cambridge, UK) 23, 1 (2016): 21–46.

99 Turley-Ewart, "Gentlemen Bankers," 294–99.

100 This trend is traced in Frank Albert Knox, "Canadian War Finance and the Balance of Payments, 1914–1918," *Canadian Journal of Economics and Political Science* 6, 2 (1940): 242–44, 257.

101 Graham Neale, "Dominion of Canada War Loan Bonds," *Canadian Paper Money Journal* (Vancouver) 11, 1 (1975): 19–20, 32.

102 The source for the publicity and advertising amounts is Canada, Parliament, *Sessional Papers,* 1921, no. 2, 46. Different figures appear in other government accounts: unpublished *Sessional Papers,* 1920, no. 109, 2; and unpublished *Sessional Papers,* 1920, no. 33 (Department of Public Printing and Stationery), 18–19. These discrepancies are possibly due to adjusted or new data or to varying accounting and auditing. *Printer and Publisher* (Toronto) 29, 6 (1920): 48, emphasized the fact that the $438,116.62 spent overall by the government on newspaper advertising in fiscal 1918–19 was a record high. With the cost of the 1918 Victory Loan removed, the biggest spender was the Department of Justice.

103 Canada, *Canada Gazette,* 5 October 1918, 1317–19.

104 Armstrong, *Blue Skies,* xxx, 72–73, 85; Michael Bliss, *Northern Enterprise: Five Centuries of Canadian Business* (Toronto: McClelland and Stewart, 1987), 383.

105 Dated essays (with proposed designs) were seen in the philatelic exhibit *Voluntary Fundraising for WW1,* by David Bartlet of Calgary, shown at a convention of the Royal Philatelic Society of Canada in Mississauga, Ontario, 21–23 June 2019.

106 The plan for thrift stamps in Canada was reportedly devised by Professor Samuel Broadfoot McCready of Ontario's Organization of Resources Committee. *Globe,* 13 May 1918.

107 Canada, Parliament, *Sessional Papers,* 1920, no. 2, xiii, 18, 205; Canada, House of Commons, *Debates,* 28 October 1919, 1498–99.

108 *Globe,* 1 July 1918; Oscar Douglas Skelton, *Canadian Federal Finance – II* (Kingston, ON: Jackson, 1918), 17–18, 25. On the stamp issues, see *Globe,* 21, 30, November, 4 December 1918.

109 Canada, House of Commons, *Debates,* 5 May 1919, 2049. The income-tax returns filed for 1918 and 1919 by Alexander Bromley, an Ottawa valley farmer, illustrate the exemption for bond interest; see "Federal Income Tax: Dominion of Canada's New Taxation Act," HWT Project, https://hwtproject.ca/rural-life/federal-income-tax. In an examination by

a group of MPs and senators, a review of the tax situation was provided by tax commissioner Robert Walker Breadner in the *Toronto Daily Star,* 8 May 1920.

110 *Globe,* 14 February, 12 June, 8 October 1919; Canada, Parliament, *Sessional Papers,* 1920, no. 2, 10, 124.

111 Tooze, *Deluge,* 212.

112 Borrowing is defined here as war-savings certificates, war-savings and thrift stamps, and the Victory Loans of 1917 and 1918; and taxation comprises customs, excise, and the various war taxes. Canada, Parliament, *Sessional Papers,* 1920, no. 2, 10.

113 On Canada's Siberian expeditionary force, see *Globe,* numerous dates, 1918–19; Robert Neil Murby, "Canada's Siberian Policy, 1918–1919" (MA thesis, University of British Columbia, 1968); Ian C.D. Moffat, "Forgotten Battlefields: Canadians in Siberia, 1918–1919," *Canadian Military Journal* (Kingston, ON) 8, 3 (2007–08): 73–86; Benjamin Isitt, *From Victoria to Vladivostok: Canada's Siberian Expedition, 1917–19* (Vancouver: UBC Press, 2010).

114 Richard H. Ullman, *Anglo-Soviet Relations, 1917–1921,* 3 vols. (Princeton, NJ: Princeton University Press, 1961–72), vol. 2, 31–32, 102.

115 Canada, House of Commons, *Debates,* 7 April 1920, 995; 29 March 1926, 1985. Fragmentary detail on the costs of the military expedition and the trade commission are found in the public accounts, estimates, and auditor general's reports. The auditor general's report for the fiscal year 1919–20 (for both the militia and the trade and commerce departments) gives the cost of the expedition as $412,213.03 (a fraction of the cost given in the Commons) and the commission as $15,794.96. Canada, Parliament, *Sessional Papers,* 1921, no. 1, part 3, ZZ-52, ZZ-226.

116 *Globe,* 15 November 1918.

117 Robert Craig Brown, "Gordon, Sir Charles Blair," *Dictionary of Canadian Biography,* vol. 16, http://www.biographi.ca/en/bio/gordon_charles_blair_16E.html.

118 Canada, Parliament, *Sessional Papers,* 1915, no. 2, xii; 1920, no. 2, xi.

119 "Change Your Victory Loan Interest Coupons into War-Savings Stamps," official ad, *Toronto Daily Star,* 14 March 1919, 12.

120 *Globe,* 20 July, 10 September, 14 November, 7 December 1918, 21 January 1919; *Commercial and Financial Chronicle,* 28 December 1918. For context, see Canada, Parliament, *Sessional Papers,* 1919, no. 2, 8; 1920, no. 2, 10, 68–69; 1920, no. 10b, Annual Report of Trade of Canada.

121 Byron Lew and Marvin McInnis, "Guns and Butter: World War I and the Canadian Economy," working paper, Department of Economics, Trent University, 2005, https://www.researchgate.net/publication/228434035_Guns_and_Butter_World_War_I_and_the_Canadian_Economy.

122 *Globe,* 2 November, 17 December 1918. On 1919 as a "war year," see, for example, White's remarks to a deputation from the Great War Veterans' Association and to MPs who had served, quoted in *Globe,* 17 May, 6 June 1919.

123 LAC, RG 14, D2, vol. 70, no. 168 (unpub. Sess. paper, 1920, no. 168).

124 Investment Industry Regulatory Organization of Canada, General Counsel's Office, Toronto, box 58516184, Bond Dealers' Association of Canada, Annual Meeting, 29 January 1919, Minutes 1917–24, 38–39; *Globe,* 4 December 1919; *Monetary Times,* 7 February 1919. For comprehensive figures on Special Committee transactions, see LAC, RG 19, E-2-e, vol. 592, file 155-28-1T, part 1. Prepared for Maclean, a memo on the Special Committee dated 20 April 1919 is in LAC, MG 27, II, D18, vol. 5, file 19(a), 3352–53.

125 *Monetary Times,* 7 January 1921, 116, 118, 120.

126 George Aylmer Macpherson, "Canadian Bonds," *Annals of the American Academy of Political and Social Science* 88 (March 1920): 139–43. Macpherson was a member of A.E. Ames and Company.

127 Janigan, *Let the Eastern Bastards Freeze,* 244.
128 Turley-Ewart, "Gentlemen Bankers," 306–12.

Chapter 4: Legacies in Peacetime, 1919–20s

1 Tim Cook and J.L. Granatstein, "Introduction," in *Canada 1919: A Nation Shaped by War,* ed. Tim Cook and J.L. Granatstein (Vancouver: UBC Press, 2020), 11.
2 Canada, Parliament, *Sessional Papers,* 1916–22, no. 2; Ernest Ludlow Bogart, *Direct and Indirect Costs of the Great World War,* 2nd ed. (New York: Oxford University Press, 1920), 51; R. Craig McIvor, *Canadian Monetary, Banking and Fiscal Development* (Toronto: Macmillan, 1958), 107.
3 Alan Bowker, "The Long 1919: Hope, Fear, and Normalcy," in *Canada 1919: A Nation Shaped by War,* ed. Tim Cook and J.L. Granatstein, 12–26 (Vancouver: UBC Press, 2020).
4 Desmond Morton and J.L. Granatstein, *Marching to Armageddon: Canadians and the Great War 1914–1919* (Toronto: Lester and Orpen Dennys, 1989), 250–59; Desmond Morton and Glenn Wright, *Winning the Second Battle: Canadian Veterans and the Return to Civilian Life, 1915–1930* (Toronto: University of Toronto Press, 1987).
5 Library and Archives Canada (LAC), RG 19, E-5-h, vol. 4011, file: Canadian Bankers' Association 1919, Ross to Boville, 13, 14 January 1919. On the visit to Ottawa of Sir Samuel Hardman Lever as co-secretary of the treasury, see University of Oxford, Bodleian Library, Brand papers, Flavelle to Brand, 7 January 1919; and LAC, MG 30, A16, vol. 25, Flavelle to Brand, 7 January 1919.
6 Robert B. Bryce, *Maturing in Hard Times: Canada's Department of Finance through the Great Depression* (Montreal and Kingston: McGill-Queen's University Press, 1986), 18, 28. Bryce points out that, in the absence of a central bank, the war loans were handled by what he calls the department's "War Finances Branch," probably the "War Loan Branch" listed in city directories for its many employees. The office of the comptroller of currency handled the monetary business of the loans. The numbers of employees, which differ from Bryce (141 in September 1912, 640-plus by March 1919), come from Canada, Parliament, *Sessional Papers,* 1913, no. 1; and LAC, RG 14, D2, vol. 70, no. 158f (unpub. Sess. paper, 1920, no. 158f).
7 The numbers of orders-in-council during the war years varied little from the immediate pre-war years – around 2,000 annually – but their import was different.
8 Canada, Parliament, *Sessional Papers,* 1914, no. 2, 16–17; 1920, no. 2, 20–21; Canada, Dominion Bureau of Statistics, *Canada Year Book, 1913* (Ottawa: Census and Statistics Office, 1914), 524; *1919* (1920), 493.
9 Frank Albert Knox, "Canadian War Finance and the Balance of Payments, 1914–1918," *Canadian Journal of Economics and Political Science* 6, 2 (1940): 244–46.
10 Canada, House of Commons, *Debates,* 4 March 1919, 210–14; 7 March 1919, 274–93; 5 June 1919, 3609–20; *Globe* (Toronto), 5 March 1919; *Le Devoir* (Montreal), 5 March 1919; Tim Cook, "The Madman and the Butcher: Sir Sam Hughes, Sir Arthur Currie, and Their War of Reputations," *Canadian Historical Review* 85, 4 (2004): 693–720.
11 Canada, House of Commons, *Debates,* 10 April 1919, 1343–66; 18 June 1919, 3614–15. Canada, Parliament, *Sessional Papers,* 1919, no. 2, xii; 1920, no. 2, xiii. The entry for shipbuilding by the Department of Naval Service refers to its problem-plagued program, begun in February 1917, of having drifters and trawlers built for the British Admiralty, with the expense to be charged to the account of the imperial government. See LAC, RG 24, D-1-a, vol. 5601, 5604–6, 5657; Canada, Parliament, *Sessional Papers,* 1919, no. 1, app. ZZ, 251–52; no. 21, 54; and Michael Moir, "Admiralty Orders for Canadian Shipyards: Trawlers, Drifters, and the Urgency of Coastal Defence during the Great War," *Northern Mariner* (Ottawa) 26, 3 (2016): 275–98. As of late 1918, none of the imperial advances for the salmon pack

had reached the canners, a delay typical of many Canadian requisitions for imperial purchases. See *British Columbia Financial Times* (Vancouver), 7 December 1918; and *Globe*, 18 February 1919.

12 LAC, RG 19, E-5-h, vol. 4011, file: Canadian Bankers' Association 1919; *Globe* (on cheese), 28 April 1917, 12 January, 26, 30 April 1918, 18 February, 10 May, 16, 28 July 1919; *Toronto Daily Star* (on cheese), 23 October 1918; Canada, Department of Agriculture, *Report of the Canada Food Board, February 11–December 31, 1918* (Ottawa: Department of Agriculture, [1919]), 14, 78, 82; Jeremy Wormell, *The Management of the National Debt of the United Kingdom, 1900–1932* (New York: Routledge, 2000), 305, 468–70; L. Margaret Barnett, *British Food Policy during the First World War* (London: Routledge, 1985).

13 Canada, House of Commons, *Debates*, 10 April 1919, 1345–55; *Globe*, 14 April 1919, 17 June 1920.

14 Morton and Granatstein, *Marching to Armageddon*, 253; S.A. Cudmore, "Reconstruction in Canada," in Canada, Dominion Bureau of Statistics, *Canada Year Book, 1920* (1921), 1–64.

15 *Toronto Daily Star*, 27 March 1920; Wormell, *Management*, 310–11; Canada, House of Commons, *Debates*, 27 April 1921, 2622, which records that, as of 31 March 1921, the amount owed to the Dominion had been reduced to $144,408,746.63.

16 *Canadian Railway and Marine World* (Toronto) 254 (April 1919): 211.

17 Canada, House of Commons, *Debates*, 19 March 1919, 633–37; *Globe*, 20 March 1919; John Anthony Turley-Ewart, "Gentleman Bankers, Politicians and Bureaucrats: The History of the Canadian Bankers' Association, 1891–1924" (PhD diss., University of Toronto, 2000), 293–98; Linda M. Grayson, "The Formation of the Bank of Canada" (PhD diss., University of Toronto, 1974), 21–49.

18 Canada, House of Commons, *Debates*, 5 June 1919, 3135–51; 18 June 1919, 3607–24; *Globe*, 19 June 1919.

19 *Globe*, 21 November 1919; Equitable Trust Company of New York, *Foreign Loans as Investments* (New York: Equitable Trust Company of New York, [c. 1920]), 42.

20 *Globe*, 8, 10 July 1919.

21 *Globe*, 10 July 1919.

22 In 1930, White stated that he had spent, during his eight years in government, $2,000 a year over and above his salary of $7,000. *Toronto Daily Star*, 30 December 1930. He would later claim that his service had cost him more than $80,000 in forfeited income from business and that, on resigning, he had had to borrow against his life-insurance policies. *Toronto Daily Star*, 11 January 1938. In 1919, Flavelle believed that White's "personal finances would not permit him to continue on the salary he was receiving." University of Oxford, Bodleian Library, Brand papers, file 7, Flavelle to Brand, 25 September 1919. What his "personal finances" were is unclear. White's salary was the same as that of most other ministers.

23 Quoted in Robert Craig Brown and Ramsay Cook, *Canada 1896–1921: A Nation Transformed* (Toronto: McClelland and Stewart, 1974), 228.

24 *Financial Post*, 22 November 1919.

25 Canada, House of Commons, Special Committee on Department of Soldiers' Civil Re-establishment Act, *Soldiers' Civil Re-establishment: Proceedings of the Special Committee ... to Whom Was Referred Bill No. 10, an Act to Amend the Department of Soldiers' Civil Re-establishment Act ...* (Ottawa: House of Commons, 1919), 5–6, 82–102, 1012 (White), 74–82, 748–57, 995–1007, 1050–57 (Boville), 74–82, 880–902 (Breadner), 4, 6, 103, 1010 (MacNeil), 1010 (Nesbitt). This report in also found in Canada, House of Commons, *Journals*, 1918–19 (3rd session), vol. 56, app. 1. See also *Globe*, 9–10, 27–28 October, 1, 18 November 1919; LAC, RG 19, E-5-h, vol. 4012, file: Conversion of bonds and treasury bills, 1919–20; Desmond Morton and Glenn Wright, "The Bonus Campaign, 1919–21: Veterans

and the Campaign for Re-establishment," *Canadian Historical Review* 64, 2 (1983): 147–67; Norman Ward, *The Public Purse: A Study in Canadian Democracy* (Toronto: University of Toronto Press, 1962), 157–58; Douglas H. Fullerton, *The Bond Market in Canada: A Study of the Institutions, Machinery, Techniques, and Problems Involved in the Issuing and Marketing of Bonds and Debentures* (Toronto: Carswell, 1962), 41; John James Deutsch, "War Finance and the Canadian Economy, 1914–20," *Canadian Journal of Economics and Political Science* 6, 4 (1940): 532; and McIvor, *Canadian Monetary*, 107.

26 LAC, RG 19, E-2-e, vol. 592, file 155-28-1T, part 1.

27 Canada, House of Commons, *Debates*, 6 April 1921, 1620; *Monetary Times* (Toronto), 8 April 1921, 7–8.

28 For an instance of market reporting, including reference to the Special Committee's asking price on bonds, see *Globe*, 11 December 1920.

29 LAC, RG 19, E-2-e, vol. 592; Investment Industry Regulatory Organization of Canada, General Counsel's Office, Toronto, box 58516184, Bond Dealers' Association of Canada, Annual Meeting, 17–19 June 1920, Minutes 1917–24, 11–12; *Globe*, 1 September, 9 October, 29 November 1920.

30 Canada, House of Commons, *Debates*, 18 May 1920, 2497, 2516–17.

31 *Vancouver Daily Star*, 18 November 1919.

32 "The Market Record of Canadian War Loan Issues," *Monetary Times*, 7 January 1921, 116, 118, 120.

33 Tracked in the *Globe*, *Toronto Daily Star*, and *Monetary Times* between December 1917 and December 1920.

34 James Powell, *A History of the Canadian Dollar* (Ottawa: Bank of Canada, 2005), 38–39, 97; Ronald A. Shearer and Carolyn Clark, "Canada and the Interwar Gold Standard, 1920–35: Monetary Policy without a Central Bank," in *A Retrospective on the Classical Gold Standard, 1821–1931*, ed. Michael D. Bordo and Anna J. Schwartz, 277–309 (Chicago: University of Chicago Press, 1984); Eric Helleiner, *Towards North American Monetary Union? The Politics and History of Canada's Exchange Rate Regime* (Montreal and Kingston: McGill-Queen's University Press, 2006), 41–43.

35 *Globe*, 13 March 1920. An inside view of the embargo and market in 1920, by John Worth Mitchell, vice-president of Dominion Securities and a former Victory Loan chairman in Toronto, appeared in the *Globe*, 3 January 1921.

36 LAC, RG 19, E-5-h, vol. 4012, file: Victory Bond Prices and Exchange, 1919–20, D.C. McIntyre to Drayton, 25 February 1920, F.A. Burlington to Drayton, 17 April 1920.

37 LAC, RG 19, E-5-h, vol. 4012, file: Victory Bond Prices and Exchange, 1919–20; Investment Industry Regulatory Organization of Canada, General Counsel's Office, Toronto, box 58516184, Bond Dealers' Association of Canada, Annual Meeting, 17–19 June 1920, Minutes 1917–24, 17–24; *Globe*, 24–28 February, 4, 13, 22 March, 26, 29 October, 17, 23 November, 2 December 1920, 15, 17 January 1921; *Canadian Annual Review of Public Affairs* (1920): 25–26; Christopher Armstrong, *Blue Skies and Boiler Rooms: Buying and Selling Securities in Canada, 1870–1940* (Toronto: University of Toronto Press, 1997), 89–90.

38 *Financial Post*, 8 November 1919; *Journal of the Canadian Bankers' Association* (Toronto) 27, 1 (1919–20): 230–31.

39 Canada, House of Commons, *Debates*, 8 March 1920, 193.

40 LAC, RG 14, D2, vol. 69, no. 108 (unpub. Sess. paper, 1920, no. 108); *Globe*, 8 April 1920.

41 W. Irwin Gillespie, *Tax, Borrow and Spend: Financing Federal Spending in Canada, 1867–1990* (Ottawa: Carleton University Press, 1991), 87, 118–19.

42 Canada, House of Commons, *Debates*, 18 May 1920, 2476–92.

43 Canada, Parliament, *Sessional Papers*, 1921, no. 2, xi, 2–3, 13–14 (national debt and funded debt). The evolution of debt on the Dominion War Loans and Victory Loans (by issue

and maturity debt) is tabulated in Marie-Michelle Pagé, "Les Emprunts de guerre et les Emprunts de la Victoire dans les comptes publics du ministère des Finances du Canada (1915–1937)," unpublished report, 2014, 11–13, 22–25.

44 A summary of this tax epiphany is found in Shirley Tillotson, *Give and Take: The Citizen-Taxpayer and the Rise of Canadian Democracy* (Vancouver: UBC Press, 2017), 51–59.

45 Canada, House of Commons, *Debates,* 19 May 1920, 2523–24; Canada, Parliament, *Sessional Papers,* 1920, no. 3, 30; *Canadian Annual Review of Public Affairs* (1920): 462–70.

46 For example, see Hector W. Charlesworth, ed., *A Cyclopaedia of Canadian Biography* (Toronto: Hunter-Rose, 1919), 13–15.

47 Canada, Parliament, *Sessional Papers,* 1922, no. 20, 165–78.

48 Canada, House of Commons, *Debates,* 27 April 1921, 2622. Free gold means nuggets or chunks, not gold embedded in ore.

49 Canada, Dominion Bureau of Statistics, *Canada Year Book, 1929* (1930), 812–13.

50 *Globe,* 8 December 1927.

51 *Globe,* 1, 5, 7, 13 May 1931.

52 *Globe,* 30 October 1937, 1 October 1934.

53 Canada, House of Commons, Select Standing Committee on Banking and Commerce, *Minutes of Proceedings and Evidence* (Ottawa: King's Printer, 1933).

54 Era Dabla-Norris, ed., *Debt and Entanglements between the Wars* (Washington, DC: International Monetary Fund, 2019); Irving Brecher, *Monetary and Fiscal Thought and Policy in Canada, 1919–1939* (Toronto: University of Toronto Press, 1957).

55 Finance through the 1920s can be followed in Canada, House of Commons, *Debates;* Canada, Dominion Bureau of Statistics, *Canada Year Book; Globe;* and *Canadian Annual Review of Public Affairs.* See also Bryce, *Maturing in Hard Times,* 28–29, 145.

56 *Globe,* 10 January 1940.

57 George S. Watts, *The Bank of Canada: Origins and Early History,* ed. Thomas K. Rymes (Ottawa: Carleton University Press, 1993), 49–50; Marc Pellerin, "The Evolution of the Government of Canada's Debt Distribution Framework," *Bank of Canada Review* (Ottawa) (Spring 2006): 38.

58 The Publishers' War Finance Committee, formed in 1940, became the National War Finance Committee the following year under banker and Victory Loan veteran George Wilbur Spinney, with an expanded mandate to direct all finance initiatives, including the Victory Loans and war savings. Spinney was succeeded in 1943 by Graham Ford Towers, governor of the Bank of Canada. Great War publicity material seen by the committee is in Bank of Canada Archives, Ottawa, National War Finance Committee fonds, First World War loans sous-fonds.

59 J.L. Granatstein, *The Ottawa Men: The Civil Service Mandarins, 1935–1957* (Toronto: Oxford University Press, 1982), 260; Robert A. Wardhaugh, *Behind the Scenes: The Life and Work of William Clifford Clark* (Toronto: University of Toronto Press, 2010), ch. 6.

60 John Frederick Parkinson, "Some Problems of War Finance in Canada," *Canadian Journal of Economics and Political Science* 6, 3 (1940): 403–33; *Globe,* 14 October 1939, 20 January 1940.

Chapter 5: The Dominion War Loans, 1915–17

1 Worth exploring in the Canadian context are the insights of Kevin Rozario, "'Delicious Horrors': Mass Culture, the Red Cross, and the Appeal of Modern Humanitarianism," in *American Quarterly* (Baltimore, MD) 55, 3 (2003): 417–55.

2 *Globe* (Toronto), 31 October 1914, 30 January, 16–18 October 1915.

3 *Globe,* 29 July, 2, 5 October 1915.

4 *Regina Morning Leader,* 22 November 1915.

5 *Globe,* 8 October 1915.
6 Toronto-Dominion Bank Archives, Toronto, Canadian Bankers' Association, Executive Council, Minutes, 2 November 1915.
7 *Globe,* 25 November 1915.
8 Robert S. Prince, "The Mythology of War: How the Canadian Daily Newspaper Depicted the War" (PhD diss., University of Toronto, 1998), 47–51.
9 David Silbey, *The British Working Class and Enthusiasm for the War, 1914–16* (New York: Frank Cass, 2005), 7–14, 108, 120, 126–27; "World War One Collections," Canadian Letters and Images Project, letters of Charles Douglas Richardson, 23 December 1915; William Roy Gullen, 17 January 1917; John William Law, 11 April, 5 October 1917; John Jackson Beck, 3 April 1917, https://www.canadianletters.ca/collections/468.
10 *Chinook Advance* (Chinook, AB), 25 November 1915.
11 Arthur Rutherford Ford, *As the World Wags On* (Toronto: Ryerson, 1950), 92, 102–4; Allan Levine, *Scrum Wars: The Prime Ministers and the Media* (Toronto: Dundurn, 1993), 79. Wellington John Jeffers of the *Globe,* who covered White during the war, later recounted his experiences in the *Globe and Mail.*
12 *Saint John Globe,* 15, 24 November 1915.
13 *L'Autorité* (Montreal), 27 November 1915; *L'Avenir du nord* (Saint-Jérôme), 26 November 1915.
14 *The Voice* (Winnipeg), 9 October 1914.
15 *British Columbia Federationist* (Vancouver), 24 December 1915.
16 Ibid.
17 Canada, House of Commons, *Debates,* 17 February 1916, 891.
18 See, for example, R. Matthew Bray, "'Fighting as an Ally': The English-Canadian Patriotic Response to the Great War," *Canadian Historical Review* 61, 2 (1980): 150.
19 *Economic Advertising* (Toronto) 8, 11 (1915): 23.
20 *Economic Advertising* 9, 3 (1916): 7.
21 *Globe,* 3 January, 16 March 1916.
22 *Gleichen Call* (Gleichen, AB), 31 August 1916.
23 *Monetary Times* (Toronto), 4 January 1916, 33; 25 June 1916, 14; *Financial Post* (Toronto), 17 June 1916; Christopher Armstrong, *Blue Skies and Boiler Rooms: Buying and Selling Securities in Canada, 1870–1940* (Toronto: University of Toronto Press, 1997), 83–84.
24 Jeffrey A. Keshen, *Propaganda and Censorship during Canada's Great War* (Edmonton: University of Alberta Press, 1996), 5; Desmond Morton, *Fight or Pay: Soldiers' Families in the Great War* (Vancouver, UBC Press, 2004).
25 McGill University Archives, Montreal, J.W. McConnell fonds, MG 4240, container 33, file 00637; *Saskatoon Phoenix,* 22 November to 1 December 1915; *Globe,* 18–29 January 1916; Philip Henry Morris, ed., *The Canadian Patriotic Fund: A Record of Its Activities from 1914 to 1919* (Ottawa: Canadian Patriotic Fund, 1920); Morton, *Fight or Pay.*
26 Duff Crerar, "Enthusiasm Embattled: Alberta 1916," in *The Frontier of Patriotism: Alberta and the First World War,* ed. Adriana A. Davies and Jeffrey A. Keshen (Calgary: University of Calgary Press, 2016), 210.
27 Library and Archives Canada (LAC), MG 27, II, D18, vol. 3, 1903–6.
28 *Northern Advance* (Barrie, ON), 3 August 1916.
29 LAC, MG 27, II, D18, vol. 4, file 14b, White to R.B. McElheran, Winnipeg, 6 September 1916.
30 LAC, RG 19, E-5-h, vol. 4005, file: Thrift Campaign, Williams to White, 18 September 1916; White to Williams, 23 September 1916.
31 LAC, MG 27, II, D18, vol. 4, 2042–44, 2047. On the management of "information-dispensing systems" and remoteness, see Keshen, *Propaganda and Censorship,* x-xii, x (quote).

32 For example, see *Farmer's Advocate* (London, ON), 1 April 1915, and the description of Toronto's Labour Day parade in *Globe,* 7 September 1915.
33 *Monetary Times,* 25 August 1916.
34 *Daily British Whig* (Kingston, ON), 14 July 1916, in *Ontario and the First World War, 1914–1918: A Collection of Documents,* ed. Barbara M. Wilson (Toronto: University of Toronto Press, 1977), 32–33.
35 On the evolution of government advertising, see Russell Johnston, *Selling Themselves: The Emergence of Canadian Advertising* (Toronto: University of Toronto Press, 2001).
36 *Globe,* 6 July 1915. A financial trail of the posters made for the Departments of Militia and Naval Service can be found in Canada, Parliament, *Sessional Papers,* 1917, no. 1, T34, T35, ZZ177, ZZ233, ZZ272; 1918, no. 1, T36–T38, T40–T41; 1919, no. 1, T37–T38, T41, ZZ9, ZZ51, ZZ147, ZZ246–ZZ247; 1920, no. 1, T35–T37, ZZ87, ZZ408.
37 *Printer and Publisher* (Toronto) 25, 4 (1916): 45; 26, 4 (1917): 41; *Economic Advertising* 9, 4 (1916): 3, 5; 9, 5 (1916): 3, 5; 9, 8 (1916): 3, 5, 7.
38 *Printer and Publisher* 25, 10 (1916): 52. By December 1916, the Gibbons firm would take on placing newspaper advertising for the Imperial Munitions Board, an arrangement made by its labour adviser Henry Edward Morgan, a former printer-comptroller and advertising agent with W.H. Smith and Sons in Britain. See *Printer and Publisher* 25, 11 (1916): 32; 25, 12 (1916): 32; and *Globe,* 30 October 1916.
39 *Montreal Daily Mail,* 23 September 1916.
40 *Farmers' Magazine* (Toronto) 9, 4 (1915–16): 61–62; 9, 9 (1915–16): 46–47; 9, 12 (1915–16): 36–37; 10, 2 (1916–17): 51; *Grain Growers' Guide* (Winnipeg), 19 August 1916.
41 *Globe,* 4 August 1916.
42 *Montreal Daily Mail,* 15 September 1916.
43 *Le Canada* (Montreal), 13, 21 September 1916; *Le Nationaliste* (Montreal), 17 September 1916.
44 *Globe,* 5 October 1916.
45 Maurice F.V. Doll, *The Poster War: Allied Propaganda Art of the First World War* (Edmonton: Alberta Community Development, Cultural Facilities and Historical Resources Division, 1993), 26.
46 LAC, RG 19, E-5-h, vol. 4010, file: Thrift Campaign 1916 Bankers, White to George W. Morley, secretary, Canadian Bankers' Association, 6 September 1916. White's sentiment about "alarming the public" could have had a censorial overtone, but it may also have reflected public consciousness of the proximity of the "war peril." See, for example, *Globe,* 27 February 1917.
47 LAC, RG 19, E-5-h, vol. 4009, file: Misc. Suggestions and Enquiries, 1916–17, *La Presse* (Montreal), 24 January 1917, 7, large ad by the Comité de recrutement canadien-français showing a German soldier looking upon a dead mother and children.
48 *Charlottetown Guardian,* 30 December 1916.
49 LAC, RG 19, E-h-5, vol. 4009, file: Misc. Suggestions and Enquiries, 1916–17, Canadian Poster Company, Montreal, to Roberts, 11 January 1917; John Nelson McKim, A. McKim Limited, Montreal, to B.J. Roberts, 15 February 1917; Roberts to McKim, 20 February 1917; M. Scarth Stevenson to White, 26 January 1917; White to Stevenson, 29 January 1917. Stevenson, of Molsons Bank in Montreal, on the request of the local French Canadian recruiting committee, urged White to take out full-page newspaper advertisements in order to reach and educate "the poorer class of French Canadians."
50 LAC, RG 19, E-h-5, vol. 4012, H.V.F. Jones to Roberts, 6, 11 January, 12 March 1917; Roberts to Jones, 26 February 1917.
51 LAC, RG 19, E-h-5, vol. 4012, Cameron to White, 17 January 1917; White to Cameron, 19 January 1917.

52 Mourad Djebabla, "'Fight the Huns with Food': Mobilizing Canadian Civilians for the Food War Effort during the Great War, 1914–1918," in *World War I and Propaganda*, ed. Troy R.E. Paddock, 65–88 (Leiden: Brill, 2014); Mourad Djebabla, "'Fight or Farm': Canadian Farmers and the Dilemma of the War Effort in World War I (1914–1918)," *Canadian Military Journal* (Kingston, ON) 13, 2 (2012–13): 57–67; Beverly Soloway, "Victory in the Kitchen: Food Control in the Lakehead during the Great War," *Papers and Records* (Thunder Bay Historical Museum Society, Thunder Bay, ON) 42 (2014): 29–44, republished at *ActiveHistory.ca*, 18 November 2014, https://activehistory.ca/2014/11/new-paper-victory-in-the-kitchen-food-control-in-the-lakehead-during-the-great-war-by-beverly-soloway/.

53 Stephen Leacock, *National Organization for War* (1917), 6–7, https://www.canadiana.ca/view/oocihm.9_91897/1.

54 Stephen Leacock, "What Are You Doing to Win the War?" in *How to Live in War Time*, 8–12 (Ottawa: National Service Board, 1917), https://wartimecanada.ca/sites/default/files/documents/How%20to%20Live_0.pdf.

55 LAC, RG 19, E-h-5, vol. 4011, Scully to White, 14 March 1917.

56 Investment Industry Regulatory Organization of Canada, General Counsel's Office, Toronto, box 58516184, Bond Dealers' Association of Canada, vol. 2, Minutes 1916–17, 79–159; vol. 3, Annual Meeting, 24 February 1917, Minutes 1917–19, 39–41.

57 *Globe*, 19 February 1917.

58 *Globe*, 27 March 1917.

59 *Saint John Globe*, 14 March 1917; *Toronto World*, 15, 17 March 1917; *Montreal Gazette*, 13 March 1917.

60 *Toronto World*, 24 March 1917.

61 Statistics Canada, salaries for 1917; Marvin L. Simner, *End of the Great War in 1918 and Its Impact on London, Ontario: Prelude, Celebrations and Aftermath* (London: London and Middlesex Historical Society, 2018), 16, https://ir.lib.uwo.ca/historybooks/4.

62 *Montreal Gazette*, 13 March 1917.

63 Johnston, *Selling Themselves*, 97.

64 *Edmonton Bulletin*, 23 March, 18 June 1917.

65 Keshen, *Propaganda and Censorship*, 117.

66 According to the *Monetary Times*, 30 March 1917, the BDAC had twenty-one members in Toronto, fifteen in Montreal, one in Halifax, one in Saint John, and one in Quebec City.

67 *Montreal Gazette*, 14 March 1917.

68 *Regina Morning Leader*, 12–24 March 1917.

69 *Marine Engineering of Canada* (Toronto) 7, 4 (1917): 83; 7, 12 (1917): 303–20; Chris Madsen and Michael Moir, "The Imperial Munitions Board and Merchant Shipbuilding in Canada," in *Turning Point 1917: The British Empire at War*, ed. Douglas E. Delaney and Nikolas Gardner, 51–77 (Vancouver: UBC Press, 2017).

70 *Saturday Night* (Toronto), 24 March 1917, 15.

71 In June 1917, Allison, a former advertising manager at the *London Times*, had told an American convention of his role in transforming government advertising for Britain's loan of 1915 from the "usual 'peace time' single column" format of "stereotyped announcement" to one that advertised the loan "like bags of flour or tins of tobacco." *Economic Advertising* 10, 6 (1917): 22–23.

72 LAC, RG 19, E-h-5, vol. 4012, Jones to Roberts, 6, 11 January 1917, 12 March 1917.

73 LAC, RG 19, E-h-5, vol. 4012, Roberts to Jones, 26 February 1917.

74 *Financial Post*, 10 March 1917.

75 *Globe*, 12, 26 February, 30 March 1917.

76 *Globe*, 27 March 1917.

77 Before the Battle of Vimy Ridge in April, there was a surge of subscriptions to the British War Loan by Canadian soldiers, some scrawled on scraps of paper: $85,000 by 2,105 noncommissioned officers and men. Subscriptions were facilitated at the front through the army pay offices. In 1915, 1,848 men invested about $100,000; in 1916, 55 invested $6,000. In the first six months of 1917, 2,443 subscribed more than $100,000. A total of 4,843 invested $250,000. *Globe,* 22 February 1918, citing "a report received by the Militia Department." Soldiers' awareness of British loans predated Vimy. The tongue-in-cheek field journal of the No. 1 Canadian Field Ambulance advised an English correspondent in 1916 not to "invest in 'Iodine Chronicle,' stock very LIMITED. The Boches [Germans] are liable to drop a 12 in foreclosure on us at any time, and then where would you be? Try a plunge into War Loan, it's safer." *Iodine Chronicle* (France), 20 January 1916, 4.

78 There are letters concerning such investment in "World War One Collections," Canadian Letters and Images Project, https://www.canadianletters.ca/collections/468.

79 *Financial Post,* 11 August 1917. Laut would follow Canada's loans, including the work of the market-stabilizing committee, in 1918. *Financial Post,* 2 November 1918.

80 *Monetary Times,* 25 August 1916, 27 July 1917. On the Liberty Loan's organization, see Edward Clifford, *Selling the First Installment of the Liberty Loan in the Seventh Federal Reserve District, May 4th to June 15th, 1917* (Chicago: Federal Reserve Bank of Chicago, 1917).

81 *Globe,* 29 December 1917.

82 Investment Industry Regulatory Organization of Canada, General Counsel's Office, Toronto, box 58516184, Bond Dealers' Association of Canada, vol. 2, Minutes 1916–17, 169–75; vol. 3, Minutes 1917–19, 3–33.

Chapter 6: The First Victory Loan, 1917

1 Investment Industry Regulatory Organization of Canada, General Counsel's Office, Toronto, box 58516184, Bond Dealers' Association of Canada, vol. 2, Minutes 1916–17, 177–[201]; *Toronto Daily Star,* 30 August 1917.

2 Serge Marc Durflinger, "Vimy's Consequence: The Montreal Anti-conscription Disturbances, May to September 1917," in *Turning Point 1917: The British Empire at War,* ed. Douglas E. Delaney and Nikolas Gardner, 160–87 (Vancouver: UBC Press, 2017).

3 *Le Nationaliste* (Montreal), 8 July, 5, 12, 19 August 1917. On Bourassa's criticism of White's handling of finance in 1915, see Geoff Keelan, "Bourassa's War: Henri Bourassa and the First World War" (PhD diss., University of Waterloo, 2015), 111, 151. Bourassa's "moderating influence in the conscription crisis" is explored in Béatrice Richard, "Henri Bourassa and Conscription: Traitor or Saviour?" *Canadian Military Journal* (Kingston, ON) 7, 4 (2006–07): 75–83, 82 (quote).

4 Library and Archives Canada (LAC), RG 19, E-h-5, vol. 4012, White to Donald A. Cameron, 19 January 1917.

5 Jeffrey A. Keshen, *Propaganda and Censorship during Canada's Great War* (Edmonton: University of Alberta Press, 1996), 55.

6 *Globe,* 14 June, 3 September, 8 October, 6 December 1917; "Bringing East and West Together," *Oyen News* (Oyen, AB), 28 November 1917, an article that appeared in many other western newspapers; David Joseph Gallant, "Armageddon: Alberta Newspapers and the Outbreak of the Great War, 1914," in *The Frontier of Patriotism: Alberta and the First World War,* ed. Adriana A. Davies and Jeffrey A. Keshen, 262–78 (Calgary: University of Calgary Press, 2016); Mark Edgar Nichols, *(CP): The Story of the Canadian Press* (Toronto: Ryerson, 1948), 126–27, 132–34; Minko Sotiron, *From Politics to Profit: The Commercialization of Canadian Daily Newspapers, 1890–1920* (Montreal and Kingston: McGill-Queen's University Press,

1997), 100–1; Gene Allen, *Making National News: A History of Canadian Press* (Toronto: University of Toronto Press, 2013), ch. 1.

7 Investment Industry Regulatory Organization of Canada, General Counsel's Office, Toronto, box 58516184, Bond Dealers' Association of Canada, vol. 3, Minutes 1916–19, 27–50; LAC, RG 19, E-5-h, vol. 4005, White to BDAC Vice-President J.H. Gundy, 14 September 1917; Dominion War Loan Chair A.E. Ames to White, 27 September 1917; White to Ames, 1 October 1917; *Financial Post* (Toronto), 18, 25 August, 15, 22 September 1917; *Globe* (Toronto), 7, 10, 11 September 1917; *Economic Advertising* (Toronto) 10, 9 (1917): 28; Russell Johnston, *Selling Themselves: The Emergence of Canadian Advertising* (Toronto: University of Toronto Press, 2001), 97–98.

8 Harold Constantine Lowrey, "Paid Advertising Carries Canada's Victory Loan to Success," *Printers' Ink* (New York) 101, 11 (1917): 87–88, original emphasis.

9 *Financial Post,* 25 August 1917.

10 Kenneth D. Garbade, *Birth of a Market: The U.S. Treasury Securities Market from the Great War to the Great Depression* (Cambridge, MA: MIT Press, 2012), 97–98. Examinations of the Liberty Loans include Julia C. Ott, *When Wall Street Met Main Street: The Quest for an Investors' Democracy* (Cambridge, MA: Harvard University Press, 2011); Richard Sutch, "Liberty Bonds: April 1917–September 1918," https://www.federalreservehistory.org/essays/liberty-bonds; Eric Hilt and Wendy M. Rahn, "Turning Citizens Into Investors: Promoting Savings with Liberty Bonds during World War I," *RFS: The Russell Sage Foundation Journal of the Social Sciences* (Baltimore, MD) 2, 6 (2016): 86–108; and James J. Kimble, *Mobilizing the Home Front: War Bonds and Domestic Propaganda* (College Station, TX: Texas A&M University Press, 2006).

11 LAC, RG 19, E-h-5, vol. 4012, file: U.S. Subscriptions, 1917.

12 LAC, RG 19, E-h-5, vol. 4008, Imrie to White, 26 September 1917.

13 Toronto-Dominion Bank Archives, Toronto, Canadian Bankers' Association, Executive Council, Minutes, 10 October 1917.

14 *Globe,* 6 June 1918.

15 *Economic Advertising* 10, 9 (1917): 28.

16 Investment Industry Regulatory Organization of Canada, General Counsel's Office, Toronto, box 58516184, Bond Dealers' Association of Canada, vol. 3, Minutes 1917–19, 35–59; *Economic Advertising* 10, 9 (1917): 28; 10, 10 (1917): 29; *Globe,* 11, 22, 25 September, 8, 13 October 1917.

17 LAC, RG 19, E-5-h, vol. 4011, file: Various Associations, Peterson to White, 22 October 1917.

18 LAC, RG 14, D2, vol. 37, no. 131a (unpub. Sess. paper, 1918, no. 131a).

19 *Bow Island Review* (Bow Island, AB), 21 December 1917.

20 LAC, RG 14, D2, vol. 37, no. 131a (unpub. Sess. paper, 1918, no. 131a). In April 1918, one insider, Thomas Bradshaw, had this proportion as high as 45 percent for 1917. See LAC, RG 19, E-5-h, vol. 4013, file: Results, 1917–21, Bradshaw to White, 13 April 1918; and file: Subscriptions over $25,000, 1917. However, if Bradshaw's figure of "approximately" $185 million for special subscriptions is correct, the proportion is closer to 33 than 45 percent.

21 LAC, RG 19, E-5-h, vol. 4012, file: Subscriptions over $25,000, 1917.

22 *Globe,* 12, 30 November 1917; *Imperial Oil Review* (Toronto) 1, 4 (1917): cover, 2–3.

23 For example, see "Launching Canada's Fourth Domestic War Loan," *Printer and Publisher* (Toronto) 26, 10 (1917): 17–18, 28; and 26, 12 (1917): 23, 32–33, 40.

24 Thunder Bay Historical Museum Society, Thunder Bay, Ontario, A 92/1/1–18, Abbott to the Mayors or Reeves, Clerks, and Treasurers of Ontario Municipalities, 26 October 1917.

25 Edward Rogers Wood, *Some Facts and Figures Regarding Canada's Victory Loan, 1917* (Ottawa: Victory Loan Committee, 1917), 3.
26 Reported in *Globe*, 26 November 1917.
27 *Edmonton Bulletin*, 22 September, 5–6 October 1917; *Munson Mail* (Munson, AB), 25 October 1917.
28 *Financial Post*, 27 October 1917; *Globe*, 24, 30 October 1917; *Toronto Daily Star*, 24 October 1917; *Monetary Times* (Toronto), 26 October 1917.
29 *Globe*, 31 October 1917.
30 *Globe*, 18 October 1917.
31 *Globe*, 13 November 1917.
32 McCord Museum/Musée McCord Archives, Montreal, P217/F, John Wardrop Ross fonds, box 15, Canada's Victory Loan 1917, City and Island of Montreal, Summary Report and Statement of Campaign, Report of the Vice-Chairman (Ross).
33 *Globe*, 27 October 1917.
34 *Globe*, 12 December 1917; LAC, Borden diaries, 25–26 November 1917.
35 *Globe*, 10 November 1917.
36 *Globe*, 1 December 1917; *Daily Times* (Moncton, NB), 1 December 1917.
37 Mary Janigan, "Treason to Their Memory," in *In Flanders Fields: 100 Years: Writing on War, Loss and Remembrance*, ed. Amanda Betts (Toronto: Knopf Canada, 2015), 74–95.
38 *Monetary Times*, 16 November 1917; McGill University Archives, Montreal, MG 4240, container 33, file 00414, J.W. McConnell fonds, *Canada's Victory Loan Montreal, 1917* (Montreal: Herald Press and Advertising Agency, 1917).
39 The question of motivation is addressed, with some resort to "educated speculation," in Sarah Glassford, "Volunteering in the First and Second World War," Wartime Canada, http://wartimecanada.ca/essay/volunteering/volunteering-first-and-second-world-war.
40 The bonds of the 1917, 1918, and 1919 Victory Loans were printed in both French and English. Canada, House of Commons, *Debates*, 8 March 1933, 2821–22. This statement by Prime Minister Richard Bedford Bennett also notes that demand for bonds in French fell off dramatically during the refunding loans of 1922 to 1923.
41 *Globe*, 3 November 1917.
42 The appearance here of the Ku Klux Klan may relate to the lasting popularity of D.W. Griffith's racist American film *The Birth of a Nation* (1915), which portrayed Klansmen galloping about during the Reconstruction era. Klan costumes also appeared at masquerades in Edmonton and York Mills, Toronto, in 1918. A Klan character was in a horse-show pageant in Edmonton in 1919, and a ranch in the area of Bassano, Alberta, took the name Ku Klux Klan Farm. Klan organizers first came to Alberta in 1924, but earlier history there is sketchy. The Canadian body appears to have been imperialist, anti-immigrant, and anti–Roman Catholic. See also Greg Marquis, "A War within a War: Canadian Reactions to D.W. Griffith's *The Birth of a Nation*," *Social History* 47, 94 (2014): 422.
43 *Truro Daily News* (Truro, NS), 13 November 1917.
44 Ames had initially asked the Canadian Bankers' Association to set up a fund of $100 million for advances to companies and individuals. On 8 November, the request was rejected by the association, which felt that loan applications should be considered by the individual banks. Canadian Bankers' Association, Annual General Meeting, Minutes, 8 November 1917. The following day, however, the association formulated a scheme for advances, which was immediately spun as an aid to the "small investor." *Globe*, 10 November 1917.
45 Garbade, *Birth of a Market*, 98; Richard N. Germain, *Dollars through the Doors: A Pre-1930 History of Bank Marketing in America* (Westport, CT: Greenwood, 1996), 140.

46 *Canadian Grocer* (Toronto) 31, 47 (1917): 31. On the soft market for small Victory Bonds in the 1930s, see for instance, *Globe*, 11 February 1932.
47 *Island Patriot* (Charlottetown), 27 September 1917. The author cannot substantiate its figures.
48 War-loan coverage in *Le Soleil* and *La Patrie* is examined in depth by Marie-Michelle Pagé in a series of unpublished reports dated 2013.
49 Shirley Tillotson, *Give and Take: The Citizen-Taxpayer and the Rise of Canadian Democracy* (Vancouver: UBC Press, 2017), 42.
50 Mourad Djebabla, "'Fight the Huns with Food': Mobilizing Canadian Civilians for the Food War Effort during the Great War, 1914–1918," in *World War I and Propaganda*, ed. Troy R.E. Paddock (Leiden: Brill, 2014), 77–78, 87–88.
51 Union Government Publicity Bureau, *Plain Facts for English-Speaking Electors* (1917), 5. The bureau appears to have been part of the publication arm of the Conservative Party, the so-called Federal Press Agency, which operated out of offices at 47 Slater Street, Ottawa. See also Keshen, *Propaganda and Censorship*, 50.
52 *Daily Mail and Empire* (Toronto), 12 December 1917.
53 *Calgary Daily Herald*, 27 November 1917.
54 *Calgary Daily Herald*, 26 October 1918.
55 Peter Ludlow, *The Canny Scot: Archbishop James Morrison of Antigonish* (Montreal and Kingston: McGill-Queen's University Press, 2015), 87–88.
56 For this expression of "deep discontent" (*vif mécontentement*), see *Le Canada* (Montreal), 17 November 1917.
57 McCord Museum/Musée McCord Archives, Montreal, P217/, John Wardrop Ross fonds, box 15, Canada's Victory Loan 1917, City and Island of Montreal, Summary Report and Statement of Campaign, Report of the Vice-Chairman (Ross); McGill University Archives, Montreal, MG 4240, container 33, file 00414, J.W. McConnell fonds, *Canada's Victory Loan Montreal, 1917* (Montreal: Herald Press and Advertising Agency, 1917). William Fong, McConnell's biographer, surmises that he "knew instinctively from his stock promotions that there was still plenty of untapped money under the beds of Canadians and that it was not being conscripted through taxation. For him as a financier, sources of funds were the tools of his profession ... In essence, the Victory Loan campaign expanded the techniques of the Patriotic Fund," in which McConnell had been involved. William Fong, *J.W. McConnell: Financier, Philanthropist, Patriot* (Montreal and Kingston: McGill-Queen's University Press, 2008), 134–39.
58 Steve Marti, *For Home and Empire: Voluntary Mobilization in Australia, Canada, and New Zealand during the First World War* (Vancouver: UBC Press, 2019), 42–45.
59 Jean-Noël Cossette, "La censure fédérale et les principaux journaux canadiens-français du Québec, 1915–1918" (MA thesis, University of Ottawa, 1971), 99–100.
60 With reference to the Unionist belief that an unofficial Bourassa-Laurier alliance was a French Canadian plot to pull Canada out of the war, *Le Canada* ran this header on page 1 on 26 November 1917: "'PULL' Is the Unionist Sticky Fly-Paper." Whereas Bourassa castigated the loan as a government trap, the French humour periodical *Le Canard enchaîné* (Paris), with reference to subscribing to France's war loan, provokingly called its citizens suckers and tightwads, despite a high rate of investments. Allen Douglas, *War, Memory, and the Politics of Humor: The Canard Enchaîné and World War I* (Berkeley: University of California Press, 2002), 230.
61 *L'Emprunt de la "Victoire": La surenchère du "bluff,"* trans. Sandy Darmagnac (Montreal: Édition du Devoir, 1917), 8, trans. Sandy Darmaganc, original emphasis.

62 LAC, RG 19, E-5-h, vol. 4012, file: Troops Subscribing to Loan, 1917. Soldiers in Europe also knew of war bonds from field journals such as the *Canadian Daily Record* (London, UK) and the *Listening Post* (7th Canadian Infantry Battalion).

63 *Globe,* 21 February 1918. Soldiers could subscribe through payroll deductions. An example from the 1918 Victory Loan is found in LAC, RG 150–3, Canadian Expeditionary Force (Siberia) personnel files, vols. 614–23, no. 4062375, Herbert McLean Bell, M.F.W. 12, Assigned Pay, "Victory Loan – 1918."

64 *Toronto Daily Star,* 23 November 1917.

65 Alan Sullivan, comp., *Aviation in Canada, 1917–1918: Being a Brief Account of the Work of the Author* (Toronto: Rous and Mann, 1919), 269.

66 The figures are given in an official advertisement that appeared, among other newspapers, in the *Moncton Daily Times* and the *Quebec Chronicle* on 15 November 1917, which had Canada at 1 in 187. The advertisement's appearance early in the campaign suggests that the figures were based on the Dominion War Loan of March 1917.

67 R.T. Naylor, *Canada in the European Age, 1453–1919* (Montreal and Kingston: McGill-Queen's University Press, 1987), 508, 515.

68 Canadian War Museum, Ottawa, Collection 58 A-1-241.3–16. The Shaw letters have been published in Marian Antliff Owens, ed., *Letters to the Front: World War I, 1916–1919* (Kamloops, BC: Antliff, 2002).

69 "World War One Collections," Canadian Letters and Images Project, https://www.canadianletters.ca/collections/468; R.B. Fleming, ed., *The Wartime Letters of Leslie and Cecil Frost, 1915–1919* (Waterloo, ON: Wilfrid Laurier University Press, 2007), 252, 263.

70 "World War One Collections," Canadian Letters and Images Project, letter of William Lowry, 20 November 1917, https://www.canadianletters.ca/collections/468.

71 *British Columbia Federationist* (Vancouver) 16, 23 November 1917.

72 LAC, RG 19, E-5-h, vol. 4013, unmarked file.

73 *Globe,* 17 November 1917, 14 August, 19 September, 9 November, 25 December 1918. Dense economic analyses of the Liberty Loans include Hugh Rockoff, "Until It's Over, Over There: The U.S. Economy in World War I," National Bureau of Economic Research, Cambridge, Massachusetts, June 2004, https://www.nber.org/papers/w10580; and Sung Won Kang and Hugh Rockoff, "Capitalizing Patriotism: The Liberty Loans of World War I," National Bureau of Economic Research, Cambridge, Massachusetts, January 2006, http://www.nber.org/papers/w11919.

74 *Manitoba Free Press* (Winnipeg), 10 November 1917.

75 McCord Museum, P217/F, Team 14 Report, by W.P. O'Brien (a stockbroker).

76 *Island Patriot,* 19 November 1918.

77 On the notions of "double duty" and "intimate fiscal relationship," see Tillotson, *Give and Take,* 43–45.

78 Olivier Zunz, *Philanthropy in America: A History* (Princeton, NJ: Princeton University Press, 2012), 60.

79 The statement on "temporary unsettlement" caused by the Victory Loan, the resumption of the campaigns for national saving and the sale of war-savings certificates, and the anticipated launch of the prepared war-savings stamps was released on 25 January. See *Globe,* 26 January 1918, *Kelowna Record* (Kelowna. BC), 31 January 1918; and *Men's Wear Review* (Toronto) 8, 1 (1918): 37.

80 For an example of scams, see LAC, MG 27, II, D18, vol. 5, file 17a, 2814–17, E.J. Chambers, Chief Press Censor, to White, 12 February 1918, where Chambers reported that Victory Bond buyers in Detroit were being victimized into selling their bonds at "absurdly low prices." *Saturday Night* (Toronto), 21 September 1918, 18, criticized the department for its

inability to control sales "at slaughter prices." An example of a department warning, dated April 1918, may be found in the New Brunswick Museum, Saint John, Stanton Family fonds, Stanton-CBDOC-8.

81 *Globe,* 31 January 1918. The director was Zebulon Aiton Lash, speaking at National Trust's annual meeting in Toronto. National Trust invested heavily in war loans: 1st ($250,000), 2nd ($650,000), 3rd ($1,250,000), 4th (Victory Loan) ($3,800,000), all new money. Variations on "Canada has found her soul" were voiced from 1916 to 1919 by politicians, churchmen, organizations such as the Imperial Order Daughters of the Empire, Bonne Entente believers, and others, with many claiming agency. National Trust's subscriptions are illustrated by a letter in Thunder Bay Historical Museum Society, Thunder Bay, Ontario, A 92/1/1–8, Vice-President, Dominion Wheel and Foundries Ltd. to James Murphy, Copp Stove Company Ltd., Toronto, 5 November 1918 (the Copp factory in Fort William had been destroyed by fire in 1917): "Mr. Kilpatrick and I called upon The National Trust Company yesterday relative to having them subscribe $50,000. to the present Victory Loan on account of funds in their hands as trustees for the bond-holders of The Copp Stove Company, Limited."

82 *Farmers' Magazine* (Toronto) 11, 6 (1917–18): 5.

83 Jim Blanchard, *Winnipeg's Great War: A City Comes of Age* (Winnipeg: University of Manitoba Press, 2010), 197.

84 *Globe,* 21 February, 27 April, 13 May 1918.

85 *Saint John Globe,* 28 September 1918; Susan R. Fisher, *Boys and Girls in No Man's Land: English Canadian Children and the First World War* (Toronto: University of Toronto Press, 2011); Sarah Glassford and Amy J. Shaw, eds., *A Sisterhood of Suffering and Service: Women and Girls of Canada and Newfoundland during the First World War* (Vancouver: UBC Press, 2012); Norah Lewis, "'Isn't this a terrible war?': The Attitudes of Children to Two World Wars," *Historical Studies in Education* (London, ON) 7, 2 (1995): 193–215; Frances Helyar, "'Gladly given for the cause': New Brunswick Teacher and Student Support for the War Effort, 1914–1918," *Journal of New Brunswick Studies* (Fredericton) 3 (2012): 82.

86 Niall Ferguson, *The Pity of War* (New York: Basic Books, 1999), 239.

87 "World War One Collections," Canadian Letters and Images Project, J.W. Law to his mother, 5 May 1918; Irving to his sister Fern ("Kid"), 5 February 1918; Nayler to his brother Walter, 8 January 1918, https://www.canadianletters.ca/collections/468.

88 Andrew Macphail, "In This Our Necessity," *University Magazine* (Montreal) 16, 4 (December 1917): 476–83; *Globe,* 8 December 1917.

89 Daniel Francis, *Selling Canada: Three Propaganda Campaigns That Shaped the Nation* (Vancouver: Stanton, Atkins and Dosil, 2011), ch. 2. On the American perspective, see Alan Axelrod, *Selling the Great War: The Making of American Propaganda* (New York: Palgrave Macmillan, 2009); Pamela Walker Laird, *Advertising Progress: American Business and the Rise of Marketing* (Baltimore, MD: Johns Hopkins University Press, 1998), 298–99, 360–61, 373, 464; Anne Classen Knutson, "Beasts, Brawn and Selling a War: American World War I Propaganda Posters, 1917–1918" (PhD diss., University of Pittsburgh, 1997); and the website for the exhibition *Advertising War: Selling Americans on World War I* (2017–19) at the National Museum of American History, Washington, DC, https://americanhistory.si.edu/exhibitions/advertising-war.

90 George Creel, *How We Advertised America: The First Telling of the Amazing Story of the Committee on Public Information That Carried the Gospel of Americanism to Every Corner of the Globe* (New York: Harper and Brothers, 1920), 4; Stewart Halsey Ross, *Propaganda for War: How the United States Was Conditioned to Fight the Great War of 1914–1918* (Jefferson, NC: McFarland, 1996); Robert H. Zieger, *America's Great War: World War I*

and the American Experience (Lanham, MD: Rowman and Littlefield, 2000), 77–83; Axelrod, *Selling the Great War*; Robert D. Hormats, *The Price of Liberty: Paying for America's Wars* (New York: Times Books, 2007), 132–33.

91 *Hardware and Metal* (Toronto) 30, 1 (1918): 35; *Dry Goods Review* (Toronto) 30, 2 (1918): 20.

92 Reconsiderations of "atrocities" in Belgium include Bobby A. Wintermute and David J. Ulbrich, *Race and Gender in Modern Western Warfare* (Berlin: De Gruyter Olderbourg, 2018), 121–25.

93 *Toronto Daily Star*, 11 December 1917.

94 Mary Rubio and Elizabeth Waterston, eds., *The Selected Journals of L.M. Montgomery*, 5 vols. (Toronto: Oxford University Press, 1985–2004), vol. 2, 232.

95 *Toronto Daily Star*, 11 December 1917, 24 January, 22 April 1918; *Globe*, 12 December 1917; *Globe and Mail*, 8 April 1953; Karen Ann Reyburn, "Blurring the Boundaries: Images of Women in Canadian Propaganda of World War I" (MA thesis, University of Guelph, 1998), 107–8, 144–51. The *Victory Telegraph* was seen at Princeton University in New Jersey, as shown in Seeley G. Mudd Manuscript Library, MC089, Liberty Loan Committee records, box 30, folder 6.

96 Advertised in *Financial Post*, 19 January 1918; *Toronto Daily Star*, 24 January 1918; and *Globe*, 23 January 1918.

Chapter 7: Pandemic and Peace, 1918

1 Nova Scotia Museum, Collections and Research, "Remembering the Forgotten Dead: Nova Scotia and the Great Influenza Epidemic of 1918–1920," virtual exhibit, https://museum.novascotia.ca/collections-research/virtual-exhibits/remembering-forgotten-dead.

2 Chris Gertridge, blog post, 28 October 2020, https://www.facebook.com/503134101/posts/10158126071129102/?d=n.

3 *Toronto Daily Star*, 9 October 1918, referencing a Department of Finance "blue book" on unclaimed bonds from Victory Loan 1917. Detailed information on unpaid subscriptions and lost or damaged bonds would emerge in the audit undertaken by Edwards, Morgan and Company in 1921–22. See also Canada, Department of Finance, *List of Lost, Stolen and Destroyed Dominion of Canada Bonds Including Bonds Issued at New York also Interim Scrip Certificates and Canadian National Railway Bonds* (Ottawa: Department of Finance, 1929). For the remarks of Walter Harris, see *Globe* (Toronto), 11 November 1955.

4 *Marketing and Business Management* (Toronto) 12, 1 (1918): 3–4; 12, 2 (1918): 16–17; 12, 3 (1918): 3–4; 12, 4 (1918): 1, 6, 7–10; 12, 5 (1918): 5–13, 22–24, 32; 12, 6 (1918): 9–18, 22–24, 26, 28–31; 12, 7 (1918): 3–4, 15–16; 12, 8 (1918): 6, 20–21, 24; Robert S. Prince, "The Mythology of War: How the Canadian Daily Newspaper Depicted the War" (PhD diss., University of Toronto, 1998), 98. On government advertising, see William Byron, "Ottawa Makes a Discovery," *Maclean's Magazine* (Toronto) 32, 1 (1919): 36–38. Still meriting examination is Harold Edward Stephenson and Carlton McNaught, *The Story of Advertising in Canada: A Chronicle of Fifty Years* (Toronto: Ryerson, 1940).

5 Library and Archives Canada (LAC), RG 14, D2, vol. 45, no. 152 (unpub. Sess. papers, 1919, no. 152); *Globe*, 10 July, 3, 23 August 1918; Jeffrey A. Keshen, *Propaganda and Censorship during Canada's Great War* (Edmonton: University of Alberta Press, 1996), 57. In an address to the Women's Good Government League of Toronto on 31 January 1918, Yeigh gave this explanation of the War Lecture Bureau's goals: "to keep up a continuous supply of war publicity propaganda to supplement the work of the press and keep Canada roused to a determination to win the war." *Globe*, 1 February 1918.

6 *Globe*, 1, 13 February, 8 March 1918. The epithets "Four-Minute" and "Five-Minute" have been explained as the gaps available for speakers between the changeover of film reels in cinemas.

7 *Carleton Observer* (Hartland, NB), 21 February 1918 (Carvell was the MP for Victoria and Carleton); *Globe,* 25 February 1918.
8 *Globe,* 11, 27 February, 14 March, 11 October 1918; Canada, Parliament, *Sessional Papers,* 1919, no. 1, part ZZ, 263–69; 1920, no. 1, part ZZ, 407–10, 482; Canada, Department of Agriculture, *Report of the Canada Food Board, February 11–December 31, 1918* (Ottawa: Department of Agriculture, [1919]); Keshen, *Propaganda,* 51–53.
9 LAC, RG 14, D2, vol. 36, no. 120; vol. 37, no. 131, 131a, 131b; vol. 44, no. 129 (unpub. Sess. papers, 1918 and 1919). Bradshaw's report is 131b. See also LAC, RG 19, E-5-h, vol. 4013, file: Results 1917–21, Bradshaw to White, 13 April 1918; Canada, House of Commons, *Debates,* 6 May 1918, 1480; and *Globe,* 9 January, 25 June 1918.
10 Ames's final report to White, 26 April 1918, is no. 131a above; LAC, RG 19, E-5-h, vol. 4013, file: Results 1917–21, Ames to Saunders, 14 January 1918.
11 Barbara Eileen Kelcey and Angela E. Davis, eds., *A Great Movement Underway: Women and the Grain Growers' Guide, 1908–1928* (Winnipeg: Manitoba Record Society, 1997), 46. Graham's letter appeared in *Grain Growers' Guide* (Winnipeg), 20 February 1918, 166.
12 *Globe,* 22 February 1918.
13 *Canadian Annual Review of Public Affairs* (1918): 462–64.
14 *The Voice* (Winnipeg), 17 May 1918.
15 *Printer and Publisher* (Toronto) 27, 4 (1918): 36.
16 LAC, RG 19, E-5-h, vol. 4006, file: Misc. 1917–20, Boville to F.C.T. O'Hara, 8 May 1918.
17 LAC, RG 19, E-5-h, vol. 4013, file: Unpaid Subscriptions 1918.
18 The Victory Loan even came up in the aftermath of the postal dispute. At the convention of the Federated Association of Letter Carriers in Hamilton, a resolution was passed calling for a pension system among the "grade men" with interest rates up to 6 percent: "As the Government was now paying nearly this rate for money which it borrowed by the Victory Loan, the postmen were of the opinion that the Government should pay the same to them." *Globe,* 6 September 1918.
19 *Commercial and Financial Chronicle* (New York), 12 October 1918; *Globe,* 13, 17, 23 September 1918; *Saint John Globe,* 20 September 1918.
20 See, for example, Adam Crerar, "Ontario and the Great War," in *Canada and the First World War: Essays in Honour of Robert Craig Brown,* ed. David MacKenzie, 236–45 (Toronto: University of Toronto Press, 2005).
21 Adam Crerar, "Ties that Bind: Farming, Agrarian Ideals and Life in Ontario, 1890–1930" (PhD diss., University of Toronto, 1999), 279.
22 *Globe,* 22 June 1918; Barbara M. Wilson, ed., *Ontario and the First World War, 1914–1918: A Collection of Documents* (Toronto: University of Toronto Press, 1977), Section D: Women.
23 Madeleine Kloske, "From Spenders to Savers: Thrift, Saving and Luxury in Canada during the First World War" (PhD diss., University of Ottawa, 2017), 191: "It is impossible to know what extent the food conservation campaign contributed to the war effort in material means." Michel S. Beaulieu, David Karl Ratz, Thorold John Tronrud, and Jenna L. Kirker, *Thunder Bay and the First World War, 1914–1919* (Thunder Bay, ON: Thunder Bay Museum Historical Society, 2018), 95: "It is debatable how well such actions [community gardens, etc.] actually worked to alleviate the high cost of living or to feed the armies overseas but maintaining morale on the home front meant finding ways for everyone to contribute, and food control was effective in that regard." Donica Belisle, *Purchasing Power: Women and the Rise of Canadian Consumer Culture* (Toronto: University of Toronto Press, 2020), 52: "Canadians' responses to federal food-control campaigns were lukewarm at best."
24 *Eastern Chronicle* (New Glasgow, NS), 25 October 1918.
25 Canadian Press Association, *Press Publicity for Canada's Victory Loan 1918* (Woodstock, ON: Sentinel-Review Press [1919]), [2], https://www.canadiana.ca/view/oocihm.9_08688/1.

This booklet contains all of the Victory Loan's official advertisements, most of them containing some illustration.

26 See, for example, *Sunday Star* (Washington, DC), 4 August 1918, part 4, 14.

27 *La Liberté* (Winnipeg), 14 November 1917; Linda J. Quiney, *This Small Army of Women: Canadian Volunteer Nurses and the First World War* (Vancouver: UBC Press, 2017), 85.

28 *Globe,* 14, 16 September 1918.

29 Janet S.K. Watson, *Fighting Different Wars: Experience, Memory, and the First World War in Britain* (Cambridge, UK: Cambridge University Press, 2004); Robert Rutherdale, *Hometown Horizons: Local Responses to Canada's Great War* (Vancouver: UBC Press, 2004), esp. ch. 6; Quiney, *This Small Army of Women.*

30 *Globe,* 6, 14 August, 9, 25, 28 October, 6, 11–12 November 1918.

31 LAC, RG 19, E-5-h, vol. 4012, file: Internal Cheques and Coupons, 1918–19, Hull to Boville, 10 September 1918; Boville to Hull, 18 September 1918; Victoria Hayward, "Indians of Alert Bay," *Canadian Magazine* (Toronto) 51, 5 (1918): 381.

32 LAC, RG 19, E-5-h, vol. 4005, file: Organization 1918–20, Richardson to White, 4 September 1918.

33 *Globe,* 9 October 1918; *Toronto Daily Star,* 9 October 1918; *Commercial and Financial Chronicle,* 12, 19 October 1918.

34 *British Columbia Federationist* (Vancouver), 18 October 1918.

35 See, for example, the pointed remarks of "Reader" (evidently a woman) on "Inequalities" in *Globe,* 23 June 1917, and those of columnist "Melinda Yonge" (Georgina Cecilia Mary White) in *Globe,* 14 October 1918: "Very reasonable criticism is being levelled at some of the thrift suggestions – sent out by men no doubt – by women who are slaving to save the pennies, while men continue to waste pounds." In the *Globe,* 10 November 1917, "Claudia" had a question about official pledge cards to save food: "Why do ladies who distribute the food pledge cards and exhort one to economy in the small matters – the cheese-parings of daily life – come in costly motors, sometimes with costly chauffeurs, and wearing costly clothes?" Writing to the leftist *Alberta Non-Partisan* (Calgary) on 20 December 1917, Robert Bentley Suthers, a British socialist who favoured conscripting wealth, did not buy into the ethos of economy behind the Victory Loans. The themes of inequality and the government's thrift program as a "project of social engineering" are taken up in Kloske, "From Spenders to Savers."

36 *Globe,* 9 September, 15 October 1918; Keshen, *Propaganda,* 56–57.

37 *Globe,* 22 January 1919.

38 Barry Ferguson, *Remaking Liberalism: The Intellectual Legacy of Adam Shortt, O.D. Skelton, W.C. Clark, and W.A. Mackintosh, 1890–1925* (Montreal and Kingston: McGill-Queen's University Press, 1993), 166–70.

39 LAC, MG 27, II, D18, vol. 5, 3160–62, Shortt to White, 13 November 1918; White to Shortt, 14 November 1918. Shortt's rewritten article appeared as "Financing After-the-War Industry," *Monetary Times* (Toronto), 3 January 1919, 75–77. There, he recognized massive domestic savings and potential investors, the need for continuing government guidance of investors, and the eventual need to refund the war loans. "Many new investors have no experience in judging safety of securities" may be part of his rewrite.

40 *Globe,* 15, 25 January, 3 August, 28 October 1918; *Okanagan Commoner* (Armstrong, BC), 16 May 1918; Cate Haste, *Keep the Home Fires Burning: Propaganda in the First World War* (London: A. Lane, 1977); Matteo Ermacora, "Civilian Morale," in *1914–1918–Online: International Encyclopedia of the First World War,* ed. Ute Daniel, Peter Gatrell, Oliver Janz, Heather Jones, Jennifer Keene, Alan Kramer, and Bill Nasson (Berlin: Freie Universität Berlin, 2018), https://encyclopedia.1914-1918-online.net/home.html.

41 Suzanne Evans, *Mothers of Heroes, Mothers of Martyrs: World War I and the Politics of Grief* (Montreal and Kingston: McGill-Queen's University Press, 2007), 81, 181n83.
42 *Globe,* 25 October 1918.
43 Julia C. Ott, *When Wall Street Met Main Street: The Quest for an Investors' Democracy* (Cambridge, MA: Harvard University Press, 2011), 96; Rohan Mascarenhas, "An Interview with Julia Ott: The Rise of Mass Investment in America," Russell Sage Foundation, 13 February 2012, https://www.russellsage.org/news/interview-julia-ott-rise-mass-investment-america.
44 *Globe,* 19 November 1917, 14 November 1918.
45 *Globe,* 18 October 1918; *Toronto Daily Star,* 18 October 1918.
46 Queen's University Archives, Kingston, Ontario, Kingston Shipyard collection, locator 2246, box 2, Shipyards, correspondence, H.B. Smith, daily and weekly reports, 1918–19; Michael Moir, "Admiralty Orders for Canadian Shipyards: Trawlers, Drifters, and the Urgency of Coastal Defence during the Great War," *Northern Mariner* (Ottawa) 26, 3 (2016): 275–96.
47 *Okanagan Commoner,* 28 November 1918; William Harold Malkin, "Report of Victory Loan 1918," in British Columbia Executive Committee, *Victory Loan 1918: Report of British Columbia Executive,* 7–11 (1919), provided by the Enderby and District Museum, Enderby, British Columbia.
48 *Globe,* 22 October 1918. For comparable instances of disputed closures, exemptions, and openings during the fourth Liberty Loan campaign in the United States in September and October 1918, see Nancy K. Bristow, *American Pandemic: The Lost Worlds of the 1918 Influenza Epidemic* (New York: Oxford University Press, 2012). For a Canadian time frame on influenza, see Janice P. Dickin McGinnis, "The Impact of Epidemic Influenza: Canada, 1918–1919," *Historical Papers* (Canadian Historical Association) 12, 1 (1977): 120–40, https://www.erudit.org/en/journals/hp/1977-v12-n1-hp1112/030824ar/.
49 *Montreal Gazette* and *Globe,* 30 October 1918; John Rankin, "The Reporting of the Influenza Pandemic, 1918–1920 in Hamilton, Ontario," *Health* (Irvine, CA) 4, 12 (2012): 1317–27.
50 *Saint John Globe,* 12, 15 October 1918.
51 *Marketing and Business Management* 15, 17 (1921): 570.
52 Canadian Press Association, *Press Publicity,* [3].
53 Nova Scotia Archives, James Fraser Paige fonds, MG 1, vol. 3305, file 4, Paige to company employees, 25 October 1918.
54 Drawing on a brochure from the dominion publicity committee, an advertisement in the *Globe* on 26 October 1918, sponsored by the local members of the Bond Dealers' Association of Canada, stated that a $1,000 bond would buy, among other quantities, 200 pairs of boots, 100 pair of socks, 450 bushels of wheat, 4,200 pounds of cheese, 40 rifles, 28,000 rifle cartridges, 40 field telephones, or 200 gas masks – equivalents that would register with the public. For another diverse list of what a $100 bond would buy, see *Calgary Daily Herald,* 5 November 1918. Other brochures accounted for the spending of the last Victory Loan and what was bought on behalf of the British government, such as $520,415,832 for foodstuffs and $325,064,237 for munitions and other war materials. The same kind of simple equivalence was used by canvassers. In Toronto, a woman who had already subscribed for $4,000 and had three sons overseas asked what it would take to bring "one boy home." Approximately $100 was the reply, whereupon she said, "Well, I'll bring 10 boys home to Canada" and subscribed for another $1,000, as reported in the *Toronto Daily Star,* 13 November 1918. Was the $100 figure pulled from the air to make sense of the need?
55 Martin Auger, "The Evolution of Defence Procurement in Canada: A Hundred-Year History," Canada, Library of Parliament, Publication No. 2020-54-E, 14 December 2020, https://lop.parl.ca/sites/PublicWebsite/default/en_CA/ResearchPublications/202054E.

56 *Globe,* 2 January 1919.
57 Enderby and District Museum, Enderby, British Columbia, Enderby and District Victory Loan Committee, Minutes, 7 October to 20 November 1918.
58 *Okanagan Commoner,* 23 January 1919.
59 *Dawson Daily News,* 13 November 1918; Michael Gates, "From the Klondike to Berlin: The Yukon in the First World War," in *The North and the First World War,* special issue of *Northern Review* (Whitehorse) 44 (2017): 9–30; Peter Kikkert and P. Whitney Lackenbauer, "'Men of Frontier Experience': Yukoners, Frontier Masculinity, and the First World War," in *The North and the First World War,* special issue of *Northern Review* (Whitehorse) 44 (2017): 209–42.
60 *Claresholm Review-Advertiser* (Claresholm, AB), 21 September 1917, 22 March, 12 July, 1, 15 November 1918.
61 Esyllt W. Jones, *Influenza 1918: Disease, Death, and Struggle in Winnipeg* (Toronto: University of Toronto Press, 2007), 51–53, 52 (quote).
62 Canada, House of Commons, *Debates,* 18 June 1919, 3612–22.
63 Raphaël Dallaire Ferland, "Patriotism and Allegiances of the 22nd (French Canadian) Battalion, 1914–1918," *Canadian Military Journal* (Kingston, ON) 13, 1 (2012): 51–60; Serge Marc Durflinger, "'L'honneur de notre race': The 22nd Battalion Returns to Quebec City, 1919," in *Canada 1919: A Nation Shaped by War,* ed. Tim Cook and J.L. Granatstein, 72–85 (Vancouver: UBC Press, 2020).
64 Marie-Michelle Pagé, "L'Emprunt de la Victoire [no. 2]: *Le Soleil,* 5 octobre–27 novembre 1918," unpublished report, 2013.
65 Mélanie Morin-Pelletier, "French Canada and the War (Canada)," in *1914–1918-Online: International Encyclopedia of the First World War,* ed. Ute Daniel, Peter Gatrell, Oliver Janz, Heather Jones, Jennifer Keene, Alan Kramer, and Bill Nasson (Berlin: Freie Universität Berlin, 2018), https://encyclopedia.1914-1918-online.net/home.html; Serge Marc Durflinger, "Vimy's Consequence: The Montreal Anti-conscription Disturbances, May to September 1917," in *Turning Point 1917: The British Empire at War,* ed. Douglas E. Delaney and Nikolas Gardner (Vancouver: UBC Press, 2017), 164; Ann P. Linder, *World War I in 40 Posters* (Mechanicsburg, PA: Stackpole Books, 2016), 27.
66 *Le Devoir* (Montreal), 14 November 1918, trans. Sandy Darmagnac, original emphasis.
67 These are the figures used for Appendices 1 and 2, but totals on any one of the war loans varied over time. For example, on the 1918 loan, different totals were compiled and issued by A.E. Ames and Company in a "comprehensive booklet of statistics," part of which was quoted in *Marketing and Business Management* 13, 4 (1919): 131.
68 *Globe,* 19 November 1918; *Toronto World,* 18 November 1918.
69 J. Garry McEachern, *If Freedom Means as Much to You* (Bloomington, IN: Xlibris, 2013), 145.
70 Canada, House of Commons, *Debates,* 27 February 1919, 93–94.
71 Morin-Pelletier, "French Canada and the War (Canada)."
72 Elgin County Archives, St. Thomas, Ontario, Storage Room 107, R5 S1 Sh2 B1 F28, Municipal World Inc. fonds, Victory Loan canvassers' sheet.
73 Shelburne County Museum, Shelburne, Nova Scotia, Shelburne Shipbuilders Ltd. fonds, acc. 2004.134.0762.
74 Thunder Bay Historical Museum Society, Thunder Bay, Ontario, B 3/2/1, Port Arthur Shipbuilding Company fonds, financial statements, 1911–20.
75 See note 45.
76 *Abbotsford Post* (Abbotsford, BC), 27 December 1918.
77 *Financial Post* (Toronto), 16 November 1918.

78 Toronto Executive Committee, *Toronto Victory Loan Campaign, 1918: A Souvenir with Views of a Remarkable Achievement* (Toronto: Toronto Executive Committee, [1918?]), https://www.canadiana.ca/view/oocihm.78194.
79 The notion of a "coping mechanism" is explored in Clémentine Tholas-Disset and Karen A. Ritzenhoff, eds., *Humor, Entertainment, and Popular Culture during World War I* (New York: Palgrave Macmillan, 2015).
80 *Globe,* 3 October 1918.
81 *Globe,* 12, 16, 20–21 November 1918; Michael Bliss, *A Canadian Millionaire: The Life and Times of Sir Joseph Flavelle, Bart., 1858–1939* (Toronto: Macmillan, 1978), 384–88. The *Toronto Daily Star,* 7 December 1918, noted that 15,000 "girls" were being discharged and that many faced difficulties adjusting as they entered domestic work.
82 Shaw Newton and Russell Motor Car Company, *The Second Line of Offence* (Toronto: Southam, 1918), 32.
83 *Globe,* 20, 23, 25 November 1918.
84 *Globe,* 2 December 1918.
85 *Globe,* 12 November 1918.

Chapter 8: Thrift, War Savings, Markets, and the Clean-Up Campaign of 1919

1 *Globe* (Toronto), 9 May 1919.
2 "Savings Movement," *Encyclopedia Britannica,* 3 vols. (London: Encyclopedia Britannica, 1922). This article notes that an important advocate of small-investment savings, in 1915, was Robert Henry Brand, the munition-funding expert encountered in Part 1 here.
3 *St. John's Daily Star* (St. John's, NL), 4 January 1919; *St. Croix Courier* (St. Croix, NB), 9 January 1919, from the *St. John Standard* (Saint John, NB); *Le Devoir* (Montreal), 14 December 1918, 28 January 1919.
4 The book appeared in New Brunswick as *The Canada War Book* in January 1919, with an introduction dated November 1918 by the chief superintendent of education, W.S. Carter, and in Ontario as *Canada War Thrift Book,* with no date. See also Susan R. Fisher, *Boys and Girls in No Man's Land: English Canadian Children and the First World War* (Toronto: University of Toronto Press, 2011), 43–45. The National War Savings Committees that operated in Britain and the United States were formed before Canada's.
5 Jonathan W. Rose, *Making "Pictures in Our Heads": Government Advertising in Canada* (Westport, CT: Praeger, 2000), 56–60.
6 Robert Craig Brown and Ramsay Cook, *Canada 1896–1921: A Nation Transformed* (Toronto: McClelland and Stewart, 1974), 315–26.
7 *Globe,* 2 January 1919.
8 Fisher, *Boys and Girls,* 45.
9 *Canadian Home Journal* (Toronto) 15, 9 (1919): 26, 49.
10 Norah L. Lewis, ed., *"I want to join your club": Letters from Rural Children, 1900–1920* (Waterloo, ON: Wilfrid Laurier University Press, 1996), 76, 139; Norah Lewis, "'Isn't this a terrible war?': The Attitudes of Children to Two World Wars," *Historical Studies in Education* (London, ON) 7, 2 (1995): 20.
11 Library and Archives Canada (LAC), RG 19, E-5-h, vol. 4012, Assistant Deputy Minister of Finance (J.C. Saunders) to W.R. Fleming (BDAC secretary), [March 1919]; Investment Industry Regulatory Organization of Canada, General Counsel's Office, Toronto, box 58516184, Bond Dealers' Association of Canada, vol. 4, Minutes 1918–20, Saunders to Fleming, 10–11 February 1919; Percy Robertson to Saunders, 10 February 1919; Central Section Executive, 19 February 1919.

12 Clarence Karr, *Authors and Audiences: Popular Canadian Fiction in the Early Twentieth Century* (Montreal and Kingston: McGill-Queen's University Press, 2000), 245n104.
13 *Globe,* 26 February 1919.
14 "World War One Collections," Canadian Letters and Images Project, Liddiard to Mother and Father, 2 February 1919, https://www.canadianletters.ca/collections/468.
15 *Globe,* 9, 25 June, 4 July, 14 August 1919; *Canadian Grocer* (Toronto) 33, 22 (1919): 35; Brown and Cook, *Canada 1896–1921,* 323–24; Michael Bliss, *Northern Enterprise: Five Centuries of Canadian Business* (Toronto: McClelland and Stewart, 1987), 383–84; Tom Traves, *The State and Enterprise: Canadian Manufacturers and the Federal Government, 1917–1931* (Toronto: University of Toronto Press, 1979), 160–64. The economics professor was William Walker Swanson, who would trace the crisis of the 1930s to wartime borrowing and the resulting debt in his book *Depression and the Way Out* (Toronto: Ryerson, 1931). See Shirley Spafford, *No Ordinary Academics: Economics and Political Science at the University of Saskatchewan, 1910–1960* (Toronto: University of Toronto Press, 2000), 67.
16 LAC, RG 19, E-5-h, vol. 4009, Makovski to White, 26 July 1919.
17 LAC, RG 19, E-5-h, vol. 4005, file: Organization 1918–20, CPA *Bulletin* no. 556, 20 August 1919; vol. 4006, file: Newspaper Advertising 1919.
18 *Toronto Daily Star,* 23 August 1919.
19 The "Make-Up" Man [pseud.], "Drayton, the Practical," *Maclean's Magazine* (Toronto) 34, 16 (1921): 13.
20 LAC, RG 19, E-5-h, vol. 4006, file: Newspaper Advertising 1919; Jeffrey A. Keshen, *Propaganda and Censorship during Canada's Great War* (Edmonton: University of Alberta Press, 1996), 201–6.
21 *Vancouver Daily Star,* 23 October 1919.
22 *Globe,* 4, 16 September, 4 October 1919.
23 *Globe,* 7, 9, 10, 15, 28 October, 18 November 1919; *Monetary Times* (Toronto), 10 October 1919.
24 Law Society of Ontario Archives, Toronto, Allen Bristol Aylesworth fonds, PF212-1, Correspondence, 2013038-116 and 2013038-119.
25 LAC, RG 19, E-5-h, vol. 4006, file: Victory Loan General 1919; vol. 4009, file: Messages 1917–20.
26 Canada, Department of Justice, Military Service Branch, *Report of the Director of the Military Service Branch ... on the Operation of the Military Service Act, 1917* (Ottawa: Department of Justice, 1919), reproduced in Terry Copp, *Montreal at War 1914–1918: A History of Canada's Metropolis at War* (Waterloo, ON: Laurier Centre for Military Strategic and Disarmament Studies, Wilfrid Laurier University, 2017), https://Montrealatwar.com.
27 LAC, RG 19, E-5-h, vol. 4006, file: Victory Loan General 1919; *Le Canada* (Montreal), 5 November 1919; *Globe,* 5 November 1919.
28 *Globe,* 6 November 1919.
29 *Vancouver Daily Sun,* 6 November 1919.
30 LAC, RG 19, E-5-h, vol. 4011, file: Correspondence October 1919.
31 Bibliothèque et Archives nationales du Québec, Montreal, Centre Vieux-Montréal, P1000, D186.
32 *Globe,* 23 October 1919.
33 Kerry Badgely, *Ringing in the Common Love of Good: The United Farmers of Ontario, 1914–1926* (Montreal and Kingston: McGill-Queen's University Press, 2000), 62.
34 *Canadian Grocer* 33, 46 (1919): 32; *Globe,* 14 August, 9 September 1919.
35 Canadian Press Association, *Plan and Organization of Press Publicity for Canada's Victory Loan, 1919* (Ottawa: Dominion Publicity Committee, 1919), [3], https://www.canadiana.ca/view/oocihm.9_08688/1.

36 *Globe,* 2 November 1918.
37 Canadian Press Association, *Plan and Organization,* [3].
38 Bank of Canada Archives, Ottawa, National War Finance Committee fonds, First World War loans sous-fonds, boxes 1, 29, 43, 44–46.
39 *Marketing and Business Management* (Toronto) 13, 10 (1919): 365–66.
40 On the American experience, see Pamela Walker Laird, *Advertising Progress: American Business and the Rise of Marketing* (Baltimore, MD: Johns Hopkins University Press, 1998), 298.
41 *Toronto World,* 24 October 1919.
42 *Canadian Machinery and Manufacturing News* (Toronto) 23, 8 (1919–20): 213.
43 Keshen, *Propaganda,* 38–39, 193; Donald E. Graves, "Booty! The Story of Canada's World War One Trophy Collection," *Canadian Journal of Arms Collecting* (Ottawa) 23, 1 (1985): 3–10; Jonathan F. Vance, "Tangible Demonstrations of a Great Victory: War Trophies in Canada," *Material History Review* (Ottawa) 42, 1 (1995): 47–56. For details from one community, Albert County in New Brunswick, see https://www.albertcountymuseum.com/world-war-1-cannons.
44 Edward Perer Soye, "Canadian War Trophies: Arthur Doughty and German Aircraft Allocated to Canada after the First World War" (MA thesis, Royal Military College of Canada, 2009), 111–12.
45 *Globe,* 28 October 1919. On wheat marketing and the imperial wheat loans, see Jeremy Wormell, *The Management of the National Debt of the United Kingdom, 1900–1932* (New York: Routledge, 2000); and Canada, Parliament, *Sessional Papers,* 1921, no. 54, Report of the Canadian Wheat Board.
46 *Calgary Daily Herald,* 16 October 1919, statement by H.W. Wood; *Manitoba Free Press* (Winnipeg), 25 October 1919; *Carleton Observer* (Hartland, NB), 13, 20 November, 4, 11, 25 December 1919.
47 *Globe,* 11 October 1919. The government's estimates for fiscal 1919–20 allowed $25 million for land settlement loans through the Soldiers' Land Settlement Board, but by 31 March 1920, the actual cost had risen to $41,735,529.83. Canada, Parliament, *Sessional Papers,* 1919, no. 3, 58; 1921, no. 2, xi.
48 Drayton would claim with some justification, but also perhaps to downplay out-of-country volumes, that Americans did not buy as many Victory Bonds "as commonly reported." Even with the Americans' advantage on the exchange rate, Britain's loan at 6 and a-quarter percent was making investors "forget Canada's offerings," he believed. *Globe,* 21 November 1919; *Truro Daily News* (Truro, NS), 21 November 1919. A rate of 6 and a-quarter was the estimated yield on Britain's five -and-a-half-percent bonds, released by J.P. Morgan and Company in New York on 6 November. *Financial Post,* 25 October, 1 November 1919. Drayton need not have looked beyond Canada for competitive offerings during and shortly after the Victory Loan campaign. Once the government's moratorium of 8 September on new releases was lifted after the loan, several new issues quickly appeared, among them the six-and-a-half-percent bonds of the Saguenay Pulp and Paper Company. *Financial Post,* 22 November 1919.
49 McCord Museum Archives, Montreal, Quebec, P217/F, John Wardrop Ross fonds, box 14, Summary Report and Statement of Campaign, City and Island of Montreal Division, 1919, original emphasis.
50 *Le Devoir,* 18 November 1919, trans. Sandy Darmagnac.
51 The executive and committee members appear at the top of a French-language circular dated 22 October 1919, a copy of which is in Bibliothèque et Archives nationales du Québec, Montreal, Centre d'archives de Montréal, Fonds Famille Papineau, P7, S8, D1, Cowans to civil engineer Louis-Gustave Papineau, 22 October 1919.

52 LAC, RG 150, acc. 1992–93/166, box 9245-38, no. 248403; box 7403-54, no. 545681.
53 City of Toronto Archives, Toronto Civic Employees, Victory Loan Ledger, 1919, fonds 200, series 486, file 34, box 152418. Ledgers have not been found for the city's other departments: audit, parks, treasury, property, law, street cleaning, and works. Another existing ledger in City of Toronto Archives, fonds 220, series 206, file 1, contains information on the Toronto Police Benefit Fund's war-bond investments and conversions, along with records of its contributions to relief and patriotic funds for the period 1916–22.
54 One such organization where funding fell off was the Toronto and York Patriotic Association, formed in 1914 (before the Canadian Patriotic Fund) to care for soldiers' dependants. By October 1915, it was posting defaults and overdue subscriptions. In 1920, it contemplated legal action to collect pledges for about $800,000 from 850 delinquents, including "several well-known firms." Commenting on the situation, Walter J. Barr believed that "the large contributor, who had received free advertising for his generosity, should be forced to pay up what he had promised." Archives of the Roman Catholic Archdiocese of Toronto, FW WE05, appeal of E.R. Wood and Sir William Mulock to subscribers, 6 October 1915; *Globe,* 30 August 1919, 20 May 1920, 11, 13 October 1922; *Cariboo Observer* (Quesnel, BC), 8 March 1919.
55 Peter E. Rider, *Charlottetown: A History* (Charlottetown: PEI Museum and Heritage, 2009), 180–81.
56 *Pictou Advocate* (Pictou, NS), 22 November 1918.
57 Robert S. Prince, "The Mythology of War: How the Canadian Daily Newspaper Depicted the War" (PhD diss., University of Toronto, 1998), 98n46.
58 *Le Canada,* 18–19 November 1919.

Chapter 9: The Aftermath, 1919–20s

1 *Financial Post* (Toronto), 8 November 1919.
2 *Globe* (Toronto), 22 November, 2, 6, 18 December 1919; *Le Devoir* (Montreal), 17 November 1919; Harold Bérubé, "Versailles, Joseph," *Dictionary of Canadian Biography,* vol. 16, http://www.biographi.ca/en/bio/versailles_joseph_16E.html.
3 Shirley Tillotson, *Give and Take: The Citizen-Taxpayer and the Rise of Canadian Democracy* (Vancouver: UBC Press, 2017), 42.
4 *Le prix courant* (Montreal) 33, 8 (1920): 79.
5 *The Tattler* (Richmond Hill, ON) 2 (March 1920): 18–19.
6 *Barrie Examiner* (Barrie, ON), 13 July 1922.
7 W.G. Cates, "Canada's War Loans," *The Rotarian* (Chicago) 16, 2 (1920): 103–4.
8 Quoted in *Maclean's Magazine* (Toronto) 32, 1 (1919): 79; see also 33, 1 (1920): 6, 95–97.
9 *Globe,* 12, 16, 23 October 1920; *Toronto Daily Star,* 30 November 1920.
10 *Globe,* 2 November 1928.
11 Queen's University Archives, Kingston, Ontario, Kingston Shipyard collection, locator 2246, box 2, Shipyards, correspondence, H.B. Smith, daily and weekly reports, 1918–19; Marine Museum of the Great Lakes, Kingston, Ontario, Canada Steamship Lines fonds, 1996.0039.0011, Port Arthur Shipbuilding Company Limited minute book, 1916–30. This company, which was majority owned by American interests, had begun investing in Victory Bonds in 1918 but disposed of its holdings in June 1920.
12 Canada, Parliament, *Sessional Papers,* 1916–22, no. 8, Report of the Superintendent of Insurance; no. 9, Abstract of Statements of Insurance Companies; *Globe,* 21 March, 14 May, 5 October 1921, 3 March, 10 April, 2 October 1922. *Canadian Annual Review of Public Affairs* (1921): 12.
13 *Monetary Times* (Toronto), 7 January 1921, 116, 118, 120.

14 John Herd Thompson, with Allen Seager, *Canada, 1922–1939: Decades of Discord* (Toronto: McClelland and Stewart, 1985), 25.
15 *Saturday Night* (Toronto), 29 September 1923, 23.
16 *Globe,* 28 July 1928.

Chapter 10: Finance in Newfoundland and the Campaign of 1918

1 Albert W. Kimber, ed., *Kimber's Record of Government Debts and Other Foreign Securities, 1922* (New York: A.W. Kimber, 1922), 307–9.
2 *Evening Telegram* (St. John's), 31 December 1914.
3 Jenny Higgins, "First World War and the Economy," in *Newfoundland and Labrador in the First World War,* Newfoundland and Labrador Heritage Web Site, 2015, https://www.heritage.nf.ca/first-world-war/articles/first-world-war-economy.php.
4 *Globe* (Toronto), 15 June 1916; *Monetary Times* (Toronto), 9 June 1916, 28; 11 April 1919, 36; 23 May 1919, 40; *Colonial Commerce* (St. John's), 29 April 1916, 20–30.
5 War finance in Newfoundland can be traced in Patrick Thomas McGrath and Charles Lucas, "Newfoundland," in *The Empire at War,* vol. 2, ed. Charles Lucas, 297–321 (London: Oxford University Press, 1923). The imperial loan is noted in David James Gill, *The Long Shadow of Default: Britain's Unpaid War Debts to the United States, 1917–1920* (New Haven, CT: Yale University Press, 2022), 203. According to the Amulree Commission, the outstanding imperial loan was valued at $1,946,666.66 in 1933. See note 14.
6 *Colonial Commerce,* 31 July 1917, 9–13; Patricia Ruth O'Brien, "The Newfoundland Patriotic Association: The Administration of the War Effort, 1914–1918" (MA thesis, Memorial University of Newfoundland, 1981), 289–94.
7 Library and Archives Canada (LAC), MG 27, II, D18, vol. 4, file 16, April–December 1917, 2583–84, Morris to Borden, 30 August 1917.
8 Sean T. Cadigan, *Death on Two Fronts: National Tragedies and the Fate of Democracy in Newfoundland, 1914–34* (Toronto: Allen Lane, 2013).
9 *Evening Telegram,* 28 November 1917.
10 LAC, RG 19, E-5-h, vol. 4006, file: Misc. 1917–20, A.E. Ames to White, 27 December 1917.
11 *Globe,* 1 June 1918; *Monetary Times,* 31 May 1918, 12; 7 June 1918, 8; 12 July 1918, 22.
12 The Rooms Provincial Archives Division, St. John's, Office of the Prime Minister fonds, William Frederick Lloyd sous-fonds, Imperial War Loan sous-fonds (hereafter cited as The Rooms), GN 8.87 (this file actually concerns Newfoundland's Victory Loan of 1918); GN 2.14.54; Newfoundland, General Assembly, *Proceedings of the House of Assembly and Legislative Council, 1918; Western Star* (Corner Brook), 21 August 1918; numerous issues of the *Globe, Evening Telegram, Daily News* (St. John's), and *St. John's Daily Star; Colonial Commerce,* 30 April 1918, 8; "The Acting Prime Minister and the Victory Loan," *Newfoundland Quarterly* (St. John's) 18, 1 (1918–19): 18; *Newfoundland Magazine* (St. John's) 1, 5 (1918): 54–55; O'Brien, "Newfoundland Patriotic Association," 293–94.
13 Newfoundland, General Assembly, *Proceedings,* 151–58; *Globe,* 10 February, 17, 20 May 1919; *St. John's Daily Star,* 16 May 1919; *Daily Telegram* (St. John's), 16 May 1919.
14 For information on wartime loans, see Great Britain, Secretary for Dominion Affairs, Newfoundland Royal Commission, 1933, *Report* (London: Secretary for Dominion Affairs, 1934). See also Higgins, "First World War"; Mike O'Brien, "Out of a Clear Sky: The Mobilization of the Newfoundland Regiment, 1914–1915," *Newfoundland and Labrador Studies* (St John's) 22, 2 (2007): 420; and Sidney John Roderick Noel, *Politics in Newfoundland* (Toronto: University of Toronto Press, 1971), 130.
15 See, for example, Canada, Parliament, *Sessional Papers,* 1920, nos. 8–9, Department of Insurance.

16 *Globe,* 28 November 1933.
17 *Globe,* 27 March 1942.
18 *Mail and Advocate* (St. John's), 8 June 1916, quoted in Cadigan, *Death on Two Fronts,* 120.
19 Cadigan, *Death on Two Fronts,* 60–73.
20 Michael R. Westcott, "Transforming the State: Gender, Class, and Ethnicity on the Newfoundland Home Front, 1914–1918" (PhD diss., Memorial University of Newfoundland, 2019), 129. Westcott gives a good account of the Victory Loan, describing the campaign as "incredibly effective" (156).
21 The Rooms, GN 8.87; GN 2.14.54; *Newfoundland Magazine* 1, 5 (1918): 54.
22 Cadigan, *Death on Two Fronts,* 183–84.
23 *Evening Telegram,* 13 June 1918; *Printer and Publisher* (Toronto) 27, 8 (1918): 42–43; 27, 9 (1918): 44–45.
24 The Rooms, GN 8.87, A.L. Barrett to Cashin, 19 June 1918.
25 *Globe,* 22 June 1918; *Evening Telegram,* 8 June 1918; *St. John's Daily Star,* 27 August 1918; Terry Bishop Stirling, "The Home Front (Newfoundland)," in *1914–1918–Online: International Encyclopedia of the First World War,* ed. Ute Daniel, Peter Gatrell, Oliver Janz, Heather Jones, Jennifer Keene, Alan Kramer, and Bill Nasson (Berlin: Freie Universität Berlin, 2018), https://encyclopedia.1914-1918-online.net/home.html.
26 *Evening Telegram,* 22, 25 July 1918.

Chapter 11: The Limits of Patriotism

1 Julia C. Ott, *When Wall Street Met Main Street: The Quest for an Investors' Democracy* (Cambridge, MA: Harvard University Press, 2011), 56.
2 Doug Owram, *The Government Generation: Canadian Intellectuals and the State, 1900–1945* (Toronto: University of Toronto Press, 1986), 94–100, 95 (quote).
3 Jeffrey A. Keshen, *Propaganda and Censorship during Canada's Great War* (Edmonton: University of Alberta Press, 1996), 61.
4 *The Voice* (Winnipeg), 9 October 1914.
5 *Globe* (Toronto), 19 April 1915.
6 *Canadian Annual Review of Public Affairs* (1916): 682; *Globe,* 13, 15 February 1918; Jonathan Swainger, "Erroneous and Detestable: Seditious Language and the Great War in Western Canada," in *Canadian State Trials,* vol. 4, *Security, Dissent, and the Llmits of Toleration in War and Peace, 1914–1939,* ed. Barry Wright, Eric Tucker, and Susan Binnie (Toronto: University of Toronto Press, 2015), 112–14; Reinhold Kramer and Tom Mitchell, *When the State Trembled: How A.J. Andrews and the Citizens' Committee Broke the Winnipeg General Strike* (Toronto: University of Toronto Press, 2010), 303–4; Desmond Morton, *Fight or Pay: Soldiers' Families in the Great War* (Vancouver, UBC Press, 2004), 82, 95, 96, 120–21; Brock Millman, *Polarity, Patriotism, and Dissent in Great War Canada, 1914–1919* (Toronto: University of Toronto Press, 2016), 65, 89, 100, 133, 139; Frances Swyripa and John Herd Thompson, eds., *Loyalties in Conflict: Ukrainians in Canada during the Great War* (Edmonton: Canadian Institute of Ukrainian Studies, 1983), 53–57.
7 Robert Teigrob, *Living with War: Twentieth-Century Conflict in Canadian and American History and Memory* (Toronto: University of Toronto Press, 2016), 205.
8 *Toronto Daily Star,* 2 November 1918.
9 Hew Strachan, *Financing the First World War* (Oxford: Oxford University Press, 2004), 115–16.
10 *Alberta Non-Partisan* (Calgary), 14, 23 November 1917.
11 John James Deutsch, "War Finance and the Canadian Economy, 1914–20," *Canadian Journal of Economics and Political Science* 6, 4 (1940): 525–42; R. Craig McIvor, *Canadian Monetary, Banking and Fiscal Development* (Toronto: Macmillan, 1958).

12 Canada, House of Commons, *Debates,* 12 September 1939, 139.

13 Library and Archives Canada (LAC), RG 19, E-5-h, vol. 4009, file: Appointments, W.R. Fleming to B.J. Roberts, 23 October 1918, Thomas Moore to White, 29 October 1918, Draper to White, 29 October 1918; *Globe,* 24, 30 October 1918.

14 Order-in-council number 1918–2525 was approved on 11 October 1918. *British Columbia Federationist* (Vancouver), 18 October 1918; *Globe,* 12, 15, 18, 22 October 1918.

15 *British Columbia Federationist,* 25 October 1918.

16 Reinhold Kramer and Tom Mitchell, "'Daniel de Leon Drew Up the Diagram': Winnipeg's Seditious-Conspiracy Trials of 1919–20," in *Canadian State Trials,* vol. 4, *Security, Dissent, and the Limits of Toleration in War and Peace, 1914–1939,* ed. Barry Wright, Eric Tucker, and Susan Binnie (Toronto: University of Toronto Press, 2015), 235.

17 *Calgary Daily Herald,* 23 November, 4 December 1917, 3, 11, 14 November 1919.

18 The ratios of subscriptions to population (from Statistics Canada) were as follows: 1915, 1 in 321; 1916, 1 in 232; 1917 (Victory Loan), 1 in 9.27; 1918, 1 in 7.2; and 1919, 1 in 10.5. After the Victory Loan of 1917, Alfred Ernest Ames calculated 1 in 193.4 for the Dominion War Loan of March 1917 and 1 in 9.62 for the Victory Loan of 1917.

19 LAC, RG 19, E-h-5, vol. 4009, Belisle to [White], 1 March 1917; Thérien to [White], 21 March 1917; vol. 4011, Cholette to Roberts, 16 April 1917; Appleton to Roberts, 5 March 1917.

20 See, for example, Alan R. Young, "L.M. Montgomery's *Rilla of Ingleside* (1920): Romance and the Experience of War," in *Myth and Milieu: Atlantic Literature and Culture, 1918–1939,* ed. Gwendolyn Davies (Fredericton, NB: Acadiensis, 1993), 97, 100 (citing Montgomery's journals).

21 *Regina Morning Leader,* 24 November 1917.

22 Lizabeth Cohen, *Making a New Deal: Industrial Workers in Chicago, 1919–1939* (Cambridge, UK: Cambridge University Press, 1990), 76–78.

23 Ibid.; John Daniels, *America via the Neighbourhood* (New York: Harper Brothers, 1920), 315–18.

24 *Daily Times-Journal* (Fort William, ON), 10 November 1919; *Port Arthur News-Chronicle,* 14 November 1918; *Vancouver Daily Sun,* 4 November 1919.

25 See Laura Madokoro, Francine McKenzie, and David Meren, eds., *Dominion of Race: Rethinking Canada's International History* (Vancouver: UBC Press, 2017).

26 *Vancouver Daily Sun,* 3 November 1918; British Columbia Executive Committee, *Victory Loan 1918: Report of British Columbia Executive* (1919), 9, provided by the Enderby and District Museum, Enderby, British Columbia.

27 *Western Lumberman* (Winnipeg), January 1918, 29; March 1918, 40; December 1918, 31–33, 38, 42.

28 Nelson's letter was seen in the *Grand Forks Sun and Kettle Valley Orchardist* (Grand Forks, BC), 28 November 1919.

29 *Globe,* 21 November 1917.

30 *Globe,* 23 November 1917.

31 Adolf Ens, *Subjects or Citizens? The Mennonite Experience in Canada, 1870–1925* (Ottawa: University of Ottawa Press, 1994), 183–88; Vanessa Quiring, "Manitoba Mennonites and the State: Wartime Measures and the Influenza Pandemic in Hanover," *Manitoba History* 82 (2016): 30–31.

32 Quiring, "Manitoba Mennonites," 30–31; Ens, *Subjects or Citizens?,* 200; LAC, RG 19, E-5-h, vol. 4012, file: Applications/Subscriptions, 1919; *Globe,* 15 November 1918.

33 Gerhard John Ens, *The Rural Municipality of Rhineland, Volost and Municipality, 1884–1984* (Altona, MB: Regional Municipality of Rhineland, [1984]), 120–22, reprinted in Manitoba Historical Society, *War Memorials in Manitoba: An Artistic Legacy* (2014), 89–93, https://www.mhs.mb.ca/docs/features/warmemorials/index.shtml.

34 On Cook, see Leslie A. Robertson, with the Kwagu'ł Gixsam Clan, *Standing up with Ga'axsta'las: Jane Constance Cook and the Politics of Memory, Church, and Custom* (Vancouver: UBC Press, 2012), 247. On Baptiste, see Canada, Parliament, *Sessional Papers*, 1920, no. 27, 27; Duncan Campbell Scott, "The Canadian Indians and the Great World War," in *Canada in the Great World War*, 6 vols. (Toronto: United Publishers of Canada, 1917–21), vol. 3, app. 1, 327; and Hester E. White, "Presentation of the Silver Jubilee Medal to Chief Baptiste by Col. Pragnall," in *Twenty-First Report of the Okanagan Historical Society* (Vernon, BC: Okanagan Historical Society, 1957), 25. On the Ojibway, see *Globe*, 17 February 1920. On the Six Nations, I have corresponded with scholars Evan Habkirk and Geoffrey Moyer; see also *Globe*, 16 November 1917; [Evan Habkirk], "Six Nations Support of WWI," Great War Centenary Association, http://doingourbit.ca/six-nations-support-war; and Katharine Albertine McGowan, "'We are wards of the Crown and cannot be regarded as full citizens of Canada': Native Peoples, the Indian Act and Canada's War Effort" (PhD diss., University of Waterloo, 2011), 52–58.

35 Timothy C. Winegard, *For King and Kanata: Canadian Indians and the First World War* (Winnipeg: University of Manitoba Press, 2012), 146–48, 197n18; Robert J. Talbot, "'It Would Be Best to Leave Us Alone': First Nations Responses to the Canadian War Effort, 1914–18," *Journal of Canadian Studies* (Peterborough, ON) 45, 1 (2011): 90–120.

36 For one examination, see Barbara M. Wilson, ed., *Ontario and the First World War, 1914–1918: A Collection of Documents* (Toronto: University of Toronto Press, 1977), Introduction and Section C: Loyalty in Question.

37 Gerald Hallowell, email correspondence with author, 7 and 9 January 2020. Hallowell is the author of *As British as the King: Lunenburg County during the First World War* (Halifax: Nimbus, 2019).

38 LAC, MG 27, II, D18, vol. 5, 3093–96.

39 *Manitoba Free Press* (Winnipeg), 16 November 1918.

40 *Morning Bulletin* (Edmonton), 13 November 1918.

41 *Calgary Daily Herald*, 20 November 1919.

42 *Toronto Daily Star*, 29 October 1919.

43 *Daily Times-Journal*, 28 October 1918; Michel S. Beaulieu, David Karl Ratz, Thorold John Tronrud, and Jenna L. Kirker, *Thunder Bay and the First World War, 1914–1919* (Thunder Bay, ON: Thunder Bay Museum Historical Society, 2018).

44 Shirley Tillotson, *Give and Take: The Citizen-Taxpayer and the Rise of Canadian Democracy* (Vancouver: UBC Press, 2017), 42–43.

45 Swyripa and Thompson, eds., *Loyalties in Conflict*; Donald Avery, *"Dangerous Foreigners": European Immigrant Workers and Labour Radicalism in Canada, 1896–1932* (Toronto: McClelland and Stewart, 1979); Jim Blanchard, *Winnipeg's Great War: A City Comes of Age* (Winnipeg: University of Manitoba Press, 2010), 23–24, 238; Bohdan S. Kordan, *No Free Man: Canada, the Great War, and the Enemy Alien Experience* (Montreal and Kingston: McGill-Queen's University Press, 2016).

46 *Port Arthur News-Chronicle*, 2, 14 November 1918; *Daily Times-Journal*, 14, 18 November 1918; Gerald Ross, "Fort William's Enemy Alien 'Problem' during the First World War," *Papers and Records* (Thunder Bay Historical Museum Society, Thunder Bay, ON) 22 (1994): 3–22; Michel S. Beaulieu, *Labour at the Lakehead: Ethnicity, Socialism, and Politics, 1900–35* (Vancouver: UBC Press, 2011), ch. 2; Beaulieu et al., *Thunder Bay and the First World War*, 129–32.

47 *Toronto Daily Star*, 13 November 1918.

48 *Strikers' Defense Bulletin* (Winnipeg), 27 August 1919.

49 Donald F. Dixon, "Advertising U.S. War Bonds in the First World War," *Journal of Nonprofit and Public Sector Marketing* (Binghamton, NY) 3, 1 (1995): 65–80.

50 See the coverage of recruitment in Paul Maroney, "'The Great Adventure': The Conduct and Ideology of Recruiting in Ontario, 1914–17," *Canadian Historical Review* 77, 1 (1996): 62–98; Ian Hugh Maclean Miller, *Our Glory and Our Grief: Torontonians and the Great War* (Toronto: University of Toronto Press, 2002); and Patrick M. Dennis, *Reluctant Warriors: Canadian Conscripts and the Great War* (Vancouver: UBC Press, 2017).
51 *Globe,* 29 May 1919.
52 *Vancouver Daily Sun,* 7 November 1918.
53 *Manitoba Free Press,* 12 November 1918.
54 *Regina Morning Leader,* 14 November 1918.
55 *Morning Bulletin,* 23 May 1918. On the United States, see American Civil Liberties Union, *War-Time Prosecutions and Mob Violence Involving the Rights of Free Speech, Free Press and Peaceful Assemblage* (New York: National Civil Liberties Bureau, 1918), 8–9, 12, 15, 20; and James J. Kimble, *Mobilizing the Home Front: War Bonds and Domestic Propaganda* (College Station, TX: Texas A&M University Press, 2006), 16–17.
56 Gary Gerstle, *Working-Class Americanism: The Politics of Labor in a Textile City, 1914–1960* (Princeton, NJ: Princeton University Press, 2002), 44; *La Grande Observer* (La Grande, OR), 16 October 1917.
57 *Le Devoir* (Montreal), 5, 13 December 1917.
58 LAC, RG 19, E-5-h, vol. 4010, file: Circulars to Bank Managers, 1917.
59 *Vancouver Daily Sun,* 16–17 November 1918.
60 *British Columbia Federationist,* 18 October 1918.
61 *Canadian Mining Journal* (Gardenvale, QC) 40, 34 (1919): 647, https://www.canadiana.ca/view/oocihm.8_06967_317/1.
62 *Globe,* 29 December 1917, 1–5, 8–9, 19, 23–24 January, 9 February, 5 March, 12 April, 10 June 1918, 21 August, 10 October 1922; *Toronto Daily Star,* 29, 31 December 1917, 2, 4–5, 7, 23 January, 8–9, 14 February, 4 March, 10 June 1918, 9 October 1922. On the suppression of the *Sault Express* (Sault Ste. Marie, Ontario), see *Globe,* 26, 29 June 1916; and *Toronto Daily Star,* 28 June, 10 July 1916.
63 *Calgary Daily Herald,* 13 November 1918; *Edmonton Bulletin,* 15 November 1918, 21 January 1919; *Red Deer News,* 20 November 1918; *Western Globe* (Lacombe, Alberta), 20 November 1918; *Globe,* 15 November 1918; *Toronto Daily Star,* 14 November 1918, 21 January 1919; "Arnold Tried for Murder Following WWI Victory Celebrations: Stories of the Century," *Drumheller Mail,* 18 March 2011, https://www.drumhellermail.com/featured/9625-arnold-tried-for-murder-following-wwi-victory-celebrations-stories-of-the-century; David C. Jones, *Feasting on Misfortune: Journeys of the Human Spirit in Alberta's Past* (Edmonton: University of Alberta Press, 1998), 170–71.
64 *Western Globe,* 20 November 1918; *Claresholm Review-Advertiser* (Claresholm, AB), 1, 8, 20 November 1918.
65 Hamilton Public Library, Hamilton, Ontario, RG 10, series K, Hamilton Police Court proceedings, 1 November 1918; *Hamilton Spectator,* 1 November 1918; *Globe,* 1–2 November 1918; Daniel Francis, *Seeing Reds: The Red Scare of 1918–1919, Canada's First War on Terror* (Vancouver: Arsenal Pulp, 2010); Melissa Turkstra, "Social Gospel in the City: Rev. W.E. Gilroy and Hamilton Clergymen Respond to the Labour Issues, 1911–1918," *Urban History Review* (Ottawa) 37, 2 (2008–09): 42.
66 *Globe,* 30 October 1918; *Toronto Daily Star,* 13 November 1918, 29 October 1919.
67 LAC, RG 150, acc. 1992-93/166, box 4342-32, item 459205; box 4343-20, item 459252; *Globe,* 16, 19 November 1917, 3, 5 April, 15, 19, 26, 28 November, 5 December 1918; Amy J. Shaw, *Crisis of Conscience: Conscientious Objection in Canada during the First World War* (Vancouver: UBC Press, 2009), 144–46; Canada's Penitentiary Museum, Kingston, Ontario,

no. CG-92-001, Cameron Willis, research report on convict G-849, 28 September 2018, with reference to Convict Register and Description Book, 1890–1935.

68 Archives of Ontario, Toronto, RG 4-32, file 1918, no. 2343, barcode B420025.

69 Sarah Glassford, email correspondence with author, 31 January 2020. Glassford is the author of *Mobilizing Mercy: A History of the Canadian Red Cross* (Montreal and Kingston: McGill-Queen's University Press, 2017).

Chapter 12: Selling through Posters, Cartoons, and Illustrations

1 *Globe* (Toronto), 14 August 1914.

2 *Globe*, 29 December 1914, 5 January 1915; *Canadian War* (Toronto), 23 January 1915, 27 February 1915, 20 March 1915.

3 Maurice F.V. Doll, *The Poster War: Allied Propaganda Art of the First World War* (Edmonton: Alberta Community Development, Cultural Facilities and Historical Resources Division, 1993), 14–18, 18 (quote); Pier Paolo Pedrini, *Propaganda, Persuasion and the Great War: Heredity in the Modern Sale of Products and Political Ideas*, trans. Stephen Smith (London: Routledge, 2018), 3 (quote), 83–127; Jonathan W. Rose, *Making "Pictures in Our Heads": Government Advertising in Canada* (Westport, CT: Praeger, 2000).

4 Stephanie Gibson, "'Confronting Their Gaze in All Directions' – First World War Posters in New Zealand," unpublished research paper, Museum of New Zealand Te Papa Tongarewa, Wellington, New Zealand (c. 2015), 5; Stephanie Gibson, "First World War Posters at Te Papa," *Tuhinga: Records of the Museum of Te Papa Tongarewa* (Wellington, New Zealand) 23 (2012): 69–84; *Munson Mail* (Munson, AB), 1 June 1916; James Taylor, *"Your Country Needs YOU": The Secret History of the Propaganda Poster* (Glasgow: Saraband, 2013), 101–2.

5 Pre-war poster collecting is traced in Ruth E. Iskin, *The Poster: Art, Advertising, Design, and Collecting, 1860s–1900s* (Hanover, NH: Dartmouth College Press, 2014).

6 Jeffrey A. Keshen, *Propaganda and Censorship during Canada's Great War* (Edmonton: University of Alberta Press, 1996), 35–38, 77–78.

7 Ibid., 19–20.

8 Nicholas Hiley, "'Kitchener Wants You' and 'Daddy, What Did You Do in the Great War?': The Myth of British Recruiting Posters," *Imperial War Museum Review* (London) 11 (1997): 40–58.

9 *Toronto Daily Star*, 8 February 1917; *Globe*, 9 February 1917; *Punch*, 17 January 1917, 41.

10 *Printer and Publisher* (Toronto) 25, 4 (1916): 45; *Economic Advertising* (Toronto) 9, 8 (1916): 3, 5, 7; 10, 1 (1917): 23–25.

11 Library and Archives Canada (LAC), RG 19, E-h-5, vol. 4009, file: Misc. Suggestions and Enquiries, 1916–17; vol. 4011, two files: Distribution of Material through Business Firms.

12 *Economic Advertising* 10, 1 (1917): 23–25, 26–29; *Globe*, 22 January 1917. On Beal's drawings for the 109th Regiment, see *Globe*, 27 February to 15 March 1917. The drawings and underlying messages are examined further in Nathan Smith, "Comrades and Citizens: Great War Veterans in Toronto, 1915–1919" (PhD diss., University of Toronto, 2012), 105–8.

13 "Stereotyped" here means the method of printing.

14 Mora Dianne O'Neill, *Collective Remembrance: Propaganda Posters from the Great War* (Halifax: Art Gallery of Nova Scotia, 2014), 9.

15 Robert Stacey, *The Canadian Poster Book: 100 Years of the Poster in Canada* (Toronto: Methuen, 1979), 15.

16 O'Neill, *Collective Remembrance*, 33; James Aulich and John Hewitt, *Seduction or Instruction? First World War Posters in Britain and Europe* (Manchester, UK: Manchester University Press, 2007), 200. See also Pearl James, ed., *Picture This: World War I Posters and Visual Culture* (Lincoln: University of Nebraska Press, 2009); and James Aulich,

"Graphic Arts and Advertising as War Propaganda," in *1914–1918–Online: International Encyclopedia of the First World War,* ed. Ute Daniel, Peter Gatrell, Oliver Janz, Heather Jones, Jennifer Keene, Alan Kramer, and Bill Nasson (Berlin: Freie Universität Berlin, 2018), https://encyclopedia.1914-1918-online.net/home.html.

17 Terry Crowley, "The Propaganda Poster," in *The Power of the Poster,* ed. Margaret Timmers (London: Victoria and Albert, 1998), 114–15.

18 Jane Potter, *Boys in Khaki, Girls in Print: Women's Literary Responses to the Great War, 1914–1918* (Oxford: Clarendon, 2005), 73.

19 James, ed., *Picture This,* 20.

20 With reference to Liberty Loan campaigns in the United States, a similar conclusion is reached in Kelly LaBreque, "Persuasion by Design: World War I, the Committee on Public Information, and the Effectiveness of Good Poster Design" (MA thesis, University of New Hampshire, 2008), 54: "The posters used seem to have created an atmosphere of 'peer pressure' for people to donate to the campaigns."

21 *Globe,* 7 May, 4, 14 July 1917.

22 Examples of advertising by the National Service Board can be seen in *Economic Advertising* 10, 3 (1917): 31–32; 10, 6 (1917): 33; 10, 7 (1917): 9, 11, 18–19, 22; 10, 11 (1917): 15.

23 Ann P. Linder, *World War I in 40 Posters* (Mechanicsburg, PA: Stackpole Books, 2016), 8, 10; Pedrini, *Propaganda,* 113, 114, 116.

24 Linder, *World War I,* 27. The attention to language by Linder is a perspective missing in most studies on propaganda and posters in Canada. The literature on propaganda is vast. A starting point is James Aulich, "Graphic Arts and Advertising as War Propaganda," cited above. See also Trevor Wilson, *The Myriad Faces of War: Britain and the Great War, 1914–1918* (Cambridge, UK: Polity, 1986), 731.

25 LAC, RG 19, E-5-h, vol. 4005, file: Dominion Victory Loan Committee 1917, B.J. Roberts to Durantel, 27 November 1917, Durantel to Roberts, 8 December 1917; *Le Devoir* (Montreal), 6 November 1917. On another Victory Loan translation, see *Le petit canadien* (Montreal) 14, 11 (November 1917): 336.

26 *Globe,* 19 May, 25 September, 25 October, 3 November 1917; *Toronto Daily Star,* 18, 21 May, 12–13, 19 June 1917; Nicholas Reeves, "Film Propaganda and Its Audience: The Example of Britain's Official Films during the First World War," *Journal of Contemporary History* (London) 18, 3 (1983): 463–94.

27 Ralph A. Stephenson, "The Publicity Campaign," in Edward Rogers Wood, *The Story of Canada's Victory Loan, 1917: A Slight Appreciation of a Remarkable Event* (Toronto: Southam, 1918), 23.

28 Aulich and Hewitt, *Seduction or Instruction?*

29 George Edward Creel, *How We Advertised America: The First Telling of the Amazing Story of the Committee on Public Information That Carried the Gospel of Americanism to Every Corner of the Globe* (New York: Harper and Brothers, 1920), 133, 162; Eric Van Schaack, "The Division of Pictorial Publicity in World War I," *Design Issues* (Cambridge, MA) 22, 1 (2016): 32–45.

30 Stacey, *Canadian Poster Book,* 19. Here, Stacey mentions a "War Poster Service" but offers no evidence to support its existence.

31 Ibid., 21, 23. See also Princeton University, Princeton, New Jersey, Seeley G. Mudd Manuscript Library, MC089, Liberty Loan Committee records, box 30, folder 6, which contains a bundle of Victory Loan publicity sent to the Liberty Loan Committee.

32 Canadian War Museum, Ottawa, Collection 58 A-1-241.3-16, Ruth Caroline Antliff to William Shaw Antliff, 11 November 1917.

33 Lennox and Addington County Museum and Archives, Napanee, Ontario, Misc. Small Record Group, the Fourth War Loan 1917, also known as the Victory Loan.

34 Pedrini, *Propaganda,* 2.

35 Herbert Andrew Williams, "Canada's Flaming War Posters Stirred the Dominion to Action," in *The Poster: War Souvenir Edition,* ed. Roy O. Randall (Chicago: Poster Advertising Association, 1919), 59.

36 *Calgary Daily Herald,* 10 November 1917.

37 Nina Kruglikova, "Weapons of Mass Persuasion: The First World War in Posters," World War I Centenary, http://ww1centenary.oucs.ox.ac.uk/?p=3920.

38 One notable exception is the series of recruiting posters done in 1914 by Stone Limited of Toronto for the Central Recruiting Committee, No. 2 Military Division, Toronto. Some of these posters verge on art deco, in the view of curator Mora Dianne O'Neill, correspondence with author, 2019–20.

39 Thomas Row, "Mobilizing the Nation: Italian Propaganda in the Great War," *Journal of Decorative and Propaganda Arts* 24 (2002): 141–69; Taylor, *"Your Country Needs YOU,"* ch. 1 and 133–34, 142; David Bownes and Robert Fleming, *Posters of the First World War* (Oxford: Shire, 2014).

40 Large billboards produced by the E.L. Ruddy Company, featuring the pointing finger, are seen in photographs in City of Toronto Archives, fonds 1488, series 1230, items 1190, 1347, and 1350.

41 Each of the three Victory Loan campaigns had a numbering system for posters starting with "W.P.1." An illustrated catalogue is being prepared by the author.

42 Pedrini, *Propaganda,* 78.

43 Marc H. Choko, *Canadian War Posters: 1914–1918, 1939–45* (Laval, QC: Canada Communication Group, 1994), 30.

44 *Toronto Daily Star,* 4–5 December 1917; *Globe,* 4–5 December 1917; *Toronto Star,* 8 June 2006, R10; Wood, *Story,* 20.

45 *Le Canada* (Montreal), 26 November 1917; *Manitoba Free Press* (Winnipeg), 26 November 1917.

46 *Intelligencer* (Belleville, ON), 13 November 1917.

47 Fred Landon, "A Special Duty for Every Public Library in War-Time," *Ontario Library Review and Book-Selection Guide* (Toronto) 2, 2 (November 1917): 51–52.

48 *Vancouver Daily Sun,* 17–18 November 1917.

49 *Dry Goods Review* (Toronto) 30, 9 (1918): 112.

50 *Printer and Publisher* 27, 11 (1918): 38, which was also reported in the *Western Canada Press* (Winnipeg). Jeffrey A. Keshen, "From Local to National: Pictorial Propaganda in Alberta during the First World War," in *The Frontier of Patriotism: Alberta and the First World War,* ed. Adriana A. Davies and Jeffrey A. Keshen, 297–306 (Calgary: University of Calgary Press, 2016).

51 Bank of Canada Archives, Ottawa, National War Finance Committee fonds, First World War loans sous-fonds, box 43, 1918 scrapbook; *Globe,* 6 July 1918; *Toronto Daily Star,* 6 July, 13, 15 August 1918; *Saint John Globe,* 10 July 1918. None of the publicity committee's advance sketches has been located.

52 *Globe,* 23 July 1918, indicated that the poster submissions would be part of the art exhibit at the Canadian National Exhibition, which would run from 26 August to 7 September.

53 *Marketing and Business Management* (Toronto) 12, 7 (1918): 4.

54 The 600 figure may be a gross exaggeration. There is an "Item of Interest," noting that there were 180 designs, in the McCord Museum Archives, Montreal, Quebec, P217/F, John Wardrop Ross fonds, box 15, page 27.

55 LAC, R1185-67-0-E, acc. 1983-028-1019, 4045, 4046, 4047, 4049, 4051, 4052, 4053, 4055, 4056, 4057, 4058. Except for 1019, these posters are contained in two large folders: bar codes 2000818308 and 2000818309. The submission by Hilda Neville is held in the

Canadian War Museum, Ottawa, Collection 58B 1 1.1, control 19770066–003. On "baby-killers," a term being used in Canada from at least mid-1915, see "Babies and 'War-Babies': Writing Language in History in 1914–15," in *English Words in War-Time: Tracking Language on the Move in WW1*, 16 June 2015, https://wordsinwartime.wordpress.com/2015/06/16/babies-and-war-babies-writing-language-in-history-in-1914-15/; and "Alien Enemies: The Politics of Being Frightful," in *English Words in War-Time: Tracking Language on the Move in WW1*, 16 March 2015, https://wordsinwartime.wordpress.com/?s=Alien+Enemies%3A+The+Politics+of+Being+Frightful.

56 LAC, R1185-67-0-E, box A177/X2, e010696993. Part of this poster design appears on the cover of this book.

57 For poster W.P.2., CWM 19850475-034, see Canadian War Museum, https://www.warmuseum.ca/cwm/exhibitions/propaganda/poster7_e.html.

58 Linda J. Quiney, "'Bravely and Loyally They Answered the Call': St. John Ambulance, the Red Cross, and the Patriotic Service of Canadian Women during the Great War," *History of Intellectual Culture* (Calgary) 5, 1 (2005): 14; Linda J. Quiney, "Gendering Patriotism: Canadian Volunteer Nurses as the Female 'Soldiers' of the Great War," in *A Sisterhood of Suffering and Service: Women and Girls of Canada and Newfoundland during the First World War,* ed. Sarah Glassford and Amy J. Shaw (Vancouver: UBC Press, 2012), 118; Karen Ann Reyburn, "Blurring the Boundaries: Images of Women in Canadian Propaganda of World War I" (MA thesis, University of Guelph, 1998), 145.

59 *Globe,* 2 July, 30 August, 2 September 1918; *Le Canada,* 2 July 1918. Gordon Williams, "'Remember the *Llandovery Castle*': Cases of Atrocity Propaganda in the First World War," in *Propaganda, Persuasion and Polemic,* ed. Jeremy Hawthorn, 19–34 (London: Edward Arnold, 1987); Daniel J. Demers, "The Sinking of *Llandovery Castle,*" *Canadian Naval Review* (Halifax) 11, 2 (2015): 25–28.

60 "Marketing Canada's Victory Loan 1918," *Marketing and Business Management* 12, 9 (1918): 13, 16–17.

61 Pedrini, *Propaganda,* 97 (quote), 106–20.

62 Context is provided in Sarah Glassford and Amy J. Shaw, eds., *A Sisterhood of Suffering and Service: Women and Girls of Canada and Newfoundland during the First World War* (Vancouver: UBC Press, 2012).

63 *Globe,* 16 June 1915; Livio Di Matteo, "Wealth and Gender in Ontario, 1870–1930," in *Men, Women, and Money: Perspectives on Gender, Wealth and Investment 1850–1930,* ed. David R. Green, Alastair Owens, Josephine Maltby, and Janette Rutterford, 125–55 (Oxford: Oxford University Press, 2011).

64 Lynn Dumenil, *The Second Line of Defense: American Women and World War I* (Chapel Hill: University of North Carolina Press, 2017).

65 Nellie McClung, "Men and Money," *Maclean's Magazine* 32, 1 (1919): 15–17, 99–100, reprinted in *Evening Telegram* (St John's), 28 November 1919, 12.

66 *Canadian Food Bulletin* (Ottawa), 13 April 1918, 3. The *Bulletin* promoted the Victory Loan and saw conservation as a large part of the loan's "Food Side," as in the issue of November 1918, 20. This *Bulletin* was published in French as *Bulletin canadien des vivres,* with the translation done by the board's "office staff."

67 *Omineca Miner* (Hazelton, BC), 1 June 1918.

68 Linder, *World War I,* 26–27.

69 *Globe,* 9 October 1918, original emphasis.

70 Mike Chasar, "Remembrance Day and the Case of the $400,000,000 Poem," in *Arcade: The Humanities in the World,* 2 November 2013, https://arcade.stanford.edu/blogs/remembrance-day-and-case-400000000-poem.

71 Joel Baetz, *Battle Lines: Canadian Poetry in English and the First World War* (Waterloo, ON: Wilfrid Laurier University Press, 2018), 62–63.

72 See, for example, *Canada Lancet* (Toronto) 51, 7 (1918): 333; and *Pictou Advocate* (Pictou, NS), 30 November 1917.

73 *Globe,* 26 October, 2 November 1918; *Winnipeg Free Press,* quoted in "McCrae's Winged Words," *Globe,* 19 June 1918, 6.

74 *Globe,* 30 November 1917.

75 Donna Coates, "War," in *Encyclopedia of Literature in Canada,* ed. William H. New (Toronto: University of Toronto Press 2002), esp. 1188–91; Amanda Betts, ed., *In Flanders Fields: 100 Years: Writing on War, Loss and Remembrance* (Toronto: Knopf Canada, 2015); Nancy Holmes, "'In Flanders Fields' - Canada's Official Poem: Breaking Faith," *Studies in Canadian Literature* (Fredericton) 30, 1 (2005): 11–33; Amanda Lowry French, "Refrain, Again: The Return of the Villanelle" (PhD diss., University of Virginia, 2004), 129–41.

76 *Globe,* 7 December 1918.

77 *Calgary Daily Herald,* 28 October 1918.

78 *Globe,* 2 November 1918; *Le Canada,* 11 November 1918; *Daily Times-Journal* (Fort William, ON), 26 October 1918.

79 *Marketing and Business Management* 12, 9 (1918): 17. The stamp stickers are illustrated in Ronald G. Lafrenière, *Field Guide to the Cinderella Stamps of Canada,* 2nd ed. (Montreal: Bird Bear, 2015). Such stickers were not a novelty; indeed, Murray Printing Company of Toronto advertised its interest in preparing them as "Miniature Posters and Art Stamps," *Globe,* 2 October 1915.

80 See, for example, the crowded Victory Bond advertisement sponsored by the Prudential Insurance Company of America, replete with its logo, the sticker image, a photo of Sir Thomas White, and one of his promotional quotations, in the *Evening Citizen* (Ottawa), 8 November 1918.

81 Canadian War Museum, Ottawa, Collection 58 A-1-241.3-16, Ruth Caroline Antliff to William Shaw Antliff, 31 October 1918.

82 Ronald G. Lafrenière, email correspondence with author, 11 January 2020, contained a copy of a letter dated 7 March 1918 from an official in Australia's treasury department to R.J. Murphy of the defence department, with the Canadian stamp attached and marked up.

83 This attribution to John Hassall comes from Doll, *Poster War,* 49. Gillett also used the billboard in a visually gripping advertisement in *Canadian Home Journal* (Toronto), including vol. 15, nos. 3 and 11, in 1918. Billed as "England's foremost poster artist," Hassall wrote, "Both newspapers *and* posters are good advertising methods, and each of them is necessary to the other." John Hassall, "What I Think about Posters," *Economic Advertising* 7, 3 (1913): 33–35, original emphasis.

84 On humour, see Pedrini, *Propaganda,* 98–99; and Clémentine Tholas-Disset and Karen A. Ritzenhoff, eds., *Humor, Entertainment, and Popular Culture during World War I* (New York: Palgrave Macmillan, 2015).

85 *Marketing and Business Management* 12, 9 (1918): 13; *Printer and Publisher* 27, 10 (1918): 45; *Toronto Daily Star,* 16 November 1927.

86 Aulich and Hewitt, *Seduction or Instruction?* 98.

87 *American Printer* (New York) 68, 3 (1919): 58.

88 *The Poster* (Chicago) 10, 8 (August 1919): 45.

89 *Globe,* 14 March 1919; *Toronto World,* 14 March 1919.

90 Wright's collection is the basis for the exhibition publication by Doll, *Poster War.* The information on Violet Black comes from the exhibition catalogue by curator Mora Dianne O'Neill, *Collective Remembrance: Propaganda Posters from the Great War* (Halifax:

Art Gallery of Nova Scotia, 2014); and from Mora Dianne O'Neill, correspondence with author, 2019.

91 Brett Bowles, "Aesthetics, Ethics, and Poster Art in World War I France and the United States," *South Central Review* (Baltimore, MD) 34, 3 (2017): 73–102.

92 *Globe,* 14 February 1918; St. George Burgoyne, "Some Canadian Illustrators, Article II," *Canadian Bookman* (Montreal), n.s., 1, 2 (1919): 27–30. The cover of the program for the Canadian Corps's athletic meet in France in September 1917, designed by English artist Lionel Hayes, featured a busty lady amidst a wheat field and produce.

93 *Globe,* 23 July 1915.

94 Several of these posters are reproduced in Stacey, *Canadian Poster Book;* Choko, *Canadian War Posters: 1914–1918;* and Marc H. Choko, *Canadian War Posters: Posters from the First and Second World Wars* (Cambridge, UK: Worth, 2012). The Food Board and the posters for war-savings stamps had their own W.P. numberings, not to be confused with the war-loan series. Some of the artists are the same. One poster for war-savings stamps featured the golden-haired girl seen in 1917 and later in 1919. Choko, *Canadian War Posters: Posters,* 128.

95 *Globe,* 23 August 1919. The reviewer was Melvin Ormond Hammond, the *Globe*'s financial editor, who had a strong interest in Canadian art.

96 Maria Tippett, *Art at the Service of War: Canada, Art, and the Great War* (Toronto: University of Toronto Press, 1984), 89–90, 92; Keshen, *Propaganda,* 194–95.

97 LAC, RG 19, E-5-h, vol. 4009, file: Advertising 1919–20, numerous letters and McIlwraith's report.

98 Bank of Canada Archives, Ottawa, National War Finance Committee fonds, First World War loans sous-fonds, box 43.

99 Desmond Morton and J.L. Granatstein, *Marching to Armageddon: Canadians and the Great War 1914–1919* (Toronto: Lester and Orpen Dennys, 1989), 42.

100 Eric Van Schaack, "The Division of Pictorial Publicity in World War I," *Design Issues* 22, 1 (2016): 40–43.

101 This point is developed in Jonathan F. Vance, *Death So Noble: Memory, Meaning, and the First World War* (Vancouver: UBC Press, 1997), 98–99.

102 Mourad Djebabla, "'Fight the Huns with Food': Mobilizing Canadian Civilians for the Food War Effort during the Great War, 1914–1918," in *World War I and Propaganda,* ed. Troy R.E. Paddock (Leiden: Brill, 2014), 77–78, 82; Caroline Durand, "L'alimentation moderne pour la famille traditionnelle: Les discours sur l'alimentation au Québec," *Revue de Bibliotheque et Archives nationales du Québec* (Montreal) 3 (2011): 62–3.

103 Stacey, *Canadian Poster Book,* 19. The style of this poster, particularly the streaming smoke and Miss Canada overseeing marching soldiers, reflects the styling in official ad number 51.

104 *Marketing and Business Management* 13, 11 (1919): 423; 13, 12 (1919): 455.

105 *Toronto World,* 24 October 1919.

106 *Marketing and Business Management* 13, 11 (1919): 422.

107 Jennifer Wellington, *Exhibiting War: The Great War, Museums, and Memory in Britain, Canada, and Australia* (Cambridge, MA: Cambridge University Press, 2017).

108 *Marketing and Business Management* 15, 9 (1921): 314. For an examination of the placement of posters and the dynamics of human observation, see Iskin, *Poster,* esp. ch. 5. In urban streets, passing notice and frequency of suggestion rather than close study were the norms, hence her conclusion that posters as a street museum for the masses is a "worn-out cliché" (175). Postermen in Canada understood the difference, and they placed Victory Bond posters outdoors and in windows where fleeting sightings were most frequent, with wordy posters going into stationary placements such as banks and post offices.

109 See Herbert Andrew Williams, *How England Raised an Army of Five Million Men and Floated Her Big War Loans* (Montreal: Canadian Poster Company, 1917), which is illustrated with British posters; and Williams, "Canada's Flaming War Posters," 56–61.
110 *Globe*, 22 December 1919.
111 *Marketing and Business Management* 14, 10 (1920): 486–88.
112 Martin Hardie and Arthur Knowles Sabin, eds., *War Posters Issued by Belligerent and Neutral Nations, 1914–1919* (London: A. and C. Black, 1920), 49–50, 74.
113 Crowley, "Propaganda Poster," 114.
114 Donald F. Dixon, "Advertising U.S. War Bonds in the First World War," *Journal of Nonprofit and Public Sector Marketing* (Binghamton, NY) 3, 1 (1995): 65–80; Daniel Pope, "The Advertising Industry and World War I," *Public Historian* (Oakland, CA) 2, 3 (1980): 4–25.
115 Lucinda Gosling, *Brushes and Bayonets: Cartoons, Sketches and Paintings of World War I* (Oxford: Osprey, 2008), 8, 11.
116 Tippett, *Art at the Service of War.*
117 *British Columbia Federationist* (Vancouver), 8 November 1918.
118 Suzanne Evans, *Mothers of Heroes, Mothers of Martyrs: World War I and the Politics of Grief* (Montreal and Kingston: McGill-Queen's University Press, 2007), 60–65.
119 *Punch*, 5 May 1915, 351; *Globe*, 28 June 1915.
120 *Globe*, 10 November 1917, 19 March, 24 October 1918; *Toronto World*, 20 October 1918.
121 David Bartlet's exhibit, *Voluntary Fundraising for WW1*, featured thrift and war-savings stamps (from early designs to final issues), promotional labels (including the Victory Bond stickers), slogans used in postal cancellations, and advertising materials. See David Bartlet, "WWI War Savings Stamps and Promotions," *BNA Topics* 71, 1 (2014): 11–17.
122 *Globe*, 24 February, 17 March, 18 July 1917.
123 *Punch*, 7 February 1917, 87.
124 Peter Desbarats and Terry Mosher, *The Hecklers: A History of Canadian Political Cartooning and a Cartoonists' History of Canada* (Toronto: McClelland and Stewart, 1979), 78–80.
125 *Toronto World*, 14, 19 March 1917; *Grain Growers' Guide*, 20 September 1916, 7 March 1917; *Montreal Daily Mail*, 15 March 1917.
126 Canada, House of Commons, *Debates*, 1 May 1918, 1320; United States, Department of State, *Papers Relating to the Foreign Relations of the United States, 1918: Supplement 1, the World War*, 2 vols. (Washington, DC: Government Printing Office), vol. 1, 536–50.
127 "Fitz Fights the War at Home," in *Fitz and the Great War*, 17 July 2019, https://robinanderson.opened.ca/fitz-fights-the-war-at-home/.
128 *Canadian Courier* (Toronto), 4 July 1914; Robyn Fowler, "'A New Canadian National Spirit': Allegorical Miss Canada and the Occult Canadian State," in *Culture and the State: Nationalisms*, ed. James Gifford and Gabrielle Zezulka-Mailloux, 40–52 (Edmonton: CRC Humanities Studio, 2003).
129 *Le Canard* (Montreal), 17 November 1918, trans. Sandy Darmagnac.
130 *Toronto World*, 14 March 1917.
131 Evans, *Mothers of Heroes*, 181n83.
132 *Island Patriot* (Charlottetown), 25 October 1919.
133 *Cartoons Magazine* (Chicago) 14, 1 (July 1918): 135–36.
134 *Toronto Daily Star*, 7 November 1918.
135 Eberhard Demm, "Caricatures," in *1914–1918–Online: International Encyclopedia of the First World War*, ed. Ute Daniel, Peter Gatrell, Oliver Janz, Heather Jones, Jennifer Keene, Alan Kramer, and Bill Nasson (Berlin: Freie Universität Berlin, 2018), https://encyclopedia.1914-1918-online.net/home.html; Lucy Shelton Caswell, "Drawing Swords: War in American Editorial Cartoons," *American Journalism* (Philadelphia) 21, 2 (2004): 13–45.

136 Burgoyne, "Some Canadian Illustrators," 30.

137 Edward B. Moogk, *Roll Back the Years: History of Canadian Recorded Sound and Its Legacy: Genesis to 1930* (Ottawa: National Library of Canada, 1975); Glenn Watkins, *Proof through the Night: Music and the Great War* (Berkeley: University of California Press, 2002).

Chapter 13: Selling through Film, Theatre, Music, and Words

1 Fabrice Lyczba, "Hoaxes, Ballyhoo Stunts, War, and Other Jokes: Humor in the American Marketing of Hollywood War Films during the Great War," in *Humor, Entertainment, and Popular Culture during World War I*, ed. Clémentine Tholas-Disset and Karen A. Ritzenhoff (New York: Palgrave Macmillan, 2015), 68.

2 Tim Travers, "Canadian Film and the First World War," in *The First World War and Popular Cinema, 1914 to the Present*, ed. Michael Paris, 96–114 (Edinburgh: Edinburgh University Press, 1999); George Robb, *British Culture and the First World War* (London: Palgrave Macmillan, 2015), 145–48.

3 Mourad Djebabla, "'Silence, on tourne': Les films de fiction sur la guerre diffusés au Québec et en Ontario durant le Guerre de 1914–1918," *Bulletin d'histoire politique* 20, 3 (2012): 10.

4 Robb, *British Culture*, 146.

5 Larry Wayne Ward, *The Motion Picture Goes to War: The U.S. Government Film Effort during World War I* (Ann Arbor, MI: UMI Research, 1985), 49–52, 138.

6 *Printer and Publisher* (Toronto) 26, 4 (1917): 44; Jeffrey A. Keshen, *Propaganda and Censorship during Canada's Great War* (Edmonton: University of Alberta Press, 1996), 19–20.

7 See Clémentine Tholas-Disset, "Mary Pickford's WWI Patriotism: A Feminine Approach to Wartime Mythical Americanness," in *Heroism and Gender in War Films*, ed. Karen A. Ritzenhoff and Jakub Kazecki, 9–21 (New York: Palgrave Macmillan, 2014); and Christel Schmidt, ed., *Mary Pickford: Queen of the Movies* (Lexington: University Press of Kentucky, 2012).

8 Peter Morris, *Embattled Shadows: A History of Canadian Cinema, 1895–1939* (Montreal and Kingston: McGill-Queen's University Press, 1978); Paul S. Moore, *Now Playing: Early Moviegoing and the Regulation of Fun* (Albany: State University of New York Press, 2008); Dominique Brégent-Heald, *Borderland Films: American Cinema, Mexico, and Canada during the Progressive Era* (Lincoln: University of Nebraska Press, 2015); Leslie Midkiff DeBauche, *Reel Patriotism: The Movies and World War I* (Madison: University of Wisconsin Press, 1997); Robert Morris Seiler and Tamara Palmer Seiler, *Reel Time: Movie Exhibitors and Movie Audiences in Prairie Canada, 1896 to 1986* (Edmonton: Athabasca University Press, 2013); Manjunath Pendakur, *Canadian Dreams and American Control: The Political Economy of the Canadian Film Industry* (Toronto: University of Toronto Press, 1990).

9 Charles Tepperman, "Digging the Finest Potatoes from Their Acre: Government Film Exhibition in Rural Ontario, 1917–1934," in *Hollywood in the Neighborhood: Historical Case Studies of Local Moviegoing*, ed. Kathryn H. Fuller-Seeley (Berkeley: University of California Press, 2008), 130–48.

10 Library and Archives Canada (LAC), RG 19, E-5-h, vol. 4008, file: Prospectus 1917, Victory Loan film, 17 December 1917; *Globe* (Toronto), 6, 9–10, 21 November 1917; *Toronto Daily Star*, 5, 10 November 1917; *Ottawa Journal*, 5 November 1917; *Winnipeg Tribune*, 7 November 1917; *Nanaimo Daily News* (Nanaimo, BC), 13 November 1917; *Winnipeg Free Press*, 17 November 1917; *Canadian Statesman* (Bowmanville, ON), 22 November 1917; *Moving Picture World* (New York), 1 December 1917, 1362; Edward Rogers Wood, *The Story of Canada's Victory Loan, 1917: A Slight Appreciation of a Remarkable Event* (Toronto: Southam, 1918), 19.

11 *Daily Colonist* (Victoria), 10 November 1917; *Truro Daily News* (Truro, NS), 12 November 1917; *Calgary Daily Herald*, 8 November 1917; *Intelligencer* (Belleville, ON), 13–14 November 1917; *Globe*, 12–13 November 1917.
12 *Canadian Moving Picture Digest* (Toronto) 4, 13 (1918): 20; Canada, House of Commons, *Debates*, 2 May 1918, 1407; 8 May 1918, 1681–82; 20 May 1918, 2267–68. The cost of the Regal film was taken from a statement of expenses approved by the dominion publicity committee and presented in the Commons. LAC, RG 14, D2, vol. 37, no. 131 (unpub. Sess. paper, 1918, no. 131.)
13 Aaron Barlow, ed., *Star Power: The Impact of Branded Celebrity*, 2 vols. (Santa Barbara, CA: Praeger, 2014), 1.
14 Matthew Kennedy, *Marie Dressler: A Biography* (Jefferson, NC: McFarland, 1999), 99.
15 Schmidt, ed., *Mary Pickford*, 151.
16 LAC, RG 19, E-5-h, vol. 4008, file: Organization, 1918–20; *Calgary Daily Herald*, 6 November 1918.
17 Brégent-Heald, *Borderland Films*, 275–77.
18 LAC, RG 19, E-5-h, vol. 4006, file: Organization, 1918–20. For an example of the recording's use, see *Island Patriot* (Charlottetown), 28 October 1918.
19 LAC, RG 19, E-5-h, vol. 4005, file: Organization, 1918–20; *Moving Picture World*, 12 October 1918, 270.
20 *Globe*, 23, 31 October, 2 November 1918, 18 November 1919; *Toronto Daily Star*, 19 November 1918; *Moving Picture World*, 19 October 1918, 353; 26 October 1918, 50.
21 Julia C. Ott, *When Wall Street Met Main Street: The Quest for an Investors' Democracy* (Cambridge, MA: Harvard University Press, 2011), 71.
22 *Intelligencer*, 7 November 1918; *Moving Picture World*, 5 October 1918, 123; *Canadian Home Journal* (Toronto) 15, 6 (1918): 15–68.
23 *Globe*, 30 October, 7, 9, 11–13 November 1918.
24 Moore, *Now Playing*, 202.
25 Ott, *When Wall Street*.
26 *Globe*, 13 March 1918.
27 *Motion Picture News*, 5 April 1919, 2104; 10 May 1919, 3012; *Exhibitors Herald and Motography* (Chicago), 5 April 1919, 49.
28 *Globe*, 4 December 1918.
29 *Toronto Daily Star*, 1, 18 February, 12 May 1919.
30 LAC, RG 19, E-5-h, vol. 4009, file: Moving Pictures, 1919–20, H.B. Housser to B.J. Roberts, 16 September 1919; vol. 4009, file: Advertising, 1919–20, W.N. McIlwraith to E.R. Wood, 20 August 1919; vol. 4013, file: Flag, 1919–20, McIlwraith to J.C. Saunders, 29 August 1919.
31 *Calgary Daily Herald*, 4 October 1919.
32 *Calgary Daily Herald*, 22 November 1919.
33 *Globe*, 4 November 1919.
34 *Daily Times-Journal* (Fort William, ON), 1 November 1919.
35 *Variety* (New York), 21 November 1919, 7.
36 *Globe*, 1, 8, 15 November, 13 December 1919.
37 *Globe*, 31 December 1919.
38 James Aulich and John Hewitt, *Seduction or Instruction? First World War Posters in Britain and Europe* (Manchester, UK: Manchester University Press, 2007), 67; Adrian Gregory, *The Last Great War: British Society and the First World War* (Cambridge, UK: Cambridge University Press, 2008), 173; Catriona Pennell, "Presenting the War in Ireland, 1914–1918," in *World War I and Propaganda*, ed. Troy R.E. Paddock (Leiden: Brill, 2014), 42, 63; Nicholas Reeves, *The Power of Film Propaganda: Myth or Reality?* (London and New York: Cassell, 1999), vii, ch. 1; George Robb, *British Culture and the First World War* (London:

Palgrave Macmillan, 2015), 148; David Silbey, *The British Working Class and Enthusiasm for the War, 1914–16* (London and New York: Frank Cass, 2005), 120; Eberhard Demm, *Censorship and Propaganda in World War I: A Comprehensive History* (London: Bloomsbury Academic, 2019), 180, 185.

39 "Songs," in *Canada and the First World War*, Canadian War Museum, https://www.warmuseum.ca/firstworldwar/history/life-at-the-front/trench-culture/songs/. For parallels in Britain, see Roger Foss, *Till the Boys Come Home: How British Theatre Fought the Great War* (Stroud, UK: History, 2018), and Jeffrey A. Keshen, "The First World War in Print," in *History of the Book in Canada: 1840–1918*, 3 vols., ed. Yvan Lamonde, Patricia Lockhart Fleming, and Fiona A. Black (Toronto: University of Toronto Press, 2004–07), vol. 2, 352.

40 Emma Hanna, *Sounds of War: Music in the British Armed Forces during the Great War* (Cambridge, UK: Cambridge University Press, 2020), 37–38.

41 Robb, *British Culture*, 187; Sara Karn, "Canadian Songs of the First World War," *The Canadian Encyclopedia*, 3 November 2018, https://www.thecanadianencyclopedia.ca/en/article/canadian-songs-of-the-first-world-war; Barbara Norman, "Music on the Home Front: Canadian Sheet Music of the First World War," Library and Archives Canada, https://www.bac-lac.gc.ca/eng/discover/films-videos-sound-recordings/sheet-music-collection/Pages/articles.aspx#TOC3; "Listening to 1918: Popular Songs on Canada's Home Front," Great War Centre, 25 May 2018, https://greatwarcentre.com/2018/05/25/listening-to-1918-popular-songs-on-canadas-home-front/.

42 *Western Clarion* (Vancouver), 1 July 1917.

43 *The Week* (Victoria), 23 March 1918.

44 On the perception of exploitation, see David Monger, *Patriotism and Propaganda in First World War Britain: The National War Aims Committee and Civilian Morale* (Liverpool, UK: Liverpool University Press, 2012), 266.

45 *Truro Daily News*, 13 November 1917.

46 *Globe*, 26 November 1917; Arthur E. Zimmerman and Betty Minaker Pratt, "Frank Oldfield: The McCormack of Baritones (1882–1956)," *Antique Phonograph News* (Toronto), January–February 2010, https://www.capsnews.org/apn2010-1.htm; "Sussex by the Sea," 1917, Dr. Danny O. Crew Theodore Roosevelt Sheet Music Collection, Dr. Danny O. Crew Collection of American Political Sheet Music, Theodore Roosevelt Digital Library, Dickinson State University, https://www.theodorerooseveltcenter.org/Research/Digital-Library/Record?libID=0292766.

47 *Calgary Daily Herald*, 23 November 1917.

48 *Truro Daily News*, 23 November 1917; *Regina Morning Leader*, 16 November 1917.

49 *Daily Times-Journal*, 7 November 1918; *Saint John Globe*, 7 November 1918; *Regina Morning Leader*, 9 November 1918; Robert Ungar, "Victory Loan Chorus," *YouTube*, 9 April 2023, https://youtu.be/J795oNvhL8o.

50 *Globe*, 5 July 1919.

51 *Toronto World*, 24 October 1919.

52 Bank of Canada Archives, Ottawa, National War Finance Committee fonds, First World War loans sous-fonds, box 43.

53 "A Poetic War Fund Raising Invitation Postcard 1917," *Canadian War Poetry WW1 Era 1900 1950*, 13 March 2015, https://canadianwarpoetryww1.wordpress.com/2015/03/13/a-poetic-war-fund-raising-invitation-postcard-1917/.

54 Joel Baetz, *Battle Lines: Canadian Poetry in English and the First World War* (Waterloo, ON: Wilfrid Laurier University Press, 2018), 6–8.

55 *Maclean's Magazine* and *Saturday Night* are noted in Rebecca Campbell, "We Gave Our Glorious Laddies: Canadian Women's War Poetry, 1915–20" (MA thesis, University of British Columbia, 2007), 34.

56 Mark W. Van Wienen, *Partisans and Poets: The Political Work of American Poetry in the Great War* (Cambridge, UK: Cambridge University Press, 1997), 143. The perspective here can apply to Canadian propaganda poetry.
57 *Vancouver Daily Sun*, 18 November 1917.
58 *Everywoman's World* (Toronto), 8, 6 December 1917, 33; *Le Canada* (Montreal), 15 November 1917.
59 *Evening Telegram* (St. John's), 11 July 1918; *Globe*, 23 November 1917.
60 Alan Sullivan of the Royal Air Force base in Leaside is noted in *Globe*, 2 November 1918.
61 Ibid.
62 John William Garvin, *Canadian Poems of the Great War* (Toronto: McClelland and Stewart, 1918), 3. See also Jonathan F. Vance, *Death So Noble: Memory, Meaning, and the First World War* (Vancouver: UBC Press, 1997), 174–75.
63 *The Civilian* (Ottawa) 12, 11 (1919): iv. This same official advertisement (no. 10-P) appeared on 18 October 1919 in newspapers in Charlottetown, Ottawa, Brandon, Vancouver, and likely elsewhere.
64 *Grand River Sachem* (Caledonia, ON), 16 January 1918; *Globe*, 17 October 1918, 15 April 1919; *The School: A Magazine Devoted to Elementary and Secondary Education* (Toronto), September 1918 to June 1919, 204, 206.
65 *Globe*, 9 November 1918.
66 *Toronto Daily Star*, 29 October 1918.
67 See, for example, Silas Wegg [a Dickensian pseudonym], "The Women and the War," in *The Civilian* 11, 10 (1918): 248–49; and mention of "bonds" in *The Civilian* 12, 1 (1918): 15.
68 William T. Allison, "Introduction," in Robert J.C. Stead, *Kitchener and Other Poems* (Toronto: Musson Book Co., 1917), viii.
69 Clarence Karr, *Authors and Audiences: Popular Canadian Fiction in the Early Twentieth Century* (Montreal and Kingston: McGill-Queen's University Press, 2000), 105.
70 Arthur Stringer, *The Stranger* (Ottawa: Dominion Publicity Committee, 1919), 16, https://archive.org/details/cihm_99118.
71 Lance E. Davis and Robert E. Gallman, *Evolving Financial Markets and International Capital Flows: Britain, the Americas, and Australia, 1865–1914* (Cambridge, UK: Cambridge University Press, 2001), 464–65.
72 *The ABC of the Victory Loan, 1918* (Ottawa: Dominion Publicity Committee, 1918), 11.
73 This version of the letter comes from the *Cumberland Islander* (Cumberland, BC), 14 August 1920, with this editorial quip: "Otherwise everything seems to be alright!"
74 Keshen, *Propaganda*, 15–18.
75 On *Rilla of Ingleside*, see Alan R. Young, "L.M. Montgomery's *Rilla of Ingleside* (1920): Romance and the Experience of War," in *Myth and Milieu: Atlantic Literature and Culture, 1918–1939*, ed. Gwendolyn Davies, 95–122 (Fredericton, NB: Acadiensis, 1993); and Erika Rothwell, "Knitting Up the World: L.M. Montgomery and Maternal Feminism in Canada," in *L.M. Montgomery and Canadian Culture*, ed. Irene Gammel and Elizabeth Epperly, 133–44 (Toronto: University of Toronto Press, 1999).
76 See, for example, White's entry in *A Cyclopaedia of Canadian Biography*, ed. Hector W. Charlesworth (Toronto: Hunter-Rose, 1919), 13–15.
77 Gilbert Edward Jackson, untitled, *Canadian Historical Review* 2, 3 (1921): 297–99, 298 (quote).
78 *Monetary Times* (Toronto), 7 January 1921, 116, 118, 120.
79 Ott, *When Wall Street*, 54, 58, 69.
80 This account appeared in three locations: Sir Thomas White, "Federal Financial Administration and the Banks," *Journal of the Canadian Bankers' Association* 5, 29 (1922): 350–62; as a booklet, *Federal Financial Administration and the Banks* (Toronto: Toronto Bankers'

Educational Association, 1922); and as "The War Finance of Canada," *Annals of the American Academy of Political Science* (Philadelphia) 107 (May 1923): 209–15.

81 Winston Churchill, *The World Crisis*, 6 vols. (London: Thornton Butterworth, 1923–31), vol. 4 (i.e., vol. 3, part 2), 20, 31–35; *Globe*, 9–10, 14 March, 1 June 1927.

82 *Globe*, 5 December 1932, 3 January 1933.

83 Robert B. Bryce, *Canada and the Cost of World War II: The International Operations of Canada's Department of Finance, 1939–1947*, ed. Matthew J. Bellamy (Montreal and Kingston: McGill-Queen's University Press, 2005).

Conclusion

1 Adam Tooze, *The Deluge: The Great War, America and the Remains of the Global Order, 1916–1931* (New York: Viking, 2014), 215–16.

2 *Globe*, 9 November 1918.

3 Kenneth D. Garbade, *Birth of a Market: The U.S. Treasury Securities Market from the Great War to the Great Depression* (Cambridge, MA: MIT Press, 2012), 98; Richard N. Germain, *Dollars through the Doors: A Pre-1930 History of Bank Marketing in America* (Westport, CT: Greenwood, 1996), 108.

4 Hans-Peter Ullmann, "Financing Global War," in *The Cambridge History of the First World War*, 3 vols., ed. Jay M. Winter (Cambridge, UK: Cambridge University Press, 2013–14), vol. 2, 419–20; Aris Gaaff, *Debts without Redemption: Cultural Difference in First World War Finance* (Soesterberg, Netherlands: Aspekt, 2017), 179–85.

5 Harvey Edward Fisk, *The Inter-Ally Debts: An Analysis of War and Post-war Public Finance, 1914–1923* (New York: Bankers Trust Company, 1924), 147.

6 Shirley Tillotson, *Give and Take: The Citizen-Taxpayer and the Rise of Canadian Democracy* (Vancouver: UBC Press, 2017), 23.

7 John James Deutsch, "War Finance and the Canadian Economy, 1914–20," *Canadian Journal of Economics and Political Science* 6, 4 (1940): 537.

8 Livio Di Matteo, *A Federal Fiscal History: Canada, 1867–2017* (Vancouver: Fraser Institute, 2017), 33.

9 Ibid., 16, 33.

10 Shirley Tillotson, *Contributing Citizens: Modern Charitable Fundraising and the Making of the Welfare State, 1920–66* (Vancouver: UBC Press, 2014).

Selected Bibliography

Armstrong, Christopher. *Blue Skies and Boiler Rooms: Buying and Selling Securities in Canada, 1870–1940*. Toronto: University of Toronto Press, 1997.

Aulich, James, and John Hewitt. *Seduction or Instruction? First World War Posters in Britain and Europe*. Manchester, UK: Manchester University Press, 2007.

Avery, Donald. *"Dangerous Foreigners": European Immigrant Workers and Labour Radicalism in Canada, 1896–1932*. Toronto: McClelland and Stewart, 1979.

Axelrod, Alan. *Selling the Great War: The Making of American Propaganda*. New York: Palgrave Macmillan, 2009.

Baetz, Joel. *Battle Lines: Canadian Poetry in English and the First World War*. Waterloo, ON: Wilfrid Laurier University Press, 2018.

Bartlet, David. "WWI War Savings Stamps and Promotions." *BNA Topics* 71, 3 (2014): 11–17.

Bliss, Michael. *A Canadian Millionaire: The Life and Times of Sir Joseph Flavelle, Bart., 1858–1939*. Toronto: Macmillan, 1978.

Bogart, Ernest Ludlow. *Direct and Indirect Costs of the Great World War*. 2nd ed. New York: Oxford University Press, 1920.

Bownes, David, and Robert Fleming. *Posters of the First World War*. Oxford: Shire, 2014.

Broadberry, Stephen, and Mark Harrison, eds. *The Economics of World War I*. Cambridge, UK: Cambridge University Press, 2005.

Brown, Frank Herbert, James Douglas Gibson, and Arthur Fitzwalter Wynne Plumptre. *War Finance in Canada*. Toronto: Ryerson, 1940.

Brown, Robert Craig, and Ramsay Cook. *Canada 1896–1921: A Nation Transformed*. Toronto: McClelland and Stewart, 1974.

Burk, Kathleen. *Britain, America and the Sinews of War, 1914–1918*. Boston: Allen and Unwin, 1985.

Butkiewicz, James L., and Mihaela Solcan. "The Original Operation Twist: The War Finance Corporation's War Bond Purchases, 1918–1920." *Financial History Review* (Cambridge, UK) 23, 1 (2016): 21–46.

Cadigan, Sean T. *Death on Two Fronts: National Tragedies and the Fate of Democracy in Newfoundland, 1914–34*. Toronto: Allen Lane, 2013.

Caswell, Lucy Shelton. "Drawing Swords: War in America Editorial Cartoons." *American Journalism* (Philadelphia) 21, 2 (2004): 13–45.

Choko, Marc H. *Canadian War Posters: Posters from the First and Second World Wars*. Cambridge, UK: Worth, 2012.

Clark, William Clifford. "Financing the War." Part 1 of *Economic Aspects of the War*, 1–64 (Kingston, ON: Queen's University, 1916).

Cook, Tim, and J.L. Granatstein, eds. *Canada 1919: A Nation Shaped by War.* Vancouver: UBC Press, 2020.

Curtis, Clifford Austin. "The Canadian Banks and War Finance." *Contributions to Canadian Economics* (Toronto) 3 (1931): 7–40.

Daniel, Ute, Peter Gatrell, Oliver Janz, Heather Jones, Jennifer Keene, Alan Kramer, and Bill Nasson, eds. *1914–1918–Online: International Encyclopedia of the First World War.* Berlin: Freie Universität Berlin, 2018. https://encyclopedia.1914-1918-online.net/home.html.

DeBauche, Leslie Midkiff. *Reel Patriotism: The Movies and World War I.* Madison: University of Wisconsin Press, 1997.

Delaney, Douglas E., and Nikolas Gardner, eds. *Turning Point 1917: The British Empire at War.* Vancouver: UBC Press, 2017.

Demm, Eberhard. *Censorship and Propaganda in World War I: A Comprehensive History.* London: Bloomsbury Academic, 2019.

Desbarats, Peter, and Terry Mosher. *The Hecklers: A History of Canadian Political Cartooning and a Cartoonists' History of Canada.* Toronto: McClelland and Stewart, 1979.

Deutsch, John James. "War Finance and the Canadian Economy, 1914–20." *Canadian Journal of Economics and Political Science* 6, 4 (1940): 525–42.

Di Matteo, Livio. *A Federal Fiscal History: Canada, 1867–2017.* Vancouver: Fraser Institute, 2017.

Dixon, Donald F. "Advertising U.S. War Bonds in the First World War." *Journal of Nonprofit and Public Sector Marketing* (Binghamton, NY) 3, 1 (1995): 65–80.

Djebabla, Mourad. "'Fight or Farm': Canadian Farmers and the Dilemma of the War Effort in World War I (1914–1918)." *Canadian Military Journal* (Kingston, ON) 13, 2 (2012–13): 57–67.

Doll, Maurice F.V. *The Poster War: Allied Propaganda Art of the First World War.* Edmonton: Alberta Community Development, Cultural Facilities and Historical Resources Division, 1993.

Donald, William John Alexander. "Canadian Financial Problems." *Journal of Political Economy* (Chicago) 23, 8 (1915): 753–90.

Dutil, Patrice, and David MacKenzie. *Embattled Nation: Canada's Wartime Election of 1917.* Toronto: Dundurn, 2017.

Eckardt, Homer Mark Philip. "The War Loan." *Journal of the Canadian Bankers' Association* (Toronto) 24, 3 (1916–17): 251–53.

Ens, Adolf. *Subjects or Citizens? The Mennonite Experience in Canada, 1870–1925.* Ottawa: University of Ottawa Press, 1994.

Evans, Suzanne. *Mothers of Heroes, Mothers of Martyrs: World War I and the Politics of Grief.* Montreal and Kingston: McGill-Queen's University Press, 2007.

Ferland, Raphaël Dallaire. "Patriotism and Allegiances of the 22nd (French Canadian) Battalion, 1914–1918." *Canadian Military Journal* (Kingston, ON) 13, 1 (2012): 51–60.

Fisher, Susan R. *Boys and Girls in No Man's Land: English Canadian Children and the First World War.* Toronto: University of Toronto Press, 2011.

Fullerton, Douglas H. *The Bond Market in Canada: A Study of the Institutions, Machinery, Techniques, and Problems Involved in the Issuing and Marketing of Bonds and Debentures.* Toronto: Carswell, 1962.

Gaaff, Aris. *Debts without Redemption: Cultural Differences in First World War Finance.* Soesterberg, Netherlands: Aspekt, 2017.

Garbade, Kenneth D. *Birth of a Market: The U.S. Treasury Securities Market from the Great War to the Great Depression.* Cambridge, MA: MIT Press, 2012.

Gilbert, Charles. *American Financing of World War I.* Westport, CT: Greenwood, 1970.

Gillespie, W. Irwin. *Tax, Borrow and Spend: Financing Federal Spending in Canada, 1867–1990*. Ottawa: Carleton University Press, 1991.

Glassford, Sarah, and Amy J. Shaw, eds. *A Sisterhood of Suffering and Service: Women and Girls of Canada and Newfoundland during the First World War.* Vancouver: UBC Press, 2012.

Gosling, Lucinda. *Brushes and Bayonets: Cartoons, Sketches and Paintings of World War I.* Oxford: Osprey, 2008.

Great Britain, Ministry of Munitions. *History of the Ministry of Munitions.* 8 vols. in 4. London: His Majesty's Stationery Office, 1922.

Gregory, Adrian. *The Last Great War: British Society and the First World War.* Cambridge, UK: Cambridge University Press, 2014.

Heaman, Elspeth A. *Tax, Order, and Good Government: A New Political History of Canada, 1867–1917.* Montreal and Kingston: McGill-Queen's University Press, 2017.

Horn, Martin, *Britain, France, and the Financing of the First World War.* Montreal and Kingston: McGill-Queen's University Press, 2002.

James, Pearl, ed. *Picture This: World War I Posters and Visual Culture.* Lincoln: University of Nebraska Press, 2009.

Johnston, Russell. *Selling Themselves: The Emergence of Canadian Advertising.* Toronto: University of Toronto Press, 2001.

Keelan, Geoff. "Bourassa's War: Henri Bourassa and the First World War." PhD diss., University of Waterloo, 2015.

Kershaw, Ian. *To Hell and Back: Europe, 1914–1949*. New York: Viking, 2015.

Keshen, Jeffrey A. *Propaganda and Censorship during Canada's Great War.* Edmonton: University of Alberta Press, 1996.

Kimble, James J. *Mobilizing the Home Front: War Bonds and Domestic Propaganda.* College Station, TX: Texas A&M University Press, 2006.

Knox, Frank Albert. "Canadian War Finance and the Balance of Payments, 1914–1918." *Canadian Journal of Economics and Political Science* 6, 2 (1940): 244–46.

Koske, Madeleine. "From Spenders to Savers: Thrift, Saving and Luxury in Canada during the First World War." PhD diss., University of Ottawa, 2017.

Lafrenière, Ronald G. *Field Guide to the Cinderella Stamps of Canada.* 2nd ed. Montreal: Bird Bear, 2015.

Linder, Ann P. *World War I in 40 Posters.* Mechanicsburg, PA: Stackpole Books, 2016.

Lucas, Charles, Sir, ed. *The Empire at War,* 5 vols. Oxford: H. Milford, 1921–26.

McGinnis, Janice P. Dickin. "The Impact of Epidemic Influenza: Canada, 1918–1919." *Historical Papers* (Canadian Historical Association) 12, 1 (1977): 120–40.

McIvor, R. Craig. *Canadian Monetary, Banking and Fiscal Development.* Toronto: Macmillan, 1958.

Moogk, Edward B. *Roll Back the Years: History of Canadian Recorded Sound and Its Legacy: Genesis to 1930.* Ottawa: National Library of Canada, 1975.

Morris, Peter. *Embattled Shadows: A History of Canadian Cinema, 1895–1939*. Montreal and Kingston: McGill-Queen's University Press, 1978.

Morris, Philip Henry, ed. *The Canadian Patriotic Fund: A Record of Its Activities from 1914 to 1919*. Ottawa: Canadian Patriotic Fund, 1920.

Morton, Desmond. *Fight or Pay: Soldiers' Families in the Great War.* Vancouver: UBC Press. 2004.

Morton, Desmond, and J.L. Granatstein. *Marching to Armageddon: Canadians and the Great War 1914–1919*. Toronto: Lester and Orpen Dennys, 1989.

Neilson, Keith. "R.H. Brand, the Empire and Munitions from Canada." *English Historical Review* (Oxford) 126, 523 (2011): 1430–55.

Nichols, Mark Edgar. *(CP): The Story of the Canadian Press.* Toronto: Ryerson, 1948.
O'Neill, Mora Dianne. *Collective Remembrance: Propaganda Posters from the Great War.* Halifax: Art Gallery of Nova Scotia, 2014.
Ott, Julia C. *When Wall Street Met Main Street: The Quest for an Investor's Democracy.* Cambridge, MA: Harvard University Press, 2011.
Owram, Doug. *The Government Generation: Canadian Intellectuals and the State, 1900–1945.* Toronto: University of Toronto Press, 1986.
Parkinson, John Frederick. "Some Problems of War Finance in Canada." *Canadian Journal of Economics and Political Science* 6, 3 (1940): 403–33.
Pedrini, Pier Paolo. *Propaganda, Persuasion and the Great War: Heredity in the Modern Sale of Products and Political Ideas.* London: Routledge, 2018.
Perry, J. Harvey. *Taxes, Tariffs, and Subsidies: A History of Canadian Fiscal Development.* 2 vols. Toronto: University of Toronto Press, 1955.
Powell, James. *A History of the Canadian Dollar.* Ottawa: Bank of Canada, 2005.
Prentice, James Stuart. *Canadian Federal Finance.* Kingston, ON: Jackson, 1928.
Prince, Robert S. "The Mythology of War: How the Canadian Daily Newspaper Depicted the War." PhD diss., University of Toronto, 1998.
Rankin, John. "The Reporting of the Influenza Pandemic, 1918–1920, in Hamilton, Ontario." *Health* 4, 12 (2012): 1317–27.
Reeves, Nicholas. "Film Propaganda and Its Audience: The Example of Britain's Official Films during the First World War." *Journal of Contemporary History* (London) 18, 3 (1983): 463–94.
Reyburn, Karen A. "Blurring the Boundaries: Images of Women in Canadian Propaganda of World War I." MA thesis, University of Guelph, 1998.
Richard, Béatrice. "Henri Bourassa and Conscription: Traitor or Saviour?" *Canadian Military Journal* (Kingston, ON) 7, 4 (2006–07): 75–83.
Rider, Peter E. "The Imperial Munitions Board and Its Relationship to Government, Business, and Labour, 1914–1920." PhD diss., University of Toronto, 1974.
Robb, George. *British Culture and the First World War.* London: Palgrave Macmillan, 2015.
Rose, Jonathan W. *Making "Pictures in Our Heads": Government Advertising in Canada.* Westport, CT: Praeger, 2000.
Ross, Gerald. "Fort Williams's Enemy Alien 'Problem' during the First World War." *Papers and Records* (Thunder Bay Historical Museum Society, Thunder Bay, ON) 22 (1994): 3–22.
Sandwell, Bernard Keble. "Canada's Financial Condition in Its Bearing on the War." In *Canada in the Great World War,* 6 vols., vol. 2, 106–15. Toronto: United Publishers of Canada, 1917–21.
–. "Canadian Industry and the Call for Munitions." In *Canada in the Great World War,* 6 vols., vol. 2, 116–27. Toronto: United Publishers of Canada, 1917–21.
–. "Financial Measures." In *Canada in the Great World War,* 6 vols., vol. 2, 128–43. Toronto: United Publishers of Canada, 1917–21.
Schmidt, Christel, ed. *Mary Pickford: Queen of the Movies.* Lexington: University Press of Kentucky, 2012.
Shortt, Adam. *Early Economic Effects of the War upon Canada.* New York: Oxford University Press, 1918.
Shortt, Adam, and Royal Society of Canada. *The Economic Effect of War upon Canada: Presidential Address.* Ottawa: Royal Society of Canada, 1916.
Silbey, David. *The British Working Class and Enthusiasm for War, 1914–16.* Abingdon, UK: Routledge, 2005.
Skelton, Oscar Douglas. *Canadian Federal Finance – II.* Kingston, ON: Jackson, 1918.

–. "Canadian War Finance." *American Economic Review* 7, 4 (1917): 816–31..
–. *Federal Finance.* Kingston, ON: Jackson, 1915.
Sotiron, Minko. *From Politics to Profit: The Commercialization of Canadian Daily Newspapers, 1890–1920.* Montreal and Kingston: McGill-Queen's University Press, 1997.
Stacey, Robert. *The Canadian Poster Book: 100 Years of the Poster in Canada.* Toronto: Methuen, 1979.
Stephenson, Harold Edward, and Carlton McNaught. *The Story of Advertising in Canada: A Chronicle of Fifty Years.* Toronto: Ryerson, 1940.
Strachan, Hew. *Financing the First World War.* Oxford: Oxford University Press, 2004.
Swyripa, Frances, and John Herd Thompson, eds. *Loyalties in Conflict: Ukrainians in Canada during the Great War.* Edmonton: Canadian Institute of Ukrainian Studies, 1983.
Talbot, Robert J. "'It Would Be Best to Leave Us Alone': First Nations Responses to the Canadian War Effort, 1914–18." *Journal of Canadian Studies* (Peterborough, ON) 45, 1 (2011): 90–120.
Taylor, James. *"Your Country Needs YOU": The Secret History of the Propaganda Poster.* Glasgow: Saraband, 2013.
Tholas-Disset, Clémentine, and Karen A. Ritzenhoff, eds. *Humor, Entertainment, and Popular Culture during World War I.* New York: Palgrave Macmillan, 2015.
Tillotson, Shirley. *Give and Take: The Citizen-Taxpayer and the Rise of Canadian Democracy.* Vancouver: UBC Press, 2017.
Tooze, Adam. *The Deluge: The Great War, America and the Remains of the Global Order, 1916–1931.* New York: Viking, 2014.
Turley-Ewart, John Anthony. "Gentleman Bankers, Politicians and Bureaucrats: The History of the Canadian Bankers' Association, 1891–1924." PhD diss., University of Toronto, 2000.
Ward, Norman. *The Public Purse: A Study in Canadian Democracy.* Toronto: University of Toronto Press, 1951.
Westcott, Michael R. "Transforming the State: Gender, Class, and Ethnicity on the Newfoundland Home Front, 1914–1918." PhD diss., Memorial University, 2019.
White, Thomas, Sir. *The Story of Canada's War Finance.* Montreal: Canadian Bank of Commerce, 1921.
Winegard, Timothy C. *For King and Kanata: Canadian Indians and the First World War.* Winnipeg: University of Manitoba Press, 2012.
Wood, Edward Rogers. *The Story of Canada's Victory Loan, 1917: A Slight Appreciation of a Remarkable Event.* Toronto: Southam, 1918.
Wormell, Jeremy. *The Management of the National Debt of the United Kingdom, 1900–1932.* New York: Routledge, 2000.
Yates, Joshua J., and James Davison Hunter, eds. *Thrift and Thriving in America: Capitalism and Moral Order from the Puritans to the Present.* New York: Oxford University Press, 2011.

Index

Note: "(f)" after a page number indicates a figure; "(t)" after a page number indicates a table

Studies in Canadian Military History

John Griffith Armstrong, *The Halifax Explosion and the Royal Canadian Navy: Inquiry and Intrigue*
Andrew Richter, *Avoiding Armageddon: Canadian Military Strategy and Nuclear Weapons, 1950–63*
William Johnston, *A War of Patrols: Canadian Army Operations in Korea*
Julian Gwyn, *Frigates and Foremasts: The North American Squadron in Nova Scotia Waters, 1745–1815*
Jeffrey A. Keshen, *Saints, Sinners, and Soldiers: Canada's Second World War*
Desmond Morton, *Fight or Pay: Soldiers' Families in the Great War*
Douglas E. Delaney, *The Soldiers' General: Bert Hoffmeister at War*
Michael Whitby, ed., *Commanding Canadians: The Second World War Diaries of A.F.C. Layard*
Martin F. Auger, *Prisoners of the Home Front: German POWs and "Enemy Aliens" in Southern Quebec, 1940–46*
Tim Cook, *Clio's Warriors: Canadian Historians and the Writing of the World Wars*
Serge Marc Durflinger, *Fighting from Home: The Second World War in Verdun, Quebec*
Richard O. Mayne, *Betrayed: Scandal, Politics, and Canadian Naval Leadership*
P. Whitney Lackenbauer, *Battle Grounds: The Canadian Military and Aboriginal Lands*
Cynthia Toman, *An Officer and a Lady: Canadian Military Nursing and the Second World War*
Michael Petrou, *Renegades: Canadians in the Spanish Civil War*
Amy J. Shaw, *Crisis of Conscience: Conscientious Objection in Canada during the First World War*
Serge Marc Durflinger, *Veterans with a Vision: Canada's War Blinded in Peace and War*
James G. Fergusson, *Canada and Ballistic Missile Defence, 1954–2009: Déjà Vu All Over Again*
Benjamin Isitt, *From Victoria to Vladivostok: Canada's Siberian Expedition, 1917–19*
James Wood, *Militia Myths: Ideas of the Canadian Citizen Soldier, 1896–1921*
Timothy Balzer, *The Information Front: The Canadian Army and News Management during the Second World War*
Andrew B. Godefroy, *Defence and Discovery: Canada's Military Space Program, 1945–74*
Douglas E. Delaney, *Corps Commanders: Five British and Canadian Generals at War, 1939–45*
Timothy Wilford, *Canada's Road to the Pacific War: Intelligence, Strategy, and the Far East Crisis*
Randall Wakelam, *Cold War Fighters: Canadian Aircraft Procurement, 1945–54*

Andrew Burtch, *Give Me Shelter: The Failure of Canada's Cold War Civil Defence*
Wendy Cuthbertson, *Labour Goes to War: The CIO and the Construction of a New Social Order, 1939–45*
P. Whitney Lackenbauer, *The Canadian Rangers: A Living History*
Teresa Iacobelli, *Death or Deliverance: Canadian Courts Martial in the Great War*
Graham Broad, *A Small Price to Pay: Consumer Culture on the Canadian Home Front, 1939–45*
Peter Kasurak, *A National Force: The Evolution of Canada's Army, 1950–2000*
Isabel Campbell, *Unlikely Diplomats: The Canadian Brigade in Germany, 1951–64*
Richard M. Reid, *African Canadians in Union Blue: Volunteering for the Cause in the Civil War*
Andrew B. Godefroy, *In Peace Prepared: Innovation and Adaptation in Canada's Cold War Army*
Nic Clarke, *Unwanted Warriors: The Rejected Volunteers of the Canadian Expeditionary Force*
David Zimmerman, *Maritime Command Pacific: The Royal Canadian Navy's West Coast Fleet in the Early Cold War*
Cynthia Toman, *Sister Soldiers of the Great War: The Nurses of the Canadian Army Medical Corps*
Daniel Byers, *Zombie Army: The Canadian Army and Conscription in the Second World War*
J.L. Granatstein, *The Weight of Command: Voices of Canada's Second World War Generals and Those Who Knew Them*
Colin McCullough, *Creating Canada's Peacekeeping Past*
Brandon R. Dimmel, *Engaging the Line: How the Great War Shaped the Canada–US Border*
Meghan Fitzpatrick, *Invisible Scars: Mental Trauma and the Korean War*
Patrick M. Dennis, *Reluctant Warriors: Canadian Conscripts and the Great War*
Frank Maas, *The Price of Alliance: The Politics and Procurement of Leopard Tanks for Canada's NATO Brigade*
Geoffrey Hayes, *Crerar's Lieutenants: Inventing the Canadian Junior Army Officer, 1939–45*
Richard Goette, *Sovereignty and Command in Canada–US Continental Air Defence, 1940–57*
Geoff Jackson, *The Empire on the Western Front: The British 62nd and Canadian 4th Divisions in Battle*
Steve Marti and William John Pratt, eds., *Fighting with the Empire: Canada, Britain, and Global Conflict, 1867–1947*
Steve Marti, *For Home and Empire: Voluntary Mobilization in Australia, Canada, and New Zealand during the First World War*
Douglas E. Delaney and Serge Marc Durflinger, *Capturing Hill 70: Canada's Forgotten Battle of the First World War*
Peter Kasurak, *Canada's Mechanized Infantry: The Evolution of a Combat Arm, 1920–2012*

Sarah Glassford and Amy Shaw, eds., *Making the Best of It: Women and Girls of Canada and Newfoundland during the Second World War*
Alex Souchen, *War Junk: Munitions Disposal and Postwar Reconstruction in Canada*
George Belliveau and Graham W. Lea, eds., *Contact! Unload: Military Veterans, Trauma, and Research-Based Theatre*
Tim Cook and J.L. Granatstein, eds., *Canada 1919: A Nation Shaped by War*
Arthur W. Gullachsen, *An Army of Never-Ending Strength: Reinforcing the Canadians in Northwest Europe, 1944–45*
Peter Farrugia and Evan J. Habkirk, eds., *Portraits of Battle: Courage, Grief, and Strength in Canada's Great War*
Andrew L. Brown, *Building the Army's Backbone: Canadian Non-Commissioned Officers in the Second World War*
Matthew Barrett, *Scandalous Conduct: Canadian Officer Courts Martial, 1914–45*
Alex Souchen and Matthew S. Wiseman, eds., *Silent Partners: The Origins and Influence of Canada's Military-Industrial Complex*

Studies in Canadian Military History
Published by UBC Press in association with the Canadian War Museum

Printed and bound in Canada by Friesens

Set in Swiss Condensed and Minion by Artegraphica Design Co Ltd.

Copy editor: Robert Lewis

Proofreader: Sophie Pouyanne

Cover design: George Kirkpatrick

Cover illustration: Top: "Lives or Dollars? Buy Victory Bonds," design by A.M. Goodden, 1918, R1185-67-0-E, box no. A177/X2 (reduced from the original) | Courtesy of Library and Archives Canada; bottom: Victory bond posters in Regina, R B8132 48 (modified from the original) | Courtesy of the Provincial Archives of Saskatchewan